I0213026

The Complete Works Of Thomas Brooks

Volume 6 of 6 Volume Set

Sovereign Grace Publishers, Inc.
P.O. Box 4998
Lafayette, IN 47903

The Complete Works of Thomas Brooks, Volume 6

Volume 6 = ISBN 1-58960-250-1

6 Volume Set ISBN 1-58960-251-X

Printed In the United States of America
By Lightning Source, Inc.

THE COMPLETE WORKS

OF

THOMAS BROOKS.

Edited, with Memoir,

BY THE REV. ALEXANDER BALLOCH GROSART,

LIVERPOOL.

VOL. VI.

CONTAINING:

LONDON'S LAMENTATIONS ON THE LATE FIERY DISPENSATION—THE GLORIOUS DAY OF THE SAINTS' APPEARANCE—GOD'S DELIGHT IN THE PROGRESS OF THE UPRIGHT—HYPOCRITES DETECTED—A BELIEVER'S LAST DAY IS HIS BEST DAY—A HEAVENLY CORDIAL—THE LEGACY OF A DYING MOTHER AND MRS BELL'S EXPERIENCES—INDICES, ETC.

EDINBURGH: JAMES NICHOL.

LONDON: JAMES NISBET AND CO. DUBLIN: G. HERBERT.

M.DCCC.LXVII.

EDITORIAL POSTSCRIPT.

FOLLOWING the last of his larger treatises—'London's Lamentations'—there will be found in the present concluding volume certain minor writings of Brooks, of some of which the Editor had despaired securing copies—having searched in vain for most of them in all our great Libraries, and applied with similar result to innumerable book-lovers and booksellers. He has not anywhere chanced upon another copy besides his own of either the 'Heavenly Cordial' or of 'The Legacy of a Dying Mother;' while years since the learned editor of the 'Depositions from the Castle of York, relating to Offences committed in the Northern Counties in the Seventeenth Century,' for the Surtees Society—James Raine, Esq.,—with reference to the Funeral Sermon of Colonel Rainsborough, designated it '*a very rare tract*,' and congratulated himself that by the kindness of a local Bibliopole he was 'able to give a copy of the title.'[1] Apart from the intrinsic worth of these excessively scarce, if not unique tractates, it is exceedingly satisfactory to the Editor that he has been enabled by lucky chances to present the ENTIRE writings of Brooks in this—like Sibbes'—first collective edition. As simple matter of fact, the Works given n these six volumes could not be purchased in the market in the original and early editions for as many pounds as the shillings they cost in this form: and it is ventured to indulge a hope that the accuracy of our reprint from a genuine and unmutilated text, the careful verification of the numerous Bible quotations and references, the annotation of names, &c., and the Glossary and marking of Shakesperean words—these sometimes explaining obscurities—will be accepted as additions to their value. The Editor may be permitted to notice the copious Indices. Ordinarily it is to be feared that labour spent on such work is ill appreciated, too many, as rare Thomas Fuller complained, regarding an index as 'the bag and baggage of a book, of

[1] Publications of the Surtees Society, vol. xl. p. 17.

more use than honour, even to such who, seemingly slighting, secretly use it, if not for need, for speed of what they desire to find.'[1] But he has so constructed these—incorporating the full 'Tables' of Brooks himself wherever prepared by him—as to render any preliminary essay here unnecessary, inasmuch as, well used, they will guide readily the reader of our Worthy to his wealth of fine thought, of priceless insight into the 'mind of the Spirit' and human nature, as well unrenewed as gracious, of definite doctrinal statement, of rich spiritual-mindedness, of tender and yet pungent appeal, of happy allusion, of brilliant, rapid wit, of racily-put, telling anecdote and *asides*, of recondite reading and multifarious lore unexpectedly turned to account, with many a pat, almost sly foot-note, 'You know how to make the application'—in a way hitherto impossible.

With such a 'Cabinet of Jewels'—to appropriate one of his own titles[2]—as these Works present, one can read with a smile the depreciatory estimate of Brooks as of Bunyan, formed by High Church contemporaries, and later. One of these is so characteristic, and serves as so excellent an illustration of the apothegm, that the eye sees what it brings with it, that it must find a place here, especially as it has not before been published: it was come upon by us in an examination of the MSS. of Walker, of the 'Sufferings,' folio, preserved in the Bodleian. This 'character' of Brooks occurs in a letter from Luke Milbourne. It is literally as follows—the name, to start with, being misspelled—'Mr Tho. Brook was another of those 'pleasant preachers' whose sermons would require a man of a very staunch temper to preach them over again without smiling. Abundance of 'fine metaphors' and 'charming similitudes' a man may meet with in his Works, fit only to debase Divinity, or to dress it up in a ffool's Coat; and I'm afraid such jingling Preachers turn'd men from Truth to ffables [rather] than from sin to righteousness. Souls are no more to be taken with chaff than old Birds are. His stile is neither prophetical nor Apostolical, nor were any of ye antient fathers guilty of such Trifling; and *indeed it would be well if all such Preachers were silenced.* A sound Christian, though he be no Critic, loves plain Truth delivered in good words, but always hates jesting in a serious matter.'[3] The italicised sentence reveals the *animus* of these small sarcasms and smaller comparisons with 'antient fathers,'—of whom the writer was evidently as ignorant as he was of the preacher and author

[1] Pisgah-sight of Palestine in 'Necessary Directions for use of the Index' at end.

[2] Works, vol. iii.

[3] From Miscellaneous Papers in Quarto. From these Walker MSS.—which lie unread and uncared, for apparently—we hope to use effectively elsewhere not a few letters, anecdotes, &c., &c. of the Puritan 'Worthies.'

he misjudges. Yet is it almost wholly from such witnesses that too many even now express their opinions on the Writings of the Puritans and Nonconformists; and perchance it must be admitted that the anti-Puritans and High Churchmen have been too much read at second-hand and controversially. In the present instance, it is ludicrous to find one so inane and sand-barren as Milbourne sitting in judgment upon a nature so rich and so much larger than his own; but it is a typical and hence valuable example of how an over-dainty culture may be offended by superficial faults, so as to be stone-blind to the preciousness of the substance of the works which these blemish; it being granted that occasionally Brooks is homely to excess, in common with the greatest divines of his age.

Calamy's summary of the 'character' of Brooks—inadequate though it be—may fitly accompany the preceding:—'He was a very affecting preacher, and useful to many; and tho' he us'd many homely phrases and sometimes too familiar resemblances, which to nice criticks appear ridiculous; yet he did more good to souls than many of the exactest composers; and let the wits of the age pass what censures they please, 'he that winneth souls is wise.'[1]

In characterising Sibbes generally, we selected the epithet universally applied to him, '*heavenly;*' and in like manner, the word '*useful*' is the one word which accurately expresses the position of Brooks among his contemporaries. His slightest 'Epistle' is 'Bread of Life:' his most fugitive 'Sermon' a full cup of 'Living Water;' the very foliage of his exuberant fancies 'Leaves' of the Tree of Life: his one dominating aim to make dead hearts warm with the Life of the Gospel of Him who is Life; his supreme purpose to 'bring near' the very Truth of God. Hence his directness, his urgency, his yearning, his fervour, his fulness of Bible citation, his wistfulness, his intensity, his emotion, and that fine passion of enthusiasm sprung of compassion, and his iteration and forgetfulness,[2] and Pauline accident of choice words or melody of sentence. His desire to be 'useful' to souls, to achieve the holy success of serving Christ, to win a sparkling crown to lay at His feet, breathes and burns from first to last. Everything is subordinated to '*usefulness;*' and while he gathered around him the cultured and the titled—who all but worshipped the 'good old man'—it was his chief rejoicing that, like his Master, 'the common people' heard and read him 'gladly.' In loving association with Sibbes and Sheffield, Baxter and Bunyan, Brinsley and Samuel

[1] Account, vol. ii. p. 27.

[2] This forgetfulness reveals itself in the repeated recurrence of the same anecdotes and sayings and names. Perhaps nothing more shews Brooks' one thought to have been present 'usefulness,' not at all literary fame.

Richardson, his books were well thumbed in the hamlets of his own England, and, in quaint 'Glasgow' editions, among the godly peasantry of Scotland, and gained wide and long-sustained welcome in Germany and Holland, as Brooks gratefully acknowledges repeatedly.[1] But more cannot be needed: and so—in the words of the loving biographer of good Bishop Lake—" I will detain thee no longer, gentle Reader, at this time, from the reading of so useful and precious works—only thus much I will promise thee for thine encouragement before thou begin, that if thou take the pains to go through with attention these . . . . *first*, Thou shalt gain thereby an exact knowledge of the meaning of the text he handles, and of every particular word and phrase in it; *secondly*, Thou shalt meet with a great variety of choice observations, both theological and moral, aptly deduced, and methodically laid down, as thou art like to find anywhere in so few leaves again; *lastly*, If thou be endued, as I hope thou art, with the same spirit of grace and regeneration that the author was, thou shalt find thine affections kindled and stirred up thereby to a real practice of piety and good works, more than by a great many more flourishing discourses than these at first sight seem to be." [2]

May this complete edition of these inestimable Works be used at this 'later day' to cause him, 'being dead, yet to speak' for that dear Lord Jesus he loved and served so well!

ALEXANDER B. GROSART.

LIVERPOOL.

[1] Among our Brooksiana is a Dutch translation of the 'Apples of Gold,' of which the following is the title-page, 'Gouden' Appelen Voor Iongh-Mans ende Ionge-Dochters, Als ook eene Kroone der Heerlykheyt Voor Oude-Mannen ende Oude-Vrowen. Ofte De Geluksaligheyt van by tijts goet te ziyn, ende de Eere van een oudt Discipel te wesen. Klaarlijk en ten vollen outdekt, ende beknooptelijk, ende getrouwelijk toegepast. Middsgaders Der Iongen Tegenworpingen beautwoordt Ende der Ouden Twijsselingen opgelost. Door Thomas Brooks, Prediker des Euangelium tot Margarets New Fish-street-hill binnen London: Uyt het Engelsch Verduytst Door D. Montanus, Dienaar des Goddelijcken Woordts tot Sluys in Vlanderen. Tot Uytrecht. By Johannes Ribbius. 1667. 12mo.' Ribbius dedicates it in highly appreciatory words to a great lady, 'Anna Elisabeth van Reede, van Nederhorst,' &c. Appended are two religious poems in Dutch.

[2] Prefixed to his 'Sermons and Divine Meditations.' 1629. Folio.

CONTENTS.

LONDON'S LAMENTATIONS.

NOTE.

'London's Lamentations,' as it is the largest, so it is perhaps the most remarkable contemporary memorial of the 'Great Fire.' It seems singular that Defoe does not appear to have known it, else his well-known compilation might have been enriched by its vivid and powerful incidental notices of public opinion and feeling during and subsequent to the direful calamity. Reeve's 'Plea for Nineveh'—by Nineveh, London being intended—may be compared with the present work. Royalist and Puritan alike give terrible pictures of the licentiousness and general wickedness of the 'great city.' The title-page will be found below.*

* *LONDON'S*

LAMENTATIONS:

OR,

A serious Discourse concerning that late fiery Dispensation that turned our (once renowned) City into a ruinous Heap. Also the several Lessons that are incumbent upon those whose Houses have escaped the consuming Flames.

By *THOMAS BROOKS, late Preacher of the Word at* S. Margarets *New-Fish-street,* where that Fatal Fire first began that turned *London* into a ruinous Heap.

Una dies interest inter magnam Civitatem & nullam.
There is but the distance of one day between a great City and none, said *Seneca* when a great City was burnt to Ashes.

Come, behold the Works of the Lord, what Desolations he hath made in the Earth. Psal. 46. 8.

LONDON,

Printed for *John Hancock* and *Nathaniel Ponder,* and are to be sold at the first Shop in *Popes-Head-Alley* in *Cornhil,* at the Sign of the *Three Bibles,* or at his Shop in *Bishopsgate-street,* and at the Sign of the *Peacock* in *Chancery-lane.* 1670.

[4to.—G.]

THE EPISTLE DEDICATORY.

To the Right Honourable Sir WILLIAM TURNER, Knight, Lord Mayor of the City of London.[1]

RIGHT HONOURABLE,—It is not my design to blazon your worth, or write a panegyric of your praises. Your brighter name stands not in need of such a shadow as men's applause to make it more renowned in the world. Native worth is more respected than adventitious glory. 'Your own works praise you in the gates,' Prov. xxxi. 31. It is London's honour and happiness, tranquillity and prosperity, to have such a magistrate, that 'bears not the sword of justice in vain,' Rom. xiii. 4, and that hath not brandished the sword of justice in the defence of the friends of Baal, Balaam, or Bacchus. My Lord, had your sword of justice been a sword of protection to desperate swearers, or to cruel oppressors, or to deceitful dealers, or to roaring drunkards, or to cursing monsters, or to gospel despisers, or to Christ contemners, &c., might not London have lain in her ashes to this very day? yea, might not God have rained hell out of heaven upon those parts of the city that were standing monuments of God's mercy, as once he did upon Sodom and Gomorrah? Gen. xix. Woe to that sword that is a devouring sword to the righteous, to the meek, to the upright, and to the peaceable in the land, Ps. xxxv. 19, 20. O happy sword! under which all sorts and ranks of men have worshipped God in peace, and lived in peace, and rested in peace, and traded in peace, and built their habitations in peace, and have grown up in peace. Sir, every man hath sat, under your sword, as under his own vine and fig-tree, in peace. Words are too weak to express how great a mercy this hath been to London, yea, I may say, to England. The ancients set forth all their gods with harps in their hands, the hieroglyphic of peace. The Grecians had the statue of Peace, with Pluto, the god of riches, in her arms. Some of the ancients were wont to paint peace in the form of a woman with a horn of plenty in her hands, viz., all blessings. The orator hit it when he said, *Dulce nomen pacis*, The very name of peace is sweet. No city so happy as that wherein the chief magistrate has been as 'eyes to the

[1] Of the Guild of Merchant Tailors: son of John Turner of Kirk-Leedham in Cleveland, Yorkshire. See Herbert's History of the Companies, ii. 426. This admirable magistrate won the praise of Richard Baxter: Reliquiæ Baxterianæ, *s. n.*—G.

blind, legs to the lame, ears to the deaf, a father to the fatherless, a husband to the widow, a tower to the righteous, and a terror to the wicked,' Job xxxi.

Certainly rulers have no better friends than such as make conscience of their ways; for none can be truly loyal but such as are truly religious. Witness Moses, Joseph, Daniel, and the three children.[1] Sincere Christians are as lambs amongst lions, as sheep amongst wolves, as lilies amongst thorns. They are exposed more to the rage, wrath, and malice of wicked men, by reason of their holy profession, their gracious principles and practices, than any other men in all the world. Now did not God raise up magistrates, and spirit magistrates, to own them, to stand by them, and to defend them in all honest and just ways, how soon would they be devoured and destroyed! Certainly the sword of the magistrate is to be drawn forth for the natural good, and civil good, and moral good, and spiritual good, of all that live soberly and quietly under it. Stobæus[2] tells us of a Persian law, that after the death of their king every man had five days' liberty to do what he pleased, that by beholding the wickedness and disorder of those few days, they might prize government the better all their days after. Certainly had some hot-headed, and little-witted, and fierce-spirited men had but two or three days' liberty to have done what they pleased in this great city during your lordship's mayoralty, they would have made sad work in the midst of us. When a righteous government fails, then (1.) Order fails; (2.) Religion fails; (3.) Trade fails; (4.) Justice fails; (5.) Prosperity fails; (6.) Strength and power fails; (7.) Fame and honour fails; (8.) Wealth and riches fails; (9.) Peace and quiet fails; (10.) All human converse and society fails. To take a righteous government out of the world, is to take the sun out of the firmament, and leave it no more a *κοσμὸς*, a beautiful structure, but a *χαὸς*, a confused heap. In such towns, cities, and kingdoms where righteous government fails, there every man's hand will be quickly engaged against his brother, Gen. xxvi. 12. Oh the sins, the sorrows, the desolations, and destructions that will unavoidably break in like a flood upon such a people!

Public persons should have public spirits; their gifts and goodness should diffuse themselves for the good of the whole. It is a base and ignoble spirit to pity Cataline more than to pity Rome, to pity any particular sort of men more than to pity the whole. It is cruelty to the good to justify the bad; it is wrong to the sheep to animate the wolves; it is danger, if not death, to the lambs not to restrain or chain up the lions; but, Sir, from this ignoble spirit God has delivered you. The ancients were wont to place the statues of their princes by their fountains, intimating that they were, or at least should be, fountains of the public good. Sir, had not you been such a fountain, men would never have been so warm for your continuance. My Lord, the great God hath made you a *κοινὸν ἀγαθὸν*, a public good, a public blessing; and this hath made your name precious, and your govern-

[1] The three things which God minds most, and loves best below heaven, are his truth, his worship, and his people.

[2] Stobæus, serm. xlii. p. 294. [*i.e.*, his Florilegium or Sermones, otherwise Ανθολόγιον.—G.]

ment desirable, and your person honourable in the thoughts, hearts, and eyes of all people.[1] Many—may I not say most?—of the rulers of this world are, as Pliny speaks of the Roman emperors, *Nomine dii, naturâ diaboli*, Monsters, not men; murderers, not magistrates. Such a monster was Saul, who hunted David as a partridge, slew the innocent priests of the Lord, ran to a witch, and who was a man of so narrow a soul that he knew not how to look or live above himself, his own interests and concernments. The great care of every magistrate should be to promote the public interest more than their own, as you may see by comparing the scriptures in the margin together.[2] It was Cæsar's high commendation, that he never had himself after the world had him for a governor; his mind was so set on the public, that he forgot his own private affairs. The stars have their brightness, not for themselves, but for the use of others. The application is easy.

My Lord, several philosophers have made excellent and elegant orations in the praise of justice. They say that all virtues are comprehended in the distribution of justice.[3] Justice, saith Aristotle, is a synopsis and epitome of all virtues. All I shall say is this, the world is a ring, and justice is the diamond in that ring; the world is a body, and justice is the soul of that body. It is well known that the constitution of a man's body is best known by his pulse: if it stir not at all, then we know he is dead; if it stir violently, then we know him to be in a fever; if it keep an equal stroke, then we know he is sound, well, and whole. So the estate and constitution of a city, kingdom, or commonweal is best known by the manner of executing justice therein; for justice is the pulse of a city, kingdom, or commonweal. If justice be violent, then the city, kingdom, or commonweal is in a fever, in a very bad estate; if it stir not at all, then the city, kingdom, or commonwealth is dead; but if it hath an equal stroke, if it be justly and duly administered, then the city, kingdom, or commonweal is in a good, a safe, and a sound condition. When Vespasian asked Apollonius what was the cause of Nero's ruin, he answered, that Nero could tune the harp well, but in government he did always wind up the strings too high or let them down too low. Extremes in government are the ready way to ruin all. The Romans had their rods for lesser faults, and their axe for capital crimes. Extreme right often proves extreme wrong. He that will always go to the utmost of what the law allows, will too too often do more than the law requires. A rigid severity often mars all. Equity is still to be preferred before extremity. To inflict great penalties and heavy censures for light offences, this

[1] There is a great truth in that old maxim, *Magistratus virum indicat.* In my epistle to my treatise called 'A Cabinet of Choice Jewels,' the ingenious reader may find six arguments to encourage magistrates to be men of public spirits. [Vol. iii. pp. 235, *seq.*—G.]

[2] Exod. xxxii. 10, 11, 32; Neh. v. 6–19; Ps. cxxxvii. 5, 6; Acts xiii. 36.

[3] Carneades, Aristotle, Socrates, &c. The Roman orator hath long since observed, that the force of justice is such, and so great, that even thieves and robbers, both by sea and land, who live upon injustice and rapine, yet cannot live upon their trade without some practice of it among themselves. Cleobulus, one of the seven sages, was wont to say that mediocrity was without compare. The very heathen could set so much divine glory in the face of a magistrate, that he styled him ἔμψυχος εἰκων θεοῦ, The living image of the ever-living God. [Cf. Plato: Tim. 92 C.—G.]

is to kill a fly upon a man's forehead with a beetle.[1] The great God hath put his own name upon magistrates: Ps. lxxxii. 6, 'I said that ye are gods.' Yet it must be granted that you are gods in a smaller letter: mortal gods—gods that must die like men. All the sons of *Ish* are sons of Adam. Magistrates must do justice impartially; for as they are called gods, so in this they must be like to God, who is no accepter of persons, Deut. i. 17; Lev. xix. 15. He accepts not of the rich man because of his robes, neither doth he reject the poor man because of his rags. The magistrates' eyes are to be always upon causes, and not upon persons. Both the statues of the Theban judges and the statues of the Egyptian judges were made without hands and without eyes, to intimate to us that, as judges should have no hands to receive bribes, so they should have no eyes to see a friend from a foe, or a brother from a stranger, in judgment.[2] And it was the oath of the heathen judges, as the orator relates, *Audiam accusatorem et reum sine affectibus, et personarum respectione:* I will hear the plaintiff and the defendant with an equal mind, without affection and respect of persons. In the twelfth Novel of Justinian you may read of an oath imposed upon judges and justices against inclining or addicting themselves to either party; yea, they put themselves under a deep and bitter execration and curse in case of partiality, imploring God in such language as this: 'Let me have my part with Judas, and let the leprosy of Gehazi cleave to me, and the trembling of Cain come upon me, and whatsoever else may astonish and dismay a man, if I am partial in the administration of justice.' The poet in the Greek epigram taught the silver axe of justice that was carried before the Roman magistrates to proclaim, 'If thou be an offender, let not the silver flatter thee; if an innocent, let not the axe affright thee.' The Athenian judges judged in the night, when the faces of men could not be seen, that so they might be impartial in judgment. My Lord, your impartiality in the administration of justice in that high orb wherein divine providence hath placed you, is one of those great things that hath made you high and honourable in the eyes and hearts of all that are true lovers of impartial justice. Some writers say, that some waters in Macedonia, being drunk by black sheep, change their fleece into white. Nothing but the pure and impartial administration of justice and judgment can transform black-mouthed, black-handed, and black-hearted men into white. There is nothing that sweetens, satisfies, and silences all sorts of men like the administration of impartial justice. The want of this brought desolation upon Jerusalem and the whole land of Jewry, Isa. i. 23, 24, and upon many other flourishing kingdoms and countries, as all know that have but read anything of Scripture or history. St Austin plainly denies that ever the Roman polity could be called properly a commonwealth, upon this ground, that *Ubi non est justitia, non est republica.*

[1] Peter Lombard. Cf. Sibbes, vol. i. 101.—G.

[2] Magistrates are, as Nazianzen expresses it, pictures drawn of God. Every magistrate, though in never so low a place, bears the image of God. A penny bears the image of the prince as well as a shilling. Magistrates are not immortal deities, neither have they everlasting godheads. Those gods, as they had a beginning, so they must have an end. *Quicquid oritur, moritur.* There is a 'Mene, mene' on them; their days are numbered their time is computed. Hercules his pillar stands in their way. *Non datur ultra.*

He calls commonwealths without justice but *magna latrocinia;* or in Lipsius his language, *congeries, confusio, turba.*[1] It is but an abuse of the word *respublica*—commonwealth—where the public good is not consulted by an impartial justice and equity; it is but a confused heap, a rout of men; or if we will call it so at present, it will not be so long without impartial justice, partly because injustice and oppression makes the multitude tumultuous, and fills the people's heads with dangerous designs, as you may see by comparing the scriptures in the margin together;[2] and partly because it lays a nation open and obnoxious to the wrath and vengeance of God, as might easily be made good by scores of scriptures. Impartial justice is the best establishment of kingdoms and commonwealths. 'The king by judgment establisheth the land,' Prov. xxix. 4: see Num. xxv. 11; 2 Sam. xxi. 14. It is the best security against desolating judgments. 'Run ye through the streets of Jerusalem, and seek in the broad places thereof, if ye can find a man, if there be any that executeth judgment, and I will pardon it,' Jer. v. 1.

My Lord, as it is the honour of a magistrate to do justice impartially, so it is the honour and glory of a magistrate to do justice speedily: Jer. xxviii. 12, 'O house of David, thus saith the Lord, Execute judgment in the morning, and deliver him that is spoiled out of the hand of the oppressor, lest my fury go out like fire, and burn that none can quench it, because of the evil of your doings.'[3] After examination, execution is to be done with expedition. When men cry out for Justice, Justice, magistrates must not cry out, *Cras, Cras*—to-morrow, to-morrow. Magistrates must do justice in the morning. Neither noon-justice, nor afternoon-justice, nor evening-justice, nor night-justice is so acceptable to God, or so honourable to magistrates, or so advantageous to the people, as morning-justice is. To delay justice is worse sometimes than to deny justice. It is a very dangerous thing for magistrates to be as long a-bringing forth their verdicts as the elephant her young. Delay of justice makes many more irreconcilable; it makes many men go up and down this world with heavy hearts, empty purses, and threadbare coats. I have read of a famous passage of Theodoric, king of the Romans, who, when a widow came to him with a sad complaint, that she had a suit depending in the court three years, which might have been ended in a few days; the king demands of her the judges' names: she tells him; he sends a special command to them to give all the speedy despatch that was possible to the widow's cause, which they did; and in two days determined it to the widow's liking. This being done, the king calls for the judges, and they, supposing that they should have both applause and reward for their expedition, hastened to him full of joy; but after the king had propounded several things to them about their former delays, he commanded both their heads to be struck off, because they had spun out that cause to a three years' length, which two days would have ended. Here was royal justice, and speedy justice indeed. Ps. ci. 8,

[1] August. de Civitate Dei, lib. x. cap. 21, &c.; lib. iv. cap. 4. Lipsius de Constan., lib. ii. cap. 13.

[2] 1 Kings xii.; 1 Sam. viii. 3.

[3] God is very speedy and swift in the execution of justice, Joel iii. 4; Gen. xix.; Num. xvi.; Ezra vii. 20. In this as in other things it becomes magistrates to be like to God.

'I will early destroy all the wicked of the land;' *summo mane*, I will do morning-justice. *Festinanter*, so Genebrad, 'I will hastily do it.'[1] Justice should be on the wing; delays are very dangerous and injurious: Prov. xiii. 12, 'Hope deferred maketh the heart sick.' The Hebrew word *Memushshacah*, that is here rendered 'deferred,' is from *Mashach*, that signifies 'to draw out at length.' Men are short-breathed and short-spirited, and hope's hours are full of eternity, and when their hopes are drawn out at length, this makes their hearts sick; and, ah! what a world of such sick souls lies languishing at hope's hospital all the world over. Hope in the text is put for the good things hoped for. Now when the good things men hope for, be it justice or a quick despatch, &c., are deferred and delayed, this makes the poor client sick at heart. A lingering hope always breeds in the heart a lingering consumption; the harder travail hope hath, and the more strongly it labours to bring forth, and yet is deferred and delayed, the more deadly sick the client grows.[2] The speedy execution of justice is the very life and soul of justice: Amos v. 24, 'But let judgment run down as waters, and righteousness as a mighty stream.' The Hebrew word *Veïiggal*, that is here rendered 'run down,' is from *Galal*, that signifies to 'roll down freely, plentifully, vigorously, constantly, speedily,' as the great billows of the sea, or as waves roll speedily over the rocks. Judgment and righteousness, like a mighty stream, should bear down all before it. *Fiat justitia, ruat orbis*—Let justice be done, whatever come of it: Deut. xvi. 20, 'That which is altogether just shalt thou follow,' or rather, as the Hebrew hath it, צדק צדק, *Tsedek*, *Tsedek*, Justice, justice shalt thou follow—that is, all manner of justice thou shalt follow, and nothing but justice shalt thou follow, and thou shalt follow justice sincerely, out of love to justice; and thou shalt follow justice exactly, without turning to the right hand or the left; and thou shalt follow justice resolutely, in spite of the world, the flesh, and the devil; and thou shalt follow justice speedily, without delays or excuses. A magistrate that has the sword of justice in his hand must never plead, 'There is a lion in the way.' My Lord, this will be your honour while you live, and your comfort when you come to die, that whilst the sword was in your hand, you did justice speedily as well as impartially. You did justice in the morning, and justice at noon, and justice in the afternoon, and justice at night. What has been your whole mayoralty but one continued day of justice? Who can sum up the many thousand causes that you have heard and determined, and the many thousand differences that you have sweetly and friendly composed and ended? If the lawyers please but to speak out, they must ingenuously confess that your Lordship has eased them of a great deal of work.

My Lord, as it is the honour and glory of a magistrate to do justice speedily, so it is the honour and glory of a magistrate to do justice resolutely, courageously, valiantly. It is observable that

[1] More accurately Gilbert Genebrardus, whose Commentary on the Psalms (1577) has passed through numerous editions.—G.

[2] Julius Cæsar's quick despatch is noted in three words: *Veni, vidi, vici*—I came, I saw, I overcame.

as soon as ever Joshua came into the office of magistracy, God charges him no less than three times, in a breath as it were, to be very courageous, Josh. i. 6, 7, 9. A magistrate that is timorous will quickly be treacherous. A magistrate that is fearful can never be faithful. Solomon's throne was supported with lions, to shew that magistrates should be men of mettle and courage. The Athenian judges sat in Mars' street, Acts xvii. 22, to shew that they had martial hearts, and that they were men of courage and mettle. The Grecians placed justice betwixt Leo and Libra, to signify that as there must be indifferency in determining, so there ought to be courage in executing. Where there is courage without knowledge, there the eye of justice is blind; and where there is knowledge without courage, there the sword of justice is blunt. A magistrate's heart, a judge's heart and his robes must be both dyed in grain, else the colour of the one and the courage of the other will quickly fade. Why should not the standard be of steel, and the chief posts of the house be heart of oak? It hath been long since said of Cato, Fabricius, and Aristides, that it was as easy to remove the sun out of the firmament as to remove them from justice and equity; they were men of such courageous and magnanimous spirits for justice and righteousness. No scarlet robe doth so well become a magistrate as holy courage and stoutness doth. As bodily physicians, so state physicians should have an eagle's eye, a lady's hand, and a lion's heart. Cowardly and timorous magistrates will never set up monuments of their victories over sin and profaneness. It is very sad when we may say of our magistrates, as the heathen did of magistrates in his time, they were very good, *si audeant quæ sentiunt*, if they durst but do what they ought to do.[1] My Lord, had not the Lord of lords put a great spirit of courage, boldness, and resolution upon you, you had never been able to have managed your government as you have done, counting the various winds that have blown upon you, and the several difficulties and discouragements that have risen up before you, Rev. i. 5, 6, and xvii. 14.

My Lord, once more give me leave to say, that in a magistrate justice and mercy, justice and clemency ought to go hand in hand: Prov. xx. 28, 'Mercy and truth preserve the king, and his throne is upholden by mercy.'[2] All justice will not preserve the king, nor all mercy will not preserve the king; there must be a mixture both of justice and mercy to preserve the king, and to uphold his throne; and to shew that mercy is more requisite than justice, the word mercy is doubled in the text. Justice without mercy turns into rigour, and so becomes hateful. Mercy without justice turns into fond pity, and so becomes contemptible.[3] Look, as the rod of Aaron and the pot of manna were by God's own command laid up in the same ark; so must mercy and justice be preserved entire in the bosom of the same magistrate. Mercy and justice, mildness and righteousness,

[1] Cic. de Mil. [2] Truth in Scripture is frequently put for justice.

[3] King John thought to strengthen himself by gathering a great deal of money together; but neglecting the exercise of mercy and justice, clemency and lenity, he lost his people's affections, and so, after many endless turmoils, he came to an unhappy end.

lenity and fidelity are a safer and a stronger guard to princes and people than rich mines, munitions of rocks, mighty armies, powerful navies, or any warlike preparations. It is very observable that Christ is called but once the 'Lion of the tribe of Judah' in the book of the Revelation, and that is in chap. v. 5; but he is called a Lamb no less than nine-and-twenty times in that book. And what is this but to shew us the transcendent mercy, clemency, lenity, mildness, and sweetness that is in Jesus Christ, and to shew that he is infinitely more inclined to the exercise of mercy than he is to the exercise of justice. It is true, magistrates should be lions in the execution of justice, and it is as true that they should be lambs in the exercise of mercy and clemency, mildness and sweetness; and the more ready and inclinable they are to the exercise of mercy, where mercy is to be shewed, the more like to Christ the Lamb they are. God is slow to anger, he abounds in pity, though he be great in power, Ps. lxviii. 18, and ciii. 13, 14; Hosea xi. 8. Seneca hath long since observed, that the custom of anointing kings was to shew that kings, above all other men, should be men of the greatest sweetness and mildness, their anointing being a sign of that kingly sweetness and mildness that should be in them. Theodosius the emperor, by his loveliness and clemency, gained many kingdoms.[1] The Goths, after the death of their own king, beholding his temperance, patience, and justice mixed with mercy and clemency, gave themselves up to his government. When Cicero would claw Cæsar, he tells him that his valour and victories were common with the rest of his soldiers, but his clemency and goodness were wholly his own. Nero's speech hath great praise, who in the beginning of his reign, when he was to subscribe to the death of any condemned person, would say, *Utinam nescirem literas*, I wish I did not know how to write. I know there are a thousand thousand cases wherein severity is to be used; but yet I must say that it is much safer to account for mercy than for cruelty; it is best that the sword of justice should be always furbished with the oil of mercy. My Lord, in the management of your government you have been so assisted and helped from on high, that stoutness and mildness, justice and mercy, justice and clemency, hath like a silver thread run through all your mayoralty, and by this means you have very signally served the interest of the crown, the interest of the city, the interest of the nation, and that which is more than all the rest, the interest of your own soul. Rigour breeds rebellion. Rehoboam by his severity, by his cruelty, lost ten tribes in one day, 1 Kings xii. 16.

My Lord, your prudence, justice, and moderation, your burning zeal against the horrid, hideous, heady vices of this day; your punishing of oaths, drunkenness, and the false balance; your singular sobriety and temperance in the midst of all your high entertainments; your fidelity and activity, your eminent self-denial in respect of your perquisites; your unwearied endeavours to see London raised out of its ruins, and to see the top-stone laid; your great readiness and willingness to spend and be spent for the public good: these are the things that have made your name as a precious ointment, and

[1] *Vide* Aug. de civit. Dei, lib. v. cap. 26. Orosius, lib. vii. cap. 34.

that have erected for you a noble living monument in the breasts and hearts of all sober, serious Christians: these are the things that have made you the darling of the people.[1] Let all succeeding lord mayors but manage their own persons, families, and government as you have done, by divine assistance, and without a peradventure they will have a proportionable interest in the hearts and affections of the people. For, my Lord, it is not barely the having of a sword of justice, a sword of power, but the well management of that sword, that makes most for the interest both of prince and people, and that gives the magistrate a standing interest in the hearts and affections of the people. My Lord, the generality of people never concern themselves about the particular persuasions of this or that magistrate in the matters of religion, their eyes are upon their examples, and upon the management of their trust and power for public good; and they that do them most good shall be sure to have most of their hearts and voices, let their private opinions in the matters of religion be what they will.

My Lord, I have not so learned Christ as to give flattering titles to men, Job xxxii. 22. The little that I have written I have written in the plainness and singleness of my heart, and for your lordship's comfort and encouragement in all well-doing, and to provoke all others that shall succeed in your chair to write after that fair copy that you have set them, which will be their honour, London's happiness, and England's interest. Plutarch said of Demosthenes, that he was excellent at praising the worthy acts of his ancestors, but not so at imitating them. The Lord grant that this may never be made good of any that shall succeed your lordship! Carus the emperor's motto was, *Bonus dux, bonus comes*, A good leader makes a good follower. The complaint is ancient in Seneca, that commonly men live not *ad rationem*, but *ad similitudinem.*[2] *Præcepta docent, exempla movent*, Precepts may instruct, but examples do persuade. Stories speak of some that could not sleep when they thought of the trophies of other worthies that went before them. The highest examples are very quickening and provoking. Oh that by all that shall succeed your lordship in the chair, we may yet behold our city rising more and more out of its ashes in greater splendour and glory than ever yet our eyes have seen it, that all sober citizens may have eminent cause to call them the repairers of the breaches and restorers of our city to dwell in![3] Concerning Jerusalem burned and laid waste by the Assyrians, Daniel foretold that the streets and the walls thereof should be rebuilded, even in troublesome times, Dan. ix. 25. Though the Assyrians have laid our Jerusalem waste, yet even to a wonder how have the buildings been carried on this last year!

My Lord, the following treatise, which I humbly dedicate to your lordship, has been drawn up some years. The reasons why it has been buried so long in oblivion are not here to be inserted. The discourse is sober, and of great importance to all that have been burnt

[1] A self-seeking magistrate is one of the worst of plagues and judgments that can befall a people; he is a gangrene in the head, which brings both a more speedy and a more certain ruin than if it were in some inferior and less noble part of the body.

[2] Seneca de vita beata, cap. 1.

[3] Isa. lviii. 12, and lxi. 4; Amos ix. 14; Ezek. xxxvi. 33–36, 38.

up, and to all whose houses have escaped the furious flames. Whilst the remembrance of London's flames are kept alive in the thoughts and hearts of men, this treatise will be of use in the world. My Lord, I do not dedicate this tractate to your lordship as if it stood in need of your honour's patronage; I judge it to be of age both to plead for itself and to defend itself against all gainsayers. *Veritas vincit, veritas stat in aperto campo.*[1] Zeno, Socrates, Anaxarchus, &c., sealed the lean and barren truths of philosophy with the expense of their dearest blood, as you may see in the heathen martyrology. Oh, how much more should we be ready to seal all divine truths with our dearest blood, when God shall call us forth to such a service! My Lord, I humbly lay this treatise at your lordship's foot, to testify that love and honour that I have in my heart for you, both upon the account of that intrinsecal worth that is in you, and upon the account of the many good things and great things that have been done by you, and publicly to testify my acknowledgment of your lordship's undeserved favours towards me. My Lord, of right this treatise should have been in your hands several months since, and in that it was not it is wholly from others and not from me. If your lordship please but to favour the author so far as to read it once over for his sake, he doubts not but that your lordship will oftener read it over for your own soul's sake, and for eternity's sake, and for London's sake also. My Lord, by reason of my being remote from the city several weeks, I have had the advantage but of reading and correcting two or three sheets, and therefore must beg your lordship's pardon as to all the neglects and escapes of the press. A second impression may set all right and straight.

My Lord, that to your dying day you may be famous in your generation, and that your precious and immortal soul may be richly adorned with all saving gifts and graces, and that you may daily enjoy a clear, close, high, and standing communion with God, and that you may be filled with all the fruits of righteousness and holiness, and that your soul may be bound up in the bundle of life, and crowned with the highest glory in the other world, in the free, full, constant, and uninterrupted enjoyment of that God who is the heaven of heaven and the glory of glory, is, and by divine assistance shall be, the earnest prayers of him who is your honour's in all humble and due observance,

THOMAS BROOKS.

[1] My Lord, some sacrifice their labours to great Mæcenases, that they may be atoned to shield them from potent antagonists; but these sermons, which here I present to your honour's perusal, being only the blessed truths of God, I hope they need no arm but his to defend them.

THE FIERY JESUIT'S TEMPER AND BEHAVIOUR.

I fain would be informed by you what ails
These foxes to wear firebrands in their tails.
What! did you teach these cubs the world to burn,
Or to embottle London in its urn?
Are Huguenots as rank Philistines grown
With you, as dwelt in Gath or Askelon?
Bold wretches! must your fire thus antedate
The general doom, and give the world its fate?
Must hell's edict to blend this globe with fire
Be done at your grave nods when you require?

LONDON'S LAMENTATIONS ON THE LATE FIERY DISPENSATION.

Who gave Jacob to the spoil, and Israel to the robbers? did not I the Lord? he against whom we have sinned; for they would not walk in his ways, neither were they obedient to his law.

Therefore he hath poured upon him the fury of his anger, and the strength of battle: and it hath set him on fire round about, yet he knew not; and it burned him, yet he laid it not to heart.—Isa. XLII. 24, 25.

The Lord in this chapter, by the prophet Isaiah, doth foretell heavy things against the people, and, by the way, marks the Lord's dealings. He ever gives warnings before he sends any plagues. He lightens before he thunders, that the people might not say, they did not hear of it, and that the wicked might be the more inexcusable, and that the godly might make an ark to save themselves in. These words contain in them five several things. (1.) The author of this destruction or judgment. (2.) The causes of it. (3.) The judgment itself. (4.) Who they were on whom this judgment was inflicted. (5.) The effects of it. Now by divine permission I will open these words in order to you.

1. For the first, *The author of it.* Now this is laid down by question and answer: 'Who gave Jacob to the spoil, and Israel to the robbers?' There is the question. 'Did not I the Lord?' There is the answer. God is the author of all the plagues and judgments that befall a nation.

2. Secondly, *The causes why the Lord did this to a people that he had chosen to be a special people unto himself;* to a people upon whom he had set his love; to a people that he had owned for his portion, and that he had formerly kept as the apple of his eye, and carried as upon eagles' wings, Deut. vii. 5, 8, and xxxii. 10–12. Now the causes are set down, first, more generally, in these words, 'Because they have sinned against the Lord;' secondly, more particularly, in these words, 'For they would not walk in his ways, neither were they obedient to his law.'

3. The third thing observable in the words is, *the dreadful judgments themselves* that God inflicted upon his sinful people, his sinning people; and these you have in ver. 25.

'Therefore he hath poured upon him the fury of his anger:' not only his anger, but the fury of his anger, to shew the greatness of it, the extremity of it. Mark, he doth not say that God did drop down his anger, but he poured down his anger and indignation. This phrase, 'he poured out,' is an allusion to the clouds pouring down of water violently all at once, in an instant, as they do many times in the Levant seas, in Egypt, at the Indies, and in several other parts of the world; as they did in the deluge, when the windows of heaven were broke open, Gen. vi. 11. Now, by this similitude, the Lord shews the dreadfulness, the grievousness, the suddenness, and the vehemency of the judgments that were fallen upon them.

'And the strength of battle.' The Lord appears in arms against them in the greatness and fierceness of his wrath; he sent in a very powerful enemy upon them, that with fire and sword overran them and their country, and destroyed them on every side, as you may see by comparing 2 Kings xxiii. 33, *seq.*, with the 24th and 25th chapters following.

'And hath set him on fire round about.' That is, say some, all the countries, cities, and towns round about Jerusalem were set on fire.

'Yet he knew not.' Though God had burnt them up on every hand, yet they took no notice of it, they regarded it not, they were not at all affected with the fiery dispensations of God.[1] Oh the dulness, the insensibleness, the sottishness of the Jews under the most awakening and amazing judgments of God! 'And it burned him.' This some apply to the city of Jerusalem itself. God did not only fire the cities and towns round about Jerusalem, but he also set Jerusalem itself into a flame. Jerusalem, which was 'beautiful for situation, the joy of the whole earth,' the paradise and wonder of the world, is turned into ashes. 'Yet he laid it not to heart,' or upon his heart, as the original runs. Oh the monstrous stupidity, insensibleness, and blockishness of this people! Though God had brought them low, though their crown was fallen from their head, though their glorious city was turned into ashes, and though they were almost destroyed by many smarting miseries and dreadful calamities, yet they were not affected with the stupendous judgments of God, they were not awakened by all the flames that God had kindled about their ears, they did not lay the judgments of God to heart, nor they would not lay the judgments of God upon their hearts.

4. The fourth thing observable in the words is, *the persons, the people that were spoiled, destroyed, and consumed by fire;* and they were Jacob and Israel. 'Who gave Jacob for a spoil, and Israel to the robbers?' They were a praying people, a professing people, a fasting people, a peculiar people, a privileged people; and yet for their

[1] Diodorus Siculus writes, that in Ethiopia there is such a sottish insensible people, that if you cut them with a drawn sword, or slay their wives and children before their faces, they are not at all affected with it, nor moved at it. Such brutes were these Jews.

sins they became a destroyed people, a consumed people, a ruined people, Isa. lviii. 2; Zech. vii. 5; Exod. xix. 5.

5. The fifth thing observable in the words is, *the little effect the judgments of God had upon them.* Now they were under such monstrous stupidity that they were not [at] all awakened nor affected with the judgments of God; they regarded them not, they laid them not to heart. And as stupid and senseless were they when Titus Vespasian had laid their city desolate by fire and sword,[1] and sold thirty of them for one piece of silver, as Josephus and other historians tell us. O sirs, since their crucifying of the Lord of glory, they have never laid their finger upon the right sore; to this very day they won't acknowledge their sin in crucifying of the Lord of glory. They confess they have sinned more than ever, and therefore it is that God hath more sorely afflicted them than ever; but their cruelty to Christ, their crucifying of Christ, which ushered in the total ruin of their city and country, they cannot be brought to acknowledge to this very day, though the Lord hath burnt them up on every hand, and hath scattered them as dung all over the earth to this very day. A learned writer tells us that they call Christ *Bar-chozab*, the Son of a Lie, a Bastard, and his Gospel *Aven Gilaion*, the Volume of Lies, or the Volume of Iniquity, and us Christians *Goiim*, that is, Gentiles, Edomites. When they salute a Christian, they call him *Shed*, that is, Devil.[2] They hate all Christians, but none so much as those that are converted from Judaism to Christianity, and all this after so great a burning and desolation that the Lord has made in the midst of them. It is true the length of those heavy judgments under which they groan to this very day hath often puzzled the intellectuals of their Rabbis, and hath many times put them to a stand, and sometimes to break out into a kind of confession, that surely their judgments could not last so long, but for crucifying of one that was more than a man. There was one Rabbi Samuel, who, six hundred years since, wrote a tract in form of an epistle to Rabbi Isaac, master of the synagogue of the Jews, wherein he doth excellently discuss the cause of their long captivity and extreme misery. And after that he had proved it was inflicted for some grievous sin, he sheweth that sin to be the same which Amos speaks of, Amos ii. 6, 'For three transgressions of Israel, and for four, I will not turn away the punishment thereof, because they sold the righteous for silver.' The selling of Joseph he makes the first sin; the worshipping of the calf in Horeb, the second sin; the abusing and killing of God's prophets, the third sin; and the selling of Jesus Christ, the fourth sin. For the first they served four hundred years in Egypt, for the second they wandered forty years in the wilderness, for the third they were captives seventy years in Babylon, and for the fourth they are held in pitiful captivity even till this day. It is certain that the body of that people are under woeful blindness and hardness to this very day. And thus much for the opening of the words.

[1] By Titus Vespasian their land became a stage of blood and of all kind of barbarisms, and now their so renowned city, their temple and *sanctum sanctorum*, so famed all the world over, was turned into ashes and laid level to the ground.

[2] Buxtorf. Synag. Judaica, cap. 5 and cap 36.

The 25th verse is the scripture that I do intend to speak something to, as the Lord shall assist. Now the proposition which I only intend to insist upon is this, viz:—

That God is the author or efficient cause of all the great calamities and dreadful judgments that are inflicted upon cities and countries, and in particular, of that of fire.

Now, that God is the author or efficient cause of all the great calamities and dreadful judgments that are inflicted upon cities and countries, will evidently appear to every man's understanding, that will but take the pains to read over the 26th chapter of Leviticus, and the 28th chapter of Deuteronomy, with that 14th of Ezekiel, from ver. 13 to ver. 22.

That God is the author or efficient cause of this dreadful judgment of fire that is at any time inflicted upon cities and countries, will sufficiently appear in these following scriptures: Amos iii. 6, 'Shall a trumpet be blown in the city, and the people not be afraid? shall there be evil in the city, and the Lord hath not done it?' This is to be understood of the evil of punishment, and not of the evil of sin. Amos iv. 11, 'I have overthrown some of you, as God overthrew Sodom and Gomorrah, and ye were as a firebrand plucked out of the burnings: yet have ye not returned unto me, saith the Lord.' Here 'I' is emphatical and exclusive, as if he should say, 'I, and I alone.' Amos i. 14, 'But I will kindle a fire in the wall of Rabbah,'—that is, in the metropolis or chief city of the Ammonites,—'and it shall devour the palaces thereof.' Rabbah, their head city, was a cruel, bloody, covetous, and ambitious city, ver. 13; and therefore, rather than it should escape divine vengeance, God will kindle a fire in the wall of it, and burn it with his own hands. Ezek. xx. 47, 'And say to the forest of the south,'—that is, to Jerusalem, that did lie southwards from Chaldæa—'Hear the word of the Lord; Thus saith the Lord God, Behold, I will kindle a fire in thee, and it shall devour every green tree in thee, and every dry tree: the flaming flames shall not be quenched, and all fuel from the south to the north shall be burnt therein:' ver. 48,[1] 'And all flesh shall see that I the Lord have kindled it: it shall not be quenched.' Men shall see that it was God that kindled the fire, and not man, and therefore it was beyond man's skill or power to quench it, or to overmaster it. Jer. vii. 20, 'Therefore thus saith the Lord God, Behold, mine anger and my fury shall be poured out upon this place, upon man, and upon beast, and upon the trees of the field, and upon the fruit of the ground; and it shall burn, and shall not be quenched.' The point being thus proved; for the further opening of it, premise with me these things:—

(1.) First, *That great afflictions, dreadful judgments, are likened unto fire in the blessed Scriptures:* Ps. lxvi. 12, 'We went through fire and water:' Jer. iv. 4, 'Circumcise yourselves to the Lord, and take away the foreskins of your heart, ye men of Judah and inhabitants of Jerusalem; lest my fury come forth like fire, and burn that none can quench it, because of the evil of your doings:' Jer. xxi. 12, 'O house of David, thus saith the Lord, Execute judgment in the morning, and deliver him that is spoiled out of the hand of the

[1] You will find this scripture fully opened in the following discourse.

oppressor, lest my fury go out like fire, and burn that none can quench it, because of the evil of your doings:' Lam. ii. 3, 4, 'He hath cut off in his anger all the horn of Israel: he hath drawn back his right hand from before the enemy, and burned against Jacob like a flaming fire, which devoureth round about: he hath bent his bow like an enemy: he stood with his right hand as an adversary, and slew all that was pleasant to the eye in the tabernacle of the daughter of Zion: he poured out his fury like fire:' Ezek. xv. 7, 'And I will set my face against them; they shall go out from one fire, and another fire shall devour them: and ye shall know that I am the Lord, when I set my face against them:' Ezek. xxii. 20-22, 'As they gather silver, and brass, and iron, and lead, and tin, into the midst of the furnace, to blow the fire upon it, to melt it; so will I gather you in mine anger and in my fury, and I will leave you there, and melt you: yea, I will gather you, and blow upon you in the fire of my wrath, and ye shall be melted in the midst thereof: as silver is melted in the midst of the furnace, so shall ye be melted in the midst thereof; and ye shall know that I the Lord have poured out my fury upon you.' Thus you see that great afflictions, great judgments, are likened unto fire.

Quest. But in what respects are great afflictions, great judgments, like unto fire?

Ans. In these eight respects they are like unto fire:—

[1.] First, *Fire is very dreadful and terrible to men's thoughts, spirits, and apprehensions.* How dreadful was the fire of Sodom, and the fire of London, to all that were near it, or spectators of it! It is observable that some are set out in the blessed Scriptures as monuments of most terrible and dreadful vengeance, whom the kings of Babylon roasted in the fire; of them, it is said, shall be taken up a curse, Jer. xxix. 21, 22. When any imprecated sore vengeance from the Lord upon any one, it is said, 'The Lord make thee like Ahab and Zedekiah, whom the kings of Babylon roasted in the fire.' It is very dreadful and terrible for a man to have the least member of his body frying in the fire; but how terrible and dreadful must it be for a man's whole body to be roasted in the fire! so are the judgments of the Lord very terrible and dreadful to the children of men. 'My flesh trembleth for fear of thee; and I am afraid of thy judgments,' Ps. cxix. 120. Hab. iii. 16, 'When I heard, my belly trembled; my lips quivered at the voice: rottenness entered into my bones, and I trembled in myself, that I might rest in the day of trouble.' But,

[2.] Secondly, *Fire is very painful and tormenting*—in which respects hell-torments are compared to fire—so are great afflictions and judgments; they are very painful and tormenting, they put a land into sore travail. Next to the pangs of conscience, and the pangs of hell, there are none to those pangs that are bred and fed by terrible judgments, Isa. xxvi. 17, 18. But,

[3.] Thirdly, *Fire is of a discovering nature;* it enlightens men's eyes to see those things that they did not see before; so do the terrible judgments of God enlighten men's minds and understandings sometimes to know the Lord, Rev. xv. 4; Ezek. xxi. 3-7. Hence it is that, after judgments threatened, God doth so often tell them that they shall know the Lord. Sometimes God, by his judgments, enlightens men's minds to see such an evil in sin that they never saw before, and to see such a vanity, mutability, impotency, and uncertainty in the creature that they never saw before; and to see such a need of free-grace, of rich mercy, and of infinite favour and goodness, that they never saw before; and to see such majesty and terribleness in God that they never saw before, Ps. lxvi. 3, 5. Job xxxvii. 22, 'With God is terrible majesty.' But,

[4.] Fourthly, *Fire is probatory and refining*, and so are the judgments of God; they will try what metal men are made of; they will try whether men are sound and sincere, or hypocritical and hollow; whether men are real Christians or nominal Christians; whether they are throughout Christians or almost Christians; whether their graces are true or counterfeit, and whether they have much, or but a little, grace, Isa. i. 25; Mal. iii. 1–3; Acts xxvi. 28, 29. Isa. xxxi. 9, 'The Lord's fire is in Zion, and his furnace in Jerusalem:' Zech. xiii. 9, 'And I will bring the third part through the fire, and will refine them as silver is refined, and will try them as gold is tried:' 1 Pet. iv. 12, 'Beloved, think it not strange concerning the fiery trial which is to try you.' Stars shine brightest in the darkest night. Torches are the better for beating. Grapes come not to the proof till they come to the press. Spices smell sweetest when pounded. Young trees root the faster for shaking. Vines are the better for bleeding. Gold looks the brighter for scouring; and juniper smells sweetest in the fire. The application is easy. But,

[5.] Fifthly, *Fire is of a consuming and devouring nature*, as we have lately found by woeful experience: Ps. xviii. 8, 'There went out a smoke out of his nostrils, and fire out of his mouth devoured:' Jer. xv. 14, 'A fire is kindled in my anger, which shall burn upon you:' Ezek. xxii. 31, 'Therefore have I poured out my indignation upon them; I have consumed them with the fire of my wrath;' Isa. lxvi. 15, 16; Ps. xxi. 9; Jer. xvii. 4; Ezek. xxxviii. 19, 20. Natural fire is a great devourer, but mystical fire, the fire of divine wrath, is infinitely a greater devourer. Men may stand before a natural fire, but no man has ever been able to stand before the devouring fire of divine wrath. The anger and wrath of God against wicked men is exceeding hot; it is a burning, fiery, flaming wrath, against which they are never able to stand: Isa. xxvii. 4, 'Who would set the briers and thorns against me in battle? I would go through them, I would burn them together.' Briers and thorns are as well able to stand before a devouring fire, as wicked men are able to stand before the smoking wrath of that God which is 'a consuming fire,' Heb. xii. 29.

[6.] Sixthly, *Fire breaks out suddenly and unexpectedly;* in an hour, in a moment, when no man thinks of it, when no man looks for it; as you see by that late dreadful fire, that in a few days turned a glorious city into a ruinous heap. So the judgments of God, they come suddenly and unexpectedly upon the sons of men. Witness the judgments of God that came upon the old world, Sodom and Gomorrah, Nadab and Abihu, Korah, Dathan, and Abiram: 1 Thes. v. 3, 'For when they shall say, peace and safety, then sudden destruction cometh upon them, as travail upon a woman with child, and they shall not escape.' Security is a certain forerunner of desolation and destruction. The apostle, by the similitude he uses, shews that the destruction of the wicked is—(1.) certain, (2.) sudden, (3.) inevitable, Mat. xxiv. 37–39; Gen. xix. But,

[7.] Seventhly, *Fire is impartial;* it makes no difference between rich and poor, high and low, honourable and base, bond and free, male and female, &c. So the judgments of God are impartial, they reach all sorts and ranks of persons. But,

[8.] Eighthly and lastly, *Fire is violent and irresistible.* We have had as dreadful a proof of this in the late dreadful conflagration of London as ever any people have had since the Lord Jesus was on earth. So are the judgments of God violent and irresistible. Witness the raging pestilence and the bloody sword that, in 1665 and 1666, has sent many score thousands to their long homes. And thus you see how that metaphorically or typically great and sore judgments do resemble fire. But,

(2.) Secondly, Premise this with me: *Fire is sometimes attributed unto God:* Heb. xii. 29, 'Our God is a consuming fire.' Sometimes fire is attributed to Christ: Mal. iii. 2, 'But who may abide the day of his coming? and who shall stand when he appeareth? for he is like a refiner's fire, and like fuller's soap.' And sometimes fire is attributed to the Holy Ghost: Mat. iii. 11, 'I indeed baptize you with water unto repentance, but he that cometh after me is mightier than I, whose shoes I am not worthy to bear; he shall baptize you with the Holy Ghost and with fire'—that is, with that fiery Holy Ghost, that spirit of judgment and of burning wherewith the filth of the daughter of Zion is washed away, Isa. iv. 4. But,

(3.) Thirdly, Premise this with me: *The word fire in Scripture is sometimes used by the Holy Ghost to set forth sin by:* Isa. ix. 18, 'For wickedness burneth as the fire, it shall devour the briers and thorns, and shall kindle in the thickets of the forest, and they shall mount up like the lifting up of smoke.' So the burning lust of uncleanness: Rom. i. 27, 'They burned in lust one towards another.' So 1 Cor. vii. 9, 'It is better to marry than to burn.' And so Sodom was first in a flame of burning lusts, before it was burned with fire from heaven. But this is not the fire that is here meant in the proposition that we are upon. But,

(4.) Fourthly, Premise this with me: *Fire is sometimes taken for the blessed angels:* Ps. civ. 4, 'Who maketh his angels spirits, his ministers a flaming fire,' Heb. i. 7. Hence it is that the angels are called seraphims, which signifies burning or flaming ones, and they are set forth by this name to note their irresistible power, Isa. vi. 2; for as there is no withstanding of the furious flames, so there is no withstanding of these burning or flaming ones. Jerome, Musculus, and several others, are of opinion that the angel that destroyed of Sennacherib's host a hundred and fourscore and five thousand in one night, that he did it by fire, burning their bodies, their garments being untouched, 2 Kings xix. 35. But the fire in the proposition cannot be understood of the blessed angels, for several reasons not here to be alleged. But,

(5.) Fifthly, Premise this with me: *Fire in Scripture is sometimes taken for wars:* 'The fire of thine enemies'—that is, the wars that shall be amongst the nations—'shall devour them.' 'Thou shalt be visited of the Lord with a flame of devouring fire; but the nations that fight against the altar shall be a dream,' Isa. xxvi. 11, 12, &c., and xxix. 6, 7. Now fire in this sense is not to be excluded out of the proposition. But,

(6.) Sixthly, Premise this with me: *Fire sometimes notes the special presence of God in a way of special love and favour to his people.* In Exod. iii. 2 you read how 'the Lord appeared unto Moses in a flame of fire out of the midst of a bush; and he looked, and behold the bush burned with fire, and the bush was not consumed.' Here was a representation of the church's affliction, that was then in Egypt, a house of bondage, in the midst of a fiery furnace, Deut. iv. 20. But now the Lord was in the bush, while the bush—the dry bush, or the bramble-bush, as the Hebrew word signifies—was in a flaming fire. In that Deut. xxxiii. 16 you read of 'the good-will of him that dwelt in the bush.' God was there in a way of merciful protection and preservation. They were in the fire, but the Lord was with them in the fire; in all their fiery trials God did bear them company. But,

(7.) Seventhly, Premise this with me: In the blessed Scriptures we read of *supernal fire, of fire that came down from above*, and that first as a sign of God's anger. So fire came down from heaven on Sodom and Gomorrah, Gen. xix. 24. Also fire came down from heaven on them that offered incense in the conspiracy of Korah, Num. xvi. 35. And so fire came down from heaven on the two captains and their fifties, 2 Kings i. 10–12. Secondly, we read of fire that came down from heaven as a sign and token of God's favour. And so fire came down from heaven on the sacrifice of Solomon, and on the sacrifice of Elijah, 2 Chron. vii. 1; 2 Kings xviii. 38. God in those times did delight to shew his special love and favour to his precious servants by fire from heaven. But in the proposition we are to understand not supernal, but material fire. But,

(8.) Eighthly and lastly, Premise this with me: *Fire is sometimes taken literally for that material fire that consumes houses, towns, cities, and the most stately structures.* Jer. xxi. 10, 'For I have set my face against this city for evil, and not for good, saith the Lord; it shall be given into the hand of the king of Babylon, and he shall burn it with fire;' 2 Chron. xxxv. 13. 'And they roasted the passover with fire;' Neh. i. 3, 'And they said unto me, The remnant that are left of the captivity there in the province are in great affliction and reproach; the wall of Jerusalem also is broken down, and the gates thereof are burnt with fire;' chap. ii. 2, 3, 'Wherefore the king said unto me, Why is thy countenance sad, seeing thou art not sick? this is nothing but sorrow of heart. Then I was very sore afraid, and said unto the king, Let the king live for ever: why should not my countenance be sad, when the city, the place of my fathers' sepulchres, lieth waste, and the gates thereof are consumed with fire?' See 2 Chron. xxxvi. 19; 2 Kings xix. 18, and xxi. 6; Ps. lxxiv. 7; Deut. xiii. 16. Now this material fire is the fire that is meant in the proposition. O sirs! God is as much the author or efficient cause of this judgment of fire, as he is the author or efficient cause of sword, famine, and pestilence. This I have in part proved already; but shall more abundantly make it good in that which follows.

But you will say, Sir, we know very well that God is the author or efficient cause of this dreadful judgment of fire, as well as he is the author or efficient cause of any other judgment that we have either felt or feared; but we earnestly desire to know what the ends of God should be in inflicting this sore and heavy judgment of fire upon his poor people, and in turning their glorious city into ashes? This we are sure of, that whoever kindled the fire, God did blow the coal, and therefore we shall not now consider what there was of man's treachery concurring with God's severity in that dreadful calamity by fire; but rather inquire after the grounds, reasons, or ends that God aims at by that fiery dispensation that has lately passed upon us.

Now here give me leave to say, that so far as the late fire was a heavy judgment of God upon the city, yea, upon the whole nation, the ends of God in inflicting that judgment are doubtless such as respect both sinners and saints, the righteous and the wicked, the profane and the holy, the good and the bad. Now such as respect the wicked and ungodly I take to be these that follow:—

[1.] First, That he may evidence *his sovereignty, and that they may know that there is a God.* The profane atheist saith in his heart, 'There is no God;' but God by his terrible judgments startles and awakens the atheist, and makes him unsay what he had said in his heart.[1] When God appears in flames of fire, devouring and destroying all before him, then the proudest and the stoutest atheists in the world will confess that there is a God—yea, then they will bow and tremble under a sense of the sovereignty of God. The sovereignty of God is that golden sceptre in his hand which he will make all bow to, either by his word or by his works, by his mercies or by his judgments. This sceptre must be kissed and submitted to, or else fire and sword, desolation and destruction, will certainly follow. Jer. xviii. 2–4, 6, 'Arise, and go down to the potter's house; and there will I cause thee to hear my word. Then I went down to the potter's house; and, behold, he wrought a work on the wheels. And the vessel that he made of clay was marred in the hand of the potter: so he made it again another vessel, that seemed good to the potter to make it. O house of Israel, cannot I do with you as the potter? saith the Lord. Behold, as the clay is in the potter's hand, so are ye in my hand, O house of Israel.' The Jews were so stupid and sottish that verbal teaching without signs would not work upon them, and therefore the Lord sent Jeremiah to the potter's house, that he might see, by what the potter did, that though he had made them a people, a nation, a church, a state, yet he could as easily unmake them and mar them, as the potter marred the vessel that he had made. God would have this people to know that he had as much power over them and all they had as the potter had power over the clay that he works upon, and that he had as much both might and right also to dispose of them at his pleasure as the potter had over his clay to dispose of it as he judged

[1] Ps. xiv. 1, x. 4, 5, and l. 21; Eccles. viii. 11; Ps. xxiv. 1; Dan. vi. 25–27; Isa. xlv. 9; Ps. ii. 9–12; Hosea ii. 8, 9.

meet.[1] Nay, beloved, the potter has not such an absolute power over his pots and clay as the Lord has over the sons of men, to make them and break them at his pleasure; and that partly because that the clay is none of his creature, and partly because without God give him strength he has no power to make or break one vessel. God by the prophet would have the Jews to know that it was merely by his good pleasure and grace that they came to be so glorious and flourishing a nation as they were at this time; yea, and further to know that they were not so great, and rich, and flourishing, and settled, and built, but that he could as easily break them and mar them as the potter could the vessel that was under his hand, Isa. lxiv. 8. Ah sirs! God by that dreadful fire that has destroyed our houses, and burnt up our substance, and banished us from our habitations, and levelled our stately monuments of antiquity and glory even with the ground, has given us a very high evidence of his sovereignty both over our persons and all our concernments in this world. Ah London! London! were there none within nor without thy walls that did deny the sovereignty of God, that did belie the sovereignty of God, that did slight the sovereignty of God, that did make head against the sovereignty of God? Were there none within nor without thy walls that did say, 'We are lords, and we will come no more unto thee'? that did say, 'Is not this great Babylon, is not this great London that we have built?' that did say, 'The kings of the earth, and all the inhabitants of the world would not have believed that the adversary and the enemy, the flaming and consuming fire, should have entered into the gates of Jerusalem, into the gates of London'? that did say, 'Who is the Lord, that we should obey his voice?' that did advance a worldly sovereignty above and against the sovereignty of God and Christ? Jer. ii. 31; Dan. iv. 30; Lam. iv. 12; Exod. v. 2. Ah London! London! if there were any such within or without thy walls, then never wonder that God has in a flaming and consuming fire proclaimed his sovereignty over thee, and that he hath given such atheists to know from woeful experience that both themselves and all their concernments are in the hands of the Lord as the clay is in the hands of the potter, and that the sorest judgments that any city can fall under are but the demonstrations of his sovereign prerogative, Isa. v. 16. Ps. ix. 16, 'The Lord is known by the judgments which he executeth; the power, justice, and sovereignty of God shines most gloriously in the execution of his judgments upon the world.'

[2.] Secondly, God inflicts great and sore judgments upon the sons of men, that *the world may stand in awe of him, and that they may learn to fear and tremble before him.*[2] When he appears as a consuming fire, he expects that the nation should tremble, and that the inhabitants should fear before him: 1 Sam. xvi. 4, 'And Samuel did that which the Lord spake, and came to Bethlehem: and the elders of the town trembled at his coming, and said, Comest thou peaceably?' Shall the elders of Bethlehem tremble for fear that Samuel came to denounce some grievous judgment against them; and shall not we tremble when God has executed his terrible judgments upon us?

[1] God hath *jus ad omnia, jus in omnibus*, a right to all things, a right in all things.
[2] Consult these scriptures, Exod. xv. 14–16; Josh. ii. 10, 11; Rev. xv. 4.

Shall Ahab tremble and humble himself, and fast and lie in sackcloth when judgments are but threatened; and shall not we tremble and fear before the great God, who has actually inflicted upon us his three great judgments, pestilence, sword, and fire? Shall the Ninevites, both princes, nobles, and people, tremble and humble themselves in sackcloth and ashes when God doth but threaten to overthrow their great, their rich, their populous city; and shall not we tremble and lie low before the Lord when we see great London, rich and populous London, laid in ashes before our eyes? 1 Kings xxi. 20–24, 27–29; Jonah iii. 3–10. When the hand of the Lord was stretched out against the Egyptians, 'the dukes of Edom were amazed, and the mighty men of Moab trembled,' Exod. xv. 15, 16; 2 Kings vi. 30, and vii. 6, 7, 15; Jer. iv. 7–9. Ah, how severely has the hand of the Lord been stretched out against London and all her inhabitants! and therefore what cause have we to be amazed and to tremble before that God who has appeared in flames of fire against us! Lam. ii. 3, 4, 'He hath cut off in his fierce anger all the horn of Israel: he hath drawn back his right hand before the enemy, and he burned against Jacob like a flaming fire, which devoureth round about. He bent his bow like an enemy: and poured out his fury like fire.' God burnt down their city, their temple, their gates, their princely habitations, their glorious structures, in the fierceness of his anger and in the greatness of his wrath. O sirs! when God falls upon burning work, when he pours out his fury like fire, when like a flaming fire he devours all our pleasant things, and lays all our glory in dust and ashes, we may safely conclude that his anger is fierce and that his wrath is great against us; and therefore what eminent cause have we to fear and tremble before him! God is a great and dreadful God: Dan ix. 4, 'A mighty God and terrible;' Deut. vii. 21, 'A great and terrible God,' Neh. i. 5. He is so in himself, and he has been so in his fiery dispensations towards us, that the world by such remarkable severities may be kept in awe of him. Generally fear doth more in the world than love.[1] As there is little sincerity, so there is but little ingenuity[2] in the world; and that is the reason why many very rarely think of God but when they are afraid of him. Many times judgments work where mercies do not win. That famous Thomas[3] Waldo of Lyons, the father of the Waldenses, seeing, among many met together to be merry, one suddenly fall down dead in the street, it struck so to his heart that he went home a penitent,—it wrought to a severe and pious reformation of his life, and he lived and died a precious man. Though Pharaoh was not a pin the better for all the heavy judgments that God inflicted upon him, yet Jethro, taking notice of those dreadful plagues and judgments that fell upon Pharaoh and upon his people, and likewise upon the Amalekites, was thereby converted and became a proselyte; as Rabbi Solomon noteth upon that 19th of Prov. 25: The world is so untractable, that frowns will do more with them than smiles. That God may keep wicked men in awe and in subjection to him, he sees it very needful to bring common, and general, and over-

[1] We are worthy, saith Chrysostom, of hell, if for no other cause, yet for fearing hell and the evil of punishment more than Christ.—Chrys. Hom. 5, in Epist. ad Rom.

[2] 'Ingenuousness.'—G.

[3] Qu. 'Peter'?—ED.

spreading judgments upon them: Rev. xv. 4, 'Who shall not fear thee, O Lord, and glorify thy name? for thou only art holy: for all nations shall come and worship before thee; for thy judgments are made manifest.' O sirs! when the judgments of the Lord come to be made manifest, then it highly concerns all ranks and sorts of men to fear the Lord and to glorify his name. How manifest, how visible has the raging pestilence, and the bloody sword, and the devouring flames of London been in the midst of us! and oh that our fear, and dread, and awe of God were as manifest and as visible as his judgments have been and still are; for his hand to this very hour is stretched out against us! Isa. ix. 12. But,

[3.] Thirdly, God inflicts great and sore judgments upon the sons of men, and upon cities and countries, *to express and make known his power, justice, anger, severity, and indignation against sinners and their sinful courses, by which he has been provoked:*[1] Deut. xxxii. 19, 'And when the Lord saw it, he abhorred them, because of the provoking of his sons and of his daughters.' Ver. 21, 'They have provoked me to anger with their vanities; and I will provoke them to anger with a foolish nation.' Ver. 22, 'For a fire is kindled in my anger, and shall burn unto the lowest hell, and shall consume the earth with her increase, and set on fire the foundations of the mountains.' Ver. 24, 'They shall be burnt with hunger, and devoured with burning heat, or with burning coals, and with bitter destruction.' There is a knowledge of God by his works as well as by his word, and by his judgment as well as by his mercies. In his dreadful judgments every one may run and read his power, his justice, his anger, his severity, and his indignation against sin and sinners. It is irrevocable sins that bring irrevocable judgments upon sinners. Whilst men hold on in committing great iniquities, God will hold on in inflicting answerable severities. When God cannot prevail with men to desist from sinning, men shall not prevail with God to desist from destroying of them, their habitations, and all their pleasant things: Jer. ii. 15, 'The young lions roared upon him, and yelled, and they made his land waste: his cities are burnt without inhabitant.' Ver. 17, 'Hast thou not procured this unto thyself, in that thou hast forsaken the Lord thy God, when he led thee by the way?' When Nicephorus Phocas had built a mighty strong wall about his palace for his own security, in the night-time he heard a voice crying unto him, ὦ βασιλεῦ ὑψίοις τὰ τειχῆ, &c., O emperor, though thou buildest the wall as high as the clouds; yet if sin be within, it will overthrow all.[2] Sin, like those traitors in the Trojan horse, will do cities and countries more hurt in one night than ten thousand open enemies could do in ten years. Cities and countries might flourish, and continue as the days of heaven, and be as the sun before the Almighty, if his wrath be not provoked by their profaneness and wickedness; so that it is not any divine[3] aspect of the heavens, nor any malignant conjunction of the stars and planets, but the loose manners, the ungracious lives, and

[1] See Jer. xiv. 15, 16; Lam. iv. 11; Jer. iv. 15–19.

[2] Brooks's allusion is to the strong 'tower' built by Nicephorus II. (Phocas) in his palace. Cf. Gibbon, xlviii. *s. n.*—G.

[3] Qu. 'malign'?—ED.

the enormous sins of men, that lay cities and countries desolate: Jer xiii. 22, 'And if thou say in thine heart, Wherefore come these things upon me? wherefore hath the Lord sent plague, sword, famine, and fire to devour and destroy, and to lay all in ashes?' The answer is, 'For the greatness of thine iniquity.' God will in flames of fire discover his anger and indignation against sin and sinners. The heathen historian [Herodotus] observes in the ruin of Troy, that the sparkles and ashes of burnt Troy served for a lasting monument of God's great anger and displeasure against great sinners. The burning of Troy served to teach men that God punisheth great sinners with great plagues; and certainly London's being laid in ashes is a high evidence that God knows how to be angry with sinners, and how to punish sin with the sorest of judgments. The gods of the Gentiles were senseless stocks and stones, not able to apprehend, much less to revenge, any injury done unto them. Well therefore might the philosopher be bold with Hercules to put him to his thirteenth labour in seething of his dinner; and Martial with Priapus, in threatening him to throw him into the fire if he looked not well to his trees.[1] A child may play at the hole of a dead asp, and a silly woman may strike a dead lion; but who dare play with a living serpent? who dare take a roaring lion by the beard? Oh that Christians then would take heed how they provoke the living God, for he is 'a consuming fire,' and with a word of his mouth, yea, with the breath of his mouth, he is able to throw down, and to burn up the whole frame of nature, and to destroy all creatures from the face of the earth. Some heathen philosophers thought anger an unseemly attribute to ascribe to God, and some heretics conceived the God of the New Testament void of all anger. They imagined two Gods: the God of the Old Testament was, in their account, *Deus justus*, a Deity severe and revengeful: but the God of the New Testament was *Deus bonus*, the good God, a God made up all of mercy; they would have no anger in him. But Christians do know that God proclaims this attribute among his titles of honour: Neh. i. 2, 'God is jealous, and the Lord revengeth, and is furious; he reserveth wrath for his enemies.' It is the highway to atheism and profaneness, to fancy to ourselves a God made up all of mercy, to think that God cannot tell how to be angry and wroth with the sons of men. Surely they that have seen London in flames, or believe that it is now laid in ashes, they will believe that God knows how to be angry, and how to fix the tokens of his wrath upon us. But,

[4.] Fourthly, God inflicts great and sore judgments upon the sons of men, and upon cities and countries, *that they may cease from sin, receive instruction, and reform and return to the most High;* as you may evidently see by comparing the scriptures in the margin together.[2] God's corrections should be our instructions, his lashes should be our lessons, his scourges should be our schoolmasters, his chastisements should be our advertisements: and to note this the

[1] Epig., lib. viii.; Ep. xl.—G.

[2] Isa. xxvi. 9; Ps. xciv. 12; Prov. iii. 12, 13, and vi. 23; Job xxxvi. 8–10, and xxxiii. 19, 20; Levit. xxvi.; Deut. xxviii.; 2 Chron. vii. 13, 14; Amos iv. 6–12; Isa. ix. 13; Jer. v. 3, and vi. 29, 30; Ezek. xxiii. 25–27.

Hebrews and the Greeks both express chastising and teaching by one and the same word [מוסר, *Masar*, *παιδεία*], because the latter is the true end of the former, according to that in the proverb, 'Smart makes wit, and vexation gives understanding.' Whence Luther fitly calls affliction, *Theologiam Christianorum*, The Christian man's divinity: Jer. vi. 8, 'Be thou instructed, O Jerusalem, lest my soul depart from thee; lest I make thee desolate, a land not inhabited.' Zeph. iii. 6, 7, 'I have cut off the nations: their towers are desolate; I made their streets waste, that none passed by: their cities are destroyed, so that there is no man, that there is no inhabitant. I said, Surely thou wilt fear me; thou wilt receive instruction: so their dwellings should not be cut off, however I punished them: but they rose early, and corrupted all their doings.' By all the desolations that God had made before their eyes he designed their instruction and reformation. From those words, Judges iii. 20, 'I have a message from God unto thee, O king,' said Ehud. Lo, his poniard was God's message: from whence one well observes, That not only the vocal admonitions, but the real judgments of God are his errands and instructions to the world. God delights to win men to himself by favours and mercies; but it is rare that God this way makes a conquest upon them: Jer. xxii. 21, 'I spake unto thee in thy prosperity,' saith God; 'but thou saidst, I will not hear:' and therefore it is that he delivers them over into the hands of severe judgments, as into the hands of so many curst schoolmasters, as Basil speaks, that so they may learn obedience by the things they suffer, as the apostle speaks, Deut. xxxii. 14–17; Jer. v. 7–10; Ps. lxxiii. 1–10. It is said of Gideon, he took briers and thorns, and with them he taught the men of Succoth, Judges viii. 16. Ah, poor London! how has God taught thee with briers and thorns, with sword, pestilence, and fire! and all because thou wouldst not be taught by prosperity and mercy 'to do justice, to love mercy, and to walk humbly with thy God,' Micah vi. 8; Lam. iii. 32, 33; Isa. xxviii. 21. God delights in the reformation of a nation; but he doth not delight in the desolation of any nation. God's greatest severity is to prevent utter ruin and misery, *Schola crucis, schola lucis.* If God will but make London's destruction England's instruction, it may save the land from a total desolation. Ah, London! London! I would willingly hope that this fiery rod that has been upon thy back has been only to awaken thee, and to instruct thee, and to refine thee, and to reform thee, that after this sore desolation God may delight to build thee, and beautify thee, and make thee an eternal excellency, a joy of many generations, Isa. lx. 15. But,

[5.] Fifthly, God inflicts sore and great judgments upon the sons of men, *that he may try them, and make a more full discovery of themselves to themselves.* Wicked men will never believe that their lusts are so strong, and that their hearts are so base, as indeed they are: 2 Kings viii. 12, 13, 'And Hazael said, Why weepeth my lord? and he answered, Because I know the evil that thou wilt do unto the children of Israel; their strongholds wilt thou set on fire, and their young men wilt thou slay with the sword, and wilt dash their children, and rip up their women with child. And Hazael said, But what, is thy servant a dog that he should do this great thing? And Elisha answered, The Lord hath shewed me that thou shalt be king over Syria.' Hazael could not imagine that he should be as fierce, cruel, murderous, and merciless as a dog, that will tear all in pieces that he can come at. It could never enter into his thoughts that ever he should do such cruel, barbarous, horrid, and inhuman acts as the prophet spoke of; but he did not know the depth of his own corruption, nor the desperateness, nor deceitfulness of his own heart, Jer. xvii. 9: Isa. viii. 21, 'And they shall pass through it hardly bestead and hungry; and it shall come to pass, that when they shall be hungry they shall fret themselves, and curse their king, and their God, and look upward.' When judgments are upon them, then their wickedness appears rampant. They shall curse their own king for not defending, protecting, or relieving of them; they shall look upon him as the cause of all their wants, sorrows, and sufferings; and as men overwhelmed with misery, and full of indignation, they shall fall a-cursing of him. And they shall curse their God as well as their king; that is, say some, the true God, who deservedly brought these plagues upon them. Their God; that is, say others, their *Melchom*, to whom they had sacrificed, and in whom they see now that they vainly trusted. So those desperate wretches under the beast: Rev. xvi. 8, 9, 'And the fourth angel poured out his vial upon the sun, and power was given unto him to scorch men with fire. And the men were scorched with great heat, and blasphemed the name of God, which hath power over these plagues; and they repented not, to give him glory;' ver. 10, 'And the fifth angel poured out his vial upon the scent[1] of the beast; and his kingdom was full of darkness, and they gnawed their tongues for pain, and blasphemed the God of heaven, because of their pains and their sores, and repented not of their deeds.'[2] The top of the judgment that is and shall be upon the wicked is this, that under the sorest and heaviest judgments that shall come upon them, they shall not repent, nor give glory to God. They shall blaspheme the name of God, and they shall blaspheme the God of heaven; and they shall be scorched with great heat, and they shall gnaw their tongues for pain, but they shall not repent of their deeds, nor give glory to that hand that smites them.[3] The fierce and fiery dispensations of God upon the followers and worshippers of the beast shall draw out their sins; but they shall never reform their lives, nor better their souls. God kept the Jews forty years in the wilderness, and exercised them with many sore and smart afflictions, that he might prove them, and make a more full discovery of themselves to themselves. And did not the heavy trials that they met with in their wilderness condition make a very great discovery of that pride, that unbelief, that hypocrisy, that impatience, that discontent, that self-love, that murmuring, &c., that was wrapt up close in all their souls? O sirs! since God has turned our renowned city into ashes, what discoveries has he made of that pride, that unbelief, that worldliness, that earthliness, that self-love, that inordinate affec-

[1] Qu. 'seat'?—ED.

[2] Plutarch observes, that it is the quality of tigers to grow mad, and tear themselves in pieces, if they hear but drums or tabors to sound about them.—*Lib. de Superstitione.*

[3] This will be the case of all the worshippers of the beast one day, Deut. viii. 2, 15, 16.

tion to relations and to the good things of the world, that discontent, that disquietness, that faint-heartedness, that has been closely wrapped up in the spirits of many thousands whose habitations are now laid in ashes! We try metals by fire and by knocking, and God has tried many thousands this day by his fiery dispensations and knocking judgments that have been in the midst of us. I believe there are many thousands who have been deep sufferers by the late dreadful fire, who never did think that there had been so much sin and so little grace, so much of the creature and so little of God, so much earth and so little of heaven in their hearts, as they now find by woeful experience. And how many wretched sinners are there who have more blasphemed God, and dishonoured Christ, and provoked divine justice, and abused their best mercies, and debased and be-beasted themselves since the late fire, than they have done in many years before! But,

[6.] Sixthly, God inflicts great and sore judgments upon persons, cities, and countries, *that others may be warned by his severities to break off their sins, and to return to the most High.* God's judgments upon one city, should be advertisements to all other cities to look about them, and to tremble before him who is 'a consuming fire,' Heb. xii. 29. The flaming rod of correction that is laid upon one city, should be a rod of instruction to all other cities. Jer. xxii. 6–9, 'I will make thee a wilderness, and cities which are not inhabited. And many nations shall pass by this city, and they shall say every man to his neighbour, Wherefore hath the Lord done this unto this great city? Then shall they answer, Because they have forsaken the covenant of the Lord their God, and worshipped other gods, and served them.' God punisheth one city, that all other cities may take warning. There is no judgment of God, be it sword, pestilence, famine, or fire, upon any people, city, nation, or country, but what is speaking and teaching to all others, had they but eyes to see, ears to hear, and hearts to understand, Micah vi. 9. Thus Tyrus shall be devoured with fire, saith the prophet; Ashkelon shall see it and fear; Gaza and Ekron shall be very sorrowful, Zech. ix. 4, 5. When Ashkelon, Gaza, and Ekron shall see the destruction of Tyre by fire, it shall make them afraid of the like judgment. They shall be a little more concerned than some were at the siege of Rhodes, and than others were at the ruin and desolation of Troy by fire. London's sufferings should warn others to take heed of London's sins. London's conflagration should warn others to take heed of London's abominations. It should warn others to stand and wonder at the patience, long-suffering, gentleness, and goodness of God towards them who have deserved as hard things from the hand of God, as London have felt in 1665 and 1666, Rom. ii. 4, 5. It should warn others to search their hearts, and try their ways, and break off their sins, and turn to the Lord, lest his anger should break forth in flames of fire against them, and none should be able to deliver them, Lam. iii. 40. It should warn others to fear and tremble before that power, justice, severity, and sovereignty that shines in God's fiery dispensations towards us. Ezek. xxx. 7–9, 'And they shall be desolate in the midst of the countries that are desolate, and her cities'—meaning Egypt—'shall be in the midst of the cities that are wasted. And they shall know that I am the Lord, when I have set a fire in Egypt. In that day shall messengers go forth from me in ships, to make the careless Ethiopians afraid, and great pain shall come upon them, as in the day of Egypt; for, lo, he cometh,' Exod. xv. 14–16; Isa. xiii. 6-8. God by his secret instinct and providence would so order the matter, as that the news of the Chaldeans' inroad into Egypt, laying all their cities and towns waste by fire and sword, should be carried over into Ethiopia; and hereupon the secure Ethiopians should fear and tremble, and be in pain as a woman is that is in travail; or as the Egyptians were, when they were destroyed at the Red Sea; or as they were, when the Lord smote their firstborn throughout the land of Egypt. Now shall the Ethiopians, the poor, blind heathens, fear and tremble, and be in pain, when they hear that Egypt is laid waste by fire and sword; and shall not Christians all the world over fear and tremble, and be in pain, when they shall hear that London is laid waste, that London is destroyed by fire? What though papists and atheists have warmed themselves at the flames of London, saying, Aha! so would we have it; yet let all that have the name of God upon them fear and tremble, and take warning, and learn righteousness by his righteous judgments upon desolate London. London's murdering-piece should be England's warning-piece to awaken them, and to work them to bethink themselves, and to turn to him who is able by a flaming fire quickly to turn them out of all, Isa. xxvi. 8, 9. The Jews have a saying, that if war be begun in another country, yet they should fast and mourn because the war is begun, and because they do not know how soon God may bring it to their doors. O sirs! London is burnt, and it highly concerns you to fast, and mourn, and pray, and to take the alarm; for you do not know how soon a fire may be kindled in your own habitations. Now God has made the once famous city of London a flaming beacon before your eyes, he expects and looks that you should all fear before him. Secure your interest in him, walk humbly with him, and no more provoke the eyes of his jealousy and glory. The design of Heaven by this late dreadful fire, is not to be confined to those particular persons upon whom it hath fallen heaviest; but it is to awaken all, and warn all. When a beacon is fired, it gives warning as much to the whole country as to him who sets it on fire; or as it does to him on whose ground the beacon stands. We can neither upon the foot of reason or religion, conclude them to be the greatest sinners who have been the greatest sufferers; for many times we find that the greatest saints have been the greatest sufferers, both from God and men. Job was a non-such in his day for holiness, uprightness, and the fear of the Lord, and yet by the wind and fire from heaven on the one hand, and by the Sabeans and Chaldeans on the other hand, he is stript of all his children and of a fair estate in one day: so that in the morning it might have been said, Who so rich as Job? and in the evening, Who so poor as Job? Job was poor even to a proverb, Job i. 1–4. Look, as wicked men are very incompetent judges of divine favours and mercies, so they are very incompetent judges of divine trials and severities; and whatever they may think or say, I dare conclude that they who have drank deepest of this cup of sorrows, of this cup of desolation and fire in London, are not greater sinners than all others in England, who yet have not tasted of this bitter cup. But more of this when I come to the application of the point. O sirs! I beg upon the knee of my soul, that you will not slight this dreadful warning of God that he has given to the whole nation, in turning London into ashes. To that purpose seriously consider, *First*, Divine warnings slighted and neglected will certainly bring down the greater wrath and vengeance upon you, as you may clearly see by comparing the scriptures in the margin together.[1] *Secondly*, Slighting of judgments is the greatest judgment that can befall a people; it speaks out much pride, atheism, hardness, blindness, and desperate security, and contempt of the great God. To be given up to slight divine warnings, is a spiritual judgment, and therefore must of all judgments be the greatest judgment. To be given up to sword, famine, fire, pestilence, burning agues, and fevers, is nothing so great a judgment as to be given up to slight divine warnings; for in the one you are but passive, but in the other you are active. *Thirdly*, Heathens have trembled, and mended, and reformed, at divine warnings, Jonah iii.; and therefore for you to slight them is to act below the heathens, yea, it is to do worse than the heathens, who will certainly one day rise up in judgment against all such who have been slighters of the dreadful warnings of heaven. *Fourthly*, Slighting of divine warnings lays men open to such anger and wrath, as all the angels in heaven are not able to express, nor all the men on earth able to conceive, Prov. i. 24–32. *Fifthly*, Slighting and neglecting of divine warnings speaks out the greatest disingenuity, stoutness, and stubbornness that is imaginable. The ingenuous child easily takes warning, and to an ingenuous Christian every divine warning is as the handwriting upon the wall, Dan. v. 5. *Sixthly*, Slighting of divine warnings provokes God many times to give up men to be their own executioners, their own destroyers. Saul had many warnings, but he slighted and neglected them all; and at last God leaves him to fall on his own sword, 1 Sam. xxxi. 4. Christ cast hell-fire often into Judas his face, 'Thou hast a devil;' and 'Woe to that man by whom the Son of man shall be betrayed; it had been good for that man that he had never been born.' But Judas slights all these warnings, and betrays his Lord and Master, and then goes forth and hangs himself, John vi. 70, 71; Mat. xxvi. 21–25, and xxvii. 5. It was a strange conceit of the Cerinthians[2] that honoured Judas, the traitor, as some divine and superhuman power, and called his treason a blessed piece of service, and that he, knowing how much the death of Christ would profit mankind, did therefore betray him to death to save the race of mankind, and to do a thing pleasing to God. Judas withstood all divine warnings from within and without, and you know how the tragedy ended; he died a miserable death, he perished by his own hands, which were the most infamous hands in all the world; 'he went and hanged himself.'[3] And as Luke hath it, 'he fell headlong and burst asunder in the midst, and all his bowels

[1] Lev. xxvi. 16–18, 21, 23, 24, 27, 28; Amos iv. 7–11; Jer. xxv. 4–12; Isa. xxii. 12–14.

[2] Irenæus, &c., Aug. de Hæresi.

[3] Some report of Judas, that he slew his father, married his mother, and betrayed his Master.

gushed out.' In every passage of his death we may take notice of divine justice, and accordingly take heed of slighting divine warnings. It was but just that he should hang in the air, who, for his sin, was hated both of heaven and earth, and that he should fall down headlong, who was fallen from such a height of honour as he was fallen from; and that the halter should strangle that throat through which the voice of treason had sounded; and that his bowels should be lost who had lost the bowels of all pity, piety, and compassion; and that his ghost should have his passage out of his midst: 'he burst asunder in the midst,' saith the text, and not out of his lips, because with a kiss of his lips he had betrayed our Lord Jesus. But *Seventhly*, By slighting divine warnings you will arm both visible and invisible creatures against you. Pharaoh slights divine warnings, and God arms the winds against him to his destruction. Sisera slights divine warnings, and the stars in their course fought against Sisera. Sennacherib slights divine warnings, and an angel of the Lord destroyed a hundred fourscore and five thousand of his army in one night, 2 Kings vi. 8-11, 16, 17; Exod. xiv.; Judges v. 19, 20; Isa. xxxvii. 7-9, 36. *Eighthly*, By slighting of divine warnings you will tempt Satan to tempt your souls. He that dares slight divine warnings will stick at nothing that Satan shall tempt him to; yea, he does to the utmost what lies in him to provoke Satan to follow him with the blackest and sorest temptations. *Ninthly*, He that slights divine warnings dams up all the springs of mercy, and turns the streams of loving-kindness and favour another way. *Tenthly* and lastly, Slighting of divine warnings will be the sword that will wound you, and the serpent that will sting you, and the worm that will be still gnawing upon you; especially (1.) When your consciences are awakening; (2.) When you shall lie upon a dying bed; (3.) When you shall stand before a judgment-seat; (4.) and lastly, When you shall awake with everlasting flames about your ears, Ps. lxxxi. 11 to the end; Jer. vii. 23-29, 34; Isa. xiii. 14-16. Upon all these considerations, take heed of slighting the warnings of God that you are under this day. But,

[7.] Seventhly and lastly, God inflicts great and sore judgments upon persons, cities, and countries, *to put the world in mind of the general judgment*. Who can think upon the conflagration of our late glorious city, and not call to mind the great and terrible day of the Lord? Ps. l. 3, 'Our God shall come, and shall not keep silence: a fire shall devour before him, and it shall be very tempestuous round about him.' As God gave his law in fire, so when he comes to judgment, in fire he will require it, to shew himself a judge and revenger of it, and to bring the world to a strict account for their breaking of it, Eccles. xii. 13, 14. In the promulgation of the law a flaming fire was only on mount Sinai, Exod. xx. 18; but when Christ shall come to execute vengeance on the transgressors of it, all the world shall become a bonfire, Heb. xii. 18-21. In the promulgation of the law there was fire, smoke, thunder, and an earthquake; but when Christ shall come in flaming fire to revenge the breaches of it, 'the heavens shall be dissolved, and the elements shall melt with fervent heat,' so that not only a few cities and kingdoms, but all this lower world shall be of a flame; and therefore if any of the wicked should be so weak as to think to secure themselves by creeping behind the Lord, they will but deceive themselves; for the fire shall not only devour before him, but it shall also devour round about him. When an unquenchable fire shall be kindled above the sinner, and below the sinner, and round about the sinner, how is it possible that he should escape, though he should cry out to the rocks and the mountains to fall upon him, and to cover him from the wrath of the Lamb? Rev. vi. 15–17; Jer. v. 14. Isa. lxvi. 15, 16, 'For, behold, the Lord will come with fire, and with his chariots like a whirlwind, to render his anger with fury, and his rebuke with flames of fire. For by fire, and by his sword, will the Lord plead with all flesh: and the slain of the Lord shall be many.' There is nothing more fearful or formidable either to man or beast than fire. Now when God comes to execute his judgments, and to take vengeance on the wicked in this life, as some carry the words, or in the other life, as others carry the words, he will come in the most terrible and dreadful manner imaginable, he will come with fire, and he will render his rebuke with flames of fire, or with fiery flames, as some say, or with flaming fire, as others say: 2 Thes. i. 7, 8, 'And to you who are troubled, rest with us, when the Lord Jesus shall be revealed from heaven, with his mighty angels, in flaming fire, taking vengeance on them that know not God, and that obey not the gospel of our Lord Jesus Christ.' Beloved, that Christ will come to judgment in flaming fire is no politic invention found out to fright men from their pleasures; nor no engine of state devised to keep men tame and quiet under the civil powers; nor no plot of the minister to make men melancholy, or to hurry them into a blind obedience; but it is the constant voice of God in the blessed Scriptures: 2 Pet. iii. 10–12, 'But the day of the Lord will come as a thief in the night, in the which the heavens shall pass away with a great noise, and the elements shall melt with fervent heat, the earth also and the works that are therein shall be burnt up. Looking for and hasting unto the coming of the day of God, wherein the heavens being on fire, shall be dissolved, and the elements shall melt with fervent heat.' Pareus is of opinion[1] that that fire that shall set all the world in a flame at last will be kindled and cherished by lightning from heaven. The earth being smitten with lightning from heaven, shall be shaken and torn into ten thousand pieces, and by fire utterly consumed; now the earth shall quake, the sea roar, the air ring, and the world burn. Now you shall look no way but you shall see fire; you shall see fire above you, and fire below you, and fire round about you. Christ's first coming was attended with a general peace, and with carols of angels: he came as rain upon the mown grass, silently, sweetly into the world, Luke ii. 8–15; Ps. lxxi. 6. Then a babe cried in the manger, but now Judah's lion will roar and thunder in the heavens. Then he came riding on an ass's colt, but now on the clouds. Then he was attended with twelve poor despised apostles, but now he shall be waited on with many score millions of angels. At his first coming he freely offered grace, and mercy, and pardon to sinners; but now he will come in flames of fire to execute wrath and vengeance upon sinners, 2 Thes. i. 7; and it will be no small

[1] Pareus in Rev. xvi. 18.

honour to Christ, nor no small comfort to the saints, nor no small torment to the wicked, for Christ to come in flames of fire when he comes to judgment. Saul was astonished when he heard Jesus of Nazareth but calling unto him out of heaven, Acts xxii. 8. Herod was affrighted when he thought that John Baptist was risen again, Mat. vi. 16. The Philistines were afraid when they saw David's sword, 1 Sam. xxi. 9. The Israelites were startled when they saw Aaron's rod, Num. vii. 10. And Judah was ashamed when he saw Thamar's signet and staff; and Belshazzar was amazed when he saw the handwriting upon the wall, Dan. v. 5. The Carthaginians were troubled when they saw Scipio's sepulchre; and the Saxons were terrified when they saw Cadwallon's image.[1] Oh, how terrified, amazed, and confounded will wicked men be when they shall see that Christ, whom they have rejected, betrayed, crucified, scorned, opposed, and persecuted, come in flames of fire to pass an eternal doom upon them! I have read a story of two soldiers,[2] that coming to the valley of Jehoshaphat in Judea, and one saying to the other, Here in this place shall be the general judgment, wherefore I will now take up my place where I will then sit; and so lifting up a stone, he sat down upon it, as taking possession beforehand: but being seated, and looking up to heaven, such a quaking and trembling fell upon him, that falling to the earth, he remembered the day of judgment with horror and amazement ever after. The case of this soldier will be the case of every wicked man when Christ shall appear in flames of fire to pass an eternal sentence of condemnation upon all the goats that shall be found on the left hand, Mat. xxv. 41–46. It is strange in this so serious a business of the day of judgment, and of Christ's appearing in flaming fire, which so nearly concerns the sons of men, how men's wits will busy themselves in many nice inquiries. Ye may meet with many such questions in the schoolmen as—(1.) How long is it to the day of judgment? (2.) In what place of the world shall the judgment-day be held? (3.) What kind of fire shall then be burning? (4.) Whether Christ shall come with a cross carried before him? As if malefactors in the jail should fall a-reasoning and debating what weather it would be at the day of assizes, or of the judge's habit and retinue, and never bethink themselves how to answer their indictment, that they may escape condemnation. London's flames should put us in mind of Christ's coming in flames of fire; and the burning of London should put us in mind of the burning of the world, when Christ shall come to judge the sons of men according to their works; and the terror and dread of that fire, and men's endeavours to escape it, should put us upon all those holy ways and means whereby we may escape the fury of those dreadful flames that shall never be quenched; and the houses and estates that were consumed by the devouring fire in London streets should put us upon securing 'a house not made with hands,' but one 'eternal in the heavens,' and upon securing 'durable riches,' and 'an inheritance that fadeth not away,' and upon 'laying up for ourselves treasures in heaven, where neither moth nor rust, nor thieves,' and let me add, nor flames, 'can break through, corrupt, or steal, or burn,' 2 Cor. v. 1, 2; Prov. viii. 18; 1 Pet. i. 4; Mat. vi. 19–21.

[1] Holinshed's Chronicle.

[2] Holcot. in lib. Sap. [1483, folio.—G.]

The more general any judgment is, the more it should put us in mind of the general day of judgment. Now the burning of London was a general judgment, a judgment that reaches from one end of the land to another, as I shall more fully evidence before I close up this discourse; and therefore it should remind us of the universal conflagration of the whole world and the works thereof. And thus you see the ends that God has in respect of the wicked in inflicting great and sore judgments upon persons, cities, and countries.

Quest. But pray, sir, what are those high and holy ends, in respect of the people of God, that God aims at by his inflicting of great and sore judgments upon persons, cities, and countries? I suppose they are such as follow:

Ans. (1.) First, *To bring about those special favours and mercies that God intends them.* By the dreadful judgments that God inflicted upon Pharaoh, and upon his people, and upon his country, God brought about the freedom and liberty of his people to worship him according to his own prescriptions. The great difference and contest between God and Pharaoh was, who should have their wills. God would have his people to worship him according to his own mind; but Pharaoh was resolved to venture his all before they should have their freedom and liberty to serve their God. Upon this God follows him with plague upon plague, and never leaves spending of his plagues upon him till he had overthrown him, and through his ruin brought about the freedom and liberty of his poor people.[1] The Babylonians were cruel enemies to God's poor Israel, and kept them in bondage, yea, in a fiery furnace, seventy years. At last God stirs up the spirit of Cyrus, for his church's sake, and he, by fire and sword, lays Babylon waste, and takes them captive who had held his people in a long captivity, Jer. xi. 4, and Dan. ix. 12. Now he, by breaking the Babylonians in pieces like a potter's vessel, brought about, as an instrument in the hand of God, the freedom and liberty of God's poor people, as you may see by comparing that xlvth of Isa. 1–6, with that 1st chapter of Ezra. God stirs up the spirit of Cyrus to put forth a proclamation for liberty for the Jews to go to their own land, and to build the house of the Lord God of Israel; and then he graciously stirs up the spirits of the people wisely and soberly to improve the liberty he had proclaimed.[2] Jer. xlix. 1, 'Concerning the Ammonites, thus saith the Lord, Hath Israel no sons? hath he no heir? why then doth their king inherit Gad, and his people dwell in his cities?' When the ten tribes were carried away captive, the Ammonites who dwelt near the tribe of Gad intruded into it and the cities of it; but mark what God saith in ver. 2, 'Therefore, behold, the days come, saith the Lord, that I will cause an alarm of war to be heard in Rabbah of the Ammonites [that was their chief city]; and it shall be a desolate heap, and her daughters [that is, lesser towns] shall be burnt with fire: then shall Israel be heir unto them that were his heirs, saith the Lord.'[3] God, by fire and sword, would lay desolate the chief city of the Ammonites, and her towns and villages that did

[1] Exod. v. 1, 2, vii. 16, viii. 8, 20, 25, 27, 29, ix. 1, 13, x. 3, 7, 8, 11, 24, xii. 31.

[2] Turn to Obadiah, and read from ver. 11 to the end of the chapter.

[3] Here was *Lex talionis* observed; they that invaded the inheritance of others had their own invaded by them.

belong to her: and by these dreadful dispensations he would make way for his people, not only to possess their own land, but the Ammonites' also; and I will leave the prudent reader to make the application. We have been under greater and dreadfuller judgments than ever this poor nation hath groaned under in former times; and who can tell but that the Lord by these amazing judgments may bring about greater and better mercies and blessings than any yet we do enjoy? The Rabbins say of civil liberty, that if the heavens were parchment, the sea ink, and every pile of grass a pen, the praises of it could not be comprised nor expressed. May we not say more of a holy liberty? Liberty to serve and worship the Lord according to his own prescriptions and directions laid down in his blessed word, by which all worship and worshippers must be tried at last, is a pearl of price that none can sufficiently value. Justinus the second emperor's motto was, *Libertas res inæstimabilis*, Liberty is unvaluable. The Lord give his people holy, wise, prudent, sober, humble, and understanding hearts, that they may know both how to prize and how to improve those liberties and mercies that he has handed to them through terrible dispensations! But,

(2.) Secondly, God inflicts great trials and sore judgments upon persons and places, *that he may awaken his own people out of that deep security that oftentimes seizeth upon them:* Ps. xxx. 5–9; Mat. xxv. 5; 2 Sam. ii. 7, 15, and xxiv. 15–17; 2 Kings xiv. 25; Mat. xii. 40; Jonah i. 1–3. What deep security had seized upon David, so that God was forced to make use of the bloody sword and of the sweeping pestilence to awaken him! Jonah was a prophet, he was a servant of the Lord, he was a type of Christ, he was a good man. His name Jonah signifies a dove, though he had but little of the dove in him, being as passionate a man of an honest man as you have lightly[1] heard of, saith Luther. Now Jonah having contracted guilt upon his conscience by acting quite contrary to God's royal call, what a desperate, senseless stupidity and security had seized upon him! what a spiritual lethargy was poor Jonah in! not much unlike that of the smith's dog, whom neither the hammers above him, nor the sparks of fire falling round about him, can awake. Jonah was not in a slumber, but in a sound, heavy, deep, and dead sleep; and what a wonder, what a prodigy was here, that in all this stir and tumult and danger, the winds whistling and roaring, the sea working, raging, swelling, frothing, foaming, and boiling like a pot, the waves mounting up to heaven and sinking down again to hell, as the psalmist speaks, the ship tumbling and tossing like a tennis-ball, the mariners, as stout fellows as they were, surprised with fear, and running up and down like men at their wits' end, like men that could not look pale death in the face with blood in their cheeks, that yet Jonah should sleep, and be as secure in that dreadful danger as if he had been in his own house sleeping on a bed of down! Oh the desperate security that may seize upon the best of saints! But this security God will cure in his Jonahs by some smart trial, or by some heavy judgment or other. The lethargy is best cured by a burning ague. Absalom sends once or twice to Joab to

[1] That is, 'likely.'—G.

come and speak with him; but when he saw that Joab would not come, he commands his corn-fields to be set on fire, and this awakens him, and fetches him with a witness, 2 Sam. xiv. 30. So God, by fiery afflictions, and by burning up our comforts round about us, awakens us, and brings us to himself with a witness. When iron grows rusty, we put it into the fire to purify it; and so when the people of God grow rusty and secure, then the Lord brings them under fiery trials to awaken them, and to purify them. If Nero was so angry with Vespasian because he slept at his music, how much more may the Lord be angry with all such as sleep and are secure under the most amazing and awakening judgments? But my hope and prayer is, that the Lord has, and will more and more graciously and effectually awaken all the wise slumbering virgins upon whom this fiery dispensation has passed. And therefore,

(3.) Thirdly, In respect of his people's sins, God has several special ends that he aims at by all the fiery trials and smart providences that he exercises them and others with. As,

[1.] First, God by these means designs *a further and a fuller discovery of their sins.* In standing waters you cannot see the mud that lies at the bottom of the pool or pond; but when once the water is drawn away, then it appears, Deut. viii. 2. In times of prosperity there is a great deal of mud, a great deal of atheism, unbelief, discontent, murmuring, impatience, passion, pride, &c., that lies at the bottom of men's hearts undiscovered. Oh, but when God shall once empty them of their estates, and burn up all their outward comforts, and set them with Job upon the dunghill, then the mud appears, then a whole army of lusts discover themselves, as we see in many this day, whom you shall rarely find without tears in their eyes, sighs in their hearts, and complaints in their mouths. Severe providences are pills made purposely to clear the eyesight: 1 Kings xvii. 18, 'And she said unto Elijah, What have I to do with thee, O thou man of God? art thou come unto me to call my sin to remembrance, and to slay my son?' If God had not taken away her son, her sin had not been brought to remembrance. O sirs! if God by this late dreadful fire had not taken away your houses, your goods, your estates, your trades, many of your sins had not been brought to your remembrance, though now you have lost most or all. You may say with the psalmist, 'My sins are ever before me,' Ps. li. 3. My pride is ever before me, my unbelief is ever before me, my frowardness is ever before me, my murmuring is ever before me, my discontent is ever before me, and my impatience is ever before me, &c.[1] Good men never come to know how bad they are, till they come to be exercised with severe providences and smart trials. It was the speech of a holy man in a great sickness, In this disease I have learned how great God is, and what the evil of sin is; I never knew to purpose what God was before, nor what sin was before. Afflictions are a Christian's glass, in which they may run and read the greatness of God and the vileness of sin. But,

[2.] Secondly, By severe providences and fiery trials God designs *the preventing of sin.* Paul was one of the holiest men on earth,

[1] Turn to the scriptures, Gen. xlii. 21; Jonah iv. 8, 9; Jer. ix. 7, *seq.*

called by some an earthly angel, and yet he needed a thorn in the flesh to prevent pride: 2 Cor. xii. 7, 'And lest I should be exalted above measure through the abundance of the revelations, there was given to me a thorn in the flesh, the messenger of Satan to buffet me, lest I should be exalted above measure.' Paul was in very great danger of being exalted above measure. Witness the doubling of those words in one verse, 'Lest I should be exalted, lest I should be exalted.' Prudent physicians sometimes give physic to prevent diseases; and so does the Physician of souls, as you may see by comparing the scriptures in the margin together.[1] The burnt child dreads the fire. Sin is but a bitter sweet, it is an evil worse than hell itself. Salt brine preserves from putrefaction, and salt marshes keep the sheep from rotting; and so sharp trials, severe providences preserve the saints from spiritual putrefying, and from spiritual rotting. The Rabbins, to keep their scholars from sin, were wont to tell them that sin made God's head ache; and saints under fiery trials do find by experience that sin makes not only their heads, but also their hearts ache; and by this means God preserves his people from many sins which otherwise they would certainly fall into. Beloved, God by his fiery dispensations has destroyed many or most of your outward comforts; but little do you know the horrible sins that by this means the Lord has preserved you from. A full estate lays men most open to the greatest sins, the worst of snares, and the deadliest temptations. The best of men have fallen foulest under their highest worldly enjoyments. Witness David, Solomon, Hezekiah, &c. Under your outward fulness, how low was your communion with God! how languishing were your graces! how lean were your souls! and how was your spring of inward comforts dried up! How little had God of your thoughts, your hearts, your time, your strength! O sirs! how bad would you have been by this time if God had not removed those things that were but fuel to your lusts, and quench-coals to your grace! Well, often think of this: it is a greater mercy to be preserved from sin, yea, from the least sin, than it is to enjoy the whole world. But,

[3.] Thirdly, By severe providences and by fiery trials God designs *the imbittering of sin to his people.* When God shall come and burn up men's comforts round about them, then they will cry out, Ah! what a bitter thing is sin! That puts God upon burning work! Then they will speak that language to their own souls that the prophet once spake to the Jews: Jer. ii. 15, 'They made his land waste: his cities are burnt with fire.' Ver. 17, 'Hast thou not procured these things to thyself?' Ver. 19, 'Thine own wickedness shall correct thee, and thy backslidings shall reprove thee: know therefore and see, that it is an evil thing and bitter, that thou hast forsaken the Lord thy God, and that my fear is not in thee, saith the Lord God of hosts.' So chap. iv. 18, 'Thy way and thy doings have procured these things unto thee: this is thy wickedness, because it is bitter, because it reacheth unto thy heart.' Yea, now they will say that sin is bitterness in the abstract, and in the plural number also, according to that of the prophet Hosea, chap. xii. 14, 'Ephraim provoked

[1] Job xxxiii. 19, 17, xxxiv. 31, 32, and xl. 4, 5; Hosea ii. 6, 7.

him to anger most bitterly,' or 'with bitternesses,' as the Hebrew has it. Relations and friends may tell us that sin is a bitter thing, and conscience may tell us that sin is a bitter thing, and good books may tell us that sin is a bitter thing, and men under terrors and horrors of spirit may tell us that sin is a bitter thing, and the sore and heavy judgments of God upon others may tell us that sin is a bitter thing, and the Spirit by his secret whispers may tell us that sin is a bitter thing, and ministers may tell us that sin is a bitter thing; they may tell you that it is bitter to God, it being the only thing in all the world that he has revealed his wrath from heaven against, and that is contrary to the nature of God, the law of God, the being of God, the glory of God, and the grand designs of God. They may tell you that it is bitter to Christ. Witness his crying out in the bitterness of his soul, 'My God, my God, why hast thou forsaken me?' and witness the sorrows and heaviness of his soul, and his sweating clods[1] of blood. When he hung upon the cross they gave him gall and vinegar to drink; but no gall was so bitter to him as your sins. They may tell you that sin is bitter to the Spirit of God; for nothing grieves him and provokes him and vexes him but sin, Gen. vi. 3, and Eph. iv. 29. They may tell you that sin is bitter to the good angels. Every sin that you commit is as a dagger at their hearts: there is nothing in all the world so bitter to them as to see their Lord and Master daily, yea, hourly, crucified by sinners' sins. They may tell you that sin is bitter to the evil angels, it being the only thing for which they were banished the court of heaven, and turned down to the lowest hell, where they are kept in chains of darkness to the judgment of the great day, Jude 6. They may tell you that sin is bitter to the worst of men; witness Adam's hiding of himself, and Judas his hanging of himself, and Cain's crying out, 'My burden is greater than I am able to bear,' Gen. iii. 10; Mat. xxvii.; Gen. iv. 13. They may tell you that it is bitter to the creatures who 'groan under their burdens, and who long to be delivered from that bondage that the sin of man hath subjected them to,' Rom. viii. 20–22; and yet for all this we will not feelingly, affectionately, experimentally say that sin is bitter, till God comes and burns us up: Lam. iv. 11, 'And gives us gall and wormwood to drink.' Chap. iii. 19, 20, 'Remembering mine affliction and my misery, the wormwood and the gall. My soul hath them still in remembrance, and is humbled in me.' O sirs, how bitter should sin be to you, who have seen London all in flames! Certainly God, by burning up your sweet, pleasant, and delightful things, would teach you to taste a greater bitterness in sin than ever. O happy fire, that shall render God and Christ, and heaven, and promises, and ordinances more sweet, and sin more bitter to poor sinners' souls! Doubtless, one of God's great designs by this late judgment of fire is to imbitter sin to all sorts of men. When judgments imbitter our sins to us, then they work kindly, powerfully, effectually, and then we may conclude that there was a hand of love in those judgments, and then we shall justify the Lord, and say with the church, Lam. i. 18, 'The Lord is righteous; for I have rebelled against him:' or as the Hebrew runs, 'because I have imbittered him,' he is righteous in all the sore judg-

[1] Query, 'clots'?—G.

ments that he hath inflicted upon me; for I have imbittered him against me by my most bitter sins. But,

[4.] Fourthly, By severe providences and fiery trials, God designs *the mortifying and purging away of his people's sins:* Isa. i. 25, 'And I will turn my hand upon thee,' [to wit, to correct or chastise thee,] 'and purely purge away thy dross,' [or drosses,] 'and take away all thy tin,' or tins in the plural number. Some by dross understand gross iniquity; and by tin, glittering hypocrisy. For as tin is very like unto silver, so is hypocrisy very like unto piety. Others by dross understand persons that are openly profane; and by tin, such as are inwardly unsound. The words are a metaphor taken from them that try metals in the fire, purging from precious silver all dross and tin, Isa. xxxi. 9.[1] The Jews, who were once silver, were now turned into dross and tin; but God by fiery trials would burn up their dross and tin, their enormities and wickednesses, and make them as shining Christians in grace and holiness as ever they were. So Isa. xxvii. 9, 'By this therefore shall the iniquity of Jacob be purged; and this is all the fruit, to take away his sin.' God by the Babylonish captivity would as by fire purge away the iniquity of Jacob; and to shew the certainty of it, he instanceth in their darling sin—viz., idolatry. When he maketh all the stones of the altar as chalk-stones that are beaten in sunder, the groves and the images shall not stand up. Idolatry was the great sin for which God sent them into captivity. Now how they were purged from this sin after their return out of captivity, appears by their history. Take one instance for all: Pilate being [appointed] by Tiberius to be governor over the Jews, caused in the night-time the statue of Cæsar to be brought into Jerusalem covered, which thing within three days after caused a great tumult among the Jews; for they who beheld it were astonished and moved as though now the law of their country were profaned, for they hold it not lawful for any picture or image to be brought into the city. At their lamentation who were in the city, there was gathered together a great multitude out of the fields adjoining, and they went presently to Pilate, then at Cæsarea, beseeching him earnestly that the images might be taken away out of Jerusalem, and that the laws of their country might remain inviolated.[2] When Pilate denied their suit, they prostrated themselves before his house, and there remained lying upon their faces for five days and nights, never moving. Afterwards Pilate, sitting in his tribunal-seat, was very careful to call all the Jews together before him, as though there he would have given them an answer, when upon the sudden a company of armed soldiers, for so it was provided, compassed the Jews about with a triple rank. The Jews were hereat amazed, seeing that which they expected not. Then Pilate told them, that except they would receive the images of Cæsar, he would kill them all, and to that end made a sign to the soldiers to draw their swords. The Jews, as though they had agreed thereto, fell all down at once, and offered their necks to the stroke of the sword, crying out that they would rather lose their lives than suffer their religion to be profaned. Then Pilate,

[1] Dan. xi. 35; Mal. iii. 1–3. God's fire is in Zion, and his furnace in Jerusalem.

[2] Josephus, p. 617. The Jews hated and feared idolatry as much as the burnt child dreads the fire. [Josephus, *sub voce.*—G.]

admiring the constancy of the people in their religion, presently commanded the statues to be taken out of the city of Jerusalem. All the hurt the fire did the three children, or rather champions, was to burn off their cords, Dan. iii. 23, 24. Our lusts are cords of vanity, but by fiery trials God will burn them up: Zech. xiii. 9, 'And I will bring the third part through the fire, and will refine them as silver is refined, and will try them as gold is tried.' The best of men are but men at the best; they have much corruption and dross in them, and they need refining; and therefore God by fiery trials will refine them, but not as dross or chaff which are burnt up in the fire, but as silver and gold which are purified in the fire. He will so refine them as that they shall leave their dregs and dross behind them. Look, what the fire is to the gold, the file to the iron, the fan to the wheat, the soap to the clothes, the salt to the flesh, that shall fiery trials be to the saints. But what shall be the fruit of their refining? *Ans.* 'They shall call on my name, and I will hear them. I will say, It is my people, and they shall say, The Lord is my God.' By fiery trials God will purge out our dross and make virtue shine. All the fiery trials that befall the saints shall be as a potion to carry away ill humours, and as cold frosts to destroy the vermin, and as a tempestuous sea to purge the wine from its lees, and as the north wind that drieth up the vapours, that purges the blood, and that quickens the spirits, and as a sharp corrosive to eat out the dead flesh. The great thing that should be most in every burnt citizen's eye and heart and prayers and desires is, that the fire of London may be so sanctified as to issue in the burning up of their lusts, and in the purging away of the filth of the daughter of Zion, Isa. iv. 4. Jerome reports of Plato, how he left that famous city of Athens, and chose to live in a little ancient village almost overturned with tempests and earthquakes, that, being often minded therein of his approaching desolation,[1] he might get more power over his strong lusts, and learn to live a more virtuous life than ever he had lived before.[2] O sirs! if God by this fiery dispensation shall make you more victorious over your strong lusts, and help you to live more virtuous lives, you will have cause to bless him all your days, though he has turned you out of house and home, and burnt up all your comforts round about you. But,

(4.) Fourthly, By severe providences and fiery trials, God designs these four things, in respect of his children's graces:

[1.] First, He designs *the reviving, quickening, and recovering of their decayed graces.* By fiery trials he will inflame that love that was even key-cold, and raise that faith that was fallen asleep, and quicken up those hopes that were languishing, and put life and spirits into those joys and comforts that were withering and dying, Rev. ii. 4; James i. 2–12; 2 Cor. xii. 10. God, under fiery trials, lets his poor children see how that by their spiritual decays he has been dishonoured, his Spirit grieved, religion shamed, the mouths of the wicked opened, weak saints staggered, strong saints troubled, conscience wounded, and their souls and graces impaired; and by these discoveries he engages them to the use of all those holy and heavenly helps, whereby

[1] Query, 'dissolution'?—Ed. [2] Hieronym. contra Jovinian, lib. ii.

their decayed graces may be revived and recovered. Many creatures that have been frozen, and even dead with cold, have been revived and recovered by being brought to the fire. God by fiery trials will unfreeze the frozen graces of his people, and put new life and spirits into them. As the air is sometimes clear, and sometimes cloudy; and as the sea is sometimes ebbing, and sometimes flowing; and as the trees of the field are sometimes flowering, green, and growing, and sometimes naked, withered, and as it were even dead: so it is sometimes with the graces of the saints; but the Lord by one fiery trial or another will revive, and recover, and raise their graces again. Epiphanius makes mention of those that travel by the deserts of Syria, where are nothing but miserable marshes and sands, destitute of all commodities, nothing to be had for love or money. Now if it so happen that their fire go out by the way, then they light it again at the heat of the sun, by the means of a burning-glass[1]: and thus if the fire of zeal, if the sparks of divine grace, by the prevalency of some strong corruption, or by the violence of some dreadful temptation, should be put out, or die as to its lively operations, by a burning-glass, or by one fiery dispensation or another, God will inflame the zeal, and enliven the dying graces of his poor people. I know the saving graces of the Spirit—viz., such as faith, love, hope, &c.—cannot be finally and totally extinguished in the souls, when they are once wrought there by the Spirit; yet their lustre, their radiancy, their activity, their shine and flame may be clouded and covered, whilst the season of temptation lasteth; as living coals may be so covered with ashes, that neither light, nor smoke, nor heat may appear, and yet when the embers, the ashes, are stirred to the bottom, then live coals appear, and by a little blowing a flame breaks forth.[2] There are several cases wherein grace in a Christian's breast may seem to be hid, cold, dead, and covered over; as sap in the winter is hid in the roots of trees, or as flowers and fruits are hid in the seeds, or roots in the earth, or as sparks of fire are hid in the ashes, or as bits of gold are hid in a dust heap, or as pearls may be hid in the mire. Ay, but God by one severe providence or another, by one fiery trial or another, will blow that heavenly grace, that divine fire, into a perfect flame: he will cause their hid graces to revive as the corn, and grow as the vine, and blossom as the lily, and smell as the wine of Lebanon, Hosea xiv. 5–7. O sirs! how many Christians were there amongst us, who were much decayed and withered in their graces, in their duties, in their converses, in their comforts, in their spiritual enjoyments, in their communions with God, and with one another; and yet were not sensible of their decays, nor humbled under their decays, nor industrious to recover themselves out of their withering and dying condition! and therefore no wonder if the Lord, to recover them and raise them, hath brought fiery trials upon them.[3] But,

[2.] Secondly, God, by severe providences and by fiery trials, designs *a further exercise of his children's graces.* Sleepy habits bring him no glory, nor do us no good. All the honour he has, and all the

[1] Lib. de Anchorat. [2] 1 John iii. 9, 11; Heb. viii; 1 Pet. i. 5; John x. 28–31.
[3] As a man may take infection, or get some inward bruise, or spring a vein, and yet not know of it.

advantage we have in this world, is from the active part of grace. Consult the scriptures in the margin.[1] There is little difference—as to the comfort and sweet of grace—between grace out of exercise, and no grace at all. A man that has millions, but has no heart to use what he has, wherein is he better, as to the comfort and sweetness of his life, than a man that hath but a few mites in the world? Eccles. vi. 1–4. 'How is it that you have no faith?' saith Christ to his disciples, when they were in a dreadful storm, and in danger of drowning, and so stood in most need of their faith, yet they had then their faith to seek. They had faith in the habit but not in the exercise, and therefore Christ looks upon their faith as no faith, Mark iv. 40. How is it that you have no faith? what is the sheath without the knife? the scabbard without the sword? the musket without the match? the cannon without the bullet? the granado without powder? no more are all your graces when not in exercise. The strongest creature, the lion, and the subtlest creature, the serpent, if they are dormant, are as easily surprised and destroyed as the weakest worm; so the strongest saints, if grace be not in exercise, are as easily surprised and captivated by sin, Satan, and the world, as the weakest saints are. O sirs! if Christians will not stir up the grace of God that is in them, if they will not look to the daily exercise of grace, God, by some severe providence or other, by some fiery dispensation or other, will stir up their graces for them, Jonah i. 6. Ah sluggish, slumbering Christians, who are careless as to the exercise of your graces, how sadly, how sorely do you provoke the Lord to let Satan loose to tempt you, and corruptions grow strong to weary you, and the world grow cross to vex you, and friends turn enemies to plague you, and the Spirit withdraw to discomfit you, Lam. i. 16, and fiery trials to break in to awaken you! And all this to bring you to live in a daily exercise of grace. God was fain to be a moth, a worm, a lion, yea, a young lion to Ephraim and Judah, before he could bring them up to an exercise of grace, Hosea v. 12–14; but when he was all this to them, then they fall roundly upon a lively exercise of grace. Hosea vi. 1–3, 'Come, let us return unto the Lord: for he hath torn, and he will heal us; he hath smitten, and he will bind us up. After two days he will revive us: in the third day he will raise us up, and we shall live in his sight. Then shall we know, if we follow on to know the Lord: his going forth is prepared as the morning; and he shall come unto us as the rain, as the latter and former rain unto the earth.' Here you see their faith, their repentance, their love, their hope, all in exercise. When a soldier's courage, mettle, and gallantry, lies as it were hid, his captain will put him upon such hardships, hazards, and dangers, as shall rouse up his courage, mettle, and gallantry; if a scholar has excellent acquired parts and abilities, and will not use them nor improve them, his master will put him upon such tasks as shall draw out all his parts and abilities to the height: so when the Lord has laid into the souls of his people a stock of grace, and they grow idle and careless, and will not improve that stock for his glory and their own good, he will then exercise them with such severe pro-

[1] Job xv. 3; 2 Chron. xx. 12, 13; James i. 4, and v. 11; Hab. ii. 3, 4; Micah vii. 7–9; Rev. xiii. 10 compared with chap. xiv. 12.

vidences and fiery trials, as shall put them to a full improvement of that blessed stock of grace that he has intrusted them with. The fire that came from heaven was to be kept continually burning that it might never go out, Lev. vi. 13. God loves to see the graces of his children in continual exercise. Neglect of our graces is the ground of their decrease and decay. Wells are the sweeter for drawing, and grace is the stronger for acting; we get nothing by dead and useless habits. Talents hid in a napkin gather rust; the noblest faculties are imbased when not improved in exercise: 2 Tim. i. 6, 'Stir up the gift of God which is in thee.' It is an allusion to the fire in the temple, which was always to be kept burning. All the praise that God has from us in this life is from the actings of grace. It was Abraham's acting of faith that set the crown of glory upon the Lord's head. O sirs! look narrowly to it, that you fail not in the activity and lively vigour of your graces. Look to it that your graces be still acted, exercised, and blown up, that so they may be still flaming and shining. The more you exercise grace, the more you strengthen it, the more you increase it. Repeated acts strengthen habits; it is so in sin, and it is so in grace also. The more the little child goes, the more strong it grows by going. The more a man plays upon an instrument, the more dexterous he grows. Money is not increased by lying in a chest, but by trading, Mat. xxv. 27. The more any member is used, the stronger it is. As the right hand is most used, so it is commonly strongest. 'The diligent hand makes rich,' Prov. x. 4. A little stock well husbanded will daily increase, when a greater stock neglected shall decay and come to nothing. The exercise of grace will best testify both the truth and the life of your graces. Grace is never more evident than when it is in exercise. When I see a man rise, and walk, and work, and exercise his arms, I know he is a real man, a living man. The more the fire is blown up the sooner it is seen to be fire. There are many precious Christians, who are full of fears and doubts that they have no love to God, no faith in God, no hope of glory, &c., but the best way under heaven to put an end to these fears and doubts is to be fervent in exerting acts of love, of faith, of hope, &c. The non-exercise of grace cast Adam out of paradise; it shut Moses and Aaron out of Canaan, Num. xx. 12; it brought Jacob into fourteen years' hard service and bondage; for had he exercised faith, hope, patience, &c., as he should have done, he would never have got the blessing by indirect means as he did; it provoked the Lord to strike Zacharias dumb, Luke i. 18–20; it shut thousands of the Jews out of the land of Canaan, Heb. iii. 17, 18. I dare not be so harsh, so rash, and so uncharitable, as to think that none of those that died in the wilderness had the habits of faith, the seeds of grace in their souls; but it was their non-acting of faith that kept them out of the Holy Land, as it did Moses and Aaron, according to what I hinted but now. Beloved, by these instances, among many others that might be produced, you see that God hath dealt very smartly and severely with his choicest servants for their not exercising of their graces as they ought to have done. And though I dare not, upon many accounts, say that for the saints' not exercising and improving their graces, God has turned London into a heap of ashes;

yet I dare say that this neglect of theirs may be one thing that added fuel to that fire.[1] Well, sirs, you had not long since many outward comforts to live upon, but the Lord has now burnt them up, that so he might lead you forth to live in a daily exercise of grace upon himself, upon his power, upon his all-sufficiency, his goodness, his faithfulness, his fulness, his graciousness, his unchangeableness, his promises. And if this fiery dispensation shall be so sanctified to us as to work us to a further activity of grace, and to a further growth and increase of grace, we shall be happy citizens though we are burnt citizens. But,

[3.] Thirdly, By severe providences and by fiery trials God designs *the growth of his people in grace.* Usually the graces of the saints thrive best when they are under a smarting rod. Grace usually is in the greatest flourish when the saints are under the sorest trials, Rom. v. 3, 4; 2 Cor. i. 3-6. The snuffing of the candle makes it burn the brighter. God beats and bruises his links[2] to make them burn the brighter; he bruises his spices to make them send forth the greater aromatical savour. Fiery trials are like the tazel, which, though it be sharp and scratching, it is to make the cloth more pure and fine. God would not rub so hard, were it not to fetch out the dirt and spots that be in his people. The Jews were always best when they were in their lowest condition. Well-waters arising from deep springs are hotter in the winter than they are in the summer. Stars shine brightest in the darkest nights; and so do the graces of the saints shine brightest in the darkest nights of affliction and tribulation. God will sometimes more carry on the growth of grace by a cross than by an ordinance; yea, the Lord will, first or last, more or less, turn all fiery trials into ordinances for the helping on the growth of grace in his people's souls, Heb. xii. 10; James i. 3, 4; 1 Pet. i. 6, 7. Look, as in the lopping of a tree, there seems to be a kind of diminution and destruction; yet the end and issue of it is better growth: and as the weakening of the body by physic seems to tend to death, yet it produceth better health and more strength: and as the ball by falling downward riseth upward, and as water in pipes descends that it may ascend: so the saints' spiritual growth in grace is carried on by such divine methods and in such ways as might seem to deaden grace, and weaken it, rather than anywise to augment and increase it. We know that winter is as necessary to bring on harvest as the spring; and so fiery trials are as necessary to bring on the harvest of grace as the spring of mercy is. Though fiery trials are grievous, yet they shall make us more gracious. Though for the present we cannot see but that such and such severe providences and fiery trials as the loss of house, estate, trade, friends, will redound much to our prejudice and damage, yet in the issue we shall find that God will turn them to the internal and eternal advantage of our precious souls, Heb. xii. 11. We may in a pang of passion say, as Jacob, 'Joseph is not, and Simeon is not!' Gen. xlii. 36.[3] 'All these are against me'—children are not,

[1] Austin writ upon that day wherein he shewed no acts of grace, *Diem perdidi,* I have lost a day. Oh how many days have we lost then for which God might justly visit us!

[2] 'Torches.'—G.

[3] But yet as old as Jacob was, he lived to see all those things work for his good, which he concluded were against him.

honours are not, riches are not, habitations are not, credit is not. All these are against us; but in the close we shall find that promise made good in power upon us, Rom. viii. 28, 'We know that all things shall work together for good to them that love God, to them that are called according to his purpose.' O sirs! all the power of heaven stands engaged to make good this promise to you; and if you would but live in the daily actings of faith upon this blessed promise, you would then be able to bear up bravely under all the troubles and trials, crosses and losses that you meet with in this world; and you would then experience the truth of Samson's riddle—'Out of the eater came meat, and out of the strong sweetness,' Judges xiv. 14. What Paul said of his fiery trials, viz., 'I know that this shall turn to my salvation,' Phil i. 19, that may you safely say of all your fiery trials: We know that they shall work for our good, we know that they shall turn to our salvation. Though wicked instruments might design our destruction, yet the wise God that sits at the helm will turn all into our salvation. Those severe providences which for the present may seem very prejudicial, in the issue shall prove very beneficial. Joseph's brethren threw him into a pit, afterwards they sell him, then he is falsely accused, and as unjustly cast into prison and laid in cold iron, Ps. cv. 17, 18: yet all this issued in his good; his abasement made way for his advancement; for his thirteen years' imprisonment he reigned fourscore years like a king, Gen. l. 20, and xli. 40. David, you know, had seven years' banishment, yet it ended in a glorious reign of forty years' continuance. Job lost all that ever he had in one day; he was a man under great calamity, he was a spectacle of the highest misery, he abounded only in boils, and sores, and rags; but all this issued in the trial of his grace, in the discovery of his grace, and in the improvement of his grace, and in the close God did compensate his very great losses by giving him twice as much as ever he had before, Job xlii. 10. Dear friends, that by all severe providences and fiery trials God will turn your spark of grace into a flame, your mites into millions, and your drops into seas, is, and shall be the hearty desire of my soul. O sirs! if Christ be even ravished with one of his spouse's eyes, and with one chain of her neck, Cant. iv. 9, with the least grains and drachms of true grace, how will he be taken with abundance of grace! how will he be ravished with the flourishing estate of your souls in grace! Well, remember this, the more under all your fiery trials grace is increased, the more God is honoured, religion adorned, the mouths of the wicked stopped, the hands and hearts of weak saints strengthened and encouraged, the smarting rod sweetened, and threatened judgments prevented. Oh that those two prophecies might be made good in power upon all the burnt citizens of London! That Isa. xxxii. 15, 'Until the Spirit be poured upon us from on high, and the wilderness be a fruitful field:' and that Isa. xxxv. 1, 2, 'The wilderness and the solitary place shall be glad for them; and the desert shall rejoice, and blossom as the rose. It shall blossom abundantly, and rejoice even with joy and singing: the glory of Lebanon shall be given unto it, the excellency of Carmel and Sharon; they shall see the glory of the Lord, and the excellency of our God.'[1] Thrice happy will the burnt citizens of London be, if under all their crosses and losses they grow into a more deep acquaintance with God, the world, and their own hearts; with God and his holiness, with the world and its vanity, mutability, impotency, and uncertainty; and with their own hearts, and the deceitfulness, vileness, baseness, and wretchedness of them. If under fiery dispensations we grow more holy than ever, and more humble than ever, and more heavenly than ever, and more meek and lowly than ever, and more tender and compassionate than ever, and more faithful and fruitful than ever, and more patient and contented than ever, then we may be confident that the grand design of God in bringing all that evil that he has brought upon us was his glory and our own internal and eternal good, and accordingly we may rejoice in the Lord, though we have nothing else to rejoice in, Hab. iii. 17, 18. But,

[4.] Fourthly and lastly, By severe providences and by fiery trials, God doth design *the trial of his people's graces, and the discovery of their sincerity and integrity to the world,* 1 Pet. i. 6, 7; Rev. iii. 18. Deut. viii. 2, 'And thou shalt remember all the way which the Lord thy God led thee these forty years in the wilderness, to humble thee, and to prove thee, to know what was in thine heart, whether thou wouldest keep his commandments, or no.' God knew them well enough before, without any experimental trial of them; but that he might the better make a discovery of themselves to themselves and to others, he led them up and down in the wilderness forty years: Ps. lxvi. 10–12, 'For thou, O God, hast proved us: thou hast tried us, as silver is tried. Thou hast brought us into the net; thou hast laid affliction upon our loins. Thou hast caused men to ride over our heads: we went through fire and through water.' God proves his people, not thereby to better his own knowledge of them, but to bring them to a better knowledge both of their own vices and graces. It is not known what corn will yield till it come to the flail, nor what grapes will yield till they come to the press. Grace is hid in nature as sweet water in rose leaves; but fiery trials will fetch it out. Fire and water are merciless elements, and they note variety of sharpest trials. Now through these God led his people, that so he might discover to them and others both the strength of their graces, and the strength of their sins. God many times exercises his dearest children with fiery trials, that he may discover the sincerity and integrity of his people to the world. The profane atheistical world are apt very boldly and confidently to conclude that the people of God are a pack of hypocrites and dissemblers, and that they serve God for a livery, for loaves, and not for love, John vi. 26; and that they are mercenary in all they do, having more in their eye the hedge that he has made about them, and the gold and silver that he has bestowed upon them, than the honour and glory of the great God; just as the devil objected against Job, chap. i. 9. Now God, to convince these men, these monsters, of the integrity and sincerity of his people, he breaks down the hedge that he had made about them, and turns the wheel upon them,

[1] Pliny speaks of a golden vine which never withereth, but is always flourishing. Oh that this might be the mercy of all those Christians who have been burnt up!

and breaks them with breach upon breach; he strips them of all, and turns them out of house and home, as he did Job, chap. xx. 21; and yet this people, with Job, will still worship the Lord, and bless a taking God, as well as a giving God. They will still keep close to the Lord and his ways, whatever God doth with them or against them. Ps. xliv. 17–19, 'All this is come upon us,' [it is a terrible 'all,' as you may see from the 9th to the 17th verse;] 'yet have we not forgotten thee, neither have we dealt falsely in thy covenant. Our heart is not turned back, neither have our steps declined from thy way; though thou hast sore broken us in the place of dragons, and covered us with the shadow of death.' In spite of all the wrath and rage of Antiochus Epiphanes, that cruel and bloody persecutor of the saints, these servants of the Lord shew their sincerity by their constancy in keeping close to the Lord and his ways in the face of the greatest opposition and hottest persecution that they met withal. When the emperor sent to Basil[1] to subscribe to the Arian heresy, the messenger at first gave him good language, and promised him great preferment, if he would turn Arian; to which Basil replied, Alas, these speeches are fit to catch little children withal that look after such things; but we that are nourished and taught by the Holy Scriptures, are readier to suffer a thousand deaths than to suffer one syllable or tittle of the Scripture to be altered. The same Basil affirms that many of the heathens, seeing the heroic zeal, courage, and constancy of the primitive Christians in the face of all oppositions and persecutions, turned Christians. Justin Martyr confesseth that the constancy of the Christians in their sufferings was the chief motive that converted him to Christianity; for I myself, saith he, was once a Platonist, and did gladly hear the Christians reviled; but when I saw they feared not death, nor any of those miseries which most frighten all other men, I began to consider with myself that it was impossible for such men to be lovers of pleasure more than lovers of piety, and that made me first think of turning Christian.[2] Now by these means and methods God convinceth the blind world of the integrity and sincerity of his people. When they see those whom they have severely judged for hypocrites shall own the Lord and his ways, and cleave to the Lord and his ways, and continue to follow the Lord and his ways, and hold on in a high honouring of the Lord and his ways, when their hedge is broken down, and God has stripped them as naked as in the day wherein they were born, oh now they begin to change their note, and to conclude, surely these are the servants of the Most High God, Dan. iii. 26, and Acts xvi. 17; these are no hypocrites nor dissemblers, but true Nathanaels in whom there is no guile, John i. 47. How have the people of God in London been judged hypocrites, dissemblers, deceivers, factious, and what not! Now God, by burning up their substance, and by turning them out of house and home, and destroying all their pleasant things, doth certainly design to give those that have so deeply censured them a proof of their integrity and sincerity, by letting them see that all the changes that have passed upon them can never work them to change their Master Christ, nor to change his ways for the ways of sin, nor to change his worship for the worship of the world, nor to change their religion for the religion of Rome.

[1] Hist. Tripart., lib. vii. cap. 36. [2] As before.—G.

Certainly those that love the Lord, that delight in the Lord, and that highly prize the Lord for those infinite perfections, beauties, glories, and excellencies that are in him, they will own him, and cleave to him, and follow after him when they have little as when they had much, yea, when they have nothing of the world as when they had all the world; and by so doing, they put a padlock upon the lying lips of such, they button up the mouths of such who asperse and calumniate them as a generation that only serve God upon the account of a worldly interest.[1] There is nothing that doth more amuse,[2] amaze, and astonish wicked men, than to see the people of God keep close to him and his ways when they are in a suffering estate, yea, when they have lost all but their God and their integrity. The fire tries the gold as well as the touchstone, and diseases try the skill of the physician, and tempests try the skill of the pilot; and so do fiery trials try both the truth and the strength of a Christian's graces. Paulinus Nolanus, when his city was taken by the barbarians, prayed thus to God: Lord, let me not be troubled at the loss of my gold, silver, honour, city, &c.; for thou art all, and much more than all these to me. Here was a heroic spirit, here was grace in strength, yea, in triumph. The spirits of the men of the world usually sink under their losses. Menippus of Phenicia, having lost his goods, strangled himself.[3] Dinarcus Phiton,[4] at a certain loss, cut his own throat to save the charge of a halter. Another, being turned out of his estate, ran out of his wits. And another, for the death of his son, threw himself headlong into the sea. Augustus Cæsar, in whose time Christ was born, was so troubled and astonished at the relation of a foil and overthrow from Varus, that for certain months together he let the hair of his beard and head grow still, and wore it long; yea, and otherwhiles he would run his head against the doors, crying out, Quintilius Varus, deliver up my legions again; Quintilius Varus, deliver up my legions again.[5] Henry the Second, who was none of the best of princes, hearing that his city Mentz was taken, used this blasphemous speech: I shall never, saith he, love God any more, that suffered a city so dear to me to be taken from me. Now by all these instances you may clearly and plainly see the different temper and carriage of wicked men under their losses, crosses, trials, and sufferings, from the people of God. When they are under fiery trials, what an evil spirit, what a desperate spirit, what a sullen spirit, what a proud spirit, what a satanical spirit, what a hellish spirit, do they discover! They tell all the world that they are under the power and dominion of the god of this world; Phil. ii. 2 and 2 Tim. ii. 26. But when the people of God are under fiery trials, they make conscience of carrying of it so as that they may convince the world that God is in them of a truth, and that they are sincere and upright before the Lord, however they are judged and censured as hypocrites, deceivers, dissemblers, and what not. Oh that all that are sufferers by this fiery dispensation would make it their business, their work, their heaven, so to carry it under their present trials, as to

[1] Joshua xxiv. 15; Mat. xix. 27; Rev. xiv. 4, 5; 1 Peter iii. 16, and ii. 12, 15. *φιμοῦν* properly signifies to muzzle, or halter, or tie up, or to button up their mouths, as we say.

[2] = Cause to 'muse,' consider.—G.

[3] Diog. Laertius, ii. 99, 100.—G.

[4] Qu. 'Phyton of Rhegium'? if so, above is a myth.—G.

[5] Suetonius.

convince all gainsayers of the sincerity, integrity, and uprightness of their hearts, both towards the Lord, his people, his ways, his ordinances, his interest, and all his concernments in this world! And thus much for the gracious ends that God aims at in all those severe providences and fiery trials that of late he has exercised his people with.

The next thing we have to inquire after is those sins for which the Lord inflicts so heavy a judgment as this of fire upon the sons of men. Now for the opening of this, give me leave to propose this question—viz.,

Quest. What are those sins that bring the fiery dispensation, that bring the judgment of fire upon cities, nations, and countries? Now, that I may give a full and fair answer to this necessary and important question, will you please to premise with me these four things:—

[1.] First, We need not question but that some of all sorts, ranks, and degrees of men in and about that once great and glorious city did eminently contribute to the bringing down of that dreadful judgment of fire, that has turned that renowned city into ashes. Doubtless superiors and inferiors, ministers and people, husbands and wives, parents and children, masters and servants, rich and poor, honourable and base, bond and free, have all had a hand in the bringing down that judgment of fire that has turned London into a ruinous heap. But,

[2.] Secondly, Premise this with me—viz., That it is a greater argument of humility, integrity, and holy ingenuity to fear ourselves, and to be jealous of ourselves rather than others, as the disciples of Christ did: Mat. xxvi. 21, 22, 'And as they did eat, he said, Verily I say unto you, that one of you shall betray me. And they were exceeding sorrowful, and began every one of them to say unto him, Lord, is it I?' It is better for every man to do his best to ransack and search his own soul, Lam. iii. 40, and to find out the Achan, Josh. vii., the accursed thing in his own bosom that has brought that dreadful judgment of fire upon us, than for men, without any Scripture warrant, to fix it upon this party and that, this sort of men and that. There is no Christian to him that smites upon his own heart, his own breast, his own thigh, saying, What have I done? The neglect of this duty the prophet long since has complained of: 'No man repents himself of his wickedness, saying, What have I done?' Jer. viii. 6—that is, none comparatively. So how rare is it to find a burnt citizen repenting himself of his wickedness, and saying, What have I done? Most men are ready to blame others more than themselves, and to judge others rather than themselves to be the persons that have brought down this judgment of fire upon us, Mat. vii. 1–4. It was a good saying of one of the ancients, [Augustine,] *Amat Deus seipsos judicantes non judicare*, God loves to judge them that judge others rashly, but not those that judge themselves religiously. But,

[3.] Thirdly, Premise this with me, In times of common judgments, common calamities, and miseries, other of the saints and servants of God have looked upon their own sins as the procuring causes of the common calamity. Thus David did in that 2 Sam. xxiv. 15, 'So the Lord sent a pestilence upon Israel, from the morning even to the time appointed: and there died of the people, from Dan even to Beer-sheba, seventy thousand men.' But mark the 17th verse, 'And David spake unto the Lord, when he saw the angel that smote the people, and said, Lo, I have sinned, and I have done wickedly: but these sheep, what have they done? Let thy hand, I pray thee, be against me, and against my father's house.' And thus did good Nehemiah, chap. i. 3, 6, 7, 'And they said unto me, The remnant that are left of the captivity there in the province are in great affliction and reproach: the wall of Jerusalem also is broken down, and the gates thereof burnt with fire. Both I and my father's house have sinned. We have dealt very corruptly against thee, and have not kept thy commandments, nor the statutes, nor the judgments which thou commandedst thy servant Moses.' Now certainly it is as much our glory as our duty to write after these blessed copies that these worthies have set before us. Alexander had somewhat a wry neck, and his soldiers thought it an honour to be like him. How much more should we count it an honour to be like to David and Nehemiah in such a practice as is honourable to the Lord, and advantageous to ourselves! But what Plutarch said of Demosthenes, that he was excellent at praising the worthy acts of his ancestors, but not so at imitating them, is applicable to the present case, and to many who have been burnt up in our day. But,

[4.] Fourthly and lastly, Premise this with me, There were many sins amongst them that did profess to fear God in that great city, which may and ought to work them to justify the Lord, and to say that he is righteous in his fiery dispensations. I may well say to the burnt citizens of London what the prophet Oded to them in that 2 Chron. xxviii. 10, 'But are there not with you, even with you, sins against the Lord your God?'

But you will say, What sins were there among the professing people in London that may and ought to work them to justify the Lord, and to say that he is just and righteous, and that he has done them no wrong, though he has burnt them up, and turned them out of all?

Ans. I answer, That there were these seven sins, among others, to be found amongst many of them, I say not amongst all of them, all which call aloud upon them to lie low at the foot of God, and to subscribe to the righteousness of God, though he has turned them out of house and home, and burnt up their substance on every hand.

[1.] First, There was among many professors of the gospel in London too great *a conformity to the fashions of the world.* How many professing men in that great city were dressed up like fantastical antics, and women like Bartholomew-babies,[1] to the dishonour of God, the shame of religion, the hardening of the wicked, the grieving of the weak, and the provoking of divine justice! When Darius changed the fashion of his scabbard from the Persian manner into the mode of the Greeks, the Chaldean astrologers prognosticated that the Persian monarchy should be translated to them whose fashion he counterfeited. Certainly that nation may fear a scourge from that nation or nations whose fashion they follow: Zeph. i. 8, 'And it shall come to pass in the day of the Lord's sacrifice, that I will punish the princes, and the

[1] 'Dolls' sold at Bartholomew Fair. Cf. Morley's 'History.'—G.

king's children, and all such as are clothed with strange apparel.' This is a stinging and a flaming check against all fashion-mongers, against all such as seem to have consulted with French, Italian, Persian, and all outlandish monsters, to advise them of all their several modes and fashions of vice, and that are so dexterous at following of them, that they are more complete in them than their pattern. Certainly, if ever such wantons be saved, it will be by fire. Strange apparel is part of the old man, that must be put off, if ever men or women intend to go to heaven. What dreadful things are thundered out against those proud, curious dames of Jerusalem, by the prophet Isaiah, who being himself a courtier, inveighs as punctually against the noble vanity of apparel, as if he had even then viewed the ladies' wardrobes, Isa. xxxviii. 16, *seq*. And those vanities of theirs brought desolating and destroying judgments upon them: Isa. iii. 24–26, 'And it shall come to pass, that instead of sweet smell there shall be a stink; and instead of a girdle a rent; and instead of well-set hair baldness; and instead of a stomacher a girding of sackcloth; and burning instead of beauty. Thy men shall fall by the sword, and thy mighty in the war. And her gates shall lament and mourn; and she, being desolate, shall sit upon the ground.' As light and slight as many make of vain apparel, yet Cyrian[1] and Augustine draw up this conclusion: that superfluous apparel is worse than whoredom, because whoredom only corrupts chastity, but this corrupts nature. Seneca complained, that many in his time were more solicitous of their attire than of their good behaviour, and that they had rather that the commonwealth should be troubled than their locks and set looks. I have read of the Grecians, that when they wished a curse upon their enemies, it was this—that they should please themselves in bad customs. There are many who lift their heads high, who seem to be under this curse this day. Why doth the apostle say, saith one of the ancients, [Austin,] 'Above all things swear not'? Is it worse to swear than to steal? worse to swear than to commit adultery? worse to swear than to kill a man? No; but the apostle would fortify us as much as he could against a pestilent custom, to punish the pestilent customs and fashions that were amongst us, James v. 12. God sent the pestilence in 1665, and the fiery judgment in 1666. And the Lord grant that the bloody sword, in the hands of cruel cut-throats, that are brutish and skilful to destroy, be not sent amongst us some other year to punish the same iniquity, Ezek. xxi. 31. O sirs! what was more common among many professors in London than to be clothed in strange apparel, *à la mode de France?* Mark, those that affected the Babylonian habit were sent captives to Babylon, Ezek. xxiii. 15. They that borrowed the fashions of the Egyptians may get their boils and blotches. Certainly such as fear the Lord should go in no apparel, but, *first,* such as they are willing to die in; *secondly*, to appear before the Ancient of days in, when his judgments are abroad in the earth, Isa. xxvi. 8–10; *thirdly*, to stand before a judgment-seat. But,

[2.] Secondly, There was among many professors of the gospel in London *much lukewarmness and coldness in the things of God.* The city was full of lukewarm Laodiceans, Rev. iii. 16, 17. The love of

[1] Qu. 'Cyprian'?—G.

many to God, to his people, to his ways, and to his instituted worship, was cold, very cold, stark cold, Mat. xxiv. 12. God destroyed the old world by water for the heat of their lusts, and God has destroyed the city of London by fire for the coldness of their love that dwelt therein. I have read of Anastasius the emperor, how God shot him to death with a thunderbolt, because of his lukewarmness and formality. But,

[3.] Thirdly, *There was a great deal of worldliness and earthly-mindedness, and covetousness among the professing people of London.* O sirs! the world is all shadow and vanity; it is *filia noctis*, like Jonah's gourd. A man may sit under its shadow for a time, but it soon decays and dies. The main reason why many professors dote upon the world is, because they are not acquainted with a greater glory. Men ate acorns till they were acquainted with the use of wheat. The loadstone cannot draw the iron when the diamond is in presence; and shall earthly vanities draw the soul, when Christ, the pearl of price, is in presence? Many of the professors of London were great worshippers of the golden calf, and therefore God is just in turning their golden calf into ashes. The world may well be resembled to the fruit that undid us all, which was fair to the sight, smooth in handling, sweet in taste, but deadly in effect and operation. The world in all its bravery is no better than the cities which Solomon gave to Hiram, which he called Cabul, that is, displeasing or dirty, 1 Kings ix. 13. The whole world is circular, the heart of man triangular, and we know a circle cannot fill a triangle. If the heart of man be not filled with the three persons in Trinity, it will be filled with the world, the flesh, and the devil, 1 John v. 7. Riches, like bad servants, never stay long with one master. What certainty is there in that which one storm at sea, one treacherous friend, one false oath, one ball of fire, yea, one spark of fire may strip us of? O sirs! if you can gather grapes off thorns, and figs off thistles, then go on, and dote upon the world still. All the things of this world are vain things —they are vanity of vanities, Eccles. i. 2. All in heaven count them vain, and all in hell count them vain: a Jacobus piece is but as a chip to them; pearls are but as pebbles in their eyes. Lazarus was a preacher, as some conceive, and Dives a lawyer: sure I am, that Lazarus in heaven is now rich enough, and happy enough, and Dives in hell is now poor enough, and miserable enough. He who makes his world his god while he is in the world, what will he do for a god when he goes out of this world? Well, sirs, remember this inordinate love to the world will expose a man to seven great losses—viz.,

First, To the loss of *many precious opportunities of grace.* Rich Felix had no leisure to hear poor Paul; and Martha, busied about many things, had no time to hear Christ preach, though never man preached as he preached, Acts xxiv., Luke x., John vii. Men inordinately in love with the world have so much to do on earth, that they have no time to look up to heaven.

Secondly, To the loss of *all heavenly benefit and profit by the ministry of the word*, Ezek. xxxiii. 31–33; Mat. xiii. 22. Nothing will grow where gold grows. Where the love of the world prevails, there the ministry of the word will not prevail. If the love of the world be too hard for our hearts, then the ministry of the word will work but little upon our hearts.

Thirdly, To the loss of *the face and favour of God.* God doth not love to smile upon those who are still smiling upon the world, and still running after the world, Ps. xxx. 6, and Isa. lvii. 17. The face and favour of God are pearls of price that God bestows upon none but such whose conversation is in heaven, Phil. iii. 20, and who have the moon—viz., all things that are changeable as the moon—under their feet, Rev. xii. 1, 2. God never loves to lift up the light of his countenance upon a dunghill-spirited man. God hides his face from none so much and so long as from those who are still longing after more and more of the world.

Fourthly, To the loss of *religion, and the true worship and service of God;* as you may see by comparing of the scriptures in the margin together.[1] Many worldlings deal with religion as masons deal with their ladders when they have work to do, and to climb, &c. Oh then how they hug and embrace the ladder, and carry it on their arms and on their shoulders! but then, when they have done climbing, they hang the ladder on the wall, or throw it into a corner. O sirs, there is no loss to the loss of religion. A man were better lose his name, his estate, his limbs, his liberty, his life, his all, than lose his religion.

Fifthly, To the loss of *communion with God, and acquaintance with God*, Deut. viii. 10, 11; Jer. ii. 31, and xxii. 21; Ps. cxliv. 15. A man whose soul is conversant with God shall find more pleasure, delight, and content in a desert, in a den, in a dungeon, and in death, than in the palace of a prince. Man's *summum bonum* stands in his communion with God, as Scripture and experience evidences—nay, God and I are good company, said famous Doctor Sibbes. Macedonius the hermit, retiring into the wilderness that he might with more freedom enjoy God and have his conversation in heaven, upon a time there came a young gentleman into the wilderness to hunt wild beasts, and seeing the hermit, he rode to him, asking him why he came into that solitary place? he desired he might have leave to ask him the same question, why he came thither? I came hither to hunt, said the young gallant: and so do I, saith the hermit, *Deum venor meum*, I hunt after my God;—they hunt best who hunt most after communion with God. Urbanus Regius, having one day's converse with Luther, said, it was one of the sweetest days that ever he had in all his life.[2] But what was one day's, yea, one year's converse with Luther, to one hour's converse with God? Now an inordinate love of the world will eat out all a man's communion with God. A man cannot look up to heaven and look down upon the earth at the same time. But,

Sixthly, To the loss of *his precious and immortal soul.* Shimei, by seeking his servant, lost his life,[3] and many by an eager seeking after this world, Mat. xvi. 26, and 1 Tim. vi. 9, lose their precious and immortal souls. Many have so much to do on earth, that they have no time to look up to heaven, to honour their God, to secure their interest in Christ, or to make sure work for their souls. But,

[1] 2 Tim. iv. 10; 1 Tim. vi. 10; Jer. v. 7; Deut. xxxii. 15; Hosea iv. 7, and xiii. 6.

[2] Adam in vit. Regii, p. 78.

[3] See 1 Kings ii. 39, *seq.*—G.

Seventhly, To the loss of *the world;* for by their inordinate love of the world they highly provoke God to strip them of the world. Ah, how rich might many a man have been had he minded heaven more, and the world less! When men set their hearts so greedily upon the world, it is just with God to blast, and curse, and burn up all their worldly comforts round about them.

[4.] Fourthly, Many in London were *fallen under spiritual decays, witherings, and languishings, in their graces, in their comforts, in their communions, and in their spiritual strength.* They are fallen from their first love, Rev. ii. 4.[1] The flame of divine love being blown out, God sends a flaming fire in the midst of them. Many Londoners were fallen into a spiritual consumption, and to recover them out of it, God sent a fire amongst them. Many in London were withered in their very profession. Where was that visible forwardness, that zeal, that diligence in waiting upon the Lord in his ordinances, that once was to be found amongst the citizens of London? And many citizens were withered in their conversations and converse one with another. There was not that graciousness, that holiness, that spiritualness, that heavenliness, that fruitfulness, that exemplariness, that seriousness, and that profitableness sparkling and shining in their conversations and converse one with another, as once was to be found amongst them. And many were withered in their affections. Ah, what a flame of love, what a flame of joy, what a flame of desires, what a flame of delight, what a flame of zeal as to the best things, was once to be found amongst the citizens of London! but how were those mighty flames of affection reduced to a few coals and cinders! and therefore no wonder if God sent a flaming fire in the midst of them, and many were withered in their very duties and services. How slight, how formal, how cold, how careless, how remiss, how neglective were many in their families, in their closets, and in their church-communions, who heretofore were mighty in praying and wrestling with God, and mighty in lamenting and mourning over sin, and mighty in their groanings and longings after the Lord, and who of old would have taken the kingdom of heaven by violence! Mat. xi. 12. There were many in that great city that had lost their spiritual taste; they could not taste that sweetness in promises, in ordinances, in Sabbaths, and in the communion of saints, that once they had tasted and found, 2 Sam. xix. 35. In spiritual things, many citizens could taste no more sweetness than in the white of an egg, Job vi. 6. Many in that great city had lost their spiritual appetite, they had lost their stomachs, they did not hunger and thirst after God and Christ, and the Spirit and grace, and the light of God's countenance, and pure ordinances, and the fellowship of the people of God, as once they did. Now is there anything more contrary to the nature of God, the works of God, the word of God, the glory of God, than spiritual decays? Oh the prayers and the praises that God loses by decayed Christians! Ah, how do decayed Chris-

[1] The nutmeg-tree makes barren all the ground about it; so doth the spice of worldly love make the heart barren of grace. Ursinus observes that the sins and barrenness under the gospel in the Protestants in King Edward's days brought in the persecution in Queen Mary's days.

tians grieve the strong, and stumble the weak, and strengthen the hands of the wicked, and lay themselves open to divine displeasure! Many in London did like Mandrobulus in Lucian, who offered to his god the first year gold, the second year silver, and the third year nothing; and therefore no wonder if God sent a fire amongst them. But,

[5.] Fifthly, *Their non-improvement of the mercies and privileges that they were surrounded with, and their non-improvement of lesser and greater judgments that God had formerly inflicted on them*, and their non-improvement of their estates to that height they should have done for the supply of them whose wants, bonds, necessities, and miseries did call aloud for supplies. Many did something, a few did much, but all should have done more.

[6.] Sixthly, *Those unnatural heats, fiery contests, violent passions, and sore divisions that have been amongst them*, may well work them to justify the Lord in his fiery dispensations towards them; for a wolf to worry a lamb is usual, but for one lamb to worry another is unnatural; for Christ's lilies to be among thorns is common, Cant. ii. 16, but for these lilies to become thorns, and to tear and rend, and fetch blood of one another, is monstrous and strange. The contest that was between the birds about the rose that was found in the way, was fatal to many of them, and issued in the loss of the rose at last.

[7.] Seventhly and lastly, *There were many in London who were so very secure, and so excessively taken up with their worldly comforts, contentments, and enjoyments, that they did not lay the afflictions of Joseph* (1.) so kindly, (2.) so seriously, (3.) so affectionately, (4.) so readily, (5.) so frequently, (6.) so lamentingly, and (7.) so constantly to heart as they ought to have done, Amos vi. 6. Upon all these accounts, how well does it become the citizens of London to cry out, The Lord is righteous, the Lord is righteous in all his fiery dispensations towards us!

But to prevent mistakes, and that I may lay no heavier a load upon the people of God that truly feared him, and that had and have a saving interest in him, than is meet, and that I may give no advantage to profane persons to father the burning of the city of London wholly, mainly, or only upon the sins of the people of God, give me leave therefore to propound these four queries:—

First, Whether all these seven sins last cited, or most of them, can be justly charged upon the body of those sincere Christians who lived then in London, and whose habitations are now burnt up?

Secondly, Whether those of the people of God, upon whom any of the forementioned sins are chargeable, have not, before the city was burnt, daily lamented, bewailed, and mourned over those sins that might have been charged upon them either by their own consciences or others?

Thirdly, Where and how it doth appear by the blessed Scriptures that ever God sent so great a judgment of fire as was poured out upon London upon the account of the sins of those that truly feared him, be it those seven that have been already specified, or any others that can be now clearly and justly proved against them?

Fourthly, Whether there are not some other men's sins upon whom in the clear evidence of Scripture light this heavy judgment of fire may be more clearly, safely, and fairly fixed, than upon the sins of those who had set up God as the great object of their fear?

Now, in answer to this last query, give me leave to say,

[1.] First, *That sin in the general brings the dreadful judgment of fire upon a people.* Mark, personal afflictions and trials may come upon the people of God for trial, and to shew the sovereignty of God, as in the case of Job, whose afflictions were for trial, and not for sin, Job i. The same may be said of the man that was born blind, John ix. But general judgments, such as this fiery dispensation was, never comes upon a people but upon the account of sin. This is evident in my text, Isa. xlii. 24, 25; God set Jacob and Israel on fire, and burnt them round about; but it was because they would not walk in his ways, neither were they obedient unto his law. Jer. iv. 4, 'Circumcise yourselves to the Lord, and take away the foreskin of your heart, ye men of Judah and inhabitants of Jerusalem; lest my fury come forth like fire, and burn that none can quench it, because of the evil of your doings.' So Ps. cvii. 33, 34, 'He turneth rivers into a wilderness, and the water-springs into dry ground; a fruitful land into barrenness, for the wickedness of them that dwell therein.' The very country of Jewry, as travellers report, which flowed once with milk and honey, is now for fifteen miles about Jerusalem like a desert, without grass, tree, or shrub. Ah, what ruins doth sin bring upon the most renowned countries and cities that have been in the world! Such is the destructive nature of sin, that it will first or last level the richest, the strongest, and the most glorious cities in the world. So the prophet Amos tells us that it is sin that brings God's sorest punishments upon his people: Amos i. 3, 'For three transgressions of Damascus,' (by which we are to understand the greatness of their iniquities,) 'and for four,' (by which we are to understand the multitude of their transgressions,) 'I will not turn away the punishment thereof.' The same is said of Gaza, ver. 6, and of Tyrus, ver. 9, and of Edom, ver. 11, and of Ammon, ver. 13, and of Moab, chap. ii. 1, and of Judah, ver. 4, and of Israel, ver. 6. Now it is very observable of every one of these, that when God threatens to punish them for the greatness of their iniquities, and for the multitude of their transgressions, he doth particularly threaten to send a fire among them to consume the houses and the palaces of their cities; so he doth to Damascus: Amos i. 4, 'But I will send a fire into the house of Hazael, which shall devour the palaces of Ben-hadad.' So he doth to Gaza, ver. 7, 'But I will send a fire on the wall of Gaza, which shall devour the palaces thereof.' So he doth to Tyrus, ver. 10, 'But I will send a fire on the wall of Tyrus, which shall devour the palaces thereof.' So he doth to Edom, ver. 12, 'But I will send a fire upon Teman, which shall devour the palaces of Bozrah.' So he doth to Ammon, ver. 14, 'But I will kindle a fire in the wall of Rabbah, and it shall devour the palaces thereof, with shouting in the day of battle, with a tempest in the day of the whirlwind. So he doth to Moab, chap. ii. ver. 2, 'But I will send a fire upon Moab, and it shall devour the palaces of Kirioth; and Moab shall die with tumult, with shouting, and with the sound of a trumpet.' So he doth to Judah, ver. 5, 'But I will send a fire upon Judah, and it shall devour the palaces of Jerusalem.' By all these remarkable instances it is evident that God, by his fiery dispensations, tells all the world that the sins of that people are great and many, upon whom the dreadful judgment of fire is inflicted in its fury, and therefore it is high folly and madness in many men that makes them impute this heavy judgment of fire to anything rather than to their sins. O sirs, it is sin that burns up our habitations, and that turns flames of love into a consuming fire. And this the Parliament, in their Act for the Rebuilding of the City of London, well observes. The clause of the Act is this: 'And that the said citizens, and their successors for all the time to come, may retain the memorial of so sad a desolation, and reflect seriously upon their manifold iniquities, which are the unhappy causes of such judgments: Be it further enacted, That the second of September (unless the same happen to be Sunday; and if so, then the next day following) be yearly for ever hereafter observed as a day of public fasting and humiliation within the said city and liberties thereof, to implore the mercies of Almighty God upon the said city, to make devout prayers and supplications unto him to divert the like calamity for the time to come.' So Sir Edward[1] Turner, knight, in his speech to the king upon the prorogation of the Parliament: 'We must,' saith he, 'for ever with humility acknowledge the justice of God in punishing this whole nation by the late dreadful conflagration of London. We know they were not the greatest sinners on whom the tower of Siloam fell,' Luke xiii. 4, 'and doubtless all our sins did contribute to the filling up that measure, which being full, drew down the wrath of God upon that city.' So much the king, in his proclamation for a general fast on the 10th of October, observes. The words of the proclamation are these: 'His majesty therefore, out of a deep and pious sense of what himself and all his people now suffer, and with a religious care to prevent what may yet be feared, unless it shall please Almighty God to turn away his anger from us, doth hereby publish and declare his royal will and pleasure, that Wednesday, being the tenth of October next ensuing, shall be set apart, and kept, and observed by all his majesty's subjects of England and Wales, and the town of Berwick-upon-Tweed, as a day of solemn fasting and humiliation, to implore the mercies of God, that it would please him to pardon the crying sins of this nation, those especially which have drawn down this last and heavy judgment upon us, and to remove from us all other his judgments which our sins have deserved, and which we now either feel or fear.' Thus you see that not only the blessed Scriptures, but also king and Parliament, do roundly conclude that it was for our sins, our manifold iniquities, our crying sins, that God has sent this heavy judgment upon us. His majesty also well observes, that there are some special crying sins that bring down the fiery judgment upon us. Now this royal hint leads me by the hand to say:—

[2.] Secondly, *That though sin in the general lays people under the fiery dispensations of God, yet if we will but diligently search into the blessed book of God, which never spoke treason nor sedition, we shall*

[1] Qu. 'William'? See Epistle Dedicatory and foot-note *in loco*.—G.

find that there are several sins that brings the heavy judgment of fire upon cities and countries. As,

First, Gross atheism, practical atheism, is a sin that brings desolating and destroying judgments upon a people: Zeph. i. 12, 'And it shall come to pass at that time, that I will search Jerusalem with candles, and punish the men that are settled upon their lees, that say in their heart, The Lord will not do good, neither will he do evil.'[1] What horrid blasphemy, what gross atheism is here! How do these atheists ungod the great God! How do they deny his omnipotency and omnisciency! What a god of clouts, what an idol-god do they make the great God to be, when they make him to be such a God as will neither do good nor hurt! Epicurus denied not God's essence, but only his providence; for he granted that there was a God, though he thought him to be such a one as did neither good nor evil; but certainly God sits not idle in heaven, but has a sharp and serious eye upon all that is done on the earth: and this both saints and sinners shall find by experience, when in the great day he shall distribute both his rewards and punishments according to what they have done in the flesh. Atheism is the main disease of the soul, not only pestilent to the person in whom it is harboured, but also to the whole land where it is practised and permitted. Atheism is worse than idolatry; for idolatry only robs God of his worship, but atheism robs God both of his attributes and being; and therefore mark what follows: ver. 13, 'Therefore their goods shall become a booty, and their houses a desolation; they shall also build houses, but not inhabit them; and they shall plant vineyards, but not drink the wine thereof.' So Ezek. xx. 47–49, 'And say to the forest of the south, Hear the word of the Lord; thus saith the Lord God, Behold I will kindle a fire in thee, and it shall devour every green tree in thee, and every dry tree; the flaming flame shall not be quenched, and all faces from the south to the north shall be burnt therein. And all flesh shall see that I the Lord have kindled it; it shall not be quenched. Then said I, Ah, Lord God, they say of me, Doth he not speak parables?' Here was a pack of atheists, that did mock and scoff at the prophet and his parables; they told him that he talked like a madman, and that he spoke of such things that neither himself nor others understood; for he talked of the south, and of the forests of the south, and of fire, and of flaming fire, and of green and dry trees, and that all these things were dark and obscure to them: they put off all the prophet spoke as allegorical, as mystical, and as enigmatical, and as dark visions, and as dreams, and imaginations, and divinations of his own brain, and therefore they needed not much mind what he said. Now mark these atheists, what do they do? They provoke the Lord to kindle a fire, a universal fire, an unquenchable fire, an inextinguishable fire in the midst of Jerusalem, which is here termed a forest, by reason of its barrenness and unfruitfulness, and the multitudes that were in it; and because it was fit for nothing but the axe and the fire. Atheism is a sin that has brought the greatest woes, miseries, destructions, and

[1] Atheism denieth God either (1.) In opinion, saying there is no God; or (2.) In affection, wishing there were no God; or (3.) In conversation, living as if there were no God, Rev. xxii. 12.

desolations imaginable upon the most flourishing kingdoms and most glorious cities in the world. Holy Mr Greenham was wont to say that he feared rather atheism than Popery would be England's ruin. O sirs! were there none within the walls of London that said in their hearts with David's atheistical fool, 'There is no God'? Ps. xiv. 1. Caligula the emperor was such a one; and Claudius thought himself a god till the loud thunder affrighted him, and then he hid himself and cried, *Claudius non est deus*—Claudius is not a god. Leo X., Hildebrand the magician, and Alexander VI., and Julius II. were all most wretched atheists, and thought that whatever was said of Christ, of heaven, of hell, of the day of judgment, and of the immortality of the soul, were but dreams, impostures, toys, and old wives' fables. Pope Paul III., at the time of his death, said he should now be resolved of three questions that he had doubted of all his life. (1.) Whether the soul was immortal or no; (2.) Whether there were a hell or no; (3.) Whether there were a God or no. And another grand atheist said, I know what I have here, but I know not what I shall have hereafter. Now were there no such atheists within the walls of London before it was turned into ashes? The atheist in Ps. x. 11 says, 'He will never see;' and in Ps. xciv. 7, they rise higher; they say, 'The Lord shall not see, neither shall the God of Jacob regard it.' They labour to lay a law of restraint upon God, and to cast a mist before the eye of his providence. And in Isa. xxix. 15, they say, 'Who seeth us? who knoweth us?' And in Ezek. ix. 9, they say, 'The Lord hath forsaken the earth, and the Lord seeth not.' These atheists shut up God in heaven as a blind and ignorant God, not knowing, or not regarding, what is done on the earth; they imagine him to be a forgetful God, or a God that seeth not. Ps. lxxiii. 11, they say, 'How doth God know? and is there knowledge in the most High?' Thus they deny God's omnisciency and God's omnipresency, which to do is to ungod the great God, as much as in them lies.

Now were there no such atheists within the walls of London before it was destroyed by fire? Oh how did practical atheism abound in London! How many within thy walls, O London! did profess they knew God, but in their works did deny him, being abominable and disobedient, and unto every good work reprobate! Titus i. 16. O sirs! some there are that live loosely under the gospel, that run into all excess of riot, and that in the face of all promises and threatenings, mercies and judgments, yea, in the very face of life and death, of heaven and hell; and others there are that sin freely in secret, that can be drunk and filthy in the dark, when the eye of man is not upon them. Certainly those men's hearts are very atheistical, that dare do that in the sight of God which they tremble to do before the eyes of men. How many are there that put the evil day far from them, that flatter themselves in their sins, that with Agag conclude, surely the bitterness of death is past, and that hell and wrath is past, and that they are in a fair way for heaven, when every step they take is towards the bottomless pit, and divine vengeance hangs over their heads, ready every moment to fall upon them! Are there not many that seldom pray, and when they do, how cold, how careless, how dull, how dead, how heartless, how irreverent, are they in all their addresses to the great God? Are there not many such atheists that use no prayer, nor Bible, but make Lucian their Old Testament, and Machiavel their New? Are there not many that grant there is a God, but then it is such a God as is made up all of mercy, and thereupon they think, and speak, and do as wickedly as they please? And are there not some that look upon God as a sin-revenging God, and thereupon wish that there were no God, or else that they were above him, as Spira did? And are there not others that have very odd and foolish conceptions of God, as if he were an old man, sitting in heaven with royal robes upon his back, a glorious crown upon his head, and a kingly sceptre in his hand, and as if he had all the parts and proportion of a man, as the papists are pleased to picture him? Some there are that are so drowned in sensual pleasures, that they scarce remember that they have a God to honour, a hell to escape, a heaven to secure, souls to save, and an account to give up. And others there are who, when they find conscience begin to accuse and terrify them, then, with Cain, they go to their buildings, or with Saul to their music, or with the drunkards to their cups, or with the gamesters to their sports, Gen. iv.; 1 Sam. xviii. 6, 10; Job xxxi. 24; Phil. iii. 19. Some there are that make their gold their god, as the covetous; others make their bellies their god, as the drunkard and the glutton. Some make honours their god, as the ambitious; and others make pleasures their god, as the voluptuous. Some make religious duties their god, as the carnal gospellers; and others make their moral virtues their god, as the civil honest man, Amos vi.; Mat. xxiii. Now what abundance of such atheists were there within and without the walls of London before the fiery judgment passed upon it! The Scripture attributes the ruin of the old world to atheism and profaneness, Gen. vi.; and why may not I attribute the ruin and desolation of London to the same? Practical atheists are enough to overthrow the most flourishing nations, and the most flourishing cities that are in all the world.

But to prevent all mistakes in a business of so great a concernment, give me leave to say, that if we speak of atheists in a strict and proper sense, as meaning such as have simply and constantly denied all deity, then I must say that there was never any such creature in the world as simply and constantly to deny that there is a God. It is an inviolable principle, and indelibly stamped upon man's nature, that there is a God. They that shall deny that there is a God, must extinguish the very light of nature, by which the very heathen in all the ages of the world have acknowledged a supreme divine Being. Bion of Boristenesa[1] was a very great atheist all his lifetime; he denied the gods, despised their temples, and derided their worship; yet when death came, he would rather have endured the greatest torment than to have died, and that not so much for fear of a natural death, but for fear of what followed after, lest God, whom he had denied, should give him up into the hand of the devil whom he had served; and therefore at the time of his death he put forth his hand, crying, *Salve, Pluto, salve,* Welcome, devil, welcome—foolishly thinking

[1] Rather Borysthenes: Laert. iv. 46, &c.—G.

to pacify the devil by this flattering salutation.[1] And Tully observes of Epicurus, that though no man seemed more to contemn both God and death, yet no man feared more both the one and the other. The philosophers did, with one consent, affirm that there is a God, and they called him, *Nomine Deum, naturâ Spiritum, ordine Motorem primum*, but knew him not. He that shall deny there is a God, sins with a very high hand against the light of nature; for every creature, yea, the least gnat and fly, and the meanest worm that crawls upon the ground, will confute and confound that man that disputes whether there be a God or no. The name of God is written in such full, fair, and shining characters upon the whole creation, that all men may run and read that there is a God. The notion of a deity is so strongly and deeply impressed upon the tables of all men's hearts, that to deny a God is to quench the very principles of common nature; yea, it is formally *deicidium*, a killing of God, as much as in the creature lies. There are none of these atheists in hell; for the devils believe and tremble, James ii. 19. The Greek word φρίσσουσι, that is here used, signifies properly the roaring of the sea; it implies such an extreme fear, as causeth not only trembling, but also a roaring and screeching out, Mark vi. 49; Acts xvi. 29. The devils believe and acknowledge four articles of our faith, Mat. viii. 29, (1.) They acknowledge God; (2.) Christ; (3.) The day of judgment; (4.) That they shall be tormented then; so that he that doth not believe that there is a God, is more vile than a devil. To deny there is a God, is a sort of atheism that is not to be found in hell.

'On earth are atheists many,
In hell there is not any.'

Augustine, speaking of atheists, saith, That albeit there be some who think, or would persuade themselves, that there is no God; yet the most vile and desperate wretch that ever lived would not say, there was no God. Seneca hath a remarkable speech, *Mentiuntur qui dicunt se non sentire Deum esse: nam etsi tibi affirmant interdiù, noctu tamen dubitant*, They lie, saith he, who say they perceive not there is a God; for although they affirm it to thee in the daytime, yet by night they doubt of it. Further, saith the same author, I have heard of some that have denied that there was a God; yet never knew the man but, when he was sick, he would seek unto God for help; therefore they do but lie that say there is no God; they sin against the light of their own consciences; they who most studiously go about to deny God, yet cannot do it, but some check of conscience will fly in their faces. Tully would say that there was never any nation under heaven so barbarous as to deny that there was a God. I have seen a city without walls, but never any city but acknowledged a God. *Quicquid vides, et quicquid non vides, Deus est*, Whatsoever thou seest, and whatsoever thou seest not, is God; that is, all things visible and invisible do express unto thee a deity, and lead thee as by the hand to contemplate heavenly, spiritual, and eternal things. God is known by his effects, though not by his essence. The creation of the world is a

[1] The stoutest atheists that ever lived cannot resolutely and constantly believe there is no God; hence heathens have condemned some to death that denied there was a God.

glass, wherein, saith Paul, we may behold his eternal power and Godhead, Rom. i., which that divine poet hath well observed,

> 'The world's a school, where in a general story
> God always reads dumb lectures of his glory.'—[*Du Bartas.*]

Austin [Soliloquiis] having gone round all the creatures, and seeing in them the characters of the Godhead imprinted, and seriously inquiring of them for God, not one or two, but all made him this answer, with an audible voice, *Non sum ego, sed per ipsum sum ego quem quæris in me*, I am not he, but by him I am whom thou seekest in me. 'I have heard,' saith my author,[1] 'of some learned atheists met together to discourse of the power of nature, to prove there was no God: a poor shepherd present asked how the rain came then? they bid him look upon a still, and he might know that vapours were drawn up by the sun and let fall again, as moisture in a still; he replied, I never yet could see a still work unless some man put fire to it.' This so wrought on one in the company, that he gave glory to God, and forsook his companions. I think Zeno hit the mark when he said, To hear and see an atheist die, will more demonstrate that there is a God, than all the learned can do by all their arguments. That epitaph which was written upon Sennacherib's tomb, [Herodotus,] may well be written upon every atheist, He that looks upon us, let him believe there is a God, and learn to fear him. In all the ages of the world, God has given a most severe testimony against atheists. That Assyrian that bragged at a feast that he did never offer sacrifice to a god, was eaten up of lice. And Lucian, a great atheist, going to supper abroad, left his hounds fast when he went, and as he returned home, having railed against God and his word, his dogs fell mad, met him, and tore him in pieces. I have read of some heathens who, being at sea in a very dangerous storm, where they were like to be cast away, they began every one apart to examine themselves what should be the reason of so dreadful a storm, and after that they had all cast up their accounts by querying with themselves, What have I done, said one, and What have I done, said another, that has occasioned this storm? At last it issued thus, they remembered that they had Diagoras the atheist on board; and rather than they would all perish for that atheist's sake, they took him by the heels and hurled him overboard, and then the storm ceased, and the sea was quiet. It will be hard to name an atheist either in the Holy Scripture, or in ecclesiastical histories, or in heathen writings, which came not to some fearful end; and therefore no wonder if Austin would not be an atheist for half an hour for the gain of a million of worlds, because he knew not but God might in that time make an end of him. I have been the longer upon this head, because atheist and atheism did never so abound in this land as it hath done these last years, and that you may the clearer see who they are that have brought that sad judgment of fire upon that once glorious city of London. Ah London, London! it was the gross atheism and the practical atheist that was within and without thy walls, that has turned thee into a ruinous heap.

Mark, I readily grant that there is the seeds, relics, stirring, and moving of atheism in the best and holiest of the sons of men; but then

[1] Mr Francis Taylor on Prov. vi. 7. [On the first nine chapters. 1657, 4to.—G.]

(1.) They disallow of it, and discountenance it; (2.) It is lamented and bewailed by them; (3.) They oppose it, and conflict with it; (4.) They use all holy and conscientious means and endeavours to be rid of it; (5.) By degrees they get ground against it, and therefore God never did, nor never will, turn cities or kingdoms into flames for those seeds and remains of atheism that are to be found in the best of saints.

It is that atheism that is rampant, that reigns in the hearts and lives of sinners, as a prince reigns upon his throne, that brings desolating and destroying judgments upon the most flourishing kingdoms and the most glorious cities that are in the world. But,

2. Secondly, *Luxury and intemperance bring desolating and destroying judgments upon places and persons:* Joel i. 5, 'Awake, ye drunkards, and weep; and howl, all ye drinkers of wine, because of the new wine; for it is cut off from your mouth;' ver. 19, 'O Lord, to thee will I cry, for the fire hath devoured the pastures of the wilderness, and the flames have burnt all the trees of the field;' ver. 20, 'The beasts of the field cry unto thee; for the rivers of the water are dried up, and the fire hath devoured the pastures of the wilderness.'[1] Luxury is a sin that brings both famine and fire upon a people; it brought the Chaldeans upon the Jews, who by fire and sword laid all waste. The horses of the Chaldeans destroyed their pastures, vines, fig-trees, pomegranates, &c., which grew in many places of the land, and their soldiers set their houses on fire, and so brought all to ruin. Amos vi. 1, 'Woe to them that are at ease in Zion;' ver. 3, 'That put far away the evil day;' ver. 4, 'That lie upon beds of ivory, and stretch themselves upon their couches, and eat the lambs out of the flock, and the calves out of the midst of the stall;' ver. 5, 'That chant to the sound of the viol, and invent to themselves instruments of music, like David;' ver. 6, 'That drink wine in bowls, and anoint themselves with the chief ointments: but they are not grieved for the affliction of Joseph;' ver. 7, 'Therefore now shall they go captive with the first that go captive, and the banquet of them that stretched themselves shall be removed;' ver. 8, 'The Lord God hath sworn by himself, saith the Lord God of hosts, I abhor the excellency of Jacob, and hate his palaces: therefore will I deliver up the city, with all that is therein;' ver. 11, 'For, behold, the Lord commandeth, and he will smite the great house with breaches, and the little house with clefts.' Luxury is a sin that forfeits all a man's enjoyments, that turns him out of house and home. Samaria was a very glorious city, and a very strong city, and a very rich city, and a very populous city, and a very ancient city, &c., and yet luxury and intemperance turned it into ashes,—it brought desolating and destroying judgments upon it. The rich citizens of Samaria were given up to mirth and music, to luxuries and excesses, to riotousness and drunkenness, to feasting and carousing, and by these vanities and debaucheries they provoked the Lord to command the Chaldeans to fall on and to spoil them of their riches, and to lay their glorious city in ashes. So it was luxury and intem-

[1] In ecclesiastical history you may read of one drunkard, who, being touched with his sin, wept himself blind; but the drunkards of our days are more apt to drink themselves blind than to weep themselves blind.

perance that provoked the Lord to rain hell out of heaven upon Sodom and Gomorrah, Gen. xviii.; luxury turned those rich and populous cities into ruinous heaps. Ah London! London! the luxuries and excesses, the riotousness and drunkenness, the mad feasting and carousing that have been within and without thy walls, that have been within thy great halls, taverns, and other great houses, hath turned thee into ashes, and laid thy glory in the dust. O you burnt citizens of London! what shameful spewing hath been in some of your feasts, as if Sardanapalus, Apicius, and Heliogabalus were still alive! How often have many of you poured into your bodies such intoxicating drinks as hath many times laid you asleep, stripped you of your reason, took away your hearts, robbed you of yourselves, and laid a beast in your room! Drunkenness is so base, so vile a sin, that it transforms the soul, deforms the body, bereaves the brain, betrays the strength, defiles the affections, and metamorphoseth the whole man; yea, it unmans the man. Cyrus the Persian monarch being demanded of his grandfather Astyages why he would drink no wine, answered, For fear lest they give me poison; for, saith he, yesterday, when you celebrated your nativity, I judged that somebody had poisoned all the wine they drank, because at the taking away of the cloth not one of all those that were present at the feast arose in his right mind. [Xenophon.] Hath it not been thus with many of you? If it hath, lay your hands upon your mouths, and say, The Lord is righteous, though he hath laid your houses in ashes. Anacharsis used to say that the first cup of wine was for thirst, the second for nourishment, the third for mirth, and the fourth for madness; but what would he have said had he lived within or without the walls of London these last six years? Isa. v. 22; Hab. ii. 17. Ah London! London! were there none within nor without thy walls that were strong to drink, and that gave their neighbour drink, and that put the bottle to them to make them drunk, that they might look on their nakedness? Were there none within nor without thy walls, that with Marcus Antoninus, Darius, Alexander the Great, &c., did boast, and glory, and pride themselves in their great abilities to drink down any that should come into their company? Were there none within nor without thy walls, O London! that cried out, If you take away our liquor, you take away our lives? Austin brings in the drunkard, saying, *Malle se vitam quàm vinum eripi*, He had rather lose his life than his wine. And Ambrose speaks of one Theotimus, who being told by his physicians that much quaffing would make him blind, answered then, *Vale lumen amicum*, Farewell sweet light, farewell sweet eyes; if ye will not bear wine, ye are no eyes for me. Were there none within nor without thy walls, O London! that did abuse the good creatures of God so profusely, so prodigally, so prodigiously, as if they had been sent into the world for no other end but thus to abuse themselves, reproach their Maker, and destroy those choice blessings which God had given for more noble ends, than to be spewed against the walls, for these last six years? A drunken health, like the conclusion in a syllogism, must not upon any terms be denied, especially in the company of such grandees whose age, whose place, whose office should have taught them better things; yea, the custom of high drinking hath been these last six years so great within and without thy walls, O London! that it is no wonder if the Lord for that alone has laid thy glory in the dust; yea, and that shameful spewing is upon all thy glory, Hab. ii. 16, considering what shameful spewing have been in thy streets, taverns, halls, alehouses, and other great men's houses, where temperance, righteousness, justice, and holiness should have dwelt in glory and triumph! Ah London! how many within and without thy walls have been drinking wine in bowls, when they should have been mourning over their sins, and grieving for the afflictions of Joseph, and sighing over those distressed Christians whose drink was nothing but sorrow and blood and tears! These are the men that have kindled a burning upon all thy glory.

O sirs! that you would for ever remember that intemperance, luxury, is a sin, an enemy that,

[1.] First, *Robs God of his glory.* It denies him all service and obedience. Intemperate persons are neither fit for praying to God, nor praising of God, nor receiving from God. Intemperance turns the temple of the Holy Ghost into a sepulchre, a kitchen, a hog-stye; and what glory then can God have from an intemperate person? 1 Cor. vi. 19. But,

[2.] Secondly, *It robs both God and man of much precious time.* Time is a precious jewel, more worth than all the world.[1] One called his friends thieves, because they stole time from him; and certainly there are no worse thieves than intemperance; for that robs men of their hearing-times, and their praying-times, and their reading-times. There is so much precious time spent in the tavern and in the tippling-house, that the intemperate person cannot be at leisure to spend any time in his family or in his closet, &c., to save his own or others' souls. But there will come a time, either in this or the other world, wherein all intemperate persons will wish that they had spent that precious time in serving of God, and in saving their own and others' souls, which they have spent in luxury and excess, carousing and drinking; but all too late, all too late. Time is not only the fruit of God's indulgence, but also the fruit of Christ's purchase. That doom passed upon Adam, 'In the day thou eatest thereof, thou shalt die the death,' or dying, thou shalt die, had been put in execution immediately, had not Christ interposed immediately between man's sin and God's wrath. What can there be of more weight and moment than eternity? It is the heaven of heaven, and the very hell of hell, without which neither would heaven be so desirable, nor hell so formidable. Now this depends upon time. Time is the prologue to eternity; the great weight of eternity hangs upon the small wire of time: our time, whether it be longer or shorter, is given us by God to provide for our everlasting condition, 2 Cor. vi. 2; Isa. xlix. 8. We have souls to save, a hell to escape, a heaven to make sure, our pardon to sue out, our interest in Christ to make good; and all this must be quickly done, or we undone, and that for ever. Man's eternal weal or woe depends upon his well or ill improvement of that inch of time that is allotted to him. Now what a dreadful

[1] When Ignatius heard a clock strike, he would say, I have one hour more to answer for: so precious a jewel was time in his eye.

account will such give up at last, who have wasted away their precious time in luxury and excess. But,

[3.] Thirdly, Luxury, intemperance, it robs men *of their names.* Bonosus, a beastly drunken emperor, was called a tankard,[1] and Tiberius was surnamed Biberius for his tippling, and Erasmus called Eccius Jeccius for the same cause, and Diotimus of Athens was called a tun-dish, and young Cicero a hog's-head. But,

[4.] Fourthly, Luxury, intemperance, it robs men *of their health;* for how many are there, that by drinking other men's healths have destroyed their own! Many more perish by intemperance than by violence. Intemperance is the source and nurse of all diseases. More perish by surfeiting than by suffering. Every intemperate person digs his own grave with his own mouth and teeth, and is certainly a self-tormentor, a self-destroyer, a self-murderer. I have read of a monk at Prague,[2] who having heard at shrift the confessions of many drunkards, wondered at it, and for an experiment he would needs try his brain with this sin, so accordingly he stole himself drunk. Now after the vexation of three days' sickness, to all that confessed that sin he enjoined no other penance but this, Go and be drunk again; intimating thereby that there was no punishment, no torment that could be inflicted upon a drunkard so great as that, Go and be drunk again. Besides all other plagues that attend this sin, drunkenness is a woe to itself. Temperance is the best and noblest physic, and they that use it commonly are most long-lived. But,

[5.] Fifthly, Intemperance robs men *of their estates.* It robs the wife many times of her dowry, and the children of their portion, and the husband of his inheritance, his trade, his all. The very word ἀσωτία, luxury, properly signifies the not preventing or keeping of the good which at the present we enjoy. Solomon hit the mark when he said, 'The drunkard and the glutton shall come to poverty,' Prov. xxiii. 21. The full cup makes an empty purse, and a fat dish makes a lean bag. He that draws thee wine out of the pipe, puts thy money into his own pocket; and this Diogenes the philosopher well understood when he asked of the frugal citizen but a penny, but begged of the prodigal a talent; and being asked the reason of his practice, he answered, Because of the one he thought he might beg often, but of the other who spent so fast, he was like to receive but once. Mr Livius, (?) when he had spent a great estate in luxurious living, jesting at his own folly, he said that he had left nothing for his heir more than air and mire. Philip king of Macedon, making war upon the Persians, understood that they were a luxurious people; he presently withdrew his army, saying it was needless to make war upon them, who by their luxury would shortly overthrow themselves. But,

[6.] Sixthly, Intemperance robs men *of everlasting happiness and blessedness*, Gal. v. 19-21. It shuts them out from all the glory of that upper world, and tumbles them down to the lowest hell, as you

[1] *Not* an emperor, but servant of one—viz., of Aurelian. He was famous or infamous for the faculty which he possessed of being able to drink to excess without being intoxicated or losing his self-command.—*Vopiscus: Vit. Bonos.*—G.

[2] Radulph. Fornerius, select., lib. iii.

may see in that great instance of luxurious Dives, Luke xvi. 19–26. The intemperate man's table proves a snare to his soul; fulness breeds forgetfulness, wantonness, blockishness, and stupidity; and therefore no wonder if God shuts the gates of glory against intemperate persons. Look, as no leper might be in the camp of Israel, Num. v.; and as no Gileadite might pass over Jordan, Judges xii.; and as no fearful man might enter into the wars of Midian, chap. vii.; and as no bastard might enter into the sanctuary, Deut. xxxiii.; so no luxurious person shall enter into heaven. Of all sorts of sinners, the luxurious sinner is most rarely reformed. The adulterer may become chaste, the thief may become an honest man, the swearer may obtain a sanctified tongue; but how rare is it to see a luxurious person repent, break off his sins, close with Christ, and walk to heaven! Luxurious persons eat and drink away their Christ; yea, they eat and drink away their souls, nay, they eat and drink away their own salvation, Mat. xxi. 31, 32; Luke xxiii. 43. They that serve their own bellies, serve not the Lord Jesus Christ, and therefore they shall never reign with him in the other world. Certainly that man that makes his belly his god, shall be for ever separated from God, Phil. iii. 19. All belly-gods shall at last be found in the belly of hell. The intemperate person hath his heaven here; his hell is to come. Now he has his sweet cups, his merry cups, his pleasant cups: oh, but there is a cup of shame and sorrow, 'and this shall be their portion for ever and ever,' Ps. xi. 6. The intemperate person hath been a gulf to devour many mercies, and therefore he shall at last be cast into a gulf of endless miseries. In a word, intemperance is a mother sin, a breeding sin; it is a sin that is an inlet to all other sins; we may call it 'Gad, for behold, a troop cometh,' Deut. xxxii. 17, 24. Oh the pride, the oppression, the cruelty, the security, the uncleanness, the filthiness, the profaneness that comes trooping after intemperance, Jer. v. 7–9. And therefore Aristotle concludes, that double punishments are due to drunkards; first for their drunkenness, and then for other sins committed in and by their drunkenness. Now seeing that intemperance and luxury is so great a sin, is it any wonder to see divine justice turn the most glorious cities in the world into a ruinous heap, when this sin of intemperance is rampant in the midst of them? Ah, London! London! the intemperance and luxury that has been within and without thy walls, has brought the desolating judgment of fire upon thee, that has laid all thy glory in ashes and rubbish. How many great houses were there once within and without thy walls, that should have been public schools of piety and virtue, but were turned into mere nurseries of luxury and debauchery! How have the rules of the Persian civility been forgotten in the midst of thee! Est. i. 6, 7. How many within and without thy walls did make their belly their god, their kitchen their religion, their dresser their altar, and their cook their minister, whose whole felicity did lie in eating and drinking, whose bodies were as sponges, and whose throats were as open sepulchres to take in all precious liquors, and whose bellies were as graves to bury all God's creatures in! And how have many men been forced to unman themselves, either to please some, or to avoid the anger or wrath of others, or else to gain the honourable character of being a high boy, or of one that was strong to drink among others, or to drink down others! Oh the drunken matches that have been within and without thy walls, O London!—the Lord has seen them, and been provoked by them to kindle a fire in the midst of thee. Luxury is a sin that never goes alone; it hath many other great sins attending and waiting on it; it is as the nave in the wheel, which turning about, all the spokes turn with it. Idleness, fighting, quarrelling, jewling,[1] whoring, cheating, stealing, robbing, are the handmaids that wait on luxury, Prov. xxiii. 29–33; and therefore no wonder if God has appeared in flames of fire against it. I have been the longer upon this head, because luxury, intemperance, is one of the great darling sins of our age and day; it is grown to epidemical, not only in the city, but in the countries[2] also, and it is a very God-dishonouring, and a God-provoking, and a soul-damning, and a land-destroying sin: and oh that what I have writ might be so blessed as to put some effectual stop to those notorious public excesses and luxuries that have been and still are rampant in most parts of the land.

But now, beloved, this sin of luxury and intemperance I cannot charge with clear and full evidence upon the people of the Lord, that did truly fear him and sincerely serve him, whose habitations were once within or without the walls of London; nay, this I know, that for this very sin among others, their souls did often mourn before the Lord in secret. And truly of such Christians that live and wallow in luxury and intemperance, if we compare their lives and Christ's laws together, I think we may confidently conclude, *Aut hæc non est lex Christi, aut nos non sumus Christiani:* Either this is not Christianity, or we are not Christians. And thus Tertullian, Cyprian, Justin Martyr, and others concluded against the luxurious and intemperate Christians of their times. Salvian[3] relates how the heathen did reproach such luxurious Christians, who by their lewd lives made the gospel of Christ to be a reproach: Where, said the heathen, is that good law which they do believe? Where are those rules of godliness which they do learn? They read the holy Gospel, and yet are unclean; they hear the apostles' writings, and yet are drunk; they follow Christ, and yet disobey Christ; they profess a holy law, and yet do lead impure lives. And Panormitan having read the 5th, 6th, and 7th chapters of Matthew, and comparing the loose and luxurious lives of Christians with those rules of Christ, concluded that either that was no gospel, or the people no Christians. The loose and luxurious lives of many Christians was, as Lactantius declares, made by the heathen the reproach of Christ himself: *Quomodo bonus magister cuius tam pravos videmus discipulos?*—How can we think the master to be good whose disciples we see to be so bad? Epiphanius saith that in his days many shunned the society of the Christians because of the looseness and luxuriousness of their lives. And Augustine confessed[4] that in his time the loose and luxurious lives of many who professed the Christian religion gave a great advantage to the Manichees to reproach

[1] Rather 'jowling,' from jowl the jaw = pressing with the fists, without blows, *e.g.*, from Wright—'Did you give him a good drubbing? No; but I gin him a good tidy jowling.' Suffolk.—G.

[2] Qu. 'country'? or 'counties'?—G.

[3] Salvianus de Gratia Dei, lib. iv.

[4] August. de moribus Ecclesiæ, cap. 34.

the whole church of God and the ways of God. The Manichees were a sort of people who affirmed that there were two principles or beginnings of things—viz. a *summum bonum* and a *summum malum*—a *summum bonum*, from whence sprang all good, and a *summum malum*, from whence issued forth all evil. Now the loose and luxurious lives of such as had a profession upon them hardened these in their errors, and caused them with open mouth greatly to reproach and deeply to censure the sincerest saints. And Chrysostom preferred brute beasts before luxurious persons; for they go from belly to labour, when the luxurious person goes from belly to bed, or from belly to cards or dice, if not to something that is worse. And Augustine well observes that God hath not given to man talons and claws to rend and tear in pieces, as to bears and leopards; nor horns to push, as to bulls and unicorns; nor a sting to prick, as to wasps, and bees, and serpents; nor a bill to strike, as to eagles and ostriches; nor a wide mouth to devour, as to dogs and lions; but a little mouth, to shew that man should be very temperate both in his eating and drinking. How applicable these things are to the luxurious persons that lived within and without the walls of London before it was turned into ashes, I shall leave the wise in heart to judge. But,

3. Thirdly, *Those great and horrid sins that were to be found in many men's callings—viz., excessive worldliness, extortion, deceit, bribery, &c.—these brought the sore judgment of fire upon us*, Prov. xxviii. 20, 22, and see Josh. vii. 15, 21, 24, 25. When men are so greedy and mad upon the world that they make haste to be rich by all sinful devices and cursed practices, no wonder if God burns up their substance, and turns their persons out of house and home. The coal the eagle got from the altar—the sacrifice—and carried it to her nest, set all on fire; so that estate that men get by sinful ways and unwarrantable courses first or last will set all they have on fire. He that resolves to be evil, may soon be rich, when the spring of conscience is screwed up to the highest pin, that it is ready to crack, when religion is locked up in an out-room, and forbidden upon pain of death to look into the shop or warehouse. No wonder such men thrive and grow great in the world; but all the riches such men store up, is but fuel for the fire: Hab. ii. 9, 'Woe to him that coveteth an evil covetousness to his house, that he may set his nest on high, that he may be delivered from the power of evil!' ver. 11, 'For the stone shall cry out of the wall, the beam out of the timber shall answer it:' ver. 13, 'Behold, is it not of the Lord of hosts that the people shall labour in the very fire, and the people shall weary themselves for very vanity?'[1] They had got great estates by an evil covetousness, and God was resolved that he would make a bonfire of all their ill-gotten goods; and though they should venture their lives to save their goods and quench the flames, yet all should be but labour in vain, according to that word, Jer. li. 58, 'Thus saith the Lord of hosts, The broad walls of Babylon shall be utterly broken, and her high gates shall be burnt with fire, and the people shall labour in vain, and the folk in the fire,

[1] He, saith Chrysostom, that locks up ill-gotten riches in his counting-house, locks up a a thief in his countenance, which will carry all away, and if he look not the better to it, his precious soul also. [Qu. 'countenance,' a misprint for 'counting-house' repeated?—G.]

and they shall be weary.' Though Babylon was a city of great fame and state and riches, and deservedly accounted one of the world's nine wonders; though the compass of the walls was three hundred and sixty-five furlongs, or forty-six miles, according to the number of the days in the year, and the height fifty cubits, and of so great a breadth that carts and carriages might meet on the top of them; yea, though it was so great and vast a city, that Aristotle saith that it ought rather to be called a country than a city, adding withal, that when the city was taken, it was three days before the furthest part of the city could take notice of it; yet at last, according to the word of the Lord, it was set on fire; and though the inhabitants did weary and tire out themselves to quench the flames, and to save their stately houses and ill-gotten riches, yet all was labour in vain, and to no purpose. In the days of Pliny it was an utter desolation, and in the time of Jerome it was turned into a park, in which the king of Persia did use to hunt. So Ezek. xxviii. 18, 'Thou hast defiled thy sanctuaries by the multitude of thine iniquities, by the iniquity of thy traffic; therefore will I bring forth a fire from the midst of thee, it shall devour thee; and I will bring thee to ashes upon the earth in the sight of all them that behold thee:' ver. 19, 'All they that know thee among the people shall be astonished at thee: thou shalt be a terror, and never shalt thou be any more.' Tyrus, among the sea-bordering cities, was most famous and renowned for merchandise and trade; for thither resorted the merchants of all countries for traffic of Palestina, Syria, Egypt, Persia, and Assyria. They of Tarshish brought thither iron, lead, brass, and silver. The Syrians brought thither carbuncles, purple, broidered work, fine linen, coral, and pearl. The Jews brought thither their honey, oil, treacle, cassia, and calamus. The Arabians brought thither lambs, muttons, and goats. The Sabeans brought thither their exquisite spices and apothecary stuff, with gold and precious stones. Now by fraud and deceit they grew exceeding rich and wealthy, which in the close issued in their total ruin, according to that of the prophet: Zech. ix. 3, 4, 'And Tyrus did build herself a stronghold, and heaped up silver as the dust, and fine gold as the mire of the streets. Behold, the Lord will cast her out, and he will smite her power in the sea; and she shall be devoured with fire.' The Tyrians did hold themselves invincible, because of their situation being round about environed by the sea; but yet the prophet tells them, that though they were compassed about with deep waters, yet they should be destroyed by fire, which was executed by Alexander the Great, as historians testify.[1] It is not the strength, nor riches, nor situation, nor trade, nor honour, nor fame, nor antiquity of a city, that can preserve it, when God beforehand has by fire determined the destruction of it. Tyrus was a city of the greatest merchandising, it was a city of mighty trade, they were set upon heaping up of riches by hook or by crook; so riches came in, though it were at the door of oppression, violence, or injustice, all was well, Ezek. xxvii.; Isa. xxiii. 5-9. The traffic of Tyrus was great, and the sins that attended that traffic were very great, and for these God sent a devouring fire amongst them, which

[1] Curtius, lib. iv., and Diod. Siculus, lib. xvii.

destroyed their palaces and treasuries, and reduced their glorious city to ashes. By the iniquity of their traffic they had built palaces and stately houses, and filled their shops and warehouses and cellars with rich and choice commodities; but when God brought Nebuchadnezzar upon them, what the Chaldeans could not destroy by the sword they consumed by fire, turning all their glorious palaces, and stately buildings, and costly shops, and warehouses, into ashes, as historians testify. So Nineveh, for greatness, riches, and antiquity, was one of the noblest cities in the world, it was the capital and chief city of the Assyrian empire; and though God, upon their repentance and humiliation, did spare them for a time, Jonah iii., yet afterwards, she returning to her old trade of robberies, covetousness, extortions, fraud, deceitful dealings, &c., God delivered her up as a prey into the hands of many of her enemies, who wonderfully spoiled and pillaged her; and at last God gave her into the hands of the Medes, who brought her to a final and irrecoverable desolation, according to the prophecy of the prophet Nahum, chap. ii. 10, 'She is empty, and void, and waste; and the heart melteth, and the knees smite together, and much pain is in all loins, and the faces of them all gather blackness,'—that is, such blackness as is on the sides of a pot. Ver. 13, 'Behold, I am against thee, saith the Lord of hosts, and I will burn her chariots in the smoke;' see also chap. iii. 12-15. The like judgment fell upon Sidon, [Sabel:] and upon that rich and renowned city of Corinth, which, through the commodiousness of the haven, was the most frequented place in the world for the intercourse of merchants out of Asia and Europe, and great and many were their sins about their trade and traffic; and for these she was finally destroyed, and turned into cinders and ashes by the Romans, [Thucyd.]

So bribery is a sin that brings desolating and destroying judgments both upon persons and places: Amos v. 11, 12, 'Forasmuch therefore as your treading is upon the poor, and ye take from him burdens of wheat: ye have built houses of hewn stones, but ye shall not dwell in them; ye have planted pleasant vineyards, but ye shall not drink wine of them. For I know your manifold transgressions and your mighty sins: they afflict the just, they take a bribe, and they turn aside the poor in the gate from their right.' Bribery is one of those mighty sins, or one of those bony or big-boned sins, as the Hebrew hath it, for which God threatens to turn them out of house and home. Bribery is a bony sin, a huge sin, a heinous sin, a monstrous sin, a sin that is capable of all manner of aggravations, and therefore the Lord punisheth it with desolating judgments: Job xv. 34, 'And fire shall consume the tabernacles of bribery,' or the receivers of gifts, as both the Hebrew and the Septuagint may be read. When wicked men build their houses, their tabernacles, by pilling and polling, by bribery, cheating, defrauding, or overreaching others, it is a righteous thing with God to set their houses on fire about their ears. Thus Dioclesian had his house wholly consumed by lightning and a flame of fire that fell from heaven upon it, as Eusebius tells us.[1] Upon such a generation of men as build their houses by bribery, or oppres-

[1] De vita Constant., lib. v.

sion, or deceit, &c., God many times makes good that word, Job xviii. 15, 'Brimstone shall be scattered upon his habitation;' and that word, Micah iii. 11, 12, 'The heads thereof judge for reward, and the priests thereof teach for hire, and the prophets thereof divine for money. Therefore shall Zion for your sake be ploughed as a field, and Jerusalem shall become heaps, and the mountain of the house as the high places of the forest.' Bribery and covetousness had overrun all sorts of such as were in power and authority, whether civil or ecclesiastical, and for this Zion must be ploughed as a field, and Jerusalem become heaps, and the mountain of the house as the high places of the forest. By these exquisite terms the total and dismal desolation and destruction of Zion, Jerusalem, and the temple, that famous house that was once worthily reckoned one of the seven wonders of the world, is set forth unto us, Jer. vii. 4, 5. That Jerusalem, that God's house and temple wherein they so much trusted and gloried, should become as a mountainous forest and wilderness, was incredible to them as the jumbling of heaven and earth together, or the dethroning of God by taking the crown from his head and thrusting of him from his chair of state; and yet all this was made good according to that dreadful prophecy of Christ, 'There shall not be left one stone upon another,' Luke xix. 43, 44. These are the sad effects of bribery, covetousness, &c. So Prov. xxix. 4, 'The king by judgment establisheth the land; but he that receiveth gifts, or bribes, overthrows it.'

Ah London! London! were there none within nor without thy walls that did take a gift out of the bosom to pervert the ways of judgment? Prov. xvii. 23; were there none whose right hands were full of bribes? Ps. xxvi. 10; were there none like Samuel's sons, who turned aside after lucre, and took bribes, and perverted judgment in the midst of thee? 1 Sam. viii. 3; were there no rulers nor others within nor without thy walls that did love to say with shame, Give ye? Hosea iv. 18; or that asked for a reward? Micah vii. 3; or that with Gehazi run after rewards? or that were not ready to transgress for a piece of bread? Prov. xxviii. 21; or that were not like the horse-leech's daughter, still crying out, Give, give? Prov. xxx. 15. Themistocles caused a brand of infamy to be set upon Athmius his children, and all his posterity after him, because he brought gold from the king of Persia to corrupt, bribe, and win the Grecians.[1] If all that were within and without the walls of London that received bribes, and run after rewards, had a brand of infamy set upon them, I am apt to think many of them would be ashamed to walk the streets, who have once carried it with a very high hand.

Ah London! London! were there none within nor without thy walls that had the balance of deceit in their hands, and that loved to oppress, falsifying the balances by deceit, and that had in their bags divers weights, that did sell by one measure and buy by another, that had wicked balances, and the bag of deceitful weights in their hands, their houses, their shops, their warehouses? Hosea xii. 7; Amos viii. 5; Deut. xxv. 13; Micah vi. 11. Well, suppose there were many

[2] Rather Arthmius, 'Αρθμιος.—Plutarch, 'Themistocles,' c. vi.—G.

such within and without the walls of London, what of that? why then, I would say,

[1.] First, *Such run counter-cross to divine commands:* Lev. xix. 35, 36, 'Ye shall do no unrighteousness in judgment, in meteyard, in weight, or in measure. Just balances, just weights, a just ephah, and a just hin, shall ye have.' Ezek. xlv. 10, 'Ye shall have just balances, and a just ephah, and a just bath.' Deut. xxv. 13–15, 'Thou shalt not have in thy bag divers weights, a great and a small. But thou shalt have a perfect and just weight, a perfect and just measure shalt thou have: that thy days may be lengthened in the land which the Lord thy God giveth thee;' Lev. xix. 13; Mark x. 19; 1 Cor. vii. 5. We have a common saying, Weight and measure is heaven's treasure. But,

[2.] Secondly, Such persons and such practices are *an abomination to the Lord:* Deut. xxv. 16, 'For all that do such things, and all that do unrighteousness, are an abomination unto the Lord thy God.' Prov. xi. 1, 'A false balance is abomination to the Lord;' chap. xx. 10, 'Divers weights, and divers measures, both of them are alike abomination to the Lord, and a false balance is not good.' Now mark, the very weights and measures are an abomination to the Lord; how much more the men that make use of them! But,

[3.] Thirdly, Such act counter-cross *to God's delight:* Prov. xi. 1, 'A just weight is his delight;' chap. xvi. 11, 'A just weight and balance are the Lord's.' They are commanded by the Lord, and commended by the Lord, and they are the delight of the Lord. But,

[4.] Fourthly, Such act counter-cross *to his nature*, which is holy, just, and righteous, and to all his administrations, which are full of righteousness, justice, and equity, Ezek. xviii., and xxxiii. 17, 20, 29. But,

[5.] Fifthly, Such act counter-cross to *the very light and law of nature*, by not dealing by others as they would have others deal by them, Mat. vii. 12. They are the very botches of the land, and enemies to all civil society. But,

[6.] Sixthly, Such *stir up the anger and indignation of God against themselves:* Ezek. xxii. 13, 'Behold, therefore I have smitten mine hand at thy dishonest gain which thou hast made,' or 'at thy covetousness,' as some render the Hebrew word, or 'at thy money gotten by fraud and force, and overreaching and cheating of others,' as others render it. God is here said to smite his hands at their dishonest gain, to note the greatness of his anger, wrath, and indignation against them; and his readiness and resolvedness to take vengeance on them, by animating, instigating, encouraging, and stirring up the Chaldeans to destroy their persons by the sword, and to consume their riches and houses by fire, chap. xxi. 17. God has no hand to smite; but this is spoken after the manner of men, who oftentimes express the greatness of their wrath and rage by smiting their hands one against another. God, to shew the greatness of his spleen and rage, in a holy sense, against them for their dishonest gain, expresses it by the smiting of his hands: 1 Thes. iv. 6, 'That no man go beyond or defraud his brother in any matter: because that the Lord is the avenger of all such.' First or last vengeance will reach them who make it their business, their trade, to overreach others. But,

[7.] Seventhly, Such act counter-cross *to the examples of the most eminent saints.* To the example of Moses: Num. xvi. 15, 'I have not taken an ass from them, neither have I hurt one of them.' Of Samuel, 1 Sam. xii. 3–5; of Zacharias and Elizabeth, Luke i. 5, 6; of Paul, Acts xxiv. 16; yea, to the examples of all the apostles, Judas excepted: 2 Cor. i. 12, and vii. 2, 'Receive us; we have wronged no man, we have corrupted no man, we have defrauded no man. But,

[8.] Eighthly and lastly, Such act counter-cross *to their own everlasting happiness and blessedness:* 1 Cor. vi. 8, 9, 'Nay, you do wrong, and defraud, and that your brethren. Know ye not that the unrighteous shall not inherit the kingdom of heaven?' Unrighteous persons may hear much of heaven, and talk much of heaven, and set their faces towards heaven; but they shall never inherit the kingdom of heaven. God himself has locked fast the gate of blessedness against the unrighteous; and therefore all the world shall never be able to open it. Heaven would be no heaven, but a hell, if the unrighteous should inhabit there. To sum up all: If such persons run counter-cross to God's commands, if their persons and practices are an abomination to the Lord, if they act counter-cross to God's delight and to his nature, yea, to the very light and law of nature, to the best examples, and to their own happiness and blessedness, is it any wonder then to see divine justice set such men's houses on fire about their ears, and to see the flames consume such estates as were got either by fraud or force, by craft or cruelty, &c.?

Now the gaining of the things of this world by hook or by crook, or by such wicked courses and cursed practices that we have been discoursing on, I cannot charge upon the people of God, that did truly fear him, whose habitations were once within or without the walls of London, because such practices would neither stand with grace, nor with the honour of God, nor with the credit of religion, nor with the law of God, nor with the law of nature, nor with the peace of a saint's soul. Besides, it is very observable to me, that those that have the balances of deceit in their hand, are called Canaanites in that 12th of Hosea 7th verse, 'He is a merchant; the balances of deceit are in his hand; he loveth to oppress'—Heb., he is Canaan, that is, a mere natural man, that hath no common honesty in him, a money-merchant, one that cares not how he comes by it, so he may have it; one that counts all good fish that comes to his net, though it be through cunning contrivances or violent practices. But,

4. Fourthly, *Desperate incorrigibleness and unreformedness under wasting and destroying judgments, brings the desolating judgment of fire upon a people,* Lev. xxvi.; Deut. xxviii.; turn to that Jer. xxx. 23, 24. Isa. xlii. 24, 25, 'Who gave Jacob for a spoil, and Israel to the robbers? did not the Lord, he against whom we have sinned? for they would not walk in his ways, neither were they obedient unto his law. Therefore he hath poured upon him the fury of his anger, and the strength of battle: and it hath set him on fire round about, yet he knew not; and it burned him, yet he laid it not to heart.' Lev.

xxvi. 27, 28, 31–33, 'And if ye will not for all this hearken unto me, but walk contrary unto me; then will I walk contrary unto you also in fury; and I, even I, will chastise you seven times for your sins. And I will make your cities waste, and bring your sanctuaries unto desolation. And I will bring the land into desolation; and your enemies which dwell therein shall be astonished at it. And I will scatter you among the heathen, and will draw out a sword after you; and your land shall be desolate, and your cities waste.' Isa. i. 5, 7, 8, 'Why should you be stricken any more? ye will revolt more and more. The whole head is sick, and the whole heart faint. Your country is desolate, your cities are burnt with fire: your land, strangers devour it in your presence, and it is desolate, as overthrown by strangers. And the daughter of Zion is left as a cottage in a vineyard, as a lodge in a garden of cucumbers, as a besieged city.' Amos iv. 7–11, 'And I also have given you cleanness of teeth in all your cities, and want of bread in all your places: yet have ye not returned unto me, saith the Lord. And also I have withholden the rain from you, when there were yet three months to the harvest: and I caused it to rain upon one city, and caused it not to rain upon another city: one piece was rained upon, and the piece whereupon it rained not withered. So two or three cities wandered unto one city to drink water; but they were not satisfied: yet have ye not returned unto me, saith the Lord. I have smitten you with blasting and mildew: when your gardens, and your vineyards, and your fig-trees, and your olive-trees increased, the palmer-worm devoured them: yet have ye not returned unto me, saith the Lord. I have sent among you the pestilence, after the manner of Egypt; your young men have I slain with the sword, and have taken away your horses, and I have made the stink of your camps to come up unto your nostrils: yet have ye not returned unto me, saith the Lord. I have overthrown some of you, as God overthrew Sodom and Gomorrah, and ye were as a firebrand plucked out of the burning: yet have ye not returned unto me, saith the Lord.' By all these scriptures it is most evident that desperate incorrigibleness and unreformedness under wasting and destroying judgments brings the fiery dispensations of God upon a people. Ah London, London! how long has the Lord been striving with thee by his Spirit, by his word, by his messengers, by his mercies, and by lesser judgments, and yet thou hast been incorrigible, incurable, and irrecoverable under all! God looked that the agues, fevers, small-pox, strange sicknesses, want of trade, and poverty that was coming on like an armed man upon thee, with all the lesser fires that have been kindled in the midst of thee, should have awakened thee to repentance; and yet under all, how proud, how stout, how hard, how obdurate hast thou been! God looked that the bloody sword that the nations round hath drawn against thee should have humbled thee, and brought thee to his foot: and yet thou hast rejected the remedy of thy recovery. God looked that the raging, devouring pestilence that in 1665 destroyed so many ten thousands of thy inhabitants should have astonished thee, and have been as a prodigy unto thee, to have affrighted thee out of thy sins, and to have turned thee to the Most High: but yet after so stupendous and amazing judgments, thou wast hardened in thy sins, and refusedst to return. By all these divers kinds of judgments, how little did God prevail with thy magistracy, ministry, or commonalty to break off their sins, to repent, and to abhor themselves in dust and ashes! Hath not God spent all his rods in vain upon thee? Were not all sorts of men generally seven times worse after those wasting judgments than they were before? Jer. xxiv. 2, 3. And therefore thou hast cause to fear that this is that which hath kindled such a devouring fire in the midst of thee, and that hath turned thy glory into shame, thy riches, palaces, and stately houses into ashes. When after the raging pestilence men returned to the city, and to their estates and trades, &c., they returned also to their old sins; and as many followed the world more greedily than ever, so many followed their lusts, their sinful courses, more violently than ever; and this has ushered in thy desolation, O London! The physician, when he findeth that the potion which he hath given his patient will not work, he seconds it with one more violent; and thus doth the chirurgeon too. If a gentle plaster will not serve, then he applies that which is more corroding; and to prevent a gangrene, he makes use of his cauterising knife, and takes off the joint or member that is so ill affected. So doth the great God; when men are not bettered by lesser judgments, he sends greater judgments upon them. God was first as a moth to Ephraim, which consumed him by little and little; but when that would not better him, and reform him, then the Lord comes as a lion upon him, and tore him all to pieces, Hosea v. 12, 14. If the dross of men's sins will not come off, he will throw them into the melting-pot again and again, he will crush them harder and harder in the press of his judgments, and lay on such irons as shall enter more deep into their souls. If he strikes, and they grieve not; if he strikes again, and they tremble not; if he wounds, and they return not; then it is a righteous thing with God to turn men out of house and home, and to burn up their comforts round about them. Now this has been thy case, O London! and therefore God has laid thee desolate in the eyes of the nations.

Now this desperate incorrigibleness and unreformedness under wasting and destroying judgments I cannot groundedly fix upon those who did truly fear the Lord within and without the walls of London, because they made it their business, according to the different measures of grace they had received, to mourn under wasting judgments, and to lament after the Lord under wasting judgments, and to be bettered and reformed under wasting judgments, and not only to understand, but also to obey the voice of the rod. Their earnest prayers, strong cries, bitter tears, sad sighs, and heavy groans under wasting judgments, may sufficiently evidence that they were not incorrigible under wasting judgments. But,

5. Fifthly, *Insolent and cruel oppressing of the poor is a sin that brings desolating and destroying judgments upon a people.* God sent ten wasting judgments one after another upon Pharaoh, his people, and land, to revenge the cruel oppression of his poor people, Exod. iii. 9. Prov. xxii. 22, 23, 'Rob not the poor, because he is poor; neither oppress the afflicted in the gate: for the Lord will plead their cause.' To rob and oppress the rich is a great sin; but to rob and oppress the

poor is a greater; but to rob and oppress the poor, because he is poor, and wants money to buy justice, is the top of all inhumanity and impiety. To oppress any one is a sin; but to oppress the oppressed is the height of sin. Poverty and want and misery should be motives to pity; but oppressors make them the whetstones of their cruelty and severity, and therefore the Lord will plead the cause of his poor oppressed people against their oppressors without fee or fear; yea, he will plead their cause with pestilence, blood, and fire. Gog was a great oppressor of the poor, Ezek. xxxviii. 8–14, and God pleads against him with pestilence, blood, and fire: ver. 22, 'And I will plead against him with pestilence and with blood; and I will rain upon him, and upon his bands, and upon the many people that are with him, an overflowing rain, and great hailstones, fire, and brimstone.' Such as oppress a man and his house, even a man and his heritage, they take the surest and the readiest way to bring ruin upon their own houses, Micah ii. 1, 2. Isa. v. 8, 'Woe unto them that join house to house, and field to field, till there be no place, that they may be placed alone in the midst of the earth!' But mark what follows: ver. 9, 'In mine ears said the Lord of hosts, Of a truth many houses shall be desolate, even great and fair, without inhabitants; of a truth many houses shall be desolate.' This is an emphatical form of swearing; it is as if the Lord had said, 'Let me not live, or let me never be owned or accounted a God, or let me never be looked upon as a God of truth, a God of my word; let me never be believed nor trusted more for a God, if I do not lay desolate the houses of oppressors, the great houses of oppressors, the fair houses of oppressors; yea, the multitude and variety of the houses of oppressors.' So Amos iii. 9–11, 'Publish in the palaces at Ashdod, and in the palaces in the land of Egypt, and say, Assemble yourselves upon the mountains of Samaria, and behold the great tumults in the midst thereof, and the oppressed,' or oppressions, 'in the midst thereof. For they know not to do right, saith the Lord, who store up violence and robbery in their palaces. Therefore thus saith the Lord God, An adversary there shall be even round about the land; and he shall bring down thy strength from thee, and thy palaces shall be spoiled.' Now mark the 15th verse, 'And I will smite the winter-house with the summer-house; and the houses of ivory shall perish, and the great houses shall have an end, saith the Lord.' In their palaces, and in their winter and summer houses, they stored up all the riches, preys, and spoils that they had got by oppression. But God tells them that their palaces should be spoiled, and that he would smite the winter-house upon the summer-house—so the Hebrew runs. God was resolved that he would dash one house against the other, and lay them all on heaps. Though their palaces and houses were never so rich, and strong, and stately, and pompous, and glorious, and decked, and adorned, and enamelled, and checkered, yet they should all down together. So Zech. vii. 10, 11, 14, 'Oppress not the widow, nor the fatherless, the stranger, nor the poor; and let none of you imagine evil against his brother in your heart. But they refused to hearken, and pulled away the shoulder, and stopped their ears, that they should not hear.' Well now, mark what follows: ver. 14, 'But I scattered them with a whirlwind among all the nations whom they knew not. Thus the land was desolate after them, that no man passed through nor returned: for they laid the pleasant land' (or as the Hebrew has it, the second land of desire) 'desolate.' Palestine was a very pleasant land—a land which flowed with milk and honey, a land which was the glory of all lands; God had made it as his paradise, and enriched it with all plenty and pleasure, and, above all, with his presence and residence in his city and temple; but they by oppressing the poor, the widow, and the fatherless, laid all desolate: Jer. xii. 12, 'O house of David, thus saith the Lord, Execute judgment in the morning, and deliver him that is spoiled out of the hand of the oppressor, lest my fury go out like fire, and burn that none can quench it.' Oppression lays a people open to God's fury, it provokes the Lord to turn their all into unquenchable flames: Ps. xii. 5, 'For the oppression of the poor, for the sighing of the needy, now will I arise, saith the Lord; I will set him in safety from him that puffeth at him.' Upon these words Chrysostom saith, *Timete quicunque pauperem injuriâ afficitis; habetis vos potentiam et opes, et judicum benevolentiam; sed habent illi arma omnium validissima, luctus et ejulatus, quæ à cœlis auxilium attrahunt. Hæc arma domus effodiunt, fundamenta evertunt, hæc integras nationes submergunt:* Fear ye, whosoever ye be, that do wrong the poor, you have power and wealth, and the favour of the judges; but they have the strongest weapons of all, sighings and groanings, which fetch help from heaven for them. These weapons dig down houses, throw up foundations, overthrow whole nations.[1] Thus you see by all these clear scriptures that oppression is a sin that brings wasting and destroying judgments upon a people.

Ah, London! London! was there no oppression and cruelty to be found within and without thy walls? Eccles. iv. 1, 'So I returned, and considered all the oppressions that are done under the sun: and behold the tears of such as were oppressed, and they had no comforter; and on the side of their oppressors there was power; but they had no comforter.' And behold the tears of such as were oppressed. The original word signifies *lachrymam, non lachrymas*, a tear, not tears; as if the oppressed had wept so long, and wept so much, that they could weep no longer, nor weep no more, having but only one tear left them. Were there not, O London! many of thy poor oppressed inhabitants that wept so long, that they could weep no longer; and that wept so much, that they had but one tear left? Oh, the cries and tears of the oppressed within and without thy walls did so pierce God's ears, and so work upon his heart, that at last he comes down in flames of fire to revenge the oppressed. Were there no rich citizens that did rack their tenants, and grind the faces of the poor, that took an advantage from their necessities to beat down the price of their commodities, that so they might raise themselves on the poor's ruin? Were there no false weights, false wares, false lights, false measures to be found within and without thy walls by which the poor has been cheated, cozened, and oppressed?[2] Oh how did the rich work upon

[1] Chrys. in Psalm xii.

[2] Were there none within nor without thy walls, O London, that used his neighbour without wages, and gave him no reward for his work? that kept back the hire of the

the necessities of the poor, bringing them to such under-prices as hath undone both them and their making good that word, Amos viii. 4, 'They swallow up the needy, and make the poor of the land to fail!' Oh the heavy burdens that have been laid upon the poor by their Egyptian taskmasters! what overreaching of the poor, and what overrating of the poor have been within and without thy walls, O London! Thy poor, O London, did rise early and go to bed late; they did fare hard, and lie hard, and work hard; and yet by reason of the cruelty, oppression, and unmercifulness of many of thy wealthy citizens, they were hardly able to make any convenient supplies for themselves and their families. Oppression turns princes into roaring lions, and judges into evening wolves: it is an unnatural sin, it is a sin against the light of nature. No creatures do oppress them of their own kind. Look upon the birds of prey, as upon eagles, vultures, hawks, and you shall never find them preying upon their own kind. Look upon the wild beasts of the forest, as upon the lion, the tiger, the wolf, the bear, &c., and you shall find them favourable to them of their own kind; and yet men unnaturally prey upon one another—like the fish in the sea, the great swallowing up the small. It is a sin against that great and common rule of equity, Mat. vii. 12, 'All things whatsoever ye would that men should do unto you, do ye even so to them.' Now no man in his wits would have another to wrong and oppress him in his estate, name, or conscience: and therefore he should not wrong or oppress others in their estates, names, or consciences: and therefore no wonder if God punishes this sin with flames of fire. It is thy oppressors, O London, that has turned thy glory into ashes.

Now this insolent oppressing of the poor is a sin that I cannot make good against the people of God that did truly fear him in that great city. It is a sin they have often bewailed and lamented before the Lord in their solemn addresses to God. Where this sin is rampant, where it rules as a prince upon the throne, it is a clear evidence that the fear of the Lord is not in such men's hearts: Lev. xxv. 17, 'Ye shall not oppress one another, but thou shalt fear thy God.' Now this lies fair in the words,—viz., that such as do oppress others, they do not fear God: and such as do fear God, they will not oppress others. Amalek was a great oppressor of the poor people of God, and the Holy Ghost hath set this black brand of infamy upon him, that he feared not God, Deut. xxv. 18.[1] Had Amalek feared the Lord, he would have been so far from oppressing the poor people of God, that he would have comforted them, and succoured them, and relieved them in the midst of their necessities, miseries, and distresses. The Jews oppressing one another is attributed to their not fearing of God, Neh. v. 9. Oppression is so crying a sin against the law of God, the law of grace, the law of nature, and the law of nations, that certainly it cannot be justly charged upon such as have set up God in their hearts as the great object of their fear. The word for oppression in

labourer, and that were the poor labourer's purse-bearers and cofferers, whether they would or no? that fleeced the poor to feather their own nests? Deut. xxiv. 14, 15; Exod. xxii. 22, 23; Zeph. iii. 3.

[1] Oppressors are persons destitute of the fear of God; and the want of the fear of the Lord is the spring and fountain of the worst of sins, and that against which the Lord will come near in judgment, Mal. iii. 5.

the Hebrew is *mispach*, which signifies a scab, a wound, a leprosy. Now oppression is such a scab, a wound, a leprosy as is not to be found upon those that have fellowship with the Father and the Son. Oppressors may boast of their profession, and call themselves saints, or the people of God, but God accounts them worse than Scythians. Witness those dreadful woes that God has denounced against them in the blessed Scriptures: Zeph. iii. 1, 'Woe to the oppressing city!' Jer. xxii. 13, 'Woe unto him that buildeth his house by unrighteousness, and his chambers by wrong: that useth his neighbour's service without wages, and giveth him not for his work!' Isa. x. 1-3, 'Woe unto them that decree unrighteous decrees. To turn aside the needy from judgment, and to take away the right from the poor of my people, that widows may be their prey, and that they may rob the fatherless! And what will ye do in the day of visitation, and in the desolation which shall come from far? to whom will ye flee for help? and where will ye leave your glory?' Micah ii. 1, 2, 'Woe to them that devise iniquity, and work evil upon their beds! when the morning is light they practise it, because it is in the power of their hand. And they covet fields, and take them by violence; and houses, and take them away: so they oppress a man and his house, even a man and his heritage.' Now by all these dreadful woes it is further evident that this horrid sin of insolent oppression cannot be charged upon the called and chosen of God; for where do you find in all the Scriptures the vessels of glory under those woes that are denounced against the ungodly? But,

6. Sixthly, *Rejecting the gospel, contemning the gospel, and slighting the free and gracious offers of Christ in the gospel, brings the fiery dispensation upon a people, and causes the Lord to lay their cities desolate:* Mat. xxii. 2-7, 'The kingdom of heaven is like unto a certain king which made a marriage for his son. And he sent forth his servants to call them that were bidden to the wedding: and they would not come. Again he sent forth other servants, saying, Tell them which are bidden, Behold, I have prepared my dinner: my oxen and my fatlings are killed, and all things are ready; come unto the marriage. But they made light of it, and went their ways, one to his farm, another to his merchandise: and the remnant took his servants, and entreated them spitefully, and slew them. But when the king heard thereof, he was wroth: and sent forth his armies, and destroyed those murderers, and burnt up their city.' In this parable the vocation of the Gentiles and the rejection of the Jews is set forth.[1] The Jews have the honour to be first called to the marriage-feast—they are invited by the prophets, and afterwards by the apostles to partake of Christ, and of all his royal benefits and favours which are displayed in the gospel, Isa. xxv. 8, 9; Prov. ix. 1-6; Isa. lv. 1-3. God the Father was very willing and desirous to make up a match between Christ and the Jews, and between Christ and the Gentiles; and he is here called a King, to declare his divine majesty, and to set forth the stateliness and magnificence of the feast. Marriage-feasts that are usually made by kings are full of joy, and full of state, full of splendour and glory. Who can sum up the variety of dishes and

[1] Calvin, Chrysostom.

dainties that then the guests are feasted with? The variety of the glorious excellencies, favours, and mercies of Christ that are discovered and tendered by God in gospel-offers, in gospel-ordinances, is the wedding-feast to which all sorts of sinners are invited. But here you see they slight, and scorn, and contemn both the master of the feast and the matter of the feast, and all those servants that were sent to invite them to the feast; and hereupon the king was wroth, and sent forth his armies—the Romans, as most interpreters do agree—and destroyed those murderers, and burnt up their city. About forty years after the death of Christ, the Lord, to revenge the blood of his Son, the blood of his servants, and the contempt of his gospel upon the Jews, brought his armies, the Romans, against Jerusalem, who by fire demolished their temple and city, and by sword and famine destroyed eleven millions of men, women, and children; and those that escaped fire, sword, and famine, were sold for slaves, and scattered among all the nations.[1] Christ and the way of salvation by him is the subject-matter of the gospel. The word Ἐυαγγέλιον, that is rendered 'gospel,' signifies glad tidings, good news; and certainly salvation by Christ is the best news, it is the greatest and the gladdest tidings that ever was brought to sinners' ears. What the psalmist had long before said of the city of God, 'Glorious things are spoken of thee,' Ps. lxxxvii. 3, that I may truly say of the blessed gospel, 'Glorious things are spoken of thee, O thou gospel of God.' The gospel is called 'the glorious gospel of the blessed God,' 1 Tim. i. 11. The gospel is a glorious gospel in respect of the Author of it, and in respect of the penmen of it, and in respect of the glorious discoveries that it makes of God, of Christ, of the Spirit, of heaven, and in respect of its glorious effects, in turning of poor sinners 'from darkness to light, and from the power of Satan unto God,' Acts xxvi. 18, that they may receive forgiveness of sins, and inheritance among them which are sanctified. Certainly Solomon's natural history, in which he treated of all trees, 'from the cedar to the hyssop, of all beasts, fowls, and creeping things,' 1 Kings iv. 33, was a very rare and incomparable piece in its kind; yet one leaf, yea, one line of the gospel is infinitely more worth, and of greater importance to us, than all that large volume would have been.[2] For what is the knowledge of trees, and birds, and beasts, and worms, and fishes, to the knowledge of God in Christ, to the knowledge of the great things of eternity, to the knowledge of a man's sinful estate by nature, or to the knowledge of his happy estate by grace? Doubtless to a soul that hath tasted that the Lord is gracious, there is no book to this of the Bible. Acts xix. 19: When the Lord had made it the day of his glorious power to their conviction, conversion, and salvation, they burnt their costly books of curious arts. And no wonder; for they had found the power and the sweet of a better book, even of God's book, upon their hearts. Luther, speaking of the gospel, saith, 'that the shortest line, and the least letter thereof, is more worth than all heaven and earth.' He tasted so much of the sweetness of the gospel, and saw so much of the

[1] Josephus de Bell Judaic., lib. vii.

[2] Some are of opinion that it was burnt by the Chaldees, together with the temple; others think that it was abolished by Hezekiah, because the people idolised it, as they did the brazen serpent.

glory and excellency of the gospel, that he would often say to his friends, that he would not take all the world for one leaf of the Bible. Rab. Chiia, in the Jerusalem Talmud, saith, that in his account all the world is not of equal value with one word out of the law. Israel had three crowns, as the Talmud observes, (1.) of the king, (2.) of the priest, (3.) of the law; but the crown of the law was counted by them the chiefest of the three. Then what is the crown of the gospel to all those upon whom the gospel is come in power? 1 Thes. i. 5–7. How divinely did that poet speak, who said he could read God in every leaf on the tree, and that he found his name written on every green herb; and shall not we read God, and Christ, and grace, and mercy in every leaf, yea, in every line of the gospel? The Bible, saith Luther, is the only book; all the books in the world are but waste paper to it,[1] so highly did he prize it, and so dearly did he love it. Contempt of the gospel is a great indignity cast upon the great God, and a great indignity cast upon Jesus Christ; for though the law was delivered by Moses, yet the gospel was delivered by Jesus Christ. And if they escaped not who despised him that spake from earth, of how much sorer punishment are they worthy that contemn him that speaks from heaven? Heb. ii. 3, and x. 28, 29. If the book of the law happen to fall upon the ground, the Jews' custom is presently to proclaim a fast. O sirs! what cause then have we to fast and mourn, when we see the glorious gospel of God fallen to the ground, scorned, despised, contemned, and trampled upon by all sorts of sinners![2] Contempt of the gospel is a sin of the greatest ingratitude. In the gospel God offers himself, his Son, his Spirit, his grace, his kingdom, and all the glory of another world. Now for men to despise and contemn these offers, is the highest ingratitude and unthankfulness imaginable; and therefore no wonder if God burn such men up, and turn them out of house and home. Such justly deserve the worst of judgments, who despise the best of mercies. The strongest and the sweetest wine always makes the sharpest vinegar; the freest, the richest, and the choicest offers of mercy, if slighted and contemned, turn into the greatest fury and severity. Divine wrath smokes and burns against none so fiercely, as it doth against those who are despisers of gospel mercies. When gold is offered, men care not how great or how base he is that offers it: neither is it material by whom the gospel is brought unto us, whether it be brought unto us by Isaiah, as some think, a prophet of the blood-royal, or by Amos from amongst the herdmen of Tekoa. Let the hand be more noble or more mean that brings it, if it be slighted and contemned, provoked justice will revenge it. Such as slight the gospel, and contemn the gospel, they sin with a high hand against the remedy, against the means of their recovery. 'This is the condemnation,' John iii. 19, this is that desperate sin that hastens judgments upon cities and countries, as Jewry, Asia, Bohemia, and other parts of the world have sadly experienced. He that hath

[1] Luther, Com. in Gen., cap. 19.

[2] Jerome reports of Uzzah, that his shoulder was shrunk up and withered; he carted the ark when he should have carried it on his shoulder: therefore that part was branded for it.

eat poison, and shall despise the means of his recovery, must certainly die for it. He who, when he hath committed treason against his prince, shall not only refuse, but scorn and slight his prince's favour and pardon, and fling it from him with disdain, is assuredly past all help and hope. Sins against the gospel are sins of a greater size, of a louder cry, and of a deeper dye, than sins against the law are, and accordingly God suits his judgments. Where the gospel shines in power, it will either mend a people or mar a people: it will either better them or worsen them; it will either fit them for the greatest good, or it will bring upon them the greatest evils: where it doth not reform, there it will destroy. And this London hath found by woeful experience. Slighting and contemning of the offers of grace in the gospel, is a sin that is not chargeable upon the greatest part of the world, who 'lieth in wickedness,' and who 'sit in darkness, and in the region and shadow of death,' 1 John v. 19; Mat. iv. 16; yea, it is a sin that is not chargeable upon the devils themselves, and therefore the more severely will God deal with those that are guilty of it. The gospel hath for above this hundred years shined forth out of the dark and thick clouds of popery and antichristianism which had overspread the nation. And in no part of the land hath the gospel been preached with more clearness, spiritualness, life, power, and purity than in London. And oh that I had not cause to say that there was no part of the nation where the gospel was more undervalued, slighted, and contemned by many than in London! For,

[1.] First, *Where the faithful and painful ministers of the gospel are slighted and contemned as ministers of the gospel, there the gospel is slighted and contemned*, Mat. xxiii. 37, and Luke x. 16. Now were there none within nor without thy walls, O London! that did slight, scorn, reproach, and contemn the ambassadors of Christ, who were faithful to their light, their Lord, their consciences, and the souls of their hearers? But,

[2.] Secondly, *Where the ministrations of the gospel, where the ordinances of the gospel are slighted and contemned, there the gospel is slighted and contemned;* yea, where any one ordinance of the gospel is slighted and contemned, there the gospel is slighted and contemned: where baptism is slighted and contemned, there the gospel is slighted and contemned; where the Lord's supper is slighted and contemned, there the gospel is slighted and contemned; where the offers of the gospel are slighted and contemned, there the gospel is slighted and contemned; where the commands of the gospel are slighted and contemned, there the gospel is slighted and contemned; where the threatenings of the gospel are slighted and contemned, there the gospel is slighted and contemned; where the promises of the gospel are slighted and contemned, there the gospel is slighted and contemned; and where the comforts of the gospel are slighted and contemned, there the gospel is slighted and contemned.[1] Now were there none within nor without thy walls, O London! that did slight and contemn the ministrations of the gospel, 'the ordinances

[1] A man upon whom the gospel hath wrought savingly, he will, (1.) Prize all the ordinances; (2.) Practise all the ordinances; (3.) Praise the Lord for all the ordinances.

of the gospel'? Luke i. 5, 6. When old Barzillai had lost his taste and hearing, he cared not for David's feasts and music, 2 Sam. xix. 35. There were many within and without the walls of London that had lost their spiritual taste and hearing, and so cared not for gospel ministrations, for gospel ordinances. There were many who, under a pretence of living above ordinances, lived below ordinances, and made light of ordinances; yea, who scorned, vilified, and contemned the precious ordinances of Christ. 'Thou art to them as a lovely song,' saith the prophet, Ezek. xxxiii. 31, 32. In the Hebrew it runs thus, 'Thou art to them as one that breaks jests.' The solemnity and majesty of the word was but as a dry jest unto them. Ordinances were but as dry jests to many within and without the walls of London; and therefore no wonder if God hath been in such good earnest with them who have made but a jest of those precious ordinances, that are more worth than heaven and earth. Many came to the ordinances too much like the Egyptian dog, which laps a little as he runs by the side of Nilus, but stays not to drink. But,

[3.] Thirdly, *Such as are weary of the gospel, such slight the gospel, such contemn the gospel.* Never were the Israelites more weary of manna, than many within and without the walls of London were weary of the plain and powerful preaching of the gospel, Num. xi. 6; Amos viii. 5. We were better have a biting gospel than a toothless mass, said blessed Bradford. But were there not some that had rather have a toothless mass than a biting gospel? Were there not many that were willing to let God go, and gospel go, and ordinances go, and all go, so they might be eased of their burdens and taxes, and greaten their relations, and have peace with all nations, and enjoy a sweeping trade, and every one sit under his vine and under his fig-tree, eating the fat, and drinking the sweet, and enjoy liberty to dishonour the Lord, to gratify their lusts, to damn their own souls, and to bring others under their feet, so weary were they of the blessed gospel?

[4.] Fourthly, *Such as have but a low and mean opinion of the gospel, such are slighters and contemners of the gospel.* Such as prefer every toy, and trifle, and fashion, and sinful custom, and base lust above the light of the gospel, the power of the gospel, the purity and simplicity of the gospel, the holiness and sweetness of the gospel, such are slighters and contemners of the gospel, 1 Cor. i. 23. Though it be better to present truth in her native plainness than to hang her ears with counterfeit pearls, yet there were many that set a greater price upon the arts, the parts, the gifts, the studied notions and seraphical expressions of their ministers, than they did upon the gospel itself; and what was this but to prefer the handmaid before the mistress, the servant before his lord, the flowers about the dish before the meat that was in the dish, the chaff before the wheat, and pebbles before the richest pearls? The gospel is the field, and Christ is the treasure that is hid in that field; the gospel is a ring of gold, and Christ is the pearl in that ring of gold; and yet how many were there within and without the walls of London that put no considerable price or value upon the gospel! But,

[5.] Fifthly, *Such as wilfully disobey the gospel, and live and walk in ways quite cross and contrary to the gospel, such are slighters and contemners of the gospel, and accordingly the Lord will deal with them.* Take one text for all, 2 Thes. i. 7–9, 'And to you who are troubled rest with us, when the Lord Jesus shall be revealed from heaven with his mighty angels, in flaming fire, taking vengeance on them that know not God, and that obey not the gospel of our Lord Jesus: who shall be punished with everlasting destruction from the presence of the Lord, and from the glory of his power.' This is a more terrible text against all such as are either ignorant of the gospel or that disobey the gospel, than any is to be found in all the Old Testament. In the last day Christ will take vengeance in flaming fire on them that disobey his gospel, and that walk contrary to the rules of his gospel; and therefore no wonder if before that day he lays their habitations desolate by a flaming fire, whose lives give the lie to his glorious gospel. These men above all others expose the gospel to the derision and contempt of the basest and vilest men. When some of the heathens have looked upon the loose lives of professors, they have said, *Aut hoc non est evangelium, aut hi non sunt Christiani*, Either this is not the gospel, in which there is so much goodness, or these are not Christians, in whom there is none at all. Did you never hear nor read of one who, eyeing the loose conversations of professors, cried out, *Sit anima mea cum philosophis*, Let my soul be rather with the honest philosophers—who were heathen—than with these wicked lewd men that are called Christians? Now were there none within nor without the walls of London that did wilfully disobey the gospel, and that walked in ways quite cross and contrary to the gospel? Surely there were; and therefore at their doors we may safely lay the burning of London. But,

[6.] Sixthly and lastly, *Such as slighted, scorned, and contemned the faithful, sincere, serious, gracious, and conscientious professors of the gospel, such slighted, scorned, and contemned the gospel itself.* When the Jews were in prosperity, it was the manner of the Samaritans to repute themselves their nearest cousins. When the Jews were in a thriving and flourishing condition, then the Samaritans could derive their pedigree from Ephraim and Manasseh, the sons of Joseph; but when the Jews were in any great affliction, or under persecution, then they would deny all acquaintance with them and all relation to them.[1] When profession was in fashion and religion was in credit, how many were there within and without the walls of London that did pretend to be kin, to be cousins to the serious, conscientious, and sincere professors of the gospel, who since the day of their affliction have not only denied all acquaintance with them, and renounced all relation to them, but also are turned slighters, scorners, and contemners of them! If these may not be reckoned among the slighters, scorners, and contemners of the gospel, I do not know who may. To sum up all, I have shewed you that slighting, scorning, and contemning of the gospel, is a sin of that high nature that it provokes the Lord to lay cities desolate. I have shewed you the greatness of that sin, and the persons that are guilty of it; so that now you may point with a finger to those persons that have laid London in ashes.

[1] Joseph. Antiq., lib. xi. cap. 8.

But before I close up this particular, give me leave to say, that this sin of slighting, scorning, and contemning of the gospel, I dare not charge upon those that truly fear the Lord, and that have found the gospel to be a gospel of power upon their own souls, turning them from darkness to light, and from the power of Satan to Jesus Christ, 1 Thes. i. 5–7; Acts xxvi. 18. And I shall freely give you my reasons, that you may be the better satisfied that it was not so much their sins as your own that has brought down that heavy judgment of fire upon the city, wherein once you and they had your respective habitations. My reasons are these:—

[1.] First, Those that did truly fear the Lord, and that had experienced the power of the gospel in a saving way upon their own souls, they did frequently before the Lord *bewail and mourn over—both together and apart—that heinous sin of slighting, scorning, and contemning of the gospel, which many were guilty of, whose habitations were then some within, and others without the walls of London*, Ezek. ix. 4, 6. The Jews have a law which enjoins them to take up any paper which they see lying on the ground, and the reason is, lest haply the name of God be written in the paper, and ignorantly trodden under foot. Though Christians ought to be free from such superstitious curiosities, yet they ought to be very careful that the least tittle of the gospel, the least command of the gospel, be not trod under foot. Now the saints who once lived within and without the walls of London, who through grace have experienced the saving power of the gospel upon their own souls, how have they mourned and lamented to see that glorious gospel of Christ trod under foot, which they have laid so near their hearts! and therefore I cannot fairly charge this sin upon them. But,

[2.] Secondly, Slighting, scorning, and contemning of the gospel, *is a great step towards the sin against the Holy Ghost, and a sin of so great a cry, and so deep a dye, that I cannot at present find where it is in Scripture charged upon such as truly fear the Lord, and that have really experienced the power of the gospel in a saving way upon their own souls*, Heb. ii. 3, and x. 28, 29; and therefore I cannot fairly charge this sin upon them.

[3.] Thirdly, *Next to God, the gospel is the most sweet and delightful thing in all the world to gracious souls, who have experienced the saving power of it upon themselves.*[1] Luther found so much sweetness in it, that it made him say, that he would not live in paradise if he might without the word, *at cum verbo etiam in inferno facile est vivere*—but with the word he could live in hell itself. Dolphins, they say, love music, and so do gracious souls love the music of the gospel. The gospel is like the stone *garamantides,* that hath drops of gold within itself, enriching all that will embrace it and conform to it: and this the saints have found by experience, and therefore they cannot but delight in it, and draw sweetness from it. Aglutuidas[2] never relished any dish better than what was distasted by others: so

[1] Ps. xix. 10, 11, and cxix. 72, 103, 127; Job xxiii. 12. Austin cries, Away with our writings, that room may be made for the book of God.

[2] Query, Aglaus of Psophis, so renowned for his contentedness? Val. Max. vii. 1, § 2: Pliny H. N. vii. 47.—G.

do the saints relish that gospel best that others distaste most; and therefore I cannot charge this sin fairly upon them. But,

[4.] Fourthly, *There are none that do so highly prize the gospel, and that set so high a value upon the gospel, as those do who have experienced the saving power of the gospel upon their own souls*, Rev. xii. 11, and ii. 12, 13; Heb. xi. 33, 38. Such prefer the gospel before all their nearest and dearest concernments and enjoyments that they have in this world; as might be made evident from their practice in the primitive times, and in the Marian days, and in those late years that are now passed over our heads.[1] The tabernacle was covered over with red, and the purple feathers[2] tell us, they take that habit for the same intent, to note that we must defend the truth of the gospel, even to the effusion of blood: and this they have made good in all the ages of the world, who have found the saving power of the gospel upon their own souls. Tertullian concludes, that the gospel must needs be a precious thing, because Nero hated it; and indeed it was so precious to the saints in his days, that they very willingly and cheerfully laid down their lives for the gospel's sake.[3] Now the same spirit rests upon the saints in our days, and therefore upon this ground I cannot charge that horrid sin of slighting, scorning, and contemning of the gospel upon them. Israel had three crowns, as the Talmud observes, (1.) of the king, (2.) of the priest, (3.) of the law; but the crown of the law, that was the chief of the three.

[5.] Fifthly, *Who were so ready and free to countenance the gospel, and to maintain the gospel, and to encourage the faithful and painful preachers of the gospel, as those that had found the sweet of the gospel, and the saving power of the gospel, upon their own souls?* They like well of religion without expense in Basil, and a gospel without charge in Nazianzen; but if it grow costly, it is no commodity for their money. Now this was the very frame and temper of many thousands in London, who never experienced the saving work of the gospel upon their poor souls: but they were of another frame and temper of spirit in London upon whom the gospel was fallen in power; and therefore I may not charge upon them this odious sin of slighting, scorning, and contemning the gospel. But,

[6.] Sixthly, *Who were there within or without the walls of London that were so much in a hearty and serious blessing, praising, and admiring of the Lord and his goodness for bringing them forth in gospel times, as those that had a saving work of the gospel upon their own souls?* When Alexander was born, his father Philip blessed such gods as he had, not so much that he had a son, as that he had him in Aristotle's days; he was thankful for natural and moral discoveries. The clearest, the choicest, the fullest, and the sweetest visions and discoveries that we have of God on this side eternity, we have in the gospel, and this they frequently experience who have found the gospel falling in power upon their souls; and therefore they cannot but always have harps in their hands, and hallelujahs in their mouths, upon this

[1] Luther, speaking of the gospel, saith, that the shortest line and the least letter thereof is more than all heaven and earth.

[2] That is, the Romish priests.—G.

[3] Tertul. Apol. cap. v.

very account, that they have lived under the warm sunshine of the gospel, Rev. xiv. 1–4, and xix. 1–8. And therefore I shall not charge this vile sin of slighting, scorning, and contemning the gospel upon them who, above all other men, were most exercised in a serious and hearty blessing and praising of God for his glorious gospel. Some there were that blessed God for their yearly incomes, and others there were that blessed God for their prosperous relations and friends, and many there were that blessed God for their deliverance from various perils and dangers; but those that had the gospel working in power upon them, they made it their business and work above all to bless the Lord for the gospel; and therefore who dare charge upon them the contempt of the gospel? But,

[7.] Seventhly and lastly, *There were none within nor without the walls of London that have suffered so many things and such hard things, for the enjoyment of the gospel in its power and purity, as they have done who have found the powerful and saving work of the gospel upon their own souls.* Such have been as signs and wonders in Israel, in London, Isa. viii. 18. Now what folly and vanity would it be to charge them with slighting, scorning, and contemning of the gospel, who have been the only sufferers for the gospel's sake. And thus much for the twelfth[1] sin that brings the fiery dispensation upon cities and people.

7. *The sin that brings the fiery dispensation upon a people, and that provokes the Lord to lay their cities desolate, is a course, a trade of lying:* Nahum iii. 1, 'Woe to the bloody city, it is full of lies;' ver. 7, 'And it shall come to pass, that all they that look upon thee shall flee from thee, and say, Nineveh is laid waste, who will bemoan her? whence shall I seek comforters for thee?' ver. 13, 'Behold, thy people in the midst of thee are women: the gates of thy land shall be set wide open to thine enemies: the fire shall devour thy bars,' that is, thy strongholds; for so the word *bars* is frequently taken, as you may see by comparing the scriptures in the margin.[2] Nineveh was a great city, a rich city, a populous city, a trading city, it was a city that was wholly made up of fraud and falsehood; it was all full of lies, or it was full of all sorts of lies; there was no truth to be found either in her private contracts or in her public transactions and capitulations with other nations; and therefore the Lord resolves to lay her desolate, and to consume her with fire. So Jer. ix. 3, 'And they bend their tongues like their bow for lies;' ver. 5, 'And they will deceive every one his neighbour, and will not speak the truth: they have taught their tongue to speak lies, and weary themselves to commit iniquity;' ver. 9, 'Shall I not visit for these things? saith the Lord: shall not my soul be avenged on such a nation as this?' ver. 10, 'For the mountains will I take up a weeping and wailing, and for the habitations of the wilderness a lamentation, because they are burnt up; so that none can pass through them, neither can men hear the voice of the cattle; both the fowl of the heavens and the beasts are fled, they are gone;' ver. 11, 'And I will make Jerusalem heaps,' (as London is this day,) 'and a

[1] Qu. 'sixth?'—ED.

[2] 1 Sam. xxiii. 7; 1 Kings iv. 13; 2 Chron. viii. 5, and xiv. 7; Jer. xlix. 31, and li. 30; Lam. ii. 9; Amos i. 5.

den of dragons; and I will make the cities of Judah desolate, without an inhabitant;' ver. 12, 'Who is the wise man that may understand this? and who is he to whom the mouth of the Lord hath spoken, that he may declare it, for what the land perisheth, and is burnt up like a wilderness that none passeth through?' Jer. xiii. 23. The Jews had so inured and accustomed their tongues to speak lies, they had got such a haunt, a habit, and custom of lying, that they could not leave it; and this was the procuring cause of that dreadful and utter devastation that befell their city and country: Hosea iv. 1–3, 'Hear the word of the Lord, ye children of Israel, for the Lord hath a controversy with the inhabitants of the land, because there is no truth, nor mercy, nor knowledge of God in the land. By swearing, and lying, and killing, and stealing, and committing adultery, they break out, and blood toucheth blood. Therefore shall the land mourn, and every one that dwelleth therein shall languish, with the beasts of the field, and with the fowls of heaven; yea, the fishes of the sea also shall be taken away.' This people made it their common practice to lie; they were given up to a course, a trade of lying, which God here threatens to punish with an extreme and universal desolation. A lie is a voluntary and wilful telling of an untruth, with a purpose to deceive; so that three things are required to the nature of a lie: (1.) There must be an untruth and falseness in the thing; (2.) This untruth must be known to be so, he must be conscious to himself that it is false; (3.) He must have an intent and purpose to utter this falsehood with a desire or design to deceive another by it. Augustine makes eight sorts of lies, but the schoolmen reduce all to three: 1. Is *jocosum*, the sporting lie; 2. Is *officiosum*, the helpful lie; 3. Is *perniciosum*, the pernicious and hurtful lie.

(1.) First, *There is mendacium jocosum, the sporting lie;* and this is when men will lie and tell untruths to make men sport, to make men merry. Of this sin the prophet Hosea complains, chap. vii. 3, 'They make the king glad with their wickedness, and the princes with their lies.'[1] Courtiers frame fictions, and tell ridiculous stories to delight princes. Among many courtiers loud lies are esteemed ornaments and elegancies of speech; and none are accounted so sweet and pleasant in their discourse as those that can tell the most pleasing lies; but such mirth-mongers and mirth-makers may do well to remember that such kind of mirth will bring bitterness in the end. If for 'every idle word that men shall speak, they must give an account in the day of judgment,' Mat. xii. 36, then surely much more for every lying word. And if foolish talking and jesting be condemned, then surely lying talking and jesting shall be much more condemned, if not here, yet in the great day, when all lying jesters shall hold up their hands at Christ's bar. Now were there none within nor without the walls of London that were guilty of merry lies, of sporting lies? But,

(2.) Secondly, *There is mendacium officiosum, the officious lie, the helpful lie;* and that is when a man lies to help himself or others at a pinch, at a dead lift. When men lie, either to prevent some danger they fear, or else to bring about some good they desire, then they tell an officious lie. Thus the Egyptian midwives lied, and thus Rahab

[1] It is a received opinion in these days, that, *Qui nescit dissimulare, nescit vivere.*

lied, and thus the old prophet lied, who, contrary to the command of God, persuaded the man of God to go back and eat bread with him under the pretence of a divine revelation, Exod. i. 15–20; Josh. ii. 1–9; 1 Kings xiii. 14–27. And thus Jacob told his father an officious threefold lie, Gen. xxvii. 19, but he hardly ever had a merry day, a good day after it; for God followed him with variety of troubles, and his sorrows, like Job's messengers, came posting in one after another, even to his dying day, that both himself and others might see what bitterness is wrapped up in officious lies. Solon, reproving Thespis the poet for lying, Thespis answered him, That it was not material, seeing it was but in sport; then Solon, beating the ground with his staff, said, If we commend lying in sport, we shall find it afterwards in good earnest. In all our bargains and dealings let us make it our wisdom and our work to remember, 'That we must not do evil, that good may come,' Rom. iii. 8; yea, we must not tell a lie to save all the souls under heaven. The Priscillianists in Spain, a most pestilentious sect, taught in Augustine's time that it was lawful to lie for the helping of a good cause, and for the propagating of the gospel, and for the advantage of religion. But Augustine confuted them, and stoutly asserts in two books that we are not to tell an officious lie, to tell a lie for no hurt but for good, though it were to save all the world. 'Will ye speak wickedly for God, and talk deceitfully for him?' saith Job, chap. xiii. 7, to his friends. A man may as well commit fornication with the Moabites to draw them to our religion, or steal from the rich to give to the poor, as lie to do another man a good turn. Nepos reporteth of Epaminondas, a nobleman of Thebes, and a famous warrior, that he would never lie in jest nor in earnest, either for his own or another's gain. This refined heathen will one day rise in judgment against such kind of Christians who take a great pleasure in officious lies. Now were there none within or without the walls of London that delighted themselves in officious lies? But,

(3.) Thirdly, and to come closer to our work, *There is mendacium perniciosum, the pernicious and hurtful lie;* and this of all lies is the worst, Gen. xxxix. 13–20, and 2 Kings v. 22, 23. When men will lie out of a design to hurt, to cheat, to defraud, or to make a prey of those they deal with, this is the sorest of all lies. Now, how rampant was this sort of lying among all sorts of citizens before London was in flames! What a common trade of lying did many, I say not all, drive in their buying and selling! The trade of lying was got into every trade, as if there had been no living but by lying. Many sellers had their lies to set off their commodities. It is good, it is very good, it is special good, it is the best of its kind, when it was naught, very naught, yea, stark naught: of this sort there are none so good in the city, when their consciences told them that they had much better in their own shops; that their commodity cost them so much, and that they could not abate, nor would not abate anything of that price they had pitched, though it were to their own father or mother; and yet, rather than they would lose a good customer, they presently agree at a lower price. And so when poor workmen came to their shops, and offered their commodities to sell, being forced thereunto for the relief of themselves and their miserable families, they slighted their commodities, telling them that they had no need of them, and that they had much of those commodities upon their hands already, and that they had no way to vend them; and all to beat down the price, and to make a prey of their pressing necessity; and all this when they wanted those very commodities, and had more vend for them than they knew how to supply. Now, as the seller abounded with his lies, so the buyer had his lies too, and all to bring down the price: It is naught, it is naught, it is very naught, saith the buyer. I will not give you your price, and yet gives it before he goes out of the shop or warehouse. I have bought as good, yea, better for a lower price than what I offer you, saith the buyer, when yet he had never bought of that commodity before. Use me well, saith the buyer, and you shall have my custom another time, when in his heart he resolves never to come into the seller's shop more. Ah, London! London! it is these lies and liars that have made thee desolate, and that have laid thy glory in the dust. O sirs! a man were better be a loser than a liar; a man were better, much better, to keep his commodity than to sell his conscience with his commodity. We hate the Turks for selling of Christians for slaves; and what shall we then think of those citizens, who by lying sell themselves and their precious souls for half a crown, yea, oftentimes for a penny? I have read that there was a time when the Romans did wear jewels on their shoes; but liars do worse, for they trample that matchless jewel, viz., their precious souls, under feet. Doubtless the lies that were told in London, and the liars that lived in London, did more than a little help on the ruin of London. Now, that you may the better read and understand the righteousness of God in his highest acts of severity against lies and liars, premise with me briefly these four things:—

[1.] First, *That lying is a very great sin.* It is a transgression not of one, but of many of the royal laws of heaven: Lev. xix. 11, 'Ye shall not lie one to another;' Zech. viii. 16, 'Speak ye every man the truth to his neighbour;' Eph. iv. 25, 'Wherefore putting away lying, speak every man truth with his neighbour, for we are members one of another.' In the body of man one member will not lie to another; the hand will not lie, in telling what it toucheth; the tongue will not lie, in telling what it tasteth; the eye will not lie, in telling what it seeth; but every member is a true witness to another, a true witness to his neighbour: and so it should be both in the politic body and in the mystical body of Christ, seeing we are members one of another. Every one should speak the truth with his neighbour. One member in the natural body will not mock another, nor make a fool of another; and why then should one Christian by lying mock another, or make a fool of another? Tremellius translates it thus: *Ne fatuum agito*, Do not play the fool with him. For certainly he is the veriest fool who by lying thinketh to make a fool of another: Col. iii. 9, 'Lie not one to another, seeing that ye have put off the old man with his deeds.' God's commands are not like those that are easily reversed, but they are like those of the Medes, that cannot be changed, Dan. vi. To act or run cross to God's express command, though under pretence of revelation from God, is as much as a man's life is worth, as you may see in that sad story, 1 Kings xiii. It is a dangerous thing for a man to neglect one of his commands, who by another is able to command him into nothing, or into hell. What God commands must be put in speedy execution, without denying, or delaying, or disputing the difficulties that attend it.[1] The great God will not endure to be called to an account by the poor creature concerning his royal commands; but expects that with all readiness and cheerfulness we should obey what he requires, even when the reason of our obedience is hid from our eyes; for then grace shines most transparently and gloriously, Gen. xxii. I have read of one Johannes Abbas, who being commanded by his confessor to go some miles every day to water a dry stick, which he accordingly did out of a pure respect to the command of his superior, without disputing the reason of it.[2] Oh, how much more then should we readily obey divine commands, which are all holy, spiritual, just, and good, considering the authority, sovereignty, and majesty of the great God, without disputing the reasons of our obedience; for let a man's reasons, though never so many and weighty, be put into one scale, and God's absolute command weighed against them in the other, the man may well write TEKEL, 'They are weighed in the balance, and found too light,' Dan. v. 27. O sirs! (Ps ciii. 20,) 'the angels that excel in strength do his commandments;' and shall the peasant scorn that work in which the prince himself is engaged? The commands of God, both in the Old and New Testament, lie fair and full against lying; and therefore no wonder if God revenge the habitual breach of them in flames of fire. The Holy Ghost in the Hebrew tongue calleth a lie *aven*, which also signifieth iniquity, implying that all lies are iniquity, and that all iniquity is after a sort included in a lie, which doth sufficiently evidence that lying is no small sin. I might further argue thus, that which is contrary to God, who is the choicest and the chiefest good, yea, who is goodness and truth itself, that must needs be the greatest evil: but lying is contrary to the nature, essence, and being of God. Witness the description that he gives of himself, both in the Old and New Testament: Exod. xxxiv. 6, 'And the Lord passed by before him, and proclaimed, The Lord, the Lord God, merciful and gracious, longsuffering, and abundant in goodness and truth.' So Moses in his song, 'He is a God of truth, and without iniquity, just and right is he.' Deut. xxxii. 4. So Isaiah, 'He who blesseth himself in the earth, shall bless himself in the God of truth; and he that sweareth in the earth, shall swear by the God of truth,' Isa. lxv. 16. So the psalmist, 'Thou hast redeemed me, O Lord God of truth,' Ps. xxxi. 5. Again, 'Thou, O Lord, are plenteous in mercy and truth,' Ps. lxxxvi. 15. So in the New Testament, 'Let God be true, and every man a liar,' Rom. iii. 4. Again, 'They themselves shew how ye turned to God from idols, to serve the living and true God,' Acts xiv. 15. Though God can make a world with a word of his mouth, Gen. i., and mar a world with a word of his mouth, chap. vi., yet he can neither die nor lie: Tit. i. 2, 'In hope of eternal life, which God, that cannot lie, promised before the world began;' yea, it is impossible for God to

[1] Obedientia non discutit Dei mandata, sed facit.—*Prosper*.
[2] Cassianus, lib. iv. cap. 24.

lie: Heb. vi. 18, 'That by two immutable things, in which it was impossible for God to lie.' Now by all these plain pregnant texts it is most evident that lying is most opposite and contrary to the very nature, essence, and being of God; and therefore no wonder if the anger and wrath of God rises high against it. But,

[2.] Secondly, Consider this, *That pernicious lies and liars are very destructive to all human societies, kingdoms, and commonwealths.* Lying destroys all society, all commerce and converse among the sons of men. Man, as the philosopher observeth, is ζῶον πολιτικὸν, a sociable creature. Speech is the means whereby men have society and commerce one with another. Now lying perverts that order which the God of truth hath appointed to be among the sons of men. It is the will and pleasure of God that the sons of men, conversing together, should by their words and speeches and discourses impart and communicate their minds, designs, intentions, and meanings one to another, for the mutual good of one another, and for the profit and benefit of the whole. Now if there be nothing in men's words but lying, deceit, and fraud, instead of truth, what can follow but confusion and desolation? When the language of men was confounded, so that one could not tell what another spake, then presently followed the dissolution of their combination; for the Lord scattered them abroad from thence upon the face of all the earth, and they left off to build the city, Gen. xi. 7, 8. When one asked brick, saith a Rabbin,[1] another brought clay, and then they fell together by the ears, and one dashed out the other's brains; and by this means their communion was dissolved, and God brought on them the evil which they sought to prevent, ver. 4. But surely a lying tongue is a far worse enemy to society than an unknown tongue; and much better it is for a man to have no society at all, than with such as he cannot believe what they say, or if he do, he shall be sure to be deceived by them. Concerning such we may well take up the words of Jacob: 'O my soul, come not thou into their secret; unto their assembly, mine honour, be not thou united,' Gen. xlix. 6. And pray with David: 'Deliver my soul, O Lord, from lying lips, and from a deceitful tongue,' Ps. cxx. 2. Jeremiah did so loathe and abominate the society of liars, that he had rather live in a wilderness than live among them, or have anything to do with them, Jer. ix. 1–6. Liars destroy that communion and society that by the law of God, nature, and nations they ought to preserve and maintain. Lying dissolves that mutual trust that we should have with one another; for hereby all contracts, covenants, and intercourse of dealings between man and man, which is, as it were, the life of the kingdom or commonwealth, are quite overthrown.[2] When men make no conscience of lying, nor of keeping their word any further than either fear of loss or force of law compelleth them, all civil communion is at an end. There can be no trust where there is no truth, nor no commerce with those that cannot be trusted. The Scythians had a law, that if any man did, *duo peccata contorquere*, bind two sins together, a lie and an oath, he was

[1] R. Salomon. The Hebrew doctors say that at this dispersion there were seventy nations, with seventy sundry languages.

[2] Mendax hoc lucratur, ut cum vera dixerit, ei non credatur.

to lose his head, because this was the way to take away all faith and truth among men. Had this law been put in execution in London, I have reason enough to fear that many citizens would have lost their heads long before they had lost their houses by the late dreadful fire. Now, seeing that pernicious lying, a course, a trade of lying, is so destructive to human society, why should we wonder to see the Lord appear in flaming fire against it? But,

[3.] Thirdly, Consider, *That lying is a sin that is most odious and hateful to God; yea, a sin that makes men odious and hateful to him.* Lying is repugnant unto God; for God is ἀψευδὴς, one that cannot lie, Titus i. 2. He is אלהי אמן, the God of truth, Isa. lxv. 16, and therefore lying cannot but be odious to him. God is said not only to forbid a lie, but to hate a lie. A lie, it is an abomination. Now we abominate that which is contrary to our natures. Amongst those things that are an abomination to the Lord, a lying tongue is reckoned: Prov. vi. 16, 17, 'These six things doth the Lord hate: yea, seven are an abomination to him: a proud look, a lying tongue,' or as the Hebrew runs, 'a tongue of lying,' that is, a tongue that hath learned the trade, and can do it artificially; a tongue that is accustomed to lying, a tongue that is delighted in lying. So ver. 19, 'A false witness that speaketh lies, and him that soweth discord among brethren.' Among these seven things abominated by God, lying is twice repeated, to note how great an abomination lying is in the eye and account of God: Prov. xii. 22, 'Lying lips are an abomination to the Lord;' not only offensive or odious, but abominable. Liars pervert the end for which God created speech, which was to give light to the notions of the mind, and therefore the Lord loathes them, and plagues them in this life with great severity, as you may see in those sad instances of Gehazi, whose lie was punished with a perpetual leprosy upon himself and his posterity, 2 Kings v. 20 to the end; and of Ananias and Sapphira, who for their lying were punished with present and sudden death, Acts v. 5–11; and of Haman, who slandering Mordecai and the Jews, and by his lies plotting their ruin, was taken in the same snare that he had laid for them, and both he and his sons hanged upon the same gallows which he had made for innocent Mordecai, Esther iii. 8–11. The same liar that was feasting with the king one day was made a feast for crows the next day, chap. vii. 9, and ix. 13, 14. Dreadful are the threatenings that the great God has given out against liars: Ps. v. 6, 'Thou shalt destroy them that speak leasing.' Such as lie in jest will, without repentance, go to hell in earnest: Ps. xii. 3, 'The Lord shall cut off all flattering lips, and the tongue that speaketh proud things.' God, by one judgment or another, in one way or another, will cut off all flattering lying lips, as a rotten member is cut off from the body, or as a barren tree that is stocked up, that it may cumber the ground no more: Ps. cxx. 2–4, 'Deliver my soul, O Lord, from lying lips, and from a deceitful tongue. What shall be given unto thee—or what shall be done unto thee, thou false tongue? Sharp arrows of the mighty'—God will retaliate sharp for sharp—'with coals of juniper.' The coals of juniper burn hot and last long, some say a month and more, and smell sweet. Now upon these coals will God broil lying lips and a deceitful tongue, pleasing himself and others in the execution of his wrath upon a lying tongue: Prov. xix 5, 'A false witness shall not be unpunished, and he that speaketh lies shall not escape.' Though men sometimes by lying may escape the displeasure of men, yet they shall never by lying escape the wrath and displeasure of God. Wrath is for that man, and that man is for wrath, who hath taught his tongue the trade of lying: Hosea xii. 1, 'Ephraim daily increaseth lies and desolation.' Desolation is the fruit and consequent of lying. Sin and punishment are inseparable companions. They who heap up lies hasten desolation, both upon themselves and the places where they live. Now, if lying be a sin so hateful and odious to God, no wonder if God appears in flaming fire against it. But,

[4.] Fourthly and lastly, *Lying is a sin against the light and law of nature.* It is a sin against natural conscience, and therefore it is that a little child will blush many times when he tells a lie. It was observed of Pomponius Atticus, Cicero's great friend, that he never used lying, neither could he with patience lend his ear to a liar. Tennes, the son of Cycnus,[1] who was worshipped as a god, was so strict in judgment that he caused an axe to be held over the witnesses' head to execute them out of hand if they were taken with falsehood or a lie. Among the Scythians, when their priests foretold an untruth, they were carried along upon hurdles full of heath and dry wood, drawn by oxen, and manacled hand and foot, and burnt to death. Aristotle saith, by the light of natural reason, that a lie is evil in itself, and cannot be dispensed withal, it being contrary to the order of nature; for, saith he, we have tongues given us to express our minds and meanings one to another by. Now, if our tongues tell more or less than our minds conceive, it is against nature.[2] It is said of Epaminondas, a heathen, that he abhorred *mendacium jocosum*, a jesting lie. Plutarch calls lying a tinkerly sin, a sin that is both hateful and shameful. Euripides saith, that he is unhappy who rather useth lies, though seemingly good, than truths when he judgeth them evil. To think the truth, saith Plato, is honest; but a filthy and dishonest thing to lie. I could, saith my author, both sigh and smile at the simplicity of some pagan people in America, who having told a lie, used to let their tongues bleed in expiation thereof,—a good cure for the squinancy,[3] but no satisfaction for lying. These heathens will one day rise in judgment against such amongst us as make no conscience of lying. To bring things close, those that lived within and without the walls of London, that were given up to a trade, a course of lying, those persons sinned with a high hand, not only against the light of nature, but also against as clear, as glorious a gospel-light as ever shined round a people since Christ was upon the earth; and therefore no wonder if God hath laid their city in ashes. He that shall seriously dwell upon these four things—viz., (1.) That lying is a very great sin; (2.) That lies and liars are very destructive to all human societies, kingdoms, and commonwealths; (3.) That lying is a sin most hateful and odious to God; (4.) That lying is a sin against the light and law of nature,—he will see cause enough to justify the Lord in that late dreadful fire that has thus been amongst us.

[1] Misprinted Cyrnus.—G.

[2] Arist. Ethic., lib. iv. cap. 7.

[3] 'Quinsy.'—G.

But before I close up this particular, give me leave to say, that this trade, this course of lying that brings that sore judgment of fire upon cities and countries, I cannot charge with any clear evidence upon those that did truly fear the Lord, whose habitations were once within or without the walls of London before it was turned into a ruinous heap; and that upon these grounds:—

[1.] First, *Because a trade, a course of lying is not consistent with the truth or state of grace*, Ps. cxxxix. 23, 24; 1 John iii. 6–10. A trade, a course of drunkenness, of whoring, of swearing, of cursing, is as inconsistent with a state of grace, as a trade, a course of lying is. I know Jacob lied, and David lied, and Peter lied, but none of these were ever given up to a trade of lying, to a course of lying. The best saints have had their extravagant motions, and have sadly miscarried as to particular actions; but he that shall judge of a Christian's estate by particular acts, though notorious bad, will certainly condemn where God acquits: *una actio non denominat.* We must always distinguish between some single evil actions and a serious course of evil actions. It is not this or that particular evil action, but a continued course of evil actions, that denominates a man wicked, as it is not this or that particular good act, but a continued course of holy actions, that denominates a man holy. Every man is as his course is; if his course be holy, the man is holy; if his course be wicked, the man is wicked. There is a maxim in logic, viz., That no general rule can be established upon a particular instance; and there is another maxim in logic, viz., That no particular instance can overthrow a general rule. So here, look, as no man can safely and groundedly conclude from no better premises than from some few particular actions, though in themselves materially and substantially good, that this or that man's spiritual estate is good; so, on the other hand, no man ought to conclude, because of some particular sinful actions and extravagant motions, that this or that man's spiritual estate is bad. A trade of lying can never stand with a trade of holiness; a course of lying can never stand with a course of godliness. Though the needle of the seaman's compass may jog this way and that way, yet the bent of the needle will still be northward; so though a Jacob, a David, a Peter may have their particular sinful joggings this way or that way, yet the bent of their hearts will still be God-wards, Christ-wards, heaven-wards, and holiness-wards. But,

[2.] Secondly, Such as did truly fear the Lord within or without the walls of London, such did in their solemn addresses to the Lord, both together and apart, *lament and bewail that trade, that course of lying that was predominant among many that day;* and therefore I dare not charge the trade, the course of lying upon their scores. But,

[3.] Thirdly, *A lie draws its pedigree from the devil, and such as make a trade of lying, such are certainly Satan's children*, 1 Kings xxii. 22; Acts v. 3–10; John viii. 44, 'Ye are of your father the devil, and the lusts of your father ye will do: he was a murderer from the beginning, and abode not in the truth, because there is no truth in him.' 'When he speaketh a lie, he speaketh of his own: for he is a liar, and the father of it,' Gen. iii. Satan is the father of all sins, as well as the father of lies; but here he is said to be a liar and the father of it, because by lying he first brought sin into the world. Satan began his kingdom by a lie, and by lies he still labours to uphold it. He is the inventor and author of all the lies that be in the world. The devil's breasts, says Luther, are very fruitful with lies. Liars are the devil's children by imitation. There are none that resemble him so much to the life as liars do. They are as like him as if they were spit out of the very mouth of him. Lying is a part of the devil's image. Other sins make men like beasts; but this of lying makes men like devils. Leo, speaking of lying, saith: *Totam vim suam in mendacio diabolus collocavit, omniaque deceptionum genera de hoc venenatissimo artis suæ fonte produxit:* The devil hath placed his whole strength in lying, and from this most poisoned fountain of his craft hath he brought forth all kinds of deceit.[1] Now upon this account also I dare not charge the trade of lying upon such who feared the Lord within or without the walls of London. Though many that make a profession of Christ are no more like Christ than Michal's image of goats'-hair was like David; yet all such as are really united to Christ, they are like to Christ, they bear upon them the image of Christ, they resemble him to the life. Jesus Christ is such a fountain, in which whosoever bathes, and of which whosoever drinks, they shall be sure to be changed into the same likeness from glory to glory, that is, from a lower degree of grace to a higher degree, even as by the Spirit of the Lord, 2 Cor. iii. 18. Such as truly fear the Lord have an image of righteousness and holiness stamped upon them, and do more resemble Christ than Satan, Phil. iv. 23, 24; and therefore the trade of lying may not be charged upon them. But,

[4.] Fourthly, *Have they not chosen rather to suffer, than by lying either to free themselves from sufferings, or to secure themselves against sufferings?* Jerome writes of a brave woman, that being upon the rack, bade her persecutors do their worst; for she was resolved rather to die than to lie. Has not much of this spirit been upon them? and therefore I dare not charge the trade of lying upon them. But,

[5.] Fifthly, *Such as truly fear the Lord, they hate lying:* Ps. cxix. 163, 'I hate and abhor lying.' David hated lying as he hated hell itself. So Prov. xiii. 5, 'A righteous man hateth lying.' Lying is a noisome, stinking weed, and therefore a righteous man abhors to touch it, he hates to come near it, and can by no means endure the scent of it in others, least of all in himself. Justin Martyr, speaking of the persecuted Christians, hath this memorable saying: *In nostra est potestate, ut quum inquirimur negemus; sed vivere nolumus mendaciter quicquam loquentes,* It is in our power, when we are sought for and examined, to deny what we are, what we believe; but we will not live speaking anything untruly.[2] These blessed souls so hated and abhorred lying, that they would rather die than lie. A lie, saith Plato, is odious not only to the gods, but also to every wise man. Cleobulus, another heathen, affirmeth that every wise prudent man hateth a lie. Erasmus had such an antipathy against lying, that from his youth he would usually tremble at the sight of a noted liar. Now upon this

[1] Leo de Eleemos., serm. 4.
[2] Justin Martyr, Apol. 2, pro Christianis.

account also I dare not charge the trade of lying upon their score that truly fear the Lord. But,

[6.] Sixthly, *Lying is that sad character and black brand that the Lord hath only put upon wicked and ungodly men:* Ps. iv. 2, 'O ye sons of men,'—ye grandees who are potent at court,—'how long will ye turn my glory into shame? how long will ye love vanity and seek after leasing?' Ps. lviii. 3, 'The wicked are estranged from the womb; they go astray as soon as they be born, speaking lies;' no sooner could they do anything, but they were doing evil, lisping out lies even as soon as they were born. Isa. xxx. 8, 9, 'Now go, write it before them in a table, and note it in a book, that it may be for the time to come for ever and ever.' Why, what must he write? mark ver. 9, 'That this is a rebellious people, lying children, children that will not hear the law of the Lord.' Now upon this account also I dare not charge the trade of lying upon them that feared the Lord in that great city before it was laid in ashes. But,

[7.] Seventhly, *A trade of lying is inconsistent with the relation of children:* Isa. lxiii. 8, 'Surely they are my people, children that will not lie: so he was their Saviour.' God makes this the ear-mark of his people, that they are children that will not lie, Col. iii. 9. When the heathen philosopher was asked in what things men were most like unto God, he answered, In their speaking of truth. Not lying is one of the choice characters by which the Lord doth difference and distinguish his own peculiar people from other men: Zeph. iii. 13, 'The remnant of Israel shall do no iniquity, nor speak lies; neither shall a deceitful tongue be found in their mouth.' In the primitive times this was a common saying, *Christianus est, non mentietur*, He is a Christian, he will not lie: Rev. xiv. 5, 'And in their mouth was found no guile: for they are without fault before the throne of God.' Now upon this account also I dare not charge the trade of lying upon those gracious souls that feared the Lord within or without the walls of London, before it was turned into a ruinous heap. But,

[8.] Eighthly and lastly, *Liars are reckoned amongst the basest and the worst of sinners that you read of in all the book of God:* Lev. xix. 11, 'Ye shall not steal, neither deal falsely, neither lie one to another.' Prov. vi. 16–19, 'These six things doth the Lord hate; yea, seven are an abomination to him: a proud look, a lying tongue, and hands that shed innocent blood, an heart that deviseth wicked imaginations, feet that be swift in running to mischief, a false witness that speaketh lies, and him that soweth discord among brethren.' So the apostle Paul, setting down a catalogue of the basest and worst of sinners, he ranks liars in the rear of them: 1 Tim. i. 9, 10, 'Knowing this, that the law is not made for a righteous man, but for the lawless and disobedient, for the ungodly and for sinners, for unholy and profane, for murderers of fathers and murderers of mothers, for manslayers, for whoremongers, for them that defile themselves with mankind, for men-stealers, for liars, for perjured persons.' So John numbers them amongst the damned crew that shall be sent to hell, and that must perish for ever: Rev. xxi. 8, 'But the fearful, and unbelieving, and the abominable, and murderers, and whoremongers, and sorcerers, and idolaters, and all liars, shall have their part in the lake which burneth with fire and brimstone: which is the second death.' In this catalogue of the damned crew, the 'fearful' are placed in the front, and the 'liars' in the rear. See once more how the Holy Ghost couples liars: Rev. xxii. 15, 'For without are dogs, and sorcerers, and murderers, and whoremongers, and idolaters, and whosoever loveth and maketh a lie.' Thus you see in all these scriptures that liars are numbered up among the rabble of the most desperate and deplorable wretches that are in the world; and therefore upon this account also I cannot charge the trade of lying upon them that feared the Lord, whose habitations were once within or without the walls of London.

8. *The eighth sin that brings the judgment of fire, is men's giving themselves over to fornication, and going after strange flesh:* Jude 7, 'Even as Sodom and Gomorrah, and the cities about them, in like manner, giving themselves over to fornication, and going after strange flesh, are set forth for an example, suffering the vengeance of eternal fire.' In these words there are these three things observable:—

[1.] First, *The places punished, and they are Sodom and Gomorrah, and the cities about them*, which were Admah and Zeboiim, Deut. xxix. 23; Hosea xi. 8. Hegesippus and Stephanus say that ten cities were destroyed, and some say thirteen cities were destroyed when Sodom was destroyed; but these things I shall not impose upon you as articles of faith. The overthrow of Sodom and Gomorrah and the cities about them was total, both in respect of the inhabitants, and the places themselves. Their sin was universal, and their punishment was as universal. That pride, idleness, and fulness of bread that is charged upon them by the prophet Ezekiel, did usher in those abominable wickednesses that laid all waste and desolate, Ezek. xvi. 49, 50.

[2.] Secondly, *The sins that brought these punishments*—viz., 'The giving themselves over to fornication, and going after strange flesh.' The first is, 'Giving themselves over to fornication.' Now the word 'fornication' is not to be taken properly and strictly for that act of uncleanness that is often committed between persons unmarried; but it is here to be taken for all sorts of carnal uncleanness. The heathen thought fornication no vice, and therefore they made it a common custom, and were wont to pray thus: 'The gods increase the number of the harlots.' The second sin that is charged upon them is, 'Their going after strange flesh:' *σαρκὸς ἑτέρας*, 'another flesh,' as the words in the original run. The apostle in this modest and covert expression, 'Going after strange flesh, or other flesh, or another flesh,' doth hint to us their monstrous and unlawful lusts, that were against the course, light, and law of nature. They gave themselves up to such filthiness as is scarce to be named among men; they went after other flesh than what nature or the God of nature had appointed. The great God never appointed that male and male, but only that male and female should be one flesh; it is impossible that man and man in that execrable act should make one flesh, as man and woman do: Gen. ii. 21, *seq.* The flesh of a male to a male must needs be another flesh. The apostle Paul expresseth their filthiness thus, 'For even their women did change the natural use into that which is against nature: and likewise also the men, leaving the natural use of the women, burned in their lust one toward another; men with men working that which is unseemly,' Rom. i. 26, 27. Chrysostom well observes on these words, that 'whereas by God's ordinance in lawful copulation by marriage, two became one flesh, both sexes were joined together in one; by Sodomitical uncleanness the same flesh is divided into two, men with men working uncleanness as with women, of one sex making as it were two.' The Gentiles had left the God of nature, and therefore the Lord in his just judgment left them to leave the order of nature, and so to cast scorn and contempt upon the whole human nature.

Again, there is another sort of pollution by strange flesh, and that is a carnal joining of a man with a beast, which is prohibited: 'Neither shalt thou lie with any beast,' Lev. xviii. 23. Oh what a sink of sin is in the nature of man, the heart of man! And as this pollution is prohibited, so it is punished with death: 'And if a man lie with a beast, he shall surely be put to death, and ye shall slay the beast,' chap. xx. 15. The Lord, to shew the horridness and the heinousness of this beastly sin, commands that even the poor, harmless, innocent beast, that is neither capable of sin, nor of provoking or enticing man to sin, must be put to death. Oh how great is that pollution that pollutes the very beasts, and that makes the unclean more unclean, and that doth debase the beast below a beast! Now to this sort of pollution the beastly Sodomites had without doubt given up themselves.

[3.] The third thing observable in the words is, *the severity of their punishment:* 'Suffering the vengeance of eternal fire.' We commonly say that fire and water have no mercy, and we have frequently experienced the truth of that saying. When God would give the world a proof of his greatest severity against notorious sinners and notorious sins, he doth it by inflicting the judgment of fire. When the Sodomites burned in their lusts one towards another, 'Then the Lord rained upon Sodom and Gomorrah brimstone and fire from the Lord out of heaven.' 'The Lord rained brimstone and fire from the Lord;' that is, by an elegant Hebraism, from himself, it being usual with the Hebrews to put the noun for the pronoun, as you may see by comparing the scriptures in the margin together.[1] Now this fiery vengeance came not from any inferior cause, but from the supreme cause, even God himself. This brimstone and material fire that was rained by the Lord out of heaven, was not by any ordinary course of nature, but by the immediate almighty power of God. Doubtless it was the supernatural and miraculous work of the Lord, and not from any natural cause, that such showers, not of water,—as when the old world was drowned,—but of material fire and brimstone, should fall from heaven upon Sodom and Gomorrah—to which add Admah and Zeboiim, for all these four cities were burned together. God rained, not sprinkled, yea, he rained not fire only, but fire and brimstone for the increase of their torment, and that they might have a hell above-ground, a hell on this side hell. They had hot fire for their burning lusts, and stinking brimstone for their stinking brutishness. They burned with vile and unnatural lusts,

[1] Gen. i. 27; 1 Sam. xv. 22; 2 Chron. vii. 2; 1 Kings viii. 1.

and therefore against the course of nature fire falls down from heaven and devours them, and their stinking abominable filthiness is punished with the stench of brimstone mingled with fire. Thus God delights to suit men's punishments to their sins; yea, that temporal fire that God rained out of heaven upon Sodom and Gomorrah was but a forerunner of their everlasting punishment in that lake which burns with fire and brimstone for evermore, Rev. xxi. 8. The temporal punishment of the impenitent Sodomites did but make way to their eternal punishments, as Jude tells us, ver. 7. I readily grant that the fire of hell was typified by that fire which fell from heaven upon Sodom and Gomorrah; but I cannot conceive that the apostle Jude, in the place last cited, doth intend or design to prove that the Sodomites were destroyed by hell-fire; for in the history of Genesis, to which the apostle alludes, there is no mention at all of hell-fire or of eternal fire. And doubtless the example that should warn sinners to repent of their sins, and to turn to the Most High, is to be taken from the history in Genesis. I cannot at present see how Sodom and Gomorrah can be set forth as an example to sinners by suffering the punishment of hell-fire, when the history is wholly silent as to any such fire. Some, to mollify the seeming austerity of that phrase which Jude uses, viz., 'eternal fire,' read the words thus, 'were made an example of eternal fire, suffering vengeance;' by which construction they gather that the fire which hath irreparably destroyed Sodom and Gomorrah was a type and figure of that fire of hell, of that eternal fire that is reserved for wicked men, and by which sinners ought to be warned. Others by 'eternal fire' understand the duration of the effects of the first temporal punishment, the soil thereabout wearing the marks of divine displeasure to this very day. Several authors write,[1] that the air there is so infectious, that no creature can live there; and though the apples and other fruit that grow there seem pleasant to the eye, yet if you do but touch them, they presently turn into cinders and ashes. The stinking lake of asphaltes near to Sodom is left as a perpetual monument of God's vengeance, killing all fish that swimmeth in it, and fowls that fly over it. Others by eternal fire understand an utter destruction, according to that 2 Peter ii. 6, 'And turning the cities of Sodom and Gomorrah into ashes, condemned them with an overthrow,' that is, utterly destroyed them, 'making them an ensample unto those that after should live ungodly.' God hangs them up in gibbets, as it were, that others might hear and fear, and not dare to do wickedly as they had done.

What though it be said that the fire wherewith these Sodomites were destroyed was eternal, yet there is no necessity to understand it of hell-fire; for even that very fire which consumed those cities may be called eternal, because the punishment that was inflicted on Sodom and Gomorrah by fire was a punishment that should last as long as the world lasted. God resolved those cities should never be rebuilt, but remain perpetual desolations in all generations. Now, in this sense, the word 'eternal' is often used in the Scripture. Again, the fire and brimstone that fell upon Sodom and Gomorrah was a type and figure of that eternal fire, or those eternal torments that shall be inflicted

[1] Josephus, Tertullian, Augustine, &c.

upon all impenitent sinners for ever and ever. The sum of all is this, that the Sodomites, by giving themselves over to fornication, and by going after strange flesh, did provoke the Lord to rain hell out of heaven upon them; they did provoke the Lord to rain material fire and brimstone both upon their persons and their habitations. Now give me leave to say, that doubtless the body of the inhabitants of that famous city, which is now laid in ashes, were as free from giving themselves over to fornication, and going after strange flesh, as any in any part of the nation; yea, more free than many in some parts of the nation; yea, give me leave to say, that I cannot see how these sins that are charged upon the Sodomites can be clearly or groundedly charged upon any of the precious servants of the Lord, that did truly fear him in that renowned city; and my reasons are these:—

[1.] First, Because in all their solemn and secret addresses to the Lord they have *seriously lamented and mourned over these crying abominations.*

[2.] Secondly, Because men's giving themselves over to fornication, and going after strange flesh, are such *high and horrid sins against the light and law of nature, that God commonly preserves his chosen from them.* He shall be an Apollo to me that can produce any one instance in the Old or New Testament of any one person that, after real and through conversion, did ever give himself over to fornication, and to go after strange flesh. Aristotle calls beastiality a surpassing wickedness. By the laws of those two emperors, Theodosius and Arcadius, Sodomites were adjudged to the fire. In the Council of Vienna the templars who were found guilty of this sin were decreed to be burnt. And among the Romans, it was lawful for him who was attempted to that abuse to kill him who made the assault. Tertullian brings in Christianity triumphing over paganism, because this sin was peculiar to heathens, and that Christians never changed the sex, nor accompanied with any but their own wives. This and such like, as Tertullian speaks, being not so much to be called offences as monsters, and not to be named without holy detestation by saints, though they be committed without shame by Sodomites. The Saxons, who of old inhabited this land, strangled the adulteress being taken, and then burnt her body with fire, and hanged the adulterer over a flaming fire, burning him by degrees till he died, [Boniface.] Opilius Macrinus, an emperor, caused the body of the adulterer and the whore to be joined together, and so burnt with fire, [Julius Capitolinus.] Aurelianus caused the adulterer's legs to be bound to the boughs of two trees bent together, and then violently being lifted up again, his body was torn asunder. And the Julian law, among the Romans, punished adultery with death, by cutting off the heads of those that were guilty of that fact. And the Turks stone adulterers to death. Zaleucus, king of the Locrians, ordained that adulterers should have their eyes put out; and therefore, when his son was taken in adultery, that he might both keep the law and be compassionate to his son, he put forth one of his own eyes to redeem one of his son's.[1] I have read of some heathens that have punished this sin with a most shameful death, and the death was this: they would have the adulterer's or

[1] Aelian V. H. xiii. 24; Val. Max. V. v. § 3.—G.

adulteress's head to be put into the paunch of a beast, where lay all the filth and uncleanness of it, and there to be stifled to death. This was a fit punishment for so filthy a sin. In old time the Egyptians used to punish adultery on this sort: the man with a thousand jerks with a reed, and the woman with cutting off her nose; but he who forced a free woman to his lusts, had his privy members cut off, [Diodorus.] But,

[3.] Thirdly, Such who give themselves over to fornication, *overthrow the state of mankind, while no man knoweth his own wife, nor no wife knoweth her own husband, and while no father knows his own children, nor no children know their own father.* Affinities and consanguinities are the joints and sinews of the world; lose[1] these and lose[1] all. Now what affinities or consanguinities can there be when there is nothing but confusion of blood—the son knoweth not his father, nor the father the son? But,

[4.] Fourthly, These expressions of giving themselves over to fornication, and going after strange flesh, implies—

First, Their making constant provisions for their base lusts, Rom. xiii. 14. Oh the time, the pains, the cost, the charge that such are at to make provision for their unsatiable lusts!

Secondly, It implies *an excessive violent spending of their strength beyond all measure and bounds in all lasciviousness and Sodomitical uncleanness.* Pliny tells of Cornelius Gallus and Q. Elerius (?) two Roman knights, that died in the very action of filthiness.[2] Theodebert, the eldest son of Glotharius, died amongst his whores; so did Bertrane Ferrier at Barcelona, in Spain; Giachet Geneve of Saluces, (?) who had both wife and children of his own, being carnally joined with a young woman, was suddenly smitten with death; his wife and children wondering why he stayed so long in his study, when it was time to go to bed called him, and knocked at his door very hard, but when no answer was made, they broke open the doors, that were locked on the inner side, and found him lying upon the woman stark dead, and her dead also.[3] Claudus of Asses, (?) counsellor of the parliament of Paris, a desperate persecutor of the Protestants, whilst he was in the very act of committing filthiness with one of his waiting-maids, was taken with an apoplexy, which immediately after made an end of him. Many other instances might be produced, but let these suffice.

Thirdly, It implies *their impudency and shamelessness in their filthiness and uncleanness.* They had a whore's forehead; they proclaimed their lasciviousness before all the world; they were not ashamed, neither could they blush: hence it is that the men of Sodom are said to be sinners before the Lord—that is, they sinned openly, publicly, and shamelessly, without any regard to the eye of God at all, Jer. iii. 3, and vi. 15; Isa. iii. 10; Gen. xiii. 13. 'Bring them out to us, that we may know them,' Gen. xix. 5. Oh faces hatcht[4] with impudency! they shroud not their sins in a mantle of secrecy, but proclaim their filthiness before all the world, they had out-sinned all shame: and therefore they gloried in their shame: they were so

[1] Query, 'loose?'—ED.
[2] Pliny, lib. vii.
[3] Pontanus. Fulgos, lib. vi. c. 12.
[4] 'Lined' or marked.—G.

arrogant and impudent in sinning, that they proclaimed their filthiness upon the house-top. But,

Fourthly, It implies *their resolvedness and obstinacy in sinning in the face of all the terrible warnings and alarms that God had formerly given them by a bloody war, and by the spoiling and plundering of their cities, and by taking away of their victuals—'fulness of bread' was a part of their sin, and now 'cleanness of teeth' is made a piece of their punishment in God's just judgment—and by Lot's admonition and mild opposition*, Gen. xiv. 10–12, and xix. 11. It is observable, that when they were smitten with blindness, they wearied themselves to find the door. God smote them with blindness, both of body and mind; and yet they continued groping to find the door, being highly resolved upon buggery and bestiality, though they died for it. Oh the hideous wickedness and prodigious madness of these Sodomites, that when divine justice had struck them blind, their hearts should be so desperately set upon their lusts, as to weary themselves to find the door! But what will not Satan's bond-slaves and firebrands of hell do? Sottish and besotted sinners will never tremble when God strikes, Phil. ii. 12. But,

Fifthly, These expressions of giving themselves over to fornication, and going after strange flesh, implies *the delight, pleasure, content, and satisfaction that they took in those abominable practices:* Rom. i. 32, 'They have chosen their own ways, and their souls delight in their abominations.' 'They had pleasure in unrighteousness,' Isa. lxvi. 3; 2 Thes. ii. 12; 2 Pet. ii. 13. Luther tells us of a certain grandee in his country, that was so besotted with the sin of whoredom, that he was not ashamed to say, that if he might ever live here, and be carried from one whore-house to another, there to satisfy his lusts, he would never desire any other heaven. This filthy grandee did afterwards breathe out his wretched soul betwixt two notorious harlots. All the pleasure and heaven that these filthy Sodomites look after, was to satisfy their brutish lusts. Hark, scholar, said the harlot to Apuleius, it is but a bitter-sweet that you are so fond of; and this the Sodomites found true at the long run, when God showered down fire and brimstone upon them. But,

Sixthly and lastly, These words of giving themselves over to fornication, and going after strange flesh, implies *their great settled security in those brutish practices.* The old world was not more secure when God swept them away with a flood, Gen. vi., than the Sodomites were secure when God rained fire and brimstone out of heaven upon them, Gen. xix. 14. Mercury could not kill Argus till he had cast him into a sleep, and with an enchanted rod closed his eyes. No more could the devil have hurt these Sodomites, if he had not first lulled them asleep in the bed of security. Carnal security opens the door for all impiety to enter into the soul. Pompey, when he had in vain assaulted a city, and could not take it by force, devised this stratagem in way of agreement; he told them he would leave the siege, and make peace with them, upon condition that they would let in a few weak, sick, and wounded soldiers among them to be cured. They let in the soldiers, and when the city was secure, the soldiers let in Pompey's army. A carnal settled security will let in a whole army of lusts into the soul; and this was the Sodomites' case. To sum up all, those expressions in Jude, (ver. 7,) of giving themselves over to fornication, and going after strange flesh, do imply or take in these six things last mentioned, which things will not stand with the truth of grace or state of grace; and therefore those sins that are specified by Jude cannot be charged with any clear, fair, or full evidence upon the people of God, who did truly fear him within or without the walls of London. But should this treatise fall into any of their hands who have given themselves over to fornication, or to go after strange flesh, then I would say that it very highly concerns all such persons to lay their hands upon their loins, and to say, we are the very men, the sinners, the monsters that have turned a rich and populous city into a ruinous heap. But,

9. *The ninth sin that brings the sore judgment of fire upon a people, is profanation of the Sabbath:* Jer. xvii. 27, 'But if you will not hearken unto me to hallow the sabbath-day, and not bear a burden, even entering in at the gates of Jerusalem on the sabbath-day; then will I kindle a fire in the gates thereof, and it shall devour the palaces of Jerusalem, and it shall not be quenched.' In this memorable scripture you may observe—(1.) A specification of the judgment that God will punish profaners of his Sabbath with, and that is fire; (2.) The specification of the object that this fire shall fall upon, viz., a city, not a town, a village, or any other mean place, but a city, a stately city, a populous city, a trading city, a secure city; (3.) Here is the specification of the city, viz., not every city neither, but Jerusalem, the city of cities, the best of cities, the beloved city, the joyous city, the glorious city, the renowned city, the crowned city, the metropolitan city, the city of God, the wonder of the world, the joy of the whole earth, Isa. lii. 1; Ps. xlviii. 1–8, and lxxxvii. 3; Jer. xxii. 8; yet God threatens to destroy this Jerusalem with fire and flames for profaning of his Sabbath. But did God only threaten Jerusalem? No, for he executed his threatenings upon it, as you may see in that 2 Kings xxv. 8–10:[1] 'And in the fifth month, on the seventh day of the month, (which is the nineteenth year of Nebuchadnezzar king of Babylon,) came Nebuzar-adan, captain of the guard, a servant of the king of Babylon, to Jerusalem: and he burnt the house of the Lord, and the king's house, and all the houses of Jerusalem, and every great man's house burnt he with fire. And all the army of the Chaldees, that were with the captain of the guard, brake down the walls of Jerusalem round about.' The same you have Jer. lii. 12–14. The Jews were great profaners of the Sabbath: Neh. xiii. 15–18, 'In those days saw I in Judah some treading wine-presses on the sabbath, and bringing in sheaves, and lading asses; as also wine, grapes, and figs, and all manner of burdens, which they brought into Jerusalem on the sabbath-day: and I testified against them in the day wherein they sold victuals. There dwelt men of Tyre also therein, which brought fish, and all manner of ware, and sold on the sabbath unto the children of Judah, and in Jerusalem. Then I contended with the nobles of Judah, and said unto them, What evil thing is this that ye do, and profane the sabbath-day? Did not your fathers thus, and did not our God bring all this evil upon us, and upon this city? yet ye bring

[1] So 2 Chron. xxxvi. 17–19; Ps. lxxiv. 4–8.

more wrath upon Israel by profaning the sabbath.'[1] Now this is observable, that as they had profaned the Sabbath, so Nebuzar-adan set their temple on fire, and their noblemen's houses on fire, and all the considerable men's houses in Jerusalem on fire on their Sabbath-day. I know Jeremiah saith it was on the tenth day, Jer. lii. 13, which several of the learned thus reconcile—viz., That on the seventh day, which was their Sabbath, Nebuzar-adan kindled a fire in their habitations, and burnt them all quite down on the tenth. Now Calvin upon the text gives these reasons of God's severity against them for profaning his Sabbath:—(1.) Because it was an easy precept to cease from labour one day in seven, and therefore they that would not herein obey were worthy of all severity, as Adam for eating the forbidden fruit; (2.) Because the Sabbath was a sign of God's people by him peculiarly chosen, and therefore not to rest now was a gross neglect of upholding the memorial of the greatest privilege that ever was bestowed upon mortal men, Exod. xxxi. 13, 17; (3.) Because the Lord would, by their keeping of a rest now from servile works, draw them to a rest from the servile works of sin, as he rested from the works of creation. To which others add a fourth—viz., That it might always be remembered that the whole world was created by God, that we might acknowledge his infinite power and wisdom herein appearing. And others add a fifth—viz., Because by keeping the Sabbath-day, it being the day wherein all religious duties were done, all the exercises of religion is meant, which if it had been purely upheld, both princes, nobles, priests, and people should have flourished for ever, and never have known what it was to have their houses set on fire about their ears. Now is not famous London the sad counterpane of desolate Jerusalem? a sore and unquenchable fire hath turned England's metropolis into ashes and rubbish. But,

That the Lord may appear most just and righteous in inflicting this dreadful judgment of fire upon those that profaned his Sabbaths in London, consider seriously with me these twelve things:—

(1.) First, *That God hath fenced this command more strongly about than he has any other, and all to prevent our transgression of it, and the more effectually to engage us to the keeping of it holy.* Now here observe,

[1.] First, *It is marked with a memento above all other commands.* Exod. xx. 8, 'Remember the sabbath-day to keep it holy,' and that partly because we are so desperately apt and prone to forget it; and partly because none can keep it holy when it comes that do not remember it before it comes; and partly because this is one of the greatest, if not absolutely the greatest, of all the commandments. It is sometimes put for all the ten. It is the synopsis of them all. And partly because the observation of all the commandments depends chiefly upon the observation of this fourth.[2] None walk so much after the Spirit on other days, as they who are most in the Spirit on the Lord's day. There are none that walk so close with God all the six

[1] Those Chaldeans that set Jerusalem on fire came from literal Babylon, and whether those Chaldeans that first set London in flames come not from mystical Babylon, I shall not here inquire nor dispute.

[2] Philo Judæus saith, that the fourth commandment is a famous precept, and profitable to excite men to all kind of virtue and piety.

days, as those that keep closest to God on the seventh day. In the due observation of this command, obedience to all the rest is comprised. And partly because this command has least light of nature to direct us to the observation of it; and partly because the forgetting of this duty, and profaning of this day, is one of the greatest sins that a people can be guilty of. It is a violation of all the decalogue at once; it is a sin against all the concernments and commandments of God at once. But,

[2.] Secondly, *It is delivered both negatively and affirmatively*, which no other command is, to shew how strongly it binds us to a holy observation of it.

[3.] Thirdly, *It hath more reasons to enforce it than any other precept*—viz., its equity, God's bounty, his own pattern, and the day's benediction.

[4.] Fourthly, *It is put in the close of the first, and beginning of the second table*, to note that the observation of both tables depends much upon the sanctification of this day.

[5.] Fifthly, *It is very considerable also, that this command is more frequently repeated than others of the commands are:* Exod. xx. 31, xiv. 34, and xxiv. 35; Lev. xix. 3, and xxviii. 30. God would have Israel know in these scriptures last cited, that their busiest times, as earing and harvest, yea, and the very building of the tabernacle, must give way to this precept.

(2.) Secondly, Consider *that God is highly pleased and delighted with the sanctification of his Sabbaths*, Jer. xvii. 24, 25. Now in this promise he shews that the flourishing estate both of church and state depends greatly upon the sanctification of this day. Two things are observable in this promise. (1.) The duty unto which the promise is made, and that is in ver. 24. (2.) Observe the reward that is promised, and that is twofold: [1.] The first concerns the commonwealth and civil state, ver. 25, as if he should say, I will maintain the honour and dignity, the wealth and strength, the peace and safety of this nation. [2.] The second blessing that is promised concerns the church, and state of religion, ver. 26. As if he should say, My solemn assemblies shall be duly frequented, and I will continue my own worship in the purity, liberty, and power of it. But,

(3.) Thirdly, Consider *that all public judgments and common calamities that ever befell the people of God, are imputed by the Holy Ghost to no sin more than to the profanation of the Sabbath*,[1] 2 Chron. xxxvi. 17–21, turn to it. So Neh. xiii. 15–18; Ezek. xxii. 26–31, 'Her priests have violated my law, and have profaned my holy things: they have put no difference between the holy and profane, neither have they shewed difference between the unclean and the clean, and have hid their eyes from my sabbaths, and I am profaned among them. Therefore have I poured out my indignation upon them; I have consumed them with the fire of my wrath: their own way have

[1] Profaners of the Sabbath were to be put to death, they were to be cut off, Exod. xxxi. 14, 15. This scripture includes not only death inflicted by the magistrate, according to that Num. xxxv. 36, but also the immediate stroke of God when that was neglected. If you turn to that Ezek. xx. 13, 21, you shall find that God threatens Sabbath profanation with his consuming fire. Now what city, gates, palaces, stately structures, strongholds, can stand before divine fury?

I recompensed upon their own heads, saith the Lord God.' Lev. xxvi. 31–33, 'And I will make your cities waste, and bring your sanctuaries unto desolation, and will not smell the savour of your sweet odours. And I will bring the land into desolation; and your enemies which dwell therein shall be astonished at it. And I will scatter you among the heathen, and will draw out a sword after you; and your land shall be desolate, and your cities waste.' Ay, but what is the reason why God brings those two terrible judgments of fire and sword upon them? The resolution of this question you have in ver. 34, 35, 'Then shall the land enjoy her sabbaths, as long as it lieth desolate, and ye be in your enemies' land; even then shall the land rest, and enjoy her sabbaths. As long as it lieth desolate it shall rest; because it did not rest in your sabbaths, when ye dwelt upon it.' The land did not rest in your sabbaths, saith the Lord, when ye dwelt upon it. But when it is eased from the wicked weight of such inhabitants, which brought upon it heavy curses, and toiled and tired it out with continual tillage, it shall then rest and be at quiet. According to the law of God, the land should have rested every seventh year, Lev. xxv. 4. But they got out the very heart of the land to spend on their lusts: but, saith God, I will ease the land of such inhabitants, and then it shall in a manner take its recreation, then it shall rest, and take its own pleasure, Lam. i. 7. Where there is not a resting from sin, there Sabbaths are not truly kept. Profaning the Sabbath brings most desolating and destroying judgments upon a professing people. The first blow given to the German churches was on the Sabbath-day; for on that day Prague was lost. The Sabbaths were woefully profaned amongst them; their nobility thought it was for their not trimming and beautifying of their churches; but better and wiser men concluded it was for their profaning of the Lord's day. Some are of opinion that the flood began on the Lord's day, from that Gen. vii., they being grown notorious profaners of the Sabbath. The Council of Matiscon, in France, attributed the irruption of the Goths and Vandals to their profanation of the Sabbath. But,

(4.) Fourthly, Consider *there are singular blessings which the sanctifying of the Sabbath will crown us with:* Ezek. xx. 12, 'Moreover also, I gave them my sabbaths, to be a sign between me and them, that they may know that I am the Lord that sanctify them.' The singular blessings that the right sanctifying of the Sabbath will bring upon us, are, (1.) *Spiritual.* They that conscientiously sanctify the Sabbath, they shall see and know the work of God, the work of grace, upon their own souls. There are many precious Christians that have a work of God, a work of grace upon their own souls, who would give ten thousand worlds, were there so many in their hands to give, to see that work, to know that work. Oh! but now they that sanctify the Sabbath, they shall both see and know the work of God upon their own souls! And they shall find the Lord carrying on the work of grace and holiness in their souls; they shall find the Lord destroying their sins, and filling their hearts with joy, and with a blessed assurance of his favour and love: Isa. lvi. 6, 7, 'Also the sons of the stranger, that join themselves to the Lord, to serve him, and to love the name of the Lord, to be his servants, every one that keepeth the sabbath from polluting it, and taketh hold on my covenant; even them will I bring to my holy mountain, and make them joyful in my house of prayer: their burnt-offerings and their sacrifices shall be accepted upon my altar; for mine house shall be called an house of prayer for all people.' So Isa. lviii. 13, 14, 'If thou turn away thy foot from the sabbath, from doing thy pleasure on my holy day; and call the sabbath a delight, the holy of the Lord, honourable: and shalt honour him, not doing thine own ways, nor finding thine own pleasure, nor speaking thine own words: then shalt thou delight thyself in the Lord.' (2.) Now, in the second place, the other blessings that the right sanctifying of the Sabbath will invest us with, are *temporal blessings;* for so they follow in the scripture last cited: 'And I will cause thee to ride upon the high places of the earth;'—here is honour, and esteem, and safety;—'and feed thee with the heritage of Jacob thy father.' Now the land of Canaan was the inheritance which God promised to Jacob, Gen. xxviii. 13, and xlviii. 4. Hereby is noted that comfortable provision that God would make for them that sanctified his Sabbaths. Such as make the Sabbath their delight, they shall never want protection nor provision. God will be a wall of fire about them, and a Canaan to them. But,

(5.) Fifthly, Consider *that our Lord Jesus, who is the Lord of the Sabbath, and whom the law itself commands us to hear, did alter it from the seventh day to the first day of the week, which we now keep,* Mat. xii. 8; Deut. xviii. 18, 19. For the holy evangelists note that our Lord came into the midst of the assembly on the two first days of the two weeks immediately following his resurrection, and then blessed the church, breathing on them the Holy Ghost: John xx. 19–26, 'Then the same day at evening, being the first day of the week, when the doors were shut where the disciples were assembled for fear of the Jews, came Jesus and stood in the midst, and saith unto them, Peace be unto you.' 'And after eight days, again his disciples were within, and Thomas with them, then came Jesus, the doors being shut, and stood in the midst, and said, Peace be unto you.' Look, as Christ was forty days instructing Moses in Sinai what he should teach, and how he should govern the church under the law: so he continued forty days teaching his disciples what they should preach, and how they should govern the church under the gospel: Acts i. 2, 3, 'Until the day in which he was taken up, after that he through the Holy Ghost had given commandments unto the apostles whom he had chosen. To whom also he shewed himself alive after his passion by many infallible proofs, being seen of them forty days, and speaking of the things pertaining to the kingdom of God.' And it is not to be doubted, but that within those forty days he likewise ordained on what day they should likewise keep the Sabbath; and it is observable that on this first day of the week he sent down from heaven the Holy Ghost upon his apostles: Acts ii. 1–4, 'And when the day of the Pentecost was fully come, they were all with one accord in one place. And they were all filled with the Holy Ghost, and began to speak with other tongues, as the Spirit gave them utterance.' So that on that day they first began, and ever after continued, the public exercise of their ministry. Christ who was Lord of the Sabbath—Mark ii. 28—

had a sovereign right to change and alter it to what day he pleased. But,

(6.) Sixthly, Consider that *according to the Lord's mind and commandment, and the direction of the Holy Ghost, the apostles in all the Christian churches ordained that they should keep the holy Sabbath upon the first day of the week:* 1 Cor. xvi. 1, 2, 'Now concerning the collection for the saints, as I have given order to the churches of Galatia, even so do ye. Upon the first day of the week let every one of you lay by him in store, as God hath prospered him, that there be no gathering when I come.' In which words you may observe these five things.

[1.] First, That the apostles ordained this day to be kept holy; therefore it is of a divine institution.

[2.] Secondly, That the day is named the first day of the week; therefore not the Jewish seventh, or any other.

[3.] Thirdly, Every first day of the week, which sheweth its perpetuity.

[4.] Fourthly, That it was ordained in the churches of Galatia, as well as of Corinth, and he settled one uniform in all the churches of the saints; therefore it was universal: 1 Cor. xiv. 33, 'For God is not the author of confusion, but of peace, as in all churches of the saints.'

[5.] Fifthly, That there should be collections for the poor on that day, after the other ordinances were ended. Now why should the apostles require collections to be made on the first day of the week, but because on that day of the week the saints assembled themselves together in the apostles' time? And in the same epistle he protesteth that he delivered them no other ordinance or doctrine but what he had received from the Lord: 1 Cor. xi. 23, 'For I have received of the Lord that which also I delivered unto you, that the Lord Jesus, the same night in which he was betrayed, took bread:' 1 Cor. xiv. 37, 'If any man think himself to be a prophet, or spiritual, let him acknowledge that the things that I write unto you are the commandments of the Lord.' Now mark, he wrote to them, and ordained among them to keep their Sabbath on the first day of the week, therefore to keep the Sabbath on that day is the very commandment of the Lord. But,

(7.) Seventhly, Consider *the apostles on that day ordinarily dispensed the holy ordinances*, John xx. 19–26. Acts xx. 7, 'And upon the first day of the week, when the disciples came together to break bread, Paul preached unto them, ready to depart on the morrow, and continued his speech until midnight.' 1 Cor. xvi. 1, 2, and xi. 23. But,

(8.) Eighthly, Consider *such things as are named the Lord's in Scripture, are ever of the Lord's institution:* as 'the word of the Lord,' 1 Tim. vi. 3, 'the cup of the Lord,' 1 Cor. xi. 27; 'the supper of the Lord,' 1 Cor. xi. 20; and so 'the Lord's day': Rev. i. 10, 'I was in the Spirit on the Lord's day.' Now why does John call it the Lord's day, but because it was a day known to be generally kept holy, to the honour of the Lord Jesus, who rose from death to life upon that day, throughout all the churches which the apostles had planted, which

St John calls the Lord's day, that he might the better stir up Christians to a thankful remembrance of their redemption by Christ's resurrection from the dead? But,

(9.) Ninthly, Consider *that a right sanctifying of the Sabbath is one of the best signs in the Bible that God is our God, and that his sanctifying work is passed in power upon us:* Ezek. xx. 20, 'And hallow my sabbaths; and they shall be a sign between me and you, that ye may know that I am the Lord your God.' So Exod. xxxi. 13, 'Speak thou also unto the children of Israel, saying, Verily my sabbaths shall ye keep: for it is a sign between me and you throughout your generations; that ye may know that I am the Lord that doth sanctify you.'[1] Look, as circumcision and the passover were signs that the Jews were in covenant with God; so likewise was the Sabbath, Ezek. xxxi. 13; and because it was a sign of the covenant between God and them. Ver. 16, 'Wherefore the children of Israel shall keep the sabbath, to observe the sabbath throughout the generations for a perpetual covenant.' God tells them that they must observe it for a perpetual covenant; and hence it was that when they violated the Sabbath, God accounted it the violation of the covenant between him and them. The sanctifying of the Sabbath in the primitive times was the main character by which sincere Christians were differenced from others; they judged of men's sanctity by their sanctifying of the Sabbath. And, indeed, as there cannot be a greater argument or evidence of a profane heart than the profaning the Sabbath, so there cannot be a greater argument or evidence of a gracious heart than a right sanctifying of the Sabbath. But,

(10.) Tenthly, Consider *a right sanctifying of the Sabbath will be a most sure and certain pledge, pawn, and earnest of our keeping of an everlasting Sabbath with God in heaven*: Heb iv. 9, 'There remaineth therefore a rest to the people of God'—*Gr.* 'A sabbatism, an eternal rest, a Sabbath that hath no evening.' Now mark, if this Sabbath be a sign and pledge of heaven, then we must keep it till we come there. For if we lose the pledge of a benefit, we lose the evidence of that benefit whereof it is a pledge. A man that is in the Spirit on the Lord's day, Rev. i. 10, he is in heaven on the Lord's day. There cannot be a more lively resemblance of heaven on this side heaven than the sanctifying of the Sabbath in a heavenly manner. What is heaven but an eternal Sabbath? And what is a temporal Sabbath but a short heaven, a little heaven on this side heaven? Our delighting to sanctify God's Sabbath on earth gives full assurance to our faith, grounded upon God's infallible promise that we shall enter into God's eternal rest in heaven; for so runs the promise: Isa. lviii. 14, 'Then shalt thou delight thyself in the Lord; and I will cause thee to ride upon the high places of the earth, and feed thee with the heritage of Jacob thy father: for the mouth of the Lord hath spoken it.' The former part of the verse relates to earthly blessings; but these words, 'I will feed thee with the heritage of Jacob thy father,' that is, with a heavenly inheritance; for what is the

[1] When the primitive Christians had this question put to them, *Servasti Dominicum?* Hast thou kept the Lord's day? they answered, *Christianus sum, omittere non possum;* I am a Christian, I cannot but keep it.

heritage of Jacob, but Canaan in the type and heaven itself in the antitype? But should I thus sanctify the Sabbath, should I be sure of going to heaven? Yes; for so it roundly follows in the next words, 'The mouth of the Lord hath spoken it.' But,

(11.) Eleventhly, Consider, *that of all days God hath put the highest honour upon his Sabbaths, by appointing his precious ordinances in a special manner to be used on those days.* The Sabbath is a gold ring, and the ordinances are as so many costly sparkling diamonds in that ring. All the works of the new creation are commonly wrought on this day. This is the joyful day wherein ordinarily God gives spiritual sight to the blind, and spiritual ears to the deaf, and spiritual tongues to the dumb, and spiritual feet to the lame. That Exod. xii. 42, is here applicable. It is a night to be much observed to the Lord, for bringing them out from the land of Egypt; this is that night of the Lord to be observed of all the children of Israel in their generations. Those that are new born are commonly new born on this day; and therefore it is a day to be much observed to the Lord. Those that are converted are ordinarily converted on this day; and therefore it is that day of the Lord that ought to be observed by all the converted Israel of God. Those that are edified are commonly most edified on this day. Oh the sweet communion! oh the choice converse! oh the singular discoveries! oh the blessed manifestations! oh the excellent enjoyments that Christ vouchsafes to his people on this day! Oh the discoveries of grace! oh the exercise of grace! oh the increase of grace, the progress in grace! oh the comforts of grace that God vouchsafes to his chosen on this day! Experience shews that the right sanctifying of the Sabbath is a powerful means under Christ to sanctify us, and to increase our faith, and raise our hope, and inflame our love, and to kindle our zeal, and to enlarge our desires, and to melt our hearts, and to weaken our sins. But,

(12.) Twelfthly and lastly, Consider this, *that a right sanctifying of the Sabbath will cross Satan's grand design, it will spoil his plot, his masterpiece.* Satan is a deadly enemy to the right sanctifying of the Sabbath. Witness the many temptations that many Christians are more troubled with on this day than they are on any other day in the whole week; and witness the many vain, wandering, and distracting thoughts that many precious Christians are more afflicted with on this day than they are on all the days of the week beside; and witness that high and hot opposition that he in his instruments makes against the strictest observers of that day, Rev. ii. 10; and witness his constant prompting and spurring such on to the profanation of the Sabbath, whose examples are most dangerous and encouraging to wicked men, as magistrates, ministers, parents, and masters, &c.; and witness his strong endeavours, constant attempts, crafty devices, and deep policies that he has made use of in all the ages of the world, to keep people off from a religious observation of the Sabbath; yea, and to make them more wicked on that day than on any other day of the week—may I not say than on all other days of the week? I have been the longer upon this ninth particular, partly because of the weightiness of it, and partly to encourage the reader to a more close and strict observation of the Sabbath, and partly to justify those that are conscientious observers of it, and partly to justify the Lord in turning London into ashes for the horrible profanation of his day.

The Sabbath-day is the queen of days, say the Jews. The Sabbath-day among the other days is as the Virgin Mary among women, saith Austin.[1] Look, what the phœnix is among the birds, the lion among the beasts, the whale among the fishes, the fire among the elements, the lily among the thorns, the sun among the stars, that is the Sabbath-day to all other days; and therefore no wonder if God burn such out of their habitations who have been profaners of his day. Ah London! London! were there none within nor without thy walls that made light of this institution of God, and that did offer violence to the queen of days by their looseness and profaneness, by their sitting at their doors, by their walking in Moorfields,[2] by their sportings and wrestlings there, and by their haunting of alehouses and whorehouses, their tossing of pots and pipes, when they should have been setting up God and Christ and religion in their families, and mourning in their closets for the sins of the times, and for the afflictions of poor Joseph? How did the wrath and rage of king Ahasuerus smoke against Haman, when he apprehended that he would have put a force upon the queen! Esther vii. 8–10. And why then should we wonder to see the wrath of the Lord break forth in smoke and flames against such a generation, that put a force upon his day, that profaned his day, the queen of days? Ah sirs! you have greatly profaned and abused the day of the Lord; and therefore why should any marvel that the Lord has greatly debased you, and laid your glory in dust and ashes? In these late years how has profaneness, like a flood, broke in upon us on the Lord's-day! and therefore it highly concerns all the profaners of the day of the Lord to lay their hands upon their hearts, and to say, The Lord is righteous, the Lord is righteous, though he has laid our habitations desolate. Who is so great a stranger in our English Israel as not to know that God was more dishonoured on the Sabbath-day, within and without the walls of London, than he was in all the other six days of the week? and therefore let us not think it strange that such a fire was kindled on that day as has reduced all to ashes. What antic habits did men and women put on, on this day! what frothy, empty, airy discourses and intemperance was to be found at many men's tables this day! how were alehouses, stews, and Moorfields filled with debauched sinners this day! No wonder then if London be laid desolate. Now this abominable sin of open profaning the Sabbaths of the Lord, I cannot with any clear evidence charge upon the people of God that did truly fear him within or without the walls of London. For, first, They did lament and mourn over the horrid profanation of that day. Secondly, I want eyes at present to see how it will stand, either with the truth of grace, or state of grace, for such as are real saints to live in the open profanation of God's Sabbaths. Thirdly, Because an ordinary profaning of the Lord's Sabbaths is

[1] The Sabbath-day differs as much from the rest of the days, as the wax doth, to which a king's great seal is put, from ordinary wax.

[2] Now the centre of the city of London: but still so named.—G.

as great an argument of a profane heart as any that can be found in the whole book of God. Fourthly, Because Sabbath-days are the saints' market-days, the saints' harvest-days, the saints' summer-days, the saints' seed-days, and the saints' feasting-days, Prov. x. 5, and xvii. 16; Isa. xxv. 6; and therefore they will not be such fools as to sleep away those days, much less will they presume to profane those days, or to toy and trifle away those days of grace. Fifthly, What singular thing do they more than others, if they are not strict observers and conscientious sanctifiers of the Lord's-day? Mat. v. 47. Sixthly and lastly, Of all the days that pass over a Christian's head in this world there are none that God will take such a strict and exact account of as of Sabbath-days; and therefore it highly concerns all people to be strict observers and serious sanctifiers of that day. Now, upon all these accounts, I cannot charge such throughout saints as lived within or without the walls of London with that horrid profanation of the Sabbath as brought the late fiery dispensation upon us, and that turned a glorious city into a ruinous heap. Whatever there was of the hand of man in that dreadful conflagration, I shall not now attempt to divine, but without a peradventure, it was Sabbath-guilt which threw the first ball that turned London into flames and ashes. When fire and smoking was on mount Sinai, God was there, Exod. xix. 18; but when London was in flames and smoke, Sabbath-guilt was there. Doubtless all the power of Rome and hell should never have put London into flames, had not London's guilt kindled the first coal. But,

We come now to the use and application of this important point.

10. Tenthly, *The profaneness, lewdness, blindness, and wickedness of the clergy, of them in the ministry, brings the judgment of fire, and provokes the Lord to lay all waste before him:* Zeph. iii. 4-6, 'Her prophets are light and treacherous persons: her priests have polluted the sanctuary, they have done violence to the law. I have cut off the nations: their towers are desolate; I have made their streets waste, that none passeth by: their cities are destroyed, so that there is no man, that there is none inhabitant.' Their prophets and priests were rash, heady, and unstable persons,—they were light, faithless men, or men of faithlessness, as the Hebrew runs. They were neither faithful to God, nor faithful to their own souls, nor faithful to others' souls. They invented and feigned prophecies of their own, and then boldly maintained them, and imposed them upon their hearers; they were profane and light in their carriages, they fitted their doctrines to all fancies, humours, parties, and times; they betrayed their trust, they betrayed the lives of men into the hand of divine justice, and the souls of men into the hands of Satan; they polluted the sanctuary, they polluted the holy things of God, by managing of his worship and service in a profane carnal way, and with a light, slight, perfidious spirit, and by perverting the true sense of the law in their ordinary teaching of the people. They did violence to the law, or they contemned, removed, or cast away the law, as the original runs: the Hebrew word here used signifies also to ravish, Ps. l. 17. Their prophets and priests did ravish the law of God by corrupting the law, and

by putting false glosses upon it, and by turning of it into such shapes and senses as would best suit the times, and please the humours of the people. Now for these abominations of their prophets and priests, God denounces a dreadful woe against the city of Jerusalem in ver. 1, 'Woe to her that is filthy and polluted, to the oppressing city:' Lam. iv. 11–13, 'The Lord hath accomplished his fury: he hath poured out his fierce anger, and hath kindled a fire in Zion, and it hath devoured the foundation thereof. For the sins of her prophets, and the iniquity of her priests, that have shed the blood of the just in the midst of her.' God sent a consuming flame into Jerusalem, which did not only burn the tops of their houses, but also the foundations themselves, leaving no mark whereby they might know where their houses stood, nor any hopes of building them up again. But why did God kindle such a devouring fire in Jerusalem, which was one of the world wonders, and a city that was not only strong in situation and building, and deemed impregnable, but a city that was God's own seat, the palace of his royal residence; yea, a city that the Lord had for many years, to the admiration of all the world, powerfully and wonderfully protected against all those furious assaults that were made upon her by her most potent and mighty adversaries? *Ans.* For the sins of her prophets, and the iniquities of her priests, as God himself testifies, who can neither die nor lie. You may see this further confirmed, if you please but seriously to ponder upon these scriptures, Ezek. xxii. 25, 26, 31; Jer. xxiii. 11, 14, 15, 39, 40.[1] Look, as the body natural, so the body politic cannot be long in a good constitution, whose more noble and essential parts are in a consumption. The enormities of ministers have the strongest influence upon the souls and lives of men, to make them miserable in both worlds. Their falls will be the fall and ruin of many; for people are more prone to live by examples than by precepts, and to mind more what the minister does than what he says: *Præcepta docent, exempla movent,* Precepts may instruct, but examples do persuade. The complaint is ancient in Seneca,[2] that commonly men live, not *ad rationem,* but *ad similitudinem.* The people commonly make the examples of their ministers the rules of their actions; and their examples pass as current among them as their prince's coin. The common people are like tempered wax, easily receiving impressions from the seals of their ministers' vices. They make no bones of it to sin by prescription, and to damn themselves by following the lewd examples of their ministers. The vulgar unadvisedly take up crimes on trust, and perish by following of bad examples. I will leave the serious reader to make such application as in prudence and conscience he judges meet. But,

11. Eleventhly, *Sometimes the sins of princes and rulers bring the fiery dispensations of God upon persons and places:*[3] Jer. xxxviii. 17, 18, 23, 'Then said Jeremiah unto Zedekiah, Thus saith the Lord, the God of hosts, the God of Israel, If thou wilt assuredly go forth unto the king of Babylon's princes, then thy soul shall live, and this city

[1] Micah ii. 11; Isa. xxx. 10, 11; Jer. v. 31; Hosea iv. 9; Isa. ix. 16; Lam. ii. 14; Ezek. iii. 18.

[2] Seneca, *de vita beata,* cap. 1.

[3] It is a strange saying in Lipsius, viz., that the names of all good princes may easily be engraven or written in a small ring.—Lipsius, *de Constantia,* lib. ii. cap. 25.

shall not be burned with fire, and thou shalt live, and thine house. But if thou wilt not go forth to the king of Babylon's princes, then shall this city be given into the hands of the Chaldeans, and they shall burn it with fire, and thou shalt not escape out of their hand, but shalt be taken by the hand of the king of Babylon, and thou shalt cause this city to be burned with fire;' or, as the Hebrew runs, 'thou shalt burn this city with fire;' that is, thou, by thy obstinacy, wilt be the means to procure the burning of this city, which by a rendition of thyself thou mightest have saved. So Jer. xxxiv. 2, 8–11, compared with chap. xxxvii. 5–22. Judges and magistrates are the physicians of the state, saith B[ishop] Lake in his sermon on Ezra,[1] and sins are the diseases of it. What skills it whether a gangrene begins at the head or the heel, seeing both ways it will kill, except this be the difference, that the head being nearer the heart, a gangrene in the head will kill sooner than that which is in the heel; even so will the sins of great ones overthrow a state sooner than those of the meanest sort, 2 Sam. xxiv. 9–18. But,

12. Twelfthly, *The abusing, mocking, and despising of the messengers of the Lord is a sin that brings the fiery dispensation upon a people*, 2 Chron. xxxvi. 15–19; Mat. xxiii. 34, 37, 38, 'Behold, your house is left unto you desolate.'[2] Here is used the present for the future, to note the certainty of the desolation of their city and temple, and their own utter ruins; and about forty years after the Romans came and burned their city and temple, and laid all waste before them. They had turned the prophets of the Lord out of all, and therefore the Lord resolves to turn them out of all. O sirs! will you please seriously to consider these six things: (1.) That all faithful, painful, conscientious ministers or messengers of the Lord, are great instruments in the hand of the Lord for stopping or stemming the tide of all profaneness and wickedness in a land, which bring all desolating and destroying judgments upon cities and countries, Isa. lviii. 1. (2.) For converting souls to God, for turning poor sinners from darkness to light, and from the power of Satan to Jesus Christ, Acts xxvi. 15–18, and Dan. xii. 3. (3.) For promoting of religion, holiness, and godliness in men's hearts, houses, and lives, which is the only way under heaven to render cities, countries, and kingdoms safe, happy, and prosperous. (4.) For the weakening of the kingdom of Satan and antichrist, the weakening of whose kingdom is the glory, safety, and security of the land. (5.) For the turning away of wrath, either felt or feared. (6.) For the bringing down of the greatest, weightiest, and noblest of temporal favours and blessings upon cities and countries, as might be proved from scores of scripture, James v. 16–18. And therefore never marvel if God revenges the abuses done to them in flames of fire. It was on a Sabbath that the public liberty of the painful, faithful ministers of London was terminated and came to an end, and it was on a Sabbath that London was burned.[3]

13. Thirteenthly, *Shedding of the blood of the just is a crying sin,*

[1] Viz., on Ezra vii. 26, in Sermons; folio, 1629, pp. 273, *seq.*, part iii.—G.

[2] Turn to these two pregnant texts, and ponder seriously upon them; for they speak close in the case.

[3] The first on the 24th of August, and the other on the 2d of September. [The reference is to the 'Ejectment' of the 'Two Thousand' in 1662.—G.]

that brings the judgment of fire, and lays all desolate:[1] Ezek. xxxv. 4, 5, 7, 'I will lay thy cities waste, and thou shalt be desolate, and thou shalt know that I am the Lord. Because thou hast had a perpetual hatred,' or hatred of old, 'and hast shed the blood of the children of Israel by the force of the sword in the time of their calamity, in the time that their iniquity had an end. Thus will I make mount Seir most desolate, and cut off from it him that passeth out, and him that returneth;' ver. 10, 'Because thou hast said, These two nations and these two countries shall be mine, and we will possess it, whereas the Lord was there;' ver. 11, 'Therefore as I live, saith the Lord God, I will even do according to thine anger, and according to thine envy, which thou hast used out of thy hatred against them: and I will make myself known among them when I have judged thee:' ver. 12, 'And thou shalt know that I am the Lord, and that I have heard all thy blasphemies which thou hast spoken against the mountains of Israel, saying, They are laid desolate, they are given us to consume or devour:' ver. 13, 'Thus with your mouth you have boasted against me, and have multiplied your words against me: I have heard them:' ver. 14, 'Thus saith the Lord God, When the whole earth rejoiceth I will make thee desolate:' ver. 15, 'As thou didst rejoice at the inheritance of the house of Israel, because it was desolate, so will I do unto thee: thou shalt be desolate, O mount Seir, and all Idumea, even all of it: and they shall know that I am the Lord.' The Edomites were deadly enemies to the Israelites—their hatred was old and strong, and active against them; and they took hold on all occasions wherein they might express their rage and cruelty against them, both in words and works. And therefore when the Babylonians took Jerusalem, they cried, Rase it, rase it, even to the foundation thereof, Ps. cxxxvii. 7. When the Babylonians entered Jerusalem, many of the Jews fled to the Edomites for succour, they being their brethren; but instead of sheltering them, they cruelly destroyed them, and greatly insulted over them, and were glad of all opportunities wherein they might vent all their rage and malice against them, that so they might the better ingratiate themselves with the Babylonians. Now for these cruel practices and barbarous severities of theirs towards the poor, afflicted, and distressed Israel of God, God is resolved to bring utter desolation upon them: ver. 3, 'Thus saith the Lord God, Behold, O mount Seir, I am against thee, and I will stretch out my hand against thee, and I will make thee most desolate:' or as the Hebrew is, *Shemamah Umeshammah*, desolation and desolation. Now this doubling of the Hebrew word shews the certainty of their desolation, the speediness of their desolation, and the greatness and throughness of their desolation: Jer. xxvi. 14, 15; see ver. 8, 9, 11, 'As for me, behold, I am in your hand, do with me as seemeth good and meet unto you. But know ye for certain, that if you put me to death, ye shall surely bring innocent blood upon yourselves, and upon this city, and upon the inhabitants thereof.' That was good counsel which Tertullian gave Scapula, a pagan persecutor: God will surely make inquisition for our blood, therefore, saith he, if thou wilt not spare us, yet spare thyself; if not thyself, yet spare thy country, which must be responsible when God comes to visit for

[1] See Ezek. xxi. 28, 31, 32, and xxv. 3–5.

blood: so Lam. iv. 11–13, 'The Lord hath accomplished his fury; he hath poured out his fierce anger, and hath kindled a fire in Zion, and it hath devoured the foundations thereof. The kings of the earth, and all the inhabitants of the world, would not have believed that the adversary and the enemy should have entered into the gates of Jerusalem. For the sins of her prophets, and the iniquities of her priests, that have shed the blood of the just in the midst of her.' The prophets and the priests enraged the people against them, and engaged the civil power against the just and the innocent, to the shedding of their blood. But this innocent blood could not be purged away but by fire. To shed the blood of the just is a most crying sin, and that for which God has turned the most glorious cities in the world into ashes. Jerome upon the text saith, that the prophets and priests shed the blood of the just in the midst of Jerusalem, by drawing them into error, which is to the destruction of the soul. But Calvin upon the text well observes this cannot stand, because just men are not so destroyed; but the wicked only, that take no heed to their false teaching. Therefore, saith he, the true prophets of God are meant by the just, for whom they had prisons, dungeons, and stocks to put them into; and sometimes stoning, or otherwise tumults, which they stirred up among the people, whereby their blood was shed.

Rome has much of the blood of the saints upon her skirts, and for this very sin she shall be utterly burnt with fire, as you may see at large, if you will please to read the 18th chapter of the Revelation at your leisure, Rev. xvi. 6, xvii. 6, xix. 2, and xviii. 24. Though Rome was a cage of unclean birds, and full of all manner of abominations, yet the sin that shall at last burn her to ashes, is the blood of the saints. Mark, though the people of God are in Babylon, and may partake of her plagues, and fall under the fiery dispensation with her, it is not the sins of the saints, but the sins of Babylon that bring the judgment of fire upon Babylon. Mark, the people of God may live in a city that may be burnt to ashes, and yet their sins may not be the procuring causes of that judgment. Lot lived in Sodom, and had his failings and infirmities as well as other saints, Gen. xix; but it was not his sins that brought the judgment of fire upon that city, but the sins of the citizens, as the Scripture assures us.

But you may say, Pray, sir, why is God so severe as to turn stately cities, rich and populous cities, great and glorious cities, into a ruinous heap, for shedding the blood of the just? *Ans.* Because, next to the blood of Christ, the blood of the just is the most precious blood in all the world. Mark, There are these nine things that speak out the preciousness of the blood of the just:—

[1.] First, *Clear and plain scriptures speak out the blood of the saints to be precious:* 'He shall redeem their soul from deceit and violence, and precious shall their blood be in his sight.' And so Ps. cxvi. 15, 'Precious in the sight of the Lord is the death of his saints;' Ps. lxxiii. 32, 33, and lxxii. 14. But,

[2.] Secondly, *The cry of their blood reaches as high as heaven, and this speaks it out to be precious blood*, Gen. iv. 10, 11. The blood of one Abel had so many tongues as drops, and every drop a voice to cry for vengeance, and the cry of his blood did strongly engage the justice of God to punish it:[1] Rev. xvi. 6, 'Give them blood to drink, for they are worthy.' But,

[3.] Thirdly, *God's cursing their blessings, who have shed the blood of his saints, speaks out their blood to be precious blood:* Gen. iv. 10, 11, 'And now art thou cursed from the earth, which hath opened her mouth to receive thy brother's blood from thy hand.' Now this is added by the way—1. To aggravate the sin of Cain; 2. To shew the fitness of the punishment: it is as if he had said the earth did, as it were, in compassion receive into her bosom that blood which thou didst cruelly and wickedly shed; and therefore out of the earth, which hath sucked in by the pores thereof thy brother's blood, shall spring a curse that shall plague thee for shedding that blood. The earth, which was created for thy blessing and service, shall execute this curse against thee in vengeance, not yielding thee the fruits which otherwise it would have done. As is expressed in ver. 12, 'When thou tillest the ground, it shall not henceforth yield unto thee her strength'—*Heb.*, 'It shall not go on to give thee its ability.' This was a second curse, whereby the earth became worse for Cain's sin than it was for Adam's. Now if this curse were not general, yet doubtless it was a particular curse upon Cain's portion, so that wheresoever or whensoever he should till the earth as a husbandman, the earth by its barrenness should upbraid him as a murderer. But,

[4.] Fourthly, *God's pouring out of the blood of the wicked as water is poured out upon the ground, to prevent the effusion of his children's blood, speaks out their blood to be precious blood,* Isa. xliii. 4, 5. At the Red Sea, God made way not only through the sea, but also through the blood of the Egyptians, to preserve the blood and lives of his poor people, Exod. xiv. God, to preserve the lives and blood of his people, destroys a hundred fourscore and five thousand of Sennacherib's army by the hand of his angel in one night, Isa. xxxvii. 36. And you know in Esther's time, Esth. ix., how God made way for the preservation of the lives and blood of his people through the blood of Haman, his sons, and the rest of their enemies that hated them. I might give you twenty other scriptures to the same purpose, but enough is as good as a feast. But,

[5.] Fifthly, *The strict inquisition that God has made after the blood of the just in all ages of the world, argues the preciousness of their blood:* Ps. ix. 12, 'When he maketh inquisition for blood, he remembereth them, he forgetteth not the cry of the humble.' Did not Pharaoh, Ahab, Jezebel, Haman, Herod, Amalek, Moab, Ammon, Sennacherib, &c., find by woeful experience that God did make a strict inquisition after the blood of the just? And so did those men of violence who shed the blood of the just in the primitive times, &c. But,

[6.] Sixthly, *The speedy and dreadful vengeance of God upon such as have shed the blood of the just, speaks out their blood to be precious in his eyes:* Ps. lv. 23, 'But thou, O God, shalt bring them down into the pit of destruction: bloody and deceitful men shall not live out half their days;' Ps. xciv. 21, 23, 'They gather themselves together'—*Heb.*, 'run by troops, as thieves do'—'against the soul of the righteous, and condemn the innocent blood. He shall bring upon them

[1] Crying is ascribed to blood by a figurative speech.

their own iniquity, and shall cut them off in their own wickedness: yea, the Lord our God shall cut them off.' Richard III. and Queen Mary were cruel princes, and shed the blood of the just, and they had the shortest reign of any since the Conquest.

Charles IX. was a great shedder of the blood of the just.[1] He had a deep hand in the massacre of the protestants in Paris, and in other parts of his kingdom he glutted himself with the blood of the just, and gloried greatly in their ruins. In his latter days he was surprised with a great debility and tormenting pains in his body; after a great effusion of blood, which issued out by all the passages of his body, he breathed forth his wretched soul.[2] Oh the horrid butcheries that were committed and commanded by this bloody prince his reign, throughout his whole realm! But at last divine vengeance overtook him, and he died wallowing in his own blood, &c.

The Duke of Guise, next to the king,[3] had the greatest hand in the massacre of the protestants. He was a most barbarous prince, and at last he falls by barbarous hands; for he being called by [Louis] Revol, secretary to Henry III., to come to the king into his cabinet, as he lifted up the tapestry with one hand to enter, he was charged with swords, daggers, and partisans,[4] and so died by the hands of murderers. He that had murdered many thousands of the protestants was at last murdered by men of his own religion.[5]

Henry III., king of France, was a most cruel enemy to the protestants, and he was by James Clemmont, a monk, stabbed in the same chamber, and on the same day wherein he had helped to contrive the French massacre.[6] Doubtless God will one day reckon with France for all that protestant blood that they have shed.

Maximinus was a great persecutor of the people of God; he set forth a proclamation, engraven in brass, for the utter abolishing of Christ and his religion; he was at last eaten up of lice.[7] The same judgment befell Philip king of Spain, who swore he had rather have no subjects than Lutheran subjects; and when he had narrowly escaped drowning in a shipwreck, he said he was delivered of God to rout off Lutheranism, which he presently began to do, but God soon cut him off.

Thomas Blavar,[8] one of the privy counsellors of the king of Scots, was a sore persecutor of the people of God in that land; when he lay on his dying-bed he fell into despair, and cried out that he was damned, he was damned: and when the monks came about him to comfort him, he cried out upon them, saying, 'that their masses and other trash would do him no good; for he never believed them, but all that he did was for love of money, and not of religion, not respecting or believing that there was either a God or a devil, a hell or a heaven; and therefore he was damned, there was no remedy but

[1] History of France, pp. 791–798. [2] *Ibid.*, pp. 808, 809,

[3] *Ibid.*, pp. 793, 794. [The Duke of Guise here referred to was Louis de Lorraine, who was lieutenant-general of the kingdom under Charles IX. He was murdered at the door of the closet of Henry III. in 1588. Anquetil, Hist. de France, vii. 193.—G.]

[4] 'Pikes.'—G. [5] History of France, p. 867.

[6] *Ibid.*, pp. 879, 880. [Clement, *not* Clemmont. Aug. 1, 1589.—G.]

[7] History of the Council of Trent, p. 417.

[8] Query, 'Blair'? Cf. Vol. I. p. 252.—G.

he must go to hell, and in this case without a sign of repentance he died.'[1]

A popish magistrate having condemned a poor protestant to death, before his execution he caused his tongue to be cut out, because he should not confess the truth: but the Lord did retaliate it upon him; for the next child he had was born without a tongue.

Cardinal Crescentius [Anno 1552] was a most desperate persecutor of the people of God. He was the pope's ambassador to the Council of Trent, and being one night busy in writing to his master the pope, a huge black dog, with great flaming eyes, and long ears dangling down to the ground, appeared to him in his chamber, and went under the table where he sat. Upon which the cardinal was amazed; but as soon as he had recovered himself, he called his servants to put out the black dog that was come into his chamber; but they looked round about his chambers, and the next chambers, but could find no black dog: upon which the cardinal fell presently sick with a strong conceit, which never left him till his death, still crying out, Drive away the black dog, drive away the black dog, which seemed to him to be climbing up his bed; and in that humour he died.

After the martyrdom of Gregory, the bishop of Spoleta, Flaccus the governor, who was the author thereof, was struck with an angel,[2] and vomited up his entrails at his mouth, and died.[3]

Mammea Agrippitus, when he was fifteen years old, because he would not sacrifice to their idols, was apprehended at Preneste, and whipped with scourges, and hanged up by the heels, and at last slain with the sword; in the midst of whose torments the governor of the city fell down dead from the tribunal-seat.[4]

Gensericus, king of the Vandals, an Arian, was a most cruel persecutor of the orthodox Christians; he was possessed of the devil, and died a most miserable death in the year 477.[5]

Herod the Great, who caused the babes of Bethlehem to be slain, hoping thereby to have destroyed Christ, shortly after was plagued by God with an incurable disease, having a slow and slack fire continually tormenting of his inward parts; he had a vehement and greedy desire to eat, and yet nothing would satisfy him; his inward bowels rotted, his breath was short and stinking, some of his members rotted, and in all his members he had so violent a cramp, that nature was not able to bear it, and so, growing mad with pain, he died miserably.[6]

Herod Antipas, who beheaded John Baptist, not long after, falling into disgrace with the Roman emperor, with his incestuous Herodias, the suggester of that murder, they were banished, and fell into such misery and penury that they ended their wretched lives with much shame and misery.[7]

Herod Agrippa was a great persecutor of the saints, Acts xii.; he was eaten up of worms in the third year of his reign, as Josephus observes.[8] He went to Cæsarea to keep certain plays in the honour of Cæsar; the gown he was in, as the same author relates, was a gown

1 Theatrum Historicum. 2 Query, 'ague'?—G. 3 Phil. Lonicer.
4 Cent. iii. cap. 12. [Rather Agapetus: Clarke, as before, p. 36.—G.]
5 Sigeb. in Chron. 6 Euseb. Hist. 7 *Ibid.*
8 Joseph. Antiq., lib. xix. cap. 7.

of silver wonderfully wrought, and the beams of the sun reflecting upon it, made it so glister, that it dazzled the eyes of the beholders; and when he had made an end of his starched oration in this his bravery, his flatterers extolled him as a god, crying out, It is the voice of a god, and not of a man, Acts xii. 21–23: whereupon he was presently smitten by the angel of the Lord, and so died with worms that ate up his entrails.[1] The blow the angel gave him was an inward blow, and not so visible to others; and his torments more and more increasing upon him, the people put on sackcloth, and made supplication for him, but all in vain; for his pains and torments growing stronger and stronger every day upon him, they separated his wretched soul from his loathsome body within the compass of five days.[2]

Caiaphas the high priest, who gathered the council, and suborned false witness against the Lord Christ, was shortly after put out of his office, and one Jonathan substituted in his room, whereupon he killed himself.[3]

Not long after Pontius Pilate had condemned our Lord Christ, he lost his deputyship and Cæsar's favour; and being fallen into disgrace with the Roman emperor, and banished by him, he fell into such misery that he hanged himself.

Oh the dreadful judgments that were inflicted upon the chief actors in the ten persecutions! Shall I give you a brief account of what befell them?

Nero, that monster of men, who raised the first bloody persecution, to pick a quarrel with the Christians, he set the city of Rome on fire, and then charged it upon them; under which pretence he exposes them to the fury of the people, who cruelly tormented them, as if they had been common burners and destroyers of cities, and the deadly enemies of mankind; yea, Nero himself caused them to be apprehended and clad in wild beasts' skins, and torn in pieces with dogs; others were crucified, some he made bonfires of to light him in his night-sports. To be short, such horrid cruelty he used towards them, as caused many of their enemies to pity them. But God found out this wretched persecutor at last; for being adjudged by the senate an enemy to mankind, he was condemned to be whipped to death, for the prevention whereof he cut his own throat.

Domitian, the author of the second persecution against the Christians, having drawn a catalogue of such as he was to kill, in which was the name of his own wife and other friends; upon which he was, by the consent of his wife, slain by his own household servants with daggers in his privy-chamber; his body was buried without honour, his memory cursed to posterity, and his arms and ensigns were thrown down and defaced.

Trajan raised the third persecution against the church; he was continually vexed with seditions, and the vengeance of God followed him close. For, first, he fell into a palsy, then lost the use of his senses; afterwards he fell into a dropsy, and died in great anguish.

Adrian being vexed with great and perpetual commotions in his life, died with much anxiety.

[1] Joseph. Antiq., lib. xviii. cap. 13. [2] Euseb. Hist. [3] *Ibid.*, lib. ii. cap. 7.

Maximinus being declared an enemy by the senate, was killed in his own tent.

Decius, by the Goths, in their first invasion of the empire, with his whole army was cut off.

Valerianus was overcome by the Persians, and made use of by Sapor as a stirrup for his foot when he went to take horse.

Julian, in his height of contempt against Christ, was deadly wounded in battle against the Persians, and throwing his blood in the air, died with that desperate expression in his mouth, *Vicisti tandem Galilœe.*[1]

Valentius, being a great favourer of the Arians, and a great persecutor of the orthodox—the Arians exceeding the heathens in cruelty —was in battle against the Goths in Thracia wounded, and being carried to a house that was near, it was set on fire by the enemy, in which he miserably perished.

Maxentius and his chief officers being put to flight on the other side of the river Tiber, by Constantine, was necessitated to return by a bridge, whereupon he had made devices in a secret way to have drowned Constantine, by which he and those that were with him were drowned in the river;[2] upon which occasion the Christians took occasion to sing that word, Ps. ix. 16, 'The Lord is known by the judgments which he executeth: the wicked is snared in the work of his own hand:' and that word, Ps. vii. 15, 'He made a pit and digged it, and he himself is fallen into it.'

Dioclesian being sent for by Constantine, upon suspicion, chose rather to poison himself than to see him.

Maximianus Herculeus, endeavouring again to recover his authority, was discovered in his design by his daughter, Constantine's wife: whereupon he was pursued and besieged by Constantine, and was either killed, or during the siege hanged himself, as is diversely reported by several writers.

Maximinus Jovius, through intemperance, becoming corpulent, was smitten with boils in the secret parts, out of which issued abundance of vermin; his physicians were either suffocated by the odious smell of his loathsome disease, or else they were killed by him because they could not cure him. One of his physicians told him that it was God's judgment on him for persecuting the Christians, which no man could cure. At last he fell under such convictions, as forced him to confess that the wrongs and injuries that he had done to the people of God were the cause of that plague; and therefore being struck with terror and horror, gave out edicts that the persecution should cease, and that churches should be builded, and that in their meetings prayers should be put up for him, as formerly used to be: which edict is to be found in Eusebius.[3] The other tyrant in the east, to wit, Maximinus, who was called Cæsar, had been industrious to invent cruel tortures for the Christians, especially to pull out their eyes; but at last he was defeated, and in a base habit made to hide himself, and afterwards he was pursued by such a sickness which made both his eyes to drop out of his head, by which judgment he was necessitated to confess that

[1] As before.—G.

[2] Euseb. Hist., lib. ix. cap. 8. The Christians compared his destruction in the water to Pharaoh's drowning in the Red Sea.

[3] Euseb. Hist., lib. viii. cap. 29.

the God of the Christians was the only true God, and that he had been mistaken concerning the gods whom he chose to worship; which words were uttered by him when he was even expiring, as Eusebius testifies.[1] By all these dreadful instances, you may run and read that heavy vengeance that has been inflicted upon those who have shed the blood of the just.

Fœlix, Earl of Wurtemburg, was a great persecutor of the saints, and did swear that ere he died he would ride up to the spurs in the blood of the Lutherans: but the very same night wherein he had thus sworn and vowed, he was choked with his own blood.

The judgments of God were so famous and frequent upon those that did shed the blood of the saints in Bohemia, that it was used as a proverb among the adversaries themselves, That if any man be weary of his life, let him but attempt against the Picardines—so they called the Christians—and he should not live a year to an end.

Sir Thomas More, once Lord Chancellor of England, was a sworn enemy to the gospel, and persecuted the saints with fire and faggot; and among all his praises he reckons this as the chiefest—that he had been a persecutor of the Lutherans, *i.e.*, the saints. But what became of him? he was first accused of treason, and then condemned, and at last beheaded.

Judge Morgan was a great persecutor of the people of God; but shortly after he had passed the sentence of condemnation upon that virtuous lady, the Lady Jane Grey, he fell mad, and in his mad raving fits, he would continually cry out, 'Take away the Lady Jane, take away the Lady Jane from me!' and in that horror he ended his wretched life.

Drahomiza, after the death of her husband, usurped the government of Bohemia, and was a cruel persecutor of the people of God; but by a righteous hand of God it so fell out, that on that very place where the ministers' bones lay unburied, the earth opened of itself, and swallowed her up alive with her chariot, and those that were in it; which place is now to be seen before the castle of Prague. There is no end of instances of a later date. But,

[7.] Seventhly, *The strange, miraculous, and wonderful preservation of the lives and blood of the just*, speaks out their blood to be precious blood.[2] Who can sum up the many miracles of divine love, power, wisdom, and care, &c., that God manifested in the preservation of Joseph in the prison, Jeremiah in the dungeon, Daniel in the den, and the three children in the fiery furnace, and not say, Surely the blood of the saints is very precious in the eyes of the Lord? I have read of a certain witch that sent her spirits to kill Ambrose; but they returned her this answer, that God had hedged him in, as he did Job, and therefore they could not touch him, they could not hurt him. Another came with a drawn sword to his bedside to have killed him, but he could not stir his hand, till, repenting, he was by the prayer of Ambrose restored to the use of his hand again. For Luther, saith my author,

[1] Euseb. de vita Constantini, lib. ii. cap. 52.

[2] Hesiod speaks of thirty thousand demi-gods that were keepers of men; but what are so many thousand gods to that one God, that neither slumbers nor sleeps, but day and night keeps his people as the apple of his eye, Zeph. v. 8; as his jewels, Mal. iii. 17; that keeps them in his pavilion, as a prince his favourite? Ps. xxxi. 20.

a poor friar, to stand it out against the pope and all the power of Rome, was a great miracle; and that he should prevail against all that power, was greater; and that after all he should die in his bed, was the greatest of all. There are many thousand instances more of the like nature, but enough is as good as a feast.

[8.] Eighthly, *The spiritual judgments that God hath given such up to, who have shed the blood of the just*, speaks out their blood to be precious blood. Oh the dreadful horrors and amazing terrors of conscience that such have been given up to! Take a few instances among the many that might be given. The *Vaivod* that had betrayed Zegedine, a godly man, professed to Zegedine that he was so haunted with apparitions and the furies of his own conscience, that he could not rest day nor night. Dionysius, a cruel tyrant, a bitter enemy to all good men and good things, was so troubled with fear and horror of conscience, that, not daring to trust his best friends with a razor, he used to singe his beard with burning coals [Cicero.] A sleepy conscience, when awakened, is like a sleepy lion; when he awakes he roars and tears his prey. It is like Prometheus' vulture, it lies ever gnawing.[1] Sin brings a stain and a sting. Horror of conscience meets a man in the dark, and makes him leap in the night, and makes him quake in his sleep, and makes him start in every corner, and makes him think every bush is a man, every man a devil, and every devil a messenger to fetch him quick to hell. By this Theodoric saw the face of a man in the mouth of a fish; Nessus heard the noise of murder in the voice of birds; Saundes(?) ran distracted over the Irish mountains. This made Cain wander, Saul stab himself, Judas hang himself, Arius empty his bowels at the stool, Latomus cry desperately, he was damned, he was damned, and Julian confess that he was conquered. It makes man, the lord of all, to be slave to all. Lord, what is man? Certainly it is better with Evagrius to lie secure on a bed of straw, than to have a turbulent conscience on a bed of down, having curtains embossed with gold and pearl. But,

[9.] Ninthly and lastly, *The shedding of the blood of the just is a sin of so high a cry, and so deep a dye, that for it God is resolved, except men repent, that he will shut them out of the highest heaven, and cast them down to the lowest hell;* as you may see by comparing the scriptures in the margin together;[2] and therefore certainly the blood of the just is most precious blood. Now, seeing that the blood of the just is such precious blood, who will wonder if God sets such cities and towns and countries into a flame about their ears, upon whose skirts the blood of the just is to be found? Josephus, speaking of the desolation of Jerusalem, saith, Because they have sinned against the Lord God of their fathers, in shedding the blood of just men and innocents that were within thee, even in the temple of the Lord, therefore are our sorrowful sighings multiplied, and our weapons[3] daily increased. It was the blood of the just, the blood of the innocents, that turned Jerusalem into ashes.

[1] Conscience is God's preacher in the bosom. Conscience is *mille testes*, a thousand witnesses for or against a man. Conscience hath a good memory.

[2] Gal. v. 21; Rev. xxi. 8, and xxii. 15; 1 John iii. 15; Mat. xxii. 7.

[3] Query, 'weepings'?—ED.

I have read of one Rabbi Samuel, who six hundred years since writ a tract in form of an epistle to Rabbi Isaac, master of the synagogue of the Jews, wherein he doth excellently discuss the cause of their long captivity and extreme misery, and after that he had proved that it was inflicted for some grievous sin, he sheweth that sin to be the same which Amos speaks of: 'For three transgressions of Israel, and for four, I will not turn away the punishment thereof, because they sold the righteous for silver, and the poor for a pair of shoes.' The selling of Joseph he makes the first sin; the worshipping of the calf in Horeb, the second sin; the abusing of God's prophets, the third sin; and the selling of Jesus Christ, the fourth sin. For the first, they served four hundred years in Egypt; for the second, they wandered forty years in the wilderness; for the third, they were captives seventy years in Babylon; and for the fourth, they are held in pitiful captivity even till this day.

When Phocas, that bloody cut-throat, sought to secure himself by building high walls, he heard a voice from heaven telling him, that though he built his bulwarks never so high, yet sin within, blood within, would soon undermine all. Shedding the blood of the just is a sin that hath undermined the strongest bulwarks, and that hath blown up, and burnt up, the most glorious cities that have been in the world. And who can tell but that the blood of the just that was shed in the Marian days, might now come up into remembrance before the Lord?[1] For in four years of her reign there were consumed in the heat of those flames two hundred and seventy-seven persons—viz., five bishops, one-and-twenty ministers, eight gentlemen, eighty-four artificers, one hundred husbandmen, servants, and labourers, six-and-twenty wives, twenty widows, nine virgins, two boys, and two infants. I say, who can tell but that the blood of these precious servants of the Lord hath cried aloud in the ears of the Lord for vengeance against that once glorious, but now desolate city? Men of brutish spirits, and that are skilful to destroy, make no more of shedding the blood of the just, than they do of shedding the blood of a swine; but yet this hideous sin makes so great a noise in the ears of the Lord of hosts, that many times he tells the world by his fiery dispensations that it cannot be purged away but by fire. And thus much for the sins that bring the fiery judgment: our way now to the application is plain.

[1] Speed's Chronicle in Queen Mary.

THE FIRST PART OF THE APPLICATION.

1. *To see the hand of the Lord in it. Ten considerations to work to this.*

2. *To mourn under the sense of so great a judgment.*

WE come now to the use and application of this important point. The explication of a doctrine is but the drawing of the bow: the application is the hitting of the mark, the white, &c.

Is it so, that God is the author or efficient cause of all the great calamities and dreadful judgments that are inflicted upon cities and countries, and, in particular, of that of fire? Then,

Use 1. First, *Let us see the hand of the Lord in this late dreadful fire that hath been upon us;* for certainly God is the author, permissively at least, he is the great agent in all those terrible judgments that befall persons, cities, and kingdoms, Ruth i. 13, 21; Ps. xxxix. 9; 1 Sam. iii. 18. Whosoever or whatsoever be the rod, it is his hand that gives the stroke. The power of bringing judgments upon cities God challengeth to himself: Amos iii. 6, 'Shall there be evil in a city, and the Lord hath not done it?' Whatever the judgment be that falls upon a city, God is the author of it; he acts in it and orders it according to his own good pleasure. There is no judgment that casually falls upon any person, city, or country. Every judgment is inflicted by a divine power and providence. The Chaldeans could never have burned Jerusalem, if the Lord had not granted them a commission. Hence saith the prophet, 'Evil came down from the Lord unto the gate of Jerusalem,' Micah i. 12. It was a sore evil that Jerusalem, which was one of the world's wonders, should be destroyed by fire; but this evil was determined at the council-board in heaven.[1] Jerusalem was burned by a commission signed in heaven, both when the Chaldeans under Nebuchadnezzar, and when the Romans under Titus Vespasian, laid it in ashes. All sorts of judgments are more at the beck of God, and under the command of God, than servants are under the commands of their masters, or soldiers under the commands of their general, or children under the command of their parents, Mat. viii. 5, 11. Whatever judgment God commands to destroy a person, a city, or country, that judgment shall certainly and effectually accomplish the command of God, in spite of all that creatures can do.[2] God, as he is our Creator, Preserver, and sovereign Lord, has an absolute power both over our persons, lives, estates, and habitations: and when we have transgressed his righteous laws, he may do with us, and all we have, as he pleases; he may turn us out of house and home, and burn up all our comforts round about us, and yet do us no wrong. Those things which seem accidental and casual unto us are ordered by the wise

[1] The soldier's firebrand, by which was fired the famous temple of Jerusalem, was commissionated by a divine command.

[2] Whatever miscreants made the fire-balls, yet God did blow the fire, and so turned London into a ruinous heap. Certainly there was much of God's hand, whatever there was of men's heads, in this fatal fire.

counsel, power, and providence of God. Instruments can no more stir till God gives them a commission, than the axe or the knife can cut of itself, without a hand. Job eyed God in the fire that fell from heaven, and in all the fiery trials that befell him. And therefore, as one observes, [Austin,] he doth not say, the Lord gave, and the devil took away; nor the Lord gave, and the Chaldeans and Sabeans took away; but 'the Lord hath given, and the Lord hath taken; and blessed be the name of the Lord,' Job i. 20, 21. Certainly without the cognisance and concurrence of a wise, omniscient, and omnipotent God, no creatures can move; nor without his foresight and permission no event can befall any person, city, or country: Acts xvii. 28, 'For in him we live, move, and have our being.' No man can put forth a natural action without him. Whatever the means or instruments of our misery be, the hand is God's; and this the saints in all the ages of the world have confessed. It becomes us, in every judgment, to see the hand of the Lord, and to look through visible means to an invisible God, Lev. x. 1–4, and Heb. xi. 25, 26; for though the Lord may, and many times does, make use of Satan and his instruments to scourge his dearest children, yet it is but one hand, and many instruments, that he smites us with. God makes use of what second causes he pleases for the execution of his pleasure. And many times he makes the worst of men the rod of his indignation to chastise his people with, Isa. x. 5–20. Witness Pharaoh, Ahab, Haman, Herod, and the Assyrian kings, with scores of other instances that the Scripture affords. And all histories abound in nothing more than in instances of this nature, as all know that have read anything of history. The conclave of Rome, and the conclave of hell can do nothing without a commission from heaven. They cannot make a louse, nor burn a house, nor drown a pig, without a commission under the broad seal of heaven. A sparrow lights not upon the ground, nor a hair falls not from our heads, no, nor a bristle from a sow's back, saith Tertullian, but by a divine providence.[1] All created creatures, both in that upper and in this lower world, depend upon God for their being, motion, and several activities. Now in that God did not exert his power, neither to prevent nor check those furious flames, which he knew, without his interposure, would lay all in ashes; it is evident that it was his divine pleasure that London should be turned into a ruinous heap. God's not hindering the desolation of London was a tacit commissioning of the flames to burn down all that stood in their way. That such are under a high mistake that ascribe the burning of London so to second causes as that they will allow no more judgment of God in it than that which accompanies common casualty, I shall sufficiently evidence before I have finished this first use. But I hope the prudent reader will make it his business to see the signal hand of God in this late fiery dispensation, and to remember that the scribe is more properly said to write than the pen; and he that maketh and keepeth the clock is more properly said to make it go and strike than the wheels and poises that hang upon it; and every workman to effect his work, rather than the tools which he useth as instruments. So the Lord of hosts, who is the chief agent and

[1] Exod. viii. 18; Jer. xxi. 10; Mat. viii. 32, and x. 30; Luke xxi. 18.

mover in all things, and in all actions, may more fitly and properly be said to effect and bring to pass all judgments, yea, all things that are done in the earth, than any inferior or subordinate causes—seeing they are but his tools and instruments, which he rules and guides according to his own will, power, and providence. At this some of the more civilised heathen hath long since hammered, viz., that the same power dispenseth both comforts and crosses, when they painted Fortune in two forms, with two faces of contrary colours, the foremost white, the hindermost black, to signify that both good and evil came from the goddess Fortune. When it was told prince Henry, that *delicia generis humani*, that darling of mankind, 'that the sins of the people caused that affliction that was upon him;' 'Oh no,' said he, 'I have sins enough of mine own to cause that.' So should we all confess, that though God take occasion by another man's sin, or by another man's hand, to fire my house, yet the cause is just that it should be so, and that I myself have deserved it, whatsoever the occasion or the instrument be. God had matter enough against the seventy thousand that died of the plague; though David's sin were the occasion, yet the meritorious cause was in them. Certainly there is no man that hath been a sufferer by this late dreadful fire, but upon an easy search into his own heart and life, he may find matter enough to silence himself, and to satisfy himself that, though God has turned him out of his habitation, and burnt up all his comforts round about him, yet he has done him no wrong. Surely in the burning of the city of London there was more of the extraordinary hand of God than there was of the hand of papist or atheist, Ezek. xxi. 31. God, if he had pleased, could have prevented brutish and skilful men to destroy and burn, by discovering of their hellish plots before they had taken effect, as he did Ahithophel's, 2 Sam. xvii. 10–24; and as he did Tobiah's and Sanballat's, Neh. iv. 7–16; and as he did the Jews' who took counsel to kill Paul, Acts ix. 23–25, and xxiii. 12–25; and as he did that of the Gunpowder treason. And God could have directed and spirited men to the use of the means, and then have given such a blessing to the means, as should have been effectual to the quenching of it when it was first kindled; but he would not, which is a clear evidence that he had given from heaven a commission to the fire to burn with that force and violence as it did, till all was laid in ashes.

Now that you may the better see and acknowledge the hand of the Lord in the late dreadful fire that has been amongst us, consider seriously with me these ten following particulars:—

[1.] First, Consider *the intemperate heat, the drought of the season.* Such a hot and dry summer as that was has not been known for many years; how by this means every man's habitation was as stubble, fully dry, prepared and fitted for the burning flames.[1] Before God would strike fire he made our houses like tinder. When fuel is wet and green, what puffing and blowing must there be to kindle a fire, and to make it burn! but when fuel is light and dry, it is so conceptive of fire, that even the very smell of fire puts it into a flame. And this

[1] Nahum i. 10; Joel ii. 5. By this parching season every man's house was prepared for fuel.

was poor London's case; for every man's house had lain long a-sunning under the scorching beams of the sun and much brightness of weather, which made everything so dry and combustible that sparks and flakes of fire were sufficient to set men's houses all in a flame about their ears. Now this finger of God we are neither to overlook nor yet deny; it is our wisdom, as well as our work, to see not only the finger, but the hand of the Lord in every circumstance that relates to that sore judgment of fire that we are still sighing under, Exod. viii. 19. It is God that withholds seasonable showers, and that causeth it to rain upon one city and not upon another, Amos iv. 7. The earth cannot open her bowels, and yield seed to the sower, and bread to the eater, if not watered from above, 1 Kings xvii. 1, 2; nor the heaven cannot drop down fatness upon the earth if God close it up, and withhold the seasonable showers. This the very heathens acknowledged in their fictions of Jupiter and Juno. God only can make the heavens as brass, and the earth as iron, and restrain the celestial influences. 'Can man bind the sweet influences of Pleiades? or loose the bonds of Orion?' Job xxxviii. 31. Can any but God forbid the clouds to drop fatness? Surely no. Beloved, drought and scantness of water upon a land, a city, &c., is a judgment of God. It is no small misery to have the streams dried up, when the fire is at our doors:[1] Jer. l. 38, 'A drought is upon her waters; and they shall be dried up: for it is the land of graven images, and they are mad upon their idols:' Jer. li. 35, 36, 'The violence done to me and to my flesh be upon Babylon, shall the inhabitant of Zion say; and my blood upon the inhabitants of Chaldea, shall Jerusalem say. Therefore thus saith the Lord; Behold, I will plead my cause, and take vengeance for thee; and I will dry up her sea, and make her springs dry.' Now mark what follows: ver. 37, 'And Babylon shall become heaps, a dwelling-place for dragons, an astonishment, and an hissing, without an inhabitant.' When God comes to plead the cause of Zion against Babylon, not by words but by deeds, by blows, by terrible judgments—when he comes to burn up the inhabitants of Babylon, and to turn them out of house and home, he first dries up her sea, and makes her springs dry: Haggai i. 11, 'And I called for a drought upon the land, and upon the mountains, and upon the corn, and upon the new wine, and upon the oil, and upon that which the ground bringeth forth, and upon men, and upon cattle, and upon all the labour of the hands.' It is God that brings droughts and rain, and that opens and stops the clouds, the bottles of heaven, at his pleasure: Jer. xiv. 2–4, 'Judah mourneth, and the gates thereof languish; they are black unto the ground; and the cry of Jerusalem is gone up. And their nobles have sent their little ones to the waters: they came to the pits, and found no water; they returned with their vessels empty: they were ashamed and confounded, they covered their heads'—they muffled up their heads and faces as a token of great

[1] Doubtless there was much wrath in this, that the water-house which served much of the city with water should be burnt down in a few hours after the fire first began. To want a proper remedy when we are under a growing misery is no small calamity. It is sad with the people that have nothing to quench the furious flames but their own tears and blood. To be stripped of water when God strikes a people with that tremendous judgment of fire is wrath to the utmost.

grief and sorrow, as close mourners do with us. 'Because the ground is chapt, for there was no rain in the earth, the plowmen were ashamed, they covered their heads.' There are many calamities that are brought upon us by human means, that are also avoidable by human helps; but drought and want of water, especially when a devouring fire is kindled in the midst of a people, is no small judgment of heaven upon that people. To want water when the house is all in flames, is a high evidence of divine displeasure. We had no rain a long time before the fire, and the springs were low, and the waterworks at the Bridge-foot, which carried water into that part of the city that was first in flames, were burnt down the first day of the fire. And was there not wrath from heaven in this? Surely yes. Look, as it is a choice mercy to have God at hand, and the creatures at hand, when we most need them, so it is a sore judgment to have God at a distance, and the creatures remote, when they should be of most service and use unto us. Certainly God's arming of the elements of fire against us, and his denying at the same time water unto us, cannot but be a signal of his great indignation against us; and therefore it highly concerns us to see the hand of the Lord in that late lamentable fire that has been amongst us. But,

[2.] Secondly, Consider *the suddenness and unexpectedness of this judgment.* Who among all the burnt citizens did ever expect to see London laid in ashes in four days' time? God's judgments many times seize upon men's persons, houses, and estates, as the soldiers did Archimedes whilst he was busy in drawing lines in the dust. Isa. lxiv. 3, 'When thou didst terrible things which we looked not for.' When the citizens saw London in flames, they might truly have said, This is a terrible thing, which we looked not for; we were minding our business, our shops, our trades, our profits, our pleasures, our delights; we were studying, and plotting, and contriving how to make ourselves and our children great and rich, and high and honourable in the earth, and it never entered into our thoughts that the destruction of London by fire was so near at hand as now we have found it to be. Isa. xlvii. 7-9, 11, 'Thou saidst, I shall be a lady for ever: so that thou didst not lay these things to thy heart,' (which things were the judgments of God that were threatened:) 'neither didst remember the latter end of it. Therefore hear now this, thou that art given to pleasures, that dwellest carelessly; that sayest in thine heart, I am, and none else besides me; I shall not sit as a widow, neither shall I know the loss of children: but these two things shall come to thee in a moment, in one day, the loss of children and widowhood: they shall come upon thee in their perfection. Evil shall come upon thee; and thou shalt not know from whence it riseth: and mischief shall fall upon thee; thou shalt not be able to put it off: and desolation shall come upon thee suddenly, which thou shalt not know.'[1] Was not London the lady-city of our land? Did the inhabitants of London lay those judgments of God to heart that they either felt or feared? Did London remember her latter end? Were not most of the inhabitants of London given to sinful pleasures and delights? Did they not

[1] Babylon bore itself bold upon the seventy years' provision laid up beforehand to stand out a siege, and upon its strength and riches, but for all this it was taken by Cyrus.

live carelessly and securely? Were they ever so secure and inapprehensive of their danger than at this very time when the flames broke forth in the midst of them? They had newly escaped the most sweeping plague that ever was in the city and suburbs, but instead of finding out the plague of their hearts, and mourning over the plague of their hearts, and repenting of the evil of their doings, and returning to the Most High, 1 Kings viii. 37, 38; Isa. ix. 13–15; Jer. viii. 6, they returned to their sins and their trades together, from both which for a time the plague had frighted them, concluding in themselves that surely the bitterness of death was past, 1 Sam. xv. 32. They thought that the worst was past, and that after so dreadful a storm they should have a blessed calm; and dreamed of nothing but peace, and quiet, and safety, and trade, striving with all their might to make up those losses that they had sustained by the pestilence. They having escaped the grave when so many score thousands were carried to their long homes, were very secure; they never thought that the city, which had been so lately infected by a contagious plague, was so near being buried in its own ruins; they never imagined that the whole city should be put in flames to purge that air that their sins had infected.[1] And therefore no wonder if desolation came upon them suddenly, in a moment, in one day. No marvel that so great a fire was kindled in the very heart of the city, and they not see the hand that kindled it, nor have no hands nor hearts to quench it. Judgments are never so near as when men are most secure, 1 Thes. v. 3. The old world was very secure until the very day that Noah entered into the ark: Luke xvii. 27, 'They did eat, they drank, they married wives, they were given in marriage, until the day that Noah entered into the ark, and the flood came and destroyed them all.' Luther observeth that it was in the spring that the flood came, when everything was in its prime and pride, and nothing less looked for than a flood. They neither believed nor regarded Noah's preaching, nor his preparations for his own and his children's security, but merrily passed without intermission from eating to drinking, and from drinking to marriage, till the very day that the flood came and swept them all away. Their destruction was foretold them to a day, but they were drowned in security, and would take no notice of Noah's predictions nor their own peril. They had made their guts their god; they had buried their wits in their guts, and their brains in their bellies, and so were neither awakened nor bettered by anything that either Noah said or did; and so they perished suddenly and unexpectedly. So Sodom was very secure till the very day that fire and brimstone was rained from heaven about their ears, ver. 28, 29. 'Likewise also as it was in the days of Lot, they did eat, they drank, they bought, they sold, they planted, they builded; but the same day that Lot went out of Sodom, it rained fire and brimstone from heaven and destroyed them all,' Gen. xix. 23, 24. Lot was no sooner taken out of Sodom, but Sodom was as soon taken out of the

[1] In the month of September the plague was at the highest, and in the same month the flames of London were at highest. Doubtless there is some mystery in this sad providence. London was judgment-proof, plague-proof in September '65, and therefore God set London in flames in September '66.

world. Their fair sunshine morning had a foul dismal evening; they had a handsel of hell on this side hell. They passed through fire and brimstone here to an eternal fire in hell, as Jude speaks, ver. 7. So the Jews were deadly secure before the first and latter destruction both of their city and country by sword and fire. All the world could not persuade them that their temple and city should be laid in ashes, till the Chaldeans at one time, and the Romans at another, had set both their city and temple in a flame before their eyes. Compare these together: Amos vi. 3; Lam. iv. 11, 12; Ezek. xii. 22, 27, 28; Hab. i. 7; Luke ii. 19, 41–44. Now mark, sudden and unexpected judgments do always carry a great deal of the anger and severity of God in them: Deut. vii. 4, 'So will the anger of the Lord be kindled against you, and destroy thee suddenly.' God being greatly angry with Jerusalem, Isa. xxix. 1–4, he tells her that her judgment should be at an instant, suddenly, ver. 5. Ps. lxiv. 7, 'But God shall shoot at them with an arrow; suddenly shall they be wounded;' Hab. ii. 7, 'Shall they not rise up suddenly that shall bite thee, and awake that shall vex thee, and thou shalt be for booties unto them?' Prov. vi. 14, 15, 'Frowardness is in his heart; he deviseth mischief continually, he soweth discord. Therefore shall his calamity come suddenly; suddenly shall he be broken without remedy.' Here is a dismal doom; not bruised, but broken—yea, suddenly broken, when they least dream or dread the danger. And this without remedy; there shall be no possibility of piecing them up again, or putting them into a better condition: chap. xxiv. 22, 'Their calamity shall rise suddenly.' When they think that they have made all cock-sure, then ruin and desolation lies at their door. Certainly there are no judgments so dreadful and amazing as those which come most suddenly and unexpectedly upon the sons of men; for these cut off all hope, they hinder the exercise of reason, they cloud men's minds, they distress men's spirits, they mar men's counsels, and they weaken men's courage, and they daunt men's hearts so, that they can neither be serviceable to themselves, nor their friends, nor the public. All this was evidently seen upon the body of the citizens when London was in flames. The more eminent cause have we to take notice of the hand of the Lord in that late fiery dispensation that has passed upon us. The year 1666, according to the computation of several sober, wise, learned men, should have been the Christian's jubilee. Many men's expectations were high that Rome that year should be laid in ashes; but it never entered into any of our hearts or thoughts that this very year London should be laid in ashes. O unexpected blow! Berlin in Germany [Scultet. Annal.] who in the pulpit charged the apostle Paul with a lie, was suddenly smitten with an apoplexy, while the words were yet in his mouth, and fell down dead in the place. The parson of Chrondall (?) in Kent, having got a pardon from Cardinal Pole, as the pope's substitute in that work, the next Lord's day in his own parish presses all his people to do the like, with this argument, that he was now so free from all his sins, that he could die presently; and God presently so struck him in his pulpit, that he died, and never spoke more. As Bibulus, a Roman general, was riding in triumph in all his glory, a tile fell from the house in the street, and knocked out his brains. Otho the emperor slew himself with his own hands, but slept so soundly the night before, that the grooms of his chamber heard him snort. And Plutarch reporteth the like of Cato. Lepidus and Aufidius stumbled at the very threshold of the senate and died; the blow came in a cloud from heaven. Sophocles died suddenly by excessive joy, and Homer by immoderate grief. Mr Perkins speaks of one who, when it thundered, scoffingly said it was nothing but *Tom Tumbril* a-hooping his tubs, and presently he was struck dead with a thunderbolt. Olympus, the Arian heretic, bathing himself, uttered sad words against the blessed Trinity, but suddenly a threefold thunderbolt struck him dead in the same place.[1] Attilus, king of the Huns, proudly gave out that the stars fell before him, and the earth trembled at his presence, and how he would be the scourge of all nations; but soon after he died by a flux of blood breaking out of his mouth, which choked him on his wedding-day. King Henry the Second of France, upon the marriage of his sister with the king of Spain, was so puffed up, that he called himself by a new title, *Tres heureux roi*, The thrice happy king; but, to confute him, in solemnising that marriage, he was slain at tilt by the captain of his guard, though against his will, but not without God's determinate counsel, in the very beginning of his supposed happiness. Now every one that is a man either of reason or religion, will certainly say that in these sudden judgments that befell these persons there was the angry and displeased hand of God to be seen. Oh how much more, then, should we see the angry and displeased hand of the Lord in that sudden, dreadful fire, that has turned our once renowned city into a ruinous heap, Jer. viii. 15. In this year 1666 many thought that there had been many great and glorious things in the womb of providence that would have been now brought forth, but they were mistaken; for unexpectedly London is laid in ashes. But,

[3.] Thirdly, Consider *the force, violence, vehemency, and irresistibleness of it, despising and triumphing over all those weak endeavours that were used.*[2] This fire broke forth with that violence, and raged with that fury, and appeared in that dreadfulness, and spread itself with that dismalness, and continued for so long a time with that irresistibleness, that discouraged hearts and weak hands, with their buckets, engines, ladders, hooks, opening of pipes, and sweeping of channels, could give no check to it. This fire broke in upon the inhabitants like an arm of the sea, and roared and raged like a bear robbed of her whelps, until it had laid our glory in ashes. When the fire was here and there a little allayed or beaten down, or put to a stand, how soon did it recover its force and violence, and make the more furious onsets, burning down water-houses, engines, churches, and the more strong, pleasant, and stately houses, nothing being able to stand before its rage! How soon did the flames mount up to the tops of the highest houses,

[1] Beard's Theatre of God's Judgments, lib. i. cap. 9, p. 64.

[2] Many authors speak much of the Greek fire, some of which burned the Saracen's fleet, to be of such force, that the ancients accounted no other means would extinguish it but vinegar. And certainly several fires that have been enkindled by Romish Jesuits have not been less furious. Stone walls and brick walls, and those noble and strong pieces of architecture, were all but fuel to those furious flames.

and as soon descend down to the bottom of the lowest vaults and cellars! How did they march along, Jehu-like, on both sides of the streets, with such a roaring, dreadful, and astonishing noise, as never was heard in the city of London before! London's sins were now so great, and God's wrath was now so hot, that there was no quenching of the furious flames. The decree for the burning of London was now gone forth, and none could reverse it. The time of London's fall was now come. The fire had now received its commission under the broad seal of heaven, to burn down the city and to turn it into a ruinous heap; and therefore it defied and contemned all remedies, and scorned to be suppressed by human attempts. Whoever kindled this fire, God blew the coal; and therefore no arts, counsels, or endeavours of men were able to quench it. If God commission the sword to walk abroad, and to glut itself with blood, who can command it into the scabbard again? No art, power, or policy can cause that sword to lie still that God has drawn in the nations round us, until it hath accomplished the ends for which he has drawn it. As to our present case, when I weigh things in the balance of right reason, I cannot but be of opinion that, had magistrates and people vigorously and conscientiously discharged their duties, much of London, by the blessing of God upon their endeavours, that is now ruined, might happily have been preserved. When in a storm, the ship and all the vast treasure that is in it, is in danger to be lost, it is sad to see every officer and mariner to mind more, and endeavour more the preservation of their chests, cabins, and particular interests, than the preservation of the ship, and the vast treasure that is in it. Now this was just our case. Cicero in his time laughed at the folly of those men, who conceited that their fish-ponds and places of pleasure should be safe when the commonwealth was lost.[1] And we may well mourn over the folly and vanity of those men who were so amazed, confounded, distracted, besotted and infatuated, if not worse, as not to improve all heads, hands, hearts, counsels, and offers that were made for the preservation of the city. This is, and this must be for a lamentation, that in the midst of public dangers, all ranks and sorts of men should take more care for the preservation of their trifling fardels — for so is any particular man's estate, though never so great, when compared with the riches of a rich, trading, populous city—than they do for the preservation of the public good. That there might have been rational and probable anticipations of those dreadful conflagrating progresses, I suppose all sober men will grant: that these were either hid from some men's eyes, and seen by others and not improved, was London's woe. When London was almost destroyed, then some began to blow up some houses for the preservation of that little that was left, and God blessed their endeavours; but had some had encouragement, who long before were ready for that work, and who offered themselves in the case, it is very probable that a great part of London might have been preserved. But what shall I say, divine justice does as eminently sparkle and shine in the shutting of men's eyes, and in the stopping of men's ears, and in the hardening men's hearts against the visible and probable

[1] Lib. i. Ep. 15, ad Atticum.

means of their outward preservation, as in any one thing. This we must seriously consider, and then lay our hands upon our mouths, and be silent before the Lord. The force and violence of this fire was so great, that many that removed their goods once, twice, thrice, yea, and some oftener, yet lost all at last. The fire followed them so close from place to place, that some saved but little, and others lost all. Now how well does it become us, in the rage and fury of the flames, to see the hand of the Lord, and to bow before him, as this fire being like time, which devours all before it.[1] Jerusalem was the glory and beauty of the whole earth; and the temple was one of the world's wonders; but when Titus Vespasian's soldiers had set it on fire, it burnt with that rage and fury that all the industry and skill that ever could be used, imagined, or thought on, could not quench it, though Titus would gladly have preserved it as a matchless monument. They threw both the water and the blood of the slain into it, but it burnt with that violence that nothing could extinguish it. King Herod, for eight years together, before the ruin of it, had employed ten thousand men at work to beautify it; but when once it was on fire, it burnt with that fierceness, that there was no preserving of it, the decree of heaven being gone out against it, &c. But,

[4.] Fourthly, Consider *the swiftness of it.* It flew upon the wings of the wind, that it might the sooner come to its journey's end. It ran along like the fire and hail in Egypt, destroying and consuming all before it, Ps. xviii. 10; Exod. ix. 23, 24. The apostle James speaks of fierce winds, James iii. 6, 2. The wind was so boisterous, that it scattered and carried the fire, the flames, sometimes one way, sometimes another, in despite of all the restraints, resistances, and limits that the amazed citizens could have set to it. I shall not trouble you with the various notions of philosophers concerning the wind, partly because they will do no service in the present case, and partly because our work is to look higher than all natural causes.[2] All that either is or can be said of the wind, I suppose, may be thus summed up: that it is a creature that may be (1.) Felt; (2.) Heard; and (3.) Little understood. Very wonderful is the rise of the winds; when it is so calm and still upon the seas, that scarce a breath of air is perceivable, upon a sudden the wind is here and there, and everywhere: Eccles. i. 6, 'The wind goeth toward the south, and turneth about unto the north: it whirleth about continually; and the wind returneth again according to his circuits.' Ps. cxxxv. 7, 'He bringeth the wind out of his treasuries.' But what those treasuries are, and where they are, no man on earth can certainly tell us. The wind is one of the great wonders of the Lord, in which, and by which the Lord's name is wonderfully magnified: Ps. cvii. 24, 25, 'They that go down to the sea, see the works of the Lord, and his wonders in the deep.' What wonders? 'He commandeth and raiseth the stormy wind.' Although something may be known of this creature in the

[1] Ungrammatical, but the meaning plain.—G.

[2] The winds are the fan of nature to cool and purge the air. But at this time God brought the winds out of his treasury, to scatter the flames of his indignation, that so London might become a desolation.

natural causes of it; yet it is a wonder above all that we can know of it, John iii. 8. What the wind is, and from whence it comes, and whither it goes, none can tell.

God is the great generalissimo and sovereign commander of the winds, so that a blast of wind cannot pass without his leave, licence, and cognizance: Jonah i. 4, 'But the Lord sent a great wind into the sea, and there was a mighty tempest in the sea.' The winds are God's posts[1]—they are sometimes messengers of mercy, and sometimes messengers of wrath: Ps. cxlvii. 18, 'He causeth his wind to blow.'[2] The winds are at God's command, to come and go, and go and come at his pleasure. When there is nothing but a sweet, smooth, and silver calm on the seas, if God does but give forth a word of command, how soon are they thrown into hills and mountains, and how dreadfully do the waves dash and clash one against another! Ps. cxlviii. 8, 'Fire and hail, snow and vapours, stormy wind fulfilling his word.' Sometimes the word that God has to fulfil is a saving word, and sometimes it is a destroying word, a drowning word, a sinking word. Now according to the word that God has to fulfil, so do the winds always blow. The Lord hath the winds at command, to be his executioners and administrators, either of destruction or preservation. What are stormy winds at sea or ashore but the utterings of God's voice in wrath and judgment? Sometimes God is said to 'fly upon the wings of the wind,' Ps. xviii. 10; and sometimes he is said to 'ride upon the wings of the wind,' 2 Sam. xxii. 11; and sometimes he is said to 'walk upon the wings of the wind,' Ps. civ. 3. Now these things are spoken after the manner of men, to shew that the winds are continually acted and governed by a divine power. God flies upon the wings of the tempestuous winds, speedily to execute the vengeance written: and he rides and walks upon the wings of the more soft, easy, and gentle gales of the wind, that he may make good the mercies promised, Exod. xv. 10, and xiv. 21. No creatures in heaven or on earth hath the winds at command but God solely and properly. Every wind that blows has a commission under the great seal of heaven to bear it out in all it does. If the winds should be examined, questioned, and required to give in a full and exact account of the many thousand mariners that they have drowned, and of the many thousand ships that they have spoiled and destroyed, and of the many ten thousand houses that they have blown down at some times, and of the many score thousand houses that, when the fire has been kindled, they have helped to consume and reduce to ashes at other times, they would shew you the hand and seal of heaven for all they have done. The sovereignty and greatness of God doth eminently shine and sparkle in this, that the winds are originally in his hand. 'He gathereth the wind in his fist,' Prov. xxx. 4. God keeps the royalty of all the creatures in his own hand. The winds are greater or lesser, of a longer or shorter continuance, according to the will and pleasure of the great God, and not according to the workings of second causes. The more civilised heathens had this notion amongst them, 'that the winds were under the dominion of one supreme power,' and therefore, dividing the world

[1] 'Runners.'—G.

[2] Mat. viii. 27; Num. xi. 31; Isa. xxvii. 8; Gen. viii.; Exod. i. 10, and xiii.

among sundry gods, they gave the honour of the winds to Æolus, whom they ignorantly suppose had a power to lock them fast, or to let them loose at his pleasure. These poor besotted heathens thought that their feigned god Æolus had power to govern and bridle the winds, and to turn them this way and that way, as a man governs the chariot in which he rideth. And many ignorant atheistical wretches, when the winds are boisterous and violent, they are ready to say, that there is conjuring abroad, and that the devil is at work; but they must know that the devil has not power of himself to raise one blast of wind, no, nor so much wind as will stir a feather. I know that the devil is 'the prince of the power of the air,' Eph. ii. 2, and that when God will give him leave to play *rex* for ends best known to himself, he can then raise such storms and tempests, both at sea and ashore, as shall dash the stoutest ships in pieces, and remove mountains, and make the most glorious cities in the world a ruinous heap; he can easily and quickly raze the foundations of the fairest, the richest, the strongest, and the renownest, and the oldest buildings in the world, if God will but permit him, Job i. 19. But without divine permission, no angel in heaven, no devil in hell, nor no witch on earth, can raise or continue the winds one moment. Satan's power over the wind is only a derivative power, a permissive power; but the Lord's power over the wind is a supreme power, an absolute power, an independent power. Now, oh what eminent cause have we to see the hand of the Lord in that boisterous wind that continued four days and nights, and that carried the fire to all points of the compass, to all parts of the city, if I may so speak, till our glorious city was laid in ashes! Oh how great were the sins of that people! Oh how great was the anger of that God, who united two of the most dreadfullest elements, fire and wind, to destroy our city, and lay our glory in the dust! When the Romans put fire to the walls of Jerusalem, at first the north wind blew it furiously upon the Romans themselves, but suddenly the wind changing and blowing from the south, as it were by God's providence, saith my author,[1] it turned the fire again upon the wall, and so all was consumed and turned into ashes. And this Eleazar, in his oration to his companions, takes special notice of, where he saith, 'Neither hath our castle, by nature inexpugnable, anything profited us to our preservation; but we having store of victuals and armour, and all other necessaries, have lost all hope of safety, God himself openly taking it from us. For the fire that once was carried against our enemies, did not of itself[2] return against us, and unto the wall we built.' Suppose the Romans, or some set on by the conclave of Rome, did at first set our city on fire, by casting their firebrands, for by that means Jerusalem was set on fire, or fire-balls here and there; yet how highly does it concern us, when we consider the furious wind that helped on the fury of the fire, to lay our hands upon our loins, and to say, The Lord is righteous; and that our present ruin is but the product of incensed justice, &c.

When the Lord hath any service for the wind to do, it is presently upon the march, to run and despatch his errands, whether of indignation or of mercy. If the Lord-General of heaven and earth, the great,

[1] Joseph. Antiq., lib. vii. cap. 28. [2] 'But by God's appointment.'—G.

the supreme commander of the winds, will have them to destroy a people, and to help on the destruction of their houses, when the flames are kindled, or to break and dash in pieces their ships at sea, it shall soon be accomplished: 2 Chron. xx. 37, 'Because thou hast joined thyself with Ahaziah, the Lord hath broken thy works. And the ships were broken, that they were not able to go to Tarshish.' Boisterous winds at sea or ashore are the arrows of God shot out of the bended bow of his displeasure; they are one of the lower tier of his indignation that is fired upon the children of men: Nahum i. 3, 'The Lord hath his way in the whirlwind and in the storm, and in the clouds are the dust of his feet.' The great Spanish Armada that came to invade our land in [15]88, were broken and scattered by the winds: so that their dice-games were frustrated, and they sent into the bottom of the sea, if not into a worse bottom. And when Charles V. had besieged Algiers, that pen of thieves, both by sea and by land, and had almost taken it, by two terrible tempests the greatest part of his great fleet were destroyed, as they did lie in the harbour at anchor.[1] Ships, houses, trees, steeples, rocks, mountains, monuments cannot stand before a tempestuous wind: 1 Kings xix. 11, 'A great strong wind rent the mountains, and brake in pieces the rocks.' What more strong than rocks and mountains? and yet they were too weak to stand before the strength of a tempestuous wind. Oh the terrible execution that God doth many times by the winds both at sea and ashore! Ps. xviii. 7, 'The earth shook and trembled; the foundations of the hills moved and were shaken, because he was wroth;' ver. 8, 'There went up a smoke out of his nostrils, and fire out of his mouth devoured: coals were kindled by it;' ver. 10, 'He rode upon a cherub, and did fly; yea, he did fly upon the wings of the wind;' ver. 12, 'His thick clouds passed; hailstones and coals of fire;' ver. 13, 'The Lord also thundered in the heavens, and the Highest gave his voice; hailstones and coals of fire,' &c. The fire in London carried the noise of a whirlwind in it: and that made it so formidable and terrible to all that beheld it, especially those that looked upon it as a fruit of God's displeasure. The wind was commissionated by God to join issue with the raging fire, to lay the city desolate. I think the like dreadful instance cannot be given in any age of the world. We cannot say of the wind that blew when London was in flames, that God was not in the wind, as it is said in that 1 Kings xix. 11. For assuredly, if ever God was in any wind, he was remarkably in this wind. Witness the dismal effects of it amongst us to this very day! Had God been pleased to have hindered the conjunction of these two elements, much of London might have been standing which now lies buried in its own ruins. I grant that it is probable enough that those that did so long before prophesy and predict the burning of London, before it was laid in ashes, were the prime contrivers and furtherers of the firing of it: but yet when they had kindled the fire, that God by the bellows of heaven should so blow upon it as to make it spread, and turn, like the flaming sword in paradise, every way, Gen. iii. 24, till by its force and fury it had destroyed above two third parts in the midst of the city, as the phrase is, Ezek. v. 2, 'This is, and this must be for a sore

[1] Val. Max. Christian., p. 132.

lamentation.' God, who holds the winds in his fist, who is the true Æolus, could either have locked them up in his treasures, or have commanded them to be still; or else have turned them to have been a defence to the city, Ps. xiii. 5; Mark iv. 39. God, who holds the bottles of heaven in his hand, Gen. vii. 11, could easily have unstopped them; he could with a word of his mouth have opened the windows of heaven, and have poured down such an abundance of rain upon the city, as would quickly have quenched the violence of the flames, and so have made the conquest of the fire more easy. But the Lord was angry, and the decree was gone out that London should be burnt; and who could prevent it?

To close up this particular, consider much of the wisdom, power, and justice of God shines in the variety of the motions of the wind: Eccles. i. 6, 'The wind goeth toward the south, and turneth about unto the north; it whirleth about continually, and the wind returneth again according to his circuits.' The wind hath its various circuits appointed by God. When the wind blows southward, northward, westward, or eastward, it blows according to the orders that are issued out from the court of heaven. Sometimes the wind begins to blow at one point of the compass, and in a short time whirls about to every point of the compass, till it comes again to the same point where it blew at the first; yet in all this they observe their circuits, and run their compass, according to the divine appointment. As the sun, so the winds have their courses ordered out by the wise providence of God. Divine wisdom much sparkles and shines in the circuits of the winds; which the Lord brings out of his treasure, and makes them serviceable, sometimes to one part of the world, and at other times to other parts of the world. It is the great God that appoints where the winds shall blow, Exod. xiv. 24; Jonah i. 4, and iv. 8, and when the winds shall blow, and how long the winds shall blow, and with what force and violence the winds shall blow. The winds in some parts of the world have a very regular and uniform motion, in some months of the year blowing constantly out of one quarter, and in others out of another. In some places of the world where I have been, the motions of the wind are steady and constant, which mariners call their trade-wind. Now by these stated or settled winds, divine providence does very greatly serve the interest of the children of men. But now in other parts of the world, the winds are as changeable as men's minds. The laws that God lays upon the winds in most parts of the world are not like the laws of the Medes and Persians, 'which alter not,' Dan. vi. 8. One day God lays a law upon the winds to blow full east, the next day to blow full west, the third to blow full south, the fourth to blow full north; yea, in several parts of the world I have known the winds to change their motions several times in a day. Now in all these various motions of the winds, the providence of God is at work for the good of mankind. That there is a dreadful storm in one place, and at the same time a sweet calm in another,—that a tempestuous storm should destroy and dash in pieces one fleet, and that at the same instant, and in one and the same sea, a prosperous gale should blow another fleet into a safe harbour,—that some at sea should have a stiff gale of wind, and others within sight of them should lie becalmed,—that some ships should come into harbour top and top-gallant, and that others should sink down at the same harbour's mouth before they should be able to get in, is all from the decree of God, and that law that he has laid upon the winds. That terrible tempestuous wind that affrighted the disciples, and that put them not only to their wits' end, but also to their faith's end, was allayed by a word of Christ's mouth: Mat. viii. 26, 'He arose and rebuked the winds and the sea, and there was a great calm.' O sirs! when London was in flames, and when the winds were high and went their circuits, roaring and making a most hideous noise, how easy a thing had it been with Jesus by a word of his mouth to have allayed them! but he was more angry with us than he was with his disciples who were in danger of drowning, or else he would as certainly have saved our city from burning by rebuking the winds and the flames, as he did his disciples from drowning by rebuking the winds and the seas. I have been the longer upon this fourth particular, that you may the more easily run and read the anger of the Lord in those furious flames, and in that violent wind that has laid our city desolate. It is true astrologers ascribe the motions of the winds to special planets. The east wind they ascribe to the sun, the west wind to the moon, the south wind to Mars, and the north wind to Jupiter; but those that are wise in heart, by what I have said concerning the winds, may safely and groundedly conclude that God alone hath the supreme power of the winds in his own hand, and that he alone orders, directs, and commands all the motions of the winds. And therefore let us look to that terrible hand of the Lord that was lifted up in that fierce wind, that did so exceedingly contribute to the turning of our city into a ruinous heap. But,

[5.] Fifthly, Consider *the extensiveness of it.*[1] How did this dreadful fire spread itself, both with and against the wind, till it had gained so great a force as that it despised all men's attempts! It quickly spread itself from the east to the west, to the destruction of houses of state, of trade, of public magistracy, besides mines of charity. It spread itself with that violence that it soon crumbled into ashes our most stately habitations, halls, chapels, churches, and famous monuments. Those magnificent structures of the city that formerly had put stops and given checks to the furious flames, falls now like stubble before the violence of a spreading fire. This fire like an arm of the sea, or like a land-flood, broke in suddenly upon us, and soon spread itself all manner of ways amongst us. It ran from place to place like the fire and hail in Egypt, Exod. ix. 23: now it was in this street, and anon in that; now this steeple is on fire, and then that; now this place of judicature is laid in ashes, and then that; now this hall is in flames, and then that; now this parish is burnt down to the ground, and then that; now this ward is turned into a ruinous heap, and then that; now this quarter of the city is level with the ground, and then that; now this gate of the city is demolished and consumed, and then that. 'The adversary hath spread out his hand upon all her pleasant things,' saith the prophet lamentingly, Lam. i. 10; and we may say sighingly, the fire hath spread out its hand upon all our pleasant

[1] Within the walls of the city there were eighty-one parishes consumed. For every hour the fire lasted, there was a whole parish consumed.

things, upon all our pleasant houses, shops, trades, gardens, walks, temples, &c. The plague, the year before, did so rage and spread, that it emptied many thousand houses of persons; and now this dreadful fire hath so spread itself that it has not left houses enough for many thousands of persons to dwell in, there being more than thirteen thousand houses destroyed by the furious flames. Sin is of a spreading nature, and accordingly it had spread itself over all parts of the city; and therefore the Lord, who delights to suit his judgments to men's sins, sent a spreading fire in the midst of us. The merciless flames spreading themselves every way, in four days' time laid the main of our once glorious city in ashes: a judgment so remarkable and past precedent, that he that will not see the hand of the Lord in it, may well be reckoned amongst the worst of atheists. But,

[6.] Sixthly, Consider *the impartiality of it.* It spared neither sinners nor saints, young nor old, rich nor poor, honourable nor base, bond nor free, male nor female, buyer nor seller, borrower nor lender. God making good that word, Isa. xxiv. 1, 2, 'Behold, the Lord maketh the earth empty, and maketh it waste, and turneth it upside down, and scattereth abroad the inhabitants thereof. And it shall be as with the people, so with the priest,'—or with the prince, for the Hebrew word signifies both;—'as with the servant, so with his master; as with the maid, so with the mistress; as with the buyer, so with the seller; as with the lender, so with the borrower; as with the taker of usury, so with the giver of usury to him.' In the day of the Lord's wrath that was lately upon us, all orders, ranks, and degrees of men suffered alike, and were abased alike; the furious flames made no difference, they put no distinction between the russet coat and the scarlet gown, the leathern jacket and the gold chain, the merchant and the tradesman, the landlord and the tenant, the giver and the receiver.

'There is no difference: fire hath made
Equal the sceptre and the spade.'

Ezek. xx. 47, 'Behold, I will kindle a fire in thee, and it shall devour every green tree in thee, and every dry tree: the flaming flame shall not be quenched, and all faces from the south to the north shall be burnt therein.' I have, in the former part of this treatise, given some light into these words. The fire, the flames in the text, takes hold of all sorts of people, rich and poor, lord and lad, high and low, great and small, strong and weak, wise and foolish, learned and ignorant, commanders and soldiers, rulers and ruled. So did the late lamentable fire in London take hold of all sorts and degrees of men, as the citizens have found by sad experience. The fire, like the duke of Parma's sword, knew no difference betwixt robes and rags, betwixt prince and peasant, betwixt honourable and vile, betwixt the righteous and the wicked, the clean and the unclean, betwixt him that sacrificed and him that sacrificed not, betwixt him that sweareth and him that feareth an oath, Eccles. ix. 1, 2. The judgment was universal, the blow reached us all, the flames brake into every man's house; such a dreadful, impartial, universal fire, eyes never saw before, nor ears never heard of before, nor tongues never discoursed of before, nor pens never writ of before. Beloved, you know that it is our duty to take serious notice of the hand of the Lord in the least judgment, and in every particular judgment. Oh how much more then does it highly concern us to take serious notice of the hand of the Lord that has been lifted up against us, in that late dreadful, impartial, universal fire, that has burnt us all out of our habitations, and laid our city desolate! But,

[7.] Seventhly, Consider *the greatness of it, the destructiveness of it.* Oh the many thousand families that were destroyed and impoverished in four days' time! Of many it might have been said the day before the fire, who so rich as these? and the very next day it might have been said of the same persons, who so poor as these? as poor as Job; yea, poor to a proverb: Jer. xxi. 13, 14, 'Behold, I am against thee, O inhabitant of the valley, and rock of the plain, saith the Lord; which say, Who shall come down against us? or who shall enter into our habitations? But I will punish you according to the fruit of your doings, saith the Lord: and I will kindle a fire in the forest thereof, and it shall devour all things round about it.'[1] Some by the forest understand the fair and sumptuous buildings in Jerusalem, that were built with wood that was hewn out of the forest of Lebanon, and stood as thick as trees in the forest. Others by the forest understand the whole city of Jerusalem with the country round about it, that was as full of people as a forest is full of trees. Others by forest understand the house of the Lord, and the king's house, and the houses of the great princes, which were built with excellent matter from the wood of Lebanon. Jerusalem was so strongly defended by nature that they thought themselves invincible, as once the Jebusites did, 2 Sam. v. 6: they were so confident of the strength of their city, that they scorned the proudest and the strongest enemies about them. But sin had brought them low in the eye of God, so that he could see nothing eminent or excellent among them; and therefore the Lord resolves by the Chaldeans to fire their magnificent buildings in which they gloried, and to turn their strong and stately city into a ruinous heap. Though Jerusalem stood in a vale, and was environed with mountains, yet the upper part of it stood high, as it were upon a rocky rising hill, Ps. cxxv. 2. Now the citizens of Jerusalem trusted very much in the situation of their city; they did not fear their being besieged, straitened, conquered, or fired; and therefore they say, 'Who shall come down against us? Who shall enter into our habitation? Where is the enemy that has courage or confidence enough to assault our city, or to enter into our habitations?' but God tells them that they were as barren of good fruit as the trees of the forest were barren of good fruit; and therefore he was resolved by the hand of the Chaldeans to hew them down, and to fire their most stately structure, and to turn their glorious city, in which they greatly trusted and gloried, into a ruinous heap. All which accordingly was done, not long after, by Nebuzar-adan and his army; as you may see in Jer. lii. 12–15. How often hath the citizens of London been alarmed with the cry of fire; which hath been as often extinguished before they could well

[1] London was the lady-city where the riches of many nations were laid up. I would rather be bound to weep over London, than be bound to sum up the losses of London by this dreadful fire.

know where it was, and how it began! but all former fires were but small fires, but bonfires, to this dreadful fire that has been lately amongst us.

In the twentieth year of the reign of William the First,[1] so great a fire happened in London, that from the West gate to the East gate it consumed houses and churches all the way. This was the most grievous fire that ever happened in that city, saith my author. And in the reign of King Henry the First, a long tract of buildings, from West Cheap in London to Aldgate, was consumed with fire. And in King Stephen's reign, there was a fire that began at London Stone, and consumed all unto Aldgate. These have been the most remarkable fires in London. But what were any of these, or all these, to that late dreadful fire that has been amongst us? London in those former times was but a little city, and had but a few men in it, Eccles. ix. 14, in comparison of what it was now. London was then but as a great banqueting-house, to what it was now, Cant. ii. 4. Nor the consumption of London by fire then was nothing proportionable to the consumption of it by fire now. For this late lamentable devouring fire hath laid waste the greatest part of the city of London within the walls by far, and some part of the suburbs also. More than fourscore parishes, and all the houses, churches, chapels, hospitals, and other the great and magnificent buildings of pious or public use, which were within that circuit, are now brought into ashes, and become one ruinous heap. This furious raging fire burnt many stately monuments to powder; it melted the bells in the steeples, it much weakened and shattered the strongest vaults under ground. Oh, what age or nation hath ever seen or felt such a dreadful visitation as this hath been! Nebuzar-adan, general to the king of Babylon, first sets the temple of Jerusalem on fire, and then the king's royal palace on fire, and then by fire he levels all the houses of the great men; yea, and all the houses of Jerusalem are by fire turned into a ruinous heap, according to what the Lord had before foretold by his prophet Jeremiah,[2] chap. lii. 12–14. Now this was a lamentable fire. Some hundred years after the Roman soldiers sacked the city, and set it on fire, and laid it desolate, with their temple, and all their stately buildings and glorious monuments.[3] Three or four towers and the wall that was on the west side they left standing as monuments of the Romans' valour, who had surprised a city so strongly fortified. All the rest of the city they so plained, that they who had not seen it before, would not believe that it had ever been inhabited.[4] Thus was Jerusalem, one of the world's wonders, and a city famous amongst all nations, made desolate by fire, according to the prediction of Christ some years before, Luke xix. 41–44. There was a great fire in Rome in Nero's time; it spread itself with that speed, and burnt with that violence, till of fourteen regions in Rome, there were but four left entire.[5] I know there are some who would make the world believe that this fire began casually,—as many now would persuade us that the late fire in London did,—but I rather join issue with them who conclude that Nero set Rome on fire, and when

[1] Sir Richard Baker's Chronicle, pp. 31, 47.
[2] Jos. Ant., p. 255, A. M. 3356.
[3] Jos. Ant., p. 741, A. M. 4034.
[4] Jos. Ant., p. 745.
[5] Tacit. An. 15.

he had done, he laid it upon the Christians, and thereupon grounded his persecution—as all know that have read the history of those times, [anno 64.] Anno 80, Rome was set on fire by fire from heaven, say some: it burned three days and nights, and consumed the capitol, with many other stately buildings and glorious monuments; it burnt with that irresistible fury, that the historian concludes that it was more than an ordinary fire. And in the time of Commodus the emperor, there happened such a dreadful fire in Rome, as consumed the temple of Peace, and all the most stately houses, princely palaces, glorious structures, and rare monuments that were in the city.

In the reign of Achmat, the eighth emperor of the Turks,[1] about the beginning of November, a great fire arose at Constantinople, wherein almost five hundred shops of wares, with many other fair buildings, were destroyed by fire; so that the harm that was then done by fire was esteemed to amount to above two millions of gold. But alas! what was this fire and loss to the fire of London, and the loss of the citizens in our day?

In Constantinople in A.D. 465, in the beginning of September, there brake forth such a fire by the water-side, as raged with that dread force, and fury, and violence, four days and nights together, that it burnt down the greatest part of the city, the strongest and the stateliest houses being but as dried stubble before it. It bid defiance to all means of resistance; it went on triumphing and scorning all human helps, till it had turned that great and populous city, once counted by some the wonder of the world, into a ruinous heap. This of all fires comes nearest to the late fire of London: but what is the burning of a thousand Romes, and a thousand Constantinoples, or the burning of ten thousand barbarous cities, to the burning of one London, where God was as greatly known, and as dearly loved, and as highly prized, and as purely served, as he was in any one place under the whole heavens? O sirs, it is our duty and our high concernment to see the hand of the Lord, and to acknowledge the hand of the Lord in the least fires: how much more then does it become us to see the hand of the Lord lifted up in that late dreadful fire that has laid our city desolate? But,

[8.] Eighthly, Consider how *all sorts, ranks, and degrees of men were terrified, amused, amazed, astonished, and dispirited in the late dreadful fire that was kindled in the midst of us.* When men should have been a-strengthening of one another's hands, and encouraging of one another's hearts, to pull down and blow up such houses as gave life and strength to the furious flames, how were their hearts in their heels, every one flying before the fire, as men fly before a victorious enemy! What a palsy, what a great trembling had seized upon the heads, hands, and hearts of most citizens, as if they had been under Cain's curse! Most men were unmanned and amazed; and therefore no wonder if the furious flames received no check. In former fires, when magistrates and people had resolved hearts and active hands, how easily, how quickly were those fires quenched![2] But now our rulers'

[1] Knolles' General History of the Turks, p. 1275.

[2] Deut. xxviii. 65; 1 Sam. xiii. 7, 14, 15; Acts i. 12. Why stand ye gazing? Oh the feebleness, the frights, the tremblings, the distractions, that was then in every house, in

minds were darkened and confused, their judgments infatuated, their souls dispirited, and their ears stopped, so that their authority did only accent their misery: and this filled many citizens' hearts with fear, terror, amazement, and discontent. These things being done, the city quickly was undone. Had the care and diligence both of magistrates and people been more for the securing of the public good than it was for securing their own private interest, much of London, by a good hand of providence upon their endeavours, might have been standing, that is now turned into a ruinous heap. Troy was lost by the sloth and carelessness of her inhabitants; and may I not say that much of London was lost by the sloth and carelessness of some, and by the fears, frights, and amazement of others, and by others endeavouring more to secure their own packs and patrimonies than the safety of the whole? When London was in flames, men's courage did flag, and their spirits did fail, the strong helpers stood helpless. Some stood looking on, others stood weeping, and shaking their heads, and wringing their hands, and others walked up and down the streets like so many ghosts: Ps. lxxvi. 5, 'The stout-hearted are spoiled,'—or as the Hebrew runs, 'The stout-hearted have yielded themselves up for a prey;' which the Rabbins thus expound, 'They are spoiled of their understandings and infatuated,'—'and none of the men of might have found their hands;' or as some read the words, 'None of the men of riches,' that is, rich men, 'have found their hands;' or as others carry the words, 'God took away their courage, and their wonted strength failed them.' So when London was in flames, how were high and low, rich and poor, honourable and base, spoiled of their understanding and infatuated! The Lord took away all wisdom, courage, counsel, and strength from them. So Judges xx. 40, 'But when the flames began to arise out of the city with a pillar of smoke, the Benjamites looked behind them, and, behold, the flame of their city ascended up to heaven. And when the men of Israel turned again, the men of Benjamin were amazed; for they saw that evil was come upon them.' These Benjamites were the very picture of our citizens; for when they saw the flame begin to arise out of the city with a pillar of smoke, when they saw the flame of the city ascend up to heaven, oh how amazed and confounded were they! All wisdom, courage, and counsel was taken away, both from magistrate and people, and none of them could find either heads, hands, or hearts to prevent London's desolation, Job xxxiv. 19, 20, 24. In Ps. lxxvi. 12, God is said 'to cut off the spirits of princes;' or as the Hebrew runs, 'He shall slip off the spirits of princes,' as men slip off a bunch of grapes, or a flower between their fingers, easily, suddenly, unexpectedly, as he did by Sennacherib's princes, 1 Kings xix. 36. Princes usually are men of the greatest spirits, and yet sometimes God does dispirit them; he slips off their spirits, as men do a flower, which soon withereth in their hand. How soon did God slip off the spirit of that great, proud, debauched monarch Belshazzar, who, when he was in the midst of his cups, bravery, and jollity, with all his great princes, lords, ladies, and concubines about him, saw a hand writing upon the wall, which did so amaze him and terrify him

every heart. When a ship is sinking, it is sad to see every man run to his cabin, when every one should be at the pumps, or a-stopping of leaks.

that his 'countenance was changed, and his thoughts troubled, and the joints of his loins loosed, and his knees dashed one against another,' Dan. v. 1–6. But you may say, What was the reason that so great a prince should be so greatly astonished? *Ans.* The text tells you, 'he saw a hand.' What hand? even the hand of a man. What! could one hand of a man, saith one,[1] terrify and startle so great a monarch? Had he seen the paws of a lion, or the paws of a bear, or the paws of a dragon, there had been some cause of terror. But what need such a puissant prince fear the hand of a man so much, at whose command and beck a hundred troops of armed horse would presently fly to his assistance? What terrible weapons could that one hand wield or manage? none but a pen, with which it wrote. But will any man, much less a king, be afraid of a writing pen? Had he beheld the three darts of Joab, 2 Sam. xviii. 14, or the fiery flaming sword of the cherub, Gen. iii. 24, brandished directly against him, he had then had some argument of astonishment; but one hand, one pen, one piece of writing which he understood not: this was that which daunted him. Many citizens were as much amazed, astonished, terrified, and startled when they saw London in flames, as Belshazzar was when he saw the hand writing upon the wall. Ahab trembled like a shaken leaf, and so did his grandson Manasseh, he that faced the heavens, and that dared God in the day of his prosperity; when troubles came thick, and his fears rise high, he hides his head among the bushes, Isa. vii. 1, 2; 2 Chron. xxxiii. 11, 12. Such a fear and trembling was upon many citizens when London was in flames. Though Tullius Hostilius, the third king of the Romans, had a great warlike spirit, as Lactantius notes, yet he carried in his bosom two new gods, *Pavorem* and *Pallorem*, fear and paleness, which he could not possibly shake off. Oh the fear that was in the citizens' hearts, and the paleness that was upon the citizens' cheeks, when London was in flames! Now excessive fear fills the heart with all confusion; they strip a man of his reason and understanding, they weaken his hands, and they do so suddenly and totally dispirit and unman a man, that he is not able to encounter with those visible dangers that threaten his utter ruin; and this the poor citizens found by woeful experience when London was in flames.[2] At the sight of this fire, how were the citizens' hearts melted, their hands feeble, their spirits faint, and their knees weak! Oh the horror, the terror, the amazement, the confusion that had now seized upon the spirits of all sorts of citizens! How were the thoughts of men now distracted, their countenances changed, and their hearts overwhelmed! Oh the sad looks, the pale cheeks, the weeping eyes, the smiting of breasts, and the wringing of hands that were now to be seen in every street and in every corner! What a universal consternation did my eyes behold upon the minds of all men in that day of the Lord's wrath! There is no expressing of the sighs, the tears, the fears, the frights, and the amazement of the citizens, who were now compassed about with flames of fire! Oh the cries, the tumults,

[1] Drexellius's School of Patience, p. 150–152.

[2] Till London was laid in ashes, that effectual means of preservation, viz., the blowing up of houses, was either greatly hid or sadly gainsaid. When the disease had killed the patients, then the physicians agreed upon a remedy. When the ladder was turned, then the pardon came.

the hurries, and the hindrances of one another that was now in every street, every one striving, with his pack at his back, to secure what he could from the rage and fury of the flames! Now one cries out, Five pound for a cart, another cries out, Ten pound for a dray; in one street one cries out, Twenty pound for a cart, and another in the next street cries out, Thirty pound for a cart; here one cries out, Forty pound for a cart, and there another cries out, Fifty pound for a cart. Many rich men, that had time enough to have removed their goods, their wares, their commodities, flattered themselves that the fire would not reach their habitations. They thought they should be safe and secure; but when the flames broke in upon them, oh then any money for a cart, a coach, a dray, to save some of their richest and choicest goods! Oh what fear were many parents now in that their children would either be now trod down in the press, or lost in the crowd, or be destroyed by the flames! And what fear were many husbands now in concerning their wives, who were either weak, or sick, or aged, or newly delivered! Words are too weak to express that distraction that all men were under when the fire went on raging and devouring all before it. And this was an evident token to me that the hand of the Lord was eminent in the fire, and that the decree was gone forth that dear London must now fall. But,

[9.] Ninthly, Consider *the time that the fire began.* It began on the Lord's day, being the second of September, about one or two of the clock in the morning. Our fears fell upon us on the Lord's day, Rev. i. 10; on that day that should have been a day of joy and delight unto us, Isa. lviii. 13, 14. On this day our singing was turned into sighing, our rejoicing into mourning, and all our praisings into tremblings. Oh the fears, the frights, the distresses that men were now under! Oh the amazed spirits, the bedewed cheeks, the faint hearts, the feeble knees, the weak hands, and the dejected countenances that were now to be seen everywhere! O sirs! the time when this fatal fire first began was very ominous, it being at a time when most citizens were but newly fallen into a dead sleep, being wearied out in their several employments, several days before, but especially on Saturday, or the last day of the week, that being with very many the most busiest day in all the week. And of all mornings, most citizens did usually lie longest in bed Sabbath-day mornings. Such as used to rise early every morning in the week to gain the meat that perisheth, to make sure and to treasure up for themselves and theirs the things of this world, Ps. cxxvii. 1, 2, and John vi. 27; such commonly made most bold with the Lord's day, and would frequently be in their beds when they should have been either instructing of their families, or at prayers in their closets, or else a-waiting upon the Lord in his public ordinances. Fire in the night is terrible to all, but mostly to such whose spirits and bodies were tired out in the preceding day. Wasting and destroying judgments are sad any day, but saddest when they fall on the Lord's day. For how do they disturb, distress, and distract the thoughts, the minds, the hearts, and the spirits of men! so that they can neither wait on God, nor wrestle with God, nor act for God, nor receive from God, in any of the duties or services of his day. And this the poor citizens found by sad experience, when London was in flames about their ears. Certainly the anger and wrath of God was very high and very hot when he made his day of rest to be a day of labour and disquiet—when his people should have been a-meeting, hearing, reading, praising, praying. For the Lord now to scatter them, and to deliver them, their substance and habitations, as a prey to the devouring fire, what does this speak out but high displeasure? That the fire of God's wrath should begin on the day of his rest and solemn worship, is and must be for a lamentation. In several of those churches where some might not preach, there God himself preached to the parishioners in flames of fire. And such who 'loved darkness rather than light, because their deeds were evil,' John iii. 19, might now see their churches all in a flaming fire. What a terrifying and an amazing sermon did God preach to his people of old in mount Sinai, when the mount burned with fire! Exod. xix. 16–18. And so what terrifying and amazing sermons did God preach to the citizens on his own day, when their temples and their habitations were all in flames! Instead of holy rest, what hurries were there in every street, yea, in the spirits of men! Now instead of taking up of buckets, men in every street take up arms, fearing a worse thing than fire. The jealousies and rumours that fire-balls were thrown into several houses and churches, by such that had no English tongues but outlandish hands, to make the furious flames flame more furiously, were so great, that many were at a stand, and others even at their wits' end. Now relations, friends, and neighbours hastened one another out of their houses, as the angels hastened Lot out of Sodom, Gen. xix. 15–17. Such were the fears and frights and sad apprehensions that had generally seized upon the citizens. Not many Sabbaths before, when men should have been instructing of their families, what bonfires, what ringing of bells, and what joy and rejoicing was there in our streets, for burning the Dutch ships in their harbour, where many English and others were highly concerned as well as the Dutch! Little did they think, who were pleasing and warming themselves at those lesser fires, that the great God would in so short a time after kindle so great a fire in the midst of their streets as should melt their bells, lay their habitations in ashes, and make their streets desolate, so that those that were so jolly before might well take up that sad lamentation of weeping Jeremiah, Lam. ii. 2, 3, 'The Lord hath swallowed up all the habitations of Jacob, and hath not pitied; he hath thrown down in his wrath the strongholds of the daughter of Judah; he hath brought them down to the ground. He burned against Jacob like a flaming fire, which devoureth round about.' May we not soberly guess that there were as many strict observers and sanctifiers of the Lord's day who did turn away their feet from doing their pleasure on God's holy day, and that did call the Sabbath a delight, the holy of the Lord, and honourable, Isa. lviii. 13, within the walls of London, as in a great part of the nation besides? Now for the Lord of the Sabbath to kindle such a devouring fire in such a city, and that on his own day, oh what extraordinary wrath and displeasure does this speak out! When God by his royal law had bound the hands of his people from doing their own works, for him now to fall upon his strange work, and by a flaming, consuming fire to turn a populous city, a pious city, an honourable city, and an ancient city into a ruinous heap, what indignation to this indignation! O sirs! it highly concerns us to take notice of the judgments of the Lord that fall upon us on any day, but especially those that fall upon us on his own day, because they carry with them more than a tincture of God's deep displeasure.

In the Council of Paris,[1] every one labouring to persuade unto a more religious keeping of the Sabbath-day, when they had justly complained that as many other things, so also the observation of the Sabbath was greatly decayed, through the abuse of Christian liberty, in that men too much followed the delights of the world, and their own worldly pleasures, both wicked and dangerous, they further add, 'For many of us have been eyewitnesses, many have intelligence of it by the relation of others, that some men upon this day being about their husbandry have been stricken with thunder, some have been maimed and made lame, some have had their bodies, even bones and all, burned in a moment with visible fire, and have consumed to ashes; and many other judgments of God have been and are daily inflicted upon Sabbath-breakers.'

Stratford-upon-Avon[2] was twice on the same day twelvemonth, being the Lord's day, almost consumed with fire, chiefly for profaning the Lord's day, and contemning his word in the mouth of his faithful minister. Feverton[3] in Devonshire, whose remembrance makes my heart bleed, saith my author, was oftentimes admonished by her godly preachers, that God would bring some heavy judgment on the town for their horrible profanation of the Lord's day, occasioned chiefly by their market on the day following. Not long after his death, on the third of April 1598, God, in less than half an hour, consumed with a sudden and fearful fire the whole town, except only the church, the court-house, and the alms-houses, or a few poor people's dwellings, where a man might have seen four hundred dwelling-houses all at once on fire, and above fifty persons consumed with the flames. And on the fifth of August 1612, fourteen years since the former fire, the whole town was again fired and consumed, except some thirty houses of poor people, with the school-house and alms-houses. Now certainly they must be much left of God, hardened in sin, and blinded by Satan, who do not, nor will not see the dreadful hand of God that is lifted up in his fiery dispensations upon his own day. But,

[10.] Tenthly and lastly, Consider that the burning of London is *a national judgment.*[4] God, in smiting of London, has smitten England round: the stroke of God upon London was a universal stroke. The sore strokes of God, which have lately fallen upon the head city, London, are doubtless designed by heaven for the punishment of the whole body. In the sufferings of London the whole land suffers. For what city, county, or town in England was there that was not one way or other refreshed and advantaged, if not enriched, with the silver

[1] Concil. Paris, lib. i. cap. 50.

[2] The Theatre of God's Judgments, pp. 419, 420. [Misprinted 'Sluon.'—G.]

[3] Query, 'Tiverton'?—G.

[4] When one member in the natural body suffers, all the members of the body suffer: it is so in the politic body, &c. Look, as all rivers run into the sea, and all the lines of the circumference meet in the centre, so did the interests of the most eminent persons in the whole nation meet in London, &c. Now London is laid in ashes, we may write Ichabod upon poor England. By the flames that have been kindled in London God hath spit fire into the face of England.

streams of London that overflowed the land, as the river Nilus doth the land of Egypt? Doubtless there are but few in the land but are more or less concerned in the burning of London. There are many thousands that are highly concerned in their own particulars; there are many thousands concerned upon the account of their inward friends and acquaintance: and who can number up the many score thousands employed in the manufactures of the land, whose whole dependence, under God, was upon London? What lamentation, mourning, and woe is there in all places of the land for the burning of London, especially among poor tradesmen, innkeepers, and others, whose livelihoods depended upon the safety and prosperity of London! Certainly he is no Englishman, but one who writes a Roman hand, and carries about him a Romish heart, who feels not, who trembles not under this universal blow! Many years' labour will not make up the citizens' losses to them. Yea, what below the riches of the Indies will effectually make up every man's losses to him? He shall be an Apollo to me, that can justly sum up the full value of all that have been destroyed by those furious flames, that has turned the best, if not the richest, city in the world into a ruinous heap. Now their loss is a loss to the whole nation; and this the nation already feels, and may yet feel more and more, if God in mercy does not prevent the things that we have cause to fear. It is true, London is the back that is smitten; but what corner is there in all the land that hath not more or less, one way or another, contributed to the burning of London. Not only those that lived in Jerusalem, but also those that came up to Jerusalem, and that traded with Jerusalem, they, even they did by their sins contribute to Jerusalem's ruin. They are under a high mistake that think it was only the sins of the city which brought this sore desolation upon her: doubtless, as far as the judgment extends and reaches, so far the sins extend and reach which have provoked the Lord to make poor London such an astonishing example of his justice. How are the effects of London's ruin already felt and sighed under all the nation over! The blood and spirits which this whole nation hath already lost by this late lamentable fire will not be easily nor suddenly recovered. The burning of London is the herald of God to the whole nation, calling it to repentance and reformation; for the very same sins that have laid London in ashes are rampant in all parts of the nation, as you may easily perceive, if you please but to compare that catalogue that in this book I put into your hands with those sins that are most reigning and raging in all places of the land; by which you may also see that they were not the greatest sinners in England upon whom the fire of London fell, no more than they were the greatest sinners in Jerusalem upon whom the tower of Siloam fell, Luke xiii. 4, 5. That the burning of London is a national judgment, is evident enough to every man that has but half an eye. But if any should doubt of it, or dispute it, the king's proclamation for a general fast on that account puts it beyond all dispute. The words of the proclamation that are proper to my purpose are these, 'A visitation so dreadful,' speaking of the burning of London, 'that scarce any age or nation hath ever seen or felt the like; wherein although the afflicting hand of God fell more immediately upon the inhabitants of this city, and the parts adjacent, yet all men ought to look upon it as a judgment upon the whole nation, and to humble themselves accordingly.' O sirs, you are to see and observe and acknowledge the hand of the Lord in every personal judgment, and in every domestical judgment. Oh how much more then in every national judgment that is inflicted upon us! And thus I have done with those ten considerations, that should not only provoke us, but also prevail with us, to see and acknowledge the hand of the Lord in that late dreadful fire that has laid our city desolate.

Use 2. The second use is a use *of lamentation and mourning.* Is London laid in ashes? Then let us all lament and mourn that London is laid desolate. Shall Christ weep over Jerusalem, Luke xix. 41–44, when it was standing in all its glory, knowing that it would not be long before it was laid even with the ground; and shall not we weep over London, whose glory is now laid in the dust? Who can look upon London as the ancient and noble metropolis of England, and not lament and mourn to see it laid in ashes? It might have been said not long since, 'Walk about Sion,' Ps. xlviii. 12, 13,—walk about London,—'and go round about her; tell the towers thereof. Mark ye well her bulwarks, consider her palaces:' look upon her stately houses, halls, and hospitals, take notice of her shops, and fair warehouses, and Royal Exchange, &c., and lo, the glory of all these things is now buried in a common ruin![1] Oh the incredible change that a devouring fire hath made in four days' time within thy walls, O London! so that now we may [say] lamentingly, Alas, poor London! 'Is this the joyous city whose antiquity is of ancient days?' Isa. xxiii. 7, 8. Is this the crowning city, whose merchants were princes, and whose traffickers were the honourable of the earth? Who can but weep to see how the Lord 'hath made a city an heap, and a ruin of a defenced city, and a palace to be no city'? Isa. xxv. 2. Who can look upon naked steeples, and useless chimneys, and pitiful fragments of ragged walls—who can behold stately structures, and noble halls, and fair houses, and see them all laid in ashes, or turned into a heap of rubbish, without paying some tears as due to the sadness of so dreadful a spectacle? Who can with dry eyes hear London thus speaking out of its ruins: 'Is it nothing to you, all ye that pass by? behold, and see if there be any sorrow like unto my sorrow, which is done unto me, wherewith the Lord hath afflicted me in the day of his fierce anger'? Lam. i. 12. Who can look upon the Lord as making London empty, as laying it waste, as turning it upside down, and as scattering abroad the inhabitants thereof, and not mourn?[2] Isa. xxiv. 1. Beloved, under desolating judgments God does expect and look that his people should lament and mourn: Jer. iv. 7, 8, 'The lion is come up from his thicket, and the destroyer of the Gentiles is on his way; he is gone forth from his place to make thy land desolate; and thy city shall be laid waste, without an inhabitant. For this gird you with

[1] London, the crown of England, hath lost its jewel of wealth and beauty.

[2] Sir Edward Turner, in his speech to the king on Friday the 18th day of January, hath these words:—'They find'—meaning the parliament—'your majesty engaged in a sharp and costly war, opposed by mighty princes and states that are in conjunction against us, they see with sorrow the greatest part of your metropolitan city buried in ashes.' [Query, Sir William Turner? See Epistle Dedicatory.—G.]

sackcloth, lament and howl: for the fierce anger of the Lord is not turned back from us.' Under wasting judgments God expecteth not only inward, but also outward, expressions and demonstrations of sorrow and grief. Shall our enemies rejoice over the ruins of London, and shall not we mourn over the ruins of London? Shall they that are afar off lament over London's desolation; and shall not we lament over London's desolation, who are every day a-walking up and down in London's ruins and rubbish? O sirs! as ever you would see London's breaches repaired, her trading recovered, her beauty restored, her riches augmented, her glory advanced, and her inhabitants rejoiced, make conscience of mourning over London's ruins. After Jerusalem was destroyed by the Romans, many of the Jews obtained leave of the Roman emperors, once a year—viz., on the 10th of August, which was the day whereon their city was taken[1]—to enter into Jerusalem, and bewail the destruction of their city, temple, and people, bargaining with the soldiers who waited on them to give so much for so long abiding there, and if they exceeded the time they conditioned for, they were to stretch their purses to a higher rate, which occasioned Jerome to say, 'that they who bought Christ's blood were then glad to buy their own tears.' O sirs, what cause have we once a year, yea, often in a year, to bewail the desolation of London! The statue of Apollo is said to shed tears for the afflictions of the Grecians, though he could not help them. Though we could not prevent the burning of London, yet let us weep over the ruins of London. The leprosy of the citizens' sins had so fretted into London's walls, that there was no cleansing of them but by the furious flames of a consuming fire, Lev. xiv. 35–46. In the law you know that when the old fretting plague of leprosy was so got into the house, and spread in the walls, that no scraping within or without could cleanse it away, then the house was to be pulled down. This seems to be London's case. God by former judgments laboured to scrape away the leprosy of sin out of London, but that deadly leprosy was so got into men's hearts and houses that there was no getting of it out but by pulling them down. This is, and this must be for a lamentation. Now the better to work you to lament and mourn over the ruins of London, consider with me these ten following particulars:—

[1.] First, *Who can look upon the burning of London, as ushered in by such sad prodigies and dreadful forerunners as it was, and not lament and mourn over its ruins?* By what a bloody sword, and by what a dreadful plague, was this late judgment of fire ushered in! First, God sends his red horse amongst us, Rev. vi. 4, 8—viz., a cruel, bloody war; and then he sends his pale horse amongst us—viz., a noisome, sweeping pestilence. Oh the garments that were rolled in blood! Oh the scores of thousands that were by the hand of the destroying angel sent to their long homes, to their eternal homes! Now in the rear of these judgments follows such a devouring fire, as hath not been known in any ages past. Not long before Vespasian came against Jerusalem,[2] there happened divers prodigies: (1.) There was a comet in form of a fiery sword, which for a year together did hang over the city. (2.) There was seen a star on the temple so

[1] Josephus. [2] Josephus, pp. 738, 739.

bright, as if a man had so many drawn swords in his hands. (3.) At the same time that this star appeared, which was the solemn passover, that whole night the temple was light and clear as mid-day, and continued so seven days together. (4.) At the same time also they brought a heifer for a sacrifice, which when she was knocked down, she calved a lamb. (5.) The inner gate of the temple, on the east side, being of massive brass, that was never opened nor shut but twenty men had enough to do about it, this gate was seen at the first hour of the night to open of its own accord, and they could not shut it till a great number joined their strength together. (6.) There was discerned on the *sanctum sanctorum*, a whole night long, the face of a man very terrible. (7.) At the same time, before the sunset, there were seen in the air iron chariots, all over the country, and an army in battle array, passing along the clouds, and begirting the city. (8.) Upon the feast day, called pentecost, at night the priests going into the inner temple, to offer their wonted sacrifice, at first they felt the place to move and tremble, and afterward they heard a man walking in the temple, and saying with a great and wonderful terrible voice, 'Come let us go away out of this temple, let us depart hence.' But (9.) Ninthly and lastly, that which was most wonderful of all, was this, that there was one Jesus the son of Ananus, a countryman, of the common people, who four years before the wars began, when the city flourished in peace and riches, coming to the celebration of the feast to Jerusalem, which we call the feast of tabernacles, suddenly began to cry out thus, 'A voice from the east, a voice from the west, a voice from the four winds of the heavens, a voice against Jerusalem, a voice against the temple, a voice against the bridegroom, a voice against the bride, and a voice against the whole people:' and thus crying day and night, he went about all the streets of the city. The nobility scourged him, yet still he cried, 'Woe, woe unto Jerusalem:' he did never curse any one, though every day he was beaten by one or other: neither did he thank any one that offered him meat. All that he spake to any man, was this heavy prophecy, 'Woe, woe unto Jerusalem.' He never went to any citizens, neither was he seen to speak to any one, but still, as it were, studying of some speech, he cried 'Woe, woe unto Jerusalem.' Thus for four years space, say some—for seven years and five months, saith Josephus—his voice never waxed hoarse nor weary, till in the time of the siege, beholding what he foretold them, as he was walking upon the walls, crying 'Woe to Jerusalem, woe to the temple, woe to all the people,' he added, 'and woe to myself;' and as soon as the words were out of his mouth, a stone came out of an engine from the camp, that dashed out his brains. These prodigies were forerunners of Jerusalem's desolation. What comets, what blazing stars, what sheets of fire have been seen fly over London, and what flames of fire have been seen over the city, a little before it was laid in ashes, I shall not now insist upon. Certainly when a consuming fire shall be ushered in by other dreadful judgments and amazing prodigies, it highly concerns us to sit down and mourn. But,

[2.] Secondly, Who can look upon London *as an ancient city, as a city of great antiquity, and not mourn over the ruins of it?* Isa. xxiii. 7; Jer. v. 15. Our chronologers affirm that the city hath stood two thousand seven hundred and seventy odd years. It is recorded by some, that the foundation of London was laid in the year of the world 2862. London by some antiquaries is called *Troynovant*, as having been first founded by the Trojans. London is thought by some to be ancienter than Rome. That London was a very ancient city, might several ways be made good; but what should I spend time to prove that which every one is ready to grant? Josephus,[1] speaking of Jerusalem, saith, 'That David the king of the Jews having driven out the Caneans, gave it unto his people to be inhabited, and after four hundred threescore and four years and three months, it was destroyed by the Babylonians. And from King David, who was the first Jew that reigned there, until the time that Titus destroyed it, were a thousand one hundred seventy and nine years; and from the time that it was first erected until it was by him destroyed, were two thousand one hundred and seventy-seven years; yet neither the antiquity, nor riches, nor the fame thereof, now spread all over the world, nor the glory of religion, did anything profit or hinder it from being destroyed.' So it was neither the antiquity, nor the riches, nor the fame, nor the greatness, nor the beauty, nor the glory, nor the religion that was there professed, that could prevent London's being turned into a chaos in four days' time. London, that had been climbing up to its meridian of worldly greatness and glory above two thousand years, how is she made desolate in a few days, and of a glorious city become a ruinous heap! Physicians make the threescore and third year of a man's life a dangerous climacterical year to the body natural; and statists make the five hundredth year of a city or kingdom as dangerous to the body politic, 'beyond which,' say they, 'cities and kingdoms cannot stand.' But Jerusalem and London, and many other cities, have stood much longer, and yet in the end have been laid desolate! Now what true Englishman can look upon London's antiquity, and not mourn to see so ancient a city turned into a ruinous heap? But,

[3.] Thirdly, What true Englishman did ever look upon London, *as an honourable city, as a renowned city, as a glorious city, that will not now mourn to see London laid in ashes?* London was one of the wonders of the world; London was the queen city, the crowning city of the land, a city as famous as most cities for worldly grandeur and glory, Isa. xxiii. 8; yea, a city more famous and glorious than any city under heaven for gospel light, and for the power of religion and real holiness:[2] Ps. lxxvi. 1, 2, 'In Judah is God known: his name is great in Israel. In Salem also is his tabernacle, and his dwelling-place in Zion.' In London was God known, his name was great in London; and in London also was his tabernacle and his dwelling-place. And as God was known in Judah, not only by his word, but also by his glorious works; so God was known in London, not only by his word, but also by his glorious works. And as God was known in Judah, first by the multitude of his mercies, but afterwards by the severity of his judgments; so God was known in London, first by the

[1] Joseph., p. 745.

[2] It is an Italian proverb, He who hath not seen Venice will not believe, and he who hath not lived some time there doth not understand what a city is. I shall leave the application to the prudent reader.

multitude of his mercies, but afterwards by the severity of his judgments: witness the sweeping pestilence and the devouring fire that he sent amongst us! And as God was known in Judah, first by lesser judgments and then by greater—for he first lashed them with rods, and then with scourges, and at last with scorpions; so God was first known in London by lesser judgments: witness the violent agues, strange fevers, small-pox, and small fires that broke forth in several places of the city and suburbs; but these having no kind, no effectual operation upon us, God at last made himself known in the midst of us by such a pestilence, and by such a fire, that the like was never known in that city before. We were once the objects of his noble favours, but we made ourselves at last the subjects of his fury. And as the philosopher tells us, *corruptio optimi, est pessima;* or as we find that the sweetest wines become the tartest vinegar, so God's heavenly favours and indulgences being long abused, they at last turned into storms of wrath and vengeance. What Englishman did look upon London as the city of the great God, as a holy city, as that city wherein God was as gloriously made known, and wherein Christ was as much exalted, and religion was as highly prized, as in any part of the world beside, and not mourn over it, now it is laid desolate?[1] It was long since said of Athens and Sparta, that they were the eyes of Greece. Was not London the eyes of England?[2] And who then can but weep to see those eyes put out? Great and populous cities are, as it were, the eyes of the earth; and when these eyes are lost, who can but sit down and sigh and mourn? London was the joyous city of our solemnities, it was the royal chamber of the King of kings, it was the mart of nations, it was the lofty city, it was the top-gallant of all our glory. Now, who can but shed tears to see this city laid even to the ground—to see this city sit like a desolate widow in the dust? Such a sight made Jeremiah to lament: Lam. i. 1, 'How doth the city sit solitary,' speaking of Jerusalem's ruin, 'that was full of people! How is she become as a widow! she that was great among the nations, and princess among the provinces, how is she become tributary!' Let profane, ignorant, superstitious, and popish defamers of London say what they please, yet doubtless God had more of his mourning ones, and of his marked ones in that city, than he had in a great part of the nation beside, Jer. ix. 1–3; Ezek. ix. 4, 6. There was a time when London was a faithful city, a city of righteousness, a city of renown, a city of praise, a city of joy; yea, the paradise of the world, in respect of the power and purity of gospel ordinances, and that glorious light shined in the midst of her. Who can remember those days of old, and not mourn to see such a city buried in its own ruins? Under the whole heavens there were not so many thousands to be found that truly feared the Lord, in so narrow a compass of ground, as was to be found in London; and yet, lo, London is laid in the dust, and the nations round gaze and wonder at her desolation! Who can but hang down his head and weep in secret for these things? But,

[4.] Fourthly, Who did look upon London *as the bulwark, as the*

[1] Ps. ci. 8; Isa. lx. 14; Ps. xlviii. 1, 8, &c.; Neh. xi. 1; Isa. xviii. 52; Dan. i. 9, 24.

[2] Look, what the face is to the body, that London was to England, the beauty and glory of it.

stronghold of the nation, that cannot mourn to see their bulwark, their stronghold, turned into a ruinous heap? Ps. xlviii. 12, 13, 'Walk about Zion, and tell the towers thereof. Mark ye well her bulwarks, consider her palaces; that ye may tell it to the generation following.' Zion had her bulwarks, her towers, her palaces; but at last the Chaldeans at one time, and the Romans at another, laid them all waste, Jer. lii. 12, 13; Luke xix. 41, 45. So London had her bulwarks, her towers, her palaces, but they are now laid desolate, and many fear, and others say, by malcontent villains and mischievous foreigners of a Romish faith. London was once terrible as an army with banners, Cant. vi. 10. How terrible were the Israelites, encamped and bannered in the wilderness, unto the Moabites, Canaanites, &c.! Exod. xv. 14-16. So was London more than once terrible to all those Moabites, Canaanites, that have had thoughts to swallow her up, and to divide the prey among themselves. How terrible were the Hussites in Bohemia to the Germans, when all Germany were up in arms against them, and worsted by them! London hath been as terrible to those that have been cousin-Germans to the Germans. London was once a battle-axe and battle-bow in the hand of the Almighty, which he has wielded against her proudest, strongest, and subtlest enemies, Jer. li. 20; Zech. ix. 10, and x. 4; Ezek. xxi. 31. Was not London the head city, the royal chamber, the glory of England, the magazine of trade and wealth, the city that had the strength and treasure of the nation in it? Were there not many thousands in London that were men of fair estates, of exemplary piety, of tried valour, of great prudence, and of unspotted reputation? and therefore why should it seem impossible that the fire in London should be the effect of desperate designs and complotments from abroad, seconded and encouraged by malcontents at home? London was the great bulwark of the Reformed religion, against all the batteries of popery, atheism, and profaneness; and therefore why should any Englishman wonder if these uncircumcised ones should have their heads and their hands and their hearts engaged in the burning of London?[1] Such whose very principles leads them by the hand to blow up kings, princes, parliaments, and reformed religion, to make way for their own religion, or for the good old religion, as some are pleased to call it; such will never scruple to turn such cities, such bulwarks, into a ruinous heap, that either stands in their way, or that might probably hinder their game, Dan. xi. 24, 39. In all the ages of the world wicked men have designed the ruin and laying waste of Christians' bulwarks and strongholds, in order to the rooting out of the very name of Christians, as all know that have read anything of Scripture or history; and therefore why should any men think it strange if that spirit should still be at work? Was ever England in such imminent danger of being made a prey to foreign power, or of being rid by men of a foreign religion, and whose principles in civil policy are very dangerous both to prince and people, as it hath been since the firing of London, or since that bulwark has been turned into a ruinous heap? Had not the great God, who laid a law of restraint upon churlish Laban,

[1] The French were then drawn down to the sea-side, and great were the fears of many upon that account. Remember the Gunpowder plot.

and upon bloody Esau and his four hundred bloody cut-throats, and upon proud, blasphemous Sennacherib, Gen. xxxi. 24, 29, and xxxiii. 1, 4; 2 Kings xix. 27, 28, 32, laid also a law of restraint upon ill-minded men, what mischief might they not then have done, when many were amazed and astonished, and many did hang down their heads, and fold their hands, crying, Alas! alas! London is fallen! and when many had sorrow in their hearts, paleness upon their cheeks, and trembling in all their joints! yea, when the flames of London were as terrible to most as the hand writing upon the wall was to Belshazzar! Dan. v. 5, 6. How mightily the burning of London would have retarded the supplies of men, money, and necessaries which would have been needful to have made opposition against an invading enemy, had we been put to it, I shall not here stand to dispute. Whilst London was standing, it could raise an army, and pay it when it had done. London was the sword and sinews of war; but when London was laid in ashes, the citizens were like Samson when his hair was cut off, Judges xvi. 18–20, and like the Shechemites when they were sore, Gen. xxxiv. 25. Beloved, the people of God have formerly made the firing of their strongholds matter of bitter lamentation, as you may see in 2 Kings viii. 11, 12, 'And he settled his countenance steadfastly, until he was ashamed;' (till Hazael blushed to see the prophet look so earnestly upon him,) 'and the man of God wept. And Hazael said, Why weepeth my lord? And he answered, Because I know the evil that thou wilt do unto the children of Israel: their strongholds wilt thou set on fire,'—[Well! and what will he do when their strongholds are in flames or turned into a ruinous heap? Why, this you may see in the following words,]—'and their young men wilt thou slay with the sword, and wilt dash their children, and rip up their women with child.' Other kings of Syria had borne an immortal hatred against the children of Israel, and the prophet knew by revelation from heaven that he should be king over Syria, and that he had as cruel and as bloody a mind against God's Israel as any of the former kings of Syria had. Now to evidence this, the prophet instances in those particular excessive acts of cruelty that he should practise upon the children of Israel—'their strongholds wilt thou set on fire.' Hazael would not think it enough to enter into their strong towns, and cities, and forts, and castles, and other strongholds, and spoil and plunder them of their treasure and goods, but he would burn all down to the ground, that so he might daunt them, and weaken them, and render them the more uncapable of making any resistance against him. But now mark what follows burning work—'their young men wilt thou slay with the sword.' Such as make no conscience of burning Israel's strongholds, such will never scruple the slaying of Israel's young men with the sword. When their strongholds were set on fire, Hazael would give them no quarter for their lives,—such as had escaped the furious flames should be sure to fall by the bloody sword. 'And wilt dash their children,'—their poor, innocent, harmless children, that never thought amiss nor never spoke amiss of Hazael, these must have their brains dashed out against the stones, Ps. cxxxvii. 9. Men that are set upon burning work are men of no bowels, of no compassion. 'And rip up their women with child.' He would destroy the very infants in the womb, that so he might cause to cease the very name of Israel. Such Hazaels as are resolute by fire to lay our cities and strong bulwarks desolate, such will be ready enough to practise the most barbarous cruelties imaginable upon our persons and relations when a fit opportunity shall present. When Israel was weary, and faint, and feeble, then Amalek fell upon them, Deut. xxv. 17-19. It was infinite mercy that the Amalekites of our day did not fall upon the amazed and astonished citizens when they were feeble, and faint, and weary, and tired out with hard labour and want of rest. O sirs! shall the prophet Elisha weep, foreseeing that Hazael would set Israel's strongholds on fire; and shall not we weep to see London, our stronghold, our noblest bulwark, turned into a ruinous heap? So Lam. ii. 2, 5, 'The Lord hath swallowed up all the habitation of Jacob, and hath not pitied: he hath thrown down in his wrath the strongholds of the daughter of Judah; he hath brought them down to the ground. The Lord was an enemy: he hath swallowed up Israel, he hath swallowed up all her palaces; he hath destroyed his strongholds, and hath increased in the daughter of Judah mournings and lamentation.' These two words, 'mourning and lamentation,' are joined together to note the great and eminent lamentation of the daughter of Judah upon the sight and sense of God's destroying, razing, and levelling to the ground, by the hand of the Chaldeans, &c., all the strongholds and fortresses that were built for the defence of the Israelites. Now shall the daughter of Judah greatly lament to see her strongholds laid desolate; and shall not we at all lament to see London, to see our strongholds, turned into a ruinous heap? But,

[5.] Fifthly, Who did ever look upon London as *a fountain, as a sanctuary, and as a city of refuge to the poor, afflicted, distressed, and impoverished people of God*, that is not now free to weep to see such a city laid in ashes? Who can number up the distressed strangers that have been there courteously entertained and civilly treated? Exod. xxii. 12; 2 Sam. xvi. 14. Who can number up the many thousand families that have been preserved, relieved, revived, and refreshed with the silver streams that has issued from that fountain London, and not mourn to see it laid desolate? Ps. xlvi. 4, 'There is a river, the streams whereof shall make glad the city of God;' Isa. viii. 6. It is an allusion to the river Siloah, which ran sweetly, softly, quietly, pleasantly, constantly, to the refreshing of all that were in need. London was a river, a fountain, whose silver streams ran sweetly, quietly, pleasantly, constantly, to the refreshing of many thousand needy ones in the land. Now who can but weep to see such a fountain, such a river, not only stopped, but dried up by a devouring fire? But,

[6.] Sixthly, Who did ever look upon London *as a city compact, a city advantageously situated for trade and commerce, yea, as the great mart town of the nation, that has not a heart to weep over it, now it lies in ashes?* Isa. xxiii. 3; Ezek. xxvii. 1; Rev. viii. 11. London was the mart of the nation's trade, and the magazine of the nation's wealth. London was that great storehouse, in which was laid up very much of the riches and glory of the land. London was the very heart of England; it was as useful every way to England's security and felicity, as the heart is useful in the natural body: and therefore no wonder if such as envy at England's greatness, grandeur, and glory, have made London, England's mart-town, to bear the marks of their displeasure. Who is so great a stranger in our English Israel, as not to know how rarely well London was situated as to trade, and as not to know how London was surrounded with plentiful store of all creature-comforts? If London had not been so nobly situated and surrounded, its desolation had not been so great a judgment; nor, it may be, the designs of men so deeply laid, as to its ruin. They that did look upon England as rich, could not but look on London as the exchequer of it. But,

[7.] Seventhly, *Who are they that have looked upon London as a city, that hath for many hundred, yea, some thousands of years, been very strangely and wonderfully preserved by the admirable wisdom, constant care, and almighty power of God—notwithstanding all the wrath, rage, malice, plots, and designs of wicked men to lay it waste, and to turn it into a ruinous heap—and not have a heart to weep over its desolation?* Isa. xxvii. 3, 4; Ps. cxxi. 4, 5. The great preservations, the singular salvations, that God hath wrought for London, many hundred years together, renders the desolation of London the more terrible. And accordingly it concerns all that are well affected to weep over its ashes. But,

[8.] Eighthly, *Who can look upon the ashes of London, as those ashes in which England's worst enemies, both abroad and at home, do daily triumph and rejoice, and not weep over London's desolation?* Obad. 10–16. Shall the vilest of men glory that England's glory is laid in the dust; and shall not we lament, when our crown is fallen from our head? Lam. v. 16. The more wicked men rejoice in our misery, the greater obligation lies upon us to lie low and mourn at the foot of God. London, like Job, lies on its dunghill, Job ii. 8. London, like the Jews, lies in its ashes, Esther iv. 3. And therefore it highly concerns all Londoners to put on sackcloth and ashes. But,

[9.] Ninthly, *Surely such as have looked upon London as the city of their solemnities—such cannot but weep to see the city of their solemnities laid desolate:* Isa. xxxiii. 20, 'Look upon Zion the city of our solemnities,' or meetings. Zion is here called a city, because it stood in the midst of the city. The city of Jerusalem was very large, and Zion stood in the midst of it; and it is called a 'city of solemnities,' because the people flocked thither to hear the law, to renew their covenant with God, to call upon his name, and to offer sacrifices. O sirs! was not London the city of our solemnities? the city where we solemnly met to wait upon the Lord, in the beauty of holiness? 1 Chron. xvi. 29; the city where we offered prayers and praises? the city where we worshipped the Lord in spirit and in truth? Ps. xxix. 2; the city wherein God, and Christ, and the great things of eternity, were revealed to us? the city wherein many thousands were converted and edified; walking in the fear of the Lord, and in the comforts of the Holy Ghost? Acts ix. 31; the city where we had the clearest, the choicest, and the highest enjoyments of God that ever we had in all our days? the city wherein we have sat down under Christ's 'shadow with great delight; his fruit has been sweet unto our taste'? the city in which

Christ has 'brought us to his banqueting-house, and his banner over us has been love'? the city in which Christ has 'staid us with flagons, and comforted us with apples'? the city in which Christ's 'left hand hath been under our heads, and his right hand hath embraced us'? Cant. ii. 3-6; the city wherein the Lord of hosts hath 'made unto his people a feast of fat things, a feast of wines on the lees, of fat things full of marrow, of wines on the lees well refined'? Isa. xxv. 6. London, the city of our solemnities, is now laid desolate: and therefore for this why should not we be disconsolate, and mourn in secret before the Lord? This frame of spirit hath been upon the people of God of old: Zeph. iii. 18, 'I will gather them that are sorrowful for the solemn assembly, who are of thee, to whom the reproach of it was a burden.' By 'solemn assemblies' are meant their several conventions, at those set times which God had appointed them, viz., on the weekly Sabbath, the new moons, the stated feasts and fasts, which they were bound to observe, Deut. xvi. Now for the want, the lack, the loss of those solemn assemblies, such as did truly fear the Lord were solemnly sorrowful. Of all losses, spiritual losses are most sadly resented by gracious souls. When they had lost their houses, their estates, their trades, their relations, their liberties, and were led captive to Babylon, which was an iron furnace, a second Egypt to them, then the loss of their solemn assemblies made deeper impressions upon their hearts than all their outward losses did. The Jews were famous artists. They stand upon record for their skill, especially in poetry, mathematics, and music: but when their city was burnt, and their land laid desolate, and their solemn assemblies broken in pieces, then they could sing none of the songs of Zion, Ps. cxxxvii. 1-5; then they were more for mourning than for music, for sighing than for singing, for lamenting than for laughing. Nothing goes so near gracious hearts as the loss of their solemn assemblies, as the loss of holy ordinances. Health, and wealth, and friends, and trade, are but mere Ichabods to the saints' solemn assemblies, and to pure ordinances. When the ark was taken, Eli could live no longer: but whether his heart or his neck was first broken upon that sad tidings, is not easy to determine, 1 Sam. iv. 17, 18. When Nehemiah understood that the walls of Jerusalem were broken down, and that the gates thereof were burnt with fire, and that the whole city was laid desolate by Nebuzar-adan and his Chaldean army, he sits down and weeps and mourns, and fasts and prays, 2 Kings xxv. 8-10; he did so lay the burning of the city of their solemnities to heart, that all the smiles of King Artaxerxes could not raise him nor rejoice him, Neh. i. 3, 4, and ii. It was on the tenth day of the fifth month that Jerusalem was burnt with fire; and upon that account the Jews fasted upon every tenth day of the fifth month, Jer. lii. 12-14. Now shall the Jews solemnly fast and mourn on the tenth day of the fifth month during their captivity, Zech. vii. 3, because their city and temple and solemn assemblies were on that day buried in ashes, and turned into a ruinous heap; and shall not we fast and mourn to see the city of our solemnities buried in its own ruins? But,

[10.] Tenthly and lastly, *That incendiary, that mischievous villain Hubert, confessed the fact of firing the first house in Pudding Lane, though he would not confess who set him at work, and accordingly was executed at Tyburn for it.*[1] Now who can look upon the dreadful consequences, the burning of a renowned city, that followed upon the firing of the first house, and not mourn over London's desolations? Hubert did confess to several persons of note and repute that he was a Catholic; and did further declare that he believed confession to a priest was necessary to his salvation. And being advised, by a chaplain to a person of honour, to call upon God, he repeated his *Ave Mary*, which he confessed was his usual prayer. Father Harvey confessed him, and instructed him, and we need not doubt but that he absolved him also, according to the custom of the Romish Church. Hubert died in the profession of the Romish faith, stoutly asserting that he was no Hugonite.[2] I know that men of the Romish religion, and such who are one in spirit with them, would make the world believe that this Hubert, who, by order of law, was executed upon the account of his own public and private confessions, was mad, distracted, and what not. But what madmen do these make the judge and jury to be? for who but madmen would condemn to such a shameful death a madman, for confessing himself guilty of such a heinous and horrid fact, which he had never committed? Doubtless both judge and jury were men of more wisdom, justice, and conscience, than to hang a madman upon his own bare confession. The German histories tell us[3] what encouragement men of a Romish faith have had from Rome to make way for their religion throughout Germany, by fire and sword; and when some of those incendiaries have been taken in setting houses on fire, they have confessed that there have been many more in combination with them, who, by all the ways they could, were to consume Silesia and other parts with firings. When the Spanish Armada came against this nation in 1588 with an invincible navy, as they counted it, they had two thousand eight hundred and forty-three great ordnance, twenty-eight thousand eight hundred and forty mariners, soldiers, and slaves, rowing in galleys, with innumerable fire-balls and granadoes, in order to the making of England desolate by fire and sword.[4] Did not F. Parsons, Doleman, and Holt the Jesuit draw other incendiaries into a combination to fire the royal navy with wildfire in Queen Elizabeth's reign, for which they were stretched at Tyburn, A.D. 1595?[5] On that very day when King James was crowned, when the generality of the people were intent upon that noble spectacle, five were suborned by the Jesuits to set London on fire in several places, but were frustrated, as is evident upon record.[6] Mr Waddesworth did depose, both in writing and *viva voce* at the Lords' bar, that one Henry, *alias* Francis Smith, *alias* Lloyd, *alias* Rivers, *alias* Simons, before the beginning of the Scotch wars, did tell him in Norfolk, where he met him, 'That the popish

[1] There were some ministers, and several other sober prudent citizens, who did converse again and again with Hubert, and are ready to attest that he was far from being mad; and that he was not only very rational, but also very cunning and subtle, and so the fitter instrument for the conclave of Rome, or some subtle Jesuit to make use of to bring about our common woe. It was never known that Rome or hell did ever make use of madmen or fools to bring about their devilish plots.

[2] Query, 'Huguenot'?—G. [3] Luc. Hist., pp. 613, 519, 520. [4] Hisp. F. 184, 185.

[5] Speed's Hist., p. 1178; Luc. Hist., pp. 298, 299. [6] Luc. Hist., pp. 509–511.

religion was not to be brought in here by disputing, or books of controversy, but with an army, and with fire and sword.'[1] Pope Martin the Fifth sent Cardinal Julian, who was namesake and near of kin to Julian the apostate, with an army of fourscore thousand, to root out Hussites or protestants in Bohemia, where they burnt up their towns; and at the same time Albertus, his assistant, burnt up five hundred of their villages. It was Philip the Second of Spain who said, [Thuanus,] 'That he had rather lose all his provinces than seem to grant or favour anything which might be prejudicial to the Catholic religion.' It was Cardinal Granveilanus[2] who was wont to say, [Gasper,] 'That he would reduce the Catholic religion in all places, though one hundred thousand men were to be burned in an hour.' It was the Spanish ministers of state who declared openly in the pacifica- of Colen,[3] [Anno 1586,] 'That the Protestants would be very well served if they were stripped of all their goods, and forced to go seek new countries like Jews and Egyptians, who wander up and down like rogues and vagabonds.' The Duke of Alba, a bloody papist,[4] sitting at his table, said, 'That he had taken diligent pains in rooting out the tares of heresies, having delivered eighteen thousand men in the space of six years only to the hands of the hangman.' From the beginning of the Jesuits to 1580, being the space of thirty years, there were almost nine hundred thousand protestants put to death in France, Spain, Italy, Germany, England, and other parts of Christendom.[5] Men of that religion, that burnt the martyrs in Queen Mary's days, are men of such bloody, desperate principles, that they will stick at nothing that may be a means to advance the Romish religion. Some men, besides the Romans, have practised most prodigious things, and all to raise themselves a name in the world. Servetus,[6] at Geneva, gave all his goods to the poor, and his body to be burnt, and all for a name, for a little glory among men. The temple of the great goddess Diana, which was one of the world's wonders, was set on fire when Alexander was born, by Erostratus, a base fellow; and this he did, 'that he might be talked of when he was dead.' So Judas and Sadoc, with their seditious sect, burnt down the temple of Jerusalem, and all the beautiful buildings in the city.[7] And at another time, when the Romans had set the temple on fire, Titus, by entreaties and threatenings, did all he could to persuade the soldiers to extinguish the fire, but could not prevail with them. They, seeing the gates of the inward temple to be gates of gold, thought that the temple was full of money, and that they might have a rich booty, and therefore regarded not their general's commands. Titus did all he could to quench the flames; but a certain soldier fired the posts about the doors of the inward temple, and presently the flame appearing within, Titus and his captains departed; and so every one stood looking upon it, and no man sought to extinguish it. Thus the temple was burnt by the hand of a single soldier, against Titus his

[1] Compl. Hist., pp. 443, 449; Roy. Favour., pp. 54, 55; Rom. Mr Pecce, 31.
[2] Qu. 'Cardinal Anthony Perrenot Granvella'?—G. [3] Query, 'Cologne'?—G.
[4] Meter. Hist. de reb. Belg., lib. xv. [Query, 'Alva'?—G.
[5] The fact of Faux was horrid and sanguinary; and you know who set him on work
[6] Anno 1555, Calvin. [Misprinted Serustus.—G.]
[7] Josephus, Ant., lib. xviii. cap. 1, p. 463.

mind.[1] One man that is of a cruel spirit, and of cruel principles, may do a world of mischief. Take that instance of Nero, who maliciously raised the first persecution against the Christians, pretending that they were incendiaries, and authors of the burning of Rome; whereas he himself had most wickedly done it. But this barbarous act of his was fathered upon the Christians; and accordingly they suffered severely for it.[2] Another author saith,[3] Nero succeeded Caligula in the government, and in no less fierceness and cruelty, because he was a man in whom, if possible it might be, all the other cruelties were enclosed, and all else that could by men be imagined; for, without any regard of sanctified things, or persons of like quality, private or public, he caused the city of Rome to be set on fire, with express prohibition not to quench it, or any man to make safety of his own goods: so the fire continued seven days and seven nights burning the city; and he being on a high tower some small distance off, clapped his hands, and joyed to behold this dismal spectacle, so far exceeding all humanity. The wisest prince that ever swayed a sceptre hath told us, 'That one sinner destroyeth much good,' Eccles. ix. 18. Who can sum up the mischief that a few ill-minded men may do in a little time? The same devil, the same lusts, the same wrath, the same rage, the same revenge, the same ends, the same motives that have put others upon burning work in former times, may probably have put some upon the same work in our time. Burning work is so odious and abominable, so destructive, hateful, and hurtful a thing in the eyes of all true Englishmen who have any sense of honour or conscience, that I shall never wonder to see such who have either had a head, or a hand, or a heart in it, of arts and crafts, to bury for ever the remembrance of it. Was not London the glory of England? Was not London England's treasury, and the protestants' sanctuary? Was not London as terrible to her enemies abroad, as she was joyous to her friends at home? Has not London been as dreadful to her foreign foes, as the hand-writing upon the wall was to Belshazzar? Dan. v. 5, 6. Was not London the great mountain that her enemies feared would be most prejudicial to their pernicious designs? Zech. iv. 7. Was not London that great rock against which many have dashed themselves in pieces?[4] Was not London as briers and thorns, as goads and gulfs and two-edged swords, to all her enemies, more remote and nearer home? Had the French invaded us when London was in flames, as many feared they would, or had such risen up at that time, in the bowels of the nation, whose very principles lead them by fire and sword to make way for their religion, what doleful days had we seen, and to what a low ebb might the protestant interest have then been brought! What greater encouragement could be given to French, Dutch, Dane, and all of the old religion, as they call it, to make desperate attempts upon us, than the laying of the city desolate by fire? But it is the glory of divine power to daunt and overrule all hearts and counsels, and to turn that to his people's greatest good

[1] Lib. vii. de Bello Jud. cap. 10, p. 737.
[2] Pareus on the Revelation, p. 110.
[3] The Treasury of Ancient and Modern Times, pp. 321, 322.
[4] The French, the Dutch, the Dane, the Spaniard, &c., have at times experienced what London's treasure and force have been able to do, &c.

which their enemies design to be their utter ruin, Ps. lxxvi. 5, 10; Gen. xxxi. 24, 29, and xxxiii. 3, 4. We know papists are no changelings; their cruel, bloody, fiery spirits and principles are still the same.[1] Both king and parliament have taken notice how vigilant and active they have been of late, by what hath been discovered, confessed, proved, printed, &c. Is it not more than probable that some influenced from Rome have kindled and promoted that dreadful fire that hath laid our city desolate? The statue of Apollo is said to shed tears for the afflictions of the Grecians, though he could not help them. Though none of us could prevent the desolation of London, yet let us all be so ingenuous as to weep over the ashes of London. Who can look upon London's glory, as now sacrificed to the flames, and made a burnt-offering to appease the wrath and fury, as many say, of a papist conclave, and not mourn?

Obj. Sir, we readily grant that it is our duty to lament and mourn over the ruins and desolations of London; yea, some of us have so lamented and mourned over London's dust and ashes, that we have almost reduced ourselves to dust and ashes; and therefore, what cordials, what comforts, what supports can you hand out to us that may help to cheer up our spirits, and to bear up our hearts, so as that we may not utterly faint and sink, neither under the sight of London's ruins, nor yet under a deep sense of our many great and sore losses?

Now that I may be a little serviceable and useful to you in the present case, give me leave to offer to your most serious consideration these following particulars by way of support:—

(1.) First, Consider, for your support and comfort, *That the great God might have burned up all;* he might not have left one house standing, nor one stone upon another. It is true the greatest part of the city is fallen; but it is rich mercy that the whole is not consumed, Luke xix. 41, 44. Though most of the city within the walls be destroyed, yet it is grace upon the throne that the suburbs are standing. Had not God spared some houses in the city, and the main of the suburbs, where would thousands have had a livelihood? How would any trade have been maintained? yea, how would the lives of many thousands have been preserved? It is true the fire was very dreadful, but God might have made it more dreadful; he might have laid every house level; he might have consumed all the goods and wealth that was there treasured up; and he might have refused to have plucked one man 'as a brand out of the fire,' Zech. iii. 2. He might have suffered London to have been as totally destroyed as Jerusalem was: Mat. xxiv. 1, 2, 'And Jesus went out, and departed from the temple: and his disciples came to him to shew him the buildings of the temple. And Jesus said unto them, See ye not all these things? verily, I say unto you, There shall not be left here one stone upon another that shall not be thrown down.' In these words Christ doth foretell the utter destruction and devastation of Jerusalem, which came to pass by Titus and the Roman army; wasting all with fire and sword, and evening with the ground that magnificent temple and city, which was the glory of the world. Though

[1] The woeful desolations that the popish party made by fire and sword amongst the protestants in Ireland is written with the pen of a diamond.

Titus, by a strict edict at first storming of the city, forbade the defacing of the temple, yet the soldiers burned it and the city. The temple was burned, say some, August 10th, when it had stood five hundred [and] eighty-nine years; and the city was burned September 8th, in the year of our Lord seventy-one.[1]

Quest. But why did Christ's disciples shew him the buildings of the temple, which they knew were not unknown unto him?

Ans. To move him to mercy, and to moderate the severity of that former sentence, of leaving their houses desolate unto them, Mat. xxiii. 38. Herod had been at a wonderful charge in building and beautifying the temple. Josephus tells us,[2] that for eight whole years together he kept ten thousand men at work about it: and that for magnificence and stateliness it exceeded Solomon's temple. The disciples might very well wonder at these stately buildings, at these goodly, stately, fair stones, which were, as Josephus writeth, fifteen cubits long, twelve high, and eight broad. Now the disciples fondly thought that Christ, upon the full sight of these stately, glorious buildings, which to see laid waste was pity, might have been so worked upon as to reverse his former sentence of laying all desolate. But here they were mistaken; for 'his thoughts were not as their thoughts.' Others think that the disciples shewed Christ the stately buildings of the temple, that upon a serious consideration of the strength, pomp, stateliness, greatness, and magnificence of the buildings, he might be the more careful to preserve them from destruction. Others think that the disciples shewed him these strong and stately buildings, to insinuate secretly thereby how difficult, yea, impossible, it was for them to be destroyed, especially considering the strength of the city also. And hence our Saviour seems to answer, 'See ye not all these things? verily I say unto you, There shall not be left here one stone upon another, that shall not be thrown down,' &c.

Quest. But when was this prediction fulfilled, that not one stone should be left upon another, which should not be thrown down, &c.?

Ans. This was fulfilled forty years after Christ's ascension, by Vespasian the emperor, and his son Titus, as Eusebius and Josephus do declare. Yea, this prophecy was not only accomplished in the destruction of the old temple, but then also, when in Julian the apostate's time, the Jews, to spite the Christians, were by him encouraged to build the temple at his charge; and they attempting it accordingly, were hindered from heaven by a mighty earthquake, which cast down that in the night which was built in the day: and besides, a fire from heaven, that consumed the work and workmen's instruments; which Cyrillus, bishop of Jerusalem, then seeing, applied unto that event this prediction of our Saviour, 'There shall not be left one stone upon another, that shall not be thrown down.'[3] Ah London, London! this might have been thy doom, that there should not have been one house standing, neither within nor without thy walls; yea, this might have been thy doom, that there should not have been 'one stone left upon another that should not have been thrown down.' In that it is other-

[1] See Joseph., lib. vii. cap. 9, 10, 18, de Bel. Jud.
[2] Joseph., lib. xv., Antiq., cap. 14.
[3] Socrat., lib. iii. cap. 17.

wise with thee, thou hast cause, O London, to cry, Grace, grace, to him that sits upon the throne, and is blessed for ever, &c.

Carthage was a noble city, mistress of Africa, and paragon to Rome. She made her part good against Rome for many years, but at length, by means of her own inward civil jars, she was utterly destroyed by them, [Oros. Eutrop.] For the inhabitants being not able to stand any longer in their own defence, were constrained to yield themselves to the mercy of their enemies—the women, to the number of five and twenty thousand, marching first forth, and after them the men, in number thirty thousand, following, all which poor captives were sold for bond-slaves, a few only of the principal excepted: and then fire was put to the city, which burnt seventeen days without ceasing, even till it was clean consumed. This might have been thy doom, O London, but God in the midst of judgment hath remembered mercy.

Athens was once the most famous flourishing city of Greece, for her fair buildings, large precincts, and multitude of inhabitants; but especially for her philosophy, by means whereof recourse was made from all parts to her, as the fountain and well-spring of arts, and the school and university of the whole world: whose policy and manner of government was so much esteemed by the Romans, that they drew from thence their laws: but now she lies dead and buried in the ashes of forgetfulness, not carrying any of her former proportion or appearance. If this had been thy doom, O London, we must all have set to our seals that the Lord had been righteous; but blessed be the Lord, London is not, and I hope never shall, let Rome and hell do their worst, be buried in the ashes of forgetfulness, &c. But,

(2.) The second support to bear up the hearts and to cheer up the spirits of all that has smarted by the late fiery dispensation, is this, viz., *That God has given them their lives for a prey.* O sirs, what a mercy is it, that though the fire has reached your houses, your shops, your goods, your commodities, your warehouses, your treasure, that yet it has not reached your lives, nor the lives of your relations or friends! though your habitations are consumed, and your losses have been great, yet that in the midst of so many deaths and dangers by the flames, and by the press of the people, and notwithstanding all the confusions that was in all parts of the city, you should have your lives for a prey, and be snatched as so many 'firebrands out of the burning'! Oh how should this miraculous providence of God be owned and admired by you! The devil hit the mark when he said, 'Skin for skin; yea, all that a man hath, will he give for his life,' Job ii. 4.[1] Men's estates in those times did lie mostly in cattle. Now, saith Satan, Job is a very great life-lover, he is fond of life, and afraid of death; and therefore he will give skin upon skin to save his life: he will give many skins, abundance of skins, yea, all his skins, to save his life: he will give his cattle's skins, and his servants' skins, and his sons' skins, to save himself in a whole skin.[2] By this proverbial speech, 'Skin for skin,' &c., Satan intimates that Job cared not for the loss of his cattle, nor for the loss of his servants, nor for the loss of his

[1] The philosopher saith that a fly is more excellent than the heavens; because the fly has life, which the heavens have not.

[2] *Proximus quisque sibi:* Every man is nearest to himself.

children, so he might secure his own life. Job set a higher price upon his own life than he did upon all other lives: let others sink or swim, so he might escape, all was well. Natural life is a precious jewel; a man will cast all overboard, when he is in danger of drowning, to save his life. A man will hold up his arms to save his head, or suffer the loss of a limb to save his life. Men will bleed, sweat, vomit, purge, part with an estate, yea, with some of their limbs, to preserve their lives. As he who cried out, 'Give me any deformity, any torment, any misery, so you spare my life.' 'Wherefore doth a living man complain,' or murmur, 'a man for the punishment of his sin?' Lam. iii. 39. Oh what a simple, senseless, brutish, blockish thing is it for a man, a mortal man, a sinful man, a man on this side the grave, on this side hell, to complain or murmur against a holy and righteous God! He that is alive on this side everlasting burnings, Isa. xxxiii. 14, on this side a devouring fire, has no just cause to complain, whatever his losses, crosses, or sufferings are. He that has deserved a hanging, if he escape with a whipping, has no cause to complain or murmur. Men that have deserved a damning, if they escape with the loss of house, goods, estates, &c., they have no cause to complain or murmur. Mark, at this time Jerusalem was burnt, city and temple was laid in ashes, the citizens were turned out of house and home, and stripped of all their comforts and contentments. 'They that did feed delicately, were desolate in the streets: they that were brought up in scarlet, embraced dunghills.' 'They were scattered among the heathen, who did mock at their Sabbaths, and who trod their mighty men under foot; yea, they sought their bread with the peril of their lives.' And yet, saith the prophet, 'Why doth the living man complain?' Lam. iv. 5, and v. 9. Though city, and temple, and goods, and estates were all consumed in the flames, yet some had their lives for a prey; and upon that very account they ought not to complain. God might have turned them into ashes, as he had turned their houses into ashes, and it was mere grace that he did not; which the church wisely and ingenuously observes, when she saith, 'It is of the Lord's mercy that we are not consumed,' chap. iii. 22. She doth not say, it is of the Lord's mercy that our houses are not consumed; but it is of the Lord's mercy that *we* are not consumed: nor she does not say, it is of the Lord's mercy that our goods are not consumed; but it is of the Lord's mercy that *we* are not consumed. The church saw mercy, much mercy, tender mercy, yea, bowels of mercy, as the word there imports, that a remnant had their lives given them, when their city and substance was turned into ashes. O sirs! others have lost their goods and their lives together, and it is miraculous mercy that you have not; when men's wits were puzzled, their hearts discouraged, and their industry tired out; when the wind was at the highest, and the fire at the hottest, and the hopes of most at the lowest, that then you should be as brands plucked out of the fire, was glorious mercy, &c.

In the reign of Achmat, the eighth emperor of the Turks,[1] a great fire arose in the city of Constantinople, wherein many, both men and women, perished, with above five hundred shops and warehouses full of rich merchandise, most of which belonged unto the Jews, of whom

[1] Knolles his General History of the Turks, p. 1244.

almost two hundred were said to be burned. These lost their goods and their lives together, but so have not you; the greater obligation lies upon you, both to think well of God, and to speak well of God, and to lay out your lives to the uttermost for God.

Certain Tartars at Constantinople in their insolency set fire upon a certain Jew's house, whereof arose such a terrible fire, as burned not only many houses, but a great many of the Jews themselves.[1] Here lives and estates went together. Though outlandish hands have set our city, our houses on fire, yet God has preserved our lives in the midst of the flames; and this is a mercy more worth than all we have lost, &c.

There was a stately palace in Jerusalem that Solomon had built, which joined near to the temple. This palace the Jews abundantly anointed all over with brimstone and pitch, so that when the Romans pursued the Jews unto this palace, they entered the palace after the Jews, who went out again another way, and shut up the palace, and set fire on the gates, which they had before anointed with brimstone and pitch; and straightway the side walls of the house, and the whole building, began to be on a-light fire, so that the Romans had no way to escape, because the fire compassed the house on every side. The Jews also stood round about the palace, with their drawn swords, to cut off any that should attempt to escape the flames. Now there was two and twenty thousand of the Romans destroyed in this fire. Titus, hearing the lamentable cry of the Romans that were compassed about in flames of fire, made speed with all his army to come and rescue them; but the fire burned so vehemently that he could save none of them. Upon which Titus and his army wept bitterly, [Josephus.] O sirs! when London was in flames, if men of a Romish faith had compassed the city round about with their drawn swords that none should have escaped the furious flames, how dreadful would such a day have been! Whether such a thing was intended or designed, and by any strange providence prevented, we shall know in the fittest season.

Numantium,[2] a city in Spain, being besieged by the Romans, and after it had borne the brunt of war a long time, and made many desperate sallies upon their enemies, and were almost consumed with famine, rather than they would bow their necks to the Roman yoke, they barred their gates, and set all on fire, and so burned themselves in the flames of their city, that so they might leave the enemy nothing but ashes for his prey and triumph. Here city and citizens are destroyed together; and it is infinite mercy that this was not the fate, the doom of the citizens of London. They and their city might have fallen together; 'but God was good, and a very present help in time of trouble,' Ps. xlvi. 1. O sirs! if not only your houses, your shops, your goods, your wares, but also your persons, had been enclosed with flames, and no possibility of escape, how dreadful would the fire have been then! Oh, what tongue can express, or heart conceive, the sighs, the groans, the cries, the tears, the gashful[3] looks, the horrible shrieks, the dreadful amazement, and the matchless astonishment that would have been upon all sorts and ranks of people, that had been compassed

[1] Knolles, p. 1266. [2] Numantia.—G. [3] 'Ghastly.'—G.

round about with flames, and could see no door of deliverance open to them! Oh what a mercy is it that we are yet alive, though we are stripped of many comforts and contentments which formerly we have enjoyed! Now here give me leave to open myself a little in these following particulars:—

[1.] First, *What a mercy was this to all unregenerate and unconverted persons, that they have had their lives for a prey when London was in flames!*[1] Had God by the flames or any other accident put an end to their natural days, they might at this time have been a-rolling up and down in unquenchable flames. Sinners, sinners, the greatest weights hang upon the smallest wires. Eternity, eternity depends upon your improvement of that time, that life, and those seasons and opportunities of grace that yet you do enjoy. That Rabbi hit it who said, *Nemo est cui non sit hora sua*, Every man hath his hour. He who overslips that season, may never meet with the like again all his days. O sirs! to have a little more time to believe, to repent, to secure your interest in Christ, a changed nature, a sanctified frame of heart, a pardon in the bosom, is a mercy more worth than ten thousand worlds. To have a little more time to make your calling and election sure, and to get the new name and white stone that none knows but those that are the favourites of heaven; to have time to make sure a city that hath foundations, a kingdom that shakes not, riches that corrupt not, an inheritance that fadeth not away, a house not made with hands, but one eternal in the heavens; to have time to make sure to yourselves a crown of righteousness, a crown of life, a crown of glory, a crown of immortality, are mercies beyond all the expressions, and above all the valuations of the sons of men.[2] The poets paint time with wings, to shew the volubility and swiftness of it. *Sumptus pretiosissimus tempus*, Time is of precious cost, saith Theophrastus. Know time, lose not a minute, saith Psittacus. Ælian gives this testimony of the Lacedæmonians, 'That they were hugely covetous of their time, spending it all about necessary things, and suffering no citizen either to be idle or play.' Titus Vespasian having spent a day without doing any man any good, as he sat at supper he uttered this memorable and praiseworthy apophthegm, *Amici, diem perdidi*, My friends, I have lost a day, [Suetonius.] O sirs! will not these poor heathens rise in judgment against all those that trifle and fool and sin away their precious time? Take heed of crying *Cras, cras*, To-morrow, to-morrow. Oh play not the courtier with your precious souls! The courtier doth all things late: he rises late, and dines late, and sups late, and goes to bed late, and repents late. Remember that manna must be gathered in the morning. The orient pearl is generated of the morning dew. There is nothing puts a more serious frame into a man's spirit than to know the worth of his time. It is very dangerous putting off that to another day which must be done to-day, or else undone to-morrow. *Nunc aut nunquam*, Now or never, was the saying of old. If not done now, it may never be done,

[1] Austin saith that he would not be a wicked man one half hour for all the world, because he might die in that half hour, and then he was undone for ever.

[2] 2 Peter i. 10; Rev. ii. 17; Heb. xi. 10, and xii. 28; 1 Peter i. 4; 2 Cor. v. 1; 2 Tim. iv. 8; Rev. ii. 10; James i. 12; 1 Peter v. 4.

and then undone for ever. Eternity depends on this moment of time. What would not many a man give for a day when it is a day too late?[1] Whilst many blind Sodomites have been groping to find a door of hope, God has rained hell out of heaven upon them. The seasons of grace are not under your locks and keys. Many thousand poor sinners have lost their seasons and their souls together. Judas repented and Esau mourned, but neither timely nor truly; and therefore they perished to all eternity. The damned in hell may weep their eyes out of their heads, but they can never weep sin out of their souls, nor their souls out of hell, &c.

Oh that the flames of London might be so sanctified to every poor sinner, who have had their lives for a prey, in that doleful day, that they may no longer neglect those precious seasons and opportunities of grace that yet are continued to them, lest God should swear in his wrath, 'that they should never enter into his rest!' Heb. ii. 3, and iii. 18. O sirs! yet you have a world of gracious opportunities, and oh that God would give you that heavenly wisdom, that you may never neglect one gracious opportunity, though it were to gain a whole world! God by giving you your lives in the midst of those furious and amazing flames, has given you time and opportunity to secure the internal and the eternal welfare of your precious and immortal souls, which is a mercy that can never be sufficiently prized or improved. But,

[2.] Secondly, *What a mercy was this to poor doubting, staggering Christians, that they have had their lives for a prey when London was in flames!* For by this means they have gained time to pray down their doubts, and to argue down their doubts, and to wrestle and weep down their doubts, &c. Christ ascended to heaven in a cloud, and the angel ascended to heaven in the flame of the altar, Acts i. 9, 10; Judges xiv. 20. It is ten to one but this had been the case of many doubting, trembling Christians, had they died when London was in flames. I know it is good getting to heaven any way, though it be in a whirlwind of affliction, or in a fiery chariot of temptation, or in the flames of persecution, or in a cloud of fears, doubts, and darkness; but yet that man is more happy that gets to heaven in a quiet calm of inward peace, and in the fair sunshine of joy and assurance.[2] It is a good thing for a man to get into a safe harbour, though it be in a winter night, and through many storms and tempests, hazards, dangers, and deaths, with the loss of masts, cables, and anchors; but yet he is more happy that gets into a safe harbour in a clear, calm, fair, sunshiny day, top and top-gallant, and with colours flying and trumpets sounding. The prudent reader knows how to apply it. Oh that all poor doubting Christians would seriously lay this to heart, viz., That for them to have time, to have their judgments and understandings enlightened, their doubts resolved, their objections answered, their consciences settled, and their souls assured that all is well, and shall be for ever well between God and them, is a mercy more worth than all the world. But,

[1] Beroaldus speaks of a fool who cried out, O repentance, repentance! where art thou, where art thou, repentance?

[2] The whole Scripture, saith Luther, doth principally aim at this thing, that we should not doubt, but that we should hope, that we should trust, and that we should believe, that God is a merciful, a bountiful, a gracious and patient God to his people.

[3.] Thirdly, *What a mercy was this to poor languishing, declining, and decaying Christians, that they have had their lives for a prey when London was in flames!* There were a great many in London who were 'fallen from their first love,' and whose sun was set in a cloud. There were many whose graces were languishing, whose comforts were declining, whose souls were withered, and whose communion with God was greatly impaired, Rev. ii. 4. Many within and without the walls of London had a worm gnawing at the root of their graces. They had lost their spiritual relish of God, of Christ, of ordinances, as dying men lose their relish. Dying men can relish nothing they sip, or eat, or drink. They had lost their spiritual strength, and they knew it not, as Samson had lost his natural strength and knew it not, Judges xvi. 20. Oh what an image of death was upon their highest professions! Now for these men to live, for these men to have time to get their graces repaired, their comforts revived, their spiritual strength restored, their souls fattened, and their communion with God raised, oh what a matchless, what an incomparable mercy is this! But,

[4.] Fourthly, *What a mercy was this to poor clouded, deserted, and benighted Christians, that they have had their lives for a prey when London was in flames!* Beloved, it is sad dying under a cloud; it is sad dying, when he who should comfort a man's soul stands afar off, Lam. i. 16. Some think that the face of God was clouded when David thus prayed, 'O spare me, that I may recover strength, before I go hence, and be no more,' Ps. xxxix. 13. And some think Hezekiah's sun was set in a cloud, and God had drawn a curtain between Hezekiah and himself, when, being under the sentence of death, Isa. xxxviii. 1–3, 'He turned his face toward the wall, and prayed unto the Lord, and said, Remember now, O Lord, I beseech thee, how I have walked before thee in truth and with a perfect heart, and have done that which was good in thy sight. And Hezekiah wept sore;' or with great weeping, as the Hebrew runs.[1] It is with clouded and deserted Christians as it was with Samson when his locks were cut off, 'his strength was gone;' and therefore, though he thought to go out and do wonders, as he had formerly done, yet by sad experience he found himself to be but as another man, Judges xvi. 18–21. So when God does but withdraw, the best of saints have their locks cut; their strength, which lieth not in their hair, but in their head Christ Jesus, Phil. i. 22, 23, is gone, and they are but like other men. They think, they speak, they act, they walk like other men. Christians under real desertions commonly fall under sore temptations, great indispositions, barrenness, flatness, dulness, and deadness of spirit. And is this a fit season for such to die in? Christians under a cloud usually have their joys eclipsed, their comforts damped, their evidences for heaven blotted, their communion with God impaired, and their title to heaven is by themselves, in such a day, much questioned. And is this a case for them to die in? O clouded and deserted Christians, who have had your lives for a prey in the midst of London's flames! and ever since those flames, what a great, what a glorious obligation has the blessed God put upon you, to labour to

[1] See more of this in my 'Mute Christian under the Smarting Rod,' pp. 279–304. [Vol. i. pp. 385–397.—G.]

recover yourselves from under all clouds and desertions, and to spend your days in a serious and deep admiration of that free, that rich, that infinite, and that sovereign grace that spared you, and that was active for you, in that day when you were compassed about with flames of fire on every hand! But,

[5.] Fifthly, *What a mercy was this to poor solicited, tempted Christians, that they have had their lives for a prey when London was in flames!*[1] For by this means they have gained time to strengthen themselves against all Satan's temptations. The daily bills that were given in, to pray for poor tempted Christians, did sufficiently evidence how active Satan was to distress and perplex poor Christians with all sorts of hideous and blasphemous temptations. Were there not many tempted to distrust the power of God, the goodness of God, the faithfulness of God? Were there not many tempted to deny God, to blaspheme God, and to turn their backs upon God? Were there not many tempted to slight the Scriptures, to deny the Scriptures, and to prefer their own fancies, notions, and delusions above the Scriptures? Were there not many tempted to have low thoughts of ordinances, and then to leave ordinances, and then to vilify ordinances, and all under a pretence of living above ordinances? Were there not many tempted to presume upon the mercies of God; and others tempted to despair of the grace of God? Were there not many tempted to destroy themselves, and others tempted to destroy their relations? Were there not many tempted to draw others to sin, and to uphold others in sin, and to encourage others in sin, and to be partners with others in sin? Were there not many tempted to have hard thoughts of Christ, and others to have low thoughts of Christ, and others to have no thoughts of Christ? Now for these poor tempted souls to have their lives for a prey, and to have precious seasons and opportunities to recover themselves out of the snares of the devil, and to arm themselves against all his fiery darts, is a comprehensive mercy, a big-bellied mercy, a mercy that has many thousand mercies in the womb of it. But,

[6.] Sixthly and lastly, *What a mercy was this to all slumbering, slothful, sluggish, lazy Christians, who had blotted and blurred their evidences for heaven, and who, instead of running their Christian race*, Heb. xii. 1, *were either at a stand, or else did but halt in the way to heaven, that they have had their lives for a prey when London was in flames; and that they have had time to clear up their evidences for heaven, and to quicken up their hearts, to run the ways of God's commands!* Ps. cxix. 32. Surely, had all the world been a lump of gold, and in their hands to have been disposed of, they would have given it for a little time to have brightened their evidences, to have got out of their sinful slumber, and to have set all reckonings even between God and their poor souls. And let thus much suffice for this second support.

(3.) The third support to bear up the hearts and to cheer up the spirits of all that have suffered by the late fiery dispensation, is this—viz., *That this has been the common lot, the common case, both of saints*

[1] See my 'Mute Christian,' pp. 260–279. [As before, Vol i. pp. 366–371.—G.] Our whole life is nothing but a temptation, saith Austin.

and sinners. God has dealt no more severely with you than he has with many others. Have you lost much? so have many others.[1] Have you lost half? so have many others. Have you lost all? so have many others. Have you lost your trade? so have many others. Have you lost your goods? so have many others. Have you lost your credits? so have many others. Have you lost many friends, who before the fire were very helpful to you and yours? so have many others. Have you lost more than your all? so have many others. This very cordial the apostle hands out to the suffering saints in his time: 1 Cor. x. 13, 'There hath no temptation taken you, but such as is common to man.' By temptation, he means affliction; as the word is used, James i. 2; 1 Peter i. 6—that is, there hath no affliction befallen you but that which is incident either to men as men, or to saints as saints: or thus, there hath no affliction befallen you but such as is common to man—that is, there is no affliction that hath befallen you but such as men may very well bear without murmuring or buckling under it. So 1 Peter v. 9, 'Knowing that the same afflictions are accomplished,' or finished, 'in your brethren, that are in the world': or in your brotherhood, that is, in the world. Afflictions are the common lot of the saints; and who shrugs, repines, complains, murmurs, or faints under a common lot, it is at the sun because it scorches, &c., John xvi. 33; Acts xiv. 22. There are none of the brotherhood but, first or last, they shall know what the fiery trial, what the fiery furnace means. Jerome, writing to a sick friend, hath this expression, 'I account it a part of unhappiness not to know adversity. I judge you to be the more miserable, because you have not been miserable:' it being the common lot of the people of God to be exercised with adversity and misery. I think he hit it who said, [Bernard,] *Impunitas securitatis mater, virtutum noverca, religionis virus, tinea sanctitatis: i.e.*, Freedom from punishment is the mother of security, the stepmother of virtue, the poison of religion, the moth of holiness. *Nihil est infelicius eo, cui nil unquam contigit adversi*, There is nothing more unhappy than he who never felt adversity, said the refined heathen [Seneca]; and shall not grace rise as high as nature? The calamity has been common, therefore wipe your eyes, and do not say, There is no sorrow to my sorrow, no loss to my loss, no ruin to my ruin, Lam. i. 12. Under common calamities, men should neither groan nor grumble. Look, as no man may conclude, upon the account of common mercies, that he is really beloved of God; so no man may conclude, upon the account of common calamities, that he is really hated of God, Eccles. ix. 1, 2. And therefore bear up sweetly, bear up cheerfully, under your present trials. In the common calamity of the plague, the destroying angel, perceiving the blood of sprinkling upon the posts of your doors, and upon the doors of your hearts, passed you by, and said unto you, 'Live,' Exod. xii. 7, 13. But by the common calamity of the fire, the Lord has turned you out of house and home, and burnt up your substance before your eyes. Now do but lay your hands seriously upon your hearts, and tell me whether you have not more cause to admire at the mercy of God towards you in '65, than

[1] The commonness of our sufferings doth somewhat mitigate the sharpness of our sufferings, &c.

you have cause to complain of the severities of God towards you in '66.

(4.) The fourth support to bear up the hearts and to cheer up the spirits of the people of God who have been sufferers, deep sufferers, under the late fiery dispensation, is this—viz., *That though they have lost much as they are men, as they are citizens, merchants, tradesmen; yet they have lost nothing as they are Christians, as they are saints, as they are the called and chosen of God.* Though they have lost their goods, yet they have not lost their God, Rev. xvii. 14. Though they have lost their shops and chests, yet they have not lost their Christ. Though they have lost their outward comforts, yet they have not lost the comforts of the Holy Ghost. Though they have lost their houses made with hands, yet they have not lost their 'house not made with hands, eternal in the heavens,' John xiv. 16, 26; 2 Cor. v. 1. Though they have lost their earthly inheritance, yet they have not lost their heavenly inheritance, 1 Pet. i. 4. Though they have lost their temporal portions, yet they have not lost their eternal portions, Ps. lxxiii. 25. Though they have lost their open public trade, yet they have not lost their secret trade, their private trade to heaven, Mat. vi. 6. I readily grant that your stately houses and your well-furnished shops are turned into ashes, and that your credit is gone, and your trading gone, and your money gone, and you utterly undone as to this world; and yet in all this God has done you no hurt, he has done you no wrong, Gen. xviii. 25: and though this at first sight may seem to be a great paradox, a very strange assertion, yet I shall thus evidence it to be an unquestionable truth. The happiness of man in this life consists, (1.) In his union with God; (2.) In his communion with God; (3.) In his conformity to God; and (4.) fourthly and lastly, In his spiritual fruition and enjoyment of God. Now none of those losses, crosses, and afflictive dispensations that have passed upon you, have or can make any breach upon your happiness, or upon any one of those four things of which your happiness is made up. The top of man's happiness in heaven lies in his near union with God, and in the beatifical vision of God, and in his full communion with God, and in his exact and perfect conformity to God, and in his everlasting fruition and enjoyment of God. Now the more of these things any Christian enjoys in this world, the more of heaven he enjoys on this side heaven, the more happiness he has on this side happiness; and therefore I would willingly know how it is possible for any outward troubles or trials to make a breach upon a Christian's happiness. Doubtless Job was as happy when he sat upon the dunghill, Job ii., without a rag on his back or a penny in his purse, as he was when he sat chief, and dwelt as a king in the army, chap. xxix. 25. If God be the most perfect being, then to enjoy him and resemble him is our greatest perfection. If God be the best of beings, then our communion with him and fruition of him must be our greatest glory and highest felicity, *omne bonum in summo bono.* Let what will befall our outward man, as long as our union and communion with God holds good, as long as our precious and immortal souls are in a safe and flourishing condition, as long as the springs of grace, of holiness, of comfort, of assurance rises in our souls, we are happy, and no outward miseries can make us miserable. There is, saith one, [Augustine,] *bona throni*, and there is *bona scabelli*, There is goods of the throne, as God, Christ, the Spirit, grace, the favour of God, pardon of sin, peace of conscience, &c.; and there is goods of the footstool, as food, raiment, house, honours, riches, trade, credit, and all bodily conveniences and accommodations. Now it was not in the power of the flames to burn up the goods of the throne; they still remain safe and secure to you. All that the flames could reach to, was only the goods of the footstool, the lumber of this world. And therefore what cause have you to bear up cheerfully, quietly, sweetly, and contentedly under all your crosses and losses, trials and troubles! 'They which adorn themselves with gold,' saith one, [Clemens Alexandrinus,] 'and think themselves bettered thereby, are worse than gold, and no lords of it, as all should be.' 'He is poor,' saith another, [Gregory the Great,] 'whose soul is void of grace, not whose coffers are empty of money.' By these short hints, you may clearly see that the people of God are never the worse for all their losses. They are as happy now they are houseless, moneyless, breadless, friendless, tradeless, as ever they were when they were most surrounded with all the comforts of this life. Woe, woe would be to the people of God, if their happiness should hang upon the comforts of this world, which like a ball are tossed from man to man. A ball of fire, a storm at sea, a false oath, a subtle enemy, a treacherous friend may easily deprive a man of all his earthly blessings at a clap. Now who so miserable as that man whose blessedness lies in earthly blessings? But,

(5.) The fifth support to bear up the hearts of the people of God under the late fiery dispensation, is this—viz., *That the Lord will certainly, one way or another, make up all their losses to them.* Sometimes God makes up his people's outward losses by giving them more of himself, more of his Son, more of his Spirit, more of his favour, more of his grace, as he did by the disciples of Christ, John xvi. When God takes away your carnals and gives you more spirituals, your temporals, and gives you more eternals, your outward losses are made up to you. Now this was the very case of those believing Hebrews, who were turned out of house and home; and who were driven to live in holes and caves and dens of the earth, and who had lost all their goods; not having a bed to lie on, or a stool to sit on, nor a dish to drink in, and who had lost all their apparel, not having a rag to hang on their backs, and therefore clothed themselves in sheep-skins and goat-skins. 'They took joyfully the spoiling of their goods, knowing in themselves that they had in heaven a better and an enduring substance,' Heb. x. 34. When under outward losses, God shall seal to his people a bill of exchange of better and greater things than any they have lost; their losses then are made up to them.[1] If a man should lose several bags of counters, and have a bill of exchange sealed to him for the receiving of so many bags of gold, would not his loss be abundantly made up to him? When God takes away our earthly treasures, and seals up in our hearts a bill of exchange, to receive all again with interest upon interest in eternal treasures,

[1] When God takes away a Christian's estates in this world, *Manet altera Cœlo*, he looks for a better in heaven.

then certainly our losses are abundantly made up to us. If men should take away your old clothes, and give you new; your rags, and give you robes; your chaff, and give you wheat; your water, and give you wine; your tin, and give you silver; your brass, and give you gold; your pebbles, and give you pearls; your cottages, and give you royal palaces, certainly you would have no cause to complain, you would have no cause to cry out, Undone! undone! If God takes away your houses, your goods, your trades, your honours, and gives you more of himself, and more grace, and more assurance of glory, he does you no injury. It is an excellent change, to get eternals for temporals. If God takes away your earthly riches, and makes you more rich in grace, in spiritual comforts, in holy experiences, in divine employments, then you are no losers, but great gainers. What are all the necessary comforts of this life to union and communion with God, to interest in Christ, to pardon of sin, to peace of conscience, and to that loving-kindness that is better than life, or better, *Chaiim*, than lives, as the Hebrew runs? Ps. lxiii. 3. If you put many lives together, there is more excellency and glory in the least discovery of divine love than in them all. Many a man has been weary of his life, but never was any man yet weary of the love and favour of God. The least drop of grace, the least smile from heaven, the least cast of Christ's countenance, the least kiss of his mouth, the least embrace of his arm, the least hint of his favour, is more worth than ten thousand worlds, Cant. ii. 3-7. That Christian cannot be poor that is rich in grace; nor that Christian cannot be miserable that has God for his portion. That Christian cannot be unhappy who hath a mansion prepared for him in heaven, though he hath not a cottage to hide his head in, in this world; nor that Christian has no cause to complain of want of food for his body whose soul is feasted with manna, with the dainties of heaven, with those rarities that are better than angels' food.[1] He that hath but rags to cover his nakedness, if his soul be clothed with the garments of salvation, and covered with the robe of Christ's righteousness, he has no reason to complain, Isa. lxi. 10. When Stilpo the philosopher had his wife, and children, and country all burnt up before him, and was asked by Demetrius what loss he had sustained, answered, 'That he had lost nothing; for he counted that only his own which none could take from him—to wit, his virtues. Shall blind nature do more than grace? Shall the heathen put the Christian to a blush?

Again, sometimes God makes up his people's outward losses, by giving in greater outward mercies than those were that he took from them; as you may see by comparing the first chapter of Job and the last chapter of Job together: Job had all doubled to him. I have read of Dionysius, [Plutarch,] how he took away from one of his nobles almost his whole estate, and seeing him as cheerful and contented as ever, he gave him all that he had taken from him again, and as much more. God many times takes away a little, that he may give more; and sometimes he takes away all, to shew his sovereignty, and then he gives them all back again with interest upon interest, to

[1] Rev. ii. 8, 9; Lam. iii. 24; John xiv. 1-4; Heb. xi. 37, 38; Rev. ii. 17; John iv. 30, 31.

shew his great liberality and noble bounty. That is a lovely loss, that is made up with so great gain.

Quest. But, sir, how shall we know, or probably conjecture, whether in this world God will make up our worldly losses to us or not? If you please to speak a little to this question, it may be many ways of use unto us.

Now that I may give you a little light to the question, give me leave to put a few questions to such who have been sufferers by the late fiery dispensation:—

[1.] First, *Did you make conscience of improving your estates to the glory of God, and the good of others, when you did enjoy them; or did you only make them subservient to your lusts?* If you have laid out your estates for God, and for his children's good, it is ten to one but that the Lord, even in this world, will make up your losses to you, Deut. xxxii. 15, 16; Hosea iv. 7; James iv. 3. But if you misimproved your estates, and turned your mercies into encouragements to sin, then you have more cause to fear that the Lord may further blast you, than you have to hope that God will make up your losses to you. But,

[2.] Secondly, *Did you daily and seriously labour to enjoy much of God in all those worldly enjoyments which formerly you were blest withal?* If so, it is very probable that the Lord may make up all your losses to you; but if you made a god of your worldly enjoyments—if they had more of your thoughts, and hearts, and time, than God himself had, then you have more cause to fear a further curse, than to expect a future blessing, Prov. iii. 33; Mal. ii. 2. But,

[3.] Thirdly, *Did your hearts commonly, ordinarily, habitually lie low under your worldly enjoyments?* Abraham, under all his worldly enjoyments, was but 'dust and ashes;' and Jacob under his was 'less than the least of all mercies,' Gen. xviii. 27, and xxxii. 10; and so David, under all God's royal favours, his heart lies low: Ps. xxii. 6, 'But I am a worm, and no man.' David in the Arabic tongue signifies a worm, to which he seems to allude. The word in the Hebrew for worm is *tolagnath*, which signifies such a very little worm that a man can very hardly see it or perceive it. Though David was high in the world, yet he was little, yea, very little, in his own eyes. Was it commonly, mostly thus with you when your comforts compassed you round about? If so, then it is very probable that the Lord in this world will make up all your losses to you. But if your blood did commonly rise with your outward goods, and if your hearts did usually so swell under your worldly enjoyments as to say with Pharaoh, 'Who is the Lord that I should obey his voice?' Exod. v. 2; or to say with Nebuchadnezzar, 'Who is that God that can deliver you out of my hands?' Dan. iii. 15; or to say with those proud atheists, 'Who is Lord over us?' Ps. xii. 4; or to say with those proud monsters, 'We are lords, we will come no more unto thee,' &c., Jer. ii. 31, then you have great cause to fear that God that hath yet some further controversy with you, and, 'except you repent,' will rather strip you of what you enjoy, than multiply further favours or blessings upon you. But,

[4.] Fourthly, *Since God has burnt up your worldly goods, have you been fervent and frequent with God that he would burn up those lusts that have burnt up your comforts before your eyes?* Have you pleaded hard with God that a spirit of burning might rest upon you, even that spirit of burning which alone can burn up your sins, your dross? Isa. ix. 2, and iv. 4. Since London hath been laid in ashes, have you made it your great business to treat and trade with God about the destruction of those sins that have laid all desolate? If so, then you have cause to hope that God will turn your captivity, and make up all your losses to you, Job xlii. 10. But,

[5.] Fifthly, *Since God has turned you out of all, are you turned nearer and closer to himself?* Though you have been prodigals, yet have you in the light of London's flames seen and found your way to your Father's house? Luke xv. Then God will make up all your losses to you. When judgments are so sanctified as to bring a people nearer to himself, then God will drop down mercies upon them, Hosea ii. 18, 20. But,

[6.] Sixthly, *Has the fire of London been as a pillar of fire to lead you Canaan-wards, heaven-wards?* Exod. xiii. 21, 22. Has God, by burning up the good things of this world, caused you to set your hearts and affections more than ever upon the great things of another world? If so, then it is a hundred to ten but that the Lord will make up all your losses to you. But,

[7.] Seventhly, *Are your hearts, under this fiery dispensation, brought into such a quiet submission to the good will and pleasure of God, as that you can now be contented to be at God's finding, at God's allowance?* Phil. iv. 12–14. Can you now be contented to be rich or poor, to have much or little, to be high or low, to be something or nothing, to have all again or to have nothing but necessaries again? Are you now willing that God shall choose for you? Can you sit down satisfied with God's allowance, though it be far short of what once you had? Content is the deputy of outward felicity, and supplies the place where it is absent. A contented frame of heart, as to all outward occurrences, is like ballast to a ship, which will help it to sail boldly and safely in all waters. When a man's mind is conformable to his means, all is well. One [Augustine upon Ps. xii.] brings in God rebuking a discontented Christian thus: 'What is thy faith? Have I promised thee these things? What! wert thou made a Christian that thou shouldst flourish here in this world?' It is an excellent expression that Bellarmine hath in his Catechism: 'Suppose,' saith he, 'a king, having many children of several ages, should apparel them in cloth of gold: now he that is sixteen years old hath more gold in his robe than the child that is but five or six years old, yet the child would rather have his own garment than his elder brother's, because it is fitter for him.' Surely the fittest estate is the best estate for us. Look, as a great shoe fits not a little foot, nor a great sail a little ship, nor a great ring a little finger, so a great estate is not always the fittest for us. He that hath most, wants something; and he that hath least, wants nothing, if he wants not a contented spirit. O sirs! let not heathens put you to a blush.

'He that can be content to be at God's finding, as a guest at a table, that takes what is carved for him, and no more, he needs not fawn upon any man, much less violate his conscience for the great things of the world.'[1] When a man's heart is brought down to his condition, he is then temptation-proof. When one told the philosopher, that if he would but please Dionysius, he need not feed upon green herbs; the philosopher replied, 'If thou wert but content to feed upon herbs, thou needest not flatter Dionysius.' A man that can be contented with a little, will keep his ground in an hour of temptation.

Diogenes the cynic, housed in his tub, and making even with his victuals and the day together, being invited to a great feast, could say, 'I had rather lick salt at Athens, than feast with Craterus.' Diogenes had more content with his tub to shelter him from the injuries of the weather, and with his wooden dish to eat and drink in, than Alexander had with the conquest of half the world, and the fruition of all the honours, pomps, treasures, and pleasures of Asia.

'The way to true riches,' saith Plato, 'is not to increase our heaps, but to diminish the covetousness of our hearts.'

And saith Seneca, *Cui cum paupertate bene convenit, pauper non est*, A contented man cannot be a poor man.

I have read of another philosopher, who seeing a prince going by, with the greatest pomp and state imaginable, he said to some about him, 'See how many things I have no need of.'

And saith another, 'It were well for the world if there were no gold in it.' But since it is the fountain whence all things flow, it is to be desired, but only as a pass, to travel to our journey's end without begging.

When Crœsus, king of Lydia, asked Solon, one of the seven wise men of Greece, who in the whole world was more happy than he? Solon answered, 'Tellus, who though he was a poor man, yet he was a good man, and content with that which he had.'

So Cato could say, as Aulus Gellius reports of him, 'I have neither house, nor plate, nor garments of price, in my hands; what I have, I can use: if not, I can want it. Some blame me because I want many things; and I blame them because they cannot want.' Now shall nature do more than grace? Shall the poor blinded heathen outstrip the knowing Christian? O sirs, he that can lose his will in the will of God, as to the things of this world; he that is willing to be at God's allowance; he that has had much, but can now be satisfied with a little; he that can be contented to be at God's finding—he is of all men the most likely man to have all his losses made up to him. But,

[8.] Eighthly and lastly, *Are your hearts more drawn out to have this fiery dispensation sanctified to you, than to have your losses made up to you?* Do you strive more with God to get good by this dreadful judgment, than to recover your lost goods, and your lost estates? Is this the daily language of your souls, Lord, let this fiery calamity be so sanctified as that it may eminently issue in the mortifying of our sins, in the increase of our graces, in the mending of our hearts, in the reforming of our lives, and in the weaning of our souls from everything below thee; and in the fixing of them upon the great things of eternity! If it be thus with you, it is ten to one but God even in this world will make up your losses to you. But,

[1] Epictetus Enchirid., cap. 21.

(6.) The sixth support to bear up the hearts of the people of God under the late fiery dispensation, is this—viz., *That by fiery dispensations, the Lord will make way for the new heavens and the new earth:* he will make way for the glorious deliverance of his people, Isa. ix. 5, 6; Ps. lxvi. 12. Isa. lxvi. 15, 16, 22, 'For, behold, the Lord will come with fire, and with his chariots like a whirlwind, to render his anger with fury, and his rebuke with flames of fire. For 'by fire and by his sword,' or by his sword of fire, 'will the Lord plead with all flesh: and the slain of the Lord shall be many. For as the new heavens and the new earth, which I will make, shall remain before me, saith the Lord, so shall your seed and your name remain.' The great and the glorious things that God will do for his people in the last days are set forth by new heavens and new earth; and these God will bring in by fiery dispensations.[1] The glorious estate of the universal church of Jews and Gentiles on earth is no lower an estate than that of a new heaven and a new earth. Now this blessed church-state is ushered into the world by fiery judgments. By fiery dispensations God will put an end to the glory of this old world, and bring in the new. Look, as God by a watery deluge made way for one new world, so by a fiery deluge, in the last of the last days, he will make way for another new world, wherein 'shall dwell righteousness,' as Peter speaks, 2 Pet. iii. 10–13. All men in common speech call a new great change a new world.[2] By fiery dispensations God will bring great changes upon the world, and make way for his Son's reign in a more glorious manner than ever he has yet reigned in the world, Rev. xviii., xix., xx., and xxi. The sum of that I have, in short, to offer to your consideration out of these chapters is this:—'Babylon the great is fallen, is fallen. How much she hath glorified herself, so much sorrow and torment shall be given her. Her plagues come in one day, death and mourning and famine, and she shall be utterly burnt with fire. Rejoice over her, thou heaven, and ye holy apostles and prophets; for God hath avenged you on her. And after these things, I heard a great voice of much people, &c., saying, Alleluiah; Salvation, and glory, and honour, and power unto the Lord our God: for true and righteous are thy judgments; for he hath judged the great whore that hath corrupted the earth, and hath avenged the blood of his saints. And again they said, Alleluiah. And the four and twenty elders said Amen; Alleluiah. And I heard as it were the voice of a great multitude, and as the voice of many waters, and as the voice of mighty thunderings, saying, Alleluiah: for the Lord God omnipotent reigneth. And the beast and the false prophet were cast into the lake of fire. And the rest were slain with the sword. But the saints reigned with Christ a thousand years in the new heavens and new earth, to whom the kings of the earth and nations of the world bring their honour.' God, by his fiery dispensation upon Babylon, makes way for Christ's reign, and the saints' reign in the new heavens and new earth. But,

[1] Isa. lxv. 17; Joel ii. 1–5, 30–32; Zeph. iii. 8, 9.

[2] Gen. ix. See our new 'Annotationists' [as before] on Isa. lxv. and xvii.; on chap. lxvi. 15, 16, 22, and on Rev. xxi. 1.

(7.) The seventh support to bear up the hearts of the people of God under the late fiery dispensation, is this—viz., *That by fiery dispensations God will bring about the ruin and destruction of his and his people's enemies*, Ps. l. 3. Ps. xcvii. 3, 'A fire goeth before him, and burneth up his enemies round about.' Hab. iii. 5, 'Before him went the pestilence, and burning coals went forth at his feet.' Ver. 7, 'I saw the tents of Cushan in affliction; and the curtains of the land of Midian did tremble.' Ver. 12, 'Thou didst march through the land in indignation, thou didst thresh the heathen in anger.' Ver. 13, 'Thou wentest forth for the salvation of thy people, even for salvation with thine anointed; thou woundedst the head out of the house of the wicked, by discovering the foundation even to the neck. Selah.' Jer. l. 31, 32, 'Behold, I am against thee, O thou most proud, saith the Lord God of hosts: for thy day is come, the time that I will visit thee. And the most proud shall stumble and fall, and none shall raise him up: and I will kindle a fire in his cities, and it shall devour all round about him.' There is nothing more fearful or formidable, either to man or beast, than fire: and therefore by fiery dispensations God will take vengeance on the wicked. This will be the more evident, if you please but to consider to what the wicked are compared in Scripture.

[1.] First, They are compared *to stubble and chaff, which the fire doth easily consume:* Isa. v. 24, 'Therefore as the fire devoureth the stubble, and the flame consumeth the chaff, so their root shall be as rottenness, and their blossom shall go up as dust.' Nahum i. 10, 'For while they be folden together as thorns, and while they are drunken as drunkards, they shall be devoured as stubble fully dry.' Mark that word 'fully dry,' and so as it were prepared and fitted for the flame.

[2.] Secondly, The wicked are compared *to thorns:* and how easily doth the flaming fire consume them! Isa. xxvii. 4, 'Fury is not in me: who would set the briers and thorns against me in battle? I would go through them, I would burn them together.' Chap. xxxiii. 12, 'And the people shall be as the burnings of lime: as thorns cut up shall they be burnt in the fire.' Mark, it is not said as thorns standing and rooted in the earth, and growing with their moisture about them; but as thorns cut up, as dead and dry thorns, which are easily kindled and consumed, &c.

[3.] Thirdly, The wicked are compared *to the melting of wax before the fire, and to the passing away of smoke before the wind*, Micah i. 4; Ps. viii. 2.

[4.] Fourthly and lastly, The sudden and certain ruin of the wicked is set forth by *the melting of the fat of lambs before the fire:* Ps. xxxvii. 20, 'But the wicked shall perish, and the enemies of the Lord shall be as the fat of lambs,' (which of all fat is the most easiest melted before the fire:) 'they shall consume; into smoke shall they consume away.' The fat of lambs in the sacrifices was wholly to be burnt and consumed, Lev. iii. 15–17. Thus you see, by the several things to which wicked men are compared, that God by fiery calamities will bring ruin and destruction upon his and his people's enemies. Such as have burnt the people of God out of house and home, may in this world have burning for burning. God loves to retaliate upon his people's enemies, Judges i. 6, 7. Such as have clapped their hands at the sight of London's flames, may one day lay their hands upon their loins, when they shall find divine justice appearing in flames of fire against them. But,

(8.) The eighth support to bear up the hearts of the people of God under the late fiery dispensation, is this—viz., *That all shall end well, all shall work for good.*[1] God, by this fiery dispensation, will do his people a great deal of good. God cast Judah into an iron furnace, into a fiery furnace, but it was for their good. Jer. xxiv. 5, 'Like these good figs, so will I acknowledge them that are carried away captive of Judah, whom I have sent out of this place into the land of the Chaldeans for their good.' Ps. cxix. 71, 'It is good for me that I have been afflicted.' Though afflictions are naturally evil, yet they are morally good; for by the wise, sanctifying, overruling providence of God, they shall either cure the saints of their spiritual evils, or preserve them from spiritual evils. Though the elements are of contrary qualities, yet divine power and wisdom hath so tempered them, that they all work in a harmonious manner for the good of the universe. So, though sore afflictions, though fiery trials seem to work quite cross and contrary to the saints' prayers and desires, yet they shall be so ordered and tempered by a skilful and omnipotent hand, as that they shall all issue in the saints' good. At the long run, by all sorts of fiery trials, the saints shall have their sins more weakened, their graces more improved, and their experiences more multiplied, their evidences for heaven more cleared, their communion with God more raised, and their hearts and lives more amended. God, by fiery trials, will keep off from his people more trials. God loves by the cross to secure his people from the curse; and certainly it is no bad exchange, to have a cross instead of a curse. God led the Israelites about and about in the wilderness forty years together, but it was to humble them, and prove them, and do them good in their latter end, Deut. viii. 2, 16. God led them through fire and water, Ps. lxvi. 12; that is, through variety of sore and sharp afflictions, but all was in order to his bringing them forth into a wealthy place. God stripped Job to his shift, but it was in order to his clothing of him in scarlet: he brought him low, but it was in order to his raising him higher than ever: he set him upon a dunghill, that he might the better fit him to sit upon a throne.[2] 'Joseph is not, and Simeon is not, and ye will take Benjamin away: all these things are against me,' saith old Jacob, Gen. xlii. 36; but yet as old as he was, he lived to see all working for his good, before he went to his long home. Under all fiery dispensations, God will make good that golden promise, Rom. viii. 28, 'And we know that all things work together for good to them that love God.' Mark, the apostle doth not say, we suppose, or we hope, or we conjecture, but we know, I know, and you know, and all the saints know by daily experience, that all their sufferings and afflictions work together for their good: the apostle doth not say *de futuro*, they shall

[1] Consult these scriptures, Isa. i. 25, and xxvii. 8-11; Zech. xiii. 9; Heb. xii. 10; Hosea ii. 6; Acts xiv. 22; John xvi. 33; Jer. xxix. 11.
[2] Compare the first and last chapter of Job together.

work, but *de præsenti*, they do work. All second causes work together with the first cause for their good who love God, and who are called according to his purpose. The Greek word συνεργεῖ, 'work together,' is a physical expression. Look, as several poisonful ingredients put together, being well tempered and mixed by the skill and care of the prudent apothecary, makes a sovereign medicine, and work together for the good of the patient; so all the afflictions and sufferings that befall the saints, they shall be so wisely, so divinely tempered, ordered, and sanctified by a hand of heaven, as that they shall really and signally work for their good. Those dreadful providences which seem to be most prejudicial to us, shall in the issue prove most beneficial to us, Gen. l. 20. Look, as vessels of gold are made by fire, so by fiery dispensations God will make his people vessels of gold, vessels of honour, 2 Tim. ii. 20, 21. Commonly the most afflicted Christians are the most golden Christians: Zech. xiii. 9, 'And I will bring the third part through the fire, and will refine them as silver is refined, and will try them as gold is tried: they shall call on my name, and I will hear them: I will say, It is my people; and they shall say, The Lord is my God.' The fire of London was rather physic than poison. There was more of a paternal chastisement, than there was of an extirpating vengeance in it; and therefore certainly it shall work well, it shall issue well.

(9.) The ninth support to bear up the hearts of the people of God under the late fiery dispensation, is this—viz., *That there was a great mixture of mercy in that dreadful judgment of fire that has turned London into a ruinous heap.* At the final destruction of Jerusalem there was not one stone left upon another, Luke xix. 41, 45. This might have been thy case, O London, had not mercy triumphed over justice, and over all the plots and designs of men. Though many thousand houses are destroyed, yet to the praise of free grace, many thousand houses in the city and suburbs have been preserved from the rage and violence of the flames. What a mercy was that, that Zoar should be standing, when Sodom was laid in ashes! Gen. xix. And what a mercy was this, that your houses should be standing, when so many thousand houses have been laid desolate! Is more than a third part of the city destroyed by fire? Why, the whole city might have been destroyed by fire, and all the suburbs round about it. But in the midst of wrath, God has remembered mercy, Ps. cxxxvi. 23: in the midst of great severity, God has exercised great clemency. Had the fire come on with that rage, fury, and triumph, as to have laid both city and suburbs level, we must have said with the church, 'The Lord is righteous,' Lam. i. 18. Had the three children their songs in the midst of the fiery furnace; and why should not they have their songs of praise, whose houses, by a miraculous providence, were preserved in the midst of London's flames? O sirs, what a mixture of mercy was there in this fiery calamity, that all your lives should be spared, and that many of your houses should be preserved, and that much of your goods, your wares, your commodities, should be snatched as so many firebrands out of the fire! If ever there were an obligation put upon a people to cry, Grace, grace, grace! the Lord has put one upon you, who have been sharers in that mixture of mercy that

God has extended to the many thousand sufferers by London's flames. Had this judgment of fire been inflicted when the raging pestilence swept away some thousands every week, and when the city was even left naked as to her inhabitants, and when the whole nation was under a dreadful fear, trembling, and dismayedness of spirit, Josh. ii. 9–11, might there not have been far greater desolations, both of houses, goods, and lives, in the midst of us? Had God contended with London by pestilence and fire at once, who would have lodged your persons in their beds, or your goods in their barns? Had these two dreadful judgments met, Londoners would have met with but few friends in the world. Well, when I look upon London's sins and deserts on the one hand, and upon the principles, old hatred, plots, designs, rage, and wrath of some malicious persons, on the other hand, Ezek. xxv. 15, instead of wondering that so much of the city and suburbs is destroyed, I rather wonder that any one house in the city or suburbs is preserved.[1] Whilst London was in flames, and all men under a high distraction, and all things in a sad confusion, a secret, subtle, designing, powerful enemy might have risen up in the midst of you, that might have spoiled your goods, ravished your wives, deflowered your daughters, and after all this have sheathed their swords in all your bowels: and in that it fell not out thus, what cause have Londoners to bow for ever before preventing and restraining grace! Since the creation of the world, God has never been so severe in the execution of his most dreadful judgments as not to remember mercy in the midst of wrath. When he drowned the old world, who before were drowned in lusts and pleasures, he extended mercy to Noah and his family. When he rained hell out of heaven upon Sodom and Gomorrah, turning those rich and pleasant cities into ruinous heaps, he gave Lot and his daughters their lives for a prey. And when by fire and sword he had made Jerusalem a dreadful spectacle of his wrath and vengeance, yet then a remnant did escape, Isa. vi. 11–13; Jer. v. 10, 18. This truth we citizens have experienced, or else we and our all before this day had been destroyed. Every citizen should have this motto written in characters of gold on his forehead, 'It is of the Lord's mercies that we are not consumed,' Lam. iii. 22. God might have made London like Sodom and Gomorrah; but in the day of his anger some beams of his favour darted forth upon your London. By which means the hopes of some are so far revived as to expect that London yet may be rebuilt and blessed. That is a dreadful word, 'When he begins he will make an end; and the fire of his wrath shall burn, and none shall quench it,' 1 Sam. iii. 12; Jer. iv. 4, and xxi. 12. These eradicating judgments had certainly fallen upon London, had not the Lord in the midst of his fury remembered mercy. 'If the Lord had not been on our side,' Ps. cxxiv. 1–3, may London now say, 'if the Lord had not been on our side when the fire rose up against us, then the fire had swallowed us up quick, when its rage was kindled against us.' Doubtless God never mingled a cup of wrath with more mercy than this.

[1] Tacitus, writing of Rome, saith, *Sequitur clades, omnibus quæ urbi per violentiam ignium acciderant gravior atque atrocior.*—Annal., lib. xv. p. 791. It was rich mercy that it was not so with London.

Though the fire of London was a very great and dreadful fire, yet it was not so great nor so dreadful a fire as that of Sodom and Gomorrah was: for that fire of Sodom and Gomorrah,

[1.] First, *It was a miraculous fire*—a fire that was, besides, beyond and against the course of nature.[1] Gen. xix. 24, 'Then the Lord rained upon Sodom and Gomorrah brimstone and fire from the Lord out of heaven.' Fire mingled with brimstone hath been found, (1.) Most obnoxious to the eyes; (2.) Most loathsome to the smell; and (3.) Most fierce in burning. He hit the mark who, speaking of fire and brimstone, said, *Facillime incenditur, pertinacissime fervet, et difficillime extinguitur*, It is easily kindled, violently swelled, and hardly extinguished. Brimstone and all that vast quantity of sulphureous fiery matter, by which those rich and populous cities were turned into ruinous heaps, were never produced by natural causes, nor after a natural manner, no culinary fire being so speedy in its consumptions, but immediately by God's own miraculous power and almighty arm. But the fire that has laid London in ashes was no such miraculous or extraordinary fire, but such a fire which divine providence permitted and suffered to be kindled and carried on, by such means, instruments, and concurring circumstances as hath buried our glory under heaps of ashes. But,

[2.] Secondly, The fire that fell upon Sodom and Gomorrah consumed not only *the greater part of those cities, but the whole cities:* yea, and not only Sodom and Gomorrah, but all the cities of the plain, except Zoar, which was to be a sanctuary to Lot. But the fire of London has not destroyed the whole city of London; many hundred —may I not say thousands?—houses are yet standing, as monuments of divine power, wisdom, and goodness: and the greatest part of the suburbs are yet preserved; and all the rest of the cities of England are yet compassed about with loving-kindness and mercy; and I hope will be reserved, by a gracious providence, as shelters, as sanctuaries, and as hiding-places to poor England's distressed inhabitants. But,

[3.] Thirdly, The fire that fell upon Sodom and Gomorrah did consume not only *places but persons, not only houses but inhabitants*. But in the midst of London's flames, God was a wall of fire about the citizens, Zech. ii. 5; in that day of his fiery indignation, he was very tender of the lives of his people. Though the lumber was burnt, yet God took care of his treasure, of his jewels—to wit, the lives of his people. But having spoken before more largely of this particular, let this touch now suffice.

[4.] Fourthly, Sodom and Gomorrah were destroyed by fire *suddenly and unexpectedly—they were destroyed by fire in a moment:* Lam. iv. 6, 'For the punishment of the iniquity of the daughter of my people is greater than the punishment of the sin of Sodom, that was overthrown as in a moment, and no hands stayed on her.'[2] Sodom and Gomorrah sustained no long siege from foreign forces, neither were they kept long in sorrows and sufferings, in pains and misery,

[1] They sinned against the light and course of nature; and therefore they were destroyed against the course of nature by fire from heaven.

[2] The judgments of God upon the Jews were so great, that they exceeded all credit amongst their neighbour nations.

but they were quickly and suddenly and instantly despatched out of this world into another world. Men had no hand in the destroying of Sodom; no mortal instrument did co-operate in that work. God by his own immediate power overthrew them in a moment. Sodom was very strangely, suddenly, and unexpectedly turned upside down, as in a moment, by God's own hand, without the help of armed soldiers: whereas the Chaldeans' armies continued for a long time in the land of Judah, and in Jerusalem, vexing and plaguing the poor people of God. Now in this respect, the punishment of the Jews was a greater punishment than the punishment of Sodom, that was overthrown as in a moment. But that fire that has turned London into a heap of ashes, was such a fire that was carried on gradually, and that lasted four days, God giving the citizens time to mourn over their sins, to repent, to lay hold on everlasting strength, and to make peace with God. But,

[5.] Fifthly and lastly, Sodom's and Gomorrah's judgment is termed *eternal fire*, Jude 7, which expression, as it refers to the places themselves, do import that they were irrecoverably destroyed by fire; so as that they shall lie eternally waste. Those monstrous sinners of Sodom had turned the glory of God into shame, and therefore God will turn them both into a hell here, and a hell hereafter. God will punish unusual sinners with unusual judgments. The punishment by this fire is lasting, yea, everlasting: it is a standing monument of God's high displeasure, Deut. xxix. 23. We never read that ever God repented himself of the overthrow of Sodom and Gomorrah. Those cities are under a perpetual destruction, and so shall continue to the end of the world, if we will give credit to authors of great credit and reputation.[1] It well becomes the wisest and best of Christians seriously to consider how God setteth forth the destruction of his church's enemies: Isa. xxxiv. 8–11, 'For it is the day of the Lord's vengeance, and the year of recompenses for the controversy of Zion. And the streams thereof shall be turned into pitch, and the dust thereof into brimstone, and the land thereof shall become burning pitch. It shall not be quenched night nor day; the smoke thereof shall go up for ever: from generation to generation it shall lie waste; none shall pass through it for ever and ever. But the cormorant and the bittern shall possess it; the owl also and the raven shall dwell in it: and he shall stretch out upon it the line of confusion, and the stones of emptiness.' In these words you have a rhetorical description of that extreme devastation that God will bring upon the enemies of the church, in way of allusion to the destruction of Sodom and Gomorrah. But I hope London's doom is not such; for God has given to thousands of her inhabitants a spirit of grace and supplication, Zech. xii. 10; which is a clear evidence that at the long run they shall certainly carry the day with God. I have faith enough to believe that God will give London's mourners 'beauty for ashes, the oil of joy for mourning, and the garment of praise for the spirit of heaviness,' Isa. lxi. 3. And that London may yet be called 'a city of righteousness, the planting of the Lord, that he may be glorified.' I hope that God will one day say to London, 'Arise, shine; for thy light is come,

[1] Strabo, Solinus, Tacitus, Plinius, Josephus, &c.

and the glory of the Lord is risen upon thee. The Lord shall arise upon thee, and his glory shall be seen upon thee,' Isa. lx. 1, 2. By what has been said, it is evident enough that there has been a great mixture of mercy in that fiery dispensation that has passed upon London. And therefore why should not this consideration bear up the hearts of the people of God from fainting and sinking under their present calamity and misery? But,

(10.) The tenth support to bear up the hearts of the people of God under the late fiery dispensation, is this—viz., *That there are worse judgments than the judgment of fire which God might, but has not, inflicted upon you.* Let me evidence the truth of this in these five particulars:—

[1.] First, *The bloody sword is a more dreadful judgment than that of fire.* Fire may consume a man's house and his estate, but the sword cuts off a man's life. Now at what a poor rate do men value the whole world, when it stands in competition with their lives. He very well knew that man was a very great life-lover, who said, 'Skin for skin,' or skin upon skin, 'and all that a man hath will he give for his life,' Job ii. 4. God might have brought upon England, ay, and upon London too, the sword of a foreign enemy, as he did upon Jerusalem and the land of Judea. In that one only city of Jerusalem, during the time of the siege by Vespasian's armies, which were made up of Romans, Syrians, and Arabians, there died and were killed a thousand thousand.[1] At this time there were slain in all Judea in several places to the number of twelve hundred and forty thousand Jews. The whole city of Jerusalem flowed with blood, insomuch that many parts of the city that were set on fire were quenched by the blood of them that were slain. In seventeen years' time the Carthaginian war only in Italy, Spain, and Sicily, consumed and wasted fifteen hundred thousand men. The civil wars between Pompey and Cæsar swallowed down three hundred thousand men. Caius Cæsar did confess it, and gloried in it, that eleven hundred ninety and two thousand men were killed by him in wars. Pompey the Great writ upon Minerva's temple that he had scattered, chased, and killed twenty hundred eighty and three thousand men. Q. Fabius killed a hundred and ten thousand of the Gauls. C. Marius put to the sword two hundred thousand of the Cimbrians. Ætius, in that memorable battle of Catalonia,[2] slew a hundred sixty and two thousand Huns. Who can number up the many thousands that have fallen by the bloody sword in Europe, from the year 1620 to this year 1667? Ah London! London! thy streets might have flowed with the blood of the slain, as once the streets of Jerusalem, Paris, and others have done. Whilst the fire was a-devouring thy stately houses and palaces, a foreign sword might have been a-destroying thine inhabitants. Whilst the furious flames were a-consuming thy goods, thy wares, thy substance, thy riches, a close and secret enemy, spirited, counselled, and animated from Rome and hell, might have risen up in the midst of thee, that might have mingled together the blood of husbands and wives, and the blood of parents and children,

[1] Josephus, de Bello Jud.

[2] Chalons: Greg. Turon. ii. 7; Jornandes de Rebus Get. 36.—G.

and the blood of masters and servants, and the blood of rich and poor, and the blood of the honourable with the blood of the vile. Now had this been thy doom, O London! which many feared, and others expected, what a dreadful day would that have been! It is better to see our houses on fire than to see our streets running down with the blood of the slain. But,

[2.] Secondly, God might have inflicted *the judgment of famine upon London*, which is a more dreadful judgment than that of fire.[1] How sad would that day have been, O London! if thou hadst been so sorely put to it, as to have taken up that sad lamentation of weeping Jeremiah: Lam. ii. 11, 12, 19, 20, iv. 4, 5, 7–10, and v. 4, 6, 9, 10, 'Mine eyes do fail with tears, my bowels are troubled, my liver is poured upon the earth, for the destruction of the daughter of my people; because the children and the sucklings swoon in the streets. They say to their mothers, Where is corn and wine? when they swooned as the wounded in the streets of the city, when their soul was poured into their mother's bosom. Arise, cry out in the night; in the beginning of the watches pour out thine heart like water before the face of the Lord: lift up thy hands towards him for the life of thy young children, that faint for hunger in the top of every street. Shall the woman eat her fruit, and children of a span long? The tongue of the suckling child cleaveth to the roof of his mouth for thirst: the young children ask bread, and no man breaketh it unto them. They that did feed delicately are desolate in the streets: they that were brought up in scarlet embrace dunghills. Her Nazarites were purer than snow, they were whiter than milk, they were more ruddy in the body than rubies, their polishing was of sapphire. Their visage is blacker than a coal; they are not known in the streets: their skin cleaveth to their bones; it is withered, it is become like a stick. They that be slain with the sword are better than they that be slain with hunger; for these pine away, stricken through for want of the fruits of the field. The hands of the pitiful women have sodden their own children; they were their meat in the destruction of the daughter of my people. We have drunken our water for money; our wood is sold unto us. We have given the hand to the Egyptians and Assyrians, to be satisfied with bread. We gat our bread with the peril of our lives, because of the sword of the wilderness. Our skin was black like an oven, because of the terrible famine.' So great was the famine in Jerusalem,[2] that a bushel of wheat was sold for a talent, which is six hundred crowns, and the dung and raking of the city sinks was held good commons; and such pinching necessities were they under, that they acted against all piety, honesty, humanity, &c. Women did eat their children of a span long; yea, the hands of pitiful women did boil their own children, and men eat one another; yea, many did eat the flesh of their own arms, according to what the Lord had long before threatened: Isa. ix. 19, 20, 'Through the wrath of the Lord of hosts is the land darkened, and the people shall be as the fuel of the fire: no man shall spare his brother. And he shall snatch on the right hand, and be hungry; and he shall eat on the left hand, and

[1] Gen. xlv. 46; Joel i. 2, and ii. 3; Jer. xxiv. 10; Ezek. vi. 11; 2 Sam. xxi. 1.
[2] Josephus, lib. vi. cap. 16, de Bello Judaico.

they shall not be satisfied: they shall eat every man the flesh of his own arm.' In the reign of William the First[1] there was so great a dearth and famine, especially in Northumberland, that men were glad to eat horses, dogs, cats, and rats, and what else is most abhorrent to nature. In Honorius's reign there was such a scarcity of all manner of provision in Rome, that men were even afraid of one another; and the common voice that was heard in the kirk was *Pone pretium humanæ carni*, Set a price on man's flesh. In Italy, when it was wasted by the Goths under Justinian, the famine was so great, that in Picene[2] only, fifty thousand persons died with hunger, and not only man's flesh was made meat of, but the very excrements of men also. In the reign of Hubid, king of Spain, there was no rain for six and twenty years together, so that the drought was so great that all the fountains and rivers, except Iber and Betis, [Baetis,] were dried up; so that the earth gaped in several places, that whole fields were parted, and that many who had thought to have fled into other parts were hindered, and could not get passage over these fearful openings of the earth. Hereby Spain, especially those places nearest the Mediterranean Sea, being stripped naked of all herbs, and the glory of trees being dried up, except a few trees which were preserved upon the banks of the river Betis, men and beasts being consumed with thirst and famine, was turned by this judgment into a miserable solitude and wilderness. The royal line of the kings was by this means extinct; and the poorer sort of men, whose means were short and provision small, went into other places as they could conveniently and with all speed, not being able to stand or stay out this six and twenty years' misery.[3] In the Peloponnesian war, at Potidæa, men ate one another, [Thucydides.] When Utica was besieged by Hamilcar, the father of Hannibal, men ate one another, the famine was so great amongst them, [Polybius.] At Antioch in Syria many of the Christians, in the holy war, through famine devoured the dead bodies of the late slain enemies.[4] At the siege of Scodra, horses were dainty meat; yea, they were glad to eat dogs, cats, rats, and the skins of beasts sod. A little mouse, and puddings made of dogs' guts, was sold at so great a price as exceeds all credit. When Hannibal besieged Casilinum, the famine was so great, that a mouse was sold for two hundred groats, that is, for three pounds eighteen shillings and eight pence.[5] That was a sore famine in Samaria when an ass's head was sold for eighty pieces of silver—that is, say some, for four or five pound, 2 Kings vi. 25; others say ten, for a shekel of silver was with the Jews as much as two shillings and sixpence with us. By this account an ass's head was sold for ten pounds sterling. In Edward the Second's time, *anno* 1316, there was so great a famine, that horses, dogs, yea, men and children, were stolen for food; and the thieves newly brought into the jails were torn in pieces and eaten presently, half alive, by such as had been longer there.[6] In war, oppression, captivity, and many other

[1] Sir Richard Baker's Chronicle, p. 26.
[2] Pisa of the Peloponnesus, or Pissæ (spelled *Pisanus*) or Etruria ?—G.
[3] All these things do the histories of Spain report.
[4] [Knolles] Turk. Hist. fol. 18.
[5] Val. Max. lib. vii. cap. 6. Turk. Hist. [Livy, xxiii. 17, 19.—G.]
[6] Purch. Pilgrim., p. 289. Speed, vi. 4.

calamities, much of the hand of man is to be seen; but famine is a deep, evident, and apparent judgment, which God himself brings upon the sons of men by his own high hand. Many or most of those calamities that are brought upon us by human means are avoidable by human helps; but famine is that comprehensive judgment, that the highest power on earth cannot help against: 'If the Lord do not help thee, whence shall I help thee? out of the barn-floor, or out of the wine-press?' said the king of Israel in the famine of Samaria, 2 Kings vi. 27. Ah London, London! if the Lord had inflicted upon thy inhabitants this sore judgment of famine, making 'the heavens as iron, and the earth as brass;' if the Lord had cut off all thy delightful and necessary provisions, and thy citizens had been forced to eat one another, or every one to eat the flesh of his own arms, and the fruit of his own body, how dismal would thy condition have been! Lev. xxvi. 19; Hab. iii. 17; Deut. xxviii. 23. Certainly such as have been swept away by the raging pestilence ashore, and such as have been slain by the bloody sword at sea, might very well be counted happy, in comparison of those who should live and die under that lingering judgment of a famine. Doubtless famine is a sorer judgment than either sword, fire, or pestilence. There be many deaths in a dearth. Famine is the top of all human calamities, as Basil termeth it. Extreme hunger hath made mothers murderers, and so turned the sanctuary of life into the shambles of death.

[3.] Thirdly, God might have overturned London and her inhabitants in a moment by *some great and dreadful earthquake*, as he hath done several great, rich, strong, and populous cities and towns in former times, Isa. xiii. 13, and Ps. xviii. 7. Under Tiberius the emperor thirteen cities of Asia fell down with an earthquake, and six under Trajan, and twelve under Constantine. In Campania, Ferrara in Italy, 1569,[1] in the space of forty hours, by reason of an earthquake, many palaces, temples, and houses were overthrown, with the loss of many a man, the loss amounting to forty hundred thousand pounds. In the year 1171, there was such a mighty earthquake that the city Tripoli, and a great part of Damascus in Antiochia, and Hulcipre (?), the chief city in the kingdom of Loradin (?), and other cities of the Saracens, either perished utterly or were wonderfully defaced. In the year 1509, [Bodin,] in the month of September, there was so great an earthquake at Constantinople, that there were thirteen thousand men destroyed by it, and the city miserably shattered and ruined by it. In the reign of Henry the First,[2] the earth moved with so great a violence, that many buildings were shaken down; and Malmesbury saith, 'That the house wherein he sat was lifted up with a double remove, and at the third time settled again in the proper place.' Also in divers places it yielded forth a hideous noise, and cast forth flames. In Lombardy [Hoveden] there was an earthquake that continued forty days, and removed a town from the place where it stood a great way off. In the eleventh year of the reign of King Henry the Second,[3] on the six and twentieth day of January, was so great an earthquake in Ely, Norfolk, and Suffolk, that it overthrew them that stood upon their feet, and made the bells to ring in the steeples. In the four and twentieth

[1] Fardentius. [2] Sir Richard Baker's Chronicle, p. 47. [3] *Ibid.* p. 65.

year of his reign, in the territory of Darlington, in the bishopric of Durham, the earth lifted up herself in the manner of a high tower, and so remained unmovable from morning till evening, and then fell with so horrible a noise, that it frighted the inhabitants thereabouts, and the earth, swallowing it up, made there a deep pit, which is seen at this day; for a testimony whereof, Leland saith he saw the pits there, commonly called hell-kettles. In the year 1666,[1] the city of Raguza was overthrown by a most dreadful earthquake, and all the inhabitants, which were many thousands, except a few hundred, were destroyed, and buried in the ruins of that city. At Berne, anno 1584,[2] near unto which city a certain hill, carried violently beyond and over other hills, is reported by Polanus, who lived in those parts, to have covered a whole village, that had ninety families in it, one half house only excepted, wherein the master of the family, with his wife and children, were earnestly calling upon God. Oh the terror of the Lord! and oh the power of fervent prayer! At Pleures (?) in Rhetia, anno 1618, Aug. 25,[3] the whole town was over-covered with a mountain, which with its most swift motion oppressed fifteen hundred. In the days of Uzziah king of Judah, there was such a terrible earthquake, that the people with fear and horror fled from it: Zech. xiv. 5, 'Yea, ye shall flee, like as ye fled from before the earthquake in the days of Uzziah king of Judah,' Amos i. 1. The Jewish doctors affirm that this amazing earthquake fell out just at that instant time when Uzziah offered incense, and was therefore smitten with a leprosy: but this is but their conjecture. However, this dreadful earthquake was a horrible sign and presage of God's wrath to that sinful people. Josephus tells us[4] that by it half a great hill was removed out of its place, and carried four furlongs another way, so that the highway was obstructed, and the king's gardens utterly marred. The same author further tells us,[5] that at that time that Cæsar and Anthony made trial of their titles in the Actian war, and in the seventh year of the reign of king Herod, there happened such an earthquake in the country of Judea, that never the like was seen in any other place; so that divers beasts were slain thereby, and that ten thousand men were overwhelmed and destroyed in the ruins of their houses. The same author saith[6] that in the midst of the Actian war, about the beginning of the spring time, there happened so great an earthquake, as slew an infinite multitude of beasts, and thirty thousand people; yet the army had no harm, for it lay in the open field. Upon the report of this dreadful earthquake, and the effects of it, the Arabians were so highly encouraged, that they entered into Judea, supposing that there were no men left alive to resist them, and that they should certainly conquer the country; and before their coming, they slew the ambassadors of the Jews that were sent unto them. Ah London, London! if the Lord had by some terrible earthquake utterly overthrown thee, and buried all thy inhabitants under thy ruins, as he hath dealt by many cities and citizens, both in former and in these latter times, how dreadful would thy case then have been over what now it is! Certainly such earthquakes as

[1] See the relation in print.
[2] Polan. Syntag. 841.
[3] Alst. Chronol.
[4] Antiq., lib. ix. cap. 11
[5] Lib. xv. cap. 7.
[6] Josephus, lib. i. cap. 14, de Bello Judaico.

overwhelm both cities and citizens are far greater judgments than such a fire or fires, that only consumes men's houses, but never hurts their persons. God might have inflicted this sore judgment upon thee, O London, but he has not; therefore it concerns thee to be still a-crying, Grace, grace! But,

[4.] Fourthly, God might have inflicted *that judgment, both upon city and citizens, that he did upon Korah, Dathan, and Abiram, and all that appertained to them:* Num. xvi. 31–34, 'And it came to pass, as he had made an end of speaking all these words, that the ground clave asunder that was under them: and the earth opened her mouth, and swallowed them up, and their houses, and all the men that appertained unto Korah, and all their goods. They, and all that appertained to them, went down alive into the pit, and the earth closed upon them: and they perished from among the congregation. And all Israel that were round about them fled at the cry of them: for they said, Lest the earth swallow us up also.'[1] Whilst Moses spake these words, saith Josephus,[2] and intermixed them with tears, the earth trembled, and, shaking, began to remove, after such a manner as when, by the violence of the wind, a great billow of the sea floateth and is tossed hither and thither; hereat all the people were amazed, but after that a horrible and shattering noise was made about their tents, and the earth opened and swallowed up both them and all that which they esteemed dear, which was after a manner so exterminate as nothing remained of theirs to be beheld. Whereupon in a moment the earth closed again, and the vast gaping was fast shut, so as there appeared not any sign of that which had happened. Thus perished they all, leaving behind them an example of God's power and judgments. And this accident was the more miserable, in that there were no one, no, not of their kinsfolks or allies, that had compassion of them; so that all the people whatsoever, forgetting those things which were past, did allow God's justice with joyful acclamations, esteeming them unworthy to be bemoaned, but to be held as the plague and perverters of the people. Oh what a dreadful judgment was this, for persons to be buried alive; for houses and inhabitants, and all their goods, to be swallowed up in a moment! What tongue can express, or heart conceive, the terror and astonishment that fell upon Korah, Dathan, and Abiram, when the earth, which God had made firm, and established by a perpetual decree to stand fast under men's feet, was weary of bearing them, and therefore opened her mouth and swallowed them and all their concernments up! Ah London, London! if the earth had opened her mouth and swallowed up all thy houses and inhabitants, with all thy goods and riches in a moment; would not this have been ten thousand thousand times a greater judgment than that fiery dispensation that has passed upon thee? But,

[5.] Fifthly and lastly, God might have *rained hell out of heaven upon you, as he did upon Sodom and Gomorrah, and this would have been a sorer judgment than what he has inflicted upon you,* Gen. xix. If God, by raining fire and brimstone from heaven, had consumed your persons, houses, riches, and relations, would not this have been the

[1] Such virgins that had been deflowered, the heathen buried alive, accounting that the sorest of all punishments.

[2] Josephus, Antiq., lib. iv. cap. 3.

height of judgment, and infinitely more terrible and dreadful to you than that fiery dispensation that has consumed part of your estates, and turned your houses into ashes? Now by these five things it is most evident that there are worse judgments than the judgment of fire, which God in justice might have inflicted upon you. But free mercy has so interposed, that God has not stirred up all his wrath; and though he has severely punished you, yet it is less than your iniquities have deserved, Ezra ix. 13; and therefore let this consideration support and bear up your hearts under all your present sorrows and sufferings. But,

(11.) Eleventhly, *Though your houses are burnt, and your habitations laid desolate, yet your outward condition is not worse than Christ's was when he was in the world.* The estate and condition of Christ was low, yea, very low and mean in this world. Witness his own relation when he was upon the earth: 'The foxes have holes, and the birds of the air have nests,' Mat. viii. 20,—or resting-places where they go to rest, as under a tent, like as the Greek word properly imports,—'but the Son of man hath not where to lay his head.' He doth not say, Kings have palaces, but I have none; nor he does not say that rich men have houses and lands and lordships to entertain their followers, but I have none; but, 'The foxes have holes, and the birds of the air have nests, but the Son of man hath not where to lay his head.' Christ was willing to undeceive the scribe, and to shew him his mistake. Thou thinkest, O scribe, by following of me to get riches, and honour, and preferment, and to be somebody in the world, but thou art highly mistaken; for I have neither silver nor gold, lands nor lordships, no, not so much as a house to put my head in. When I was born, I was born in a stable and laid in a manger, Luke ii. 17; and now I live upon others, and am maintained by others, Luke viii. 3. I am not rich enough to pay my tribute, and therefore do not deceive thyself, Mat. xvii. 27. The great Architect of the world had not a house to put his head in, but emptied himself of all, and became poor to make us rich, not in goods, but in grace, not in worldly wealth, but in the treasures of another world, Phil. ii. 7; 2 Cor. viii. 9.[1] He that was heir of both worlds had not a house of his own to put his head in. Christ lived poor and died poor. As he was born in another man's house, so he was buried in another man's tomb. Austin observes, when Christ died he made no will, he had no crown-lands, only his coat was left, and that the soldiers parted amongst themselves. Are you houseless, are you penniless, are you poor, and low, and mean in this world? So was Christ. Remember 'the servant is not greater than his lord,' John xiii. 16. It is good seriously to ponder upon that saying of Christ, 'The disciple is not above his master, nor the servant above his lord. It is enough for the disciple that he be as his master, and the servant as his lord,' Mat. x. 24, 25. If Joab the lord-general be in tents, it is a shame for Uriah to take his ease at home in a soft bed. It is unseemly to see the head all begored with blood and crowned with thorns, and the members to be decked with roses and jewels, and to smell of rich odours, spices, and perfumes. Art thou in a worse condition than Christ was in this

[1] Christi paupertas meum est patrimonium.—*Ambrose.*

world? Oh no, no! Why then dost thou murmur and complain? Why dost thou say there is no sorrow to thy sorrow, nor no suffering to thy suffering? O sirs! it is honour enough for the disciples of Christ to fare as Christ fared in this world. Why should the servant be in a better condition than his lord? Is not that servant happy enough that is equal with his lord? Did the burnt citizens but seriously and frequently meditate and ponder upon the poverty and low estate of Christ whilst he was in this world, their hearts would be more calm and quiet under all their crosses and losses than now they are. But,

(12.) Twelfthly, *Though your houses are burnt, and your habitations laid desolate, and you have no certain dwelling-place, &c., yet your outward condition in this world is not worse than theirs was* 'of whom this world was not worthy:' Lam. v. 2, 'Our inheritance is turned to strangers, our houses to aliens;' Ps. cvii. 4, 5, 'They wandered in the wilderness in a solitary way; they found no city to dwell in. Hungry and thirsty, their souls fainted in them;' 1 Cor. iv. 11, 'Even unto this present hour we both hunger and thirst, and are naked, and are buffeted, and have no certain dwelling-place;' Heb. xi. 37, 38, 'They wandered about in sheep-skins and goat-skins, being destitute, afflicted, tormented. They wandered in deserts, and in mountains, and in dens, and in caves of the earth.' Some of the learned, by their wandering up and down in sheep-skins and goat-skins, do understand their disguising of themselves for their better security. One well observes from the words, [Chrysostom,] that they did not only wander and were removed from their own habitation, but that they were not quiet even in the woods, deserts, mountains, dens, and caves of the earth, but were hunted by their persecutors from desert to desert, and from mountain to mountain, and from den to den, and from one cave to another.

But hereupon some might be ready to object and reply,

Obj. These were the very worst of the worst of men. Surely these were very vile, base, and unworthy wretches, these were the greatest of sinners, &c.

Ans. Oh no; they were such, saith the Holy Ghost, 'of whom the world was not worthy.' The heathenish world, the poor, blind, ignorant, atheistical world, the profane, superstitious, idolatrous, oppressing, and persecuting world was not worthy of them—that is, they were not worthy, (1.) Of their presence and company. (2.) They were not worthy of their prayers and tears. (3.) They were not worthy of their counsel and advice. (4.) They were not worthy of their gracious lives and examples. In this scripture you may plainly see that their wandering up and down in deserts, and on the mountains, and in dens, and in the caves of the earth, is reckoned up amongst those great and dreadful things that the saints suffered in that woeful day. Those precious souls that dwelt in caves and dens, and wandered up and down in sheep-skins and goat-skins, might have rustled in their silks, satins, and velvets; they might, Nebuchadnezzar-like, have vaunted themselves on their stately turrets and palaces, if they would have wounded their consciences and have turned their backs upon Christ and religion. Now if the burnt-up citizens of London would but seriously lay to heart the sad dispensations of God towards his choicest worthies, then their hearts would neither faint nor sink under their present losses, crosses, and sufferings. But,

(13.) Thirteenthly and lastly, *There is a worse fire than that which has turned London into a ruinous heap—viz., the fire of hell, which Christ has freed believers from.* There is 'unquenchable fire:' Mat iii. 12, 'He will burn up the chaff with unquenchable fire.' There is 'everlasting burnings:' Isa. xxxiii. 14, 'The sinners in Zion are afraid; fearfulness hath surprised the hypocrites. Who among us shall dwell with the devouring fire? who among us shall dwell with everlasting burnings?[1] Luke iii. 17; Mat. xviii. 8. Wicked men, who are now the only burning jolly fellows of the time, shall one day go from burning to burning; from burning in sin, to burning in hell; from burning in flames of lusts, to burning in flames of torment, except there be found repentance on their sides, and pardoning grace on God's. O sirs! in this devouring fire, in these everlasting burnings, Cain shall find no cities to build, nor his posterity shall have no instruments of music to invent there; none shall take up the timbrel or harp, or rejoice at the sound of the organ. There Belshazzar cannot drink wine in bowls, nor eat the lambs out of the flock, nor the calves out of the midst of the stall. In everlasting burnings there will be no merry company to pass time away; nor no dice to cast care away; nor no cellars of wine wherein to drown the sinner's grief, Gen. iv. 17; Amos vi. 5; Job xxi. 12; Dan. v. 23 Amos vi. 4. There is everlasting fire: Mat. xxv. 41, 'Then shall he say also unto them on the left hand, Depart from me, ye cursed, into everlasting fire, prepared for the devil and his angels.' This terrible sentence breathes out nothing but fire and brimstone, terror and horror, dread and woe. The last words that ever Christ will speak in this world will be the most tormenting and amazing, the most killing and damning, the most stinging and wounding, 'Depart from me.' There is rejection: pack, begone, get you out of my sight, let me never see your faces more! It was a heavy doom that was passed upon Nebuchadnezzar, Dan. iv. 25, that he should be driven from the society of men, and, in an extremity of a sottish melancholy, spend his time among the beasts of the field; but that was nothing to this soul-killing word, 'Depart from me.' It was nothing to men's being cast out of the presence of Christ for ever. The remembrance of which made one to pray thus, 'O Lord, deliver me at the great day from that killing word DEPART.[2] And what saith another?—

> 'This word *depart*, the goats with horror hears;
> But this word *come*, the sheep to joy appears.'[3]

Basil saith, 'That an alienation and utter separation from God is more grievous than the pains of hell.'[4] Chrysostom saith,[5] 'That the torments of a thousand hells, if there were so many, comes far short of this one—to wit, to be turned out of God's presence with a

[1] Some devout personages caused this scripture to be writ in letters of gold upon their chimney-pieces.—*B. of Betty in France, in his Draught of Eternity.* [Camus, Bishop of Belly, *not* Betty.—G.]

[2] Bernard. in Ps. xci.

[3] Sphynx.

[4] Basil. Asc. Etic., cap. 2.

[5] Chrysost. in Mat., hom. xxiv.

Non novi vos, I know you not.' What a grief were it here to be banished from the king's court with Absalom, or to be turned out of doors with Hagar and Ishmael, or to be cast out of God's presence with cursed Cain! But what is all this to a man's being excommunicated, and cast out of the presence of God, of Christ, of the angels, and out of the general assembly of the saints and congregation of the firstborn? To be secluded from the presence of God is of all miseries the greatest, Heb. xii. 22, 23. The serious thoughts of this made one say, 'Many do abhor hell, but I esteem the fall from that glory to be a greater punishment than hell itself; it is better to endure ten thousand thunder-claps than be deprived of the beatifical vision.' Certainly the tears of hell are not sufficient to bewail the loss of heaven. If those precious souls wept because they should see Paul's face no more, Acts xx. 38, how deplorable is the eternal deprivation of the beatifical vision! 'Depart from me,' is the first and worst of that dreadful sentence which Christ shall pass upon sinners at last. Every syllable sounds horror and terror, grief and sorrow, amazement and astonishment to all whom it doth concern.

'Ye cursed:' there is the malediction. But Lord, if we must depart, let us depart blessed.[1] No, 'depart ye cursed:' you have cursed others, and now you shall be cursed yourselves; you shall be cursed in your bodies, and cursed in your souls; you shall be cursed of God, and cursed of Christ, and cursed of angels, and cursed of saints, and cursed of devils, and cursed of your companions. Yea, you shall now curse your very selves, your very souls, that ever you have despised the gospel, refused the offers of grace, scorned Christ, and neglected the means of your salvation. O sinners, sinners, all your curses, all your maledictions shall at last recoil upon your own souls! Now thou cursest every man and thing that stands in the way of thy lusts, and that crosses thy designs; but at last all the curses of heaven and hell shall meet in their full power and force upon thee. Surely that man is cursed with a witness that is cursed by Christ himself!

But, Lord, if we must depart, and depart cursed, oh let us go into some good place! No, 'Depart ye into everlasting fire.'[2] There is the vengeance and continuance of it. You shall go into fire, into everlasting fire, that shall neither consume itself, nor consume you. Eternity of extremity is the hell of hell. The fire in hell is like that stone in Arcadia, which being once kindled, could never be quenched. If all the fires that ever were in the world were contracted into one fire, how terrible would it be! Yet such a fire would be but as painted fire upon the wall to the fire of hell. If it be so sad a spectacle to behold a malefactor's flesh consumed by piecemeals in a lingering fire, ah, how sad, how dreadful, would it be to experience what it is to lie in unquenchable fire, not for a day, a month, or a year, or a hundred or a thousand years, but for ever and ever! If it were, saith one, [Cyril,] but for a thousand years, I could bear it; but seeing it is for eternity, this amazeth and affrighteth me! I am

[1] Cursings now are wicked men's hymns; but in hell they shall be their woes, Rev. xvi. 9, 11, 21.

[2] Of this fire you had need of some devil or accursed wretch to descant, saith one.

afraid of hell, saith another, [Isidore,[1]] because the worm there never dies, and the fire never goes out. For to be tormented without end, this is that which goes beyond all the bounds of desperation. Grievous is the torment of the damned for the bitterness of the punishments, but it is more grievous for the diversity of the punishments, but most grievous for the eternity of the punishments.[2]

To lie in everlasting torments, to roar for ever for disquietness of heart, to rage for ever for madness of soul, to weep, and grieve, and gnash the teeth for ever, is a misery beyond all expression, Mat. xxv. 46. Bellarmine out of Barocius[3] tells of a learned man who, after his death, appeared to his friend complaining that he was adjudged to hell-torments, which, saith he, were they to last but a thousand thousand years, I should think it tolerable, but, alas, they are eternal! And it is called 'eternal fire,' Jude 7. I have read of a prison among the Persians which was deep, and wide, and dark, and out of which the prisoners could never get, and therefore it was called by them *Lethe*, Forgetfulness: this prison was a paradise to hell. Mark, everything that is conducible to the torments of the damned is eternal. (1.) God that damns them is eternal, Isa. xxxiii. 14; Rom. xvi. 26. (2.) The fire that torments them is eternal, Isa. xxx. 33, and lxvi. 24; Jude 7.[4] (3.) The prison and chains that holds them are eternal, Jude 6, 7, 13; 2 Pet. ii. 17. (4.) The worm that gnaws them is eternal, Mark ix. 44. Melanchthon calls it a hellish fury. (5.) The sentence that shall be passed upon them shall be eternal, Mat. xxv. 41, 42. The fire of hell is called a burning lake: Rev. xx. 15, 'Whosoever was not found written in the book of life, was cast into the lake of fire.' You shall[5] know that fire is the most tormenting element. Oh the most dreadful impressions that it makes upon the flesh! The schoolmen distinguish thus of fire—they say there is *ignis ardoris, fœtoris, et terroris*, fire of heat, of stench, and of terror: of heat, as in Mount Etna; of stench, as in Mount Heda;[6] of terror and fear, as *ignis fulguris*, the fire of lightning in America: all these fires they say are in hell. But to let the schoolmen pass. It is disputed among many of the learned whether there be material fire in hell or no. That it is very probable that there is material fire in hell, or that which is full as terrible, or more terrible, may, I suppose, be thus evidenced:—

[1.] First, *The fire of hell is frequently mentioned in the blessed Scripture.* 'Who shall say to his brother, Thou fool! shall be in danger of hell-fire.' At the day of judgment the tares are burnt in the fire, Mat. xiii. 40. Into this fire offending members are cast, Mat. xviii. 18, 19. To this everlasting fire the goats are adjudged, Mat. xxv. 41. In this fire those that worship the beast are tormented, Rev. xiv. 10. And the Sodomites at this very day suffer the vengeance of eternal fire, Jude 7. Into this fire shall all barren and unfruitful Christians be cast: Mat. iii. 10, 'And now also the axe is laid unto the root of the trees, therefore every tree which bringeth not forth good fruit is

[1] Cl. Orat. 12. [2] Dionys. in 18 Apocalyps., fol. 301. [3] De arte moriendi.

[4] 1 Pet. iii. 19. Lucian saith that it was the common opinion among them that the wicked were held in chains by Pluto, (so they call the prince of devils,) in chains, which cannot be loosed. [5] Query, 'all'?—G. [6] Query, 'Hecla'?—G.]

hewn down, and cast into the fire.' Negative goodness will never secure a man either from the axe or from the fire. Yea, every man and woman under heaven that keeps off from Christ, and that lives and dies out of Christ, and that are never entered into a marriage union with Christ, they shall all be cast into this fire: John xv. 6, 'If a man abide not in me, he is cast forth as a branch that is withered; and men gather them, and cast them into the fire, and they are burned.' Thus you see how the Scripture runs. Now you know that it is safest for us to adhere to the very letter of the Scripture, unless evident and necessary occasion draw us from a literal interpretation of it. But,

[2.] Secondly, *To this fire is ascribed sulphur, flames, wood:* Isa. xxx. 33, 'For Tophet is ordained of old,' that is, hell; those terrible allusions to Tophet, to the shrieks and yellings of those children that were sacrificed there, are but dark representations of the pain and miseries of the damned: 'yea, for the king it is prepared;' if princes be wicked, it is neither their power nor their policy, their dignity or worldly glory, that can secure them from Tophet. 'He hath made it deep and large; the pile thereof is fire and much wood; the breath of the Lord, like a stream of brimstone, doth kindle it;' 2 Kings xxiii. 18. Now he shall be an Apollo to me that can shew me where the Lord in his word gives such properties to immaterial fire that are here given in the text. But yet remember this, that that God that makes the damned live without food, is able to maintain this fire without wood. But,

[3.] Thirdly, *Fire is the most furious of all elements, and therefore the bodies of men cannot be more exquisitely tormented than with fire.*[1] The bodies that sinned on earth shall be punished and tormented in hell. Now what can be more grievous and vexatious, more afflicting and tormenting to the bodies of men, than material fire? Bilney the martyr could not endure to hold his finger in the flame of a candle for a little while, for a quarter of an hour, though he tried to do it before he burnt at the stake. Oh, then, how will the bodies of men endure to dwell in unquenchable fire, to dwell in everlasting burnings! The brick-kilns of Egypt, the furnace of Babel, are but as the glowing sparkle, or as the blaze of a brush-faggot, to this tormenting Tophet, that has been prepared of old to punish the bodies of sinners with. But,

[4.] Fourthly, *Several of the fathers and schools generally agree that the fire which shall torment the wicked in hell shall be material fire; but yet they say that this material fire shall wonderfully exceed ours, both in degree of heat and fierceness of burning.*[2] Our elementary or culinary fire is no more to be compared with the fire of hell, than fire painted upon the wall is to be compared with fire burning in our chimneys. *Si igne damnabit reprobos, quare non in igne cruciabit damnatos*, says one of the ancients, If he will judge the reprobates in fire, why not condemn them to fire?

Obj. But if it be material fire, then it may be quenched; besides, we see by common experience that material fire in a short time will

[1] Water doth only kill, but fire doth vex, terrify, and torment in killing.—[*Foxe,*] *Act. and Mon.*

[2] Zaach. Austin, Peter Lombard, Thos. Aquinas, Gregory, &c.

consume and spend itself. Neither can we see how material fire can make impressions upon spirits, as the devils and souls of men are.

Ans. [1.] First, *Do not we find that the bush burned and was not consumed?* Exod. iii. 2, 3. Though all clothes by daily experience wax old, yet when the Israelites were in their wilderness-condition their clothes did not wax old: Deut. viii. 4, 'Thy raiment waxed not old upon thee, neither did thy foot swell these forty years': Neh. ix. 41, 'Yea, forty years didst thou sustain them in the wilderness, so that they lacked nothing; their clothes waxed not old, and their feet swelled not.' Their clothes were never the worse for wearing. God by his almighty power kept their clothes from waxing old; and so God by his almighty power can keep the fire of hell unquenchable. But,

[2.] Secondly, Such as thus object, *draw things to the scantling of their own reason, which may be many ways of a dangerous consequence both to themselves and others.* Certainly such as go about to make the fire of hell only spiritual fire, they go about to make it no fire at all; for it passeth the natural fire to be spiritual. But,

[3.] Thirdly, We see in this life *that bodily tortures work upon the spirits in the same bodies: and why may it not be so in hell?* Do not men by their daily experience find that their souls are frequently afflicted in and under corporeal distempers, diseases, and weaknesses? Doubtless God can by his almighty power infuse such power into material fire as to make it the instrument of his dreadful wrath and vengeance, to plague, punish, scorch, and burn the souls of damned sinners. Bodies and souls are co-partners in the same sins, and therefore God may make them co-partners in the same punishments. Every creature is such as the great God will have it to be, and commands it to be; and therefore if the Lord shall lay a command upon the fire of hell to reach and burn the souls of damned sinners, it shall certainly do it. God is the God of nature as well as the God of grace; and therefore I cannot see how the fire of hell can be said now to act against its own nature, when it does but act according to the will and command of the God of nature. I readily grant that if you consider infernal fire in itself, or in its own nature, and so it cannot have any power on such a spiritual substance as the soul of man is; but if you consider infernal fire as an instrument in an almighty hand, and so it can act upon such spiritual beings as devils and damned souls are, and make the same dreadful and painful impressions upon them as it would do upon corporeal beings.[1] Though spirits have nothing material in their nature which that infernal fire should work upon, yet such is the almighty power of God that he can make spirits most sensible of those fiery tortures and torments which he has declared and appointed for them to undergo. Let them tell us, saith one, [Dr Jackson,] how it is possible that the soul of man, which is an immortal substance, should be truly wedded to the body or material substance: and I shall as easily answer them, that it is as possible for the same soul to be as easily wrought upon by a material fire. It is much disputed and controverted among the schoolmen how the devils can be tormented with corporeal fire, seeing they are spirits; and, as I

[1] *Vide* August., lib. xxi. c. 10, de Civitate Dei.

suppose, it is well concluded of them thus—1. First, That in hell there is corporeal fire, as appears thus: (1.) Because the Scripture affirms it, Mat. iii. 10, v. 22, and xxv. 41: (2.) Because the bodies sinning against God are to be vexed and tormented with corporeal pains. 2. Secondly, They conclude that the devils are tormented in that fire because Christ saith so: Mat. xxv. 41, 'Depart from me, ye cursed, into everlasting fire, prepared for the devil and his angels.' 3. Thirdly, It being demanded, How the devils are tormented in that fire? they answer, They are tormented, not only, First, With the sight of it; or Secondly, With an imaginary apprehension thereof; but Thirdly, As an instrument ordained of God for that very end; and Fourthly, *Ut locus locatum continens et cogens.*[1] Hell is a fiery region, or a region of fire; and therefore the devils being contained and included therein, must needs be tormented thereby. *Cum Dives ab igne patiatur, quis neget, animas ignibus puniri.* None must question this truth, saith my author, that souls and spirits are punished by fire, seeing our Saviour himself telleth us that Dives, who was in hell but in soul, was tormented in the flames, Luke xvi. 24.[2] But,

[4.] Fourthly, *It is not safe to leave the plain letter of the Scripture to allegorise;* and whether the opinion of metaphorical fire in hell, hath not been an introduction to that opinion that many have taken up in these days—viz., that there is no other hell but what is within us, I shall not now stand to determine. I know Calvin, and some others, are for the allegory; and they give this for a reason, that there is mention made of wood, and of a worm, as well as fire. Now these are allegorical, and therefore the fire is allegorical also. But by their favour, we find in the Scripture that those things which are spoken together are not always taken in the same nature and manner. As, for example, Christ is called, 'the rock of our salvation,' Deut. xxxii. 15, 18, 30, 31; 2 Sam. xxii. 47; 1 Cor. x. 4. Now the rock is allegorical; is our salvation therefore allegorical? So likewise Luke xxii. 30, 'Ye shall eat and drink,' saith our Saviour, 'at my table in my kingdom.' Eating and drinking is allegorical: is therefore the kingdom allegorical too? Allegories are not to be admitted but where the Scripture itself doth warrant them; and commonly where an allegory is propounded, there it is also expounded. As in Gal. iv. 24, 'Which things are an allegory; for these are the two testaments.' Many men have been too wanton with allegories. Origen, Ambrose, Jerome, and several others of the ancients, have been blamed for it by learned men. But,

[5.] Fifthly and lastly, I cannot tell but that the fire by which the damned shall be punished, *may be partly material, and partly spiritual; partly material, to work upon the body, and partly spiritual, to torment the soul.* Dr Gouge[3] puts this question, Is it a material fire wherewith the damned in hell are tormented? and gives this answer—viz., This is too curious a point to resolve to the full; but yet this answer may safely be returned, It is no wasting or consuming fire, but a torturing; and so far corporeal, as it tormenteth the body; and

[1] Tho. [Aquinas,] Supplem. lxx. cap. 3.
[2] Greg. Dial. iv., cap. 28, 29.
[3] Dr Gouge on Heb. x. 27, sec. 98.

so far incorporeal, as it tormenteth the soul. Socrates, speaking of hell, saith, I was never there myself, neither have I ever spoke with any that came from thence. Suppose, saith one, [Mr Bolton,] there be no fire in hell, yet I assure thee this, that thou shalt be scorched with fire; the fire of God's wrath shall torment thee more than bodily fire can do, and therefore it will be your wisdom not so much to question this or that about hell-fire, as to make it your work, your business, not to come there. He gave good counsel who said, [Bernard,] Let us go down to hell while we are alive, that we may not go to hell when we are dead. And so did he who, speaking of hell, said, [Chrysostom,] *Ne quœramus ubi sit, sed quomodo illam fugiamus*, Let us not seek where it is, but how we shall avoid it. The same author gives this further counsel—viz., That at all banquets, feasts, and public meetings, men should talk of hellish pains and torments, that so their hearts may be overawed, and they provoked to avoid them and secure themselves against them. Doubtless, the serious thoughts of hellish pain while men live, is one blessed way to keep them from those torments when they come to die. Another gives this pious counsel, Let us earnestly importune the Lord, that this knowledge, whether the fire of hell be material or not, be never manifested to us by experience. It is infinitely better to endeavour the avoiding hell-fire, than curiously to dispute about it. Look, as there is nothing more grievous than hell, so there is nothing more profitable than the fear of it.

Obj. But what difference is there between our common fire and hell-fire?

I answer, a mighty difference, a vast difference. Take it in these six particulars:—

[1.] First, They differ *in their heat.* No heart can conceive, nor no tongue can express the exquisite heat of infernal fire. Were all the fires under heaven contracted into one fire; yea, were all the coals, wood, oil, hemp, flax, pitch, tar, brimstone, and all other combustibles in the world contracted into one flame, into one fire, yet one spark of infernal fire would be more hot, violent, dreadful, amazing, astonishing, raging, and tormenting, than all that fire that is supposedly made up of all the combustibles the earth affords. To man's sense, there is nothing more terrible and afflictive than fire; and of all fires, there is none so scalding and tormenting as that of brimstone. Now in that lake which burns with fire and brimstone for ever and ever, shall the wicked of the earth be cast.[1] Infernal fire far exceeds ours—that are on our hearths and in our chimneys—in degree of heat and fierceness of burning. Our fire hath not that terrible power to scorch, burn, torment, as the fire of hell hath. Our fire, as Polycarpus and others say, compared to hell-fire, is but like painted fire upon the wall. Now you know a painted fire upon the wall will not hurt you, nor burn, nor affright you, nor torment you; but the fire of hell will, beyond all your conception and expression, hurt, burn, affright, and torment you. The fire of hell, for degrees

[1] Rev. xiv. 10, and xxi. 8. The fire in a landscape is but *ignis pictus*, a painted fire, and the fire of purgatory is but *ignis fictus*, feigned fire. Now what are these to hell-fire?

of heat, and fierceness of burning, must wonderfully surpass our most furious fires, because it is purposely created by God to torment the creature, whereas our ordinary fire was created by God only for the comfort of the creature. The greatest and the hottest fires that ever were on earth, are but ice in comparison of the fire of hell, [Alsted.]

[2.] Secondly, *There are unexpressible torments in hell, as well as unspeakable joys in heaven.* Some who write of purgatory, tell us that the pains thereof are more exquisite, though of shorter continuance, than the united torments that the earth can invent, though of longer duration. If the pope's kitchen be so warm, how hot is the devil's furnace?[1] A poetical fiction is but a *meiosis*, when brought to shew the nature of these real torments: the lashes of furies are but petty scourgings, when compared to the stripes of a wounded conscience. Tytius his vulture,[2] though feeding on his liver, is but a flea-biting to that worm which gnaweth their hearts and dieth not. Ixion his wheel is a place of rest, if compared with those billows of wrath, and that wheel of justice, which is in hell brought over the ungodly. The task of Danaüs his daughter is but a sport, compared to the tortures of those whose souls are filled with bitterness, and within whom are the arrows of the Almighty, the poison whereof doth drink up their spirits. Hell is called a furnace of fire, which speaketh intolerable heat; a place of torment, which speaketh a total privation of ease; a prison, which speaketh restraint, Mat. xiii. 42; Luke xvi. 28; Mat. v. 22–25: Gehenna, from the valley of Hinnom, where the unnatural parents did sacrifice the fruit of their bodies for the sin of their souls to their merciless idols,—the which word, by a neighbour nation, is retained to signify a rock,[3]—than the torture of which what more exquisite? It is called a lake of fire and brimstone; than the torment of the former, what more acute? than the smell of the latter, what more noisome? But,

[3.] Thirdly, *Our fire is made by the hand of man, and must be maintained by continual supplies of fuel.* Take away the coals, the wood, the combustible matter, and the fire goes out; but the infernal fire is created, and tempered, and blown by the hand of an angry, sin-revenging God: Isa. xxx. 33, 'For Tophet is ordained of old; yea, for the king it is prepared; he hath made it deep and large: the pile thereof is fire and much wood, and the breath of the Lord, like a stream of brimstone, doth kindle it;' and therefore the breath of all the reprobates in hell shall never be able to blow it out.[4] Our fire is blown by an airy breath, but the infernal fire is blown by the angry breath of the great God, which burns far hotter than ten thousand thousand rivers of brimstone. The breath of God's mouth shall be both bellows and fuel to the infernal fire; and therefore, oh how terrible and torturing, how fierce and raging will that fire be! If but three drops of brimstone should fall upon any part of the flesh of a man, it would fill him so full of torment, that he would not be able to forbear roaring out for pain and anguish. Oh how dreadful and

[1] Bellarm. de Purg., lib. ii. c. 14; Bellarm. de Æter. Fæli. Sanct., lib. i. c. 11.
[2] Prometheus, as before.—G. [3] Query, 'rack?'—ED.
[4] A river of brimstone is never consumed by burning.

painful will it be then for damned sinners to swim up and down in a lake or river of fire and brimstone for ever and ever! There is no proportion between the heat of our breath and the fire that it blows. Oh then, what a dreadful, what an amazing, what an astonishing fire must that needs be which is blown by a breath dissolved into brimstone! God's wrath and indignation shall be an everlasting supply to hell's conflagration. Ah sinners, how fearful, how formidable, how unconceivable will this infernal fire prove! Surely there is no misery, no torment to that of lying in a torrent of burning brimstone for ever and ever! Mark, this infernal fire is a fire prepared by God himself, to punish and torment all impenitent persons and reprobate rebels, who scorned to submit to the sceptre of Christ. 'Depart from me, ye cursed, into everlasting fire, prepared for the devil and his angels,' Mat. xxv. 41. The wisdom of God hath been much exercised in preparing and devising the most tormenting temper for that formidable fire, in which the devil and his angels shall be punished for ever and ever. Not as if it were not prepared also for wicked and ungodly men; but it is said to be prepared for the devil and his angels, because it was firstly and chiefly prepared for them. All impenitent sinners shall have the devil and his angels for their constant companions; and therefore they shall be sure to share with them in the extremity and inevitableness of their torments. But,

[4.] Fourthly, *Our fire when it burneth it shineth, it casts a light.* Our fire burns, and in burning shines; light is a natural property of our common fire. It is true, the elementary fire in its own sphere shineth not, because of its subtleness, and the infernal fire of hell shineth not, because of its grossness; yet our ordinary fire, being of a mixed nature, hath light as well as heat in it, and that is our comfort. It hath light to shew itself to us, and to ourselves, and it hath light to shew others to us, and us to others, &c. Some men can work as well as talk by the light of the fire. Our fires have their beams and rays as well as the sun: but the fire of hell burns, but it does not shine, it gives no light at all. Infernal fire hath no light or brightness attending of it, and therefore Christ calls it 'utter darkness,' or outer darkness, that is, darkness beyond a darkness, Mat. xxv. 30, and viii. 12. I have read of a young man who was very loose and vain in his life, and was very fearful of being in the dark, who, after falling sick and could not sleep, cried out, Oh, if this darkness be so terrible, what is eternal darkness? Hell would not be so uncomfortable a prison if it were not so dark a prison.[1] Light is a blessing that shall never shine into that infernal prison. In Jude (ver. 6) you read of 'chains of darkness.' It would be a little ease, a little comfort, to the damned in hell, if they might have but light and liberty to walk up and down the infernal coasts; but this is too high a favour for them to enjoy, and therefore they shall be chained and staked down in chains of darkness, and in blackness of darkness, that so they may fully undergo the scorchings and burnings of divine wrath and fury for ever and ever. In ver. 13 you thus read, 'To whom is reserved the blackness of darkness for ever.' The words are a

[1] Drexellius. Basil speaking of hell-fire, saith, *Vim comburendi retinet, illuminandi amisit.* It retains the property of burning: it hath lost the property of shining.

Hebraism, and signify exceeding great darkness. Hell is a very dark and dismal region, and extreme are the miseries, horrors, and torments which are there. The poets described the darkness of hell by the Cimmerian darkness. There was a territory in Italy betwixt Baiæ and Cumæ, where the Cimmerii inhabit, which was so environed with hills, and overshadowed with such hanging promontories, that the sun never comes at it. The darkness of Egypt was such a strong and horrid thick darkness, that it was palpable, it might be felt. 'Even darkness which may be felt,' Exod. x. 21.[1] The darkness that is here threatened is called 'darkness that may be felt,' either by way of a hyperbole, to signify what an exceeding great darkness it should be; or else because the air should be so thickened with gross mists and thick foggy vapours, that it might be felt; or else because this extraordinary darkness should be caused by a withdrawment of the light of the celestial bodies, or by drawing a thick curtain of very black clouds betwixt men's eyes and them. Yet this horrid darkness was nothing to the darkness of hell. The darkness of Egypt was but as an overcasting for three days: Exod. x. 22, 23, 'And there was a thick darkness in all the land of Egypt three days: they saw not one another, neither rose any from his place three days.' For three days they were deprived not only of the natural lights and lamps of heaven, but of all artificial light also. It is possible that the vapours might be so thick and moist as to put out their candles, and all other lights that were kindled by them. It is probable that they had neither light from sun, moon, or stars above, nor yet from fire or candle below; so that they were as blind men that could not see at all, and as lame men that could not move from their places; and so they sate still as under the arrest of this darkness, because they could not see what to do, nor whither to go. God would teach them the worth of light, by the want of it. Some think that by that dreadful judgment of thick darkness, they were filled with that terror and horror, that they durst not so much as move from the places where they sate down. But after these three days of darkness were over, the Egyptians enjoyed the glorious light of the sun again. Oh, but sinners [when they] are in hell, when they are in chains of darkness, when they are in blackness of darkness, they shall never see light more! Hell is a house without light. Gregory, and all other authors that I have cast my eye upon, agree in this, that though our fire hath light as well as heat, yet the infernal fire hath only heat to burn sinners; it has no light to refresh sinners; and this will be no small addition to their torment. A philosopher being asked, whether it were not a pleasant thing to behold the sun? answered, that that was a blind man's question. Surely life without light is but a lifeless life. But,

[5.] Fifthly, *Our fire burns and consumes only the body, it reaches not, it torments not the precious and immortal soul; but infernal fire burns and torments both body and soul.* Now the soul of pain is the pain of the soul: Mat. x. 28, 'And fear not them which kill the body, but are not able to kill the soul; but rather fear him which is able to destroy both body and soul in hell.' If the glutton in the historical parable, who had but one half of himself in hell, viz., his soul, Luke

[1] The words are figurative, importing extraordinary black darkness.

xvi. 24, cried out that he was horribly tormented in that flame; what tongue can express or heart conceive how great the damned's torments shall be in hell, when their bodies and souls in the great day shall be reunited for torture? Beloved, it is a just and righteous thing with God, that such bodies and souls that have sinned impenitently together should be tormented everlastingly together. To this purpose, the Hebrew doctors have a very pretty parable, [Pet. Martyr,]—viz., That a man planted an orchard, and, going from home, was careful to leave such watchmen as might both keep it from strangers and not deceive him themselves; therefore he appointed one blind, but strong of his limbs, and the other seeing, but a cripple. These two in their master's absence conspired together, and the blind took the lame on his shoulders, and so gathered the fruit; their master returning and finding out this subtlety, punished them both together. Now so shall it be with those two sinful companions, the soul and the body, in the great day of our Lord, 2 Cor. v. 10; 2 Thes. i. 7–10. With Simeon and Levi they have been brethren in iniquity, and so shall be in eternal misery. As body and soul have been one in sinning, so they shall be one in suffering; only remember this, that as the soul has been chief in sin, so it shall be chief in suffering. But, O sirs! if a consumable body be not able to endure burning flames for a day, how will an unconsumable soul and body be able to endure the scorching flames of hell for ever? But,

[6.] Sixthly, *Our fire wasteth and consumeth whatsoever is cast into it.* It turns flesh into ashes, it turns all combustibles into ashes; but the fire of hell is not of that nature. The fire of hell consumes nothing that is cast into it; it rages, but it does not waste either bodies or souls. Look, as the salamander liveth in the fire, so shall the wicked live in the fire of hell for ever. 'They shall seek for death, but they shall not find it,' Rev. ix. 6. They shall desire to die, and death shall fly from them. They shall cry to the mountains to fall upon them and to crush them to nothing, Rev. vi. 16, 17. They shall desire that the fire that burns them would consume them to nothing; that the worm that feeds on them would gnaw them to nothing; that the devils which torment them would tear them to nothing, Mark ix. 44, 46, 48. They shall cry to God, who first made them out of nothing, Gen. i. 26, to reduce them to that first nothing from whence they came; 'but he that made them will not have mercy on them, he that formed them will not shew them so much favour,' Isa. xxvii. 11. *Semper comburentur, nunquam consumentur*, They shall always be burned, but never consumed.[1] Ah, how well would it be with the damned if in the fire of hell they might be consumed to ashes! But this is their misery, they shall be ever dying, and yet never die; their bodies shall be always a-burning, but never a-consuming. It is dreadful to be perpetual fuel to the flames of hell! What misery to this? for infernal fire to be still a-preying upon damned sinners, and yet never making an end of them! The two hundred and fifty men that usurped the priest's office were consumed by the fire that came out armed from the Lord against them, Num. xvi. 35. And the fire that Elijah, by an extraordinary spirit of prayer, brought down from

[1] Augustine. This fire is *pœna inconsumpta.—Jerome.*

heaven upon the two captains and their fifties, consumed them, 2 Kings i. 10, 12. The fierce and furious flames of hell shall burn, but never annihilate, the bodies of the damned. In hell there is no cessation of fire burning, nor of matter burned.[1] Neither flames nor smoke shall consume or choke the impenitent; both the infernal fire, and the burning of the bodies of reprobates in that fire, shall be preserved by the miraculous power and providence of God. The soul through pain and corruption will lose its *beate vivere,* its happy being; but it will not lose its *essentialiter vivere*, its essential life or being. But,

[7.] Seventhly and lastly, *Our fire may be quenched and extinguished.* The hottest flames, the greatest conflagrations have been quenched and extinguished by water. Fires on our hearths and in our chimneys are sometimes put out by the sun's beams, and often they die and go out of themselves. Our fire is maintained with wood, and put out with water; but the fire of hell never goes out, it can never be quenched.[2] It is an everlasting fire, an eternal fire, an unquenchable fire. In Mark ix. from ver. 43 to ver. 49, this fire is no less than five times said to be unquenchable, as if the Lord could never speak enough of it. Beloved, the Holy Ghost is never guilty of idle repetitions; but by these frequent repetitions the Holy Ghost would teach men to look about them, and to look upon it as a real thing, and as a serious thing, and not sport themselves with unquenchable flames, nor go to hell in a dream. Certainly the fire into which the damned shall be cast shall be without all intermission of time or punishment. No tears, nor blood, nor time, can extinguish the fire of hell. Could every damned sinner weep a whole ocean, yet all those oceans together would never extinguish one spark of infernal fire. The damned are in everlasting chains of darkness; they are under the 'vengeance of eternal fire,' Jude 7; they are 'in blackness of darkness for ever.' 'The smoke of their torment ascendeth for ever and ever, and they shall have no rest day nor night,' Rev. xiv. 11.[3] The damned in hell would fain die, but they cannot. *Mors sine morte*, they shall be always dying, yet never dead; they shall be always a-consuming, yet never consumed. 'The smoke of their furnace ascends for ever and ever.' *Æternis punientur pœnis*, they shall be everlastingly punished, saith Mollerus on Ps. ix. 17. And Musculus on the same text saith, *Animi impiorum cruciatibus debitis apud inferos punientur*, The souls of the ungodly shall be punished in hell with deserved torments. *Ubi per millia millia annorum cruciandi, nec in secula seculorum liberandi*, Myriads of years shall not determine or put a period to their sufferings, saith Augustine. Plato could say that whoever are not expiated, but profane, shall go into hell to be tormented for their wickedness with the greatest, the most bitter, and terrible punishments for ever in that prison of hell. And Trismegistus could say, That souls going out of the body defiled were tossed to and

[1] Hell torments punish but not finish the bodies of men.—*Prosper.*

[2] Jerome was out when he said, *Infernum nihil esse, nisi conscientiæ horrorem.* And Tully was out, who held that there are no other hell furies than the stings of conscience.

[3] Oh that word *never*, said a poor despairing creature on his deathbed, breaks my heart! They are lying histories that tell us that Trajan was delivered out of hell by the prayers of Gregory, and Falconella by the prayers of Teclaes.

fro with eternal punishments. Yea, the very Turks, speaking of the house of perdition, do affirm,[1] That they who have turned God's grace into wantonness, shall abide eternally in the fire of hell, and there be eternally tormented. A certain religious man going to visit Olympius, who lived cloistered up in a monastery near Jordan, and finding him cloistered up in a dark cell, which he thought uninhabitable by reason of heat and swarms of gnats and flies, and asking him how he could endure to live in such a place, he answered, 'All this is but a light matter, that I may escape eternal torments. I can endure the stinging of gnats, that I might not endure the stinging of conscience and the gnawing of that worm that never dies. This heat thou thinkest grievous, I can easily endure when I think of the eternal fire of hell; these sufferings are but short, but the sufferings of hell are eternal.' Certainly infernal fire is neither tolerable nor terminable. The extremity and eternity of hellish torments is set forth by the worm that never dieth. Christ at the close of his sermon makes a threefold repetition of this worm: Mark ix. 44, 'Where their worm dieth not;' and again, ver. 46, 'Where their worm dieth not;' and again, ver. 48, 'Where their worm dieth not, and their fire goeth not out.' Certainly those punishments are beyond all conception and expression which our Lord Jesus doth so often inculcate within so small a space.

> 'In hell there 's nothing heard but yells and cries;
> In hell the fire never slacks, nor worm never dies.
> But where this hell is placed, my muse, stop there.
> Lord, shew me what it is, but never where.
> To worm and fire, to torments there
> No term he gave; they cannot wear.'[2]

If after so many millions of years as there be drops in the ocean, there might be a deliverance out of hell, this would yield a little ease, a little comfort to the damned. Oh but this word *eternity*, *eternity*, *eternity*, this word *everlasting*, *everlasting*, *everlasting*, will even break the hearts of the damned in ten thousand pieces! There is scarce any pain or torment here on earth but there is ever some hope of ease, mitigation, or intermission, there is some hope of relief or delivery; but in hell the torments there are all easeless, remediless, and endless. Here if one fall into the fire, he may like a brand be pulled out of it and saved; but out of that fiery lake there is no redemption. That majesty that the sinner hath offended and provoked is an infinite majesty. Now there must be some proportion betwixt the sinner's sin, and his punishment and torment. Now the sinner being a finite creature, he is not capable of bearing the weight of that punishment or torment that is intensively infinite, because it would be his abolishing or annihilating; and therefore he must bear the weight of that punishment or torment that is extensively infinite—namely, *duratione infinita*, infinite in the continuance and endurance. What is wanting in torment must be made up in time. Everlasting fire and everlasting punishment in the New Testament is directly opposed to eternal life, to that blessed state of the righteous which will never have an end;[3] and therefore, according to the rules and

[1] Alcoran. Mahom. cap. 14, p. 166, &c.; cap. 20, p. 193.
[2] A pentelogia dolor inferni.—*Prudentius* the poet.
[3] Mat. xxv.; 2 Thes. i. 7-10, &c. *Vide* August., lib. xxi. cap. 23, 24, *De Civitate Dei.*

maxims of right reason, doth necessarily import a punishment of the same duration that the reward is. Now the reward of the saints in that other world is granted on all hands to be everlasting, to be eternal; and therefore the punishment of the damned cannot be but everlasting and eternal too. The rewards of the elect shall never be ended, therefore the punishment of the damned shall never be ended, because as the mercy of God is infinite towards the elect, so the justice of God is infinite towards the reprobate in hell. The reprobate shall have punishment without pity, misery without mercy, sorrow without succour, crying without compassion, mischief without measure, and torment without end, [Drexelius.] All men in misery comfort themselves with hope of an end. The prisoner with hope of a jail-delivery; the mariner with the hope of his arrival in a safe harbour; the soldier with hope of victory; the prentice with hope of liberty; the galley-slave with the hope of ransom: only the impenitent sinner hath no hope in hell. He shall have end without end, death without death, night without day, mourning without mirth, sorrow without solace, and bondage without liberty. The damned shall live as long in hell as God himself shall live in heaven.[1] Their imprisonment in that land of darkness, in that bottomless pit, is not an imprisonment during the king's pleasure, but an imprisonment during the everlasting displeasure of the King of kings. Suppose, say some, that the whole world were turned to a mountain of sand, and that a little wren should come every thousandth year and carry away from that heap one grain of sand, what an infinite number of years, not to be numbered by all finite beings, would be spent and expired before this supposed mountain could be fetched away! Now if a man should lie in everlasting burnings so long a time, and then have an end of his woe, it would administer some ease, refreshment, and comfort to him. But when that immortal bird shall have carried away this supposed mountain a thousand times over and over; alas! alas! man shall be as far from the end of his anguish and torment as ever he was.[2] He shall be no nearer coming out of hell than he was the very first moment that he entered into hell. Suppose, say others, that a man were to endure the torments of hell as many years, and no more, as there be sands on the sea-shore, drops of water in the sea, stars in heaven, leaves on the trees, piles of grass on the ground, hairs on his head, yea, upon the heads of all the sons of Adam that ever were, or are, or shall be in the world, from the beginning of it to the end of it; yet he would comfort himself with this poor thought, Well, there will come a day when my misery and torment shall certainly have an end! But woe and alas! this word *never*, *never*, *never*, will fill the hearts of the damned with the greatest horror and terror, wrath and rage, amazement and astonishment. Suppose, say others, that the torments of hell were to end after a little bird should have emptied the sea, and only carry out her billful once in a thousand years;—suppose, say others, that the whole world, from the

[1] There is not a Christian which doth not believe the fire of hell to be everlasting.—*Dr Jackson on the Creed*, lib. xi. cap. 23.

[2] If the fire of hell were terminable, it might then be tolerable; but being endless, it must needs be caseless and remediless. We may well say of it, as one doth, Oh killing life! oh immortal death!—*Bellar. de Arte Moriendi*, lib. ii. cap. 3.

lowest earth to the highest heavens, were filled with grains of sand, and once in a thousand years an angel should come and fetch away one grain, and so continue till the whole heap were spent;—suppose, say others, if one of the damned in hell should weep after this manner —viz., that he should only let fall one tear in a hundred years, and these should be kept together till such time as they should equal the drops of water in the sea: how many millions of ages would pass before they could make up one river, much more a whole; and when that were done, should he weep again after the same manner till he had filled a second, a third, a fourth sea, if then there should be an end of their miseries, there would be some hope, some comfort that they would end at last: but that shall never, never, never end. This is that which sinks them under the most tormenting terrors and horrors.

Drexelius makes this observation from the words of our Saviour, John xv. 6, 'If a man abide not in me, he is cast forth as a branch, and it is withered; and men gather them, and cast them into the fire, and they are burned,' where he observeth that the words do not run in the future tense,—he shall be cast forth, and shall be cast into the fire, and burned; but all in the present tense—he is cast forth, is withered; men cast them into the fire, and they are burned. This, saith he, is the state and condition of the damned; they are burned—that is, they are always burning. When a thousand years are past, as it was at first, so it is still, they are burned; after a thousand thousand years more, as it was before, so it is still, they are burned. If after millions of years the question was asked, What is now their state and condition? what do they? what suffer they? how doth it fare with them? there can be no other answer returned but they are burned, continually and eternally burning. Socinians say there will come a time when the fallen angels and the wickedest men shall be freed from infernal torments; and Augustine speaks of some such merciful men in his time; and Origen held and taught that not only impenitent Christians, but even pagans and devils, after the term of a thousand years, should be released out of hell, and become as bright angels in heaven as they were before.[1] But these dangerous fancies and ungrounded opinions fall flat before the clear evidence of those sad and serious truths that I have now tendered to your consideration. And thus I have shewed you the difference between our fire and hell-fire.

Now, O ye citizens of London who truly fear the Lord, and who are united to Christ by faith, know for your everlasting comfort and support, that Christ hath secured you from infernal fire, from everlasting fire, from unquenchable fire, from eternal fire, and from the worm that never dieth, as you may see clearly and fully by comparing the scriptures in the margin together.[2] Christ by his blood hath quenched the violence of infernal flames, so that they shall never scorch you nor burn you, hurt you nor harm you. Nebuchadnezzar's fiery furnace was a type of hell, say some. Now look, as the three children, or rather champions, had not one hair of their heads singed in that fiery

[1] Aug. lib. xxi. cap. 17–22, *De Civitate Dei.*

[2] John iii. 17, 18, 36; Luke i. 68–71, 74; Rom. vi. 23, and viii. 1, 31–35, 37; 1 Cor. iii. 21–23, and xv. 54–58; 1 Thes. i. 10; Rev. xx. 5, 6.

furnace, so hell-fire shall never singe one hair of your heads. Your interest in Christ is a noble and sufficient security to you against the flames of hell. Pliny saith, that nothing in the world will so soon quench fire as salt and blood; and therefore in many countries where they can get plenty of blood, they will use salt and blood rather than water to quench the fire. If you cast water on the fire, the fire will quickly work it out; but if you cast blood upon it, it will damp it in a moment. O sirs, Christ's blood has so quenched the flames of hell, that they shall never be able to scorch or burn those souls that are interested in him. The effusion of Christ's blood is so rich and available, saith my author,[1] that if the whole multitude of captive sinners would believe in their Redeemer, not one should be detained in the tyrant's chains. All those spots that a Christian finds in his own heart, shall first or last be washed out in the Lamb: 1 John i. 7, 'The blood of Jesus Christ his Son cleanseth us from all our sins.' Now such as are washed and cleansed from their sins in the blood of Jesus, such shall never experimentally know what everlasting burnings or a devouring fire means. Such as are washed in Christ's blood needs no purifying by hell's flames. Pliny saith of *polium* that it is a preservative against serpents. Sure I am that the blood of Christ is an effectual preservative against all infernal serpents and infernal torments.[2]

You believing citizens, who have set up God as the object of your fear, and whose hearts are inflamed with love to Christ, know, for your everlasting refreshment, that Christ has freed you, and secured you from everlasting fire, from unquenchable fire, from eternal fire; and therefore bear up sweetly, bear up cheerfully under that fiery dispensation that has passed upon you. What is the burning of your houses and substance, to the burning of bodies and souls in hell? What was the fire of London, to infernal fire? What is a fire of four or five days' continuance, to that everlasting fire, to that unquenchable fire, to that eternal fire that you have deserved, and that free grace hath preserved you from? A frequent and serious consideration of hell-fire, as I have opened it unto you, and of your happy deliverance from it, may very well bear and cheer up your hearts under all your greatest sufferings by that dreadful fire, that has turned beloved London into a ruinous heap.

Sir, you have been a-discoursing about hellish torments; but, for the further clearing up of the truth, we desire your serious answer to this sad question—viz.,

Obj. How will it stand with the unspotted holiness, justice, and righteousness of God, to punish a temporary offence with eternal punishments? for the evil of punishment should be but commensurate to the evil of sin. Now what proportion is there betwixt finite and infinite? Why should the sinner lie in hellish torments for ever and ever for sinning but a short time, a few years in this world?

Ans. I judge it very necessary to say something to this important

[1] Leo de Pas., Serm. xii. c. 4.

[2] Nero had a shirt made of a salamander's skin, so that if he did walk through the fire in it, it would keep him from burning. O sirs! Christ is the true salamander's skin that will certainly keep every gracious soul from burning in everlasting flames.

question, before I come to discourse of those duties that are incumbent upon those citizens whose houses are turned into a ruinous heap; and therefore take me thus:—

[1.] First, *God's will is the rule of righteousness, and therefore what he doth, or shall do, must needs be righteous.* He is Lord of all; he hath a sovereign right and an absolute supremacy over the creature. He is the only Potentate, King of kings, and Lord of lords; he is the Judge of the whole world; 'And shall not the Judge of all the earth do right?' 1 Tim. i. 15; Gen. xviii. 25. But,

[2.] Secondly, I answer, *There is a principle in man to sin eternally; and therefore it is but just with God if he punish him eternally.* The duration of torment respects the disposition of the delinquent. *Pœnæ singulorum inæquales intentione, pœnæ omnium æquales duratione,* [Aquinas.] If the sinner should live ever, he would dishonour God ever, and crucify the Lord of glory ever, and grieve the Spirit of grace ever, and transgress a righteous law ever; and therefore it is just with God to punish such sinners for ever. *Etsi peccator in æternum viveret, in æternum peccaret,* If the sinner might live eternally, he would sin eternally; if he might live still, he would sin still. Though the sinner loses his life, yet he does not lose his will to sin. Sinners sin as much as they can, and as long as they can, and did not the grave put a stop to their lusts, their hearts would never put a stop to their lusts. *Peccare si velis tu in æterno tuo, punire æquum est te Deum in æterno suo,* The sinner sins in his eternity, and God punishes in his eternity. The sinner never loses his will to sin. His will to sin is everlasting; and therefore it is but just with God that his punishment should be everlasting. A will to sin is sin in God's account. God looks more at the will than at the deed; and therefore that being lasting, the punishment must be so. The mind and intention of the sinner is to sin everlastingly, eternally. If the sinner should live always, he would sin always; and therefore as one saith, [Gregory,] *Quia mens in hac vita nunquam voluit carere peccato, justum est ut nunquam careat supplicio,* Because the mind of man in this life would never be without sin, it is just that it should never be without punishment in the life to come. Many of the men of the old world lived eight or nine hundred years, and yet faith and repentance was hid from their eyes: that patience, forbearance, long-suffering, gentleness, and goodness, which should have led them to a speedy repentance, 1 Pet. iii. 20, to a serious repentance, to a thorough repentance, to that repentance that was never to be repented of, was only made use of to patronise their lewdness and wickedness.[1] This is certain: wicked men left to themselves will never be weary of their sins, nor never repent of their sins; and therefore God will never be weary of plaguing them, nor never repent of punishing them. The sinner never leaves his sin till sin first leaves him: did not death put a stop to his sin, he would never cease from sin. This may be illustrated by a similitude thus, A company of gamesters resolve to play all night, and accordingly they sit down to chess, tables, or some other game; their candle accidentally or unexpectedly goes out, or is

[1] Peccant in æterno suo, ergo puniuntur in æterno Dei. The sinner always sinned in his eternity, therefore he shall always be punished in God's eternity.—*Augustine.*

put out, or burnt out; their candle being out, they are forced to give over their game, and go to bed in the dark; but had the candle lasted all night they would have played all night. This is every sinner's case in regard of sin: did not death put out the candle of life the sinner would sin still. Should the sinner live for ever, he would sin for ever; and therefore it is a righteous thing with God to punish him for ever in hellish torments. Every impenitent sinner would sin to the days of eternity, if he might but live to the days of eternity: Ps. lxxiv. 10, 'O God, how long shall the adversary reproach? shall the enemy blaspheme thy name for ever?' For ever and evermore; or for ever and yet—for so the Hebrew loves to exaggerate: as if the sinner, the blasphemer, would set a term of duration longer than eternity to sin in. The psalmist implicitly saith, Lord, if thou dost but let them alone for ever, they will certainly blaspheme thy name for ever and ever. I have read of the crocodile, that he knows no *maximum quod sic*, he is always growing bigger and bigger, and never comes to a certain pitch of monstrosity so long as he lives. *Quamdiu vivit crescit.* Every habituated sinner would, if he were let alone, be such a monster, perpetually growing worser and worser. But,

[3.] Thirdly, I answer, *That God against whom they have sinned is an infinite and eternal good.* Now a finite creature cannot bear an infinite punishment intensively, and therefore he must bear it extensively. They have sinned impenitently against an infinite majesty, and accordingly their punishment must be infinite.[1] Now because it cannot be infinite, in regard of the degree, men being but finite creatures, and so not capable of infinite torments at one time; therefore their punishment must be infinite in the length and continuance of it. What is wanting in torment must be made up in time. Every sin is of an infinite nature, because of the infinite dignity of the person against whom it is committed; and therefore it deserveth an infinite punishment; which because it cannot be infinite *secundum intensionem*, in the inattention[2] and greatness of it, it remaineth that it should be infinite *secundum durationem*, in respect of the duration and continuance of the same.[3] Mark, all punishments ought to be levied according to the dignity of him against whom the offence is committed. Words against common persons bear but common actions; words against noblemen are *scandala magnatum*, great scandals; but words against princes are treason. So the dignity of the person against whom sin is committed, does exceedingly aggravate the sin. To strike an inferior man is matter of arrest, but to strike a king is matter of death. Now what an infinite distance and disproportion is there between the Lord of hosts and such poor crawling worms as we are! he being holiness, and we sinfulness; he fulness, and we emptiness; he omnipotency, and we impotency; he majesty, and we vanity; he *instar omnium*, all in all, and we nothing at all. Now to sin against such an infinite glorious majesty, deserves infinite punishment. But,

[4.] Fourthly, I answer, *Though the act of sin be transient, yet it leaveth such a stain upon the soul as is permanent, and continueth in*

[1] Sin is *contra Deum infinitum*, against an infinite majesty.

[2] Query, 'intension'?—ED.

[3] *Vide* August., lib. xxi. cap. 14, De Civitate Dei.

it evermore, and evermore it disposeth the sinner unto sin, if it be not pardoned and purged out by mercy and grace, and therefore it is but just that this perpetual purpose of sinning should be punished with perpetuity of pain.[1] The guilt and stain of sin, of its own nature and unpardoned, endures eternally upon the soul; and therefore what can follow but eternal torments? The lasting continuance of sin is remarkably described by the prophet Jeremiah, chap. xvii. 1, 'The sin of Judah is written with a pen of iron, and with the point of a diamond: it is graven upon the table of their hearts:' not only written, but engraven, that no hand can deface it. Slight not the commission of any sin ; it perishes not with the acting. The least vanity hath a perpetuity, nay, an eternity of guilt upon it. Sin leaving a blot in the soul brings the matter of hell-fire, is eternally punished, because there is still matter for that everlasting fire to work upon. But,

[5.] Fifthly, I answer, *Though death put an end to men's lives, yet not to sins.* Hell is as full of sin as it is of punishment or torment. Though the schoolmen determine that after this life men are capable neither of merit nor demerit, and therefore by their sins do not incur a greater measure of punishment, yet they grant that they sin still. Though when the creature is actually under the sentence of condemnation, the law ceases to any further punishment, yet there is an obligation to the precepts of the law still. Though a man be bound only to the curse of the law, as he is a sinner, yet he is bound to the precept of the law, as he is a creature: so that though the demerit of sin ceaseth after death, yet the nature of sin remaineth: though by sinning they do not incur a higher and a greater degree of punishment, yet as they continue sinning, so it is just with God there should be a continuation of the punishment already inflicted. But,

[6.] Sixthly, I answer, *It is no injustice in God to punish temporal offences with perpetual torments.* God measureth the punishment by the greatness of the offence, and not by the time wherein the sin was acted. Murder, adultery, sacrilege, treason, and the like capital crimes, are doomed in the judicatories of men to death without mercy, and sometimes to perpetual imprisonment, or to perpetual banishment; and yet these high offences were committed and done in a short time. Now this bears a proportion with eternal torments. O sirs, if the offences committed against God be infinitely heinous, why may not the punishment be infinitely lasting? Sinners' offences, as Austin well observes,[2] are not to be measured *temporis longitudine*, by the length of time wherein they were done: but *iniquitatis magnitudine*, by the foulness of the crime: and if so, then God is just in binding the sinner in everlasting chains. We must remember that God is a great and a glorious God, and that he is an omniscient and an omnipotent God, and that he is a mighty, yea, an almighty God, and that he is a holy and a just God, and that he is out of Christ an incomprehensible, incommunicable, and very terrible God, and that he is an infinite, eternal, and independent God, Heb. xii. 29, 30. And we must remember that man is a shadow, a bubble, a vapour, a dream, a base, vile, sinful, worthless worm. Now these things being considered, must we not

[1] As long as the guilt of sin remains, punishments and torments will remain.
[2] Aug. de Civit. Dei., lib. i. cap. 11.

confess that eternity itself is too short a space for God to revenge himself on sinners in? But,

[7.] Seventhly and lastly, I answer, *Such sinners have but what they chose.* Whilst they lived under the means of grace, the God of grace set before them heaven and hell, glory and misery, eternal life and eternal death, so that if they eternally miscarry, they have none to blame but themselves, for choosing hell rather than heaven, misery rather than glory, and eternal death rather than eternal life.[1] Ah, how freely, how fully, how frequently, how graciously, how gloriously, hath Christ been offered in the gospel to poor sinners, and yet they would not choose him, they would not close with him, they would not embrace him, nor accept of him, nor enter into a marriage covenant with him, nor resign themselves up to him, nor part with their lusts to enjoy him: they would not come to Christ that they might have life; they slighted infinite mercy, and despised the riches of grace, and trod under foot the blood of the everlasting covenant, and scorned the offers of eternal salvation; and therefore it is but just that they should lie down in everlasting sorrows, John v. 40; Mat. xxii. 2–5; 2 Cor. iv. 3, 4. How can that sinner be saved that still refuses salvation? How can mercy save him that will not be saved by mercy? yea, how can Christ save such a man, that will not be saved by him? All the world cannot save that man from going to hell, who is peremptorily resolved that he will not go to heaven. Sinners have boldly and daily refused eternal life, eternal mercy, eternal glory, and therefore it is but just that they should endure eternal misery. And let thus much suffice for answer to the objection.

Quest. But, sir, pray what are those duties that are incumbent upon those that have been burnt up, and whose habitations are now laid in its ashes?

I answer, They are these that follow:—

1. First, *See the hand of the Lord in this late dreadful fire, acknowledge the Lord to be the author of all judgments, and of this in particular*, Lev. xxvi. 41, and Micah vii. 9. It is a high point of Christian prudence and piety to acknowledge the Lord to be the author of all personal or national sufferings that befall us: Jer ix. 12, 'Who is the wise man, that may understand this? for what the land perisheth, and is burnt up like a wilderness, that none passeth through.' It is very great wisdom to know from whom all our afflictions come, and for what all our afflictions come upon us. God looks that we should observe his hand in all our sufferings. 'Hear the rod, and who hath appointed it,' Micah vi. 9. God challenges all sorts of afflictions as his own special administration: Amos iii. 6, 'Is there any evil in the city, and the Lord hath not done it? I form the light, and create darkness; I make peace, and create evil, I the Lord do all these things,[2] Isa. xlv. 7. God takes it very heinously, and looks upon it as a very great indignity that is put upon his power, providence, and justice, when men will neither see nor acknowledge his hand in those

[1] Deut. xi. 26, 27, and xxx. 15; Heb. ii. 2, 3, and x. 28, 29; John iii. 14–17, 36, and i. 11.

[2] See this text fully opened in my first Epistle to my Treatise on 'Closet Prayer.' [Vol. I.—G.]

sore afflictions and sad sufferings that he brings upon them. Of such the prophet Isaiah complains, chap. xxvi. 11, 'Lord, when thy hand is lifted up, they will not see.' The hand, the power of the Lord was so remarkable and conspicuous in the judgments that were inflicted upon them, as might very well wring an acknowledgment out of them that it was the Lord that had stirred his wrath and indignation against them; and yet they wilfully and desperately shut their eyes against all the severities of God, and would not behold that dreadful hand of his that was stretched out against them. O sirs, God looks upon himself as reproached and slandered by such who will not see his hand in the amazing judgments that he inflicts upon them: Jer. v. 12, 'They have belied the Lord, and said, It is not he'—or, as the Hebrew runs, 'he is not.' Such was the atheism of the Jews, that they slighted divine warnings, and despised all those dreadful threatenings of the sword, famine, and fire, which should have led them to repentance, and so tacitly said, The Lord is not God. Such who either say, that God is not omniscient, or that he is not omnipotent, or that he is not so just as to execute the judgments that he has threatened; such belie the Lord, such deny him to be God. Many feel the rod, that cannot hear it; and many experience the smart of the rod, that do not see the hand that holds the rod; and this is sad. How can the natural man, without faith's prospective, look so high as to see the hand of the Lord in wasting and destroying judgments? By common experience we find that natural men are mightily apt to father the evil of all their sufferings upon secondary causes. Sometimes they cry out, This is from a distemper in nature; and at other times they cry out, This is from a bad air. Sometimes they cry out of the malice, plots, envy, and rage of men; and at other times they cry out of stars, chance, and fortune, and so fix upon anything rather than the hand of God. But now a gracious Christian under all his sufferings, he overlooks all secondary causes, and fixes his eye upon the hand of God. You know what Joseph said to his unnatural brethren, who sold him for a slave: *Non vos, sed Deus:* 'It was not you, but God that sent me into Egypt,' Gen. xlv. 7. Job met with many sore losses and sad crosses, but under them all he overlooked all instruments, all secondary causes; he overlooks the Sabeans, and the Chaldeans, and Satan, and fixes his eye upon the hand of God: 'The Lord hath given, and the Lord hath taken away; blessed be the name of the Lord,' Job i. 21. Judas, and Annas, and Caiaphas, and Pilate, and Herod, and the bloody soldiers, had all a deep hand in the sufferings of Christ, but yet he overlooks them all, and fixes his eye upon his Father's hand. 'The cup which my Father hath given me, shall I not drink it,' John xviii. 11. This cup was the cup of his sufferings. Now in all his sad sufferings he had still an eye to his Father's hand. Let us in all our sufferings write after this copy that Christ has set before us. But of this I have spoken very largely already, and therefore let this touch suffice here.

2. Secondly, *Labour to justify the Lord in all that he has done; say, the Lord is righteous, though he hath laid your city desolate.* When Jerusalem was laid desolate, and the wall thereof broken down, and the gates thereof were burned with fire, Nehemiah justifies the Lord: chap. ix. 33, 'Howbeit thou art just in all that is brought upon us;

for thou hast done right, but we have done wickedly.'[1] The same spirit was upon Jeremiah: Lam. i. 1, 4, 18, 'How doth the city sit solitary that was full of people! how is she become as a widow! she that was great among the nations, and princess among the provinces, how is she become tributary! The ways of Zion do mourn, because none come to the solemn feasts: all her gates are desolate; her priests sigh, her virgins are afflicted, and she is in bitterness. The Lord is righteous; for I have rebelled against his commandment.' The same spirit was upon David: Ps. cxix. 75, 'I know, O Lord, that thy judgments are right, and that thou in faithfulness hast afflicted me.' So Ps. cxlv. 17, 'The Lord is righteous in all his ways, and holy in all his works.' This maxim we must live and die by, though we do not always see the reason of his proceedings. It is granted on all hands that *voluntas Dei est summa, perfectissima, et infallibilis regula divinæ justitiæ, et Deus sibi ipsi lex est,* The will of God is the chiefest, the most perfect and infallible rule of divine justice, and that God is a judge[2] to himself: 'Shall not the Judge of all the earth do right?' Gen. xviii. 25. In this negative question is emphatically implied an affirmative position, which is, that God, above all others, must and will do right; because from his judgment there is no appeal. Abraham, considering the nature and justice of God, was confidently assured that God could not do otherwise but right. Hath God turned you out of house and home, and marred all your pleasant things, and stripped you naked as the day wherein you were born? Yes. Why, if he hath, he hath done you no wrong; he can do you no wrong; he is a law to himself, and his righteous will is the rule of all justice. God can as soon cease to be as he can cease to do that which is just and right. So Ps. xcvii. 2, 'Clouds and darkness are round about him; righteousness and judgment are the habitation of his throne.' Clouds and darkness notes the terribleness of God's administrations. Though God be very terrible in his administrations, yet righteousness and judgment are the habitation of his throne. It hath been a day of God's wrath in London, a day of trouble and distress, a day of wasting and desolation, a day of darkness and gloominess, a day of clouds and thick darkness, as it was once in Jerusalem, Zeph. i. 15; yet righteousness and judgment are the habitation of his throne; or, as it may be translated, are 'the foundation of his throne.' God's seat of judgment is always founded in righteousness. So Dan. ix. 12, 'And he hath confirmed his words which he spake against us, and against our judges that judged us, by bringing upon us a great evil: for under the whole heaven hath not been done as hath been done upon Jerusalem;' ver. 14, 'The Lord our God is righteous in all his works which he doeth; for we obeyed not his voice.' God is only righteous, he is perfectly righteous, he is exemplarily righteous, he is everlastingly righteous, he is infinitely righteous, and no unrighteousness dwells in him, Ps. xcii. 15; Job xxxvi. 23. There are four things that God cannot do: (1.) He cannot lie; (2.) He cannot die; (3.) He cannot deny

[1] Neh. i. 4. So Mauricius the emperor justified God when he saw his wife and children butchered before his eyes by the traitor Phocas, and knew that himself should soon after be stewed in his own broth, cried out, Just art thou, O Lord, and just are all thy judgments!

[2] Query, 'law'?—G.

himself; nor (4.) He cannot look upon iniquity and not loathe it; he cannot behold iniquity and approve of it or delight in it. God has a sovereignty over all your persons and concernments in this world, and therefore he may do with you and all that is yours as he pleaseth. Upon this account you ought to say, The Lord is righteous, though he hath laid your habitations desolate, and burned up your houses before your eyes. It is true, God has dealt severely with London; but he might have dealt more severely with it, Lam. iii. 22. He might have burnt up every house, and he might have consumed every inhabitant in London's flames. He might have made good that sad word upon them, 'They shall go from one fire, and another fire shall devour them,' Ezek. xv. 7. The citizens of London may say with good Ezra, God hath punished us less than our iniquities deserve; and therefore it highly concerns them to say, 'The Lord is righteous.' All that God doth is good. You know what Hezekiah said: 2 Kings xx. 19, 'Good is the word of the Lord.' This was a hard word, a sad word, that all his treasure should be carried into Babylon, and his sons also, and made servants there, and yet he saith, 'Good is the word of the Lord.' Whatever God doth is good. God, in that he is good, saith one—Luther in Psalm cxx.—can give nothing, do nothing, but that which is good; others do frequently, he cannot possibly. Upon this account also it concerns us to say, The Lord is righteous, though our city be laid desolate. It is better to be under a fiery rod, than to be wallowing in the mire of sin.[1] It is better that London should be laid desolate, than that God should say, England, farewell. That is a Christian worth gold who can seriously, heartily, and habitually say, The Lord is righteous, though all our pleasant things are laid desolate.

Objec. I would say, The Lord is righteous; but by this fiery dispensation I am turned out of house and home.

Now, in answer to this objection, give me leave to inquire:—

[1.] First, *Whether your house was dedicated to the Lord by fasting and prayer or not?* Deut. xx. 5. If it were only dedicated to the service of sin, Satan, or the world, no wonder if the Lord has turned it into a heap. But,

[2.] Secondly, Give me leave to inquire, *Whether you had set up Christ and holiness and holy orders in your house or no?* See Ps. ci. Did you in good earnest resolve with Joshua, 'That you and your house would serve the Lord,' Joshua xxiv. 15. If not, no wonder if the Lord has laid your habitations desolate. But,

[3.] Thirdly, Give me leave to inquire, *Whether you did labour and endeavour to the utmost of what you were able, that Christ might have a church in your house or no?* Col. iv. 15, 'Salute the brethren which are in Laodicea, and Nymphas, and the church which is in his house'; that is, saith Dr Hammond, which meets together in his house. 1 Cor. xvi. 19, 'The churches of Asia salute you. Aquila and Priscilla salute you much in the Lord, with the church that is in their house.' Phil. 2, 'And to our beloved Apphia, and Archippus our fellow-soldier, and to the church in thy house.'[2] Philemon's

[1] See more of this in my 'Mute Christian.' [Vol. I. as before.—G.]

[2] See Dr Hammond on this scripture. *Vide* Bishop Dav[enant] Cotton, Beza, Scultetus, Ambrose, &c.

house was a public meeting-house, where the faithful had their assemblies; and so continued for many years after, as Theodoret and others witnesseth. Some understand this last scripture of the church which kept their assemblies in Philemon's house. Others understand it of his household, which was as a little church in his house: Rom. xvi. 5, 'Likewise greet the church that is in their house.' Chrysostom by the church in their house understands their Christian family, who, saith he, were so godly, as to make their whole house the church. Origen interpreteth it of the faithful and ready ministry of these servants of the Lord, in entertaining of the saints in their house. Theophylact thinketh it to be called the church in their house, because the faithful were entertained there. But beside this, it seemeth that their house was a place for the saints to assemble in; there the congregation used to come together, [Martyr.] The last thing in their praise was, that they had a church in their house; either for that their family, for their godly order observed in it, seemed to be a church, or else for the faithful gathered together in their house to celebrate their assemblies; for they might not have in most places the free use of their Christian religion, through the malice of the Jews on the one hand, and the rage of the Gentiles on the other hand. Consult Acts xiii. and xiv., [Wilson.] In this great city of Rome there were divers assemblies of believers, which were held in some private men's houses, where they might meet safest—the state then, and some hundred years after, not permitting them any public temples or auditories to meet in, as our English Annotators observe upon the place. In each particular family last cited, there was a church of Christ. Now have you burnt citizens made it your business to erect a church of Christ in your particular families? if so, well it is with you, though you have lost all. If not, do not wonder that God has laid your houses desolate. Adam had a church in his house, so had Abraham, and Jacob, and Joshua, and David, and Cornelius. Well governed families may in some sense be well reputed churches. The house of George, Prince of Anhalt, for the good orders therein observed, is said to have been, *Ecclesia, academia, curia.* Ah London, London! it may be there might have been more houses standing within thy walls than now there is, if every particular house had been as a particular church to Christ. As for such houses where there were no exercises of religion; as for such houses where idleness, cheating, lying, cursing, swearing, slandering, gaming, drunkenness, uncleanness, and riotousness were rampant, they were rather the devil's chapel than Christ's church; and therefore it was just with God to lay such habitations desolate. But,

[4.] Fourthly, Give me leave to inquire, *Whether you were friends or enemies to God's house,* 2 Tim. i. 20; Num. xii. 7; Joshua i. 2. Now God's house is his church, and his church is his house: Heb. iii. 5, 6, 'And Moses verily was faithful in all his house, as a servant; but Christ as a Son over his own house; whose house are we;' 1 Pet. ii. 5, 'Ye also, as lively stones, are built up a spiritual house, an holy priesthood, to offer up spiritual sacrifices, acceptable to God by Jesus Christ;' so 1 Tim. iii. 15, 'That thou mayest know how thou oughtest to behave thyself in the house of God, which is the church of the living God, the pillar and ground of the truth;' Prov. ix. 1, 'Wisdom hath builded her house, she hath hewn out her seven pillars.' Wisdom—חכמות, *chakmoth*, the Hebrew word is plural, wisdoms: wisdoms hath built her a house. By wisdoms some understand the trinity of persons; but most conclude that by wisdoms is meant our Lord Jesus Christ, in whom are hid all the treasures of wisdom and knowledge, Col. ii. 3. The word is plural for honour's sake. As princes write, *We command*, the Lord Jesus Christ is said to be *wisdoms* in the plural number, to note that he is the sovereign and supreme wisdom, and that he is instead of all wisdoms, and comprehends all wisdoms in himself, all the world being fools in comparison of him. Wisdoms hath built her a house—(1.) Some take this house to be the human nature of Christ, but that was not then built; (2.) Others understand it of the work of grace in man's soul, but this the Spirit commonly works in this house by the ministry of the word, Gal. v. 22, 23; (3.) Others by this house understand heaven, that upper house, that house of state in which Christ saith there are many mansions, but this cannot [be it], because the house in the text is such a house to which wisdom doth immediately invite and call all her guests; but (4.) and lastly, Others by house understand the church of Christ on earth, for the church militant is a house built up of many lively stones, 1 Pet. ii. 5; and with these I close. Now by these scriptures it is very plain that God's house is his church, and his church his house. Now if you were enemies to God's house, if you hated his house, and designed and endeavoured to pull down his house, no wonder that the Lord has laid your houses desolate, Mat. xxiii. 37, 38; Zech. xii. 2, 3, 6, 9. Such who cry out concerning his house, Raze it, raze it even to the foundation thereof, Ps. cxxxvii. 7, may one day want a house to live in.

It is observable that in private houses Christ his apostles, and particular churches, and primitive Christians, frequently used to meet when the times were dangerous: John xx. 19, 'Then the same day at evening, being the first day of the week, when the doors were shut where the disciples were assembled for fear of the Jews, came Jesus, and stood in the midst, and saith unto them, Peace be unto you;' ver. 26, 'And after eight days, again his disciples were within, and Thomas with them. Then came Jesus, the doors being shut, and stood in the midst, and said, Peace be unto you,' Luke xxiv. 33. This was the usual manner of salutation among the Jews, whereby they wished one another all happiness and prosperity. The doors of the room where they were together were shut for the more secrecy and security, to avoid danger from the Jews, saith Dr Hammond on the words:[1] Acts i. 13, 14, 'And when they were come in, they went up into an upper room, where abode both Peter, and James, and John, and Andrew, Philip, and Thomas, Bartholomew, and Matthew, James the son of Alpheus, and Simon Zelotes, and Judas the brother of James. These all continued with one accord in prayer and supplication, with the women, and Mary the mother of Jesus, and with his brethren:' Acts xx. 7,[2] 'And upon the first day of the week, when the disciples came together to break bread, Paul preached unto them,

[1] See the Dutch Annotations.
[2] See the Dutch Annotations and Diodati on Acts xx. 7–12.

ready to depart on the morrow; and continued his speech until midnight;' ver. 8, 'And here were many lights' (*Gr.* many lamps) 'in the upper chamber, whither they were gathered together;' ver. 9, 'And there sat in a window a certain young man named Eutychus, being fallen into a deep sleep: and as Paul was long preaching, he sunk down with sleep, and fell down from the third loft, and was taken up dead;' ver. 10, 'And Paul went down, and fell on him, and, embracing him, said, Trouble not yourselves; for his life is in him;' ver. 11, 'When he therefore was come up again, and had broken bread, and eaten, and talked a long while, even till break of day, so he departed;' ver. 12, And they brought the young man alive, and were not a little comforted;' Acts v. 42, 'And daily in the temple, and in every house, they ceased not to teach and preach Jesus Christ;' Acts xii. 12,[1] 'And when he had considered the things, he came to the house of Mary the mother of John, whose surname was Mark; where many were gathered together praying'—or where many thronged to pray, as it runs in the original; Acts xx. 20, 'And how I kept back nothing that was profitable unto you, but have shewed you, and have taught you publicly, and from house to house;' Acts xxviii. 30, 31, 'And Paul dwelt two whole years in his own hired house, and received all that came in unto him: preaching the kingdom of God, and teaching those things which concern the Lord Jesus Christ, with all confidence, no man forbidding him;' Luke x. 38, 39, 'Now it came to pass, as they went, that he entered into a certain village: and a certain woman, named Martha, received him into her house. And she had a sister called Mary, which also sat at Jesus' feet, and heard his word.' Beloved, by these scriptures it is most evident and clear that our Lord Jesus Christ, and his disciples and apostles, and those Christians that lived in their times, did frequently meet in private houses, and there performed acts of public worship—viz., such as preaching, hearing, praying, breaking of bread, &c. How the primitive Christians in those hot times of persecution met in the nights, and in woods, and houses, and obscure places, they best understand who have read the writings of Tertullian, Cyprian, Chrysostom, Theodoret, Austin, Eusebius, Justin Martyr, Pliny, &c. But this to some being an unpleasing theme, I shall not enlarge myself upon it. Only remember this, that there was never yet any town, city, or country, kingdom or commonwealth, that did ever fare the worse for a holy praying people. Frequent and fervent prayer, be it in public or in private, in a synagogue or in an upper room, never did, nor never will, bring misery or mischief upon those places where such exercises are kept up, James v. 17, 18. Such conventicles of good fellowship, as some call them, where there is nothing but swearing and cursing, and carousing and gaming, and all manner of filthiness and profaneness, are the only conventicles that bring desolating judgments upon princes, people, and nations, as is most evident throughout the scriptures.[2]

[1] See Dr Hammond on the words and the English Annotations; *vide* Dr Hammond of Acts xxviii. 30, 31.

[2] Several hundred scriptures might be produced to make good the assertion. Remember what one Achan did, and what one Manasseh did, 2 Kings xxi. 11, 12; Eccles. ix. 18. 'One sinner destroyeth much good.' Oh, then, what a world of good will a rabble of sinners destroy!

Take two texts for all: 1 Sam. i. 12, 25, 'But if ye shall still do wickedly, ye shall be consumed, both ye and your kings.' When princes and people continue to do wickedly together, then they shall be consumed together. Zeph. i. 12, 'I will search Jerusalem with candles, and punish the men that are settled on their lees: that say in their heart, The Lord will not do good, neither will he do evil;' ver. 13, 'Therefore their goods shall become a booty, and their houses a desolation;' ver. 17, 'And I will bring distress upon men, that they shall walk like blind men, because they sinned against the Lord; and their blood shall be poured out as dust, and their flesh as the dung;' ver. 18, 'Neither their silver nor their gold shall be able to deliver them in the day of the Lord's wrath: but the whole land shall be devoured by the fire of his jealousy: for he shall make even a speedy riddance of all them that dwell in the land.' Now, if any of you whose houses are laid desolate, have had your spirits imbittered and engaged against the poor people of God, for practising as Christ and his apostles did, then lay your hands upon your mouths, and say, The Lord is righteous, though he has turned us out of house and home, and laid all our pleasant things desolate. Certainly all that legal and ceremonial holiness of places which we read of in the Old Testament did quite vanish and expire with the types, when Christ, who is the substance at which all those shadows pointed, came into the world. I have neither faith to believe, nor any reason to see that there is in any separated or consecrated places for divine worship, any such legal or ceremonial kind of holiness which renders duties performed there more acceptable unto God, than if performed by the same persons and in the like manner in any other places.[1] Doubtless Christ by his coming in the flesh hath removed all distinction of places through legal holiness. This is clear by the speech of our Saviour to the Samaritan woman, concerning the abolishing of all distinction of places for worship through a ceremonial holiness: John iv. 21, 'Jesus saith unto her, Woman, believe me, the hour cometh when ye shall neither in this mountain, nor yet at Jerusalem, worship the Father.' The public worship of God was now to be restrained to no place, as formerly it was to the temple at Jerusalem—that is, to no place for its ceremonial holiness, which may render the parts of divine worship more acceptable to God than if performed elsewhere; because those types which sanctioned the places formerly, were now to be taken away, when Christ the substance was come; and the body of the ceremonial worship being now to expire, and the partition-wall taken down, that the Gentiles might be admitted to worship God in spirit and in truth. It could not possibly be, for these reasons, that the true worship of God should be tied and fixed to any one such temple as was at Jerusalem, any more. The temple at Jerusalem was a mean of God's worship, and part of their ceremonial service, and a type of Christ; but our temples, saith my author,[2] are not a part of the worship of God, nor types of the body of Christ. Neither are we bound when we pray to set our faces towards them. They are called places of prayer only, because the saints meet there; and if the saints' meet-

[1] Merc[erus] in Rad. קדש

[2] Weemes. Vol. i., Christian Synagogue, p. 110.

ing were not in them, they were but like other common places. The temple of Jerusalem sanctified the meetings of the saints, but the meeting of the saints sanctifies our temples. Herod's temple at Jerusalem was so set on fire by Titus his soldiers, that it could not be quenched by the industry of man; and at the same time Apollo's temple at Delphi was utterly overthrown by earthquakes and thunderbolts, and neither of them could ever since be repaired. The concurrence of which two miracles, saith mine author,[1] evidently sheweth that the time was then come when God would put an end both to Jewish ceremonies and heathenish idolatry, that the kingdom of his Son might be the better established. The time of Christ's death and passion was the very time that God, in his eternal counsel, had set for the abrogation of the ceremonial law, and all ceremonial holiness of places. As soon as ever Christ had said, 'It is finished, and had given up the ghost,' John xix. 30, immediately the vail of the temple was rent from the top to the bottom, Mat. xxvii. 51; and from that very hour there was no more holiness in the temple than in any other place. By the death of Christ all religious differences of places is taken away, so that no one place is holier than another. Before the coming of Christ the whole land of Canaan, because it was a type of the church of Christ, and of the kingdom of heaven, was esteemed by God's people a better and holier place than any other in the world. And upon that ground among others, Jacob and Joseph were so desirous to be buried there, Gen. xlvii. 29, 31, and xlix. 29. And in the land of Canaan some places are said to have been more holy than others—viz., such as wherein God did manifest himself in a special and sensible manner. So the place where Christ appeared to Moses in the fiery bush is called holy ground; and so was that wherein he appeared to Joshua, Exod. iii. 5; Joshua v. 15. And the mount whereon Christ was transfigured is called by Peter the holy mount, 1 Pet. i. 18. But these places were no longer accounted holy than during the time of this special presence of the Lord in them. So Jerusalem was called the holy city, Mat. iv. 5; yea, at the very moment of Christ's death, it is called the holy city, chap. xxvii. 53, because it was a city set apart by God for a holy use, a city where he was daily worshipped, a city that he had chosen to put his name upon. Though Jerusalem was a very wicked city, yea, the wickedest city in all the world, counting the means they enjoyed, yet it is called the holy city; and so doubtless, in respect of separation and dedication, it was holier than any other city or place in the world besides. So the temple in Jerusalem is nine times called the holy temple, because it was a more holy place than any other place in Jerusalem.[2] Now mark, though all the parts of the temple were holy, yet some places in it were holier than other some. This may be made evident three ways. First, There was a place where the people stood separated from the priests, Luke i. 10. And this was so holy a place that Christ would not suffer any to carry any vessel through it, Mark xvi. 11. And secondly, There was a place where the priests executed their ministry, which was holier than that that the people stood in, and

[1] Godw. Antiq. Heb.

[2] Ps. v. 7, xi. 4, lxv. 4, lxxix. 1, and cxxxviii. 2; Jonah ii. 4, 7; Micah i. 2; Hab. ii. 20.

is therefore called the holy place, Lev. xvi. 30, *seq.* And thirdly, There was a place which the high-priest might only enter into, and that but once a year, and that is called the holy of holies, the holiest place of all, Heb. ix. 3. But now since the death of Christ, there is no place in the world that is holier than other. The prayer of faith is as powerful and as prevalent with God in one place as in another. Paul describes the faithful to be such as call upon God in every place, 1 Cor. i. 2. 'And I will,' saith he, 'that men pray everywhere,' 1 Tim. ii. 8. 'And where two or three,' saith Christ, 'are gathered together in my name, there am I in the midst of them,' Mat. xviii. 20. That every place should be free for the people of God to worship the Lord in, was foretold by the prophets, as a singular privilege that should come to the church in the days of the gospel: Zeph. ii. 11, 'And men shall worship him, every one from his place, even all the isles of the heathen;' that is, all countries, though not encompassed with the sea, for the Jews called all lands islands whither they could not come but by water. Men should worship, not only at Jerusalem, as once, but in all places; they should lift up 'pure hands and hearts without wrath or doubting,' 1 Tim ii. 8, both in church and chamber. Any place whatsoever shall be a sufficient oratory, so that God be worshipped in spirit and in truth: Mal. i. 11, 'For from the rising of the sun, even to the going down of the same, my name shall be great among the Gentiles; and in every place,' not in Judea only, 'incense shall be offered unto my name,'—here the prophet frames his words to the capacity of the people, and by the altar and sacrifices he meaneth the spiritual service of God, which should be under the gospel, when an end shall be put to all these legal ceremonies by Christ's only sacrifice—'and a pure offering: for my name shall be great among the heathen, saith the Lord of hosts.' The poor blind besotted Jews thought that God was so tied to them, that if they did not worship him at Jerusalem, he would have no service nor worship in the world. But God tells them that they were under a very high mistake, for he would take care of his own name and glory. 'For from the rising of the sun, even to the going down of the same, my name shall be great'—that is, the knowledge of it, and of the right worship of it—'among the Gentiles,' [this is an excellent prophecy of the cutting off[1] the Gentiles;]—'and in every place incense shall be offered unto my name.' My worship, saith God, shall not be confined to Judea or Jerusalem, or the temple, but in every place I will have a people that shall worship me, and that shall be still offering of prayers and praises and thanksgivings to me.[2] Christ, by his death, hath taken away all difference of places. And indeed it was but necessary that, when the body was come, the shadow should cease. Yea, since Christ's death, all difference of persons is taken away: 'For in every nation under heaven, such as fear God, and work righteousness, are accepted of him.' 'There is neither Jew nor Greek, there is neither bond nor free, there is neither male nor female: for ye are all one in Christ Jesus,' Acts x. 34, 35; Gal. iii. 28. And therefore all difference of places must needs also be taken away, for this difference of places was as a partition-wall between the Jews and

[1] Query, 'calling of'?—G.

[2] See Isa. lxvi. 19, 20, lx. 8, and xix. 19.

the Gentiles, Eph. ii. 14, 15. Now mark, since the destruction of the temple and city of Jerusalem, the Lord hath not sanctified any other place in the world, or consecrated it to a more holy use than the rest, and it is only God's institution and word that can make any thing or any place holy, 1 Tim. iv. 4, 5. Nothing can make any place or any thing else holy, but the ordinance and institution of God. It is Judaism, it is a denying of Christ to be come in the flesh, to hold or affirm that one place is holier than another. I know the papists put more holiness in some places than they do in others; for they hold that it is more advantageous to the dead to be buried in the churchyard than out of it; and in the church, more than in the churchyard; and in chancel, more than in the church; and near the high altar, more than in any other place of the chancel; and all out of a superstitious conceit, that these places are consecrated and hallowed, that they are holier than other places are. But Christians that live under a bright shining gospel understand the folly and vanity of these men's spirits, principles, and practices. Such as are wise in heart know that since Christ by his death hath taken away all religious difference of places, England is as holy as Canaan, and London as Jerusalem, and our houses as the temple.

Under the law they were wont to dedicate their houses, and consecrate them to God, before they dwelt in them: Deut. xx. 5, 'And the officers shall speak unto the people, saying, What man is there that hath built a new house, and hath not dedicated it?'—by prayers, hymns, and other holy solemnities;—'let him go and return to his house, lest he die in the battle, and another man dedicate it.' Now though this were done in those times, with sundry ceremonies which are now abolished, yet the equity of the duty still remains. And doubtless the best way for a man to bring down a blessing upon himself and his house, is to dedicate himself and his house to God: 2 Sam. vi. 11, 'And the ark of the Lord continued in the house of Obed-edom the Hittite three months: and the Lord blessed Obed-edom, and all his household:' ver. 12, 'And it was told king David, saying, The Lord hath blessed the house of Obed-edom, and all that pertaineth to him, because of the ark of God.'[1] In this scripture you see that when men do anything to the advancement of religion, or to the furtherance of God's worship and service, he takes it kindly at their hands. The meanest service that is done to Christ or his church hath a patent of eternity. Again, in this scripture you may run and read a real retribution and remuneration. God does not put off Obed-edom with a fine feather, or with empty favours, or court-compliments, but he really blesses him and all his household. Obed-edom had been at some cost and charge in giving entertainment to God's ark; but God defrays all the charges, and pays him abundantly for his kind entertainment, with interest upon interest. No man ever gave the gospel a night's lodging, that hath been a loser by it. God will pay all such with use and principal, who do anything to the furtherance of his

[1] Neh. xii. 27, 28; Ps. xxx. Title, A Psalm and Song at the Dedication of the House of David. While the ark brought the plague, every one was glad to be rid of it; but when it brought a blessing to Obed-edom, they looked upon it as worthy of entertainment. Many will own a blessing ark, a prosperous truth; but he is an Obed-edom indeed that will own a persecuted, tossed, banished ark.

worship and service. Hiram shall have corn and oil, for affording materials to the building of the temple. Cyrus shall prosper and be victorious, for breaking off the yokes that were about his people's necks, and restoring of them to their Christian liberty. Egypt fared the better for entertaining the patriarchs; God stored that country with great plenty and variety of outward blessings, because his church was to sojourn there. God blessed Obed-edom's person and possession and family for the ark's sake. The blessings that was upon Obed-edom was like the precious ointment that was shed upon Aaron's head, and that ran down to the lowest skirts of his garments. Every servant in Obed-edom's family tasted of God's noble bounty, and fared the better for the ark's sake. Let men and devils do their worst, God will certainly bless their dwellings who give entertainment to his ark, to his people that desire to worship him in spirit and in truth.

O sirs, this is and this must be for a lamentation, that there are so many ale-houses, and gaming-houses, and whore-houses, that are usually stuffed with vain persons, yea, with the very worst of the worst of men, both on the Lord's day, and on other days.[1] Certainly these houses are the very suburbs and seminaries of hell. *Ubi fuisti?* Where hast thou been? *apud inferos*, in hell, said Erasmus merrily: comparing tippling-houses to hell. Doubtless they are the nurseries of all sin, and the synagogue of devils incarnate. In the above-mentioned houses, how notoriously is the name of God blasphemed, and how shamefully are the precious fruits of the earth abused! and how many hundred families are there impoverished! and how many thousand children and servants are there impoisoned! and how is all manner of wickedness and lewdness there encouraged and increased! But when, oh when shall the sword of the magistrate be turned against these conventicles of hell? Certainly the horrid wickednesses that are daily committed in such houses, if not prevented by a faithful, zealous, and constant execution of the laws in force, will arm divine vengeance against the land. Magistrates should not bear the sword of justice in vain; for they are ministers of God to revenge and execute wrath upon them that do evil. By their office they are bound to be a terror to evil-doers, and encouragers of them that do well; and oh that all in power and authority would for ever resolve against being Satan's drudges: Rev. ii. 10, 'Fear none of these things which thou shalt suffer: behold, the devil shall cast some of you into prison, that ye may be tried; and ye shall have tribulation ten days: be thou faithful unto death, and I will give thee a crown of life.'[2] The devil by his imps and instruments whom he acts and agitates, the devil by engaging the civil and the military power of the world against the people of God, should so far prevail as to clap them up in prison. The prison in this text notes, by a synecdoche, the adjuncts and conse-

[1] Among all the Lacedæmonians you could not have seen one drunken man among them, unless it was their slaves. The Mahometans forbid any of their sect to drink wine, under pain of death; their Mussulmans and Darnisels [*sic*] affirming that there lurks a devil under every grape. [Query, 'darvishes'?—ED.]

[2] The devil in Dioclesian, say some; the devil in Trajan, say others: for he reigned next after this book was written, and was very cruel against the Christians, delivering them over to prisons and death, and all to drive them through fear from the profession of Christ.

quences—as namely, torments, punishments, and all sorts of martyrdom. This one punishment, imprisonment, saith Brightman, doth contain prescribings,[1] confiscation of goods, banishments, slaughters, fires, rackings, or whatsoever exquisite torment beside, as the story teacheth. The heathen emperors, with those wicked governors, officers, and soldiers that were under them, were the great instruments in Satan's hand, to practise the greatest cruelties upon the saints in those days. Some they cast into prisons, some they banished, multitudes they slew with the sword; some of the precious servants of Christ they beat with stripes to death, others they branded in their foreheads, others were tortured and racked. Yea, and many holy women in that day had their breasts cut off, and others of them had their breasts burnt with a hot iron, and sometimes with eggs roasted as hot as could be. These, with many other torments, the people of God were exercised with, as all know that have read the lamentable stories of those sad times.

Obj. But you may say, Why then is the imprisonment of the saints so ascribed to the devil, as if it were immediately acted by him? 'Behold, the devil shall cast some of you into prison.'

Ans. [1.] To shew what influence the devil hath in the acting of wicked men, so that in effect their deed is his deed, they are so subservient to him.

[2.] It is to shew us that the author, original, and fountain from whence all the persecutions of the saints do flow, is the devil, who was a murderer and a liar from the beginning, John viii. 44.

[3.] It is to aggravate the horribleness of this sin of persecution, as being a main piece of the devil's business, whatever the instruments are.

[4.] It is to comfort and encourage the people of God to patience and constancy in all their sufferings for Christ, seeing that it is the devil that is their grand enemy, and that makes, in his instruments, the highest opposition against them. A gracious man in the midst of all oppositions, as Chrysostom said of Peter, is as a man made all of fire walking in stubble, he overcomes and consumes all oppositions; all difficulties are but whet-stones to his fortitude. When Christians meet with great opposers and great oppositions, they should say as that noble soldier, Pædarelus, in Erasmus, did to him that told him of a numerous and mighty army which was coming against him, *Tanto plus gloriæ referemus quoniam eo plures superabimus:* The number of opposers makes the Christian's conquest the more illustrious. It is very observable, that in Dioclesian's time, under whom was the last and worst of the ten persecutions, when Christian religion was more desperately opposed than ever, yet then it prospered and prevailed more than ever [Ruffinus.] So that Dioclesian himself observing that the more he sought to blot out the name of Christ, the more legible it became, and the more he laboured to block up the way of Christ, the more passable it became.[2] And whatever of Christ he thought to root out, it rooted the deeper and rose the higher: thereupon he re-

[1] Query, 'proscribings'?—ED.

[2] As they said once of the Grecians in the epigram, whom they thought invulnerable, We shoot at them, but they fall not down, we wound them, but do not kill them. [As before.—G.] See Exod. i. 10-13, and Acts viii. and xiv.

solved to engage no further, but retired to a private life. All the oppositions that the devil and his instruments hath raised against the saints in all the ages of the world, hath not diminished, but increased their number. For the first three hundred years after Christ there was a most terrible persecution. Historians tell us that by seven and twenty several sorts of deaths they tormented the poor people of God. In these hot times of persecution many millions of Christians were destroyed. And yet this was so far from diminishing of their number, that it increased their number; for the more they were oppressed and persecuted, the more they were increased. And therefore some have well observed, that though Julian used all means imaginable to suppress them, yet he could never do it. He shut up all their schools, that they might not have learning, and yet never did learning more flourish than then. He devised all manner of cruel torments to terrify the Christians, and to draw them from their holy faith; and yet he saw that they increased and multiplied so fast, that he thought it his best course at last to give over his persecuting of the saints, not out of love, but out of envy, because that through his persecution they increased. This was represented unto Daniel in a vision, Dan. ii. 34, 35. The kingdom of Christ is set forth there by a little stone cut out of the mountain without hands, without art or industry, without engines and human helps. The stone was a growing stone, and although in all the ages of the world there have been many hammers at work to break this stone in pieces, yet they have not nor shall not prevail; but the little stone shall grow more and more, till it becomes a great mountain, and fills the whole earth.

And let this suffice for answer to the first objection.

Obj. 2. I would justify the Lord, I would say he is righteous, though my house be burnt up: but I have lost my goods, I have lost my estate, yea, I have lost my all as to this world; and how then can I say the Lord is righteous? how can I justify that God which has even stripped me as naked as the day wherein I was born? &c.

To this I answer.

[1.] First, *Didst thou gain thy estate by just or unjust ways and means?* If by unjust ways and means, then be silent before the Lord. If by just ways and means, then know that the Lord will lay in that of himself, and of his Son, and of his Spirit, and of his grace, and of heaven's glory, that shall make up all thy losses to thee. But,

[2.] Secondly, *Did you improve your estates for the glory of God, and the good of others, or did you not?* If not, why do you complain? If you did, the reward that shall attend you at the long run, may very well bear up your spirits under all your losses. Consult these scriptures: 1 Cor. i. 15; 2 Cor. ix. 6; Eccles. xi. 1; Gal. vi. 7, 8; Isa. xxxii. 20, and lv. 10; Prov. xi. 18; Rev. xxii. 12. But,

[3.] Thirdly, *What trade did you drive Christ-wards, and heaven-wards, and holiness-wards?*[1] If you did drive either no trade heaven-wards, or but a slender or inconstant trade heaven-wards, and holiness-wards, never wonder that God by a fiery dispensation has spoiled your

[1] The stars which have least circuit are nearest the pole, and men that are least perplexed with business are commonly nearest to God.

civil trade. Doubtless there were many citizens who did drive a close, secret, sinful trade, who had their by-ways and back-doors—some to uncleanness, others to merry-meetings, and others to secret gaming. Now if thou wert one of them that didst drive a secret trade of sin, never murmur because thy house is burnt, and thy trade destroyed, but rather repent of thy secret trade of sin, and wonder that thy body is not in the grave, and that thy soul is not a-burning in everlasting flames. Many there were in London, who had so great a trade, so full a trade, so constant a trade, that they had no time to mind the everlasting concernments of their precious souls and the great things of eternity.[1] They had so much to do on earth, that they had no time to look up to heaven, as once the Duke of Alva told the king of France. Sir Thomas More saith, There is a devil called *negotium*, business, that carrieth more souls to hell than all the devils in hell beside. Many citizens had so many irons in the fire, and were cumbered about with so many things, that they wholly neglected the one thing necessary; and therefore it was but just with God to visit them with a fiery rod. Look, as much earth puts out the fire, so much worldly business puts out the fire of heavenly affections. Look, as the earth swallowed up Korah, Dathan, and Abiram, so much worldly business swallows up so much precious time, that many men have no leisure to secure their interest in Christ, to make their calling and election sure, to lay up treasure in heaven, to provide for eternity; and if this have been any of your cases who are now burnt up, it highly concerns you to justify the Lord, and to say he is righteous, though he has burnt up your habitations, and destroyed your trade, Num. xxii. 32, and 2 Pet. i. 10. It is sad when a crowd of worldly business shall crowd God and Christ and duty out of doors. Many citizens did drive so great a public trade in their shops, that their private trade to heaven was quite laid by. Such who were so busy about their farm and their merchandise, see Luke xiv. 16, 22, that they had no leisure to attend their souls' concernments, had their city set on fire about their ears: Mat. xxii. 5, 'But they made light of it'—that is, of all the free, rich, and noble offers of grace and mercy that God had made to them—'and went their ways, one to his farm, another to his merchandise.' Ver. 7, 'But when the king heard thereof, he was wroth: and he sent forth his armies'—that is, the Romans—'and destroyed those murderers, and burnt up their city.' It is observable that the Jews, who were commanded six days to labour, were also commanded to offer morning and evening sacrifice daily, Exod. xx. 9. *Vide* Exod. xxix. 38, 39; Num. xxviii. 3; Deut. vi. 6-8. They had their morning sacrifice when they entered upon their work, and they had their evening sacrifice when they ended their work. Their particular callings did not steal away their hearts from their general callings. The Jews divided the day into three parts, the first, *ad Tephilla*, *orationem*, to prayer; the second, *ad Torah*, *legem*, for the reading of the law; the third, *ad Malacha*, *opus*, for the works of their lawful callings.[2] Although

[1] There were many who sacrificed their precious time either to Morpheus the minister of sleep, or to Bacchus the god of wine, or to Venus the goddess of beauty, as if all were due to the bed, the tavern, and the brothel-house.

[2] Weemse, Mor. Law, p. 223.

they were days appointed for work, yet they gave God his part, they gave God a share of them every day. God, who is the Lord of all time, hath reserved to himself a part of our time every day. And therefore men's particular callings ought to give way to their general calling. But alas! before London was in flames, many men's—Oh that I could not say most men's!—particular callings swallowed up their general calling. The noise is such in a mill as hinders all intercourse between man and man: so many of the burnt citizens had such a multitude of worldly businesses lying upon their hands, and that made such a noise, as that all intercourse between God and them was hindered. Seneca, one of the most refined heathens, could say, 'I do not give, but only lend myself to my business.' I am afraid this heathen will one day rise in judgment against those burnt citizens who have not lended themselves to their business, but wholly given up themselves to their business, as if they had no God to honour, no souls to save, no hell to escape, nor no heaven to make sure. But,

[4.] Fourthly, *Job lost all, and recovered all again: he lost a fair estate, and God doubles his estate to him.*[1] So David lost all, and recovered all again: 1 Sam. xxx. 18, 'And David recovered all that the Amalekites had carried away; and David rescued his two wives.' Ver. 19, 'And there was nothing lacking to them, neither small nor great, neither sons nor daughters, neither spoil, nor anything that they had taken to them.' David recovered all. Here the end was better than the beginning; but the contrary befell the Amalekites, who a little before had framed comedies out of poor Ziklag's tragedies. In the beginning of the chapter you may see that David had lost all that ever he had in the world, ver. 1–5. All the spoil that he had taken from others were gone—his corn gone, his cattle gone, his wives gone, and his city burnt with fire, and turned into a ruinous heap, so that he had not a house, a habitation in all the world to put his head in; he had nothing left him but a poor, grieved, madded, and enraged army. The people spake of stoning of him, ver. 6: but what was the event now? Why, David recovers all again. O sirs, when a Christian is in greatest distress, when he hath lost all, when he is not worth one penny in all the world, yet then he hath a God to go to at last. David encouraged himself in the Lord his God. A Christian's case is never so desperate but he hath still a God to go to.[2] When a Christian has lost all, the best way to recover all again is to encourage himself in the Lord his God. God sometimes strips his people of outward mercies, and then restores to them again those very mercies that he had stripped them of. I have read a story of a poor man that God served[3] faithfully, and yet was oppressed cruelly, having all his goods taken from him by an exacting knight; whereupon, in a melancholy humour, he persuaded himself that God was dead, who had formerly been so faithful to him, and now, as he thought, had left him. It so fell out that an old man met him, and desired him to deliver a letter into the hands of his oppressor; upon the receipt and perusal of which, the knight was so convinced, that immediately he confessed his fault,

[1] Compare the first and last chapters of Job together.

[2] Remember that of Zeno, who said he never sailed better than when he suffered shipwreck.

[3] Query, 'served God'?—ED.

and restored the poor man his goods; which made the poor man say, Now I see that God may seem to sleep, but can never die. If God has taken away all, yet remember that God has a thousand thousand ways to make up all thy losses to thee, which thou knowest not of; therefore do not murmur, do not fret, do not faint, nor do not limit the Holy One of Israel. If thou madest no improvement of thy house, thy estate, thy trade, then it is thy wisdom and thy work rather to be displeased with thyself for thy non-improvement of mercies, than to be discontented at that hand of heaven that hath deprived thee of thy mercies. Remember, O ye burnt citizens of London, that you are not the first that have lost your all. Besides the instances already cited, you must remember what they suffered in the tenth and eleventh chapters of the Hebrews; and you must remember that in the ten persecutions many thousands of the people of God were stripped of their all; and so were very many also in the Marian days. Who shrugs or complains of a common lot? It was grace upon the throne that thou enjoyedst thy house, thy estate, thy trade so long; and therefore it concerns thee to be rather thankful that thy mercies were continued so long unto thee, than to murmur because thou art now stripped of all. But,

[5.] Fifthly, *When all is gone, yet mercy may be near, and thou not see it.* When Hagar's bottle was empty, the well of water was near, though she saw it not, Gen. xxi. 19. Mercies many times are never nearer to us than when, with Hagar, we sit down and weep because our bottle is empty, because our streams of mercy are dried up. The well was there before, but she saw it not till her eyes were opened. Though mercy be near, though it be even at the door, yet till the great God shall irradiate both the organ and the object, we can neither see our mercies, nor suck the breasts of mercy. Christ, the spring of mercy, the fountain of mercy, was near the disciples, yea, he talked with the disciples, and yet they knew him not, Luke xxiv. 15. Look, as dangers are nearest to wicked men when they see them not, when they fear them not:—As Haman was nearest the gallows when he thought himself the only man that the king would honour, Esther vi. And so when Sisera dreamed of a kingdom, Jael was near with her hammer and her nail, ready to fasten him to the ground, Judges iv. And so when Agag said, 'Surely the bitterness of death is past, Samuel stood ready with his drawn sword to cut him in pieces in Gilgal before the Lord, 1 Sam. xv. 32, 33. So when Pharaoh said, 'They are entangled in the land, the wilderness hath shut them in. I will pursue, I will overtake, I will divide the spoil; my lust shall be satisfied upon them; I will draw my sword, my hand shall destroy them,' Exod. xiv. 3, and xv. 9, 10; but presently God blows with his wind, and the sea covered them, and they sank as lead in the mighty waters. Soon after Sennacherib had sent a blasphemous letter to king Hezekiah, 'the angel of the Lord went forth and smote in the camp of the Assyrians a hundred and fourscore and five thousand: and when they arose early in the morning, behold, they were all dead corpses,' Isa. xxxvii.: and within five and fifty days after, Sennacherib himself was butchered by his own sons, Tobit i. 21. No sooner had the people, as profane sycophants, applauded Herod, and given him the honour due to God, but he was smitten by the angel of the Lord, or eaten up of worms, or with vermin—with lice, as his grandfather Herod had been before him, Acts xii. 22, 23. Roffensis had a cardinal's hat sent him; but his head was cut off before it came: the axe was nearer his head than his hat. The heathen historian could not but observe, that as soon as Alexander the Great had summoned a parliament before him of the world, he was summoned himself by death to appear before God in the other world.—Now as you see by these instances that dangers are nearest the wicked when they see them not, when they fear them not; so mercies are very near to the people of God when they see them not, when they expect them not. The Israelites found it so in Asa his time, and in Jehoshaphat's time, and in Pharaoh's time, and in Hezekiah's time, and in Esther's time, and in the time of the judges, as is evident throughout the book of Judges.[1] When there was but a handful of meal in the barrel, and a little oil in the cruse, supply was at hand. Her barrel and cruse had no bottom, who out of a little gave a little. In all the ages of the world God has made that word good: Isa. xli. 17, 'When the poor and needy seek water, and there is none, and their tongue faileth for thirst, I the Lord will hear them, I the God of Israel will not forsake them.' Ver. 18, 'I will open rivers in high places, and fountains in the midst of the valleys: I will make the wilderness a pool of water, and the dry land springs of water.' Chrysostom observes, That it is very delightful to the mother to have her breasts drawn. Oh how much more, then, is it delightful to God to have his breasts of mercy drawn! O sirs, look, as many times the mother's breasts are drawn, and near the child, though the child sees them not; so God's breasts of mercy are many times drawn, and near his people, and yet they see them not. Geographers write that the city of Syracuse, in Sicily, is so curiously situated, that the sun is never out of sight. Certainly the mercies of God are never out of sight, though sometimes the people of God are so clouded and benighted that they cannot see their mercies, though they are near them, yea, though they stand before them. But,

[6.] Sixthly, I answer, *That God many times, by taking away some outward mercies, comforts, and contentments, does but make way for greater and better mercies to come in the room of those he has taken away.* He took from David an Absalom, and gave him a Solomon, Ps. lxxi. 20, 21; he took from him a scoffing Michal, and gave him a a prudent Abigail, 1 Sam. xxv.; he took away from Isaac his mother Sarah, and made up his loss by giving of him Rebekah to wife, Gen. xxiv. 67; he took away much from Job, but laid twice as much in the room of all the mercies that he had stripped him of. The Lord many times takes away small mercies to make room for greater mercies, and many times takes away great mercies to make room for greater mercies, yea, the greatest of mercies. But,

[7.] Seventhly and lastly, *Though thou hast lost all thy outward comforts in this world, yet if thou art a believer, there are ten choice jewels that thou shalt never, that thou canst never lose:—*

[1] Ps. cxxvi. 2, 3; 2 Chron. xiv., and xx.; Exod. xv.; 2 Kings xix.; Esther vi. 8; 1 Kings xvii. 12–16.

[1.] That thou shalt never totally or finally lose thy God, Hosea ii. 19, 20.

[2.] Thou shalt never lose thy interest in Christ. Whatever thy outward losses are, yet thy interest in Christ still holds good, Rom. viii. 33, *seq.*

[3.] Thou shalt never lose the Spirit of grace: John xiv. 16, 'And I will pray the Father, and he shall give you another Comforter, that he may abide with you for ever.'

[4.] Thou shalt never lose the seed of grace, the habits of grace: 1 John iii. 9, 'Whosoever is born of God, doth not commit sin'—that is, doth not give himself over to a voluntary serving of sin; he does not make a trade of sin; he sins not totally, finally, maliciously, habitually, studiously, resolutely, wilfully, delightfully, deadly, ἁμαρτίαν οὐ ποιεῖ, he does not make it his work to sin, he cannot follow his lusts as a workman follows his trade, 'for his seed remaineth in him.' The seed of God, the seed of grace, is an abiding seed, 1 Cor i. 8; Luke xxii. 32.

[5.] Thou shalt never lose the forgiveness of thy sins, though thou mayest lose the sense and assurance of thy forgiveness: Jer. xxxi. 34, 'For I will forgive their iniquity, and remember their sin no more;' Micah vii. 19.

[6.] Thou shalt never lose thy interest in the covenant of grace, Ps. lxxxix. 30, 35; Jer. xxxi. 31, 38; Isa. liv. 10. Once in covenant, and for ever in covenant.

[7.] Thou shalt never lose thy union with Christ, John xv. 1, 6. In John xvii., Christ prayed that we 'might be one, as he and his Father are one;' not essentially, nor personally, but spiritually, so as no other creature is united to God. There can be no divorce between Christ and the believing soul. Christ hates putting away, Mal. ii. 16. Sin may for a time seemingly separate between Christ and the believer, but it can never finally separate between Christ and the believer. Look, as it is impossible for the leaven that is in the dough to be separated from the dough after it is once mixed; for it turneth the nature of the dough into itself: so it is impossible for the saints ever to be separated from Christ; for Christ is in the saints, as nearly and as really as the leaven is in the very dough, [Luther.] Christ and believers are so incorporated as if Christ and they were one lump. Our nature is now joined to God by the indissolvable tie of the hypostatical union in the second person; and we in our persons are joined to God by the mystical indissolvable bond of the Spirit, the third person. Our union with the Lord is so near and so glorious, that it makes us one spirit with him. In this blessed union, the saints are not only joined to the graces and benefits which flow from Christ, but to the person of Christ, to Christ himself, who is first given for us and to us, and then with him we receive all other spiritual blessings and favours, 1 Cor. vi. 17; Rom. viii. 32; 1 Cor. iii. 21–23.

[8.] Thou shalt never lose thy inward peace, either totally or finally. It is true, by sin, and Satan, and the world, and divine withdrawings, thy peace may be somewhat interrupted, but it shall never be finally lost. The greatest storms in this life that beats upon a believer will in time blow over, and the Sun of righteousness, the

Prince of peace,[1] will shine as gloriously upon him as ever: John xiv. 27, 'Peace I leave with you,'—it is *bonum hæreditamentum*, a good inheritance,—'my peace I give unto you; not as the world giveth, give I unto you.' 'My peace I give unto you'—that is, that peace with God and peace with conscience that I have purchased with my blood I give unto you. Men may wish me peace, but it is only Christ that can give me peace. The peace that Christ gives is bottomed upon his blood, upon his imputed righteousness, upon his intercession, and upon a covenant of peace; and therefore it must needs be a lasting peace, an abiding peace. When a tyrant thus threatened a Christian, I will take away thy house, the Christian replied, Thou canst not take away my peace. When the tyrant threatened to break up his school, the Christian answered, I shall still keep whole my peace. When the tyrant threatened to confiscate all his goods, the Christian answered, Yet there is no *premunire* against my peace. When the tyrant threatened to banish him out of his own country, the Christian replied, Yet I shall carry my peace with me.

[9.] Thou shalt never lose thy title to heaven: Luke xii. 32, 'Fear not, little flock,'—μικρὸν ποίμνιον—here are two diminutives in the original; the word translated flock signifieth a little flock; but that the exceeding littleness of it might appear, Christ adds another word, so that the words in the fountain[2] run thus, 'Fear not, little little-flock.' And indeed in all the ages of the world the flock of Christ have been but little in their own eyes, and little in the world's eyes, and little in their enemies' eyes, and but little in comparison of that world of wolves that has still surrounded them,—'for it is your Father's good pleasure to give you the kingdom.' You need neither fear the loss of earthly things or the want of earthly things, for you have a kind, a tender, a loving Father, whose pleasure it is to give you the kingdom—that is, the heavenly kingdom that is prepared and reserved for you.

[10. and lastly], Thou shalt never lose thy crown of life, thy crown of glory, thy incorruptible crown, thy crown of righteousness, Rev. ii. 10; James i. 12; 1 Pet. v. 4; 1 Cor. ix. 25. 2 Tim. iv. 8, 'Henceforth is laid up for me a crown of righteousness, which the Lord, the righteous Judge, shall give me at that day; and not to me only, but unto all them also that love his appearance.' A crown is the top of royalty. Here it notes that everlasting glory that is laid up for the saints. Now this crown is called a crown of righteousness: partly because it is purchased by the righteousness of Christ; and partly because he is righteous that hath promised it; and partly because it is a just and righteous thing with God to crown them with glory at last, who have for his honour been crowned with shame and reproach in this world; and partly because they come to this crown in the use of righteous ways and means. And this crown is said to be laid up, to note our sure and certain enjoyment of it, as the Greek word ἀποκεῖται does import. And let thus much suffice for answer to this second objection.

[1] Ps. xxx. 5; Mal. iv. 2; Isa. ix. 6. שלום, *shalom;* under this word the Jews comprehend all peace, prosperity, and happy success.

[2] 'Original.'—G.

Obj. 3. I would justify the Lord, I would say he is righteous, though my house be burnt up, and I am turned out of all; but this troubles me, I have not an estate to do that good that formerly I have done. I was once full, but the Lord hath made me empty: I was once Naomi, *i.e.*, beautiful, but now God has made me Marah, *i.e.*, bitter, Ruth i. 20, 21; the Lord hath testified against me, and the Almighty hath afflicted me, and consumed me on every hand. I have fed the poor, I have clothed the naked, I have received them that were in bonds: the blessing of him that was ready to perish came upon me. But now I can do little or nothing for others; and this troubles me, Job xxix. 13.

[1.] I answer, *Thy condition is no lower than was the condition of Christ and his apostles in this world.* 'Silver and gold have we none,' Acts iii. 6. Salvian saith that Christ is *mendicorum maximus*, the greatest beggar in the world, as one that shareth in all his saints' necessities. Both Christ and his followers, when they were in this world, they were maintained by others. They had no lands nor lordships, but lived upon others' costs. But of this before; therefore let this touch suffice here. But,

[2.] Secondly, *God many times in this life repairs his people's charity with interest upon interest*, Mat. xix. 27-30; 2 Cor. ix. 6-14; Heb. vi. 10. Their scattering is their increasing, their spending is their lending, their layings out are but layings up for themselves: Prov. xi. 24, 'There is that scattereth, and yet increaseth;' verse 25, 'The liberal soul shall be made fat: and he that watereth shall be watered also himself.' It is fabled of Midas, that whatever he touched he turned it into gold. This is most true of charity; whatever the hand of charity toucheth it turneth it into gold, be it but a cup of cold water, Mat. x. 42; nay, into heaven itself. I have read of one who, having given somewhat to a poor man, and considering with himself whether he had not injured himself by giving beyond his ability, presently corrected himself with those thoughts, that he had lent it to one that would pay well again; and within an hour after he had it restored above sevenfold, in a way which he never thought of. However God may carry it towards his people in this world, yet he will be sure to repay their charity in that other world. It is storied of one Evagrius, in Cedrenus, a rich man, who, lying upon his deathbed, and being importuned by Synesius the bishop to give something to charitable uses, he yielded at last to give three hundred pounds; but first took bond of the bishop that it should be paid him in another world, according to the promise of our Saviour, with a hundredfold advantage, and the very next night after his departure he appeared to the bishop, delivering the bond cancelled and fully discharged, thereby acknowledging that what was promised was made good.[1] It is probable that the relation is fabulous; but this is certain, viz., that one day's being in heaven will make us a sufficient recompense for whatsoever we have given, or do give, or shall give in this world. But,

[3.] Thirdly, *If the constant frame and disposition of your hearts be to do as much good as ever you did, or more good than ever you did, then you may be confident that the Lord accepts of your will for*

[1] As before.—G.

the deed: 2 Cor. viii. 12, 'For if there be first a willing mind, it is accepted according to that a man hath, and not according to that he hath not.' God prefers a willing mind before a worthy work. God measures all his people, not by their works, but by their wills. When the will is strongly inclined and biassed to works of charity, so that a man would fain be a-giving to the poor and a-supplying the wants and necessities of the needy, but cannot for want of an estate; in this case God accepts of the will for the deed. David had a purpose and a will to build God a house, and God took it so kindly at his hands, that he despatches an ambassador to him to tell him how highly he resented his purpose and good-will to build him a house, 2 Chron. vi. 8. The widow's will was in her two mites which she cast into God's treasury, and therefore Christ sets a more honourable value upon them than he does upon all the vast sums that others cast in, Mark xii. 41–44. Many princes and queens, lords and ladies are forgotten, when this poor widow, who had a will to be nobly charitable, has her name written in letters of gold, and her charity put upon record for all eternity. The king of Persia did lovingly accept of the poor man's handful of water, because his good-will was in it, and put it into a golden vessel, and gave the poor man the vessel of gold. And do you think that the King of kings will be outdone by the king of Persia? Surely no. But,

[4.] Fourthly and lastly, *As there are more ways to the wood than one, so there are more ways of doing good to others than one.* If thou canst not do so much good to others as formerly thou hast done by thy purse, yet thou mayest do more good to others than ever yet thou hast done by thy pen, thy parts, thy prayers, thy gifts, thy graces, thy examples. Though thou art less serviceable to their bodies, yet if thou art more serviceable than ever to their souls, thou hast no reason to complain. There is no love, no compassion, no pity, no charity, no mercy to that which reaches immortal souls, and which will turn most to a man's account in the great day of our Lord Jesus.

Obj. 4. I would justify the Lord, I would say he is righteous, though my house be burned up, and I am turned out of all; but God has punished the righteous with the wicked, if not more than the wicked. This fiery rod has fallen heavier upon many saints than upon many sinners, &c. How, then, can I justify God? How, then, can I say that the Lord is righteous? &c.

Ans. [1.] *In all ages of the world God's dearest children have been deep sharers with the wicked in all common calamities.* Abraham and his family were by famine driven into Egypt as well as others, and Isaac and his family were by famine driven into the Philistines' country as well as others, and Jacob and his family by famine were driven into Egypt as well as others, and in David's time there was a famine for three years, and in Elijah's time there was a sore famine in Samaria, Gen. xxvi., and xlii.; 2 Sam. xxi. 1; 1 Kings xviii. 2; Mat. v. 4, 5. The difference that God puts between his own and others are not seen in the administration of these outward things: Eccles. ix. 2, 'All things come alike to all: there is one event to the righteous, and to the wicked; to the good and to the clean, and to the unclean; to him that sacrificeth, and to him that sacrificeth not: as is the good, so is the sinner;

and he that sweareth, as he that feareth an oath.' The privileges of the saints lie [not] in temporals, but in spirituals and eternals, else religion would not be a matter of faith, but sense: and men would serve God not for himself, but for the gay and gallant things of this world.[1] But,

[2.] Secondly, *There are as many mysteries in providences as there are in prophecies; and many texts of providence are as hard to understand as many texts of Scriptures are.* God's 'way is in the sea, his paths are in the great waters, and his footsteps are not known;' 'His judgments are unsearchable, and his ways are past finding out.' And yet when clouds and darkness are round about him, 'righteousness and judgment are the habitation of his throne,' Ps. lxxvii. 19; Rom. xi. 33; Ps. xcvii. 2, and xxxvi. 6. When his judgments are a great deep, yet then his righteousness is like the great mountains. There are many mysteries in nature, and many mysteries of state which we are ignorant of; and why, then, should we wonder that there are many mysteries in providence that we do not understand? Let a man but seriously consider how many possible deaths lurk in his own bowels, and the innumerable hosts of external dangers which beleaguers him on every side; how many invisible arrows fly about his ears continually, and yet how few have hit him, and that none hitherto have mortally wounded him; and it will doubtless so far affect his heart, as to work him to conclude, that great, and many, and mysterious are the providences that daily attend upon him.[2] Vives reports of a Jew, that having gone over a deep river on a narrow plank in a dark night, and coming the next day to see what danger he had escaped, fell down dead with astonishment. Should God many times but open to us the mysteriousness of his providences, they would be matter of amazement and astonishment to us. I have read that Marcia, a Roman princess, being great with child, had the babe in her killed with lightning, she herself escaping the danger.[3] What a mysterious providence was this! God's providence towards his servants is as a wheel in the midst of a wheel, whose motion, and work, and end in working, is not discerned by a common eye, Ezek. i. 16. The actings of divine providence are many times so dark, intricate, and mysterious, that it will pose men of the most raised parts, and of the choicest experiences, and of the greatest graces, to be able to discern the ways of God in them. There are many mysteries in the works of God as well as in the word of God. But,

[3.] Thirdly, *Sometimes God's own people sin with others, and therefore they smart with others.* Thus Moses and Aaron sinned with others, and therefore they were shut out of Canaan, and their carcases fell in the wilderness as well as others, Num. xx. Ps. cvi. 35, 'They were mingled among the heathen, and learned their works;' ver. 40, 'Therefore was the wrath of the Lord kindled against his people, insomuch that he abhorred his inheritance;' Jer. ix. 25, 26, 'Behold, the days come, saith the Lord, that I will punish all them which are circum-

[1] Communia esse voluit, et commoda prophanis, et incommoda suis.—*Tertul.*

[2] I have read of a father and his son, who being shipwrecked at sea, the son sailed to shore upon the back of his dead father. What a strange, mysterious providence was this!

[3] Plin. Nat. Hist., lib. ii. cap. 51.

cised with the uncircumcised; Egypt, and Judah, and Edom, and the children of Ammon, and Moab, and all that are in the utmost corners, that dwell in the wilderness: for all these nations are uncircumcised, and all the house of Israel are uncircumcised in their heart;' *vide* Rom. ii. 28, 29. Such as were outwardly, but not inwardly, circumcised, should be sure to be punished in the day of God's wrath, with those who were neither inwardly nor outwardly circumcised. When the good and the bad join in common provocations, no wonder if they suffer in common desolations, Ezek. ix. 6; Rev. xviii. 4; 1 Peter. iv. 17. Though gross impieties, like pitch or gunpowder, enrages the fire, yet the sins, the infirmities of God's people add to the flame. Not only Manasseh his bloodshed, but also good Hezekiah's pride and vanity of spirit, boasting and glorying in his worldly riches, brought on the Babylonish captivity upon the Jews, 2 Chron. xxxii. But,

[4.] Fourthly, *The people of God many times suffer in common calamities, as they are parts and members of that politic body that is punished*, 2 Sam. xxiv. 10–18. The sins of a city, a society, a company, or a nation, may involve all the members in the same judgment. Though Lot was not guilty of the sins of Sodom, yet Lot was carried away in the captivity of Sodom, as cohabiting with them, Gen. xiv. 12, 16.[1] And so though many of the precious servants of the Lord in London were not guilty of those gross impieties that their neighbours were guilty of, yet, cohabiting either with them or near them, they were burnt up and destroyed with them. Achan's family were not guilty of Achan's sacrilege, and yet Achan's family were destroyed for Achan's sacrilege. The burning of London was a national judgment, and this national judgment was a product of national sins, as I have formerly proved. Now mark, though the people of God may be personally innocent, yet because they are members of a nocent body, they are liable to undergo the temporal smart of national judgments. Doubtless a whole city may be laid desolate for the wickedness of one man, or of a few men, that dwelleth in it: Eccles. ix. 18, 'One sinner destroyeth much good.' But,

[5.] Fifthly, *When good men who cannot be justly charged with public sins, do yet fall with wicked men by public judgments, you must remember that God has several different ends in inflicting one and the same judgments, both upon the good and upon the bad.* The metal and the dross go both into the fire together, but the dross is consumed, and the metal refined, Zech. xiii. 9; Eccles. viii. 12, 13. The stalk and the ear of corn fall upon the threshing-floor under one and the same flail; but the one is shattered in pieces, the other is preserved. From one and the same olive, and from under one and the same press is crushed out both oil and dregs, but the one is tunned up for use, the other thrown out as unserviceable. The same judgments that befall the wicked may befall the righteous, but not upon the same account. The righteous are cast into the furnace for trial, but the wicked for their ruin. The righteous are signally sanctified by fiery dispensations, but the wicked are signally worsened by the same dis-

[1] Common calamities make no discrimination between persons and persons, or houses and houses. All common judgments work according to their commission and according to their nature, without distinguishing the righteous from the wicked.

pensations, Jer. xxiv. 1–3, 5. The very self-same judgment that is as a loadstone to draw the righteous towards heaven, will be as a mill-stone to sink the wicked down to hell. The pillar of fire that went before Israel had a light side and a dark side; the light side was towards God's people, and the dark side was towards the Egyptians, Exod. xiv. 20. The flames of London will prove such a pillar both to the righteous and the wicked. That will certainly be made good upon the righteous and the wicked, whose habitations have been destroyed by London's flames, that the Greek epigram speaks of the silver axe, the ensign of justice:—

'That sword that cuts the bad in twain,
The good doth wound and heal again.'

Those dreadful judgments that have been the axe of God's revenging justice, to wound and break the wicked in pieces, shall be righteous men's cures and their golden restoratives. But,

[6.] Sixthly and lastly, *God sometimes wraps up his own people with the wicked in desolating judgments, that he may before all the world wipe off that reproach which atheists and wicked men are apt to cast upon him, as if he were partial, as if he were a respecter of persons, and as if his ways were not just and equal*, Ezek. xviii. 25, 29, and xxxiii. 20. God, to stop the mouth of iniquity, the mouth of blasphemy, hath made his own people as desolate as others by that fiery calamity that has passed upon them. Such men that have been eye-witnesses of God's impartial dealing with his own people in those days when London was in flames, must say that God is neither partial nor fond. And let thus much suffice, by way of answer to this objection.

3. The third duty that lies upon those that have been burnt up, is for them *in patience to possess their own souls, and quietly to acquiesce in what the Lord has done*, Luke xxi. 19. O sirs! hold your peace, and bridle your passions, and quietly submit to the stroke of divine justice. When Aaron's sons were devoured by fire, Aaron held his peace.[1] And will not you hold your peace, now your houses are devoured by fire? What were your houses to Aaron's sons? All the houses in the world are not so near and dear to a man as his children are. In this story concerning Aaron and his sons, there are many things remarkable. As,

[1.] That he had lost two of his sons, yea, two of his eldest sons, together at a clap.

[2.] These two were the most honourable of the sons of Aaron: as we may see, Exod. xxiv. 1, in that they only with their father and the seventy elders are appointed to come up to the Lord.

[3.] They were cut off by a sudden and unexpected death, when

[1] Lev. x. 2, 3. The Hebrew word *damam* signifies silence or stillness; it signifies a staying of the heart, a quieting of the mind. Aaron's mind was quiet and still; all his unruly affections and passions were stilled and allayed. Oleaster observes that Joshua, in speaking to the sun, 'Stand still in Gibeon,' useth the same word, דם, that is here used, Joshua xii. 10. So that this phrase, 'Aaron held his peace,' imports thus much, That Aaron stood still, or stayed from further vexing, or troubling, or disquieting of himself; though at first his heart was in a strange violent motion, yet he recovers himself, and stands still before the Lord.

neither themselves nor their father thought their ruin had been so near. What misery to that of being suddenly surprised by a doleful death?

[4.] They were cut off by a way which might seem to testify God's hot displeasure against them; for they were devoured by fire from God. They sinned by fire, and they perished by fire. Look, as fire came from the Lord before in mercy, so now fire is sent from the Lord in judgment. Certainly the manner of their death pointed out the sin for which they were smitten. Now what father had not rather lose all his children at once, by an ordinary stroke of death, than to see one of them destroyed by God's immediate hand in such a terrible manner?

[5.] They were thus smitten by the Lord on the very first day of their entering upon that high honour of their priestly function, and when their hearts were doubtless full of joy. Now to be suddenly thunderstruck in such a sunshine day of mercy as this seemed to be, must needs add weight to their calamity and misery.

[6.] They were cut off with such great severity for a very small offence, if reason may be permitted to sit as judge in the case. They were made monuments of divine vengeance, only for taking fire to burn the incense from one place, when they should have taken it from another. And this they did, say some, not purposely, but through mistake, and at such a time when they had much work lying upon their hands, and were but newly entered upon their new employment. Now notwithstanding all this, Aaron held his peace. It may be, at first, when he saw his sons devoured by fire, his heart began to wrangle, and his passions began to work; but when he considered the righteousness of God on the one hand, and the glory that God would get to himself on the other hand, he presently checks himself, and lays his hand upon his mouth, and stands still and silent before the Lord. Though it be not easy in great afflictions, with Aaron, to hold our peace, yet it is very advantageous; which the heathens seemed to intimate in placing the image of Angeronia, with the mouth bound, upon the altar of Volupia, to shew that they [who] do prudently and patiently bear and conceal their troubles, sorrows, and anxieties, they shall attain to comfort at last. What the apostle saith of the distressed Hebrews, after the spoiling of their goods, 'Ye have need of patience,' Heb. x. 34, 36, the same I may say to you, who have lost your houses, your shops, your trades, your all—You have need, yea, you have great need of patience. Though thy mercies are few, and thy miseries are many, though thy mercies are small, and thy miseries are great, yet look that thy spirit be quiet, and that thou dost sweetly acquiesce in the will of God. Now God hath laid his fiery rod upon your backs, it will be your greatest wisdom to lay your hands upon your mouths, and to say with David, 'I was dumb, I opened not my mouth, because thou didst it,' Ps. xxxix. 9. To be patient and silent under the sharpest providences and the sorest judgments, is as much a Christian's glory as it is his duty.[1] The patient Christian feels the want of nothing. Patience will give contentment in the midst of

[1] See my 'Mute Christian under the Smarting Rod,' where the excellency of patience and the evil of impatience is largely set forth. [Vol. I., as before.—G.]

want. No loss, no cross, no affliction will sit heavy upon a patient soul. Dionysius saith that this benefit he had by the study of philosophy—viz., that he bore with patience all those alterations and changes that he met with in his outward condition. Now shall nature do more than grace? shall the study of philosophy do more than the study of Christ, Scripture, and a man's own heart? But,

4. The fourth duty that lies upon those who have been burnt up, is to *set up the Lord in a more eminent degree than ever, as the great object of their fear.* Oh how should we fear and tremble before the great God, who is able to turn the most serviceable and useful creatures to us to be the means of destroying of us! Heb. xii. 28, 'Let us have grace whereby we may serve God acceptably, with reverence and godly fear;' ver. 29, 'For our God is a consuming fire.' Here are two arguments to work the saints to set up God as the great object of their fear. The first is drawn from the terribleness of God's majesty, 'He is a consuming fire.' The second is drawn from the relation which is between God and his people, 'Our God.' What a strange title is this of the great God, that we meet with in this place! and yet this is one of the titles of God, expressing his nature, and in which he glories, that he is called 'a consuming fire.' These words, 'God is a consuming fire,' are not to be taken properly, but metaphorically. Fire, we know, is a very terrible and dreadful creature; and so may very well serve to set forth to us the terribleness and dreadfulness of God. Now God is here said to be a consuming or devouring fire. The word in the original, *καταναλίσκον*, is doubly compounded, and so the signification is augmented and increased, to note to us the exceeding terribleness of the fire that is here meant. When God would set forth himself to be most terrible and dreadful to the sons of men, he does it by this resemblance of fire, which of all things is most terrible and intolerable: Deut. iv. 24, 'For the Lord thy God is a consuming fire, even a jealous God.' The Hebrew word, אכלה, that is here rendered consuming, doth properly signify devouring or eating; it comes from אכל, which signifies to devour and eat; and by a metaphor, it signifieth to consume or destroy. God is a devouring fire, an eating fire; and sinners, and all they have, is but bread and meat for divine wrath to feed upon: Deut. ix. 3, 'Understand therefore this day, that the Lord thy God is he which goeth before thee; as a consuming fire he shall destroy them, and he shall bring them down before thy face: so shalt thou drive them out, and destroy them quickly, as the Lord hath said unto thee.' See Ps. l. 3; Isa. xxxiii. 14; Deut. xxviii. 58. What more violent, what more irresistible, what more terrible than fire! Oh how much therefore does it concern us to set up that God as the great object of our fear, who hath armed and commanded this dreadful creature, the fire, to destroy us in many or in most of our outward concernments as to this world! Jer. x. 11, 'At his wrath the earth shall tremble, and the nations shall not be able to abide his indignation:' Job xiii. 11, 'Shall not his excellency make you afraid, and his dread fall upon you?' Ps. cxix. 120, 'My flesh trembleth for fear of thee, and I am afraid of thy judgments:' Hab. iii. 5, 'Before him went the pestilence, and burning coals went forth at his feet;' ver. 16, 'When I heard, my belly trembled; my lips quivered at the voice:

rottenness entered into my bones, and I trembled in myself, that I might rest in the day of trouble.' Ah London, London! it highly concerns thee to tremble and quiver, and stand in awe of that great and glorious God who hath sent so many thousands to their long homes by a sweeping pestilence, and who hath by a dreadful fire turned thy ancient monuments and thy stately buildings into a ruinous heap. That Christian is more worth than the gold of Ophir, who fears more the hand that hath laid on the fiery rod than the rod itself. That prudent and faithful counsel which the prophet Isaiah gives, should always lie warm upon every burnt citizen's heart: Isa. viii. 13, 'Sanctify the Lord of hosts himself, and let him be your fear, and let him be your dread.' But,

5. The fifth duty that lies upon those who have been burnt up, is *to be contented with their present condition.*[1] When a man's mind is brought down to his means, all is well. Contentation of mind under all the turns and changes of this life, makes a believer master both of the little and great world of unruly desires within himself, and of temptations in the world without. Contentment in a man's present condition, will yield him a little heaven in the midst of all the great hells that he meets with in this world. Contentation is a hidden treasure, that the believer will carry with him to the third heaven, where an exceeding weight of glory and contentation, with full satisfaction to his desires, will be added to that little stock of contentment that he has obtained in this world. Contentation in every condition, is no other but the house of God, and the gate of heaven, as Jacob once speaks of that gracious manifestation of God, Gen. xxviii. God dwells in a contented heart, and a contented heart dwells in God. Contentment is that porch wherein the believer waits for an entrance into a house not made with hands, but one eternal in the heaven, 2 Cor. v. i. Oh labour much with God, that your hearts may be brought fully under the power of these divine commands:—1 Tim. vi. 8, 'Having food and raiment, let us be therewith content.' Heb. xiii. 5, 'Let your conversation be without covetousness'—or without the love of silver, as the Greek word signifies,—'and be content with such things as you have.' *Contenti præsentibus*: so Beza and others, 'Be content with things present.' The believing Hebrews had been plundered of all they had in this world, Heb. x. 34, when the apostle gave forth this royal command; and yet the apostle requires them to be content. It is as much the duty of a Christian to be content when he has nothing, as when all the world smiles upon him. Christians are soldiers, strangers, travellers, pilgrims, and therefore it concerns them to make shift with little things, yea, with anything in this world. The Israelites had no gay clothes, nor no new clothes in their wilderness condition; but God made their old clothes to be all clothes to them, and that was enough. Jacob did not indent with God for junkets[2] or ornaments, but for food and raiment: Gen. xxviii. 20, 'If God will give me bread to eat and raiment to put on, then shall the Lord be my God.' Nature is content with a little, grace with less;

[1] The poets bring in the feigned gods, each one content with his own office and estate—Mars with war, Minerva with sciences, Mercury with eloquence, Cupid with love, Jupiter with heaven, and Pluto with hell.

[2] 'Dainties.'—G.

though nothing will satisfy those men's hearts whose lusts are their lords. We shall never want a penny in our purses to bear our charges till we get to heaven; and therefore let us be content with our present portion in this world. Phil. iv. 12, 'I have learned, in whatsoever estate I am, therewith to be content. I know how to be abased, and I know how to abound: everywhere, and in all things, I am instructed both to be full and to be hungry, both to abound and to suffer need.' In these words you have first the vicissitude of Paul's outward condition: at one time he abounds, at another he is abased: at one time he is full, and at another time he suffers need. You have the sweet and gracious composure of his spirit, and this is expressed in two singular acts. The first is his contentation of mind in all conditions: 'I have learned, in whatsoever estate I am, therewith to be content.' The second is his prudent and pertinent comportment with his present condition: 'I know both how to be abased, and how to abound.' You have the way how he attained this contentation of mind in all conditions: 'I have learned,' saith he, 'I am instructed;' this lesson of contentment he did not learn at the feet of Dr Gamaliel, but in the school of Jesus Christ. Contentment in every condition is too high a lesson for any effectually to teach, but Jesus Christ. O sirs! in the grave it is all one who hath [had] all, and who hath had none. What folly is it to lay up goods for many years, when we cannot lay up one day for the enjoyment of our goods! Christ, who never miscalled any, calls him 'fool' who had much of the world under his hands, but nothing of God or heaven in his heart. Zopirus the Persian was contented to sustain the cutting off his nose, and ears, and lips, to further the enterprise of his lord, Darius, against proud Babylon.[1] So Christians should be contented to be anything, to do anything, or to suffer anything, to further or promote the glory of God in this world. All this whole world is not proportionable to the precious soul. All the riches of the Indies cannot pacify conscience, nor secure eternity, nor prevent death, nor bring you off in the day of judgment; and therefore be contented with a little. All the good things of this world are but cold comforts: they cannot stretch to eternity, they will not go with us into another world; and therefore why should the want of such things either trouble our thoughts, or break our hearts? The whole world is but a paradise for fools; it is a beautiful but deceitful harlot; it is a dreamed sweetness, and a very ocean of gall. There is nothing to be found in it that has not mutability and uncertainty, vanity and vexation stamped upon it. And therefore he cannot be happy that enjoys it, nor he miserable that wants it. And why then should not he be contented that has but a little of it? The greatest outward happiness is but honeyed poison; and therefore do not shrug nor faint because thou hast but little of the world. All thy crosses and losses shall be so tempered by a hand of heaven, as that they shall become wholesome medicines; they shall be steps to thy future glory, they are thy only hell, thy heaven is to come. And therefore be contented in the midst of all thy sorrows and sufferings. ' Remember that many times they who have most of the world in their hands, have

[1] Rather Zopyrus, whose extraordinary devotion to Darius is told by Herodotus, iii. 153–160.—G.

least of God, of Christ, of the Spirit, of grace, of heaven in their hearts.[1] And remember, that a man were better to have much of God with a little of the world, than to have much of the world with a little of God. God alone is a thousand thousand felicities, and a world of happiness, the only life and light. Algerius the martyr, being swallowed up in a sweet fruition of God, found more light in his dungeon than was without in all the world. O sirs! if upon casting up of your accounts for another world, you find that heaven is your home, the world your footstool, the angels your attendants, your Creator your father, your Judge your brother, the Holy Spirit your comforter; if you find that God is ever with you, ever before you, ever within you, ever round about you, and ever a-making of provision more or less for you, why should you not be contented with your present condition, with your present proportion, be it more or be it less? But,

6. The sixth duty that lies upon those who have been burnt up, is *to mourn, to lie low, to keep humble under this dreadful judgment of fire, under this mighty hand of God.* When Ziklag was burnt by the Amalekites, 'David and the people lifted up their voices and wept, until they had no power to weep,' 1 Sam. xxx. 1–4. They wept their utmost; they wept themselves even blind. They did not stoically slight that fiery rod, but prudently laid it to heart. Tears are called the blood of the soul. Now a shower of tears, a shower of blood, they poured out to quench those flames that the Amalekites had kindled. When they saw their city laid desolate by fire, their sorrow was so great that they were overburthened with the weight of it; and therefore they sought ease in venting their sorrow in a shower of tears. And so when Nehemiah understood that the wall of Jerusalem was broken down, and the gates thereof were burnt with fire, he sat down and wept, and mourned certain days, Neh. i. 3, 4. Some authors report [Nazianzen and Jerome, &c.] that the Jews to this day come yearly to the place where Jerusalem, the city of their fathers, stood, which was by Titus and Adrian destroyed by fire and sword, and upon the day of the destruction of it weep over it. Oh how well does it become all burnt citizens to stand and weep over the ashes of London, and greatly to abase themselves under that mighty hand of God that has been lifted up against them![2] 1 Pet. v. 6, 'Humble yourselves under the mighty hand of God, that he may exalt you in due time.' Ah London, London! how hath the mighty hand of the Lord been lifted up against thee! how hath he by flames of fire laid all thy glory in the dust! The Lord, by fire, sword, and pestilence, hath greatly humbled thee. And oh, when shall it once be that thou wilt be humble under the mighty hand of God! It is one thing to be humbled by judgments; it is another thing to be

[1] It is only an infinite good and infinite God that can fill and satisfy the soul of man. Plato could say, The mind is not satisfied nor quieted till it return thither from whence it came.

[2] Deut. viii. 16; Lev. xxvi. 40–42; Luke xiv. 11; Dan. v. 22. Augustine saith that the first, second, and third virtue of a Christian is humility. If I were asked, saith he, what is the readiest way to attain true happiness, I would answer, The first, the second, the third thing is, humility, humility, humility: as often as I was asked, I would say, Humility. Humility doth not only entitle to happiness, but to the highest degree of happiness, Mat. xviii. 4.

humble under judgments. There have been many nations, cities, and particular persons who have been greatly humbled by amazing and astonishing judgments, who yet never had so much grace as to lie humble under those judgments. When God's hand is lifted up very high, he expects that our hearts should fall very low. To be poor and proud is to be doubly miserable. If men's spirits are high when their estates are low, the next blow will be more dreadful. God has laid our habitations in dust and ashes, and he expects that we should even humble ourselves in dust and ashes. The only way to avoid cannon-shot, is to fall down flat on the ground: the application is easy. Humility exalteth: he that is most humble shall be most honourable. Moses in his wilderness-condition was the meekest man on earth, and God made him the most honourablest, calling him up unto himself in the mount, and making of him the leader of his people Israel. Gideon was very little in his own eyes, 'the least in his father's house' in his own apprehension; and God exalted him, making him the deliverer of his Israel. He that is little in his own account, is always high in God's esteem. When one asked the philosopher what God was a-doing? he answered, that his whole work was to lift up the humble and cast down the proud. Those brave creatures, the lion and the eagle, were not offered in sacrifice unto God, but the poor lamb and dove was offered in sacrifice: to note to us, that God regards not your brave, high, lofty spirits, and that he is all for such that are of a dove-like and a lamb-like spirit. They say if dust be sprinkled upon the wings of bees, their noises, humming, and risings will quickly cease. The Lord, in the late fiery dispensation, has sprinkled dust and ashes upon us all. And oh that our proud noises, hummings, and risings of heart might cease from before the Lord, who is risen out of his holy place! Ah London, London! thou hast been proud of thy trade, and proud of thy strength, and proud of thy riches, and proud of thy stately buildings and edifices, but God has now laid all thy glory in dust and ashes; and therefore it highly concerns thee to humble thyself under the mighty hand of God. God has abased thee, and therefore make it thy work to be base in thine own eyes. When Nehemiah understood that the Chaldeans, who were a generation of idolaters, had made Jerusalem desolate by fire, he greatly humbled himself under the mighty hand of God.[1] He looked through all active causes to the efficient cause, and accordingly he abased himself before the Lord: as you may see Neh. i. 3, 4, 'And they said unto me, The remnant that are left of the captivity there in the province are in great affliction and reproach: the wall of Jerusalem also is broken down, and the gates thereof are burnt with fire. And it came to pass, when I heard these words, that I sat down and wept, and mourned certain days, and fasted, and prayed before the God of heaven.' When Nehemiah heard that the wall of Jerusalem was broken down, and that the gates thereof were burnt with fire, his grief was so great that he could not stand under it, and therefore he sits down and weeps. Who is there that is a man, that is an Englishman, that is a Christian, that is a protestant, that can behold

[1] There is nothing more evident in history than this—viz., that those dreadful fires that have been kindled amongst the Christians have been still kindled by idolatrous hands.

the ruins of London, and not—at least the frame of his spirit—sit down and weep over those ruins? The way of ways to be truly, yea, highly exalted, is to be thoroughly humbled. The highest heavens and the lowest hearts do both alike please the most high God, Isa. lvii. 15. God will certainly make it his work to exalt them who make it their great work to abase themselves. Such who are low in their own eyes, and can be content to be low in the eyes of others, such are most high and honourable in the eye of God, in the esteem and account of God. The lowly Christian is always the most lovely Christian. Now God hath laid your city low, your all low, he expects that your hearts should lie low under his mighty hand. All the world cannot long keep up those men who do not labour to keep down their hearts under judgments inflicted or judgments feared. Remember the sad catastrophe of Herod the Great, of Agrippa the Great, of Pompey the Great, and of Alexander the Great. If your spirits remain great under great judgments, it is an evident sign that more reigning[1] judgments lie at your doors. But,

7. The seventh duty that lies upon those who have been burnt up, is *to bless a taking God as well as a giving God; it is to encourage themselves in the Lord their God, though he has stripped them of all their worldly goods.* Thus did Job when he had lost his all: 'The Lord gave, and the Lord hath taken away; blessed be the name of the Lord,' Job i. 21. One[2] brings in holy Job standing by the ruined house, under whose walls his ten children lay dead and buried, and lifting up his heart and hands towards heaven, saying, 'Naked came I out of my mother's womb, and naked shall I return thither: the Lord gave, and the Lord hath taken away; blessed be the name of the Lord.' *Ecce spectaculum*, says he, *dignum ad quod respiciat intentus operi suo Deus!* Behold a spectacle—a spectacle worthy of God himself, were he never so intent upon his work in heaven, yet worthy of his cognisance! When Ziklag was burnt with fire, and David plundered by the Amalekites, and his wives carried captive, yet then he 'encouraged himself in the Lord his God,' 1 Sam. xxx. 1–3, 6. 'His God' notes [1.] His nearness and dearness to God. Saints are very near and dear to God. [2.] 'His God' notes his relation to God. God is the saint's Father. [3.] 'His God' notes his rights to God. Whole God is the believer's. All he has, and all he can do, is the believer's, Ps. cxlviii. 14; Eph. ii. 13; 2 Cor. vi. 18. From these, and such other like considerations, David encouraged himself in the Lord his God when all was gone; and so should we. So the believing Hebrews 'took joyfully the spoiling of their goods'—whether by fire, or plundering, or otherwise, is not said—'knowing in themselves that they had in heaven a better and more enduring substance,' Heb. x. 34. And to this duty James exhorts: chap. i. 2, 'Count it all joy, my brethren, when you fall into divers temptations,' or tribulations, or afflictions. A Christian in his choicest deliberation ought to count it all joy when he falls into divers tribulations. The words are emphatical; the apostle doth not say, be patient or quiet when you fall into divers temptations or afflictions, but 'be joyful.' Nor the apostle

[1] Spelled 'raigning': query, 'raging'?—G.
[2] Drexelius in his *Gymnasium Patientiæ*.

doth not say, be joyful with a little joy, but be 'joyful with exceeding great joy;' the words are a Hebraism. All joy is full joy; all joy is perfect joy. And this becomes the saints when they fall, or are begirt round, not with some, but with divers, that is, with any kind of affliction or tribulation. An omnipotent God will certainly turn his people's misery into felicity; and therefore it concerns them to be divinely merry in the midst of their greatest misery. Oh that all burnt citizens would seriously consider of these three things:—

[1.] That this fiery rod has been a rod in a father's hand.

[2.] That this fiery rod shall sooner or later be like Aaron's rod, a blooming rod. Choice fruit will one day grow upon this burnt tree, London. No man can tell what good God may do England by that fiery rod that he has laid upon London.

[3.] That this fiery rod that has been laid upon London has not been laid on, 1. According to the greatness of God's anger; nor 2. According to the greatness of his power; nor 3. According to the strictness of his justice; nor 4. According to the demerits of our sins; nor 5. According to the expectations of men of a Romish faith; who, it is to be feared, did hope to see every house laid desolate, and London made an Aceldama, a field of blood, Acts i. 19; nor 6. According to the extensiveness of many of your fears; for many of you have feared worse things than yet you feel. Now, upon all these considerations, how highly does it concern the people of God to be thankful and cheerful; yea, and to encourage themselves in the Lord under that fiery dispensation that has lately passed upon them!

Quest. But what is there considerable in God to encourage the soul under heavy crosses, and great losses, and fiery trials?

Ans. [1.] First, *There is his gracious, his special, and peculiar presence*, Dan. iii. 24, 25. Ps. xxiii. 4, 'Though I walk through the valley of the shadow of death, I will fear no evil: for thou art with me; thy rod and thy staff they comfort me.' Ps. xci. 15, 'He shall call upon me, and I will answer him: I will be with him in trouble.' Oh, the precious presence of God with a man's spirit will sweeten every fiery dispensation, and take off much of the bitterness and terribleness of it. In the gracious presence of God with our spirits lies, (1.) Our greatest happiness. (2.) Our greatest honour. (3.) Our greatest profit and advantage. (4.) Our greatest joy and delight. (5.) Our greatest safety and security. The bush, which was a type of the church, consumed not all the while it burned with fire, because God was in the midst of it. The gracious presence of God with a man's spirit will make heavy afflictions light, and long afflictions short, and bitter afflictions sweet, 2 Cor. iv. 16–18. God's gracious presence makes every burden light, Ps. lv. 22. He that has the presence of God with his spirit can bear a burden without a burden, Deut. xxxiii. 27, 29. What burden can sink that man that hath everlasting arms under him, and over him, and round about him? But,

[2.] Secondly, *There is wisdom in God to encourage them under all their trials*, Jer. xxiv. 5; Rom. viii. 28. There is wisdom in God so to temper and order all judgments, afflictions, crosses, and losses, as to make them work kindly and sweetly for their good.

Whilst God is near us, wisdom and counsel is at hand. God is that wise and skilful physician that can turn poison into cordials, diseases into remedies, crosses into crowns, and the greatest losses into the greatest gains. What can hurt us, whilst an infinite wise God stands by us? But,

[3.] Thirdly, *There is strength, power, and omnipotency in God to encourage them*, Prov. xviii. 10; Ps. xlvi. 1, 2; Isa. xxvi. 4; Ps. iii. 17. There is nothing too high for him, nor nothing too hard for him: he is able easily and speedily to bring to pass all contrivances. You read of many who have been mighty, but you read but of one Almighty: Rev. iv. 8, 'Holy, holy, holy, Lord God Almighty.' Chap. xi. 17, 'We give thee thanks, Lord God Almighty.' Chap. xv. 3, 'Great and marvellous are thy works, Lord God Almighty.' Chap. xvi. 7, 'And I heard another out of the altar say, &c., even so, Lord God Almighty, true and righteous are thy judgments.' Under all your fiery trials an almighty God can do mighty things for you. And therefore it concerns you to encourage yourselves in him, even when you are stripped of all.

O Christians, it highly concerns you to bear all your losses cheerfully and thankfully, 'In everything give thanks,' saith the apostle; 'for this is the will of God in Christ Jesus concerning you,' 1 Thes. v. 18. Chrysostom speaks excellently:[1] 'This,' saith he, 'is the very will of God, to give thanks always;' this argues a soul rightly instructed. Hast thou suffered any evil? if thou wilt, it is no evil. Give thanks to God, and then thou hast turned the evil into good. Say thou as Job said when he had lost all, 'The Lord hath given, and the Lord hath taken away; blessed be the name of the Lord.' What evil hast thou suffered? What! is it a disease? This is no strange thing to us, seeing our bodies are mortal and naturally born to suffer. What! dost thou want money? this may be gotten here, and lost here. Whatsoever evils or losses therefore do oppress thee, give thou thanks, and thou hast changed the nature of them. Job then did more deeply wound the devil, when, being stripped out of all, he gave thanks to God, than if he had distributed all to the poor and needy. For it is much more to be stripped of all, and yet to bear it patiently, generously, and thankfully, than for a rich man to give alms, as it here happened to righteous Job. But hath fire suddenly taken hold upon thy house, destroyed thy house, and consumed thy whole substance? Remember the sufferings of Job. Give thanks to God, who could, though he did not, have hindered that mischance; and thou shalt be sure to receive as equal a reward, as if thou hadst put all into the bosom of the indigent. This he repeateth over again, and saith thy reward, being thankful, is equal to his who gave all he had to the poor. To wind up your hearts to thankfulness and cheerfulness under this late desolating judgment, consider (1.) God might have taken away all.[2] It is good to bless him for what he has left. (2.) He has taken away more from others than he has taken away from you—*ergo*, be thankful.

[1] Chrysost., tom. v. homil. 63.

[2] When a gentleman in Athens had his plate taken away by Ahashuerus, [?] as he was at dinner, he smiled upon his friends, saying, I thank God that his highness hath left me anything. [A curious misprint apparently, for Alcibiades. Cf. Vol. I. 348.—G.]

(3.) You are unworthy of the least mercy, you deserve to be stripped of every mercy; and therefore be thankful for anything that is left. God has a sovereign right over all you have, and might have stripped you as naked as the day wherein you were born. (4.) God has left you better and greater mercies than any those were that he has stripped you of—viz., your lives, your limbs, your friends, your relations, yea, and the means of grace, which is better than all, and more than all other mercies—*ergo*, be thankful. (5.) The Lord has given those choice things to you, as shall never be taken from you—viz., himself, his Son, his Spirit, which shall abide with you for ever; his grace, which is an abiding seed; and his peace, which none can give to you nor take from you—*ergo*, be thankful, though God has laid all your pleasant things desolate, John xvi.; 1 John iii. 9. (6.) Thankfulness under crosses and losses, speak out much integrity and ingenuity of spirit. Hypocrites and profane persons are more apt to blaspheme than to bless a taking God—*ergo*, be thankful. The ancients say, *Ingratum dixeris, omnia dixeris*, Say a man is unthankful, and say he is anything. Ingratitude is a monster in nature, say some, a solecism in manners, a paradox in grace, damming up the course of donations divine and human. If there be any sin in the world against the Holy Ghost, said Queen Elizabeth in a letter to Henry the Fourth of France, it is ingratitude. The laws of Persia, Macedonia, and Athens, condemned the ungrateful to death; and unthankfulness may well be styled the epitome of vices. Ingratitude was so hateful to the Egyptians, that they used to make eunuchs of ungrateful persons, that no posterity of theirs might remain. Well, sirs, remember this, the best way to get much, is to be thankful for a little. God loves to sow much where he reaps much. Thankfulness for one mercy makes way for another mercy, as many thousand Christians have experienced. The Lord's impost for all his blessings is our thankfulness; if we neglect to pay this impost, the commodity is forfeit, and so will take it back. Our returns must be according to our receipts. Good men should be like the bells, that ring as pleasantly at a funeral as at a wedding. They should be as thankful when it goes ill with them, as when it goes well with them. Cicero complained of old that it was a hard thing to find a thankful man. Oh how hard a thing is it to find burnt citizens really, cordially, frequently, and practically thankful that they are alive, that they are out of the grave, out of hell, and that yet they have bread to eat, and clothes to wear, though their habitations are laid in ashes, and all their pleasant things destroyed! But,

8. The eighth duty that lies upon those who have been burnt up, is *to keep in their hearts a constant remembrance of the late dreadful conflagration.* God expects that his children should commemorate his judgments as well as his mercies. The sore judgment that God inflicted upon Sodom is mentioned thirteen times in the blessed Scripture, and all to work us to mind it, and to abhor those sins that laid that city desolate, Isa. xxvi. 8, 9; Ps. cxix. 30, 120. The Lord looks that his people should keep up fresh in their memories such judgments that have been long before executed: Jer. vii. 12, 'Go to my place which was in Shiloh, where I set my name at the first, and see what I did to it for the wickedness of my people.' The ark of old stood at

Shiloh, but after it was taken and carried away by the Philistines it was never brought back, and from that time Shiloh lay ever after desolate, 1 Sam. iv. 10, 11. And this the Lord would have engraven upon their memories, and upon their hearts. Though stony hearts are bad, yet iron memories are good: Luke xvii. 32, 'Remember Lot's wife.' Consider her sin and her punishment; that so fearing the one, you may learn to take heed of the other: 2 Pet. ii. 6, 'And turning the cities of Sodom and Gomorrah into ashes condemned them with an overthrow, making them an ensample unto those that after should live ungodly.' There is much in those words, 'that after should live ungodly.' Why hath God turned those rich and populous cities into ashes, and set them up as burning beacons, but to warn all the world that they live not ungodly, and to work them to keep alive in their memories the desolating judgments of God? The Rabbins say that the Jews at this day, when they are to build a house, they are to leave one part of it unfinished and lying rude, in remembrance that Jerusalem and the temple are at present desolate. Oh let the remembrance of London's desolation by fire be for ever kept up in all your hearts. To this purpose consider,

[1.] That the burning of London is a very great judgment, as I have formerly proved. Now great judgments, like great mercies, should be always kept up fresh in our memories.

[2.] The burning of London is a national judgment, as I have formerly proved. Now national judgments should be always fresh in our memories.

[3.] It is a judgment that carries much of the wrath and anger of the Lord in it: Amos iii. 6, 'Shall a trumpet be blown in the city, and the people not be afraid? Shall there be evil in a city, and the Lord hath not done it?' Ver. 8, 'The lion hath roared, who will not fear? The Lord God hath spoken, who can but prophesy?' Now the more anger and wrath we read in any judgment, the more highly it concerns us to remember that judgment.

[4.] A serious commemoration of God's judgments is a thing that is highly pleasing to the Lord. God delights as much in the glory of his justice as he does in the glory of his mercy or grace. Now when we commemorate his judgments, we glorify his justice that has inflicted them.

[5.] Severe judgments contribute much to the enlightening of men's understandings, and to the awakening of their consciences, and the reforming of their lives, and to work men to judge them, and justify the Lord. And therefore it highly concerns you to keep up the remembrance of London's desolation by fire always fresh and flourishing in your souls, Hosea v. 14, 15, and vi. 1–3; Jer. xxiv. 1–6, and xxii. 8, 9.

[6.] Smart judgments are teaching things. All God's rods have a voice. 'Hear ye the rod, and him that hath appointed it,' Micah vi. 9. Look, as Gideon taught the men of Succoth by thorns and briers, so God, by piercing judgments, teaches both sinners and saints to take heed of despising his patience and long-suffering, and to cease from doing evil and to learn to do well, Isa. i. 16, 17; and to fear and fly from all such sinful courses or practices that bring destructive judgments upon the most glorious cities in the world. And upon this account, how deeply does it concern us to have always the late fiery dispensation in our thoughts and upon our hearts!

[7.] All God's judgments are his messengers; they are all at his command. The centurion had not such a sovereign power over his servants, as the great God hath over all sorts of judgments. If the Lord do but hiss for the fly of Egypt and the bee of Assyria, they shall come and do their office, Ezek. xiv. 13, 15, 17, 19; Mat. xxi. 8; Isa. vii. 18, 19. Now all God's messengers, as well as his mercies, should still be kept in our eye. But,

[8.] and lastly, Consider a serious commemoration of the judgments of God will difference and distinguish you from all profane persons and unsound professors: Ps. x. 5, 'Thy judgments are far above out of his sight.' Thy judgments, that is, the plagues and punishments that thou layest upon the ungodly, are high above his sight; that is, he fears them not, he thinks not of them, he minds them not, he does not seriously consider of them, he is not kindly or deeply affected with them, he regards them no more than a tale that is told, or than foreign wars wherein he is not concerned. Others carry the words thus: He casteth thy judgments out of his sight, he will not so much as once mind them; they are too high for him to set them before him; they are hidden before him; they are above the reach of his understanding and apprehension. Both mercies and judgments have much of God in them. They speak, and speak aloud; but wicked men can neither see, nor hear, nor understand the voice of God either in the one or in the other. I have read of such a pestilential disease once at Athens, as took away the memories of those who were infected with it, so that they forgot even their own names. One pestilential disease or another usually so seizeth upon wicked men, that they easily and usually forget the judgments of God. If God set in with these eight arguments, they will contribute more to the enabling of you to keep the late fiery dispensations of God fresh in your memories, than all the pillars of brass or stone in the world. Yet I am far from questioning the lawfulness of erecting a pillar of brass or stone to commemorate the late dreadful fire, according to an act of parliament [p. 108] that is now before us. But,

9. The ninth duty that lies upon those who have been burnt up, is *to see the vanity, mutability, and uncertainty of all worldly comforts and enjoyments, and accordingly to sit loose from them, and to get their affections weaned from them*, 1 Tim. vi. 17; 1 John ii. 17; Heb. xi. 25. Behold, in four days' time a glorious city is turned into a ruinous heap, and a little world of wealth is laid in ashes, and many hundreds of families almost reduced to beggary. And are not these loud sermons of the vanity, mutability, and uncertainty of all earthly things? That is good advice Solomon gives: Prov. xxiii. 4, 5, 'Labour not to be rich. Wilt thou set thine eyes upon that which is not? for riches certainly make themselves wings; they fly away as an eagle towards heaven.'[1] All certainty that is in riches is that they

[1] He saith not, they take wing, but they make them; and not the wings of a hawk, to fly away and to come again to a man's fist, but the wings of an eagle, to fly quite away.

are uncertain. Riches, like bad servants, never stay long with one master. Did not the citizens of London see their riches flying away from them upon the wings of the fire and of the wind, when their own and their neighbours' habitations were all in flames? O sirs, what certainty can there be in those things which balls of fire, storms at sea, false oaths, or treacherous friends may in a few days, yea, in a day, an hour, deprive us of? God can soon clap a pair of wings upon all a man has in this world. And therefore he acts safest and wisest who sits most loose from the things of the world. 'Riches are not for ever; and the crown doth not endure to every generation,' Prov. xxvii. 4. This Adoni-bezek, Belshazzar, and many other great princes have found by experience, as Scripture and histories do sufficiently testify. In all the ages of the world the testimony of Solomon holds good: Eccles. i. 2, 'Vanity of vanities, saith the Preacher, vanity of vanities; all is vanity.' The things of this world are not only vain, but vanity in the abstract. They are excessive vanity; vanity of vanities; yea, they are a heap of vanity; vanity of vanities.[1] And this the burnt citizens have found by sad experience. The world is all shadow and vanity: it is like Jonah's gourd, a man may sit under its shadow for a while, but it soon withers, decays, and dies. He that shall but weigh man's pains with his pay, his miseries with his mercies, his sorrows with his joys, his crosses with his comforts, his wants with his enjoyments, &c., may well cry out, Oh the vanity and uncertainty of all these earthly things! Thus[2] the world in all its bravery is no better than the cities which Solomon gave to Hiram, which he called Cabul, that is, displeasing or dirty. All the great, the gay, the glorious things of the world may fitly be resembled to the fruit that undid us all, which was fair to the sight, smooth in handling, sweet in taste, but deadly in operation. A man may be happy that is not wealthy; witness Lazarus, and those worthies of whom this world was not worthy, Heb. xi. But how hard a thing is it for a man to be happy that is wealthy: Mat. xix. 24, 'It is easier for a camel,'—or cable-rope, as some render it—'to go through the eye of a needle, than for a rich man to enter into the kingdom of God.' There are several expositions upon these words.

[1.] First, Some say that there was a little gate in Jerusalem called the Needle's-eye, which was so low and little that it was impossible for a camel to enter in at it with his burden, and therefore when camels came that way they took off their loads, and the camels themselves were forced to stoop before they could pass through the gate. Some think that our Saviour alludes to this. But,

[2.] Secondly, Others interpret it of a cable-rope or cord, and then thus they expound the words: A man cannot by any means possible put a cable through a needle's eye, but if he untwist it, he may by thread and thread put it through.

[3.] Thirdly, Others say these words are a proverbial speech, for the Talmud had a proverb, 'Are ye of Pambeditha, who can cause an

[1] All in heaven write vanity of vanities upon all sublunaries; and all in hell write vanity of vanities upon all sublunaries: and why should not all on earth write vanity of vanities upon all sublunaries? 1 Kings ix. 13; Gen. iii.

[2] Misprinted 'though.'—G.

elephant to go through a needle's eye?' Those of Pambeditha were great braggers; they would boast to others that they could do very great things and very strange things. Hence came that proverb amongst them, It is easier to cause an elephant to go through a needle's eye, than to do thus or thus. Now our Saviour useth the word camel because he was better known to them. It was usual, say others, with the Jews to say, when difficult matters were promised, Hast thou been at Pambeditha, where camels go through the eyes of needles? But,

[4.] Fourthly and lastly, The plain and simple meaning of this proverbial speech is doubtless this—viz., that it is as impossible for such a rich man to be saved, that trusteth in his riches, and that sets a higher price upon his riches than upon Christ, and that will rather part with Christ than part with his riches, and that will rather go to hell rich than to heaven poor—as it is for a camel to go through the eye of a needle. The proverbial speech, say others, notes the difficulty of rich men's being saved: Hab. ii. 6, 'Woe to him that ladeth himself with thick clay.' Thick clay will sooner break a man's back than satisfy his heart. And oh what a folly and madness is it for a man to be still a-loading of himself with the clay of this world! In Gen. xiii. 2, it is said that Abraham was very rich in cattle, in silver, and in gold; the word is כבד, *gravis fuit;* he was very heavy, to shew that riches, that gold and silver—which is the great god of the world, the paradise, the all in all, the great Diana that all the world magnifies and worships—are but heavy burdens, and rather a hindrance than a help to heaven and happiness. Though the rich man in the Gospel fared and lived like a gentleman, a gallant, a knight, a lord; yet when he died he went to hell, Luke xvi. Though *mammon*, as Aretius and many others observe, is a Syriac word, and signifies riches, yet Irenæus derives mammon of *mum*, that signifies a spot, and *hon*, that signifies riches; to shew that riches have their spots: and yet, oh how in love are men with these spots! how laborious, how industrious are men to add spots to spots, bags to bags, houses to houses, and lands to lands, and lordships to lordships, as if there were no hell to escape, nor no heaven to make sure! Isa. v. 8.

O sirs, the voice of God in that fiery dispensation that has lately passed upon us seems to be this, O ye citizens of London, whose habitations and glory I have laid in dust and ashes, sit loose from this world, and set your affections upon things above! Live in this world as pilgrims and strangers. Remember this is not your resting-place; never be inordinate in your love to the world, nor in your delight in the world, nor in your pursuit of the world any more, Col. iii. 1; Heb. xi. 13; Jer. i. 6; Micah ii. 10. Never spend so many thoughts upon the world, nor never send forth so many wishes after the world, nor never spend so much precious time to gain the world, as you have formerly done. Take off your thoughts, take off your hearts, take off your hands from all these uncertain things. Remember it will not be long before you must all go to your long home, and a little of the world will serve to bear your charges till you get to heaven. Remember I have burnt up your city, I have poured contempt upon your city, I have stained the pride and glory of your city; that so seeing you have here no continuing city, you may seek one to come, Heb. xiii. 14. Remember I have destroyed your houses, that so you may make sure a house not made with hands, but one eternal in the heavens, 2 Cor. v. 1. I have taken away your uncertain riches, that so you may make sure more durable riches, Prov. viii. 18. I have spoiled many of your brave full trades, that so you might drive a more brave full trade towards heaven, Phil. iii. 20. Oh that I had no just grounds to be jealous that many who have been great losers by the fire are now more mad upon the world, and more eagerly carried after the world, than ever they have been! as if the great design of God in setting them on fire round about was only to enlarge their desires more after the world, and more effectually to engage them to moil and toil as in the fire, to lay up treasure for another fire to consume. Before I close up this particular, let me offer a few things to your consideration:—

[1.] First, Are there none of the burnt citizens who seek the world in the first place, and Christ and heaven in the last place? that are first for earth, and then for heaven? first for the world, and then for Christ? Mat. vi. 33; John vi. 27; first for the meat that perisheth, and then for the meat which endureth unto everlasting life? The old poet's note was, first for money and then for Christ. But,

[2.] Secondly, Are there none of the burnt citizens whose love, and hearts, and affections are running more out after the world than they are after God, and Christ, and the great things of eternity? 1 Tim. vi. 9, and Jer. xvii. 11. Are there none of the burnt citizens that are peremptorily resolved to gain the world whatever it costs them? The Gnostics were a sort of professors that made no use of their religion but to their secular advantages, and therefore when the world and their religion stood in competition, they made no scruple, no bones of renouncing their profession to enjoy the world. Oh the deadness, the barrenness, the listlessness, the heartlessness to anything that is divine and heavenly, that does always attend such Christians who are resolved to be rich, or great, or somebody in the world, whatever comes on it! Oh the time, the thoughts, the strength, the spirits that these men spend upon the world, whilst their souls lie a-bleeding, and eternity is posting on upon them! Men that are highly and fully resolved to be rich by hook or by crook, will certainly forget God, undervalue Christ, grieve the Spirit, despise Sabbaths, slight ordinances, and neglect such gracious opportunities as might make them happy for ever. Rich Felix had no leisure to hear poor Paul, though the hearing of a sermon might have saved his soul, Acts xxiv. 24, *seq.* But,

[3.] Thirdly, Are there none of the burnt citizens who spend the first of their time, and the best of their time, and the most of their time about the things of the world, and who ordinarily put off Christ and their souls with the least, and last, and worst of their time?[1] The world shall freely have many hours, when Christ can hardly get one. Are there none who will have their eating times, and their drinking times, and their sleeping times, and their buying times, and their selling times, and their feasting times, and their sporting times, yea, and their sinning times, who yet can spare no time to hear, or

[1] Pythagoras saith, that time is *Anima cœli,* the soul of heaven. And we may say, it is a pearl of price that cost Christ his blood.

read, or pray, or mourn, or repent, or reform, or to set up Christ in their families, or to wait upon him in their closets? Are there not many who will have time for everything but to honour the Lord, and to secure their interest in Christ, and to make themselves happy for ever?

Look, as Pharaoh's lean kine ate up the fat, so many now are fallen into such a crowd of worldly business, as eats up all that precious time which should be spent in holy and heavenly exercises.

[4.] Fourthly, Are there none of the burnt citizens who daily prefer the world before Christ; yea, the worst of the world before the best of Christ? The Gergesenes preferred their swine before a Saviour; they had rather lose Christ than lose their hogs, Mat. viii. 28, *seq.* They had rather that the devil should still possess their souls, than that he should drown their pigs. They preferred their swine before their salvation, and presented a wretched petition for their own damnation. 'For they besought him'—who had all love, and life, and light, and grace, and glory, and fulness in himself, Col. i. 19, and ii. 3 —'that he would depart out of their coasts.' Though there be no misery, no plague, no curse, no wrath, no hell to Christ's departure from a people, yet men that are mad upon the world will desire this.[1] Bernard had rather be in his chimney-corner with Christ, than in heaven without him, at so high a rate he valued Christ. There was a good man who once cried out, I had rather have one Christ than a thousand worlds. Another mourned because he could not prize Christ enough. But how few burnt citizens are of these men's minds! It was a sweet prayer of one, 'Make thy Son dear, very dear, exceeding dear, only dear and precious to me, or not at all.' But do all burnt citizens lift up such a prayer? I suppose you have either read or heard of that rich and wretched cardinal who professed that he would not leave his part in Paris for a part in paradise.[2] But,

[5.] Fifthly, Are there no burnt citizens who follow the world so close, that they gain no good by the word? like Ezekiel's hearers, and like the stony ground, Ezek. xxxiii. 31–33, and Mat. xiii. 22. Some writers say that nothing will grow where gold grows. Certainly, where an inordinate love of the world grows, there nothing will grow that is good. A heart filled either with the love of the world, or with the profits of the world, or with the pleasures of the world, or with the honours of the world, or with the cares of the world, or with the business of the world, is a heart incapacitated to receive any divine counsel or comfort from the word. The poets tells us of Lycaon's being turned into a wolf;[3] but when a worldling is wrought upon by the word, there is a wolf turned into a man; yea, an incarnate devil turned into a glorious saint. Therefore the Holy Ghost, speaking of Zaccheus, whose soul was set upon the world, brings him in with an *Ecce*, behold, Luke xix. 2, as if it were a wonder of wonders that ever such a worldling should be subdued by grace, and brought in to Christ. But,

[1] Hosea ix. 12. The Reubenites preferred the country that was commodious for the feeding of their cattle, though it were far from the temple, far from the means of grace, before their interest in the land of Canaan.

[2] As before.—G.

[3] Pausanias, viii. 2, § 1. Ovid, *Met.* i. 237.—G.

[6.] Sixthly, Are there no burnt citizens that are very angry and impatient when they meet with opposition, disappointments, or procrastination in their earnest pursuing after the things of the world? Balaam was so intent and mad upon the world, that he desperately puts on upon the drawn sword of the angel, Num. xxii. 21–35. Are there no burnt citizens who are so intent and mad upon the world, that they will put warmly on for the world, though the Lord draws, and conscience draws, and the Scriptures draw their swords upon them? But,

[7.] Seventhly, Are there no burnt citizens who are grown cold, very cold, yea, even stark cold, in their pursuit after God, and Christ, and heaven, and holiness, who once were for taking the kingdom of heaven by violence, who were so eagerly and earnestly set upon making a prey or a prize of the great things of that upper world, that they were highly and fully resolved to make sure of them, whatever pains or perils they run through?[1] Aristotle observes, that dogs cannot hunt where the smell of sweet flowers is, because the sweet scent diverteth the smell. Ah, how has the scent of the sweet flowers of this world hindered many a forward professor from hunting after God and Christ and the great things of eternity! The Arabic proverb saith, 'That the world is a carcase, and they that hunt after it are dogs.' Ah, how many are there who once set their faces towards heaven, who now hunt more after earth than heaven; who hunt more after terrestrial than celestial things; who hunt more after nothingnesses and emptinesses, than they do after those fulnesses and sweetnesses that be in God, in Christ, in the covenant, in heaven, and in those paths that lead to happiness! When one desired to know what kind of man Basil was, there was presented to him in a dream, saith the history, a pillar of fire, with this motto, *Talis est Basilius,* Basil is such a one, all on a-light fire for God. Before London was in flames, there were some who for a time were all on a-light fire for God, who now are grown either cold, or lukewarm, like the lukewarm Laodiceans, Rev. iii. 14, 19. But,

[8.] Eighthly, Are there no burnt citizens whose hearts are filled with solicitous cares, and who are inordinately troubled, grieved, dejected, and overwhelmed upon the account of their late losses? And what does this speak out but an inordinate love of these earthly things? 2 Cor. vii. 10. When Jonah's gourd withered, Jonah was much enraged and dejected, Jonah iv. 6, *seq.* It is said of Adam that he turned his face towards the garden of Eden, and from his heart lamented his fall. Ah, how many are there in this day who, turning their faces towards their late lost mercies, their lost shops, trades, houses, riches, do so bitterly and excessively lament and mourn, that with Rachel, they refuse to be comforted, Jer. xxxi. 15, and with Jacob, they will go down into the grave mourning! Gen. xxxvii. 35.[2] Heraclitus the philosopher was always weeping; but such a frame of spirit is no honour to God, nor no ornament to religion. (1.) There

[1] Mat. xi. 12. As a castle or town is taken by storm.

[2] One cries out, How shall I live, now I have lost my trade? another cries out, What shall I do when I am old? another cries out, What shall I and my six children do when you are dead? another cries out, I have but a handful of meal in the barrel, and a little oil in the cruse, and when that is spent I must lie down and die, 1 Kings xvii. 12, &c.

is a holy sadness, which arises from the sense of our sins and our Saviour's sufferings: this is commendable. (2.) There is a natural sadness, which sometimes rises from sickness, weakness, and indisposition of body: this is to be pitied and cured. (3.) There is a sinful sadness, which usually is very furious, and hath no ears, and is rather cured by miracle than precept. This usually flows from the loss of such near and dear comforts upon which men have inordinately set their hearts, and in the enjoyment of which they have promised themselves no small felicity. Oh that such sad souls would seriously remember that there is nothing beyond remedy, but the tears of the damned! A man who may, notwithstanding all his losses and crosses, be found walking in the way to paradise, should never place himself in the condition of a little hell. And he that may or can hope for that great-all, ought not to be excessively sad for any losses or crosses that he meets with in this world. But,

[9.] Ninthly, Are there no burnt citizens who, to gain the world, do very easily and frequently fall down before the temptations of the world? And what does this speak out, but their inordinate love to the world? That man who is as soon conquered as tempted, vanquished as assaulted by the world, that man is doubtless in love with the world, yea, bewitched by the world, Num. xxii. 15–23; Josh. vii. 20–22; Jude 11. The champions could not wring an apple out of Milo's hand by strong hand, but a fair maid by fair means got it presently. The easy conquests that the temptations of the world make upon many men, is a fair and a full evidence that their hearts are greatly endeared to it. Luther was a man weaned from the world; and therefore when honours, preferments, and riches were offered to him, he despised them. So when Basil was tempted with money and preferment, he answered, 'The fashion of this world passeth away, as the waters of a river that runs by a city, or as a fair picture drawn upon the ice, that melts away with it.' *Pecuniam da quæ permaneat*, &c., Give money, said he, that may last for ever, and glory that may eternally flourish.[1] I have read of a mortified Christian, who being tempted with offers of money to desert his religion, gave this excellent answer, 'Let not any think that he will embrace other men's goods to forsake Christ, who hath forsaken his own proper goods to follow Christ.' It was an excellent answer of one of the martyrs, when he was offered riches and honours if he would recant, 'Do but offer me somewhat that is better than my Lord Jesus Christ, and you shall see what I will say to you.' Thus you see that men that are crucified to this world do not only resist, but also triumph over all the glittering temptations of a tempting and enticing world. And oh that such a spirit might rest upon all those whose habitations are laid desolate! But,

[10.] Tenthly and lastly, Are there no burnt citizens who go to the utmost of their line and liberty for the gaining of the things of this world? Ah, how near the pit's brink, how near the borders of sin, how near the flames of vengeance, how near the infernal fire, do many venture to gain the things of this world! And what does this speak out, but an inordinate love of this world? O sirs, what do all these

[1] Basil in XL. Martyrs. In Queen Mary's time, when some offered a certain martyr money, he refused it, saying, I am going to a country where money will bear no price.

things evidence, but this, that though God has fired many men out of their houses, yet the inordinate love of this world is not fired out of their hearts!

O sirs, to moderate your affections to the things of this world, and to put a stop to your too eager pursuit after earthly things, seriously and frequently dwell upon these ten maxims:—

[1.] First, *That the shortest, surest, and safest way to be rich, is to be content with your present portion*, Eccles. v. 12. The philosopher could say, 'He that is content wants nothing; and he that wants content enjoys nothing.'

'One might have riches, yet be very poor;
One might have little, yet have all and more.'

[2.] Secondly, *He who is [not] contented with a little, will never be satisfied with much.* He who is not content with pounds, will never be satisfied with hundreds; and he who is not content with a few hundreds, will never be satisfied with many thousands:[1] Eccles. v. 10, 'He that loveth silver, shall not be satisfied with silver; nor he that loveth abundance, with increase.' Money of itself cannot satisfy any desire of nature. If a man be hungry, it cannot feed him; if naked, it cannot clothe him; if cold, it cannot warm him; if sick, it cannot recover him. A circle cannot fill a triangle; no more can the whole world fill the heart of man. A man may as soon fill a chest with grace, as a heart with wealth. The soul of man may be busied about earthly things, but it can never be filled nor satisfied with earthly things. Air shall as soon fill the body, as money shall satisfy the mind. There is many a worldling who hath enough of the world to sink him, who will never have enough of the world to satisfy him. The more a hydropical man drinketh, the more he thirsteth. So the more money is increased, the more the love of money is increased; and the more the love of money is increased, the more the soul is unsatisfied. It is only an infinite God, and an infinite good, that can fill and satisfy the precious and immortal soul of man, Gen. xv. 1. Look, as nothing fits the ear but sounds, and as nothing fits the smell but odours, so nothing fits the soul but God. Nothing below the great God can fit and fill an immortal soul. Nothing can content the soul of man but the fruition of God. Nature hath taught all men to seek after a *summum bonum.* God never rested till he made man; and man can never rest till he enjoys his God. Every man has a soul within him of a vast capacity, and nothing can fill it to the brim but he that is fulness itself. Should we knock at every creature's door for happiness, they would all answer us round, that it is not in them. The man in Plutarch that heard the philosophers wrangle about *summum bonum*, one placing of it in this, and another in that, went to the market and bought up all that was good, hoping among all he should not miss of happiness; and yet he missed of it. The soul of man is of so glorious a make, that nothing below him that made it can satisfy it. The sum of all that the creatures amount to, according to Solomon's reckoning, is vanity and vexation of spirit. Vanity and vexation is the very quintessence of the creature, and all

[1] Much treasure stoppeth not a miser's mouth, saith the proverb.

that can possibly be extracted out of it. Now if vanity can satisfy, or if vexation can give content; if you can gather grapes of thorns, or figs of thistles, then go on and dote upon the world still, and be always enamoured with a shadow of perishing beauty. Oramuzes[1] the enchanter boasted that in his egg all the happiness in the world was included; but being broken, there was nothing in it but wind and emptiness. But,

[3.] Thirdly, *It is infinitely better to have much of God, of Christ, of the Spirit of holiness and of heaven in our hearts, with a little of the world in our hands, than to have much of the world in our hands, and but a little of God and Christ in our hearts*, 2 Cor. vi. 10. It is infinitely better to be rich towards God, and poor towards the world, than to be poor towards God, and to be rich towards the world. There are some very rich, who yet are very poor; there are others who are very poor, and yet are very rich, Eccles. v. 12; Prov. xi. 24. It is infinitely better to be poor men and rich Christians, than to be rich men and poor Christians. But,

[4.] Fourthly, *The best and surest way under heaven to gain much of the world, is to mind the world less, and God, and Christ, and grace, and heaven more:* 1 Kings iii. 9, 'Give therefore thy servant an understanding heart to judge thy people, that I may discern between good and bad: for who is able to judge this thy so great a people?' Ver. 10, 'And the speech pleased the Lord that Solomon had asked this thing.' Ver. 11, 'And God said unto him, Because thou hast asked this thing, and hast not asked for thyself long life; neither hast asked riches for thyself, nor hast asked the life of thine enemies; but hast asked for thyself understanding to discern judgment;' ver. 12, 'behold, I have done according to thy words: lo, I have given thee a wise and an understanding heart; so that there was none like thee before thee, neither after thee shall any arise like unto thee.' Ver. 13, 'And I have also given thee that which thou hast not asked, both riches and honours: so that there shall not be any among the kings like unto thee all thy days.' This is more generally and fully expressed in 2 Chron. i. 12, 'Wisdom and knowledge is granted unto thee: and I will give thee riches and wealth and honour, such as none of the kings have had before thee, neither shall there any after thee have the like.' Solomon desired wisdom of the Lord, and the Lord granted him his desire, and cast in riches, and wealth, and honour as an overplus, which he did not so much as once desire. God won't be wanting to them in temporals, who in their desires and prayers are most carried out after spirituals:[2] Mat. vi. 33, 'First seek the kingdom of God, and his righteousness; and all these things shall be added to you,' or over-added. He who before all, and above all other things, seeks grace and glory, shall have the things of this world cast in as an overplus, as a handful to the sack of grain, or as [an] inch of measure to an ell of cloth, or as paper and packthread is given into the bargain: 1 Tim. iv. 8, 'Godliness is profitable unto all things, having the promise of the life that now is, and of that which

[1] *Sic.*—Query, 'Ormuzd of the system of Zoroaster'?—G.

[2] The shorter cut to riches is by their contempt: it is great riches not to desire riches, and he hath most that covets least, saith Socrates and Seneca.

is to come.' There is earth as well as heaven; bread as well as grace; and raiment as well as righteousness; and the lower springs as well as the upper springs to be found in the precious promises, 2 Pet. i. 4. Abraham, and Isaac, and Jacob, and Joseph, and Job, and Nehemiah, and Mordecai, and David, and Hezekiah, and Josiah, and Jehoshaphat, and Daniel, and the three children, or rather champions, made it their business to be holy, to walk with God, to maintain communion with God, and to exalt and glorify God: and you know how the Lord heaped up the good things and the great things of this world upon them. I verily believe if men were more holy, they would be more outwardly happy; if they did but more seriously and earnestly press after the great things of that upper world, the Lord would more abundantly cast in the things of this lower world upon them. But when men are immoderately carried out in seeking after the great things of this world, it is just with God to blast their endeavours, and to curse their mercies to them, Jer. xlv. 5; Mal. ii. 2. But,

[5.] Fifthly, *It is better to get a little of the world, than to get much of the world; it is better to get a little of the world justly and honestly, than to get much of the world unjustly and dishonestly.* A little of the world blessed, is better than much of the world cursed. Solomon's dinner of green herbs, Daniel's pulse, barley loaves, and a few fishes, and John's rough garment blessed, are better and greater mercies than Dives his riches, purple robes, and dainty fare cursed, Gen. xxii.; Prov. iii. 33, and xv. 17; Dan. i. But,

[6.] Sixthly, *The greatest outward gain cannot countervail the least spiritual loss*, Ps. xxx. 6, 7; be it but a drachm of grace, or a cast of God's countenance, or an hour's communion with him, &c. Suppose a man could heap up silver as the dust, and gold as the streams of the brook, that he could gain as much as the devil promised Christ—viz., all the kingdoms of the world, and the glory of them; yet all these could not make up the least spiritual loss, Job xxii. 24, and xxvii. 16; Mat. iv. 1–11. He that shall exchange the least spiritual favour for the greatest outward good, shall but, with Glaucus and Diomedes, exchange gold for copper; he shall, with the cock in the fable, part with a pearl for a barley-corn. Chrysostom compareth such to workers in mines, who, for a little wages, do always hazard, and sometimes lose their lives. Menot, a French preacher, compareth them to a huntsman, that spoileth a horse worth many pounds, in pursuit of a hare not worth so many pence. Pareus compares them to a man that with much ado winneth Venice, and as soon as it is won, is hanged up at the gates of the city. When such a one shall at last compute what he hath gained and what he hath lost, he will certainly conclude that he hath but a miserable bargain of it. But,

[7.] The seventh maxim is this—viz., *A little that a righteous man hath is better than the riches of many wicked*, Ps. xxxvii. 16. The righteous man's mite is better than the wicked man's millions. 'A little,' that is, a competent and mean portion, though yet but very little; one little piece of gold is more worth than a bag of counters; one little box of pearls is more worth than many loads of pebbles. And so a little that a righteous man hath is better than the abundance of the wicked—is better than the riches of many wicked. *Hamon*, which is the word here used, is from *Hamah*, which signifies multitude of riches, or great plenty, or store of riches; from this Hebrew word *Hamon*, riches are called mammon, Luke xvi. 9, 11, 13. The little that the righteous man hath is better than the multitude or store of riches that the wicked have. Out of these words you may observe these following particulars:—

(1.) Here is the righteous man's portion, and the wicked man's portion, as to this world; the righteous man hath but little, the wicked has much.

(2.) The righteous man hath but little, but the wicked has riches.

(3.) The righteous man's little is a better portion than the riches of the wicked.

(4.) The righteous man's little is better than the multitude of riches that the wicked have.

(5.) The righteous man's little is better than the multitude of riches that many wicked men enjoy. Now, for their sakes who have been burnt up, and have but little of the world left them, I shall make good this blessed truth by an induction of these eleven particulars:—

[1.] First, *The righteous man hath a better tenure to his little than wicked men have to their multitude of riches.* The righteous man holds his tenure by virtue of his marriage-union with Christ, who is the heir of all things, Heb. i. 2. We had an equal right in the first Adam to all the good things of this world; but, in his fall, we lost our original right to the good things of this world. But now the righteous man, by the second Adam, has recovered his right to all he enjoys: Rom. viii. 32, 'How shall he not with him also freely give us all things?' 1 Cor. iii. 21, 'All things are yours:' ver. 22, 'Whether Paul, or Apollos, or Cephas, or the world, or life, or death, or things present, or things to come; all are yours.' But how come they to be interested in this large charter? the apostle answers it in ver. 23, 'Ye are Christ's; and Christ is God's.' All comes to us by Jesus Christ. All the corn in Egypt came through Joseph's hands, Gen. xli. So all we have, be it little or much, we have it through Christ's hands, upon the account of our marriage-union with Christ. We may say, as Hamor and Shechem said to their people, 'Shall not all their cattle, and substance, and every beast of the field, be ours?' Gen. xxxiv. 23. So being married to Christ, and become one with him, all comes to be ours, through him who is the heir of all. By virtue of our marriage-union with Christ, our title to the creatures is not only restored, but strengthened. That little we have is entailed upon us by Christ, in a more firm and better way than ever. In the first Adam our tenure was lower, and meaner, and baser, and uncertainer than now it is; for our title, our tenure by Christ, is more honourable, and stronger, and sweeter, and lastinger than ever it was before. For now we hold all we have *in capite;* Christ is our head and husband, and by him we hold all we have. But now wicked men, by the fall of Adam, have lost their original patent and charter which once they had to shew for the things of this life. By Adam's fall they have forfeited God's primitive donation of all right in the creatures. Every wicked man in the world has forfeited his right to the creatures in Adam, and lies under that forfeiture. But to the glory of divine patience be it spoken, God has not sued out his forfeiture, God has not brought a writ of ejection against him; and by this means he comes to be lawfully possessed of those earthly blessings he does enjoy; as a felon, though he hath forfeited his life and estate to the king's justice, and is still subject to ejection at the king's pleasure, yet while the king forbears him, his possession is good and lawful, and no man may disturb him. Wicked men are lawful owners and possessors of the good things God hath given them: Num. xxii. 30, 'Am not I thine ass?' whence you may observe:—

(1.) That the silliest and simplest being wronged, may justly speak in their own defence.

(2.) That they who have done many good offices and fail in one, are often not only unrewarded for former services, but punished for that one offence.

(3.) That when the creatures formerly officious to serve us start from their former obedience, man ought to reflect upon his own sin as the sole cause thereof.

(4.) That the worst men have good title to their own goods.[1] For though Balaam was a sorcerer, yet the ass confesseth twice that he was his ass. Luke xii. 33, 'sell' and 'give' are words of propriety. And God hath set the eighth commandment as a hedge, as a fence to every man's possession: Dan. iv. 17, 'This matter is by the decree of the watchers, and the demand by the word of the holy ones, to the intent that the living may know that the Most High ruleth in the kingdoms of men, and giveth it to whomsoever he will, and setteth up over it the basest of men.' He that gave Canaan to Jacob, gave mount Seir to Esau. And did not Jacob buy a burying-place of the sons of Heth? and did he not buy corn of the Egyptians? Gen. xxiii. 3–5, 9, and xlii. 3, 5. By all which they did acknowledge that those wicked men and idolaters had a lawful title to those temporal blessings that they did enjoy. Now mark, God, as he is the God of nature by common providence, allots to wicked men their lawful possessions, and this is the best tenure they hold by. Oh, but now that little that a child of God has, he holds it by a more glorious tenure and honourable title, and therefore his mite is better than a wicked man's millions. But,

[2.] Secondly, *That little a righteous man hath, he hath through the covenant and through precious promises*, 2 Peter i. 4. Now a little mercy reached out to a man through the covenant, and as a fruit of the promise, is more worth than a world of blessings that flow in upon a man merely by a general providence. There are no mercies so sweet, so sure, so firm, so lasting, as those that flow in upon us through the covenant of grace. Oh, this sweetens every drop, and sip, and crust, and crumb of mercy that a godly man enjoys: 'All the paths of the Lord are mercy and truth to such as keep his covenant,' Ps. xxv. 10. This is a sweet promise, a precious promise, a soul-satisfying promise, a promise more worth than all the riches of the Indies. Mark, all

[1] Consult these scriptures: Deut. xxxii. 8; Acts xvii. 26; Luke iii. 14.

the paths of the Lord to his people are not only mercy, but they are mercy and truth; that is, they are sure mercies that stream in upon them through the covenant.[1] Well, sirs, you must remember this, viz., that the least mercy, the least blessing flowing in upon us through the promise, is more worth than a thousand blessings that flow in upon us from a general providence. The least blessing flowing in upon us through the covenant, is better than ten thousand talents that are the mere products of a general providence. For,

First, Such as enjoy all they have only from a general providence, they enjoy their mercies from that common source or spring that feeds the birds of the air and the beasts of the field, Ps. cxlv. 15, 16. The same common bounty of God that feeds and clothes the wicked, feeds the birds and beasts that perish. But,

Secondly, There is no certainty of the continuance of such mercies that are only the product of a common providence, Isa. xxxiii. 16; but now the mercies that flow in upon the saints through the covenant of grace, they shall be sure to us so long as the continuanee of them may be for our good and God's glory, chap. lv. 3. Now the least mercies held by covenant are infinitely better than the greatest riches in the world, that only drop upon us out of the hand of a common providence.

Thirdly, The righteous man hath his little from the special love and favour of God. All his little flows in upon him from that very same love which moved the Lord to bestow Christ upon him, Ps. cxlvi. 8, and Prov. xv. 17. All the righteous man's little is from the good-will of him that dwelt in the bush, Deut. xxxiii. 16. His little comes from a reconciled God as well as a bountiful God; from a tender Father as well as a merciful Creator. A dinner of green herbs, Daniel's pulse, barley loaves, a few fishes, yea, Lazarus his scraps, crusts, and rags, and John's garment of camel's hair, from reconciled love, is infinitely better than all the riches and dainties of the wicked, which are all mixed and mingled with crosses and curses. All the mercies and abundance that wicked men have, is in wrath and from wrath; there is wrath in every cup they drink in, and in every dish they eat in, and in every bed they lie on, and in every stool they sit on, Prov. iii. 33; Mal. ii. 2; Ps. lxxviii. 30, 31. But the little the righteous man hath flows from the sweetest springs of divine love; so that they may well say as Gideon did, 'The gleanings of the grapes of Ephraim, is it not better than the vintage of Abi-ezer?' Judges viii. 2. The very gleanings of the righteous are better than the greatest vintages of the wicked. The abundance of the wicked still flows in upon them from the bitter streams of divine wrath. A little water flowing from a sweet spring is much better than a great deal that flows from the salt sea. The loving-kindness of God does raise the least estate above the greatest estate in the world; yea, it raiseth it above life itself—or lives, *chajim*—which is the best of all temporal blessings, Ps. lxiii. 3. Ten pounds given by a king out of favour and respect, is a better gift than a thousand given in wrath and displeasure. But,

Fourthly, The little that the righteous man hath is blessed and sanctified to him, as you may see by comparing the scriptures in the

[1] Consult these scriptures: Joshua xxiii. 14, 15, and 1 Tim. iv. 8.

margin together.[1] A little blessed unto a man is better than all the world cursed. Now all the blessings and mercies that the wicked do enjoy, though they are materially blessings, yet they are formally curses; as all the crosses that befalls a righteous man, though they are materially crosses, yet they are formally blessings. The habitations, relations, honours, riches, &c., of the wicked are all cursed unto them. There is poison in every cup the wicked man drinks, and snares in every dish he puts his fingers in, the plague in all the clothes he wears, and a curse upon the house in which he dwells: Zech. v. 3, 4, 'Then he said unto me, This is the curse that goeth forth over the face of the whole earth: for every one that stealeth shall be cut off as on this side, according to it; and every one that sweareth shall be cut off as on that side, according to it. I will bring it forth, saith the Lord of hosts, and it shall enter into the house of the thief, and into the house of him that sweareth falsely by my name: and it shall remain in the midst of his house, and shall consume it, with the timber thereof, and the stones thereof.' So Job xxiv. 18, 'Their portion is cursed in the earth.' A fat purse and a fat heart, a whole estate and a whole heart, a fat body and a lean soul: Ps cvi. 15, 'He sent leanness into their souls.' All the blessings of the wicked have their *but*, as the cup in Benjamin's sack, which proved a snare to him rather than a mercy. Oh the curses and vexations that attend all the blessings of the wicked! It may be said of 'the little that a righteous man hath,' Prov. iii. 33, as it was once said of Jacob's garment, 'It is like a field which the Lord hath blessed. He blesseth the habitations of the just.' Esau had a fair estate left him, and Jacob a less; yet Jacob's was a better estate than Esau's, because his little was blessed to him, when Esau's much was cursed to him. One little draught of clear water is better than a sea of brackish salt water. The application is easy. But,

Fifthly, A little improved and well husbanded, is better than a great deal that is either not improved or but ill improved. Every estate is as it is improved. A little farm well improved, is much better than a great farm that is either not improved or ill improved. A little money, a little stock in a shop well improved, is better than a great deal of money, a great stock, that is either not improved or ill improved. Now here give me leave to shew you briefly how a godly man improves his little. Take me thus—

First, A godly man improves his little to the stirring up of his heart to thankfulness, and to be much in admiring and blessing of God for a little. Every drop the dove drinks he lifts up his head to heaven. Every bird in his kind, saith Ambrose, doth chirp forth thankfulness to his Maker. So the righteous man will bless God much for a little; yea, he will bless God very much for a very little, Ps. ciii. 1–3, and cxvi. 12, 13. But,

Secondly, A righteous man improves his little to the humbling and abasing of himself before the Lord, as one that is much below the least of mercies: Gen. xxxii. 10, 'I am not worthy of the least of all the mercies which thou hast shewed unto thy servant,' 2 Sam. vii. 18.

[1] Deut. xxviii. 8, 9; Ps. iii. 8; Gen. xxii. 17, and xxvi. 12; Prov. x. 22; Deut. xxviii. 16–20; Prov. iii. 33; Mal. ii. 2.

A righteous man labours to have his heart lie low under the sense of the least sin, and under the smart of the least rod, and under the sight of the least mercy. But,

Thirdly, A righteous man improves his little to the arming and fencing of himself against sinful temptations. Little mercies are many times great arguments to keep a gracious soul from sin, Gen. xxxix. 7–10. But,

Fourthly, A righteous man improves his little to the relief and refreshing of the bowels of others that are in want, and whose pinching necessities call for supplies, 2 Cor. viii. 1–4; Heb. vi. 10. A poor man begging at a Christian's door who was very poor, he spoke to his wife to give him something; she answered that she had but threepence in the house; saith he, give him that, for if we never sow, we shall never reap. There was another Christian who having given a little of his little to a man, began to think whether he had injured himself; but presently he corrected himself with these thoughts, that he had lent it one that would pay all again with advantage, with interest upon interest; within an hour after he had it restored above sevenfold, in a way which he never thought of. The Italian form of begging is, *Do good for yourselves.* But,

Fifthly, A righteous man improves his little to the stirring up and provoking of his own heart to look after better and greater mercies—viz., spiritual and eternal favours. Oh, saith the righteous man, if there be so much sweetness in a few drops, and sips, and small draughts, and crusts, and scraps, what is in those everlasting springs of pleasure and delight that be at God's right hand! Ps. xvi. 11; John iv. 10, 11, 14, and vi. 4; Rev. xix. 8. If there be so much pleasantness in a piece of bread, and so much warmth in a coarse suit of clothes, what sweetness is there in the waters of life! and what pleasantness is there in that bread of life that came down from heaven! and what warmth is there in that fine linen that is the righteousness of the saints! &c. A righteous man looks upon his least temporals to be a strong engagement upon him to seek after eternals. But now wicked men are so far from improving their much, their riches, their great riches, that they either hide their talents, as that evil servant did his, Mat. xxv., or else they prove jailers to their mercies, and make them servants to their lusts, as pride, drunkenness, uncleanness, &c. Compare these scriptures together: Job xxi. 1–10; Amos vi. 1–7; Ps. lxxiii.; Hosea iv. 7; Jer. ii. 31, and v. 7–9; Deut. xxxii. 13–18; James v. 1–6. But,

Sixthly, The few mercies, the least mercies that the righteous man hath, are pledges and pawns and an earnest of more mercies, of better mercies, and of greater mercies than any yet they do enjoy. Now a farthing given as an earnest of a thousand a year is better than many pounds given as a present reward. Wicked men have outward blessings as their portion, their heaven, their all: 'Son, remember that thou in thy lifetime receivedst thy good things,' Ps. xvii. 14; Luke xvi. 25. But now that little that a godly man hath, he has it as a pledge of heaven, and as an earnest of eternal favours and mercies. The little mercies the saints enjoy are doors of hope to let in greater and better mercies; those mercies a righteous man has are but inlets to further mercies. When Rachel had a son, she called his name Joseph, saying, 'The Lord shall add to me another son,' Gen. xxx. 24. Every mercy that a righteous man enjoys may well be called Joseph, because it is a certain pledge of some further and greater mercy that is to be added to those the righteous man already enjoys. But,

Seventhly, The righteous man enjoys his little with a great deal of comfort, peace, quiet, and contentment. The righteous man with his little, sits Noah-like, quiet and still in the midst of all the hurries, distractions, combustions, and confusions that be in the world, Phil. iv. 12, 13; Prov. x. 22, and xv. 16, 17. Though the righteous man has but from hand to mouth, yet seeing that God feeds him from heaven as it were with manna, he is quiet and cheerful: but now wicked men have abundance of vexation with their worldly abundance: as you see in Haman, Esth. v. 9, 11-13, 'Then went Haman forth that day joyfully and with a glad heart: but when Haman saw Mordecai in the king's gate, that he stood not up, nor moved for him, he was full of indignation against Mordecai. And Haman told them of the glory of his riches, and the multitude of his children, and all the things wherein the king had promoted him, and how he had advanced him above the princes and servants of the king. Haman said moreover, Yea, Esther the queen did let no man come in with the king unto the banquet that she had prepared but myself; and to-morrow am I invited unto her also with the king. Yet all this availeth me nothing, so long as I see Mordecai the Jew sitting at the king's gate.'[1] It is seldom seen that God allows unto the greatest darlings of the world a perfect contentment. Something they must have to complain of, that shall give an unsavoury verdure[2] to their sweetest morsels, and make their felicity miserable. It was not simply Mordecai's sitting at the king's gate, but Mordecai's refusing to stand up, or to move either hat, head, or hand, or to bow any part of his body, that damped all Haman's joy, and that filled him with rage and vexation of spirit. The want of little things—viz., a knee, a hat—will exceedingly vex and discompose an ambitious spirit. So Ahab, though a king, yet when he was sick for Naboth's vineyard, his heart did more afflict and vex itself with greedy longing for that bit of earth, than the vast and spacious compass of a kingdom could counter-comfort, 1 Kings xxi. 4. And so Alexander the Great, in the midst of all his glory, he was exceedingly vexed and discontented, because he could not make ivy to grow in his garden in Babylon. Contentment is a flower that does not grow in nature's garden. All the honours, riches, pleasures, profits, and preferments of this world cannot yield a man one day's contentment; they are all surrounded with briers and thorns.[3] You look upon my crown and my purple robes, said that great king, Cyrus, but did you but know how they were lined with thorns, you would never stoop to take them up.[4]

[1] If I had an enemy, saith Latimer, to whom I might lawfully wish evil, I would chiefly wish him great store of riches; for then he should never enjoy quiet.

[2] 'Green mould.'—G.

[3] Pheraulas, a poor man, was wearied out with care in keeping those great riches which Cyrus had bestowed upon him. [Xenophon, Cyr. ii. 3, secs. 7, 8, viii. 3.—G.]

[4] As before: and ascribed to Xerxes, Themistocles, and others.—G.

Charles the Fifth, emperor of Germany, whom of all men the world judged most happy, cried out at last with grief and detestation to all his honours, pleasures, trophies, riches, *Abite hinc, abite longe:* Get you hence; let me hear no more of you! Who can sum up the many grievances, fears, jealousies, disgraces, interruptions, temptations, and vexations that men meet with in their very pursuit after the things of this world! Oh how sweet is it to want these bitter-sweets! Riches are compared to thorns; and indeed all the comforts the wicked enjoy, they have more or less of the thorn in them. And indeed riches may well be called thorns; because they pierce both head and heart—the one with care of getting, and the other with grief in parting with them. The world and all the glory thereof is like a beautiful harlot: a paradise to the eye, but a purgatory to the soul. A wicked man under all his enjoyments,

(1.) Enjoys not the peace of his conscience upon any just or solid grounds.

(2.) He enjoys not the peace of contentment upon any sober or righteous grounds. But now a righteous man, with his little, enjoys both peace of conscience and peace of contentment; and this makes every bitter sweet, and every little sweet to be exceeding sweet. A dish of green herbs, with peace of conscience and peace of contentment, is a noble feast, a continual feast to a gracious soul. But,

Eighthly, The righteous man sees God, and acknowledges God, and enjoys God in his little, Job i. 21; Gen. xxvii. 28, and xxxiii. 10, 11. Look, as he that cannot see God in the least affliction, in the least judgment, will never be truly humbled; so he that cannot see God in the least mercy will never be truly thankful nor cheerful. In every crust, crumb, drop, and sip of mercy that a righteous man enjoys, he sees much of the love of his God, and the care of his God, and the wisdom of his God, and the power of his God, and the faithfulness of his God, and the goodness of his God, in making the least provision for him. I have read of the Jews, how that when they read the little book of Esther they let fall the book on the ground, and they give this reason for that ceremony, 'because the name of God is not to be found in all that history.' So a righteous man is ready to let that mercy drop out of his hand, out of his mouth, wherein he cannot read his God, and see his God, and taste his God, and enjoy his God. But now wicked men may say, as Elisha did in another case, 'Here is the mantle of Elijah, but where is the God of Elijah? Here is abundance of riches and honours and dignities, &c., but where is the God of all these comforts?' 2 Kings ii. 14.

But alas! they mind not God, they see not God, they acknowledge not God in all they have, in all they enjoy; as you may see by comparing the scriptures in the margin together.[1] Wicked men are like the horse and the mule that drinks of the brook, but never think of the spring. They are like to the swine that eats up the mast, but never looks to the tree from whence the mast falls. They are like such barren ground that swallows up the seed, but returns nothing to

[1] Hosea ii. 5, 8, 9; Isa. i. 3, 4; Jer. ii. 6; Esther v. 10–12; Luke xii. 19.

the sower. A dunghill-spirited fellow in our days, being by a neighbour excited to bless God for a rich crop of corn he had standing on his ground, atheistically replied, 'Thank God! Nay, rather thank my dung-cart!' I have read of a great cardinal, who, writing down in his diary what such a lord did for him, and how far such a prince favoured him, and what encouragement he had from such a king, and how such a pope preferred him, but not one word of God in all: one reading of it, took his pen and wrote underneath, here God did nothing. But,

Ninthly, The little the righteous man hath is enough; enough to satisfy him, enough to content him, enough to bear his charges till he gets to heaven, Ps. xxiii. 1, 2: Phil. iv. 12, 13; 1 Tim. vi. 6: Gen. xxxiii. 11, 'I have enough,' saith Jacob to Esau: Gen. xlv. 28, 'And Israel said, it is enough; Joseph my son is yet alive.' Though the righteous man hath but little, yet he hath enough for his place and calling in which God has placed him, and enough for his charge, whether it be great or small; he has enough to satisfy nature, enough to preserve natural life, Prov. xxx. 8.[1] Agur is but for food convenient, convenient for his life, not for his lusts; he prays for enough to satisfy necessity, convenience, not concupiscence; he begs for bread, not for quails; he begs that nature may be sustained, not pampered. Though it be true that nothing will satisfy a wicked man's lusts, yet it is as true that a little will satisfy nature, and less will satisfy grace. Jacob vows that the Lord should be his God, if he would but give him bread to eat, and raiment to put on. This was the first holy vow that ever we read of; hence Jacob is called the father of vows, Gen. xxviii. 20, 21. He begs not dainties to feed him, nor silks nor satins to clothe him; but bread to feed him, though never so coarse, and clothes to cover him, though never so mean. Job is only for necessary food,[2] Job xxiii. 12. A little will satisfy a temperate Christian. Luther made many a meal of bread and a red herring; and Junius made many a meal of bread and an egg. Nature laps only, like those three hundred soldiers, Judges vii. 6. When Christ fed the people graciously, miraculously, he fed them not with manchets[3] and quails, or pheasants, &c., but with barley loaves and fishes, a frugal, temperate, sober diet. If the handful of meal in the barrel, and the oil in the cruse fail not, and if the brook and the running water fail not, Elijah can be well enough contented. But now wicked men never have enough, they are never satisfied. They are like those four things that Solomon speaks of, that are never satisfied—viz., the grave, the barren womb, the earth, and the fire. That is an observable passage of the psalmist, 'Thou fillest their bellies with thy hid treasures.' To a worldly wicked man all these outward things are but a bellyful; and how soon is the belly emptied after it is once filled! Though many rich men have riches enough to sink them, yet they have never enough to satisfy them. Like him that wished for a thousand sheep in his flock, and when he had them, he wished for other cattle without num-

[1] If thou live according to nature, thou wilt never be poor; if according to opinion, thou wilt never be rich.

[2] He is rich enough that lacketh not bread; and high enough in dignity that is not forced to serve.—*Jerome.* John vi. 9–15; 1 Kings xvii. 12, and iii. 4–6; Prov. xxx. 15, 16; Ps. xvii. 14.

[3] 'Fine bread.'—G.

ber. When Alexander had all the crowns and sceptres of the princes of the world piled up at his gates, he wishes for another world to conquer: 'The eye is not satisfied with seeing, nor the ear with hearing.' 'He that loveth silver shall not be satisfied with silver; nor he that loveth abundance with increase,' Eccles. i. 8, and v. 10. There is enough and enough in silver, in abundance of silver, to vex and fret the soul of man, but not to satisfy the soul of man. God himself is the only centre of centres, and as the soul can never rest till it return to him, as the dove to the ark, so it can never be filled, stilled, or satisfied, but in the enjoyment of him.[1] All the beauty of the world is but deformity, all the brightness of the world is but blackness, all the light of the world is but bitterness; and therefore it is impossible for all the bravery and glory of this world to give absolute satisfaction to the soul of man. Solomon, the wisest prince that ever sat upon a throne, after his most diligent, curious, critical, and impartial search into all the creatures, gives this as the *summa totalis*, and product of his inquiries, 'Vanity of vanities, all is vanity.' And how then can any of these things, yea, all these things heaped up together, satisfy the soul of man! Hab. ii. 5, 'He enlargeth his desire as hell, and is as death, and cannot be satisfied, but gathereth unto him all nations, and heapeth unto him all people.' This is spoken of the king of Babylon, who though he had gathered to him all nations and people, yea, and all their vast treasures also—Isa. x. 13, 'I have robbed their treasures:' ver. 14, 'And my hand hath found as a nest, the riches of his people: and as one gathereth eggs that are left, have I gathered all the earth; and there was none that moved the wing, or opened the mouth, or peeped'—and yet for all this was his desire enlarged as hell, and could not be satisfied. The desires of worldlings are boundless and endless, and there is no satisfying of them. It is not all the gold of Ophir, or Peru, nor all the pearls or mines of India; it is not Joseph's chains, nor David's crowns, nor Haman's honours, nor Daniel's dignities, nor Dives his riches, that can satisfy an immortal soul.

Tenthly, The little that the righteous man hath is more stable, durable, and lasting, than the riches of the wicked; and therefore his little is better than their much, his mite is better than their millions, Job v. 20-22. Ps. xxxiv. 9, 10, 'Oh fear the Lord, ye his saints: for there is no want to them that fear him. The young lions do lack, and suffer hunger: but they that seek the Lord shall not want any good thing.' Such as are separated from the world's lusts, can live with a little. Such as set up God as the object of their fear, have no cause to fear the want of anything. When David was a captive amongst the Philistines, he wanted nothing. Paul had nothing, and yet possessed all things, 2 Cor. vi. 10. A godly man may want many good things that he thinks to be good for him, but he shall never want any good thing that the Lord knows to be good for him, Heb. xiii. 5, 6; Prov. x. 3. We do not esteem of tenure for life as we do of freehold, because life is a most uncertain thing. Ten pound a year for ever is better than a hundred in hand. All the promises are God's bonds,

[1] The poor heathen could say, I desire neither more nor less than enough. For I may as well die of a surfeit as of hunger.

and a Christian may put them in suit when he will, and hold God to his word; and that not only for his spiritual and eternal life, but also for his natural life, his temporal life; but so cannot the wicked. The temporal estate of the wicked is seldom long-lived, as you may see by comparing the scriptures in the margin together.[1] Alexander the Great, conqueror of the world, caused to be painted on a table a sword in the compass of a wheel, shewing thereby that what he had gotten by the sword was subject to be turned about the wheel of providence. There is no more hold to be had of riches, honours, or preferments, than Saul had of Samuel's lap. They do but like the rainbow shew themselves in all their dainty colours, and then vanish away. There are so many sins, and so many crosses, and so many curses that usually attend the riches of the wicked, that it is very rare to see their estates long-lived. Hence their great estates are compared to the chaff, which a puff of wind disperseth; to the grass, which the scorching sun quickly withers; to the tops of corn, which are soon cut off; and to the unripe grape: Job xv. 33, 'He shall shake off his unripe grape as the vine, and shall cast off his flower as the olive.' Every day's experience confirms us in this truth. But,

Eleventhly and lastly, The little that the righteous man hath is better than the riches of the wicked, in respect of his last reckoning, in respect of his last accounts. God will never call his children in the great day, either to the book or to the bar, for the mercies that he has given them, be they few or be they many, be they great or be they small. Though the mercer brings his customer to the book for what he has, and for what he wears, yet he never brings his child to the book for what he has and for what he wears. Though the vintner or innkeeper brings their guests to the bar for the provisions they have, yet they never bring their children to the bar for the provisions they make for them. In the great day the Lord will take an exact account of all the good that his children have done for others, Mat. xxv., but he will never bring them to an account for what he has done for them. Christ in this great day will,

(1.) Remember all the individual offices of love and friendship that hath been shewed to any of his members.

(2.) He will mention many good things which his children did, which they themselves never minded, ver. 37.

(3.) The least and lowest acts of love and pity that have been shewed to Christ's suffering servants, shall be interpreted as a special kindness shewed to himself, ver. 40.

(4.) The recompense that Christ will give to his people in that day shall be exceeding great, ver. 44, 46. Here is no calling of them to the book or to the bar for the mercies that they were entrusted with. But oh the sad, the great accounts that the wicked have to give up for all their lands and lordships, for all their honours, offices, dignities, and riches! 'To whom much is given, much shall be required,' Luke xii. 48. Christ in the great day will reckon with all the grandees of the world for every thousand, for every hundred, for every pound, yea, for every penny that he has entrusted them with. All princes, nobles, and people that are not interested in the Lord Jesus,

[1] Prov. x. 3; Ps. xxxvii. 34–36; Jer. xvii. 11; Job xx. 20, *seq.*

shall be brought to the book, to the bar, in the great day, to give an account of all they have received and done in the flesh, Rev. vi. 15-17; Luke xvi. 2; Eccles. xii. 14. But Christ's darlings shall then be the only welcome guests: Mat. xxv. 34, 'Then shall the King say to them on his right hand, Come, ye blessed of my Father, inherit the kingdom prepared for you from the foundation of the world.' Before the world was founded the saints were crowned in God's eternal counsel. Here is no mention made of the book or the bar, but of a kingdom, a crown, a diadem. Now by these eleven arguments it is most evident that the little that the righteous man hath is better than the riches of the wicked. The righteous man's mite is better than the wicked man's millions.[1] But,

[8.] The eighth maxim that I shall lay down, to put a stop to your too eager pursuit after the things of this world, is this, viz., *That the life of man consists not in the enjoyment of these earthly things, which he is so apt inordinately to affect:* Luke xii. 15, 'And he said unto them, Take heed, and beware of covetousness. For a man's life consisteth not in the abundance of the things which he possesseth.' Whether we consider man's life in the length and continuance of it, or in the comfort of it, it consists not in riches; for no man lives a day longer or merrier for his riches. Though possessions are useful to sustain life, yet no man is able to prolong his life, or to make it anything more happy or comfortable to him, by possessing more than he needs or uses. It is not the golden crown that can cure the headache, nor the velvet slipper that can ease a man of the gout, nor the purple robe that can fray away a burning fever. Mark, the life of man is so far from consisting in the enjoyment of these earthly things, that many times they hasten a man to his long home, Jer. xvii. 11. Many a man's coffer has hastened him to his coffin; and as many a man has lost his finger for his ring's sake, so many a man has lost his life for his purse's sake. In all the ages of the world many a man has deeply suffered for his means. Naboth lost his life for his vineyard's sake, 1 Kings xxi. Quintus Aurelius, in the days of Sylla,[2] lost his life by reason of his lands. Many a man's means has hanged him. Many a man has deeply suffered for his means' sake. The Romans ripped up the bellies and bowels of the Jews to search for gold.[3] The Americans had been more safe had they had less gold: they thought gold was the Spaniards' god. But how the Spaniards played the devil to get their gold, I shall not at this time take pleasure to relate. Now if our temporal life consists not in any of these earthly things, then certainly our spiritual life consists not in any of these earthly things. For what religious duty is there that a believer cannot do, though he has neither money in his bag nor dainties on his table. And as our spiritual life consists not in any of these earthly things, so our eternal life consists not in any of these earthly things: for as all the treasures of this world

[1] Some of the more refined heathen have had some kind of dread and fear in their spirits upon the consideration of a day of account, as the writings of Plato and Tully, &c., do sufficiently evidence.

[2] Plutarch, *in vita Syllæ*.

[3] Josephus. When Zelimus, [?] emperor of Constantinople, had taken Egypt, he found a great deal of treasure there; and the soldiers asking of him what they should do with the citizens of Egypt, having found a great treasure among them; Oh, saith the emperor, hang them all up, for they are too rich to be made slaves.

cannot bring a soul to heaven, so they cannot keep a soul from dropping down to hell.

> 'This world's wealth that men so much desire,
> May well be likened to a burning fire,
> Whereof a little can do little harm
> But profit much our bodies well to warm:
> But take too much, and surely thou shalt burn.
> So too much wealth to too much woe does turn.'

But,

[9.] The ninth maxim that I shall lay down to put a stop to your too eager pursuit after the things of this world, is this—viz., *That there is no rest to be found in any earthly enjoyments.* Rest is the centre at which all intellectual natures, as well as natural bodies, aim at. A man that is inordinately in love with the world can never be at rest. The drunkard sometimes rests from his cups, and the unclean person from his filthiness, and the swearer from his oaths, and the idolater from his idols, but the worldling is never at rest; his head and heart are still a-plodding and a-plotting how to get, and how to keep, the things of this world: Eccles. v. 12, 'The sleep of the labouring man is sweet, whether he eat little or much; but the abundance of the rich will not suffer him to sleep.'[1] These three vultures—care of getting, fear of keeping, and grief of losing—feed day and night upon the heart of a rich and wretched worldling, so that his sleep departs from him. Sometimes his abundance lies like a lump of lead heavy upon his heart, so that he cannot rest. Sometimes his conscience does so lash, and lance, and gall him for what he has got by indirect ways and means, that he cannot sleep. Sometimes God himself will not suffer him to sleep. Sometimes God shews him the handwriting upon the wall, Dan. v. 5, 6; sometimes he terrifies him with dreams, and sometimes he throws handfuls of hell-fire in his face, as once he did into Judas's, Mat. xxvi. 24; and this hinders his rest. Sometimes by their excessive eating and drinking, their gluttony, their delicious fare, they overcharge nature, which causeth indigestion and malignant vapours, whereby sleep is wholly removed, or else much disturbed. Earthly riches are an evil master, a treacherous servant, fathers of flattery, sons of grief, a cause of fear to those that have them, and a cause of sorrow to those that want them; and therefore what rest is there to be found in the enjoyment of them? [Augustine.] The prior in Melanchthon rolled his hands up and down in a basin full of angels, thinking to have charmed his gout, but this could give him no ease, no rest.[2] Latimer, in a sermon before King Edward the Sixth, tells a story of a rich man, who, when he lay upon his sick-bed, one came to him and told him that he was a dead man, that he was no man for this world. As soon as ever the sick man heard these words, saith Latimer, he cried out, Must I die? Send for a physician! Wounds, side, heart—must I die? Wounds, side, heart—must I die? and thus he continued crying out, Wounds, side, heart—must I die? Must I die and leave these riches behind me? All the riches that he had

[1] He that is rich in conscience, saith Austin, sleeps more soundly than he that is richly clothed in purple, Luke xii. 20.

[2] Had a man as much honour and dignity, profit and pleasure, as himself could wish, or the world afford, yet within twenty-four hours he would be weary of all, and must go to sleep.

heaped together could give him no rest nor quiet when the king of terrors knocked at his doors. All the good things of this world have more or less of the thorn in them; and therefore what rest can they give? Achan's golden wedge proved a wedge to cleave him, and his garment a garment to shroud him. In Spain they lived happily until fire made some mountains vomit gold; but what miserable discords have followed ever since! It is only heaven that is above all winds and storms and tempests, neither hath God cast man out of one paradise for him to think to find out another paradise in this world. But,

[10.] The tenth and last maxim that I shall lay down to put a stop to your too eager pursuit after the things of this world, is this—viz., *That it is a very high point of Christian wisdom and prudence, always to look upon the good things and the great things of this world as a man will certainly look upon them when he comes to die.* Oh, with what a disdainful eye, with what a contemptible eye, with what a scornful eye, and with what a weaned heart and cold affections do men look upon all the pomp, state, bravery, and glory of the world, when their soul sits upon their trembling lips, and there is but a short step between them and eternity! He that looks upon the world whilst he has it under his hand, as he will assuredly look upon it when he is to take his leave of it, he will,

(1.) Never sin to get the world. Nor,

(2.) He will never grieve inordinately to part with the world. Nor,

(3.) He will never envy those who enjoy much of the world. Nor,

(4.) He will never dote upon the world, he will never be enamoured with the world. I have read of a man, who, lying in a burning fever, professed that if he had all the world at his dispose, he would give it all for one draught of beer; at so low a rate do men value the world at such a time as that is. King Lysimachus lost his kingdom for one draught of water to quench his thirst.[1] If men were but so wise to value the world at no higher a rate in health than they do in sickness, in the day of life than they do at the hour of death, they would never be fond of it, they would never be so deeply in love with it. Now, oh that these ten maxims may be so blest to the reader as to crucify the world to him, and him unto the world! Gal. vi. 14. He gave good counsel who said, [Austin,] O man, if thou be wise, let the world pass, lest thou pass away with the world. Fix thy heart on God, let him be thy portion; fix thy affections upon Christ, he is thy redemption; on heaven, let that be thy mansion. Oh take that counsel, 'Love not the world, nor the things of the world.' John ii. 15. Mark, he doth not say, have not the world, nor the things of the world, but 'love not the world, nor the things of the world:' nor he doth not say, use not the world, nor the things of the world, but '*love* not the world, nor the things of the world:' nor he doth not say, take no moderate care for the world, nor the things of the world, but 'love not the world, nor the things of the world.' But to prevent all mistakes, give me leave to premise these three things:—

[1.] First, *It is lawful to desire earthly things, so far as they may*

[1] As before.—G.

be furtherances of us in our journey to heaven.[1] As a passenger when he comes to a deep river desires a boat, but not for the boat's sake, but that he may pass over the river; for could he pass over the river without a boat, he would never cry out, A boat, a boat; or as the traveller desires his inn, not for the inn's sake, but as it is a help, a furtherance to him in his journey homewards; or as the patient desires physic, not for physic's sake, but in order to his health: so a Christian may lawfully desire earthly things in order to his glorifying of God; and as they may be a help to him in his Christian course, and a furtherance to him in his heavenly race, Heb. xii. 1. But,

[2.] Secondly, *We may desire earthly things in subordination to the will of God.* Lord, if it be thy pleasure, give me this and that earthly comfort; yet not my will, but thy will be done. Lord, thou art the wise physician of bodies, souls, and nations: if it may stand with thy glory, give thy sick patient life, health, and strength; yet not my will, but thy will be done. But,

[3.] Thirdly, *We may desire such a measure of earthly things, and such a number of earthly things, as may be suitable to the place, calling, relation, and condition wherein the providence of God has set us,* Prov. xxx. 8, 9, and 1 Tim. vi. 8: as a master, magistrate, prince, lord, gentleman, &c. A little of these earthly things, and a few of these earthly things, may be sufficient to the order, place, calling, and condition of life wherein some men are placed, but not sufficient for a king, a lord, a magistrate, a general, &c. These must have their counsellors, their guards, variety of attendance, and variety of the creatures, &c. A little portion of these earthly things is sufficient for some, and a great and large portion of these earthly things is but sufficient for others. Less may serve the servant than the master, the child than the father, the peasant than the prince, &c. The too eager pursuit of most men after the things of this world, to make up the losses that they sustained by the fire, hath been the true cause why I have insisted so largely upon this ninth duty that we are to learn by that fiery dispensation that hath passed upon us.

10. The tenth duty that lies upon those who have been burnt up, is *to be very importunate with God to take away those sins that have laid our city desolate, and to keep off from sin for the time to come, and to look narrowly to your spirits, that you do not charge the Lord foolishly, because he has brought you under his fiery rod,* Mal. ii. 15; Job i. 16, 'While he was yet speaking, there came also another, and said, The fire of God is fallen from heaven, and hath burnt up the sheep, and the servants, and consumed them, and I only am escaped alone to tell thee;' ver. 22, 'In all this Job sinned not, nor charged God foolishly.' The fire of God, that is, a great, fierce, and terrible fire that fell from heaven and consumed Job's sheep and servants, was a more terrible judgment than all the former judgments that befell them, because God seemed to fight against Job with his own bare hand by fire from heaven, as once he did against Sodom. 'In all this Job sinned not;' that is, in all this that Job suffered, acted, and uttered, there was not anything that was materially sinful. Satan he

[1] As Mr Tyndale the martyr said, I desire these earthly things so far as they may be helps to the keeping of thy commandments.

said, that if God would but touch all that he had, Job would curse him to his face; but when it came to the proof, there was no such thing. For Job had a fair and full victory over him, and Satan was proved a loud liar. For Job sinned not in thought, word, or deed; Job did neither speak nor do anything that was dishonourable to God, or a reproach to his religion, or a wound to his conscience. Under this fiery trial Job did not so much as entertain one hard thought concerning God, nor let fall one hard word concerning God. Under all the evils that befell Job, Job still thinks well of God, and speaks well of God, and carries it well towards God. Certainly Job had a great deal of God within him, which kept him from sinning under such great and grievous sufferings. O sirs, it is a far greater mercy to be kept from sinnings under our sufferings, than it is to be delivered from the greatest sufferings. Job's heart was so well seasoned with grace, that he would admit of no insolent or unsavoury thoughts of God, or of his severest providences: 'In all this Job sinned not, nor charged God foolishly,' or with folly. Some refer the former part of this verse to the mind, and the latter to the mouth; shewing that Job, though he had lost all, neither thought in his heart, nor uttered with his mouth, anything unmeet and unworthy of God. The meek, humble, patient, and gracious behaviour of Job under all his sore losses and crosses is here owned, renowned, crowned, and chronicled by God himself. O sirs, sinning is worse than suffering; it is better to see a people bleeding than blaspheming, burning than cursing; for by men's sins God is dishonoured, but by their sufferings God is glorified. Oh that the Christian reader would seriously consider of these twelve things:—[1]

(1.) That there is nothing that the great God hates, but sin.

(2.) That there is nothing that he has revealed his wrath from heaven against, but sin.

(3.) That there is nothing that crucifies the Lord of glory afresh, but sin.

(4.) That there is nothing that grieves the Spirit of grace, but sin.

(5.) That there is nothing that wounds the conscience, but sin.

(6.) That there is nothing that clouds the face of God, but sin.

(7.) That there is nothing that hinders the return of prayer, but sin.

(8.) That there is nothing that interrupts our communion with God, but sin.

(9.) That there is nothing that imbitters our mercies, but sin.

(10.) That there is nothing that puts a sting into all our troubles and trials, but sin.

(11.) That there is nothing that renders us unserviceable in our places, stations, and conditions, but sin.

(12.) That there is nothing that makes death the king of terrors, and the terror of kings, to be so formidable and terrible to the sons of men, as sin. And therefore under all your sorrows and sufferings, crosses and losses, make it your great business to arm yourselves against sin, and to pray against sin, and to watch against sin, and to turn from sin, and to cease from sin, and to get rid of sin, and to stand for ever in defiance of sin, 2 Chron. vii. 14; Isa. xvi. 17, and lv. 7;

[1] Prov. vi. 16, 17; Jer. xlix. 4; Rom. i. 18; Heb. vi. 6; Eph. iv. 30; Mat. xxvi. 15; Ps. xxx. 6, 7; Isa. xlix. 1, 2; Mal. ii. 2; Jer. iv. 18.

Hosea xiv. 8; Isa. xxx. 22. Assuredly every gracious heart had rather be rid of his sins than of his sufferings: Job vii. 21, 'And why dost thou not take away mine iniquity?'—or lift up, as the Hebrew runs, to note that though Job had many loads, many burdens upon him, yet none lay so heavy upon him as his sin; Hosea xiv. 2, 'Take away all iniquity, and receive us graciously.' It is not, take away our captivity, and receive us graciously, but take away our iniquity, and receive us graciously; nor is it to take away this or that particular iniquity, and receive us graciously, but take away all iniquity, and receive us graciously; take away stain and sting, crime and curse, power and punishment, that we may never hear more of it, nor never feel more of it, nor never be troubled any more with it. Though their bondage was great, very great, yea, greater than any people under heaven were exercised with, yet their sins were a more unsupportable burden to their spirits than their bondage was, Dan. ix. 11–13. And therefore they cry out, 'Take away all iniquity, and receive us graciously.' And this was the usual method of David;[1] when he was under sore troubles and trials, he was more importunate with God to be purged and pardoned, than he was to be eased under his troubles, or delivered from his troubles: Ps. li. 2, 'Wash me throughly from mine iniquity, and cleanse me from my sin;' ver. 7, 'Purge me with hyssop, and I shall be clean: wash me, and I shall be whiter than snow;' ver. 9, 'Hide thy face from my sins, and blot out all mine iniquities;' ver. 14, 'Deliver me from blood-guiltiness, O God.' When Pharaoh was under the hand of the Lord, he was all for removing of the plagues, the frogs, the locusts, &c., Exod. x. But when David was under the hand of the Lord, he was all for the removing of his sins, and for the cleansing, purging, and washing away of his sins. Oh that all the burnt citizens of London would be more earnest and importunate with God to pardon, and purge, and take away all those iniquities that have brought the fiery rod upon them, than they are studious and industrious to have their credits repaired, their houses rebuilded, their trades restored, and all their losses made up to them! Oh that they might all be driven by what they have felt, seriously to consider what they have done! 'No man saith, What have I done?' Jer. viii. 6; Hosea vi. 1–3; Isa. lvi. 6; Ezek. xxxvi. 33, 37. Oh that they would all blame themselves more, and their sins more, and turn to him who has so sorely smitten them, and lay hold on his strength, and make peace with him, that so he may yet build up their waste places, and make up their breaches, and repair their losses, and never turn away from doing of them good! Jer. xxxii. 41–44. But,

11. The eleventh duty that they are to learn that have been burnt up, is *to prepare and fit for greater troubles and trials.* The anger of the Lord is not yet turned away, but his hand is stretched out still, Isa. ix. 12; Rev. xi. 18. The nations are angry, the face of the times seems sorely to threaten us with greater troubles than any yet we have encountered with. Ah London, London! ah England, England! the clouds that hang over thee seem every day to be blacker and blacker, and thicker and thicker: thou hast suffered much, and thou hast cause to fear that thou mayest suffer more; thou hast been

[1] See Ps. lxxix. 1, 5, 8, xxv. 7, xxxii. 4, 5, and xxxviii. 3, 4.

brought low, yea, thou art this day brought very low in the eyes of the nations round about thee, and yet thou mayest be brought lower before the day of thy exaltation comes.[1] When God intends to raise a person, a city, a nation high, very high, he then usually brings them low, very low; and when they are at lowest, then the day of their exaltation is nearest. It is commonly darkest a little before break of day. The hand of the Lord has been lifted up high, yea, very high, over us and against us; but who repents? who reforms? who returns to the Most High? who smites upon his thigh? who says, What have I done? Jer. viii. 6; who finds out the plague of his own heart? who ceaseth from doing evil? who learns to do well? who stirs up himself to take hold of God? who stands in the gap? who wrestles and weeps, and weeps and wrestles to turn away those judgments that this day threaten us? Isa. i. 16–18; Ps. cvi.; Hosea xii. 4. So long as sin remains rampant, and men continue impenitent, there is reason to fear a worse scourge than any yet we have been under. Pharaoh's stubbornness did but increase his plagues, Exod. ix. 17; the more stout and unyielding we are under judgments, the more chains God will still put on, Eccles. v. 8. When his hand is lifted up, we must either bow or break. Such as have been under the smart rebukes of God, and will not take Christ's warning to go their way and sin no more, John v. 14, have reason to fear his inference, that a worse thing will come upon them. The face of present providences looks dismal; dreadful sufferings seem to be near, very near, even at our very doors. Yet to prevent fainting, we must remember that God never wants chambers to hide his people in till his indignation be overpast, Isa. xxvi. 20. God hath ways enough to preserve his wheat, even when the whirlwind carries away the chaff. God can find an ark for his Noahs, when a flood of wrath sweeps away sinners on every hand; and God can provide a Zoar for his Lots, when he rains fire and brimstone upon all round about them. Look, as God many times by lesser mercies fits his people for greater mercies; so God many times by lesser judgments fits his people for greater judgments: and who can tell, but that the design of God by the late judgments of fire, sword, and pestilence, is to prepare and fit his people for greater judgments? That God might have inflicted greater judgments than any yet he has inflicted upon us, I have already proved by an induction of particulars. That greater judgments may be prevented, and our present mercies continued and increased, it highly concerns us to repent, and to turn to the Most High. There are seven sorts of men who have high cause to fear worser judgments than any yet have been inflicted upon them:—

(1.) Such who scorn and deride at the judgments of God, Isa. v. 19; Jer. xvii. 15, and xx. 8; 2 Pet. iii. 3–5.

(2.) Such who put off the judgments of God to others, who cry out, Oh! these judgments concern such and such, but not us.

(3.) Such who are no ways bettered nor reclaimed by judgments.

(4.) Such as grow worser and worser under all the warnings and judgments, as Pharaoh and Ahaz did, Isa. i. 5; Jer. v. 3; 2 Chron. xxviii. 22, 23.

[1] Deut. xxviii. 43; 2 Chron. xxviii. 18, 19; Deut. xxxii. 36; Ps. lxxix. 8, cxxxvi. 23, and cxlii. 6; Isa. xxvi. 10, 11.

(5.) Such as make no preparations to meet God when he is in the way of his judgments, Amos iv. 12.

(6.) Such who are careless Gallios, that do not so much as mind or regard the warnings of God, the judgments of God, Isa. v. 12, 13.

(7.) Such as put the evil day far from them, as they did in Isa. xxii. 12, 13, and as they did in Amos vi. 3, and as the inhabitants of Jerusalem did a little before their city was laid desolate. Some writers tell us, [Hegesippus, Josephus, &c.,] that though the Jews had a great many warnings, by prodigious signs and fearful apparitions, before Jerusalem was besieged and the city destroyed, yet most of them expounded the meaning of them in a more favourable sense to themselves than ever God intended, till the dreadful vengeance of God overtook them to the utmost. It is the greatest wisdom and prudence in the world to prepare and fit for the worst. The best way on earth to prevent judgments from falling upon us, or if they do fall, to sweeten them to us, is to prepare for them. But,

12. The twelfth duty that lies upon those who have been burnt up, is *to secure the everlasting welfare of their precious and immortal souls.* O sirs, London's ashes tell you to your faces that you cannot secure your houses, your shops, your estates, your trades; but the eternal well-being of your souls may be secured. Every burnt citizen carries a jewel, a pearl of price, a rich treasure about him—viz., a divine soul, which is more worth than all the world, Mat. xvi. 26. As Christ, who only went to the price of souls, has told us, there is much of the power, wisdom, majesty, and glory of God stamped upon the stately fabric of this world, Ps. xix. 1, 2; but there is more of the power, wisdom, majesty, and glory of God stamped upon an immortal soul. The soul is the glory of the creation. What Job speaks of wisdom is very applicable to the precious soul of man, chap. xxviii. 13, 16, 17. 'Man knows not the price thereof: it cannot be valued with the gold of Ophir, with the precious onyx, or the sapphire. The gold and the crystal cannot equal it; and the exchange of it shall not be for jewels of fine gold.' The soul is a beam of God, a heavenly spark, a celestial plant; it is the beauty of man, the wonder of angels, the envy of devils, and the glory of God.[1] Oh how richly and gloriously hath God embroidered the soul. 'The king's daughter is all glorious within: her clothing is of wrought gold,' Ps. xlv. 13. The soul is divinely inlaid and enamelled by God's own hand. The soul is of an angelical nature, it is of a divine offspring; it is a spiritual substance, capable of the knowledge of God, and of union with God, and of communion with God, and of an eternal fruition of God. The soul is an immortal substance, and that not only *per gratiam*, by the grace and favour of God, as the body of Adam was in the state of innocency, and as the bodies of saints shall be at the resurrection, but *per naturam*, by its own nature, having no internal principle of corruption, so as it cannot by anything from within itself cease to be; neither can it be annihilated by anything from without. 'Fear not them which kill the body, but are not able to kill the soul.' Mat. x. 28. Some [Gregory, &c.] have observed to

[1] Epictetus, and many others of the more refined heathens, have long since said that the body was but the organ, the soul was the man, the merchandise.

my hand, that there are three sorts of created spirits: the first, of those whose dwellings is not with flesh, or in fleshly bodies; they are the angels; the second, of those which are wholly immersed in flesh, the souls of beasts, which rise out of the power of the flesh, and perish together with it; the third is of those which inhabit bodies of flesh, but rise out of the power of the flesh, nor die when the body dieth; and these are the souls of men, Eccles. xii. 7, 'When the body returneth to the earth as it was, the spirit shall return to God who gave it.' O sirs, the soul being immortal, it must be immortally happy, or immortally miserable. Certainly there is no wisdom nor policy to that of securing the everlasting welfare of your souls. All the honours, riches, greatness, and glory of this world are but chips, feathers, trifles, pebbles, to your precious and immortal souls; and therefore before all, and above all other things, make sure work for your souls. If they are safe, all is safe; but if they are lost, all is lost, and you cast and undone in both worlds. Chrysostom observeth, that whereas God hath given many other things double, two eyes to see with, two ears to hear with, two hands to work with, and two feet to walk with, to the intent that the failing of the one might be supplied by the other, he hath given us but one soul; if that be lost, hast thou another soul to give in recompense for it? If you save your souls, though you should lose all you have in this world, your loss would be a gainful loss; but if you lose your precious souls, though you should gain all the world, yet your very gains will undo you for ever. You have found, by the late dreadful fire, that there is no securing of the things of this world; and therefore make it your business, your work, to get a Christ for your souls, grace for your souls, and a heaven for your souls, that so, though all go to wreck here, yet your souls may be saved in the day of Christ. What desperate madness and folly would it have been in any, when London was in flames, to mind more and endeavour more to save their lumber than their jewels; their goods in their shops, than their children in their cradles, or their wives in their beds! But it is a thousand times greater madness and folly for men to mind more and endeavour more to secure their temporal estates, than they do to secure their eternal estates. But,

13. The thirteenth duty that is incumbent upon those who have been burnt up, is *to get a God for their portion*, Ps. xvi. 5, and lxiii. 26. You have lost your earthly portion, your earthly possessions; oh that you would now labour with all your might to get God for your portion! Ps. cxix. 57; Jer. x. 16; Lam. iii. 24. If the loss of your earthly portions shall be so sanctified to you as to work you to make God your portion, then your unspeakable losses will prove inconceivable gain unto you. O sirs, God is the most absolute, needful, and necessary portion. The want or the loss of earthly portions may afflict and trouble you, but the want of God for your portion will certainly damn you. It is not absolutely necessary that you should have a portion in gold, or silver, or jewels, or goods, or houses, or lands, or lordships; but it is absolutely necessary that you should have God for your portion. Suppose that, with the apostles, you have no certain dwelling-place, nor no gold nor silver in your purses, 1 Cor. iv. 11; Acts iii. 6; suppose, with Lazarus, you have never a rag to hang on

your backs, nor never a dry crust to put in your bellies, Luke xvi. 20, 21; suppose, with Job, you should be stripped of all your worldly comforts in a day; yet if God be your portion, you are happy, you are really happy, you are signally happy, you are greatly happy, you are unspeakably happy, you are eternally happy. However it may go with you in this world, yet you shall be sure to be glorious in that other world. To have God for thy portion, O man, is the one thing necessary; for without it thou art for ever and ever undone. If God be not thy portion, thou canst never enjoy communion with God in this world; if God be not thy portion, thou canst never be saved by him in the other world. Will you consider a little what an excellent transcendent portion God is:—

(1.) He is a present portion;[1] he is a portion in hand, he is a portion in possession.

(2.) God is an immense portion; he is a vast large portion, he is the greatest portion of all portions.

(3.) God is an all-sufficient portion.

(4.) God is a pure and unmixed portion; God is an unmixed good, he hath nothing in him but goodness.

(5.) God is a glorious, a happy, and a blessed portion; he is so in himself, and he makes them so too who enjoy him for their portion.

(6.) God is a peculiar portion—a portion peculiar to his people.

(7.) God is a universal portion, he is a portion that includes all other portions.

(8.) God is a safe portion, a secure portion, a portion that none can rob a believer of.

(9.) God is a suitable portion; no object is so suitable and adequate to the heart as he is.

(10.) God is an incomprehensible portion.

(11.) God is an inexhaustible portion; a portion that can never be spent, a spring that can never be drawn dry.

(12.) God is a soul-satisfying portion; he is a portion that gives the soul full satisfaction and content.

(13.) God is a permanent portion, an indeficient portion, a never-failing portion, a lasting, yea, an everlasting portion.

(14 and lastly.) God is an incomparable portion, God is a portion more precious than all those things which are esteemed most precious. Nothing can make that man miserable that has God for his portion; nor nothing can make that man happy that hath not God for his portion. O sirs, why do you think that God, by his late fiery dispensations, has stripped you of your earthly portions, but effectually to stir you up to make him your only portion? &c. But,

14. The fourteenth duty that is incumbent upon them that have been burnt up, is *to make God their habitation, to make God their dwelling-place:* Ps. xc. 1, 'Lord, thou hast been our dwelling-place'—or place of retreat—'in all generations'—or in generation and generation, as the Hebrew runs. It is a Hebraism, setting forth God to be the dwelling-place of his people in all generations, before the flood and

[1] See my 'Matchless Portion,' from p. 8 to 107, where all these particulars are fully proved. [Vol. II. pp. 1, *seq.*: being 'An Ark for all God's Noahs.'—G.]

after the flood.[1] The Israel of God, in all their troubles and travels in their wilderness condition, were not houseless nor harbourless. God was both their hiding-place and their dwelling-place. He that dwelleth in God cannot be unhoused, because God is stronger than all. It is brave for a Christian to take up in God as in his mansion-house. It was a witty saying of that learned man, Picus Mirandola, viz., that God created the earth for beasts to inhabit, the sea for fishes, the air for fowls, the heavens for angels and stars; and therefore man hath no place to dwell and abide in, but God alone. Now the great God has burnt up your dwelling-places, make him your dwelling-place, your habitation, your shelter, your place of retreat, your city of refuge. Certainly they dwell most safely, most securely, most nobly, most contentedly, most delightfully, and most happily, who dwell in God, who live under the wing of God, and whose constant abode is under the shadow of the Almighty. Let the loss of your habitations lead you by the hand to make choice of God for your habitation. There is no security against temporal, spiritual, and eternal judgments, but by making God your dwelling-place. How deplorable is the condition of that man that hath neither a house to dwell in, nor a God to dwell in! that can neither say, This house is mine, nor, This God is mine! that hath neither a house made with hands, nor yet one eternal in the heavens! It is a very great mercy for God to dwell with us, but it is a far greater mercy for God to dwell in us, and for we to dwell in God, 2 Cor. v. 1, 2; 1 John iv. 13, and iii. 24. For God to dwell with us, argues much happiness, but for we to dwell in God, this argues more happiness, yea, the top of happiness. There is no study, no care, no wisdom, no prudence, no understanding, to that which works men to make God their habitation. No storms, no tempests, no afflictions, no sufferings, no judgments can reach that man, or hurt that man, who has made God his dwelling-place. He that hath God for his habitation can never be miserable; and he that hath not God for his habitation can never be happy. That God that has once burnt you out of your habitations can again burn you out of your habitations; and if he should, how sad would it be that God has once and again burnt you out of your habitations, and yet you have not made him your habitation! &c. But,

15. The fifteenth duty that is incumbent upon those who have been burnt up, is *to make sure an abiding city, a city that hath foundations, whose builder and maker is God*:[2] Heb. xiii. 14, 'For here have we no continuing city, but we seek one to come.' These words are a reason of his former exhortation to the believing Hebrews to renounce the world, ver. 13, and to take up Christ's cross and follow him; as is clear by this causal particle 'for,' [γὰρ.] It is a probable conjecture made by some, as Estius observeth,[3] that St Paul speaks prophetically of the destruction of the city of Jerusalem, which was then at hand, and that in a short time neither that city, nor the country about it, would be an abiding place for them; but driven from thence they should be, and be forced to wander up and down;

[1] Ponder seriously on these scriptures, Ps. xci. 2, 9, 10, lxxi. 3, and lvii. 1; 2 Cor. vi. 8–10; Ezek. xi. 16.

[2] See my Treatise on Assurance. [Vol. II., as before.—G.]

[3] Exposit. *in loco*.

and therefore they were to look for no other abiding place but heaven; 'Here we have no continuing city.' The adverb translated 'here,' [ὧδε,] is sometimes used for *place*, and this more strictly for the *particular place* where one is—as for that place where Peter was, when he said, 'It is good for us to be here,' Mat. xvii. 4,—or more largely for the whole earth, and so it is taken hère, for it is opposed to heaven. For the present we have no abiding city, but there is an abiding city to come, and that is the city which we seek after. This earthly Jerusalem is no abiding city for us; this old world, the glory of which is wearing off, is no abiding city for us; but Jerusalem that is above, the heavenly city, the city of the great King, the city of the King of kings, Rev. xxi. 2, and i. 5, 6. This world is a wilderness, and believers, as pilgrims and strangers, must pass through it to their heavenly Canaan. This world is no place for believers to continue in; they must pass through it to an abiding city, to a continuing city, to a city that hath foundations: Heb xi. 10, 'For he looked for a city which hath foundations, whose builder and maker is God.' The plural number is here used, *foundations*, [θεμελίους,] for emphasis sake; this city is said to have foundations, to shew that it is a firm, stable, immovable, and enduring city, which the apostle opposeth to the tabernacles or tents wherein Abraham and the other patriarchs dwelt while they were on earth, which had no foundations, but were movable, and carried from place to place, and easily pulled down, or overthrown, or burnt up; but heaven is an immovable, firm, stable, and everlasting city. Heaven is a city that is built,

(1.) Upon the foundation of God's eternal good-will and pleasure.

(2.) That is built upon God's election to eternal glory.

(3.) That is built upon the foundation of Christ's eternal merits and purchase.

(4.) That is built upon the foundation of God's everlasting covenant of free, rich, infinite, sovereign, and glorious grace.

(5.) That is built upon the immutable stability of God's promise and oath.[1] Heaven is built upon the foundation of great and precious promises, and upon his oath who is faithfulness itself and cannot lie. Now, oh what a strong city, what a glorious city, what a continuing city, what a lasting, yea, what an everlasting city must heaven needs be, that is founded upon such strong and immovable foundations as they are! Heaven hath foundations, but the earth hath none: the earth hangs upon nothing, as Job speaks, chap. xxvi. 7; Nineveh, Babylon, Jerusalem, Athens, Corinth, Troy, and those famous cities of Asia, were strong and stately cities in their times; but where are they now? Both Scripture and history doth sufficiently evidence that in all the ages of the world there hath been no firm, stable, or continuing city to be found: and the divine wisdom and providence hath [so] ordered, and that partly to work the sons of men to put a difference betwixt the things of this world and the things of the world to come; and partly to wean them from the world, and all the bravery and glory thereof; and partly to awaken them and stir them up to make sure a kingdom that shakes not, riches that corrupt not, an inheritance that fadeth not

[1] Eph. i. 3–6; 2 Tim. ii. 10; 1 Pet. i. 2–5; Rom. ix. 11, and xi. 5, 7; 2 Pet. i. 4; Heb. vi. 17–20.

away, a house not made with hands, but one eternal in the heavens; and a city that hath foundations, whose builder and maker is God, Heb. ii. 5; Col. iii. 1; Heb. xii. 28; 1 Pet. i. 4; 2 Cor. v. 1, 2. Heaven is styled a city, to set out the excellency, glory, and benefits thereof. The resemblance betwixt heaven and a city holds in these respects among others:—

[1.] First, A city is a place of safety and security; so is heaven a place of the greatest safety and security, Neh. iii. 1; Jer. xxxv. 11. A soul in heaven is a soul out of gun-shot. No devil shall there tempt, no wicked men shall there assault, no fire-balls shall be there cast about to disturb the peace of the heavenly inhabitants.

[2.] Secondly, A city is compact, it is made up of many habitations; so in heaven there are many habitations, many mansions, John xiv. 2. In our common cities many times the inhabitants are much shut up and straitened for want of room; but in heaven there is elbow-room enough, not only for God and Christ and the angels, those glistering and shining courtiers, but also for all believers, for all the elect of God.

[3.] Thirdly, A city hath sundry degrees of persons appertaining unto it, as chief magistrates and other officers of sundry sorts, with a multitude of commoners; so in heaven there is God the Father, God the Son, and God the Holy Ghost, and an innumerable company of angels and saints, Heb. xii. 22, 23.

[4.] Fourthly, In a city you have all manner of provisions and useful commodities; so in heaven there is nothing wanting that is needful or useful.

[5.] Fifthly, A city hath laws, statutes, and orders for the better government thereof. It is so in heaven; and indeed there is no government to the government that is in heaven. Certainly there is no government that is managed with that love, wisdom, prudence, holiness, and righteousness, &c., as the government of heaven is managed with.

[6.] Sixthly, Every city hath its peculiar privileges and immunities; so it is in heaven. Heaven is a place of the greatest privileges and immunities, Rev. iii. 12.

[7.] Seventhly, Cities are commonly very populous; and so is heaven a very populous city, Dan. vii. 10; Rev. v. 11, and vii. 9.

[8.] Eighthly, None but freemen may trade, and keep open shop in a city; so none shall have anything to do in heaven, but such whose name are written in the Lamb's book of life, Rev. xxi. 27. Believers are the only persons that are enrolled as freemen in the records of the heavenly city.

[9.] Ninthly, Cities are full of earthly riches; and so is heaven of glorious riches: there are no riches to the riches of the heavenly Jerusalem, Isa. xxiii. 8; Rev. xxi. All the riches of the most famous cities in the world are but dross, brass, copper, tin, &c., to the riches of heaven.

O sirs, how should the consideration of these things work us all to look and long, and to prepare and fit for this heavenly city, this continuing city, this city which hath foundations, whose builder and maker is God! The Holy Ghost frequently calling believers pilgrims, sojourners, strangers, doth sufficiently evidence that there is no abiding for them in this world, Heb. xi. 13; 1 Pet. ii. 11; Ps. cxix. 54. This world is not their country, their city, their home, their habitation; and therefore they are not to place their hopes or hearts or affections upon things below, Col. iii. 1, 2. Heaven is their chief city, their best country, their most desirable home, and their everlasting habitation; and therefore the hopes, desires, breathings, longings, and workings of their souls should still be heaven-ward, glory-ward, Luke xvi. 9; Rev. xxii. 17. Oh when shall grace be swallowed up in glory? when shall we take possession of our eternal mansions? John xiv. 2-4; when shall we be with Christ, which for us is best of all? Phil. i. 23. The late fire hath turned all ranks and sorts of men out of the houses where they once dwelt, and it will not be long before death will turn the same persons out of their present habitations, and carry them to their long homes. Death will turn princes out of their most stately palaces, and great men out of their most sumptuous edifices, and rich men out of their most pleasant houses, and warlike men out of their strongest castles, and poor men out of their meanest cottages, Eccles. xii. 5. The prince's palace, the great man's edifice, the rich man's house, the warlike man's castle, and the poor man's cottage, are of no long continuance. Oh how should this awaken and alarm all sorts and ranks of men to seek after a city which hath foundations, to make sure their interest in the new Jerusalem which is above, in those heavenly mansions that no time can wear nor flames consume! But,

16. Sixteenthly and lastly, Was London in flames on the Lord's day? and was the profanation of that day one of those great sins that brought that dreadful judgment of fire upon London, that hath turned that glorious city into a ruinous heap? then *oh that all that have been sufferers by that lamentable fire, and all others also, would make it their business, their work, their heaven, to sanctify the Sabbath and to keep it holy all their days, that the Lord may be no more provoked to lay London more desolate than it is laid this day.* Let it be enough that this day of the Lord hath been so greatly profaned by sinful omissions and by sinful commissions, by the immorality, debauchery, gluttony, drunkenness, wantonness, filthiness, uncleanness, rioting, revelling, and chambering that multitudes were given up to before the Lord appeared against them in that flaming fire that hath laid our renowned city in ashes. Let it be enough that the Lord has been more dishonoured and blasphemed, that Christ hath been more reproached, despised, and refused, and that the Spirit hath been more grieved, vexed, provoked, and quenched on the Lord's day, than on all the other days of the week. Let it be enough that on this day of the Lord many have been a-playing, when they should have been a-praying; and that many have been a-sporting, when they should have been a-mourning for the afflictions of Joseph, Amos vi. 6; and that many have been a-courting of their mistresses, when they should have been a-waiting on the ordinances; and that many have been sitting at their doors, when they should have been instructing of their families; and that many have been walking in the fields, when they should have been a-sighing and expostulating with God in their closets; and that

many have made that a day of common labour, which God hath made to be a day of special rest from sin, from the world, and from their particular callings. Oh that all men who have paid so dear for profaning of Sabbaths would now bend all their force, strength, power, and might to sanctify those Sabbaths that yet they may enjoy on this side eternity! &c.

Quest. But you will reply upon me, How is the Sabbath to be sanctified?

Ans. I shall endeavour to give a clear, full, and satisfactory answer to this necessary and noble question. And therefore take me thus:—

1. First, We are to sanctify the Sabbath *by resting from all servile labour and work on that day*, Exod. xvi. 29, 30; Neh. xiii. 15-18. Exod. xx. 10, 'But the seventh day is the sabbath of the Lord thy God: in it thou shalt not do any work; thou, nor thy son, nor thy daughter, thy man-servant, nor thy maid-servant, nor thy cattle, nor thy stranger that is within thy gates.' Jer. xvii. 22, 'Neither carry forth a burden out of your houses on the sabbath-day, neither do ye any work; but hallow ye the sabbath-day, as I commanded your fathers.' Isa. lviii. 13, 'If thou turn away thy foot from the sabbath, from doing thy pleasure on my holy day; and call the sabbath a delight, the holy of the Lord, honourable; and shalt honour him, not doing thine own ways, nor finding thine own pleasure, nor speaking of thine own words.' Here are three things distinctly observable in the words:—

(1.) Words.

(2.) Works.

(3.) Pleasure.

Not doing thine own ways, that is works; not speaking thine own words; not finding thine own pleasure. Now mark, we have stronger reasons to engage us to a stricter observation and sanctification of the Lord's day than they had for their Sabbath; which may be thus evinced:—

(Not to speak of their double sacrifices, Num. xxviii. 9, 10, upon their Sabbath, which, as some think, might typify our double devotion on the Lord's day; nor yet to speak of those six lambs whereby others conjecture was fore-prophesied the abundant services in the time of the gospel, Ezek. xlvi. 1-5.)

(1.) *First, Our motives are far greater, and more efficacious;* for,

[1.] First, *Our day hath many privileges above theirs.* Witness the honourable titles given to it by holy and learned men—as the queen of days, princess, principal, primate, a royal day, higher than the highest, the first-fruits of the days; yea, saith Jerome, the Lord's day is better than any other common day, than all festivals, new moons, and Sabbaths of Moses. By these titles it is evident that the ancients had the Lord's day in very high esteem and veneration. Sirs, look, what gold is among inferior metals, and wheat among other grain, &c., the same is the Lord's day above all other days of the week.

[2.] Secondly, Their Sabbath was celebrated for *the memorial of the creation; ours for the great work of redemption.* But,

[3.] Thirdly, Theirs was celebrated for *their deliverance out of Egypt; ours for our deliverance from hell.* Now if the Jews were bound, and that for a whole day, not to do their own works, nor speak their own words, nor find their own pleasure; how much more solemnity belongs to our Lord's day! Oh, what a day is the Lord's-day! and how solemnly and devoutly ought it to be observed and sanctified! But,

(2.) Secondly, *We have greater means and helps for the sanctification of the Sabbath than the Jews had for a long time, or than the primitive Christians had for three hundred years.* Mark, the holy observation of the Sabbath among them came in by degrees, long after the day was settled; and the reason was this, because for a good while they had no word written to be read, nor no synagogues built to read it in. It was well-nigh a thousand years, or above a thousand years, after the giving of the law, before the reading of the law in synagogues came up. For a long time they had no books among them but the five books of Moses; and those books neither were not well understood by the common people. And it is further observable that the children of Israel being in Egypt under sore pressures, afflictions, and cruel bondage, &c., neither did nor could keep the Sabbath in any solemn manner, not being permitted either to rest or enjoy any solemn assemblies. And when they were in their wilderness condition, they had many stations, diversions, and incursions of enemies, so that they could not keep the Sabbath in any solemn public manner, as afterwards they did when they were settled in peace and safety in the land of Canaan. And so the primitive Christians, for three hundred years, living under very great and violent persecutions, they neither did nor could keep the Lord's day with that solemnity that they should or would; but as for place, they met not openly, but secretly in woods and deserts, and holes and caves, and dens of the earth; and so for time, sometimes they met in the day, and often they met in the night. But as for us, who have lived and do live in these days of the Son of man, what rare means and helps, what abundance of means and helps, what choice and precious means and helps have we had, and still have, in spite of all oppositions from high or low, to enable us to sanctify the Sabbath! And oh that all the means and helps that we yet enjoy may be signally blessed to that purpose! But,

(3.) Thirdly, *The heathens, by the very light of nature, held it but reasonable that the days consecrated to their gods should totally be observed with rest and sanctity.* The flamens, which were their priests, affirmed that the holy days were polluted if any work were done upon the solemn days; besides, it was not lawful for the king of the sacrifices, and the flamens, their priests, to see a work done on the holy days; and therefore by a crier it was proclaimed that no such things should be done; and he that neglected the precept was fined; and besides the fine, he which did aught unawares on such days was to offer sacrifices for expiation. And Scævola, the high priest, affirmed that the wilful offender could have no expiation.[1] Now shall heathens be so strict in the observation of their holy days, and shall not Christians be as strict in their observation of the Lord's day? These heathens will one day rise in judgment against the slight observers and the gross profaners of the Lord's day. But,

2. Secondly, We must sanctify the Sabbath *by preparing ourselves*

[1] Macrobius, lib. i., cap. 16.

beforehand for that day, and all the duties of that day, Eccles. v. 1, 2. Hence it is that God hath fixed a *memorandum* upon this command, more than he hath upon any other command: Exod. xx. 8, 'Remember the sabbath-day, to keep it holy.' Sabbath-days are our market-days. Now men that are worldly wise, they consider beforehand what to buy and what to sell. The husbandman dungs, dresses, ploughs, harrows, and all to prepare it for seed. 'I will,' saith holy David, 'wash my hands in innocency: so will I compass thine altar, O Lord,' Ps. xxvi. 6; signifying that to holy performances there ought to be holy preparations. When the temple was to be built, the stones were hewn, and the timber squared and fitted, before they were brought to the place where the temple stood. The application is easy.

[1.] First, *The Jews had their preparations:* Mark xv. 42, 'And now when the even was come, because it was the preparation,' that is, the day before the Sabbath, &c. Their preparation began at three o'clock in the afternoon, which the Hebrews called the Sabbath eve. The Jews, as I have read, were so careful in their preparation for the Sabbath, that to further it, the best and wealthiest of them, even those that had many servants, and were masters of families, would chop herbs, sweep the house, cleave wood, and kindle the fire, and do such like things, &c.

[2.] Secondly, *The heathens did use to prepare themselves by a strict kind of holiness, before they would offer sacrifices to several of their gods.* They had, as authors write, their stone pots of water set at the doors of their temples, where they used to wash before they went to sacrifice.

[3.] Thirdly, *The works of the day are great and glorious:* and what excellent works are there in nature, but requires some previous preparation? &c.

[4.] Fourthly, *Consider the dignity, majesty, authority, and purity of that God with whom you have to do in all the duties of the day.* When men are to converse and treat with earthly princes, or to give them entertainment, how do they prepare and make ready! And will you carry it worse towards the King of kings and Lord of lords, than men do carry it towards mortal princes, whose breath is in their nostrils, and whose glory shall assuredly be laid in the dust? &c., 1 Tim. vi. 15, 16.

[5.] Fifthly, *Consider, if you do not prepare yourselves beforehand for that day of the Lord, and all the duties of that day, what difference will there be between you and the worst of hypocrites, formalists, superstitious, or profane persons, who rush upon holy duties as the horse rusheth into the battle?* Dost thou dress up thy house, thy husband, thyself, thy children? so do the worst of persons. If you do not prepare for the duties of the day, and to meet with God in those duties, what singular thing do ye? Mat. v. 27.

[6.] Sixthly, *Consider what blessed earnings you have made on those Sabbaths wherein you have been prepared to meet with the Lord, and to manage the duties of those days.* Oh the joy, the peace, the comfort, the communion, the satisfaction, the enlargements, that you have then met with! And, on the other hand, consider what poor earnings you have made of it, when you have been careless and rash, and have not prepared yourselves for the duties of the day, and for the enjoyment of God in those duties. Oh how flat, how cold, how dull, how dead, how straitened, have you been on those Sabbaths wherein you have not prepared to meet with the Lord ! &c.

Quest. But you may say, Wherein doth our preparation for the Sabbath consist?

Ans. In these three things:—

[1.] First, *In a holy care, so to order all our worldly business and affairs on the day before, that they may not increase upon us on the Lord's day, to trouble us or distract us in the duties of that day.*

[2.] Secondly, *In putting iniquity far from you, in 'laying aside all superfluity of naughtiness, that you may receive the engrafted word with meekness, which is able to save your souls:'* Job xi. 14, 15; James i. 21. When the vessel is unclean, it sours quickly the sweetest liquors that are poured into it. And so when the heart is filthy and unclean, it loses all the good it might otherwise gain by ordinances. If the stomach be foul, it must be purged before it be fed, or else the meat will never nourish and strengthen nature, but increase ill humours. So the souls of men must be purged from foul enormities and gross impieties, or else they will never gain any saving good by ordinances: 2 Tim. ii. 21, 'If a man therefore purge himself from these, he shall be a vessel unto honour, sanctified and meet for the Master's use, and prepared unto every good work,' &c.

[3.] Thirdly, *In acting your graces in all the duties of the day.* Sleepy habits will do you no good, nor bring God no glory: all the honour he hath, and all the comfort and advantage you have, is from the active part of grace, Isa. l. 10, and therefore you must still be a-stirring up the grace of God that is in you: 2 Tim. i. 6, 'Stir up the gift of God that is in thee.' I know the apostle speaks of the ministerial gift; but it is as true of the work of grace: for the Greek word χάρισμα signifies grace, as well as gift. 'Stir up *the grace* of God in thee.' Mark the phrase, it is a remarkable phrase; for in the original it is to blow up thy grace, Ἀναζωπυρεῖν, just as a man blows up a fire that grows dull, or is hid under the ashes: blow up the grace of God in thee. Some think—Calvin and others—that it is a metaphor taken from a spark kept in ashes, which by gentle blowing is stirred up till it take a flame. Others say it is an allusion to the fire in the temple, which was always to be kept burning. Look, as the fire is increased and preserved by blowing, so are our graces preserved and increased by our acting of them. We get nothing by dead and useless habits. Talents hid in a napkin gather rust. Look, as the noblest faculties are imbased when they are not improved, when they are not exercised; so the noblest graces are imbased when they are not improved, when they are not exercised. Grace is bettered and made more perfect by acting. Neglect of our graces is the ground of their decrease and decay. Wells are the sweeter for drawing, and so are our graces for acting. We had need pray hard with the spouse, Cant. iv. 16, 'Awake, O north wind; and come, thou south; blow upon my garden, that the spices thereof may flow out. Let my beloved come into his garden, and eat his pleasant fruit.' Satan's grand design is not to keep men from going the round of duties, nor yet to keep men from attending on ordinances, but his grand design is to hinder the exercise of grace. All other exercises without the exercise of grace will do a Christian no good, as you may see by comparing the scriptures in the margin together.[1] The more grace is exercised, the more corruptions will be weakened and mortified. As one bucket in the well rises up, the other goes down; so as grace rises higher and higher, corruptions fall lower and lower. There was two laurels at Rome, and when the one flourished, the other withered; so where grace flourishes, corruptions wither. As the house of David grew stronger and stronger, so the house of Saul grew weaker and weaker, 2 Sam. iii. 1. So as grace in its exercise grows stronger and stronger, so sin, like the house of Saul, will every day grow weaker and weaker. If you keep not grace in exercise, it may most fail you when it should stand you most in stead, Mark iv. 40. If a man uses a knife but now and then, he may have his knife to seek when he should use it. That sword grows rusty in the scabbard that is used but now and then. You know how to apply it. But,

3. Thirdly, You must sanctify the Sabbath, *by looking upon the enjoyment of Sabbaths and ordinances as your great happiness, by looking upon every duty as your dignity, and by looking upon every work of that day as carrying a reward with it,* Prov. viii. 34, 35; Ps. xxvii. 4, xlii. 1–5, and lxiii. 1–3. Ps. xix. 11, 'And in keeping of them there is great reward:' not only *for* keeping, but also *in* keeping of God's commands there is great reward. A gracious soul would not exchange the joy, the peace, the comfort, the assurance, the communion, the delight, the satisfaction that it enjoys in the ways of obedience, before pay-day comes, before the crown be put on, before the full reward is given out, for all the crowns and kingdoms of this world. David was a king, a great and glorious king, yea, the best king in all the world, and yet he esteemed it as a very high honour to be the lowest officer, a door-keeper in God's house: Ps. lxxxiv. 10, 'A day in thy courts is better than a thousand; I had rather be a door-keeper in the house of my God'—or I had rather sit at the threshold, as the Hebrew runs—'than to dwell in the tents of wickedness.' 1 Kings x. 8, 'Happy are thy men, happy are these thy servants, which stand continually before thee, and that hear thy wisdom,' said the queen of Sheba concerning Solomon's servants. Oh, then, how many thousand times more happy are they who hear Christ in his ordinances, who see Christ in his ordinances, and who enjoy Christ in his ordinances on his own day! Of all days the Sabbath-day is the day wherein Christ carries his people into his wine-cellar, wherein he brings them to his banqueting-house, and his banner over them is love. This is the day wherein he stays his people with flagons, and comforts them with apples, and wherein his left hand is under their head, and his right hand doth embrace them, Cant. ii. 4–6. Oh the sweet communion, the sweet discoveries, the sweet incomes, and that blessed presence, and those glorious answers and returns of prayer that the saints have had on Sabbath-days! Christ in his ordinances on the Sabbath-day doth, as Mary, open a box of precious ointment, which diffuseth a spiritual savour among them that fear him. Though many slight ordinances, and many deny ordinances, and many oppose

[1] Luke xxii. 31–33; 1 Tim. iv. 8; Isa. lviii. 1–8; Neh. vii. 4–6.

ordinances, and many fall off from ordinances, and many pretend to live above ordinances, and under that pretence vilify the ordinances as poor, low, weak things, yet the beauty and glory of God's ordinances will one day convince the world of the excellency of the saints: Ezek. xxxvii. 26–28, 'I will set my sanctuary in the midst of them for evermore. My tabernacle also shall be with them; yea, I will be their God, and they shall be my people. And the heathen shall know that I the Lord do sanctify Israel, when my sanctuary shall be in the midst of them for evermore.'[1] I doubt not but there are many thousands of the precious servants of the Lord who are able to tell this poor, blind, dark world, from their experience, that they have seen, and felt, and tasted, and enjoyed more of God in his ordinances on this day than ever they have enjoyed on any other day. But,

4. Fourthly, You must sanctify the Sabbath, *by rising as early in the morning as your age, strength, health, and ability, and bodily infirmities will permit*, Ps. cxxxix 18; Gen. xxii. 3; Job i. 5. Abraham rose up early in the morning to offer up his only son; and Job rose up early in the morning to offer up burnt-offerings. So David, 'My voice shalt thou hear in the morning. O Lord, in the morning will I direct my prayer unto thee'—or marshal my prayer, as the Hebrew runs—'and will look up'—or will look out as a watchman looks out of his watch-tower to discover an approaching enemy. So Ps. cxxx. 6, 'My soul waiteth for the Lord more than they that watch for the morning: I say, more than they that watch for the morning.' Ps. lxxxviii. 13, 'In the morning shall my prayer prevent thee.' That this may the more work, and the better stick, seriously consider of these hints, &c.:—

[1.] First, *God is the first being, and therefore of right deserveth to be served first*, Dan. vii. 22, and ii. 20–22. If you can find any being before the being of that God, who is blessed for ever, let that being be served first: if not—as I am sure you cannot—then let the first being be first served. But,

[2.] Secondly, As God is the first being, so he is *the best being: he is the choicest and chiefest good;* and therefore ought to be first minded and served, Ps. iv. 6, lxxiii. 25, and cxliv. 15. But,

[3.] Thirdly, As God is the best being, so he is *the greatest being:* as he is the choicest and chiefest good, so he is the greatest good, the greatest majesty, the greatest authority; and therefore he ought to be first served, Mal. i. 14. But,

[4.] Fourthly, *God gives the greatest rewards, and the fullest rewards, and therefore he ought to be served first*, Ps. xix. 11; Mat. v. 12; 2 John 8. He gives 'a crown of righteousness,' 2 Tim. iv. 8; 'a crown of life,' Rev. ii. 10; 'a crown of glory,' James i. 12; 'a crown of immortality.' What have not men done, what won't men do, what don't men do for earthly crowns? A crown is the top of royalty; and how many princes have swam through the blood of thousands to their earthly crowns! Oh how much more active for God should that glorious crown make us, which he has laid up for all that love him! But,

[1] Many in these days are like old Barzillai, that had lost his taste and hearing, and so cared not for David's feasts and music, 2 Sam. xix. 35.

[5.] Fifthly, *Christ rose early in the morning before day, and went into a solitary place to pray; and why should not we make it our business, our work, our heaven, to write after so noble a copy?* Mark i. 35, 36. We cannot glorify Christ more than by our conformity to him, than by imitating of those blessed patterns that he hath set before us. But,

[6.] Sixthly and lastly, *The children of Israel rose up early in the morning on the Sabbath-day, to offer up burnt-offerings and peace-offerings to an idol*, Exod. xxxii. 4–6. So papists, Turks, and heathens are early in the mornings at their devotions; and the harlot rises early in the morning to trepan the lustful youth: Prov. vii. 15, 'Therefore came I forth to meet thee, diligently to seek thee'—or, as it runs in the Hebrew, 'In the morning came I forth to meet thee.' Now how should this put Christians to a holy blush, to see the very basest and worst of people to take more pains to go to hell than themselves do to go to heaven. Shall they rise early to serve their idols; and shall not we rise early to serve our God, and save our souls? O sirs, did you but love Christ more, and Sabbaths more, and duties more, you would then be more early in your communion with God, as the spouse was, Cant. vii. 11, 12. Mary Magdalene loved Christ much: Luke vii. 47, and she came early to the sepulchre to seek him. She came to look after Christ as soon as it began to dawn, Mat. xxviii. 1; Mark xvi. 1, 2; Luke xxiv. 1; John xx. 1. Men that love the world can rise early to gain the world. Now shall nature do more than grace? Shall the love of the world outdo the love of Christ? The Lord forbid. And thus I have done with those considerations that should quicken you up to sanctify the Sabbath, by rising as early in the morning as your age, health, strength, ability, and bodily infirmities will permit. But,

5. Fifthly, You must sanctify the Sabbath, *by a religious performance of all the duties of the day.*

Quest. What are they?

Ans. (1.) Public.

(2.) Private.

Quest. What are the public duties that are to be performed on that day?

[1.] First, *To assemble yourselves with the people of God to hear his word*, Neh. viii. 1-9; Mat. xiii. 54; Joel i. 13, 14; Luke iv. 16, 17; John xx. 19, 26; Acts ii. 1, 44, 46, and v. 12; 1 Cor. xi. 20.

[2.] Secondly, *Prayer*, Ps. v. 7, xlii. 4, and cxviii. 24–26; Isa. lvi. 7; Mat. xxi. 13; Acts i. 13, 14, ii. 46, 47, and xvi. 13; Heb. xiii. 15.

[3.] Thirdly, *The administrations of the seals*, Acts ii. 46, and xx. 7; 1 Cor. xi. 20, 33.

[4.] Fourthly, *Singing of psalms, hymns, or spiritual songs*, Ps. xcii. 1; Mat. xxvi. 30; 1 Cor. xiv. 15; James v. 13; Heb. ii. 12.

[5.] Fifthly, *Works of mercy and charity*, Neh. viii. 9–12; 1 Cor. xvi. 1, 2.

[6.] Sixthly and lastly, *The censures of the Church*, as casting out of communion the obstinate, and in receiving such into communion as the Lord hath received into communion and fellowship with himself, 1 Tim. v. 20, 21; 1 Cor. v. 4; 2 Cor. ii. 6, 7; Rom. xiv. 1, and xv. 7, &c.

Quest. What are the private duties that are to be performed on that day?

Ans. [1.] First, *Prayer in our families and closets*, Col. iii. 17; Luke xviii. 1, 2; 1 Thes. v. 18; Eph. vi. 18. See my treatise on Closet Prayer, &c.[1]

[2.] Secondly, *Reading of the word*, Josh. i. 8; Deut. vi. 6, 8–10, xi. 19, and iv. 10; John v. 35; Col. iii. 16; Rev. i. 3.

[3.] Thirdly, *Meditation*, Ps. i. 2, and cxix. 97; 1 Cor. xiv. 5; 1 Tim. ii. 11, 18.

Quest. But on what must we meditate?

Ans. (1.) *Upon the holiness, greatness, and graciousness of God.*

(2.) *Upon the person, natures, offices, excellencies, beauties, glories, riches, fulness, and sweetness of Christ.*

(3.) *Upon the blessed truths that we either hear or read.*

(4.) *Upon our own emptiness, nothingness, baseness, vileness, and unworthiness.*

(5.) *Upon the works of creation and redemption.*

(6.) *Upon our spiritual and internal wants.*

(7.) *Upon that eternal rest that is reserved for the people of God*, Heb. iv. 9.

[4.] Fourthly, *Instructing, examining, and preparing of your families, according to the measures of grace you have received*, Deut. vi. 7, and xi. 18, 20; Gen. xviii. 19, 20; Josh. xxiv. 15.

[5.] Fifthly, *Singing of psalms*, James v. 13; Col. iii. 16; Eph. v. 19.

[6.] Sixthly, *Holy conference upon the word*, Luke xiv. 8–12, 15, 16, and xxiv. 14, 17, 18; Col. iv. 6; Mal. iii. 16, 17, &c.

[7.] Seventhly, *Visiting and relieving the sick, the poor, the distressed, afflicted, and imprisoned saints of God*, Mat. xv. 34–40; James i. 27, &c.

Now mark, when the public ordinances may be enjoyed in Christ's way, and in their liberty, purity, and glory, it will be your wisdom so to manage all your family duties and closet duties, as that you do not shut out more public worship. It is more observable that the Sabbaths and public service are joined together: Lev. xix. 30, 'Ye shall keep my sabbaths, and reverence my sanctuary: I am the Lord.' Now what God hath solemnly 'joined together, let no man put asunder.' Every Christian should make it his great care that private duties do not eat up public ordinances, and that public ordinances do not shut out private duties. More of this you may see in my discourse on Closet Prayer.[2] But,

6. Sixthly, You must sanctify the Sabbath, *by managing all the duties of that day as under the eye of God.*[3] God's eye is very much upon his people whilst they are in religious duties and services. Therefore, in the tabernacle, the place of God's public worship, it was thus commanded, Exod. xxv. 37, 'Thou shalt make seven lamps, and they shall light the lamps, that they may give light:' to teach us that nothing there escapes his sight; for in his house there is always light: and so

[1] Vol. II., as before.—G. [2] Vol. II., as before.—G.

[3] God is *totus oculus*, all eye. As the eyes of a well-drawn picture are fastened on thee which way soever thou turnest, so are the eyes of the Lord.

when the temple was built, 'Mine eyes,' saith God, 'shall be there perpetually,' 1 Kings ix. 3. It was an excellent saying of Ambrose,[1] 'If thou canst not hide thyself from the sun, which is God's minister of light, how impossible will it be to hide thyself from him whose eyes are ten thousand times brighter than the sun!' Subjects will carry themselves sweetly and loyally when they are under their sovereign's eye; and children will carry themselves dutifully when they are under their parents' eye; and servants will carry themselves wisely and prudently when they are under their minister's[2] eye. God's eye is the best tutor to keep the soul in a gracious frame. It is good to have a fixed eye on him whose eye is always fixed on thee, Job xxxi. 5, 6; Prov. xv. 9, and v. 21. The best way on earth to keep close to God's precepts, is always to walk as in his presence. No man on earth, by day or night, can draw a curtain between God and him. There is a threefold eye of God that is present in the assemblies of his people. As,

[1.] First, There is the eye *of observation and inspection.* God seeth what uprightness and seriousness, what integrity, ingenuity, and fervency you have in his services. 'Mine eyes are upon all their ways,' Jer. xvi. 17. Ps. xvi. 8, 'I have set the Lord always before me.' Ps. cxix. 168, 'I have kept thy precepts and thy testimonies: for all my ways are before thee.' Job xxxi. 4, 'Doth not he see all my ways, and count all my steps?' O sirs, whether you are praying, or hearing, or reading, or meditating, or singing, or receiving the Lord's supper, or conferring one with another, the eye of the Lord is still upon you, Mal. iii. 17. But,

[2.] Secondly, There is an eye *of favour and benediction:* Amos ix. 4, 'I will set mine eyes upon them for good.' 2 Chron. vii. 16, 'Mine eye and my heart shall be there;' that is, in my house. God's eye is here to approve, and to bless, and to increase the graces, the comforts, the communions, and the enjoyments of his people. But,

[3.] Thirdly, There is the eye *of fury and indignation.* God's looks can speak his anger, as well as his blows. His fury is visible by his frowns. 'Mine eyes shall be upon them for evil.' God's sight can wound as deeply as his sword. 'He sharpeneth his eyes upon me,' saith Job, chap. xvi. 9. Wild beasts, when they fight, whet their eyes as well as their teeth. 'He sharpeneth his eyes upon me,' as if he would stab me to the heart with a glance of his eye. He that waits on God irreverently, or worships him carelessly, or that profaneth his day, either by corporal labour or spiritual idleness, may well expect an eye of fury to be fixed upon him, Jer. xvii. 27; Ezek. xxii. 26, 31. But,

7. Seventhly, You must sanctify the Sabbath, *by pressing after immediate communion with God and Christ in all the duties of the day,* Ps. xxvii. 4, xlii. 1, 2, xliii. 4, lxiii. 1, 2, and lxxxiv. 1, 2. Oh do not take up in duties, or ordinances, or privileges, or enlargements, or meltings, but press hard after intimate communion with God in all you do. Let no duty satisfy thy soul without communion with God in it: Cant. vii. 5, 'The king is held in the galleries,' that is, in his ordinances. The galleries, the ordinances, without King Jesus be enjoyed in them, will never satisfy the spouse of Christ, Cant. iii.

[1] Ambrose Offic., lib. i. cap. 14.

[2] Query, 'master's'?—ED.

1–4. What is a purse without money, or a table without meat, or a ship without a pilot, or a fountain without water, or the body without the soul, or the sun without light, or the cabinet without the jewels? no more are all ordinances and duties to a gracious soul without the enjoyment of God in them,[1] 2 Kings ii. 13, 14. Moses had choice communion with God in the mount, and that satisfied him. The disciples had been with Jesus, and this was a spring of joy and life unto them: John. xx. 20, 'Then were the disciples glad, when they saw the Lord.' 'Here is the mantle of Elijah, but where is the God of Elijah?' said Elisha. So saith a gracious soul, here is this ordinance and that ordinance, but where is the God of the ordinance? Ps. ci. 2, 'Oh when wilt thou come unto me?' O Lord, I come to one ordinance and another ordinance, but when wilt thou come to me in the ordinance? when shall I be so happy as to enjoy thyself in the ordinances that I enjoy? The waggons that Joseph sent to fetch his father were the means of bringing Joseph and his father together. All the ordinances should be as so many waggons, to bring Christ and our souls nearer together. Man's *summum bonum* stands in his communion with God, as Scripture and experience evidences.

8. Eighthly, You must sanctify the Sabbath, *by labouring after the highest pitches of grace and holiness on this day.* Every Christian should labour after an angelical holiness on this day; on this day every saint should walk like an earthly angel, Isa. lviii. 13. Mark, the Sabbath is not only called holy, but holiness to the Lord: Exod. xxxi. 15, 'Six days may work be done, but in the seventh is the sabbath of rest, holy to the Lord'—or as the Hebrew runs, 'holiness to the Lord;' which shews that the day is exceeding holy, and ought to be kept accordingly. The sacrifices on this day was to be double: Num. xxviii. 9, 'And on the sabbath-day two lambs of the first year without spot, and two tenth deals of flour for a meat-offering, mingled with oil, and the drink-offering thereof.' The sacrifices here appointed for every Sabbath-day are full double to those appointed for every day, ver. 3; and yet the daily sacrifices, the continual burnt-offering, ver. 10, was not omitted on the Sabbath-day neither. So that every Sabbath, in the morning, there was offered one lamb for the daily sacrifice, and then two lambs more for the Sabbath: and this was appointed,

[1.] To shew the holiness of that day above other days; and that God required more service from them on that day than he did on any other day.

[2.] Secondly, To testify their thankfulness for the world's creation, Exod. xx. 11.

[3.] Thirdly, To put them in remembrance of God's bringing them out of Egypt by a mighty hand, and by a stretched-out arm, Deut. v. 15.

[4.] Fourthly, For a sign of their sanctification by the Lord, Ezek. xx. 12; Heb. iv.

[5.] Fifthly and lastly, For to be a figure of grace, and a sign of

[1] The sea ebbs and flows, the moon increases and decreases; so it is with saints in their communion with God in ordinances. Sometimes they rise, and sometimes they fall; sometimes they have more, and sometimes less communion with God.

that rest in heaven that Christ hath purchased for his people with his dearest blood. Now mark, as this day was a sign of more than ordinary favours from the Lord, so he required greater testimonies of their thankfulness and holiness on this day than he did on any other day. Every day should be a Sabbath to the saints, in regard of their ceasing to do evil, and learning to do well, but on the seventh-day-Sabbath, our duties and services should be doubled. In Ps. xcii., which psalm is titled a Psalm for the Sabbath, there is mention made of morning and evening performances. The variety of duties that are to be performed on this day may very well take up the whole day with delight and pleasure. On this day, in a more especial manner, we should labour to do the will of God on earth, as the angels and spirits of just men made perfect do it now in heaven, Heb. xii. 22, 23—viz., wisely, freely, readily, cheerfully, faithfully, seriously, universally, and unweariedly. If we are not wanting to ourselves, God on this day will give out much of himself, and much of his Christ, and much of his Spirit, and much of his grace into our souls. But,

9. Ninthly, You must sanctify the Sabbath, *by managing all the duties of the day with inward reverence, seriousness, and spiritualness*, John iv. 23, 24. It is the pleasure of God that we reverence his sanctuary: Lev. xix. 30, 'Ye shall keep my sabbaths, and reverence my sanctuary: I am the Lord.' Twice in this chapter the observation of the Sabbath is commanded, that it may be the better remembered, and that men may know that it is not enough to rest on that day, but that rest must be sanctified by a reverent management of all their soul-concernments in all our drawings nigh to God. We must look that our hearts lie under a holy awe and dread of his presence. To the commandment of sanctifying God's Sabbath, this of reverencing his sanctuary is joined, because the Sabbaths were the chief times whereon they resorted to the sanctuary, Gen. xxviii. 16, 17.

The Jews made a great stir about reverencing the temple. They tell us that they were not to go in with a staff, nor shoes, not to spit in it, nor, when they went away, to turn their backs upon it, but go sidelong. But doubtless the great thing God points at and expects from his people's hands on this day is, that they do worship him with inward reverence, seriousness, and spiritualness. All other worship abstracted from this, will neither pleasure God nor profit us: 1 Tim. iv. 8, 'For bodily exercise profiteth little.' Oh labour to be very spiritual in all the duties of this day! Christ, the Lord of the Sabbath, was spiritual in his conception, in his life and conversation, in his death and passion, in his resurrection and ascension. He was spiritual in his words, in his works, in his ways, and in his worship; and therefore let us labour to be very spiritual in all we do on that day, Luke i. 35, 36; Mat. iii. 16; John i. 32, and vi. 36; Heb. vii. 26, and ix. 14; 1 Tim. iii. 16. Again, all the ordinances of the day are spiritual, viz., the word, prayer, sacraments, singing of psalms, &c.; and therefore we had need to be spiritual in all the services of that day. Again, the ends for which the Lord's day was appointed are all spiritual, viz., the glory of God, the illumination, conversion, and salvation of sinners, and the edification, confirmation, consolation of saints; and therefore we had need be spiritual in all the duties of the day, Eph. vi. 12. Again, the grand enemies that we are to encounter with on this day are spiritual, sin within and Satan without; and therefore we had need be spiritual in all we do. For there is no way to conquer spiritual enemies but by spiritual weapons and by spiritual exercises, 1 Cor. x. 13. Again, grace thrives most and flourishes best in their souls who are most spiritual in their duties on the Lord's day. Again, the more spiritual any man is in his duties on the Lord's days, the more secured and armed he will be against all spiritual judgments, which are the sorest and dreadfullest of all judgments. Again, the more spiritual any man is in the duties of the Lord's day, the more that man acts like the angels in heaven, and like the spirits of just men made perfect, Heb. xii. 22, 23. Again, this will difference you from hypocrites, formalists, and all profane persons. An external observation of the Sabbath will difference you from heathens; but a spiritual spending of the Sabbath will difference you from hypocrites. A hypocrite never rises so high as to be spiritual in the Sabbaths of God, Luke xiii. 14, 15. Mark, Sabbaths spiritually spent are a sure sign of a sincere heart and of a saving estate, Exod. xxxi. 13. Now, oh that all these considerations might greatly provoke you, and mightily encourage you to be very spiritual on the Lord's day, and in all the duties of that day! But,

10. Tenthly, You must sanctify the Sabbath, *by being spiritual in all natural actions, and holy and heavenly in all earthly enjoyments*, 1 Cor. x. 13. It is reported of a Scotch minister, that he did eat, drink, and sleep eternal life.[1] Luther tells us that though he did not always pray and meditate, but did sometimes eat and drink, and sometime sleep, yet all should further his account. That is a Christian worth gold that hath learned that heavenly art, so to spiritualise all his natural actions as that they shall turn to his account in the great day: Zech. xiv. 20, 21, 'In that day shall there be upon the bells,' or bridles, 'of the horses, Holiness unto the Lord. And the pots in the Lord's house shall be like the bowls before the altar; yea, every pot in Jerusalem and in Judah shall be holiness unto the Lord of hosts.'[2] Here is holiness written upon the bridles of the horses they ride on, and holiness written upon the cups and pots they drink in. A holy and heavenly heart will be holy in the use of the meanest things that are for common use. Something of sanctity should run through every piece of your civility. Something of the spirit, life, and power of religion you should shew in all parts of your common conversation on every day, but especially on the Lord's day. Tertullian, [Apolog.,] speaking of the carriage of the primitive Christians at their meals, saith,

[1.] Our table resembleth an altar, and our supper a sacrifice.

[2.] Our table hath nothing savouring of baseness, sensuality, or immodesty. We feed by measure, we drink by the rules of temperance.

[3.] We speak and converse as in the presence of God. Every one repeateth what he knoweth out of the Holy Scriptures, and his own invention, to the praise of God.

[4.] As prayer began the banquet, so prayer concludes it. If you

[1] Probably Samuel Rutherford.—G.

[2] Calvin renders it 'stables of horses,' which are the most stinking and contemptible places; and yet these should be holily used.

beheld us, you would say that we were not at supper, but at a lecture of holiness.

Should not the practice of these primitive Christians put all such Christians to a blush in our day, who on the Lord's day are so carnal in the use of spiritual things, and so earthly in the use of heavenly things?

That is a memorable expression that you have in Exod. xviii. 12, 'And Aaron came, and all the elders of Israel, to eat bread with Moses' father-in-law before God.' See Deut. xii. 5, 7; 1 Chron. xxix. 21, 22. The word *bread* is used for all meat, Gen. iii. 19, and xxxi. 14. Now mark, in these words you have,

[1.] The greatness of their courtesy: for though Jethro was a stranger and no Israelite, yet the elders honoured him with their company. 'And Aaron and all the elders came to eat bread with Moses his father-in-law.'

[2.] The graciousness of their carriage: 'They came to eat bread with him before the Lord.' That is, saith Calvin on the text, *in gloriam et honorem Dei*, To the honour and glory of God. Grace must spice every cup, and be sauce to every dish, or nothing will relish well with him whose heart is set to sanctify the Sabbath. 'Aaron and all the elders of Israel ate bread before the Lord,' that is, they ate bread as in the presence of God. Whilst they were eating of bread, their hearts were under a reverential awe of God. Diana's temple was burnt down, when she was busy at Alexander's birth, and could not be at two places together. But God is present both in paradise and in the wilderness at the same time: he is present both at board and bed, both in the family and in the closet at the same time. Oh that in all your natural, civil, and common actions you would carry it as becomes his eye, his presence, that fills heaven and earth with his glory, Ps. cxxxix. But,

11. Eleventhly, You must sanctify the Sabbath, *by managing all the duties of the Sabbath with a spirit of holy joy and delight*, Ps. xxxiii. 1, and xxxii. 11; Phil. iv. 4; 1 Thes. v. 16, 18. There is no garment that so well becomes the upright as the garment of gladness. God hath laid his royal command upon us to rejoice on this day: Isa. lviii. 13, 14, 'If thou turn away thy foot from the sabbath, from doing thy pleasure on my holy day, and call the sabbath a delight'—or as the Hebrew runs, 'delights:' and so Tremelius reads it—'the holy of the Lord, honourable, and shalt honour him,' &c.: 'then shalt thou delight thyself in the Lord,' &c.: Ps. cxviii. 24, 'This is the day which the Lord hath made, we will be glad and rejoice therein.' Now if you compare this text with Mat. xxi. 22, 23, and Acts iv. 11, you will find that the precedent verses are a prophetical prediction of Christ's resurrection; and so this verse foretells the church's joy upon that memorable and glorious day. 'A feast,' saith Solomon, 'is made for laughter,' Eccles. x. 19. Now on this day the Lord of hosts is pleased more especially and more abundantly to make for his people 'a feast of fat things, a feast of wines on the lees, of fat things full of marrow, of wines on the lees well refined,' Isa. xxv. 6. On this day we enjoy the freest, and the fullest, and the sweetest, and the choicest, and the nearest communion of saints: and what doth this call for, but

a spirit of holy joy? On this day we enjoy all the precious ordinances in a most solemn manner; and why then should we not be joyful in God's house of prayer? Isa. lvi. 7. The heavenly host sung at his birth, Luke ii. 10–14; and why should not we sing and rejoice at his second birth, his resurrection from the dead? O sirs, Sabbaths are the very suburbs of heaven; and who can be in the suburbs of heaven and not rejoice? A beautiful face is at all times pleasing to the eye, but then especially when there is joy manifested in the countenance. Joy in the face puts a new beauty upon a person, and makes that which before was beautiful to be exceeding beautiful; it puts a lustre upon beauty. And so doth holy joy put a lustre upon the day of God, the ways of God, and the people of God. It is the duty and glory of a Christian to rejoice in the Lord every day, but especially on the Lord's day. God reserves the best wine, the best comforts, and the choicest discoveries of himself, and of his love, and of his Christ, and of his glory for that day; and all to make his people 'joyful in the house of prayer,' Isa. lvi. 7. The Manichees were wont to keep their fasts upon the Lord's day, which made Tertullian say that that practice of theirs was a detestable wickedness. To fast on the Lord's day, saith Ignatius, is to kill Christ; but to rejoice in the Lord this day, and to rejoice in all the duties of this day, and to rejoice in that redemption that was wrought for us on this day, this is to crown Christ, this is to lift up Christ. But,

12. Twelfthly, You must sanctify the Sabbath, *by sanctifying of the whole day to God's service, and not by fits, and flashes, and sudden pangs.* O sirs, if the Lord was so strict that he would not lose a moment's honour in a ceremonial day of rest—Lev. xxiii. 32, 'It shall be unto you a sabbath of rest, and ye shall afflict your souls in the ninth day of the month at even: from even unto even shall ye celebrate your sabbath'—what shall we think the Lord expects upon this day, which is more? Ps. xcii. 1, 2, 'It is good to sing of his loving-kindness in the morning, and of his faithfulness every night.' Jer. xvii. 22, 'You shall do no work, but sanctify my sabbath.' Now that this may the better stick, consider,

[1.] First, *God hath given you six whole days that you may provide for yourselves and families*, and therefore do not deny him one day in seven, Exod. xx. 9, and xxiii. 12. What an unrighteous thing is it to buy by one measure which is greater, and sell by another which is lesser! Do not rob God of his time, who hath been so noble as to give you six in seven. But,

[2.] Secondly, *God rested all the seventh day:* he had finished the creation in six days, Gen. ii. 1–3. God did not rest on one part of the seventh day and work on the other part of the seventh day, but he rested all the seventh day. And doubtless it is your wisdom, duty, and glory to write after the copy that God has laid before you. But,

[3.] Thirdly, *The Sabbath is not to be an artificial day, but a natural day*, viz., twenty-four hours together: as you may see in Lev. xxiii. 32, 'From even unto even shall ye celebrate your sabbath.' The days then were so reckoned. But,

[4.] Fourthly, *You would not take it well at your servants' hands if they should only work three or four hours in a day, and either trifle away the rest of the time, or else spend it in doing their own work when they should be a-doing of yours;* and do you think that the great God will take it well at your hands, that when you have spent three or four hours in the duties of his day, that then you should either trifle away, or fool away, or play away, or sleep away, or sin away the remaining part of his day? But,

[5.] Fifthly, *This hath been the judgment of most judicious divines in all ages.* In the Council of Mexicon[1] there was an assembly of ministers out of all nations in Christendom, and they ordained a canon concerning the Lord's day. The canon runs thus: 'We ordain that people keep the whole Lord's day holy, and that they set themselves the whole day to pray to God, and delight in God, and hear his word; and if a country man's servant break this day, his punishment shall be to be beaten with severe blows,' [*ictubus gravioribus*, are the very words of the council;] 'and if a lawyer offer to plead this day, he shall not have the benefit of his pleading or case; and if a minister break this day, he shall be excommunicated half a year, and thrown out of the church, and shall not be received into the church again but upon great humiliation.' It is a good observation of Musculus upon Exod. xx. 8: God doth not say, saith he, 'remember the Sabbath, to keep it holy;' for he that keeps it an hour or two keeps it holy; but 'remember the sabbath-day to keep it holy:' he will have not a part of a day only, but a whole day kept holy. And Calvin, upon these words, 'Remember the sabbath-day to keep it holy,' saith, we are to keep this day holy, and not a part of it, but all of it. I might produce a cloud of witnesses in the case; but let these suffice. But,

[6.] Sixthly and lastly, *Consider that the very heathen have kept the whole day to their idol-gods, and not a part.* And shall we then put off God with a part of a day? Shall we be worse than the heathens? Shall we act below heathens? Shall nature, shall blind devotion do more than grace? The Lord forbid! But,

13. Thirteenthly, You must sanctify the Sabbath, *by such an abstinence or moderate use of all your lawful comforts, contentments, and enjoyments, as may render you most apt and fit for the sanctification of the Sabbath.* 'Let your moderation be known among all men' always, Phil. iv. 5; but especially on the Lord's day, be moderate in your eating, drinking, entertainments, &c. Oh how do many by their immoderate use of lawful comforts on this day, indispose and unfit themselves for the duties of the day! It is a Christian's duty every day to eat and drink soberly: Titus ii. 11, 12, 'The grace of God which bringeth salvation, hath appeared to us, teaching us to live soberly in this present world.' It is both the duty and the glory of a Christian to be temperate in his diet. A little will satisfy nature, less will satisfy grace, though nothing will satisfy men's lusts.[2] Sobriety is a gift of God, whereby we keep a holy moderation in the use of our diet: Prov. xxiii. 1, 2, 'When thou sittest to eat,' &c., 'consider diligently what is before thee, and put the knife to thy throat;' that is, be very careful and circumspect in taking thy food, bridle thine appetite, take heed thou dost not exceed measure. He may endanger

[1] *Sic:* but query 'Matiscon in France'? See before, Index *sub voce.*—G.

[2] The Greeks call sobriety the keeper and guard of wisdom.

his health, his life, his soul, that gives way to his greedy appetite. Some read the words thus: 'For thou puttest a knife to thy throat, if thou be a man given to appetite.' Thou shortenest thy life, and diggest as it were thine own grave with thine own teeth. Meat kills as many as the musket; the board as the sword, [Chrysostom.] I know that the bodies, stomachs, callings, constitutions, and climates wherein men live, differ; and therefore no such particular rules, as to eating and drinking, can be laid down as shall be binding to every one: yet this is certain, that a man that eats or drinks so much on the Lord's day as oppresses nature, and as unfits him for praying, working,[1] or hearing work, or reading work, or closet work, that man is guilty of intemperance.[2] Such who feed till they unfit themselves for service are belly-gods. Paul wept over such in his day, and so should we in ours, Phil. iii. 18, 19. Thou shouldst use thy food, O Christian, as a help, and not as a hindrance to thee in thy Christian course. A full belly never studies well, nor never prays well, nor never hears well, nor never reads well, nor never repeats well, nor never doth anything well, either on the Lord's day or any other day. What a shame is it to see a Christian a slave to his palate on any day, but especially on the Lord's day. I may use the creatures so as to support sheer nature, but not so as to clog it, and weaken it, and debase it. I may use the creatures as my servants, but I must never suffer them to be my lord. Daniel was very temperate in his diet, Dan. i. 8. Though there was not a greater born of a woman than John the Baptist, yet his fare was but locusts and wild honey, Mat. xi. 11. A little bread was Basil's provision. Hilarion did seldom eat anything till the sun went down, and then that which he did eat was very mean. Jerome lived with cold water and a few dried figs; and Augustine hath this expression concerning himself,[3] *Hoc me docuisti, Domine, &c.*, Thou Lord hast taught me this, that I should go to my meat as to a medicine. His meaning was, that he went to his meat, not to satisfy his appetite, but to repair nature. And Luther made many a meal with bread and a herring. Socrates, Anacharsis, Cyrus, Cæsar, Herodicus, Augustus, and many other heathens were very temperate in their diet. The old Gauls were very sparing in their diet, and used to fine them that outgrew their girdles. These heathens will one day rise in judgment against those nominal Christians who are intemperate, both upon the Lord's day, and other days also. But,

14. Fourteenthly and lastly, You must sanctify the Sabbath, *by abstaining from speaking your own words.* The spouse's lips are like a thread of scarlet, Cant. iv. 3. They are red like a thread of scarlet in discoursing of a crucified Christ, and they are thin like a thread of scarlet, and not swelled with frothy, empty, worldly discourses, on the Lord's days or on other days. Such words as will neither profit a man's own soul, nor better others, are not to be spoken on the Lord's day. It is God's express pleasure that we should not speak our own words on his day: Isa. lviii. 13, 'Nor speaking thine own words.' Cæsar[4] passing

[1] Query, 'praying work'?—ED.

[2] In the hot Eastern countries men have lived long with parched corn and a cake, but their example is no rule for us.

[3] Lib. x. Confessionum.

[4] Plutarch in the life of Pericles.

through the streets of Rome, and seeing many of the ladies playing with little dogs, monkeys, and baboons, asked them if the women in that country had no children? So when men spend the Lord's day in playing, sporting, toying, or talking of this or that trifle, of this or that person, of this or that fashion, of this or that vanity, we may ask them whether they have no God, no Christ, no heaven, no promises, no experiences, no evidences to talk of? There are many idle talkers: of every idle word that men shall speak they shall give an account at the day of judgment, Mat. xii. 36. An idle word is a profuse or needless word, used rashly or unadvisedly, wanting a reason of just necessity, bringing neither honour to God nor edification to others, nor conducing to any profitable end.[1] And as there are many idle talkers, so there are many over-talkers; and they are such who spend a hundred words when ten will serve the turn, Eccles. v. 2, 3. And as there are many over-talkers, so there are many that are only talkers, that can do nothing but talk, Prov. xiv. 23. To fall under the power or scourge of these men's tongues is to fall under no easy persecution. And as there are many that are only talkers, so there are many that are unprofitable talkers. 'The beginning of the words of their mouth is foolishness, and the end of his talk is mischievous madness,' Eccles. x. 13. And as there are many unprofitable talkers, so there are many unseasonable talkers, that place one word where another should stand. 'A wise man discerneth time and judgment,' Eccles. viii. 4. And as there are many unseasonable talkers, so there are many rash talkers, who speak first and think afterwards, chap. v. 2. God hath set a double bar about the tongue—the teeth and the lips,—that men should not speak rashly. Words once spoken cannot return. A man that thinks before he speaks, seldom repents of what he speaks. Silence is far better than rash speaking, or than vain speaking, &c.

O sirs, the tongue is the nimble interpreter of the heart. If there be piety or iniquity at the bottom of your hearts, your tongues will discover it, Mat. xii. 43, 44. The stream riseth not above the fountain. We know not what metal the bell is made of by[2] the clapper. What is in the well will be in the bucket. What is in the warehouse will be in the shop. So what is in the heart will be in the mouth. If there be anything of God, of Christ, of grace, of heaven, of hell, of sin, of the world, of self in the bottom of your souls, your tongues will discover it. Man, saith one, is like a bell, and his tongue like the clapper, [Plutarch.] So long as this standeth still, he may be thought to be without any flaw, craze, or crack in him; but let it once stir, and then he discovers himself presently. No man can so change himself, but his heart may sometimes be seen at his tongue's end. Men watch interpreters. Oh that, on the Lord's day especially, you would make more conscience of watching your tongues! If the tongue be not watched, it will be sin's solicitor-general; it will be a bawd to all lusts: it will plead for sin, and defend sin, and lessen sin, and provoke to sin, and shew the pleasure of the heart in sin. There are but five virtues of the tongue reckoned up by philosophers; but there are twenty several sins

[1] Alexander forgave many sharp swords, but never any sharp tongues, &c.
[2] Query, 'but by'?—G.

of the tongue reckoned up by Peraldus.[1] The Arabians have a proverb, 'Take heed thy tongue cut not thy throat.' Many a man's tongue has cut his throat; that is, it hath been his ruin.[2] Our Chronicles make mention of one Burdet, a merchant, who, living at the sign of the Crown in Cheapside, in the days of King Edward the Fourth, in the year 1483, jestingly said to his son that he would leave him heir of the crown, meaning the sign of the crown where he lived; for which he was apprehended, and within four hours hanged, drawn, and quartered. The tongue is often like a sharp razor, that, instead of shaving the hair, cuts the throat. If a man do not look well about him, he may every day be in danger of dying by his tongue. 'Life and death,' saith Solomon, 'are in the power of the tongue,' Prov. xviii. 21. Gaping-mouthed men are noted for fools by Lucian; and a better and a wiser man than Lucian hath told us that 'the lips of a fool will swallow up himself,' Eccles. x. 12. Ah, how good had it been for many that they had been born dumb! The tongue can easily travel all the world over, and wound men's names and credits in this country; and that in this city and that in this town, and that in this family, and that in a trice run from one place to another: here it bites, and there it tears: in this place it leaves a blot, and in that it gives a wound; and therefore you have cause to watch your tongues on every day, but especially on the Lord's day. There are many whose tongues do more mischief, and travel further on the Sabbath-day, than they do on all the other days of the week. You ought to keep a strict guard upon your tongues every day, but on the Lord's day you should double your guard. Satan without you, and that strong party that he hath within you, will do all they can so to oil your tongues on that day as to make you miscarry more ways than one, if you do not carefully look about you. Are there none on that day that do watch your words, to deride you and jeer you? Jer. xx. 10. Yes. Are there none on that day that do watch your words, either to ensnare you or trepan you? Yes. Are there none on that day that do watch your words, that they may find matter, if possible, either to reprove you or to reproach you?[3] Yes. Are there none on that day that do watch your words, that do hang upon your lips, expecting to be instructed, edified, confirmed, comforted, and strengthened by you? Yes. Well, then, if this be your case, how highly it doth concern you on this day to watch your words, I shall leave you to judge. O sirs, all your words, whether good or bad, are all noted and observed by God, as you may see by comparing the scriptures in the margin together.[4] If a person were by us that should book all our words from Sabbath-day morning to Sabbath-day night, and the like on other days, would we not be very careful what we spoke? Why, God is by and hears all. Athenodorus, a heathen, used to say, that all men ought to be very careful of their

[1] Qu. Pelbartus?—G.

[2] James iii. 3, 11. The Holy Ghost sheweth the mischief of the tongue by the several characters by which he brands it. He calls it the flattering tongue, the double tongue, the deceitful tongue, the lying tongue, the perverse tongue, &c., Ps. lii. 2; Prov. xviii. 21; Eccles. x. 12; Ps. xix. 4, and lxxiii. 9; Mat. xxviii. 13, 15.

[3] It is better for a man to watch and stop his own mouth by silence, than to have it stopped by others' reproofs.

[4] Ps. cxxxix. 4; Isa. lix 3; Jer. xxxiii. 24, and xliv. 25; Mal. iii. 16, 17; Job xlii. 7 Mat. xii. 37.

actions and words, because God was everywhere, and beheld all that was done and said. And Zeno, a wise heathen, affirmeth that God seeth and taketh notice of our very thoughts; how much more then of our words! O sirs, how many men and women are there that are choice of what they eat, that are not choice of what they speak—that are curious about the food which goes into their mouths, lest it should hurt or poison them, who are nowise curious about the words that go out of their mouths, lest they should hurt or poison others!

Of all the members in the body, there is none so serviceable to Satan as the tongue. And therefore Satan spares Job's tongue; his grand design being not to make Job a beggar, but a blasphemer. Job was blistered all over by Satan, only his tongue was not blistered. Satan thought by that member to work Job to fight against God, and the peace of his own soul. It is queried in the schools what was the first sin of the first angel that fell; for they assert that one fell first, then the rest. Now there are very many opinions about it. Some say it was envy, others discontent; and some say it was their refusing to undertake the charge that was given to them to minister unto man. Others think it was a spiritual luxury; others ingratitude. The most and best say pride, but wherein that pride consisted is not easily determined, nor by them unanimously resolved; and by some it is as confidently observed that it was a sin of the tongue. Now if these last have hit the mark, how highly doth it concern us all to set a watch before the door of our lips at all times, but especially on the Lord's day! Now considering how wonderful apt and prone Christians are to be speaking their own words, yea, foolish, vain, worldly, and unprofitable words on the Lord's day, give me leave to offer to your serious consideration these four things:—

[1.] First, *Where the Lord hath commanded the whole man to rest from servile works, there he commands the hand to rest from working, the foot from walking, and the tongue from talking.* But in the fourth commandment, 'Thou shalt do no manner of work,' Exod. iv. 10, the Lord hath commanded the whole man to rest from servile works. And therefore the tongue from talking of this or that worldly business. But,

[2.] Secondly, *Those things which as lets hinder the duties of the Lord's day are forbidden:* but worldly words as lets hinder the duties of the Lord's day; therefore worldly words are forbidden. But,

[3.] Thirdly, *Where bodily works are forbidden, there those things are forbidden which hinder the sanctifying of the Sabbath, as much or more than bodily works do:* but bodily works are forbidden in the fourth commandment; therefore worldly words, which hinder more the sanctifying of the Sabbath than bodily works do, are forbidden in the same commandment. That worldly words do hinder the sanctifying of the Sabbath, as much or more than bodily works, is evident by this, among other arguments that might be produced, that a man may work alone, but he cannot talk alone. But,

[4.] Fourthly, *That commandment which ties the outward man from the deed done, that commandment ties the tongue from talking of the same:* but the fourth commandment ties the outward man from worldly works; and therefore that command ties the tongue from worldly words. Certainly all those persons that make the Lord's day a reckoning-day with workmen, as some do, or a directing-day, what shall be done the next week, as others do; or a day of idle talk about this worldly business or that, or about this person or that, or about this fashion or that, or about this man's matters or that, or about this pleasure or that, or about this profit or that, or about this man's calling or that, or about this gossip's tale or that, &c., all such persons are profaners and no sanctifiers of the Lord's day.

I have been the longer upon this particular, to confute and recover those Christians who give their tongues too great a liberty on the Lord's day.

Now in these fourteen particulars I have shewed you how the Sabbath is to be sanctified. O sirs, as you desire to see London rebuilt; as you desire to see London in as great, or greater, prosperity and glory as she hath been in; as you desire to see her once more the bulwark of the nation; as you desire to see her a shield and shelter to her faithful friends at home, and a terror and dread to her proudest enemies abroad; as you desire that she may be an eternal excellency, a joy of many generations; as you desire the Lord to be for ever a wall of fire about her, and a glory in the midst of her, make conscience of sanctifying the Sabbath in a right manner; make it your business and work to sanctify the Sabbath according to those fourteen rules which I have now laid down, Ps. xlviii. 12, 13; Cant. vi. 4; Isa. lx. 15; Zech. ii. 5.

I know there is a desperate opposition and contrariety in the hearts of carnal men to the strict observation of the Sabbath. When Moses had first received a commandment concerning the observation of the Sabbath, his authority could not so prevail with the Jews, but that some of them would be gadding abroad to seek manna on the Sabbath-day, contrary to an express prohibition, Exod. xvi. 25, 31; yea, when it was death to gather sticks on that day, chap. xxxi. 13–16, yet in contempt of heaven itself one ventures upon the breach of the law. How sadly and frequently the prophets have lamented and complained of the breach of the Sabbath, I have in this treatise already discovered, and therefore need say no more of it in this place. The horrid profanation of this day in France, Holland, Germany, Sweden, and in these three nations, England, Scotland, and Ireland, and among all protestants everywhere else, is and must be for a sore lamentation. The Sabbath in all ages hath been more or less crucified between profaneness and superstition, as Christ, the Lord of the Sabbath, was crucified between two thieves. When the observation of the Sabbath came to be more sacred and solemn in public performances, which was about Nehemiah's time, as is conceived, presently after Satan stirred up some hypocrites, who run into such an extreme of superstition, that they held that they might not stir out of their places, nor kill a flea, and a thousand such like fooleries. Yea, some dangerous fooleries they laboured to distil into the people; as that they might not draw a sword to defend themselves in a common invasion, &c.

For a close, remember this, that there are no Christians in all the world comparable to those, for the power of godliness and heights of grace, holiness, and communion with God, who are most strict, serious, studious, and conscientious in sanctifying of the Lord's day. Such as are careless, remiss, light, slight, formal, and carnal upon the Sabbath-day, they will be as bad, if not worse, on every other day in the week. The true reason why the power of godliness is fallen to so low an ebb, both in this and in other countries also, is because the Sabbath is no more strictly and conscientiously observed in this land, and in those other countries where the name of the Lord is made known. The Jews were never serious in the observation of their Sabbaths, till they smarted seventy years in Babylon for their former profanation of it. And who can look upon the ashes of London, and not see how dearly the citizens have paid for their profaning of the Lord's day? And oh that all these short hints might be so blessed from heaven, as to work us all to a more strict, serious, and conscientious sanctifying of the Lord's day, according to those directions or rules that I have in this treatise laid before you.

And thus I have done with those duties that are incumbent upon those who have been burnt up by that late dreadful fire that hath turned London into a ruinous heap.

I come now to those duties that are incumbent upon those whose habitations are yet standing, as monuments of divine wisdom, power, and grace. O sirs, the flames have been near you, a devouring fire hath consumed many thousand habitations round about you, and you and your habitations have been as so many brands plucked out of the fire! Oh how highly doth it concern you seriously and frequently to lay to heart the singular goodness and kindness of God towards you, manifested in the mighty preservations, protections, and salvations that he has vouchsafed to you when you were surrounded with all manner of hazards and dangers! Oh that you would strive, as for life, to come up to duties which are certainly incumbent upon all those who have escaped the burning flames!

Quest. But you will say, What are they?

Ans. These that follow:—

[1.] First, It highly concerns you who have escaped the fiery dispensation, to *take heed of those sins which bring the fiery rod, and which have turned many of your neighbours out of house and home,* 2 Pet. ii. 6; Luke xvii. 32; Jer. vii. 12; 1 Sam. iv. 11; Ps. lxxviii. 60. What they are, I have already declared at large. If those sins that have brought the fiery judgment upon your neighbours are to be found among you, you have cause to fear the fiery rod, or else some other judgment that shall be equivalent to it. If you sin with others, you shall suffer with others, except there be found repentance on your side, and pardoning grace on God's. The Lord hath punished your neighbours with that judgment of judgments,—the fire; and he expects that you should take notice thereof, and be instructed thereby, to take heed of those sins that they have been judged for, else the same or worser judgments will certainly befall you. Because Edom made no good use of Jerusalem's sufferings, therefore the Lord threatens her that shame should cover her, and that she should be cut off for ever, Jer. iii. 8; Obad. 11–14. God expects that the judgments that he hath executed upon all round about you should awaken you out of security, and work in you a holy dread of his name, and provoke you to repentance for what is past, and engage you to a more exact walking with him for the time to come. But,

[2.] Secondly, It highly concerns you *not to think those who are burnt up to be greater sinners than yourselves who have escaped the consuming flames*, Isa. v. 22-24, and li. 17, 22, 23; Jer. xxv. 15, 30. Some there were that told Christ of certain Galileans whose blood Pilate had mingled with their sacrifices—an argument of God's sore displeasure in the eye of man, to be surprised with a bloody death even in the act of God's service—'But Jesus answered, Suppose ye that these Galileans were sinners above all the Galileans, because they suffered such things? I tell you, Nay; but, except ye repent, ye shall all likewise perish,' Luke xiii. 1-3. And Christ confirmeth it by another parallel to it, of the men upon whom the tower in Siloam fell: Luke xiii. 4, 5, 'Or those eighteen, upon whom the tower in Siloam fell, think ye that they were sinners above all men that dwell in Jerusalem? I tell you, Nay; but, except ye repent, ye shall all likewise perish.' Doubtless there are many fifties in London whose habitations are laid desolate, who were more righteous than many of those whose houses have escaped the consuming flames. Judgments many times begin at the house of God: the hand of God is many times heaviest upon the holiest of people, 1 Pet. iv. 17; Ezek. ix. 6. Job was stripped of all his earthly comforts, and set upon a dunghill to scrape his sores with potsherds, Job i.; and yet Job had not at that time his fellow in all the east country for a man fearing God and eschewing evil. Job was a perfect, peerless man, and yet had his habitation laid in ashes, and his substance destroyed, when his neighbours round about him enjoyed their all without disturbance. Doubtless many of them whose houses are turned into a ruinous heap were good people—people of unblamable lives, people of exemplary lives, yea, earthly angels, if compared with many of those who have escaped the fiery rod. Many have drunk deep of this cup of wrath, who are a people of his choicest love; and therefore do not judge all them to be greater sinners than yourselves that have not escaped the fiery rod as well as yourselves. You who have escaped the consuming flames should make other men's lashes your lessons, and their burnings your warnings. You should not so much eye what others have suffered, as what yourselves have deserved. But,

[3.] Thirdly, It concerns you *to be much in blessing of God that your habitations are standing, when others' habitations are laid desolate round about you.* But here look that your thankfulness is, (1.) Real; (2.) Great; (3.) Cordial; (4.) Practical; and, (5.) Constant. No thankfulness below such a thankfulness will become such whose habitations are standing monuments of God's free mercy. I have largely pressed this duty before, and therefore a touch here must suffice. But,

[4.] Fourthly, *Be not secure:* do not say, 'The bitterness of death is past,' as Agag did when he came before Samuel, stately and haughtily, with the garb and gait of a king, 1 Sam. xv. 32. Many times, when wicked men are in the greatest security, they are then nearest the highest pitch of misery. Is there not guilt enough upon all your hearts, and upon all your habitations, to expose them to as great a desolation as London lies under? *Ans.* Yes, yes. Why, then, do not you get off this guilt by frequent exercises of faith in the blood of Christ, or else prepare to drink of the same cup that London hath drunk of, or of a worse? Ponder seriously and frequently upon these scriptures: Isa. li. 17, 'Awake, awake, stand, O Jerusalem, which hast drunk at the hand of the Lord the cup of his fury: thou hast drunken the dregs of the cup of trembling, and wrung them out.' Ver. 22, 'Thus saith thy Lord the Lord, and thy God that pleadeth the cause of his people, Behold, I have taken out of thy hand the cup of trembling, even the dregs of the cup of my fury; thou shalt no more drink it again.' Ver. 23, 'But I will put it into the hands of them that afflict thee: which have said to thy soul, Bow down that we may go over; and thou hast laid thy body as the ground, and as the street, to them that went over.' Jer. xxv. 15, 'For thus saith the Lord God of Israel unto me, Take the wine-cup of this fury at my hand, and cause all the nations, to whom I send thee, to drink it.' Ver. 17, 'Then took I the cup at the Lord's hands, and made all the nations to drink, unto whom the Lord had sent me.' Ver. 18, 'To wit, Jerusalem, and the cities of Judah, and the kings thereof, and the princes thereof, to make them a desolation, an astonishment, an hissing, and a curse, as it is this day.' Ver. 28, 'And it shall be, if they refuse to take the cup at thine hand to drink, then shalt thou say unto them, Thus saith the Lord of hosts, Ye shall certainly drink.' Ver. 29, 'For lo, I begin to bring evil on the city which is called by my name, and should ye be utterly unpunished? Ye shall not be unpunished: I will call for a sword upon all the inhabitants of the earth, saith the Lord of hosts.' When Jerusalem hath drunk of the cup, if God be God, the nations round shall certainly drink of it.[1] God hath begun with London: poor London hath drunk deeply of the cup of God's fury; and therefore let the nations round repent, or prepare to drink of London's cup. Most of those sins that bring the fiery rod, if not all, are to be found in all the great cities of the world. And therefore let all the great cities in France, Spain, Italy, Germany, Holland, England, Ireland, Scotland, &c., take warning by London's desolation, and prepare to meet the Lord in the way of his fury: let them cease from doing evil, and learn to do well: let them repent in dust and ashes, lest they are laid in dust and ashes. Let them break off their sins, lest God throws down their walls and habitations by furious and devouring flames. Let all those whose habitations are still standing remember that the same sins, the same wrath, and the same malicious hands that has laid so many thousand habitations desolate, can lay theirs also desolate, except they reform and turn to the Most High.

[5.] Fifthly, It highly concerns you whose houses are standing monuments of God's mercy, *to shew much love, bowels, pity, and compassion to those who are burnt up and turned out of all: who are houseless, harbourless, and penniless this day*, Gen. xviii.; Ps. cii. 13; 2 Cor. xi. 29. God

[1] The particular kings and kingdoms that must drink of this cup are set down from ver 19 to ver. 28. See Lam. iv. 21, and Ezek. xxiii. 31–34.

takes it well at our hands when we pity those whom he thinks meet to punish. One of God's great ends in punishing of some is to stir up pity and compassion in others towards them. It should melt your hearts to see other men's substances melted in the flames. God hath threatened an evil, an only evil, without the least mixture of mercy, to such as shew no mercy to those in misery, Obad. 12, 13; James ii. 13. Who ever have beheld London in its former prosperity and glory, that cannot lament to see London laid desolate? The ashes of London seems to cry out, Have pity upon me, O my friends! Job vi. 14. They that will not lament upon the burnt citizens as the greatest objects of their pity, may one day be engulfed under the greatest misery. He was a Nabal, a sapless fellow, who shut up all bowels of pity against David in his misery, 1 Sam. xxv. 10, 11. They were cursed Edomites who did behold the ruin of Zion and not mourn over it, Ps. cxxxvii. 6-8. Let all burnt citizens remember, that usually God pities them most whom men pities least; but burnt citizens are not to be mocked or menaced, but mourned over.

[6.] Sixthly, It highly concerns you whose houses are standing monuments of God's mercy, *to lift up a prayer for all those as are fallen under this heavy judgment of fire*, Num. xi. 1–3; 2 Kings xix. 4. When you are in the mount, be sure you bear the sad condition of the burnt citizens upon your hearts: Neh. i. 3, 'And they said unto me, The remnant that are left of the captivity there in the province are in great affliction and reproach: the wall of Jerusalem also is broken down, and the gates thereof are burnt with fire.' Well, what doth Nehemiah do? *Ans.* He lifts up a prayer for them, ver. 5–11. O sirs, your prayers must not be pent or confined to your own private interests, but extended to the benefit of all God's suffering servants. Philo the Jew, discoursing of Aaron's ephod, which he put on when he went to pray, saith it was a representation of the whole world, having in it all colours, to represent the condition of all states of all people whatsoever. It is brave, when we are in the mount, to bear the conditions of others upon our hearts, as well as our own, especially theirs whom the hand of the Lord hath severely reached. The best of men have been much in prayer for others; witness Moses, David, Job, Jeremiah, Daniel, Paul, Rom. i. 9; 2 Tim. i. 3. And it is very observable that our Lord Jesus Christ, who is our great pattern, was very much in this noble work, for you shall find in John xvii. that he puts up but one petition for himself, in ver. 1, which petition is repeated again in ver. 5. And all the rest of his time he spent in praying both for the converted and unconverted. Now shall our Lord Jesus Christ put up many requests for others and but one for himself, and shall we put up all our requests for ourselves and not one for others? Among the Persians, he that offered sacrifice prayed for all his countrymen.[1] These Persians will one day rise in judgment against many who are called Christians, and yet make no conscience of lifting up a prayer for those that are under the afflicting hand of God. He that prayeth for himself and not for others, is fitly compared by some to a hedgehog, who laps himself within his own soft down, and

[1] Herodot., lib. i.

turns his bristles to all the world besides. The Jews have a saying, 'That since the destruction of Jerusalem, the door of prayer hath been shut up.' Oh that we had not cause to fear that, since the burning of London, the door of prayer both for ourselves and one another hath been too much shut amongst us! Oh that all you whose habitations are standing, would seriously consider—

(1.) That none need prayer more than the burnt citizens.

(2.) You do not know how soon their case may be yours; the same hand or hands that hath made them desolate, may make you desolate also.

(3.) Else what do you more than others? Mat. v. 47.

(4.) To pity and pray for those that are in misery, is honourable and commendable.

(5.) It is one of the most compendious ways in the world to prevent all those calamities and miseries that now you fear, and that you think you shall shortly feel.

(6) To lift up a prayer for those whose sufferings have been sore, is no costly nor chargeable duty, and therefore buckle to it. But,

[7.] Seventhly, It highly concerns you whose houses are standing monuments of God's mercy, seriously to consider *that some men's escaping of very great judgments is not properly a preservation, but a reservation to some greater destruction*, Gen. xiv. and xix. compared; Exod. xiv. 28; 1 Kings xix. Witness those kings who escaped the edge of the sword, and were afterwards destroyed by fire and brimstone from heaven; and witness Pharaoh, who escaped all the ten plagues of Egypt in order to his being buried with his host in the Red Sea. And witness Sennacherib, who escaped the sword of the destroying angel in order to his falling by the swords of his own sons. Upon what discontentment his sons rose up to slay him is uncertain. Some say, [Castalion,] it was because he preferred their younger brother Esharhaddon to the kingdom, who was the last of the Assyrian monarchs; for after him the monarchy was translated from the Assyrians to the Babylonians. R. Solomon, as Lyra cites him, saith that the great men of the country having lost each one his son, brother, or friend, in that expedition against Jerusalem, were so provoked that they meant to destroy him, which he hearing, fled to the idol's temple, and prayed and vowed that if his god would deliver him from this danger, he would give these two sons for sacrifice to him; then they hearing of this came and slew him there. I shall leave you to your choice whether you will give credit to this relation, or look upon it as a rabbinical invention.[1] In this judgment that fell upon Sennacherib there are these things remarkable:—

[1.] That he should see so great and well prepared an army so suddenly destroyed, Isa. xxxvii. 36.

[2.] That the storm should mainly fall upon the great ones of his army: 2 Chron. xxxii. 22, 'And the Lord sent an angel which cut off all the mighty men of valour, and the leaders and captains in the camp of the king of Assyria.' From whence we may easily gather

[1] If Tobit may be credited, he lived not fifty-five days after his return to Nineveh. Tob. ii. 24.

that some of the weaker sort, some of the refuse of the army, were spared—the prime men and great officers of his army being only smitten; upon which account the king and his ragged regiments became contemptible.[1]

[3.] That he should be forced to fly into his own country with shame and contempt; his general and great officers being destroyed, he had no heart to keep the field, having none to order the battle; and the dread and terror of the Lord and his judgments abiding upon him and his army, he provides for his own safety by fleeing home with his routed, scattered troops.

[4.] That himself should be slain, and that in the temple of his idol, and in the very act of his idolatry, and that by his own sons that came out of his own bowels, as the Holy Ghost observes, 2 Chron. xxxii. 21, 'And when he was come into the house of his god, they that came forth of his own bowels slew him there with the sword.' Certainly this was a far greater judgment than if he had fallen by the sword of the destroying angel. And witness those very persons who escaped pestilence, were now burnt in the very flames, as well as their houses and estates. O sirs, though you have escaped the burning flames, yet you do not know what other judgments you may be reserved to; and therefore be not secure, but be wakeful and watchful, and provide for the worst. Unexpected judgments many times seize upon persons, and slay them, as the soldier slew Archimedes, whilst he was busy in drawing lines in the dust. Take heed of saying, surely the worst is past.

[8.] Eighthly and lastly, *Do not rejoice in the fiery calamity that hath passed upon others: do not glory in your neighbours' ruins.* The fire-fly leaps and dances in the fire; and so do many wicked men rejoice in the sufferings of others, Prov. xxiv. 17, 18.[2] Such as rejoice in the sufferings of others, are sick of the devil's disease; but from that disease the Lord deliver all your souls! It is sad to insult over those whom God hath humbled; it is high wickedness to triumph over those to whom God hath given a cup of astonishment to drink. Such as make the desolations of their neighbours to be the matter either of their secret repast or open exultation, such may fear that the very dregs of divine wrath is reserved for them. It is bad playing upon the harp, because others have been put to hang their harps upon the willows. We must not pray with him in the tragedy, that it may rain calamities; nor with Clemens his Gnostic, 'Give me calamities that I may glory in them.' There cannot be a greater evidence of a wicked heart than for a man to be merry because others are in misery. So without repentance such may one day dance in infernal flames, who have sung and danced at the remembrance of London's flames: Prov. xvii. 5, 'He that is glad at calamities,' that is, at the calamities of others, 'shall not be unpunished.' If God be God, such as congratulate our miseries, instead of condoling them, shall be sure to be pun-

[1] The mighty monarchs of Assyria used to go forth to war with 500,000, and sometimes with 1,000,000 men; and therefore this slaughter may well be understood of the grandees of his army. Wherefore Josephus saith, he fled with his army.

[2] Seriously ponder upon chap. xxv. and xxxv. of Ezekiel, and Lam. i. 21; 2 Sam. xvi. 17, 25; and Lam. iii. 14, 45.

ished with the worst of punishments; for such do not only sin against the law of grace, but also against the very law of nature—the law of nature teaching men to sympathise with those that are in misery, and not to rejoice over them because of their miseries. O sirs, do not make others' mourning your music, do not make others' tears your wine, as you would not be made drunk at last with the wine of astonishment.

THE GLORIOUS DAY OF THE SAINTS' APPEARANCE.

NOTE.

For notices of Rainsborough—whose 'Funeral Sermon' composes the 'Glorious Day of the Saints' Appearance'—see our Memoir, Vol. I. pp. xxx., xxxi. We there state that certain contemporary broad-sheets might be given here; but on re-examining them, they prove such poor doggerel as to be unworthy of reprint. The curious in such out-of-the-way literature will find them in the British Museum. In that posthumous tractate of John Vicars, 'Dagon Demolished: or, Twenty Admirable Examples of God's severe Justice and Displeasure against the subscribers of the late Engagement against our Lawfull Soveraign, King Charles the Second, and the whole House of Peers,' . . . . [1660, 4to,] we have Rainsborough as one of the 'Examples,' as follows:—'Collonel Rainsborow, a mighty engager, and prime stickler for the power at Westminster, a desperate header of the Levellers, and Admiral of the Navy at Sea, was suddenly also assaulted by a company of cavaliers at Pomfract town, in Yorkshire, in an inne, and there murthered by them,' [p. 10.] The mistake as to the scene of the crime is only one of many blunders of all sorts; 'Pontefract' was the town whence the royalist murderers came. The item concerning Rainsborough as 'Admiral at Sea' confirms our conjecture that Brooks's sea-services were probably under him. See Memoir, as above. The title-page is given below.*—G.

* THE
Glorious day of the
SAINTS Appearance;
Calling for
A glorious conversation from all Believers.

Delivered in a Sermon
By THOMAS BROOKS,
Preacher of the Gospel at *Thomas Apostles*
at the interment of the Corps of that
renowned Commander,
Colonell *Thomas Rainsborough*
Who was treacherously murthered on the Lords day in the morning at *Doncaster*, October 29. 1648. and honourably interred the 14th of *November* following, in the Chappell at *Wapping* neare *London.*

Isa. 26. 19.
Thy dead men shall live (together with) my dead body shall they arise. Awake, and sing yee that dwell in the dust; for thy dew is as the dew of herbs, and the earth shall cast forth her dead.

2 Pet. 3. 14.
Wherefore (beloved) seeing that yee look for such things, be diligent that yee may be found of him in peace, without spot, and blameless.

London;
Printed by M. S. for *Rapha Harford,* and *Matthew Simmons,* and are to be sold at the Bible in Queens-head Alley in Pater-noster-row, and in *Aldersgate-streete.*
1648. [4to.—G.]

THE EPISTLE DEDICATORY.

To the Right Honourable THOMAS, LORD FAIRFAX, Lord General of all the Parliament's Forces in England; such honour and happiness as is promised to all that love and honour the Lord Jesus.

I purpose not, Right Honourable, to insinuate myself or my poor endeavours into your favour by fine words and feigned commendations of your virtues. A sincere heart abhors it, and a wise heart doth both suspect that art, and account it base. Right Honourable, when I preached upon this subject of the saints' glorious appearance at the last, He that knows all hearts and thoughts, knows that I had not the least thought to put it to the press. And that partly because the meditations following were not the meditations of a week, no, nor of two days, but of some few hours—I having but short warning to provide, and other things falling in within the compass of that short time that did divert my thoughts some other ways; but mainly because of that little little worth that is in it. And yet, Right Honourable, the intentions of some to put it to the press, in case I would not consent to have it printed—by which means truth and myself might have been co-partners in suffering—and the strong importunity of many precious souls, hath borne me down and subdued me to them. They besieged me so strongly that they have taken away this little thing, which they are pleased to call [a] good prize; but it will be well if they be not mistaken. I shall look upon it as free grace and mercy to them and me, if they, having made a prey of it, find it worth their having. I stood out against them, not because I prized it, but because I thought it not good enough for them. But since it is fallen into their hands, my desire is, that the rich blessing of God may so accompany it, as that it may reach their hearts, and be better to them than the choicest riches of this world.

Now may it please your Excellency, the reasons why I have gladly taken the occasion to make honourable mention of your name, are three:—

First, Because the sense of your great worth has wheeled my thoughts in this kind towards you.

Secondly, That I might testify not only to your Honour, but to all the world, my thankful remembrance and due acknowledgment of your Lordship's undeserved respect towards me.

Thirdly, Because the matter doth relate to the glorious appearing of one of England's worthies, with the rest of the saints, to one whom your Excellency did dearly love, highly prize, and greatly honour.

My noble Lord, I shall much rejoice if this poor mite may in any measure help forward your faith and joy in the Lord Jesus: which that it may, I shall humbly supplicate the throne of grace. My Lord, this is your greatest honour, that you account the opportunities of service for God and his people your greatest honour upon earth: that your Honour hath appeared, in the darkest night and in the greatest storms, for the honour, the safety, the sound peace and liberty of the saints and this kingdom—and that notwithstanding all the discouragements your Excellency hath met with, through the neutrality, apostasy, and treachery of men, high and low, in this kingdom. Ah! my Lord, what a mercy is this, that the true nobility of your Lordship's spirit, scorning such baseness, hath delivered you from those checks, wounds, and lashes of conscience which those forenamed wretches lie under, and from that shame and confusion of face which hath already begun to seize upon them here, but shall more fully and dreadfully seize on them in the great day of account, when the books shall be opened, and all the treachery and baseness to enslave the saints and this kingdom shall be discovered!

My noble Lord, through the glorious presence of God with you, you have done gloriously in endeavouring the full rescue of the people of God from the hands of cruel and unreasonable men, who have left no stone unturned, that their lusts and will upon the people of God might be satisfied. My Lord, as you have pleaded the cause of the people of God, and as you have appeared for them, do so still: for the Lord will side with those that side with his saints, and they that seek their lives seek yours also. But the comfort is, God will make Jerusalem 'a cup of poison unto all the people round about:' he will make Jerusalem 'a burdensome stone: and all that burden themselves with it shall be cut in pieces, though all the people of the earth gather together against it,' Zech. xii. 2, 3.

My noble Lord, for the great things you have already done for this kingdom, the high praises of God are in the mouths of the saints, and the children unborn shall bless you, and bless God for you. And when the name of tyrants, malignants, neuters, and apostates shall rot, the memorial of your name shall be for ever precious among the 'precious sons of Zion.' And that your Excellency may do yet more and more gloriously, the breathing and desire of my soul to God for your Lordship is, that the Lord would take up your spirit into such sweet and full enjoyment of himself and of that glory above, that may enable you divinely to trample upon all those things that may anyway hinder you from solacing and delighting your soul in the love, light, and sweetness that is in the bosom of Christ; that the Lord will take you by the hand, whenever you are in the dark, and lead out your spirit in such ways that may be for the honour of his name, for the joy of his people, and for the real happiness and welfare of this kingdom. That in all your hours of temptation you may find the power of the lively prayers of the saints—in which and in whose affection you have as great a share as any mortal that breathes—strengthening and raising you above them all. That no weapon nor device nor counsel that is formed against you may prosper; that the eternal God will be your refuge, and that under you may be his everlasting arms; that your soul may be swallowed up in the sweet enjoyment of God, that so every bitter may be made sweet unto you, and that your last days may be your best; that the longer you live, the more glorious for God and his people you may act; that God will 'guide you by his counsel here, and after all receive you to glory.'

My Lord, you know that God doth not 'despise the day of small things;' and I believe that the fear of the great God is so strong upon your Lordship's spirit that your Honour will not. I humbly crave your Excellency, and all others that shall read this sermon, to overlook the mistakes of the printer, I having no time to wait upon the press to correct what haply may be found amiss. The perusal and acceptance of what I here present in love and out of a due respect unto your Excellency, I submit to your wisdom, and humbly take my leave, remaining your Lordship's, in all humble and due observance,

THOMAS BROOKS.

CHRIST IS THE LIFE OF BELIEVERS.

When Christ, who is our life, shall appear, then shall ye also appear with him in glory.—COL. III. 4.

THE apostle, in the verse before, tells them that their 'life is hid with Christ in God.' These saints might object: but when shall that hidden life be discovered? when shall that life of glory be manifested? He answers in the text: 'When Christ, who is our life, shall appear, then shall ye also appear with him in glory.' The words do speak out the time when the glorious life of believers shall be manifested, and that is, when Christ shall appear in glory. I have in some other place observed from these words this point—namely, that *the Lord Jesus Christ is the life of believers.*

'When Christ, who is our *life*, shall appear.' Life here is, by a metonymy, put for the author of life.

We have shewed that Jesus Christ, he is first the *author* of a believer's spiritual life. In the 14th of John, 'I am the Way, the Truth, and the Life,' (ver. 6.)

Secondly, Jesus Christ, he is the *matter* of a believer's spiritual life: in John vi. 48, 'I am the bread of life.' The original hath it more elegantly, ἐγω εἰμι ὁ ἄρτος τῆς ζωῆς, 'I am the bread of that life,' that is, of that spiritual life of which before the Lord Jesus Christ had spoken.

Thirdly, Jesus Christ is the *exerciser and actor* of the spiritual life of believers: John xv. 5, 'Without me ye can do nothing.' The original is, χωρις ἐμου, *seorsim a me;* [Calvin, Cameron, &c.] separate from me, or apart from me, ye can do, &c.

Fourthly, The Lord Jesus Christ, he is *the strengthener and the cherisher* of a believer's spiritual life, Ps. cxxxviii. 3, 'In the day when I cried, thou didst answer me, and strengthen me with strength in my soul.'

Lastly, The Lord Jesus Christ, he is the *completer*, he is the *finisher* of the spiritual life of a saint, Heb. xii. 2; Phil. i. 6. We have opened this point, and have made several uses of it. There were one or two things that we could not reach nor speak to when we treated upon this subject; I will only mention them, and so I pass to that special point that I intend to speak to at this time.

Is the Lord Jesus Christ a believer's life? To pass by what we have further spoken upon this point—this same, by way of use, doth serve to bespeak all believers *not to repent of anything they have done, or suffered, or lost, for the Lord Jesus.* Oh, is the Lord Jesus Christ a believer's life? Why, then, let no believer be disquieted, nor overwhelmed and dejected, for any loss or for any sorrow or suffering that he meets with for the Lord Jesus Christ's sake. What a base and unworthy spirit is it for a man to be troubled and disquieted in himself for anything that he shall do or suffer for his own natural life! Oh, Jesus Christ is thy life; do not say this mercy is too dear for Christ, nor that comfort is too great for Christ. Christ is the life of a believer: what wilt thou not do for thy life? The devil hit right when he said, 'Skin for skin, and all that a man hath will he give for his life.' Oh, what should a man then do for Jesus Christ, who is his life! You noble hearts whose particular God hath come near in this sad loss, remember this, that Christ is a believer's life; Christ is that glorious champion's life. Therefore be not overwhelmed, for doubtless he is now triumphing in the love, in the light, in the goodness, and in the glory of him who is his life. Let the sense of this sad loss kindly affect you, but let it not discourage you.

But, secondly, If the Lord Jesus Christ be a believer's life, then this serves to bespeak all believers *highly to prize the Lord Jesus.* Oh, it is this Christ that is thy life; it is not thy husband, it is not thy child, it is not this or that thing; neither is it this ordinance or that that is a believer's life. No; it is the Lord Jesus Christ that is the author, that is the matter, that is the exerciser, that is the strengthener, that is the completer, of a believer's life. You prize great ones; the Lord Jesus Christ is great—he is King of kings, and Lord of lords. You prize others for their wisdom and knowledge: the Lord Jesus hath in himself all the treasures of wisdom and knowledge, Col. ii. 3. You prize others for their beauty: the Lord Jesus Christ is the beautifullest of ten thousand, Cant. v. 10. You prize others for their usefulness: the Lord Jesus Christ is the right hand of a believer, without which he can do nothing. The believer may say of Christ as the philosopher said of the heavens, *Tolle cœlum, nullus ero*—Take away the heavens, and I shall be nobody; so take away Jesus Christ, and a believer is nobody—nobody to perform any action, nobody to bear any affliction, nobody to conquer corruption, nobody to withstand temptation, nobody to improve mercies, nor nobody to joy in others' grace. Oh, prize Jesus Christ!

Again, Consider the Lord Jesus Christ doth highly prize you; you are as the apple of his eye; he accounts you his fulness; you are his jewels; therefore prize him who sets such a high price on you. But I hasten to what I intend—

In the last place, Remember *a Christ highly prized will be Christ gloriously obeyed.* As men prize the Lord Jesus Christ, so they will obey him. The great reason why Jesus Christ is no more obeyed, is because he is no more prized. Men look upon him as a person of no worth, no dignity, no glory; they make slight of him, and that is the reason they are so poor in their obedience to him. Oh, if the sons of men did but more divinely prize Christ, they would more purely, and more fully, and more constantly obey him. Let this bespeak all your hearts highly to prize the Lord Jesus, who is your life. But I shall pass from this, to that point that in order to this occasion I shall now speak to: 'When Christ, who is our life, shall appear, then shall ye appear also with him in glory.' The observation that I shall speak to at this time is, that *believers shall at last appear glorious.*

It is a very choice point, and a useful point, in order to the present providence. I shall not be long in the doctrinal part, because the application is that that I have my eye most upon. The scriptures that speak of this truth I will but name them; at your leisure you may read them: Judges xv. 14; 1 Cor. xv. 43, 44, 51–55; 1 Thes. iv. 13, *seq.;* Mat. xix. 26–28. These scriptures clearly speak out this truth, that the people of God shall at last appear glorious.

The reasons of this point, why they shall appear glorious, are these as follow. They shall appear glorious;—

1. First of all, because that day is *a day of solemnity; it is the marriage-day of the Lamb.* I may allude to that Rev. xix. 6–8. It is true, believers in this life, they are spiritually married to the Lord Jesus; but this marriage is not celebrated till this day, when the saints shall appear in their glory. God the Father hath put off the celebration of this glorious marriage to this last day, when believers' mourning weeds shall be taken off, and their glorious robes shall be put on; when God himself shall, as a Father, be more fully and gloriously present among all his children; whenas he shall have all his attendants visible, I mean his angels, which now are not visible, in that spiritual marriage between his Son and believers.

2. A second reason that believers at last shall appear glorious, is this, because *they shall all appear at the last as kings crowned.* Here believers are kings elected, but at that last day they shall all appear as kings crowned. Here believers have a crown in reversion, but at the last they shall have a crown in possession; the Lord will set it upon their heads: 2 Tim. iv. 7, 8, 'I have fought the good fight of faith, I have finished my course; henceforth is laid up for me'—the Greek word ἀποκειται, is 'safely laid up'—'a crown of glory which he shall give me at that day.' I have now, saith he, a crown in reversion; but at that day I shall have it in possession; then it shall be set upon my head, and then angels and devils and murderers shall say, 'Lo! here is the man that God is pleased to honour.'

3. Then a third reason why believers at the last shall appear glorious, is for *the terror and the horror of all ungodly wretches that have opposed, persecuted, and murdered them.* They shall appear glorious for the greater torment of such ungodly souls. Oh, there is nothing that will make sinners in that great day more to tear their hair, to beat their breasts, to wring their hands, and to gnaw their own hearts, than this, when they shall behold those advanced and those appearing in their glory, whom they have slighted, and despised, and most treacherously murdered, here below. I doubt not but there are some base, unworthy spirits here; but let them know that there is a day coming when the saints shall appear in glory, and then the mangled ones and this thrice-worthy champion shall appear among the rest, to the terror, horror, and confusion of these murderous wretches

that have brought the guilt of his blood upon them. It will be with you and with all ungodly wretches as it was with Haman: he, like an ungodly wretch, had plotted and contrived the destruction of the Jews; he had sold them, as it were, to bondage, tyranny, and slavery; but the Lord wheels things gloriously about, and Haman comes to the king, (Esther vi.): saith the king to him, 'What shall be done to the man whom the king is pleased to honour?' Saith he, 'Let the king's horse be brought, and glorious robes put on him, and let the chief nobles of the kingdom lead him and proclaim before him, Thus shall it be done to the man whom the king is pleased to honour.' 'Go,' saith the king, 'and do thus to Mordecai.' But mark, (ver. 11), 'Then took Haman the apparel and the horse, and arrayed Mordecai, and brought him on horseback through the streets of the city, and proclaimed before him, Thus shall it be done to the man whom the king delighteth to honour; but Haman hasted to his house, mourning and having his head covered.' This is but an emblem of the carriage of wicked men, when they shall behold the saints of God, his glorious worthy ones, in their glory at this great day. Then shall they, with Haman, have their heads covered, which was a sign of shame and confusion of face.

And it will be with all such ungodly wretches as it was with Belshazzar: Dan. v. 5, 6, 'In the same hour came forth fingers of a man's hand, and wrote over against the candlestick upon the plaster of the wall of the king's palace: and the king saw the part of the hand that wrote. Then the king's countenance was changed, and his thoughts troubled him, so that the joints of his loins were loosed, and his knees smote one against another.' Just thus shall it be with ungodly wretches, that oppose and murder and destroy the righteous ones. Oh! when they shall see them in glory—as when he saw the handwriting, his countenance was changed, his thoughts were troubled, his loins were loosed, and his knees dashed against one another—thus shall it be when the saints shall appear in glory: therefore they at last shall appear glorious, to the terror, horror, and inexpressible confusion of all ungodly, bloody wretches.

4. A fourth reason why they shall appear glorious at last, is, because their glorious appearance at the last *will make much for the honour and glory of the Lord Jesus.* The more glorious the body is, the more it makes for the glory of the head: the more glorious the bride is, the more it makes for the glory of the bridegroom: for the glory of his power, wisdom, fulness, and goodness; and therefore they shall appear glorious.

5. Then, again, they shall appear glorious at the last day, that there may be *some suitableness between the head and the members.* Oh, what an uncomely thing would it be to see the head to be all of fine gold, and the hands of iron, and the feet of clay! What an uncomely thing would it be to see the bridegroom in all his glorious apparel, and the bride in her rags, or her mourning weeds! The Lord will have it so, that his people at last shall appear glorious, that they may be suitable to their glorious head, unto their precious bridegroom.

It is true, when Christ came first, he came clothed with flesh, and was looked upon as one that had no form nor comeliness nor beauty, that men should desire him, Isa. liii. 2, 3. And such a state was the church in to whom he came. Oh! but now when he shall appear 'the second time, without sin, to salvation,' then he shall appear glorious; and so shall all his saints, that there may be a suitableness between the members and the head, between the bride and bridegroom.

6. And then, again, another reason why believers shall appear glorious, is, because that *is the very time wherein the most wicked shall justify the goodness and mercy of God in his dealings towards his own people.* Oh, here many say with those in Job xxi. 15, 'What profit is there in serving of God?' Who would be as those men are, to carry their lives in their hands? Who would run through so many miseries; and all for others? 'What profit is there in honouring of God?' Mal. iii. 14. It is a strong affirmation that there is no profit. They are ready to say, when they look upon the sorrows, miseries, and evils that attend the saints in this wilderness, that it is madness and folly to walk holily as they walk, and to do righteously as they do. Isa. lix. 15, 'Truth faileth, and he that departeth from evil maketh himself a prey,' or a proverb, as the original hath it.[1] Oh, the world accounts them a company of mad, foolish people that refrain from evil. But God will have his people at last appear glorious, that the mouths of ungodly wretches may be stopped, that they may justify God in his goodness and mercy towards his own people. When they shall see those that they accounted monsters and wonders of the world, men not worthy to live in the world, when they shall see crowns set on their heads, and glorious robes put on their backs, oh how will ungodly men gnash teeth, and say, Oh! we thought them fools and madmen, that thus waited on God, and walked with God; but now we see ourselves the only fools, the only mad ones, that have turned our backs on God, and kicked at God, and that have said, 'There is no profit in serving of God.' Therefore the saints shall appear glorious at the last.

7. Then, the last reason why they shall appear glorious, is, because *they shall be employed about glorious work:* 1 Cor. vi. 2, 3, 'Know ye not that the saints shall judge the world?' Nay, he goes higher, 'Know ye not that the saints shall judge the angels?' There is a day coming when the saints shall judge the world. They shall be employed in a glorious work. Therefore they shall appear glorious; for the work in which they shall be employed shall be glorious. They shall sit as so many fellow-judges with the Lord Jesus Christ, to say Amen to the righteous sentence that Christ shall pass upon all treacherous and bloody murderers. O ungodly souls, the day is coming when those that now you have persecuted, murdered, and destroyed, they shall sit upon thrones and shall judge you; they shall say Amen to that glorious sentence that Christ at the last day shall pass upon you. There is a day coming when all those that have rejoiced in the fall of this worthy, and those treacherous wretches that had a hand in this unparalleled butchery, when they shall hold up their hands at the bar of God's tribunal. There is a day acoming when the saints shall appear glorious, and this worthy among

[1] משׁל a משׁתולל

the rest, to pass a righteous sentence upon such unrighteous, bloody wretches. That is another reason why they shall appear in glory, because they shall be employed in a glorious service, in judging the wicked world, however they have been scoffed at and despised here.

The use of the point is the main thing I shall speak to. Is it so that the saints at last shall appear glorious?

1. First, This serves to *bespeak the people of God to be glorious.* Oh that you would strive to be glorious now, who at last shall appear so glorious! Oh that your words might be more glorious, that your thoughts of God might be more glorious, that your conversations might be more glorious, that your actings towards God and man might be more glorious! The day is coming, O blessed souls, whenas you shall appear glorious! Oh that you would labour now to shine in glory, who at the last shall transcend the sun in glory! But I shall hasten to that which I chiefly intend, and that is this: Is it so that believers at last shall appear glorious? Then,

2. Second, This serves to *bespeak all believers to do gloriously whiles you are here, for you shall appear glorious.* In this I shall endeavour these three things:—

First, To lay down some motives to move you to do gloriously here, who shall appear glorious in heaven.

Secondly, We shall shew when a man may be said to do gloriously.

Thirdly, I shall lay down some directions and helps to enable you while you are here to do gloriously; and so proceed to other things that remain.

1. For the first, to move you to do gloriously, methinks here is a motive, that *at last you shall be glorious.* But to engage you a little, consider these four or five things to move you to do gloriously:—

[1.] First, Consider *the Lord hath done already very gloriously for you; therefore do you gloriously for God.* God hath done very gloriously for you. He hath made your ugly inside glorious, and he hath made your ugly outside glorious: Ps. xlv. 13, 'The king's daughter is all glorious within, and her raiment is of embroidered gold.' God hath pardoned you gloriously, God hath justified you gloriously, God hath fenced you against corruption gloriously, God hath strengthened you against temptations gloriously, God hath supported you under afflictions gloriously, God hath delivered you from the designs and plots of treacherous, murderous wretches, gloriously and frequently. Oh, how should this engage all Christians to do gloriously for God, that hath already done gloriously for them!

[2.] But then, in the second place, To move you to do gloriously, consider that *the greatest part of the world doth basely and wickedly against God; therefore you have the more cause to do gloriously for God:* 1 John v. 19, 'The whole world,' saith he, 'lies in wickedness,' in malignity. The world lies in troublesomeness. The word πονηρῷ signifies a desire, a study and endeavour to work wickedness, a working wickedness; and in such a wickedness the world lies, and the greatest part of the great ones of this world do basely and wickedly against God. Oh the treachery and apostasy, oh the neutrality and impiety, oh the facing about of the great ones of this age! O believers, you had need to do gloriously, for great and small, honourable and base, do treacherously; and therefore this should engage you to do more gloriously. Oh, the more base and vile any are, the more glorious should the saints be!

[3.] Then, in the third place, Consider this, *the more gloriously you do for God here, the more glorious you shall be hereafter.* Suffering saints for Christ shall have weighty crowns set upon their heads. Murdered saints for Christ shall have double crowns set upon their heads. The more gloriously any man doth for Christ here, the more glorious that man shall be hereafter: 2 Cor. ix. 6, 'As a man soweth, so shall he reap. He that soweth sparingly shall reap sparingly; but he that soweth liberally shall reap liberally;' 2 John 8, 'Look to yourselves, that ye lose not the things ye have wrought, but that ye receive a full reward.' There is a reward in Scripture, and a full reward. The more glorious any soul is in doing for God here, the more glorious that soul shall be hereafter: Mat. xix. 27, 28, 'We have forsaken all, and followed thee; what shall we have? Verily,' saith Christ, 'you that have done this, shall sit upon twelve thrones, judging the twelve tribes of Israel.' Look, Christians, the more gloriously any man doth for God here, the more comfort and peace and joy that man hath on this side heaven, which is but an earnest of that happiness, of that glorious good and sweetness that the soul shall have when he shall appear in his glory. It is not the slight Christian, the light, loose, talking Christian, that hath much joy and peace, and the most full discoveries of God here, but the most glorious-doing Christian, the most acting soul; and the more gloriously any man doth for God here, the more joy and peace and comfort he shall have, which is but a pawn of that glorious joy and goodness which at last he shall receive.

[4.] And then, fourthly, To move you to do gloriously for God, you that shall be glorious at the last, consider this, *the greatest part of your time you have spent foolishly and in ways of vanity against God.* Oh, that time that is behind to spend gloriously, it is very, very little; which should bespeak you to do gloriously for God that little, little time that is allotted you. The apostle hath one argument—1 Peter iv. 3, 6, 7 compared, 'For the time past of our life may suffice us to have wrought the will of the Gentiles, when we walked in lasciviousness, lusts, excess of wine, revellings, banquetings, and abominable idolatries,' &c. 'For, for this cause was the gospel preached also to them that are dead, that they might be judged according to men in the flesh, but live according to God in the spirit. But the end of all things is at hand; be ye therefore sober, and watch unto prayer.' He tells them that the greatest part of their time was spent vainly; and in ver. 7 he tells them that the time behind was short. Upon this consideration he presseth them to do glorious things in the latter part of ver. 6. But 'live according to God in the spirit,' oh what is that but to live gloriously, to do gloriously?

[5.] Then, lastly, Consider this to move you to do gloriously for God: *if you do not gloriously for God, none in the world can do gloriously for God; if you do not, none in the world will.* Consider this, you that are believers. Of all persons in the world, you have the greatest cause to do gloriously for God; for God hath done more for you than for all the world besides. You have not only the greatest cause to do gloriously for God, but you have the choicest principles to enable you to do gloriously for God—as knowledge, and wisdom, and power, and faith, and zeal. And as you have the choicest principles, so you have the sweetest experience to engage you to do gloriously for God. How hath God knocked at your doors when he hath passed by the doors of thousands! How hath free grace saluted you, when wrath hath broken forth upon thousands! How hath God dandled you on his knee, when he hath trampled others under his feet! What is this but to engage you to do gloriously for God? If you do not, none in the world will do gloriously. And what a sad thing it is that God should make a world, and not a soul in the world to do gloriously for God, that hath made such a glorious world! So much by way of motive to move you to do gloriously.

2. The second thing I am to speak of is, *When a man may be said to do gloriously.* Haply some soul may say, We are satisfied that we shall appear glorious at last, and we would do gloriously; but when may a soul be said to do gloriously?

I answer: A soul may be said to do gloriously, *first, when their doing lies level with the glorious rule; when men do suitable to a glorious rule.* Those thoughts are glorious thoughts that are suitable to a glorious rule, and those words are glorious words that are suitable to a glorious rule, and those actions towards God and man are glorious actions that are suitable to a glorious rule. But this is too general. Therefore, *secondly*, and more particularly, men do gloriously *whenas they do such things that others refuse to do, that others have no heart to do, that others are afraid to do for God.* Oh, to do this is to do gloriously. As David, when he engaged with Goliath, he did gloriously; others were afraid to do it, others had no heart to do it. So when men engage for God when others are afraid to engage, when others dare not engage, they shall lose the smiles of this man, and procure the frowns of that; there is a lion in the way. So men turn off the work. It is too hard, saith one; it is too high, it is too rough, it is too dangerous, say others. Now to do gloriously is to do that that others refuse to do, and that others have not hearts to do. And in this respect this thrice-honoured champion hath done gloriously. The mountains that he hath gone over, the difficulties that he was engaged in, were known to thousands in this kingdom. Many worthies have done worthily for this unworthy kingdom, and this worthy hath excelled many of them. And then, in the *third* place, men do gloriously *when they hold on in the way of God, and in the work of God, notwithstanding all discouragements that befall them.* When men serve their generation, notwithstanding the discouragements that do or may befall them, blow high or blow low, rain or shine, let men smile or frown, do what they will against their persons or actions, yet for a soul to hold on and to serve his generation, against all and notwithstanding all the reproaches and dirt and scorn and contempt that is thrown on them, is to hold on in the way of God; this is to do gloriously. Thus God enabled this worthy, and many other worthies in the kingdom, in the House,[1] and in the army, to do gloriously against all discouragements and storms

[1] House of Commons.—G.

and projects of ungodly wretches. It was the glory of the church: Ps. xliv. 17–19, 'Though thou hast sore broken us in the place of dragons, and covered us with the shadow of death, yet we have not dealt falsely with thee; our heart is not turned back, neither have our steps declined from thy ways.' Oh, you have a generation that pretend much for God while they may gain by the bargain honour and riches and great places and the like; but when God brings them through the valley of darkness, that they meet with discouragements and difficulties, they throw away the bucklers, and will be no more for God, but fire about, and prove treacherous to church and kingdom. It was the glory of David, and it was a glorious speech of his in Ps. lvii. Saith David, ver. 4, 'My soul is among lions, and I lie even among them that are set on fire, even the sons of men, whose teeth are spears and arrows, and their tongue a sharp sword. They have prepared a net for my steps; my soul is bowed down; they have digged a pit before me.' Mark, what was the courage of this worthy one? He met with discouragements. Doth he grow treacherous, and give back? No: 'My heart is fixed, O God, my heart is fixed.' *Macon*, that is here rendered 'fixed,' is a Hebrew participle that signifies firm, constant, and established; and he geminates it, 'my heart is firm, constant, and established,' even then when his soul was among lions. He doth not now play the apostate and shake hands with the ways of God. No. But 'my heart is fixed.' Now a man doth gloriously when he keeps to God and his truth, and serves his generation, notwithstanding all discouragements that are thrown upon him.

I need not tell you what discouragements this noble champion met with from malignant pens, spirits, and tongues; but through all God carried out his spirit that he was able to do his master's work and to serve his generation, till he had finished that work that God had for him to do.

It is nothing for a man to serve his generation when he hath wind and tide on his side, and all the encouragements that the heart of man can desire; but it is the glory of a Christian, and then he doth gloriously, to be faithful in his generation against all discouragements. Therefore, honoured commanders and worthy members of the House of Commons, for you to do gloriously is to hold out against discouragements and to serve your generation. Though your soul may be amongst lions, and you live among them that are set on fire, as the psalmist speaks, yet say as he saith in that psalm, 'Our heart is fixed, our heart is fixed in God, we will sing and give praise.' Fixed stars are most useful, and so are fixed souls to church and state.

Then in the *fourth* place, Men may be said to do gloriously, when *the end of their doings is the glory of God and the general good.* O Christians, now you do gloriously. Those spirits will never do gloriously that make themselves the end of their actions, that make the advancing of any particular interest the end of their actions. This is not to do gloriously. Parliament-men, and soldiers, and Christians, then do gloriously, when the glory of God and the general good is the end of all their doings. But if it be yourselves, to save your own necks, and to advance your own designs, and to bring in this and that, these are base, unworthy actions, and God will so demonstrate them before angels and men. To do gloriously is to make the glory of God and the general good the end of all your doings. Then you do gloriously indeed, when you can centre and rest in the glory of God and the general good. It is a base and unworthy spirit when men make themselves the end of their actions, and the advancing of such or such a particular interest the end of their actions, and not the glory of God and the general good of his people.

And then again, *fifthly*, Men do gloriously when *they rejoice under the sufferings that befall them for Christ:* not only to bear sufferings, but to joy under sufferings, to rejoice under all afflictions and troubles that may befall them for Jesus Christ. So the apostle, 2 Cor. xii. 10, saith he there, 'I take pleasure in infirmities, in reproaches, in necessities, in afflictions, for Christ.' The original word, διὸ εὐδοκῶ, that is rendered 'I take pleasure,' is an emphatical word. It signifies the infinite delight and contentment he did take in the afflictions and persecutions that befell him. It is the same word that God the Father useth to express his unexpressible delight in his Son: Mat. iii. 17, 'This is my beloved Son, in whom I am well pleased'—or rather, as the original has it more elegantly, 'This is that, my Son, that my beloved, in whom I am infinitely delighted and contented.' The same word the apostle useth to express his delight in afflictions and persecutions for Christ. So those in Acts v. 41, 'They went away rejoicing that they were accounted worthy to suffer for Christ.' O Christians, this is to do gloriously, for a man to rejoice that he hath an estate to lay out for Christ, that he hath a life to lay down for Christ, that he hath a tongue to speak for Christ, that he hath a hand to fight for Christ. This is to do gloriously, to rejoice in anything we suffer for Christ, and in all sorts of sufferings and doings for Christ.

Then again, Men do gloriously, mark this, when *they appear for the people of God, and side with the people of God, notwithstanding any evil and danger that may befall.* Come what come can, yet they will appear for the people of God, and side with the people of God. This is to do gloriously, when come what come can, I will fall in with the saints, and be one with them that are one with God. As Esther, when they were in a sad condition, and Haman had sold them to be butchered and mangled by ungodly wretches: 'Well, I will go to the king,' saith she, though there was a command that none should, 'I will venture my life; if I perish, I perish.' Now she did gloriously. So Nehemiah: 'Shall such a man as I flee?' Shall I desert the saints, and turn my back on the saints? No; I will appear for them, and side with them, I will not desert them. So David's father and his brethren: 1 Sam. xxii. 1, 'David therefore departed thence, and escaped to the cave Adullam: and when his brethren and his father's house heard it, they went thither to him.' They did not stand disputing: we have estates to lose, and if Saul know that we join with David, and have taken part with him, we shall lose our heads, and lose our estates. The politicians of our times are wise: they will say they wish the saints well, but they dare not, they will not side with them. Ah, wretches! God will save his glory and the honour of his name, and will deliver the righteous, and leave such to deliver themselves.

God can shift well enough for his honour and for his people, and leave such wretches in a shiftless condition. So good Onesiphorus: Paul speaks of some, 2 Tim. i. 13, 14, &c., that played the apostates; ver. 15, 'This thou knowest, that all they which are in Asia are turned away from me; of whom are Phygellus and Hermogenes.' They played the apostates, and when he was to answer, left him to shift for himself. They would own him when all was clear overhead; but when he was in trouble they fall off. But Onesiphorus, he stands by him, and the apostle commends it for a glorious cause, and commends him in a particular manner to God: 'Oh that God would double his mercy on him; the Lord grant that he may find mercy of the Lord in that day; and in how many things he ministered unto me thou knowest; and he was not ashamed of my chain.' There were base spirits that were ashamed of his chain, that were ashamed to side with and to own Paul; and this world is full of such base spirits. Now this is to do gloriously—for a man to appear and side with the saints, let what will come of it. Thus Moses did very gloriously: Heb. xi. 25, 'He chose rather to suffer afflictions with the people of God, than to enjoy the pleasures of sin for a season.' But ah! Lord, in how few hearts does this brave spirit of Moses breathe!

O noble hearts, would you do gloriously? To do gloriously is to appear for the saints, and to side with the saints, let the issue be what it will. Oh, it is a sad and a base thing in those that have appeared for and sided with the saints, but now face about and prove treacherous, and leave the poor saints to shift for themselves! But it is their comfort that they have a God that will shift for his people and his own glory. And as Mordecai said to Esther, chap. iv. 14, 'If thou wilt not stir, the Lord will bring deliverance to his people some other way.' So if parliament-men, and those that have power, do not appear and side with the saints, deliverance will come another way; but they and their father's house may perish. And therefore remember to do gloriously is to appear for them; and not to appear for the saints is to betray them, and so it shall be brought in on the day of account.

Then again, in the next place, To do gloriously is *to do justice, and that impartially*. Then men do gloriously when they do justice impartially upon high and low, honourable and base, father and son, kinsman and brother; and not to dispute, this is a near kinsman, and that is my father, and the other is my brother, and that the one is too great and the other is too mean for justice, this is inglorious. The basest and unworthiest spirits on earth cannot do more basely; there is nothing of the power of the Spirit or heavenly gallantry in such. It is said, Ps. cvi. 30, 31, 'Then stood Phinehas, and executed judgment: so the plague was stayed. And that was accounted to him for righteousness to all generations for ever.' Oh this executing of justice impartially, how it makes the names of persons to live from generation to generation! If so be that the powers of this world would have their names immortal, so graven that they should never be wiped out, let them do justice. This is that Phinehas was admired for; it was 'accounted to him for righteousness, to all generations for evermore.'

And then, *lastly*, Men do gloriously when *they believe the promise and rest on the promise, notwithstanding that providence seems to cross the promise.* It is nothing, it is not to do gloriously, for a man to believe, and to love, and the like, when the promise is made good, when God is a-smiling and in a giving way; but to do gloriously is to believe the promise, to stay upon the promise, when providence in our apprehension crosseth the promise. In this respect, Abraham did very gloriously; he believed the promise though providence seemed to cross the promise. 'I will give thee a son,' saith God. Abraham was old, and Sarah was stricken in years; and yet Abraham believed, and this was such a glorious piety as God hath put it upon record. This faith of Abraham so takes God that he swears with joy, Gen. xiii. 16, 17, 'That in blessing I will bless thee.' So it was with Moses: Num. x. 29, 'And Moses said unto Hobab, the son of Raguel the Midianite, Moses' father-in-law, We are journeying unto the place of which the Lord said, I will give it you: come thou with us, and we will do thee good; for the Lord hath spoken good concerning Israel.' Mark, what could he promise in the wilderness, where the Lord exercised those poor wretches with judgment upon judgment, with misery upon misery, and one calamity upon the neck of another? Moses was confident in the promise of God, that God would do Israel good, and he adventured to engage Hobab on that consideration; 'Come, go along with us; the Lord hath spoken good, and we will do thee good.' I am confident, though providence cross the promise, and God seems to be angry, and to chide, and frown, and strike, and destroy, yet he will make good his promise, and 'we will do thee good.' Oh, this is to do gloriously, to believe the promise when providence crosseth it. Do you see heaven frown, and things to work cross to those promises that respects the joy, glory, liberty, and the exaltation of the saints? Doth providence work cross to the promise? now do gloriously, believe the promise, rest in the promise; let heaven and earth meet, devils and men combine; let men play the apostates, and turn neuters, and prove treacherous, I will rest on the promise, suck sweetness from the promise. Though all providences seem to cross it, and heaven seem to work contrary to it, I will say, I will stay upon the promise; this is to do gloriously. So much for the second thing.

Ay, but some souls will say, we see we shall be glorious, and we are willing to do gloriously; and we see reasons why we should do gloriously; but what directions and helps are there that we may do gloriously?

First, If you will do gloriously, there are some things that you must be careful to take heed of.

Secondly, There are others which you must labour to practise.

[1.] If you will do gloriously, seeing hereafter you shall be glorious, in the first place, whatever you do, *take heed of unbelief.* There is nothing in the world that more hinders men from doing gloriously, than unbelief. All other miscarriages and weaknesses have not such an influence upon the heart, to hinder it from doing gloriously, as unbelief. As it is said of Christ concerning them in Mat. xiii. 58, 'He did not many mighty works there because of their unbelief.'

Unbelief, as it were, tied the hands of Christ—'He *could* not do many mighty works because of their unbelief.' If men would do glorious things, take heed of that: unbelief ties the tongue; it causeth a damp to fall upon the heart, and binds the hands, that a man hath no tongue to speak for Christ, nor heart to act for Christ, nor hand to strike for Christ. Unbelief spoils all the strength and power by which we should be serviceable to God. What water is to fire, that unbelief is to the soul; therefore as you would do gloriously, take heed of unbelief.

[2.] *Secondly*, As you must take heed of unbelief, so, if you would do gloriously, *consult neither with the tempting nor with the persecuting world.* What hinders many men from doing gloriously, but consulting with the tempting or the persecuting world? This hath overthrown many. Nay, what hinders men in our age from doing gloriously? They are consulting with flesh and blood, with the tempting world and the frowning world. This hinders men from doing gloriously. I cannot believe but if parliament-men, and others in power and authority, did not look too much upon the tempting world when it smiles and holds forth her beautiful breasts, upon the ugly face of the world when it frowns and threatens, but that they would act more gloriously for God, and for the general good, and for the advancing of the name of the Most High in these days we live in.

[3.] If you would do gloriously, *look off from the tempting world:* it is a plague and a snare; and *look off from the frowning world*, it will discourage you; consult not with flesh and blood, with carnal reason. Looking upon the tempting or the frowning world will damp the most gallant spirits in the world, and hinder them from doing any noble service for God or his saints. And therefore, as ever you would do gloriously, look not on the tempting or on the persecuting world; look not upon it when it smiles or when it frowns; but remember you have a God to look at, a Christ to look at, and a crown to look at; that is better than all, that is more than all other things to your souls.

[4.] Then, again, If you would do gloriously, whatever you do, *take heed of base, selfish ends, take heed of self-love.* There is nothing under heaven that will disable a man more from doing gloriously, than a base spirit of self-love; such a man will never do gloriously. It may be, when he hath the wind and tide on his side, he may do something that vain men may account glorious; but this man will never do that which God and the saints call glorious, and count glorious. That base, selfish spirit, that looks no higher nor no further than self, it will never do gloriously. It may be fit for treachery, neutrality, and apostasy, but never to do gloriously.

Now as you must avoid these things so that you may do gloriously, in the next place,

[1.] *First, Labour for internal spiritual knowledge of God.* Oh, there is a great deal of notional light in the world! but if men did know God internally, if they did know God more in the mystery and light of the Spirit, if they did know God more from union and communion with God, it were impossible but they should do more gloriously. That is a brave text: Daniel xi. 32, 'And such as do wickedly against the covenant shall be corrupted by flatteries.' Mark the latter words, 'but the people that do know their God shall be strong, and do exploits.' Oh! take one that knows God internally, mystically, and spiritually, from union, and from being taken into heavenly communion with God, and he will act bravely and strongly for God. Alas! take a Christian that hath merely sucked in notions, and is only able for discourse, but hath no internal experimental knowledge of God, you shall never find him guilty of doing exploits, of doing glorious things for God and his saints. No! 'the people that know God,'—he speaks of the internal, spiritual knowledge of God, of knowledge in the mystery;—and thus to know him will enable a man to do exploits, to do glorious things. Oh, if God would raise up parliament-men, and men in the army, and in the city, and round the kingdom, to more internal knowledge, to more spiritual acquaintance with himself, we should find that they would do abundantly more gloriously. But it is for want of an internal, spiritual knowledge of God that men are treacherous, and base, and unfaithful, and prove apostates, and neuters, and anything. As you would do glorious and honourable things, look to this, that you have an internal knowledge and spiritual acquaintance with God, and this will enable you to do exploits.

And, then, If you would be enabled to do gloriously, in the second place, you should look upon those examples and worthies that have gone before you, and have done gloriously. So the apostle, Heb. xii. 1, when he would press them to do gloriously, he presseth them into this consideration of those glorious worthies that had gone before: 'Having therefore such a cloud of witnesses, let us run with patience the race that is set before us,' chap. xii. 1. Look to the cloud of witnesses, in chap. xi.; that is another means to help us to do gloriously.

Another is this, If you would do gloriously, then keep your evidences for glory always bright and shining; do not soil your evidences for glory. What made them take joyfully the 'spoiling of their goods,' Heb. x. 34, but this, that they knew in themselves that they had in heaven a better and more enduring substance? When a man's evidence is bright, that he can run and read his title to heaven, his interest in God, and the glory above, then will he be strong to do exploits; this will enable a man to do gloriously.

Then, again, If you would do gloriously, look to faith; give faith scope, give it elbow-room to work. Faith is a noble grace, and will ennoble the soul to do gloriously for God. Faith is that that will carry a man over all difficulties; faith will untie all knots; it will carry a man through the valley of darkness, though it be never so long; and over mountains of difficulties, though they be never so high. Faith will not plead 'there is a lion in the way,' and that such and such men will frown if I do this or that for God and the general good. Faith will carry a man bravely over all. You know that story in Hebrews xi.; you have several instances of the saints doing gloriously. But what enabled them? It is all along attributed to faith. By the power of faith they did gloriously: they stopped the mouths of lions; they turned to flight the armies of the aliens; they waxed valiant in fight; they refused to be delivered,—and all by the power of faith. Oh! faith will enable men to do gloriously. If parliament-men, and men in the army, and in the city, and round the kingdom, did believe more gloriously, they would do more gloriously for God, in their relations and places, than now they do. It springs from want of faith that things work thus basely. Did men believe more gloriously, things would work more gloriously. Therefore, when things work crossly, blame not so much this or that instrument, but blame thy own unbelieving heart; for glorious faith will see a smiling Father beyond a dark cloud. Though men are at a loss, yet God is not at a loss, says faith; and though the arm of man be weak, His arm is strong, says faith; and though the work be too hard for the arm of flesh, too hard for an army or parliament, it is not too hard for God, says faith. Faith carries a man gloriously through all. If you would do gloriously, abound in faith, let faith have elbow-room. I shall say no more of this. Though there be other directions, I will rather leave them.

Is it so, that the saints shall be glorious? Then this serves, in the next place, by way of use, *for singular comfort and consolation.* Shall the saints at last appear glorious? It speaks singular comfort to all believers, against all the reproaches, and contempt, and scorn that they may meet with in this world. What though you be scorned, and one saith this, and another saith that? Here is your comfort: you shall appear glorious. What though this worthy's body be mangled here and there by bloody butchers? yet this body shall appear glorious at the last. What a singular comfort is it! The apostle makes the same use from the same consideration: 1 Thes. iv. 15, 'We that are alive and remain shall not prevent them that sleep: for the Lord himself shall descend from heaven with a shout, with the voice of the archangel, and the trump of God: and the dead in Christ shall rise first. Then we which are alive and remain shall be caught up together with them in the clouds, to meet the Lord in the air, and so we shall ever be with the Lord. Wherefore comfort one another with these words.' Let the wife comfort herself with these, the brother, the kinsman, the friends of this worthy that now lies in the dust mangled. Oh, comfort yourselves with this consideration, that he shall appear glorious at last, with the rest of the glorious renowned saints! And so this may comfort us against all reproaches, and scorns, and contempts that men throw upon us: and what though the glory of the saints is now hid by prevailing distempers, and afflictions, and poverty? yet here is your comfort, the day is coming when your glory will break out, when your rags shall be taken off, and your glorious robes put on, when God will wipe away all the dirt and filth that hath been thrown on you by vain spirits. Therefore bear up, brave hearts! There is a day coming when you shall appear glorious, and it will be but as a day before that day overtake you.

Then, again, If the saints at the last shall appear glorious, then it bespeaks all, in the last place, to *long for that day.* You shall at the last appear in glory. Oh then long for that day; cry out with the church, 'Come, Lord Jesus, come quickly:' cry out again with the church in Solomon's Song, viii. 14, 'Make haste, my beloved;' or as the original has it, ברח דודי, 'Flee away speedily, my beloved, and be thou like a roe or a young hart upon the mountains of spices.' Will you remember these two things, to engage you to be much in longing for this day, wherein the saints shall appear in glory. Divers things might be said, but I shall reduce all to two things.

Till this day your happiness will not be complete, therefore long for it. Till the saints shall appear glorious, all will be incomplete; your comforts, your graces, your enjoyment of God, and of that glory that he hath provided. Till this glorious day your glory will be incomplete; therefore long for the day wherein all shall be complete.

Secondly, *Till then the innocency of the saints shall not be fully cleared:* that is another thing. Oh long for that day wherein the saints shall appear in glory, for till then the innocency of the saints shall not be fully cleared. Now I say, the devil and wicked men throw much dirt on them, and reproach and revile them, and what not, and something of that will stick; but let this bespeak all such to long for that day wherein all dirt, scorn, and filth shall be wiped off, wherein God will clear the righteousness, integrity, and innocency of his saints. Therefore seeing the saints shall appear glorious, be not discouraged, however you appear in the world to the eye of men. Now you are strangers, far from your Father's house; but it will be but as a day before the trumpet sound and the angels shall gather you, before the robes of glory shall be put on, and your mourning weeds shall be taken off, and the glorious crowns put on your heads, and your happiness shall be complete. Long for this day; for this will be a day indeed of refreshing from the Lord. I shall say no more to this point, but earnestly desire that God would please to make it take impression on your spirits. The saints shall appear glorious. Oh let it be our glory, while we are here, so to walk as they that expect to appear glorious another day!

As for this thrice-honoured champion now in the dust: for his enjoyment of God, from my own experience, being with him both at sea and land, I have abundance of sweetness and satisfaction in my own spirit, which to me exceedingly sweetens so great a loss. I shall not speak of the wife's loss, nor the brother's loss, nor the army's loss; for the loss of this worthy is a loss to the kingdom, and if they are not in a sad, sinful sleep, they will say so. And, indeed, it is with me, I ingenuously confess, as it was with him who, when he was demanded what God was; he desired three days' consideration to give an answer, and when those days were expired, three more; and then he gives this answer, 'That the more he thought of him, the further he was from discovering of him.' The more I think of the gallantry and worth of this champion, the further off I am from discovering his worth. I think he was one of whom this sinful nation was not worthy; he was one of whom this declining parliament was not worthy; he was one of whom those divided, formal, carnal, gospellers was not worthy. He served his generation faithfully, though he died by the hand of treachery. I am fully satisfied, with many more, that he is now triumphing in glory; and it will be but as a day before he shall see his enemies stand at the bar. For my own part, I can truly say that, to the best of my memory and understanding, I have not observed that the hearts of the people of God have been so generally and eminently affected with the loss of any worthy, as with the loss of this worthy; no, not for any worthy that hath fallen since the sword was drawn, though many precious worthies have fallen upon the ground; which strongly speaks out the love of the people of God to him, and their honourable esteem of him. They honoured him in his life, and they shewed no small respect to him in death. He was a joy to the best, and a terror to the worst of men. But for my part I should rather choose, I ingenuously confess, if it were possible, to weep over him with tears of blood, than to trouble you further with relating his gallant service for the good of this sinful kingdom.

We will cease from saying anything more of him, and sit down satisfied and joying in this, that the day is coming when the saints shall appear glorious; and with that we will refresh and cheer our spirits as with a cordial, that there is a day coming when we with this deceased worthy shall appear glorious. And it will be but as a day before our robes shall be put on our backs, and crowns set on our heads. I have now done; and so shall commend you 'to God and to the word of his grace, which is able to build you up, and to give you an inheritance among all them which are sanctified,' [Acts xx. 32.]

GOD'S DELIGHT

IN THE

PROGRESS OF THE UPRIGHT.

NOTE.

The title-page of 'God's Delight' will be found below.* The usual 'order' is prefixed as follows:—'Die Mercurii 30mo Decem. 1648. Ordered by the Commons assembled in Parliament that Sir John Bourchier do from this House give thanks to Mr Brooks for the great pains he took in his sermon preached at Margarets, Westminster, before the House of Commons, upon the day of their public Humiliation last preceding: and that he be desired to print his sermon, wherein he is to have the like privilege in printing of it, as others in the like kind usually have had.

'Henry Elsynge, Cer. Dom. Com.

'I appoint Rapha Harford and Thomas Brewster to print this sermon,

'Thomas Brooks.'

* GOD'S DELIGHT
IN THE PROGRESSE
OF THE UPRIGHT.

Especially
In Magistrates Uprightnesse and
constancy in wayes of justice and righte-
ousnesse in these Apostatizing Times,
notwithstanding all discouragements, oppositions, &c.

Presented in a Sermon before the Honorable
House of Commons at their last monethly
Fast, December 26. 1648.

By Thomas Brooks, Preacher of the
Gospel at *Thomas Apostles.*

Job 17. 8, 9.

The righteous shall hold on in his way, and he that hath clean hands shall be stronger and stronger.

Upright men shall be astonished at this, for the Innocent shall stirre up himselfe against the Hypocrite.

Numb. 35. 33.

Yee shall not pollute the Land wherein yee are; for bloud, it defileth the Land, and the Land cannot be cleansed of the bloud that is shed therein, but by the bloud of him that shed it.

London,
Printed by M. S. for R. Harford at the Bible in Queen's-head-alley in Paternoster-row, and *Thomas Brewster* at the West end of *Pauls*, 1649.

[4to.—G.]

THE EPISTLE DEDICATORY.

To the Honourable House of Commons in Parliament assembled.

This work was too high for me; and, as it is now done by so weak a hand, is too low for so many judicious eyes to look down to. Yet, according to your command, I have published these notes, which I humbly present to your Honours. They were once in your ear, they are now in your eye, and the Lord ever keep them in your hearts! Solomon bids us 'buy the truth,' but doth not tell us what it must cost, because we must get it though it be never so dear. *Multi amant veritatem lucentem, oderunt redarguentem*, We should love it both shining and scorching. The desire of my soul is, that you may deal so with those truths which here in all humbleness is presented to you. Oh that we may be all doers of the word, and not hearers only, lest we deceive our own souls! When I stood upon my watch to see what the Lord would say unto me, that I might speak unto you a word in season—or as the Hebrew has it, Prov. xxv. 11, עַל־אָפְנָיו, *gnal ophnau*, upon the wheels, *i.e.*, with a due concurrence and observation of all circumstances, of time, place, persons, &c., which are as the wheels upon which our words and speeches should run—He directed me to make this discovery of upright hearts' progress in the ways of God, notwithstanding all afflictions, &c., that do befall them; which gives me hope that God intended to send home into your hearts some light and influence from this truth, to encourage and keep up your spirits against all the opposition which you may find in the cause of God and the kingdom, and to maintain your zeal and forwardness therein, that justice and judgment may run down as waters, and righteousness as a mighty stream. If justice do not work the salvation of sinners' souls, yet it will work to the restraining of their sin—the measure of their wickedness will be less. That is a grave speech of Seneca's, *Ut nemo pereat, nisi quem perire etiam pereuntis intersit*, That none perish but those to whom it is an advantage to perish. And yet, Right Honourable, I desire that justice and clemency may go together. Nero's speech has great praise, who, when he was to subscribe to the death of a man condemned, would say, *Utinam nescirem literas*, I wish I did not know how to write. Right Honourable, you have the largest opportunities to honour God and to do good to his saints that ever any men had since the world began. God hath laid out works for you, fit for truly noble spirits. You have many precious saints to take care of; use them kindly, and 'the good-will of him that did dwell in the bush shall rest upon you.' Be not exasperated against any of them, by those who are so enraged, that they would have fire to come down from heaven and consume them. I hope there be a generation that will not abuse that liberty that shall be granted them according to the word, but will, in the midst of all their liberties, be faithful servants to peace and concord, according to that which Master Calvin writes to Farel, *Nos liberi servi sumus pacis et concordiæ.* I hope God will arise in you, and cause you to do his work his own way. The Lord God guide your Honours, and give every one of you to act like the angels of God, cheerfully, freely, readily, sincerely, and unweariedly in your generation, that in all your ways Christ may own you, and that all the godly of the land may rise up and call you blessed; and let the blessing of him that was in the bush be upon you and yours for ever; and let all the precious sons of Zion that loves the God of heaven, who is the Saviour of this nation, say Amen.—Honoured and worthy Senators, I am, your Honours' in all humble service for Christ,

THOMAS BROOKS.

GOD'S DELIGHT IN THE PROGRESS OF THE UPRIGHT.

Our heart is not turned back, neither have our steps declined from thy ways.—Ps. XLIV. 18.

CURIOSITY is the spiritual adultery of the soul. Curious divisions do rather affect the ear than warm the heart: they do but rack and disjoint the sense of Scripture. And therefore, as he speaks, 2 Sam. xviii. 23, 'We will run by the way of the plain.'

'Our heart is not turned back,' &c.

These words look to the front and to the rear; they look forward and backward. They look forwards upon the tossed and afflicted estate in which the church was, as you may read from ver. 9–17; and they look backward to the broken and persecuted estate of the church, expressed in ver. 19–24, 'Though thou hast sore broken us in the place of dragons, and covered us with the shadow of death, and though we be every day as sheep accounted for the slaughter; yet we have not forsaken thee, neither have we dealt falsely in the covenant. Our heart is not turned back, neither have our steps declined from thy ways.'

'Our heart,' *Libbenu*. The Hebrew word, לבב, or Greek, *καρδία*, that is rendered 'heart,' both in the Old and New Testament, doth signify the understanding, mind, will, affections, conscience, the whole soul. 'Our heart is not turned back.' Our understandings and minds are the same as they were in a summer's day, though now we be in a winter's storm—though now we be afflicted, tossed, broken, and persecuted; yet notwithstanding, 'our heart is not turned back'—our mind, will, affections, and conscience, our whole soul, is the same now as before. 'Our heart is not turned backward, neither have our steps declined from thy ways.'

'Our heart is not turned back.'

This notes their progress in the ways of well-doing; for the old saying is, *Non progredi est regredi*, Not to go forward is to go backward. 'Neither have our steps or our goings declined from thy ways.' It notes their settled course of walking in the ways of God; and, in short, the sum of all is, though we have been afflicted, tossed, broken and persecuted, yet our hearts have held on in the ways of the Lord, and we have not departed from our God. 'Our heart is not turned back, neither have our steps declined from thy ways.'

Right Honourable, there is but one observation that I shall speak to this day, and that is this: that doctrine—

Upright hearts will hold on in the ways of God, and in the ways of well-doing, notwithstanding all afflictions, troubles, and discouragements they meet withal.

That is the sum and the scope of this verse here. The church was afflicted, tossed, broken, and persecuted; and yet this is still the burden of the song, 'Our heart is not turned back, neither have our steps declined from thy ways.'

I judge it a point seasonable in every respect. I shall only eye the scriptures that prove it, and then open it to you.

The scriptures that prove it are these: Ps. cxix. 23, 24; Josh. xxiv. 15; Neh. iv. 13, 17 compared; Mal. iii. 13–17; 2 Cor. xi. 23–30. These scriptures speak out this truth, that upright hearts will hold on in the ways of God, and in the ways of well-doing, notwithstanding all the afflictions, troubles, and discouragements they meet withal.

For the opening of the point, I shall premise these three things:—

First, I shall premise something concerning upright hearts.

Secondly, I shall premise something concerning the ways of God. And,

Thirdly, The reasons why upright hearts will hold on in the ways of God, in the ways of well-doing, notwithstanding all the afflictions, troubles, and discouragements they meet withal.

Concerning upright hearts, I shall only premise these four things:—

1. First, *An upright heart hates all sins, even those which he cannot conquer; and he loves all divine truths, even those which he cannot practise.* An upright heart, he hates all sin. All sin strikes at God, at his holiness, as well as at an upright man's happiness. It strikes at God's glory, as well as at the soul's comfort; therefore the soul strikes at all. All sins, in the eye of an upright heart, are traitors to the crown and dignity of the Lord Jesus; therefore the soul riseth in arms against all. An upright heart, he looks upon sin to be *malum catholicum*—A catholic evil. An upright heart, he looks upon sin as that which hath thrown down the most righteous man in the world, as Noah; as that which hath thrown down the best believer in the world, as Abraham; as that which hath thrown down the best king in the world, as David; as that which hath thrown down the best apostle in the world, as Paul. It looks upon sin as that which hath thrown down the strongest, as Samson; and the wisest, as Solomon; and the meekest, as Moses; and the patientest, as Job; and so his soul riseth against it. In Ps. cxix. 104, 'Through thy precepts I get understanding: therefore I hate every false way.' 'Therefore I hate every false way:' *sanethi*, from *sane.* The original word, שנא, signifies to hate with a deadly and irreconcilable hatred; to hate so as that nothing will satisfy but the destruction of the thing hated. It is the same Hebrew word that is used to express Absalom's hatred of Amnon for defiling of his sister Thamar, 'My soul hates him.'

An unsound heart, a rotten heart, strikes at some sins, and yet falls in with others; he cries down pride and ignorance, and yet falls in with oppression and cruelty; he cries down tyranny and injustice in others, and yet plays the tyrant and unjust one himself. There are men who are blinded by Satan, and he hath them by the hand, and the Lord knows whither he will lead them.

And as an upright heart hates all sins, even those he cannot conquer, so an upright soul loves all truths, even those that he cannot practise. Every word of the Lord is just and righteous in the eye of an upright soul; he loves all truth strongly, though he can practise no truth but very weakly. Every word of grace is glorious, every line of grace is very glorious. Truth is homogeneal; where one truth is sweet, there every truth is sweet to an upright soul. In Ps. cxix. 127, 128, saith David there, 'I have loved thy commandments above gold; yea, above fine gold: I esteem all thy precepts concerning all things to be right.' That is the first thing.

2. Secondly, Concerning upright hearts, I shall premise this: Upright hearts, they serve God, and seek God more *for that internal worth and that eternal good that is in him, than for any external good they receive from him.* So it was with upright Job. The devil, in Job i., would fain charge Job that his heart was not right with God, that God had made a hedge about him, and therefore Job served him. The Lord therefore gives Satan liberty to break down that hedge, that Job's uprightness might appear, and that it might appear to all the world, that Job served God for that internal and eternal worth that was in him—viz., holiness, wisdom, and goodness. Therefore, when that hedge was down, and Job was stripped of all, yet in ver. 21, 'The Lord hath given,' saith he, 'and the Lord hath taken away; blessed be the name of the Lord.' Oh, upright Job served God for that internal and eternal worth that is in him; and therefore, though all his outward goods were lost, his soul could bless God.

But an unsound heart, a rotten heart, serves God and seeks good merely for some external good it hath from him, or expects to receive by him. That is a true saying, *Pauci quærunt Deum propter se, sed propter aliud*, Few men seek God for himself, but for some other thing. Like those in Hosea vii. 14, 'When they howled,' saith God, 'upon their beds, it was for corn, and wine, and oil, and they rebelled against me.' It was not for any internal or eternal worth in me, it was not for that holiness, wisdom, faithfulness, purity, and glory that is in me; but they seek me for loaves, for corn, and wine, and oil, and they rebelled against me.

3. A third thing I shall premise is this, Upright hearts are most *exercised and most busied and taken up about the inward man, about the inside, observing that, reforming that, examining that, watching that.* An upright heart knows that his soul is Christ's throne, his chamber of presence; and therefore, above all, the upright heart is most diligent to observe that none sit upon that throne but Christ, and that none come into that chamber of presence but Christ, that no sceptre be advanced there but the sceptre of Christ; he is most careful of the inside. In Ps. lxxxvi. 11, 'Incline my heart to fear thy

name;' Ps. cxix. 36, 'Let my heart be sound in thy statutes;' and so in ver. 80 and ver. 112 of the same psalm.

Now an unsound heart, a rotten heart, is most taken up about the outside,—informing that, and reforming that, and watching of that; but as for the inside, there is no eye cast to see how all stands there. The devil may bear rule; any may come into the soul and domineer and oppose the sceptre of Christ. So an unsound soul is taken up merely about the outside. That same exhortation of Solomon is strong upon an upright heart: Prov. iv. 23, 'Keep thy heart with all diligence; for out of it are the issues of life.' The original hath it more elegantly, 'Before all, or above all keeping, keep thy heart; for out of it is the goings forth of lives.'[1] This duty that Solomon presseth, is a duty that an upright heart above all endeavours to practise. Above all and before all, he guards his soul; he looks to his inward parts, how he thrives and grows, how he stands God-ward, Christ-ward, heaven-ward, and holiness-ward.

4. The last thing I shall premise is, Upright hearts in their constant course are *even-carriaged hearts*. An upright heart in his constant course is an even-carriaged heart. All the ways of an upright soul are as commentaries one upon another; and look, 'as face answereth face,' as Solomon speaketh, so the ways of an upright heart do one answer another. Christ sits at the stern of the soul, and guides the soul into those ways that are most like to himself: 2 Chron. xxxiv. 2, 'Josiah, he walked in all the ways of the Lord, as his father David did; he turned neither to the right hand nor to the left.' In all his ways he carried himself evenly. But an unsound heart, a rotten heart, is a very uneven-carriaged heart. You shall have one way wherein he walks to speak him out an angel, another to speak him a very sinful man, and a third to speak him a devil. Now he is for God, anon against God; now for justice and righteousness, anon for injustice and unrighteousness. But an upright heart is an even-carriaged heart. Let heaven and earth meet, let trials come, temptations and afflictions come, he keeps his ground, he is an even-carriaged heart. So much concerning the first thing.

For the second, concerning the ways of God, I shall briefly premise these five things:—

1. First, The ways of God are *righteous ways*, the ways of God are *blessed ways:* Prov. viii. 20, 'I lead in the way of righteousness, and in the midst of the paths of judgment;' and in the 33d verse of that same chapter, 'Hearken unto me now therefore, O ye children, for blessed are they that keep thy ways.' The ways of God are blessed ways; they bring in temporal, spiritual, and eternal blessings upon all that walk in them. They are righteous ways; they lead to righteousness, to the love of righteousness, to the practice of righteousness, to a delight in righteousness. As for the ways of profaneness, pride, hypocrisy, neutrality, formality, and apostasy, these are none of the ways of God; they are unrighteous ways, cursed ways, and they bring nothing but curses and crosses upon all that walk in them. Those that

[1] In the margin Brooks thus reads the original, *Mikkol mishmar nelsar libbecha ki memeunu lotseoth haïim.*

walk in these ways are nowhere secure, but are every moment liable to the thunderbolts of divine displeasure.

2. And secondly, The ways of God are *soul-refreshing ways*. Oh, they yield the soul abundance of refreshing and sweetness that walks in them. In Jer. vi. 16, 'Ask for the old way, the good old way, and walk therein, and ye shall find rest,'—מרגוע, *margoang*, 'ye shall find refreshing to your souls,' as the original hath it. If a man's soul be tired and weary, the ways of the Lord will refresh it; if it be dead and dull, the ways of the Lord will quicken it; if he be fainting, the ways of the Lord will be as a cordial to him.

3. And then, thirdly, The ways of the Lord, as they are soul-refreshing ways, so they are *transcendent ways*, ways that transcend all other ways. What is darkness to light? What are pebbles to pearls? What is dross to gold? No more are the choicest ways of the creature to the ways of God: Isa. lv. 8, 9, 'My ways are not as your ways, nor my thoughts as your thoughts; but as high as the heavens are above the earth, so are my thoughts above your thoughts, and my ways above your ways.' What is said of wisdom, Prov. iii. 15, 'that she is more precious than rubies, and that all the things we can desire are not to be compared to her,' the same may be affirmed of the ways of God. Oh! they are more precious than rubies, and all other ways are not to be compared to them.

4. And then, fourthly, The ways of God are *soul-strengthening ways*, ways that yield strength to the soul. In Prov. x. 29, 'The way of the Lord is strength to the upright,' ('*magnos*'): from *gnazaz*, the way of the Lord maketh strong. The original word, עוז signifies to confirm, to make strong. Oh, the ways of the Lord confirm upright hearts, they make upright hearts strong, strong to withstand temptations, strong to conquer corruptions, strong to rejoice under afflictions, strong to perform the most heavenly duties, strong to improve the most spiritual mercies. The ways of the Lord make strong, they confirm such hearts as walk in them.

5. Then, fifthly and lastly, As the ways of the Lord are soul-strengthening ways, so they are *afflicted, perplexed, and persecuted ways*. Mat. vii. 14, 'Strait is the gate,' &c. The original word, τεθλιμμένη, signifies perplexed, afflicted, persecuted; and the way is made strait by afflictions and troubles and persecutions. And so in Acts xix. 9, 'This way is everywhere evil spoken of;' and in Acts xxiv. 14, 'In the way that you call heresy, so worship I the God of my fathers.' The ways of God are afflicted, persecuted, and perplexed ways. And so much for the second thing.

The third—to make haste to what I chiefly intend—for the reasons why upright hearts will hold on in the ways of God, notwithstanding all the afflictions, troubles, and discouragements that do befall them, are these:—

1. The first is drawn from the nature of a Christian's life, which is a race; and as he that runs a race, if he holds not out, notwithstanding all discouragements, till he comes to the goal, loseth the garland; and as he that faints in wrestling loseth the crown, so do those that hold not out to the end; therefore upright hearts will hold out to the end, notwithstanding all the discouragements they meet with in the

ways of God: 1 Cor. ix. 24, 'Know ye not that they that run in a race run all, but one receiveth the crown? So run, that ye may obtain.' So in Heb. xii. 1, 'Let us with patience run the race that is set before us.'

2. A second ground of their holding out, notwithstanding all the afflictions and discouragements they meet with in the ways of God, and in the ways of well-doing, is drawn from the glorious promises of reward. For mark, as there is a comforting virtue in the promises, so there is a quickening and an encouraging virtue in all the glorious promises, as to warm the heart, so to raise and encourage the heart to run the ways of God's commandments, especially such promises as these:—Rev. ii. 10, 'Satan shall cast some of you into prison: but fear not, but be faithful unto the death, and I will give thee the crown of life.' That crown is a sure crown, a matchless crown, a glorious crown, a lasting crown: 'I will give you a crown of life;' I that am faithfulness itself, I that am truth itself, I that am goodness itself, I that am power itself, I that have all in heaven and earth at my disposing, I will give thee a crown of life. And Paul, 2 Tim. iv. 8, 'Henceforth is laid up for me a crown of righteousness.' The word that is rendered laid up [ἀπόκειται] signifies safely to lay up: it notes both a designation and a reservation. There is a crown designed and safely kept for me. And so such a promise as that, Rev. iii. 5, 'He that overcometh shall be arrayed in white: and I will not blot his name out of the book of life, but I will confess him before my Father, and before his angels.' And in ver. 21 of the same chapter, 'He that overcometh shall sit down with me in my throne, as I overcame, and sat down with my Father in his throne.' That is another reason from the promises of reward. Promises of reward to the master and mariners, oh, how do they raise up their spirits to go through any storms, to go through many dangers! and so doth the glorious promises of reward that God makes to his; they carry them bravely through all storms.

3. A third reason is, Because of all ways the ways of God are *the most honourable ways;* therefore upright hearts will hold on in them, notwithstanding all the afflictions and discouragements they meet with. The most renowned and honoured saints that ever breathed on earth, and that are now triumphant in heaven, have walked in those ways of God. The ways of sin are base, reproachful ways; but the ways of God are honourable ways.

When a man doth but fancy that the way he walks in is an honourable way, alas! how is his spirit carried on in that way against all opposition that he meets with! Oh, how much more doth the testimony that God gives of his ways, and the encouragements that he gives to his people to hold on in his ways, raise up their spirits to hold on against all discouragements.

4. But fourthly, The principal reason of upright hearts holding on in the ways of well-doing against all discouragements, is, because they are carried on in the ways of well-doing, and in the ways of God, from spiritual and internal causes, from spiritual principles, from a principle of inward life and spiritual power. It is true, if upright hearts were only carried on from fleshly, carnal, and external causes, they

would wheel about, and turn apostates, and be base, and what not. But upright hearts are carried on in the ways of God from inward principles, as in Jer. xxxii. 40, 'I will put my fear in their hearts, and they shall never depart from me;' and in Ezek. xxxvi. 26, 27, 'I will take away the heart of stone, and give them a heart of flesh. I will put my Spirit in them, and cause them to observe my statutes, and to walk in my ways.' Upright hearts are carried on by an inward principle of fear, faith, and love, and this carries them bravely on against all the discouragements they meet with. In Isa. xl. 31, 'They that wait on the Lord shall renew their strength like the eagle; they shall run and not be weary,' because they run upon another's legs—viz., the Lord Christ's; 'and they shall walk and not faint,' because they walk in the strength of Christ. That is another reason.

5. The fifth and last reason of their holding on in the ways of God, notwithstanding all the discouragements that befall them, is drawn from *the former profit and sweetness that they have found in the ways of God.* Oh! upright souls have found by experience the ways of God to be profitable ways indeed, to be the most gainful way that ever souls walked in. Upright hearts can say, We went to prayer at such a time, and we met with Christ answering us. Oh! what a mercy was that! And another time, We went to the word, and we met with Jesus Christ embracing us. Oh! what a favour was that! And another time, We went to the communion of saints, and we met with Christ warming and inflaming our hearts; and oh, what a heaven was that! as they in Luke xxiv. 32, 'Did not our hearts burn within us while he talked to us?' Oh! the remembrance of that former sweetness they have found carries them aloft against all discouragements! The kiss that the king gave one, as the story speaks, was more than the golden cup he gave to the other. Oh, the spiritual kisses that the King of kings gives upright souls when he meets them in his ways, carries their souls an-end against all afflictions and oppositions that they meet withal. David saith, in Ps. cxvi. 2, 'Because thou hast inclined thine ear to me, therefore will I call on thee as long as I live.' Therefore—wherefore? 'Because thou hast inclined thine ear to me, I will call on thee as long as I live.' In summer season and in winter season, let men smile or frown, I will call upon thee as long as I live. The sweet gain and profit that usurers and mariners have found in such and such ways, doth exceedingly carry their spirits on in those ways, notwithstanding all discouragements, reproaches, and scorns; and so doth the sweetness that upright souls have found in the ways of God. And thus much for the reasons of the point, and for the doctrinal part.

We come now to the use, which is the main thing I have my eye upon at this time.

1. And first, Is it so, that upright hearts will hold on in the ways of God and the ways of well-doing, notwithstanding all afflictions, troubles, and discouragements that may befall them? Then this, in the first place, serves to shew us that the number of upright hearts are very few; for ah! how few be there that keep close to the ways of God, and hold on in the ways of well-doing, when storms begin to rise!

Right Honourable, it is nothing for a man when he hath wind and tide on his side, when there is concurrence of all secondary causes to lift a man up and carry him bravely on; it is nothing to hold on now in the ways of God and the ways of well-doing. Oh, but when a man is tossed and afflicted, broken and persecuted, now to hold on in the ways of well-doing, this is the glory of a Christian; but how few are there that hold out in these seasons! Oh! witness the treachery, witness the apostasy, witness the neutrality of men in our days, that, when storms begins, for fleshly ends wheel about. It shews that the number of upright hearts are very few: but I will not stand on this.

2. Secondly, Is it so, that upright hearts will hold on in the ways of well-doing, notwithstanding all discouragements that befall them? Right Honourable, let me then exhort you first more particularly, and then more generally, to hold on in the ways of well-doing, notwithstanding all the afflictions, troubles, and discouragements you may meet with. You have begun to fall upon the execution of justice, which is a way wherein God delights to walk, and wherein he delights to see those that are in authority to walk impartially. I shall press this particularly, and then press the point more generally, both upon yourselves and all that hear me.

Now, Right Honourable, in this labour to hold on, you have begun in the Spirit—as to that point—do not end in the flesh, but hold on in the way of well-doing. Justice is called by Aristotle, Hesperus, the glorious star: by another, the sun of the world. Oh let this glorious sun so shine forth, that the best of men may rejoice, and the worst of men may tremble. Take to yourselves, Right Honourable, the glorious resolution of Jerome,[1] who once expressed himself thus: 'If my father should stand before me, and my brethren press about me, and my mother hang upon me, I would throw down my father, and break through my brethren, and trample upon my mother, to cleave to Jesus Christ.' O Right Honourable, take glorious resolutions to yourselves. Though your fathers may stand before you, and your brethren and friends press about you, though your mothers should hang on you, I mean the nearest relations, throw down the one, and break through the other, and trample upon the third, that your souls may cleave to the way of God, to the ways of justice and righteousness. You know the rule is, *Fiat justitia et ruat mundus*, Let justice be done, though the world be ruined. And that is a true saying, *Odia qui nimium timet regnare nescit.* Oh that upon every worthy member's heart and forehead that which once Chrysostom spake of himself might be written, *Nil nisi peccatum timeo*, I fear nothing but sin. Oh that this were every member's motto, I fear nothing but sin. I fear not the threats, the rage, the fury, nor the designs and plots of men that are turned into devils: I fear nothing but sin.

Right Honourable, that this may stick, give me leave to propound to your serious thoughts these few considerations:—

1. First, Consider this, when men do execute their just judgment, then *God will divert and turn away his judgment from a nation.* In Ps. cvi. 30, 31, 'Then Phinehas stood up and executed judgment, and the plague was stayed,' that not a man died after. When men stand

[1] Epist. ad Heliodorum I.

up to execute their just judgment, the Lord will divert and turn away his. There are a company of ignorant sottish people that think that the doing of justice will undo a land, and bring all calamities upon it; whereas there is nothing of more power to divert the judgment of God from a nation than the execution of justice and judgment: Jer. v. 1, 'Go,' saith God, 'run to and fro through the streets of Jerusalem, and see and know and seek in the broad places thereof if you can find a man'—ay, but it is not every man that will do it, but such a man—'that will execute judgment and seek truth,' and I will pardon you. 'If there be but a man that executes judgment and seeks truth, I will pardon you,' saith God, 'I will turn away my wrath.' So in Ezek. xxii. 29–31, 'The people of the land have used oppression, and exercised robbery, and vexed the poor and needy; they oppress the stranger wrongfully. And I sought for a man among you' [mark!] 'that might make up the hedge,' alluding to Moses that magistrate—'I sought for a man among you that might make up the hedge, and stand in the gap before me for the land, that I might not destroy it; but he could not be found.' And what follows? 'Therefore I poured out my indignation on them, and consumed them with the fire of my wrath; their own way have I recompensed upon their heads,' saith the Lord.

2. Secondly, Your neglect of justice will *provoke God to throw all your religious services as dung in your faces:* Isa. i. 11, 'To what purpose is the multitude of your sacrifices? I am weary of your new moons and your burnt-offerings and your sabbaths; my soul loathes them, they are an abomination to me.' What is the reason? 'Your hands are full of blood,' ver. 15—or rather, as the Hebrew hath it, דמים מלאו, 'your hands are full of bloods.' The Hebrew word is taken from a ship under full sail: your hands are full of bloods, as the sails of a ship is full of wind. There is the father's blood and the children's blood, and there is the master's blood and the servant's blood, and there is the bond-man's blood and the free-man's blood, and the wife's blood and the widow's blood; your hands are full of blood. Therefore to what purpose is the multitude of your sacrifices? God throws them as dung in their faces, because they neglected justice. You have a parallel text, Amos v. 21–24, 'I hate, I despise your feast-days, I will not smell in your solemn assemblies,' &c. What was the reason? 'Let judgment run down as water, and righteousness as a mighty stream.' Judgment did not run down, and therefore, saith God, 'I hate, I despise your fasting and prayer, and your feast-days.' Ah, Right Honourable, as you would not have your services thrown as dung in your faces, look that justice and judgment run down as a mighty stream.

3. Thirdly, Consider this, that your execution of justice and judgment *will free you from the guilt of other men's sins, and the neglect of justice and judgment will wrap you up in the guilt of other men's sins.* When those that are guilty shall be by you sinfully or wilfully acquitted, that shall be charged on your score. When justice is not executed, a land is defiled: Num. xxxv. 33, 34, 'So ye shall not pollute the land wherein ye are; for blood defileth the land, and the land cannot be cleansed of the blood that is shed therein, but by the blood

of him that shed it. Defile not, therefore, the land that ye shall inhabit, wherein I dwell; for I the Lord dwell among the children of Israel.' Oh! Right Honourable, have you not sins enough of your own to awaken you, to startle you, to trouble you, to amaze you, to afflict you, and to humble you? Have you not sins enough of your own to provoke God against you to strike you, to chide you, to wound you, and to lay you low; but will you wrap yourselves up in the guilt of other men's sins? Will you wrap yourselves up in the treachery, and murder, and blood, and cruelty, and tyranny of others? The Lord forbid!

It was an ingenuous acknowledgment of an emperor, who, when one had committed murder, and he was importuned to spare his life, and he did it; suddenly after the same person committed wilful murder again; then there was complaint made to the emperor that he had committed murder twice,—No, saith the emperor, he is guilty of the former only; I am guilty of the latter.

Right Honourable, guilty persons that be by you sinfully acquitted, their sin God will charge upon your account. And therefore as you would not have the guilt of other men's sins upon you, hold on in the way of well-doing: let justice and judgment run down as mighty streams.

4. Fourthly, Right Honourable, consider this, those persons that have neglected the execution of justice upon their implacable enemies, when God has given them into their hands, those God hath left to perish basely and miserably. See it in Ahab, 1 Kings xxi. compared with xxii. 23–37. God gives Benhadad into Ahab's hand, in ver. 40, 41, 'Because thou hast let a man go that I had appointed to destruction'—which was not signified to him by any extraordinary revelation, but by that ordinary dispensation,—'Therefore,' saith God, 'thy life shall go for his:' xxii. 31, 'Fight neither against small nor great, but against the king of Israel.' In which fight he lost his life at that time, and so perished miserably.

So concerning Saul in 1 Sam. xv. 19, compared with the last of [first] Samuel xxxi. 3, 4. Saul, he spares Agag, and he would shift off the command of the Lord; but for that God shifted him out of his kingdom. When he neglected to do justice upon an implacable enemy, when God had given him into his hands, God left him to perish and fall basely: ver. 26, 'Because thou hast rejected the word of the Lord, the Lord hath rejected thee from being king.' The Hebrew word, מאס מאסת, signifies to reject, to disdain, to cast off. The Lord rejected Saul, and he rejected the Lord; Saul disdained the Lord, and the Lord disdained Saul; he cast off the Lord, and the Lord cast off him. Saul did not do justice, therefore he shall die basely, and perish miserably upon his own sword: as he did, in 1 Sam. xxxi. 4.

5. Fifthly and lastly, Right Honourable, consider this, that your neglect of justice will *exceedingly encourage wicked persons in ways of impiety*, Eccles. viii. 11; *and discourage the godly of the nation from doing their duty.* Your neglect of justice will encourage wicked persons in the ways of impiety, and hinder the saints from a cheerful and sweet discharge of their duty.

Right Honourable, if you would sit down and study which way you might most encourage the worst of men, and discourage the best, you could not fall upon such another way, as to neglect what God and the nation calls for at your hands. Right Honourable, it is cruelty to the good to spare the bad: it is cruelty to the sheep and lambs to spare the wolves and lions. You were better a thousand times to set some of those grand malefactors a-mourning, that have caused the kingdom to mourn so many years in garments rolled in blood, by the execution of justice, than by the neglect of justice to keep a kingdom still mourning in garments of blood. I shall say no more as to that particular.

But now I shall endeavour to apply the point more generally, both to your Honours and all that hears me at this time, knowing that it is a useful point for us all, especially in these times and seasons wherein God doth exercise us with afflictions and discouragements, while we are in his own ways. The exhortation that I shall press upon you all is, that you will hold on in the ways of well-doing, notwithstanding all the afflictions, troubles, and discouragements that may befall you.

Now that you may, I shall endeavour to do these two things:—

First, To lay down some motives to encourage you.

Secondly, To premise some directions to further you.

1. For the first, by way of motive to move you to hold on against all discouragements that possibly may befall you, consider, Right Honourable, these few things, and all you that hear me this day:—

(1.) First of all, Consider this, that *all the afflictions and troubles that you meet withal shall never hurt nor harm you, but be very advantageous to you.* All the arrows that wicked men shoot at your heads shall stick fast in their own hearts: 1 Peter iii. 13, 'And who shall harm you, if ye be followers of that which is good?' Interrogations are strong affirmations. It is a strong affirmation, 'none shall harm you:' devils nor men, let them roar and rage, none shall harm you. For as one speaks truly, *Nemo proprie lœditur, nisi a seipso*, No man is properly hurt but by himself and his own fault. All the afflictions and troubles that you shall meet with in the ways of well-doing, they shall be advantageous to you; they shall be a means by which God will convey more of his grace and mercy, more of himself and his glory into your souls: Hosea ii. 14, 'I will allure her into the wilderness, and then I will speak friendly to her'—or as the Hebrew has it, ודברתי על-לבה, *uedibbarti gnal-libbah,* I will earnestly speak to her heart. God will make all afflictions, even a wilderness, to be an inlet to more of his own self. All the discouragements that you meet with in the ways of well-doing shall but rub off your dross, and empty out that filth that is in you, and so make more room for more of himself and of his glory to be communicated to you. In Heb. xii. 10, 'But he afflicts us for our profit, that we may be partakers of his holiness.' They were before partakers of his holiness. Oh, but God will make afflictions conduit-pipes, through which he will convey more of himself and of his holiness to his children's souls. That is the first thing. All the afflictions that befall you shall not harm you, but be very advantageous to you. Who would not then hold on in the ways of well-doing, notwithstanding any trouble or affliction that may befall them?

2. Secondly, Right Honourable and belovėd, let all gracious and upright hearts consider this, *that Jesus Christ hath held on in a way*

of mercy and sweetness towards you, notwithstanding all the discouragements and all the lets that have been in his way; and will not you hold on in ways of duty to Christ, who hath held on, notwithstanding all discouragements, in a way of mercy towards you? Oh consider, consider what difficulties the Lord Jesus Christ hath gone over to come to your souls. In Cant. ii. 8, it is said there, 'It is my beloved that comes leaping over the mountains and skipping over the hills.' Oh, the Lord Jesus Christ is come over mountains of wrath, and mountains of sin, and mountains of sorrow, and all that he might come to your souls. In Isa. lxiii. 3, 'I have trod the wine-press alone; and of the people there was none with me'—or as the Hebrew has it, *Umegnamium en ish itti*, ומעמים אין איש אתי, 'and of the nations, or of the peoples, there was not a man with me.' He trod the wine-press of the wrath of his Father alone. And so in Isa. l. 5, 6, 'The Lord God hath opened mine ear, and I was not rebellious, neither turned my back. I gave my back to the smiters, and my cheek to them that pluck off the hair: I hid not my face from shame and spitting.' Oh, the Lord, in a way of mercy towards you, hath come over all difficulties. Jesus Christ never pleaded, Oh this mountain of wrath, of sin, and sorrow is too high for me to go over: and these valleys of darkness are too long and too terrible for me to walk through. Oh no! but the Lord came skipping over all mountains, and all for the good of your souls. And will not you, upright hearts, hold on in ways of duty to him that hath thus carried himself in ways of mercy to you? And as he hath, so he doth still hold on in ways of mercy to you, notwithstanding all your provocations and unworthy walking of former mercies. Yet still he holds on in ways of mercy and kindness to you. Witness all those mercies that now you enjoy, the clothes that thou wearest, and the bread that thou eatest, and the house that thou lodgest in, and the bed that thou liest on, when thousands lie down in everlasting sorrow. He hath held on in ways of mercy, and he doth. Oh, this should bespeak you to hold on in his ways, notwithstanding any difficulties that you may meet withal.

3. But then, in the third place, Let all upright hearts seriously consider this, *that wicked and ungodly men do hold on in ways of impiety, notwithstanding all the discouragements that they meet with from God;* and will not you that are upright, hold on in ways of piety, notwithstanding all the discouragements and afflictions that you may meet with from men? Wicked and ungodly men, they hold on in ways of wickedness, notwithstanding all the afflictions, and troubles, and discouragements that God exerciseth them with. God lasheth their consciences, and passes the sentence of death upon all their comforts. Afflictions comes upon them as Job's messengers, one upon the neck of another; and yet they remain proud still, and formal still, and treacherous still, and apostates still, and profane still. O upright hearts, will not you hold on in the ways of piety, notwithstanding the discouragements that you meet with from men? Shall wicked men hold on in the ways of wickedness, notwithstanding all discouragements, though God chide them and set his angel in the way to draw a sword upon them, and crushes their bones against the wall, as he dealt with Balaam, Num. xxii. 25; shall wicked men,

Balaam-like, ride on though the angel of the Lord draw his sword; and will not you, when men draw their swords, hold on in the ways of well-doing?

4. Fourthly, Consider solemnly of *that agreement that you made with Jesus Christ, when you first took Jesus Christ upon the day of your marriage with Christ.* Oh, there is enough in that to engage you to hold on against all the discouragements you shall meet with! Oh remember, upright souls, in the day of your marriage with Jesus Christ, you indented with the Lord Jesus Christ to keep close to him, to hold on in his ways. Then you did say in effect to Christ what Ruth said to Naomi, Ruth i. 14–16, 'Where thou goest, I will go; where thou lodgest, I will lodge; thy God shall be my God; and nothing but death shall part between thee and me.' When you first gave your names to Jesus Christ, in that day your souls were really married to Christ, then you indented with the Lord Jesus Christ, and in effect said thus, 'O blessed Lord! I will follow thee wheresoever thou goest; where thou goest I will go; and where thou lodgest I will lodge; and thy God shall be my God; and nothing shall part between thee and my soul, between thy ways and my heart;' therefore let that bespeak you to hold on in ways of well-doing, notwithstanding all afflictions and discouragements you meet withal.

5. And then again, in the next place, Let upright hearts consider this, *that God knows how to deliver from troubles by troubles; he knows how to deliver from afflictions by afflictions; and God will by lesser afflictions that befall his people deliver them from greater afflictions; and by those troubles that befall them, he will deliver them from greater troubles.* That saying shall be found true, *Periissem nisi periissem*, I had perished, if I had not perished; I had been undone, if I had not been undone; I had been ruined, if I had not been ruined; I had been broken in pieces, if I had not been broken in pieces. I remember a saying of a philosopher, [Anaxagoras,] who seeing great possessions which he had lost, speaks thus, *Non essem ego salvus nisi istæ periissent*, Had not those things perished, saith he, I could not have been safe. God will so order all the afflictions and troubles that befall you in the ways of the Lord, that your soul shall say, Oh, had I not met with this affliction, I had been afflicted with a witness indeed; had I not been undone, I had been undone; had not these troubles and sorrows and discouragements befallen me, it had been worse with me. God will deliver his people, mark it, from spiritual afflictions and spiritual judgments, by the temporal afflictions and troubles that befall them. By those afflictions that you meet with in the ways of well-doing, God will deliver you from that security, pride, formality, dead-heartedness, lukewarmness, and censoriousness that otherwise might fall upon you.

I remember a story of a godly man, that as he was going to take shipping for France, he broke his leg; and it pleased providence so to order it, that the ship that he should have gone in at that very time was cast away, and not a man saved; so by breaking a bone his life was saved. Thus is the dealing of the Lord with his; sometimes he exerciseth them with afflictions—it may be he breaks their bones; ay, but it is in order to the saving of their lives.

6. And then again consider, *that all the afflictions, troubles, and discouragements that befall you shall never rob you of your treasure, of your jewels.* They may rob you of some slight, light things; as the sword that is by your side, the stick that is in your hand, and the flower that is in your hats; but they cannot rob you, they cannot strip you of your choice jewels and treasures. The jewels and treasures of an upright heart is the spiritual presence of God, union with Christ, communion with Christ, joy that is unspeakable and glorious, peace that passeth understanding, spiritual comfort, the least drop of which is more worth than a world. Now all the afflictions and troubles that befalls you can never rob you of your jewels; your treasure is safe. They may rob you of your sword, of your stick, of your flower; but your jewel is safe. Some slight, poor, outward comforts they may rob you of. Oh, but your jewels is safe, your treasure is still safe. What an encouragement it is to a poor traveller to hold on his way, notwithstanding there be thieves and enemies, when he remembereth that all the thieves and enemies that he meets with cannot rob him of his treasures, of his jewels, that is about him! they may take away his sword, or his stick, or his hat; but his jewel is safe. O upright hearts! your jewel is safe, your treasure is safe, and all the powers of darkness can never rob you of your God, of your Christ, of your comfort, of your inward peace; therefore hold on against all discouragements and afflictions that you shall meet with.

7. Then again, in the next place, consider that your holding on in the ways of well-doing, notwithstanding all discouragements and afflictions that may befall you, *is very acceptable to God; and [it] tends much to the glory and honour of God, for his people to hold on in the ways of well-doing against all discouragements that may befall them.* The church of Pergamos did, and the Lord was taken with it: Rev. ii. 13, 'I know thy works, and where thou dwellest, even where Satan's seat is: and thou hast held fast my name, and hast not denied my faith, even in those days wherein Antipas was my faithful martyr, who was slain among them where Satan dwelleth.'

The Lord here was much affected and taken with the constancy of the church, that it held on in his worship and ways, notwithstanding the discouragements and troubles that she met with. It is very honourable to God. Oh! it is an honour to the power of God, to the wisdom of God, to the goodness of God, by holding on in his ways against all oppositions; you declare to the world that there is no God like your God, and no ways like his ways; nor no encouragements like those that he gives; therefore hold on in the ways of well-doing against all discouragements.

8. But in the eighth and last place, do but consider *the dangerous nature of apostasy;* and if there were no other argument to move men to hold on in the ways of God, in the ways of well-doing, against all discouragements and troubles that may befall them, yet this alone may carry their hearts bravely on against all troubles and afflictions. Consider the dangerous nature of apostasy. If you would judge of the dangerous nature of apostasy aright, you may do it by these few things:—

[1.] First, *Consider what you fall from by apostatising from God, from his truth, and from his ways.* Oh! consider that of all falls, the falls of such apostates are the most dangerous falls. Thou that playest the apostate, and turnest from the ways of God, and from the ways of well-doing, thou fallest from God, who is the greatest good; thou fallest from his ways, that are the crown and the glory of the soul; and from his truth, the least tittle of which is more worth than heaven and earth. Alas! what are the falls of others to your falls! Alexander the Third, he fell from a pope to be a gardener in Venice; and Valerian fell from a golden chair to an iron cage; and Dionysius fell from a king to be a schoolmaster; and Nebuchadnezzar fell from a mighty prince to be a beast; but what are these falls to thy falls, O apostate! who fallest from heaven to hell—from the greatest good to the greatest evil!

We live in an apostatising age; men wheel and turn about as second causes work, and are not steadfast with their God. These are days wherein grapes are turned into thorns, and figs into thistles; wherein men that were persecuted by others, turn persecutors of others; and men that were smitten by others, now by their pens and tongues bitterly smite others, even their fellow-brethren. These are days wherein lambs are turned into lions, and doves are turned into serpents; and men that have acted like angels for God and his people, are turned to act like devils in respect of their rage and malice against God and his children, and against those ways wherein his people do walk. They are like the *taxus* of India, which the first year bears fruit, the second year leaves, and the third year poison. Thus it is with apostates of our time. For a time they bear fruit, a little after leaves, and now at last poison, the worst of all. Oh, consider the danger of apostasy! By apostasy you fall from the greatest good, and from the present hope of mercy, and from the future hope of glory; for there is no sin that doth so strip a man of the present hope of mercy, and the future hope of glory, as the sin of apostasy: witness Spira, Judas, &c.

[2.] Then again, in the second place, judge of the dangerous nature of apostasy by the judgments of God that have fallen upon apostates, as upon Julian, Judas, Spira, &c. I remember Mr Foxe makes mention of a smith in King Edward the Sixth's days, who was instrumental to convert a young man; the young man being clapped in prison for the gospel's sake, sent for the smith, and asked him whether he would encourage him to stand for the truth, and to burn for religion; he answered, his cause was good, and he should do well to suffer for his religion; but for *his* part he could not bring his heart over to burn for religion. But a little time after his shop was set on fire, and he was burned in the midst of it. Oh! it would take up more time than is now allotted to me to set out the judgments of God that have befallen apostates that have been treacherous and base to God, to his ways, to his saints, and to the trust reposed in them.

[3.] Again, you may judge of the danger of apostasy by *its near bordering upon the sin against the Holy Ghost, and by the exceeding difficulty of a man's recovering his ground, when he hath once played the apostate, and turned his back upon God and his ways.* Of all sins, the sin of apostasy comes nearest the unpardonable sin against the Holy Ghost. That soul that hath turned his back upon God and his truth, and the ways of well-doing, because of discouragements, is now upon the borders of that sin, that if God leave him but a little, he may fall into, and then he shall never rise again; which speaks out the dangerous nature of it.

[4.] And to shut up all, judge of the dangerous nature and evil of apostasy by this, that it renders all a man's former righteousness, doings, and sufferings invalid and lost: Ezek. xviii. 24, 'If a man forsake his righteousness, shall he live?' 'No,' saith God, 'he shall die'—ay, die with a witness: 'in his iniquity which he hath committed he shall die, and his righteousness shall be mentioned no more.' There shall be no more talk—This was a gallant man for God, and this man stood bravely up for his people and his ways, and for the liberty of the nation, suitable to the trust reposed in him. There shall be no mention of this if a man play the apostate. There shall be no pleading—This was once a worthy man, and stood gloriously to it. But now he is turned an apostate: he is turned away from God and his ways. All his righteousness, all his former actings and doings and sufferings shall be lost, and they shall never go to the grave with him, nor follow him to the judgment-seat of Christ: his apostasy shall follow him indeed, but for his former works of piety, they are all lost. As a soldier when he forsakes his colours and runs to the enemy, all his former good service is lost and buried in oblivion; so men that profess love to God and his people, and at last meet with difficulties and play the apostate, this their apostasy renders all their former service lost.

Thus much by way of motive to move you, Right Honourable, and all you that hear me this day, to hold on in the ways of well-doing, notwithstanding all the afflictions and discouragements that you may meet with in the ways of well-doing.

I shall now lay down a few directions. I shall be brief in them, and so draw towards a close.

1. First, Right Honourable, if you would hold on in the ways of well-doing, notwithstanding all discouragements and afflictions, in which you must expect to have your share as well as others, and haply the greatest, therefore it stands you the more upon to consider of those things that may be of use to bear up your spirits bravely, to carry you through all the trials and troubles you may meet with. To that purpose,

(1.) There are some things that you must carefully decline.

(2.) There are other things that you must carefully practise.

If you will hold on in the ways of well-doing against all oppositions, and notwithstanding all the afflictions and troubles that you may meet with, then,

[1.] First, *Take heed of unbelief.* There is nothing in the world that doth more damp the heart, that ties the tongue, that binds the hands, that puts fetters on the feet, that puts out the eyes, than unbelief. Unbelief, it blinds the eyes, it ties a man's hands, and causeth a sad and fearful damp to fall upon his heart. It renders the man utterly unfit to walk in the ways of God, especially when there is a lion in the way, and when the storm begins to rise: Heb. iii. 13, 'Take heed lest there be found in any one of you an evil heart of unbelief, to depart from the living God.' Unbelief will carry a man to apostasy. It hath been the great reason of many men's apostasy and backsliding from God and his ways, and that trust the nation hath put in them, that they could not hang on God and trust in God by faith; but unbelief was prevalent, and hath carried them from God and all just ways. Therefore take heed of unbelief.

[2.] Secondly, If you would hold on in the ways of well-doing, notwithstanding all the discouragements you may meet with, *take heed of an inordinate love to the things of this life.* This made Judas play and Demas play the apostate, and Spira play the apostate. 'Demas hath forsaken us' to embrace this present world. He looked upon the world in its pomp, beauty, and glory; and his heart falls off from God and his ways. I remember it is storied of Henry the Fourth of France asking the Duke of Alva whether he had seen the eclipses; he answered, he had so much business to do on earth, that he had no time to look up to heaven. A man whose heart is engaged to the love of the world, will find so much to do in the world, that, with that wicked duke, he will have no time to look up to heaven for strength, to walk in heavenly and holy ways against opposition. It was a good saying of Augustine, *Certe non amant illi Christum qui aliquid plusquam Christum amant*, Surely they do not love Christ who love anything more than Christ. If your hearts are pitched more upon the world, and are engaged more to it than to Christ, you will never be able to hold on in the ways of well-doing.

[3.] Thirdly, If you would hold on in the ways of well-doing, *take heed of consulting with flesh and blood:* take heed of listening and hearkening to carnal reason and carnal counsel; that is that that hath turned many a man out of the ways of God. When Paul was brought in to Christ—Gal. i. 14–16, 'When it pleased God, that separated me from my mother's womb, to call me by his grace,' as to send me to preach the gospel among the heathen, 'immediately I consulted not with flesh and blood.' If he had consulted with flesh and blood, he might have made several objections to have kept him off; 'but I consulted not with flesh and blood:' flesh would have told him that the work was too high, too hard, too dangerous for him. 'Oh but,' saith he, 'I consulted not with flesh and blood.'

[4.] Lastly, If you would hold on, notwithstanding all discouragements that may befall you, then *take heed of judging of the ways of God, and of the ways of well-doing, by the opinion that wicked men have of them.* Alas! wicked men are blind, and see not the beauty and loveliness that is in the ways of God. Wicked men are malicious against the ways of God, and ill-will will never suffer them to speak well of them.

But again, If you would walk in the ways of well-doing against all discouragements, then as you must labour carefully to decline all those things, so you must labour to put in practice these things:—

[1.] *Frequently and solemnly cast up what you have gained by walking in the ways of God.* Frequently and solemnly cast up your accounts, and see what you have gained by walking in the ways of God. Look over that power against corruptions, that strength to withstand temptations, that power to rejoice in afflictions, that you have gained in the ways of God. Look often over that 'peace that passeth understanding,' and that heavenly joy and those blessed consolations that you have gained in the ways of God and in the ways of well-doing. When the mariner and the shopkeeper cast their eye upon their former gains, it encourageth and enableth their spirits to hold on against all the discouragements and troubles they may meet with in their way; and so it will do with you.

[2.] In the second place, Look *that you act and walk in the ways of God, and in the ways of well-doing, from internal and spiritual principles.* Oh, I beseech you, Right Honourable, and all that hear me this day, as you would hold on in the ways of well-doing, look to your principles, that you move from spiritual and internal principles, from the power of the Spirit and the breathings of the Spirit, from love to God and a holy fear of God; and this will carry you bravely on against all discouragements you shall meet with. If you act from carnal and fleshly principles, and for carnal ends, as for honour or favour or profit, &c., you will never be constant in the ways of God; but when these ends cannot be answered, you will turn apostates, and turn back from God. Therefore, as you would hold on, look to your principles that they may be sound.

[3.] Then, in the third place, If you would hold on in the ways of well-doing and in the ways of God, notwithstanding all the afflictions and troubles that may befall you, labour *to exercise faith.* Faith is a singular means to enable us to walk in the ways of God against all the discouragements that may befall us. I shall open it in those two things, that are worthy of your consideration. Faith will carry the soul through all discouragements and difficulties that the soul can meet with in the ways of God. Thus:—

First, By being conversant about soul-greatening objects. Mark, this is one way by which faith enables the soul to hold on against all discouragements, by raising the soul to converse with soul-greatening objects, as God and Christ, and those treasures, pleasures, and sweetnesses that are in the Lord Jesus Christ. So in 2 Cor. iv. the last three verses, 'Our outward man decays, but our inward man is renewed day by day.' How comes this? 'While we look not at things that are seen, but at things which are not seen.' 'While faith is conversant about things which are not seen:' the word [σκοπούντων] signifies to look as a man looks at a mark. While we keep a fixed eye upon future glory—while our faith is conversant upon that crown that fades not, upon those robes that wither not, upon that kingdom that shakes not, 'the inward man is renewed day by day,' and heavy afflictions are made light, and long afflictions are made short. Thus faith enables the soul, and carries it bravely on against all discouragements, by conversing with soul-greatening objects. There is nothing so enables the soul, and so divinely greatens the soul and makes it too large, too wide, and too big for troubles and afflictions to bring under, than faith's conversing with those high and glorious objects.

Second, Then faith doth this, in the second place, *by appropriating all to itself that it lays hands upon.* Faith looks on God, and saith with the psalmist, 'This God is my God for ever and ever; and he shall be my guide unto death.' Faith looks on Christ, and saith with Thomas, 'My Lord and my God.' Faith looks on the promises, and saith, 'These precious promises are mine.' It casts an eye upon the crown of righteousness, and saith with Paul, 'Henceforth is laid up for me a crown of righteousness.' It looks upon all treasures, pleasures, and sweetness that is in Christ, and that are by Christ prepared for the soul, and saith faith, 'Those treasures are mine, those pleasures are mine, and all that sweetness that is in him is mine.' Thus faith carries on the soul against all discouragements that the soul can meet with.

Third, Then again, in the next place, If you would hold on in the ways of well-doing, *labour to increase and abound in love.* Oh let your love to God and love to his ways be augmented and increased! Oh look that love do its part, and then the soul will hold on! Cant. viii. 6, 7, 'Love is stronger than death: many waters cannot quench it, nor the floods drown it.' If a man would give all the substance of his house for love it would be contemned. בוז יבוזו, *boz jabuzu*, contemning it would be contemned, loathing it would be loathed, as the original hath it.

Now I shall shew you how love will enable the soul to hold out in the ways of God, and in the ways of well-doing, against all discouragements: and that it will do thus,

[1.] First, *By egging all other graces on to act and operate.* Love is a very active grace. It is the great wheel in the soul that sets all other graces on work. Love is like to the virtuous woman, Prov. ix. 3, that sets all her maidens at work. Where love is strong in the soul, there no grace shall be idle in the soul. There love will call upon faith, Faith, do you lay hold on that God and on that crown that is set before you; and, Patience, do you wait on God, &c. It calls on all, and sets all on work. And now the more grace is acted, the more its strength is increased; and the more its strength is increased, the more the soul is enabled to walk in the ways of God, against all discouragements that doth or can befall the soul. And,

[2.] Secondly, Love will enable you to hold on in the ways of God against all discouragements, *by rendering all the ways of God sweet and pleasant to the soul.* Love renders those ways sweet, that men that have no love to Christ look on as bitter ways. Every way is sweet and pleasant, saith love: his yoke is easy and his way is pleasant. As it is in Prov. iii. 17, 'Her ways are ways of pleasantness, and all her paths are peace:' in the abstract Love saith, This way is a precious way, and the other way of God, oh! it is a heavenly way: I find much sweetness in it, saith Love; and thus it encourageth the soul to hold on in the ways of well-doing. For the more sweet and lovely the ways of God are presented to the soul, the more the soul is raised and encouraged to hold on in those ways of God, notwithstanding any affliction and trouble that the soul meets withal. I remember I have read a story of a Dutch schoolmaster, who, when he was asked whether he loved not his wife and children, thus answered: Were all the world a lump of gold, and in my hand to dispose of, I would lay it down at my enemy's feet, that with freedom and liberty I might live and walk in the ways of God, they are so lovely to my soul.

[3.] And then, thirdly, Love, it will enable the soul to hold on in the ways of well-doing against all discouragements, *by making a blessed interpretation and a heavenly construction of the afflictions, sorrows, and discouragements that an upright heart can meet with in the ways of God.* All the afflictions and discouragements that upright hearts meets with, love will thus interpret and expound: Oh! saith the upright heart, all those afflictions are but means that God will use to rub off my dross and filth, to convey more of himself: they are all my friends, and shall work for my good, saith Love. All those cursings God will turn to blessings, saith Love. All these afflictions that befall me are but out of some noble design that God hath to reveal more of himself and of his glory to me. It is but that he may empty me more of myself and of the creature, that so he may communicate more of his own sweetness and fulness to my soul, saith Love. I know, though for the present it be bitter, yet, saith Love, it will be sweet in the end; I know the way to the crown by the cross, saith Love, and I know all those afflictions shall lead me to more heavenly enjoyments of God. This construction David made concerning Shimei's cursing of him, 2 Sam. xvi. 12: when Shimei cursed him, David expounds it sweetly: ver. 12, 'The Lord,' saith he, 'will look on mine affliction, and requite good for his cursing this day.' This interpretation carries David along on his way, notwithstanding Shimei's cursing of him. Oh! the Lord will turn the curse into a blessing, saith Love; and this carries him on bravely. So in that 1 Cor. xiii. 5, 'Love thinketh no evil.' It will make a sweet interpretation of all the afflictions that befalls the soul; and the more sweet and heavenly interpretation Love makes of afflictions that befall the soul in the ways of God, the more the soul is raised and encouraged. Well! saith the soul, if it be so, I will go on though the lions roar, &c. That is another means; if you will hold on in the ways of well-doing, then look that Love do its part: let Love be operative and working in your souls.

[4.] Lastly, I have but one thing more that I will press as to this, and so draw towards a close, and that is this, *Look frequently and solemnly upon that 'cloud of witnesses' that have gone before you.* It is the apostle's own argument, Heb. xii. 1, 2,—he brings down all those instances in the 11th chapter, and sets them before their eyes, and encourageth them from that very consideration—'To run the race that was set before them with patience, looking to Jesus, the author and finisher of our faith; who, for the joy that was set before him, endured the cross, and despised the shame, and is set down at the right hand of God.' Oh, look upon those glorious worthies that held on in the ways of well-doing. Look upon Nehemiah, that held on bravely, and David, who though princes scorned him and persecuted him, yet he held on in the ways of well-doing. So Paul and Jeremiah, &c., notwithstanding all their tossings, afflictions, and sufferings, yet held on in the ways of well-doing. Oh, why should you degenerate basely from those examples that are your crown and glory to follow? So much by way of direction, as to enable you to hold on in the ways of well-doing against all discouragements that may befall you.

Now, Right Honourable, give me only leave to premise a few things to your considerations, desiring that those considerations may be your daily meditations; and so I shall close at this time.

[1.] The first thing I desire to present to your Honourable considerations is this, *The doing of great things is most worthy of great men.* Great men should do great things, and account themselves little.[1] Oh, Right Honourable, that by your means 'the angel with the everlasting gospel in his hand might fly through our heavens,' Rev. xiv. 6; especially that he might fly through those dark corners of the kingdom where you will have thousands that sit in darkness, and in the region and shadow of death, that scarce know whether there be a Holy Ghost or no! O Right Honourable, God is now about a glorious design to exalt his Son, and the children unborn shall rise and call you blessed if you will be instrumental to further this design; and it were better that you had never been born, than that you should be instrumental to hinder those poor souls from enjoying the means of grace, that cry out, 'Bread, bread for our souls,' that say, 'Look upon us, and see if there be any sorrow like our souls' sorrow; if any darkness be like that darkness that is upon us; if any grievance be like that that is in us.' O Right Honourable, the doing of great things is most worthy of great men. The Lord stir up your hearts that you may further that glorious work; and the Lord direct you that you may pitch on some way or other whereby those that sit in darkness, and in the shadow of death, may be enlightened, and Christ revealed, and his kingdom exalted in this kingdom! Oh, if you do not labour to keep by the word that you have war by the sword, how long will it be before the sword be sheathed!

[2.] A second consideration that I premise for your honours' meditation is this, *That the saints are very dear and precious to the Lord Jesus Christ, and they that shelter them he will shelter.* They are his jewels, Mal. iii. 17. The word there rendered jewels, סגלה, *segulla*, signifies such particular treasures that he loves and lays up for himself, and for special use. They are 'the apple of his eye,' Zech. ii. 8; their service is precious to him, Prov. xv. 8; their voice is precious, Cant. ii. 14, 'Let me hear thy voice, for thy voice is sweet, and thy countenance is lovely;' their tears are precious, Ps. lvi. 8, 'He puts them in his bottle;' and their names are precious, for he 'writes them in his book,' Luke x. 20; their very thoughts are precious, Mal. iii. 16; and their blood is precious, Ps. cxvi. 15, 'Right dear and precious in the sight of the Lord is the death of his saints,' and they that shelter them God will shelter. Ebed-melech sheltered Jeremiah in the day of the king's wrath, and God sheltered him in the day of God's wrath; Rahab sheltered the spies, and the Lord sheltered Rahab; Obadiah sheltered the prophets, and the Lord sheltered him. Right Honourable, God hath made you in some blessed measure instrumental to shelter his people; and certainly that hath been one great reason that God hath sheltered you, notwithstanding all the designs, plots, and treacheries of men to destroy you. You have sheltered the saints, and God hath sheltered you. They are always precious to him, and they should be always precious to you.

[1] Vere magnum est magna facere et teipsum putare nihil.—*Eusebius.*

[3.] A third consideration for every day's meditation is, *That it is very destructive and dangerous for the powers of this world to engage against the saints of God.* Right Honourable, I abhor pleading for any particular interests; I plead for all saints which Jesus Christ hath stamped his image upon, that he hath taken into union and communion with himself; I plead for them all; for your Honours, and thousands more do know, that those men that go under different names, yet for abilities and holiness they are as precious as any that breathes: for those I plead. And I say it hath been an old design of the devil to dash the powers of this world in pieces, by engaging them against the saints and servants of Christ. Little did Pharaoh know that the devil was in that design when he pursued Israel, 'I will rise and pursue and overtake, my lust shall be satisfied;' but this was Pharaoh's destruction. His engaging against Israel was his overthrow. Haman engaged against the Jews, but this engagement against them was Haman's destruction, as you know.

Those princes (Dan. vi.) that engaged against Daniel, and found nothing against him but in the matter of his God, you know their very engagement against him was their destruction. It is dangerous and destructive to the powers of this world for them to engage against the saints of God. I will only point at two or three scriptures: Isa. viii. 8–10, 'Associate yourselves together, O ye people, and ye shall be broken in pieces.' *Rognu*, רעו, from *roang*, it signifies 'to be broken in pieces, as an army is shattered and broken in pieces with fear.'

The word 'broken' in your English Books[1] is twice more repeated, 'You shall be broken in pieces, you shall be broken in pieces;' but in the Hebrew it is three times more repeated, *Vahottu, vahottu, vahottu*, 'Ye shall be thrown down, ye shall be thrown down, ye shall be thrown down;' or 'Ye shall be confounded, ye shall be confounded, ye shall be confounded,'—Why? 'For God is with us,' ver. 10. So in Zech. xii. 2, 3, 'Jerusalem shall be a cup of trembling;' or 'a cup of poison to all the nations round about; and though all the people of the earth should gather together against her, they shall be dashed in pieces:' Isa. liv. 17, 'No weapon that is formed against thee shall prosper; and every tongue that riseth in judgment against thee shalt thou condemn. This is the heritage of the servants of the Lord; and their righteousness is of me, saith the Lord.'

[4.] Again, Right Honourable, a fourth consideration for your daily meditation is this, *That the power of godliness infinitely transcends and excels all forms of godliness.* Alas! what is the shadow to the substance? what is the shell to the kernel? what is the box to the jewel that is in it? No more are forms of godliness to the power of godliness. What is darkness to light? what are counters to gold? what is earth to heaven? No more are forms of godliness to the power of godliness; which doth bespeak you to cherish, nourish, and countenance the power of godliness, and not so to advance forms of godliness as to throw down the power and the glory of holiness.

Right Honourable, it is the power of godliness that is the honour of a nation, it is the power of godliness that is the beauty of a nation, it is the power of godliness that is the safety of a nation. Right

[1] Brooks's usual way of designating the 'Authorised (English) Version.'—G.

Honourable, as you would have joy in life, and peace in death, and boldness before Christ's judgment-seat, oh look to this, that you advance the power of godliness, that you countenance the power of godliness, that you cherish and nourish the power of godliness. Take heed, Right Honourable, of stamping *jus divinum* on anything that Christ hath not in capital letters stamped *jus divinum* upon. Oh take heed of giving a two-edged sword into the hands of any that are hot for forms of godliness, and that love to lord it over the faith and consciences of the saints, lest they, like the giant,[1] cut off all that are higher than themselves in spiritual enjoyments of God, and stretch out all that are shorter than themselves in forms of godliness. I am apt to think that if such men were more careful and skilful in using the sword of the Spirit, they would not be so hot for a temporal sword, neither would they be so angry for the want of it, as they are. A spiritual sword is most suitable to spiritual men, and most suitable to all that spiritual work that God requires of them.

Right Honourable, God is most exalted, Christ is most honoured, the Spirit is most rejoiced, the mouths of the wicked are most stopped, and the saints are most gladded by the power of godliness, by countenancing, advancing, and cherishing of that. Therefore, as you would have the Lord exalted and lifted up, and made famous and glorious, oh let the power of godliness be countenanced and cherished throughout the kingdom!

The way of instructing the people of the nation, I leave it with you whom it most concerns, desiring the Lord to direct you into such ways as may be most for the honour of his name, and for the happiness and comfort of the land we live in. That is another consideration.

[5.] One thing more, beloved, and so I shall draw to a close. In the next place, consider this, *God hath, and God will save his people and ruin their enemies, by very weak, unlikely, and contemptible means, and by very hidden and mysterious ways.* He hath done it: witness his leading of Israel by the hand through the Red Sea, and overthrowing their enemies in a mysterious way. Witness his destroying of that mighty army of the Midianites—which were as grasshoppers, and for multitude without number—by Gideon's three hundred that lapped water like a dog. The story you have in Judges vi. and vii., compared. Witness his delivering his people and ruining their grand enemy, Haman, by Esther's attempting that which was directly against the law of the land, Esth. iv. 10, 16. Haman had plotted the ruin of the Jews; all was agreed on; the writings were signed; there was but a step between death and the Jews. Esther adventures and throws herself upon God's providence, and comes to the court, directly cross to the law of the land, to the letter of the law; and by this untrodden way, which one would have thought might have enraged the king to have cut her and her people off, yet, by this untrodden way, God delivered his poor people. And whether he hath not done the same for his people who were sold to slavery, by poor, despised instruments, in our own land, I leave your Honours to judge. I will give you but only two or three texts: Isa. xli. 14–16, 'Fear not, thou worm Jacob, and ye men of Israel.' 'Fear not, thou worm

[1] The reference is to the famous bed of Procrustes.—G.

Jacob.' The original, *tolagnath*, signifies a little worm that springs out of a grave[1] or kernel. 'And ye men of Israel:' *methe*, 'ye dead men of Israel.' What follows? 'Behold, I will make thee a new sharp threshing instrument having teeth: thou shalt thresh the mountains, and beat them small, and shalt make the hills as chaff. Thou shalt fan them, and the wind shall carry them away, and the whirlwind shall scatter them: and thou shalt rejoice in the Lord, and shalt glory in the Holy One of Israel.'

Mountains are high, you know, and mountains are mighty, and mountains are strong; and so are the powers of the world; and yet little worms and dead men shall thresh these mountains, they shall overthrow and bring under even the powers that are high and strong and mighty against Jesus Christ and his ways, as we see this day. He will save his people, and destroy his enemies, though they be mighty and powerful, and in very untrodden and mysterious ways, by little worms, by dead men. So likewise Dan. ii. 33, 34, compared with vers. 44, 45, 'Thou sawest till that a stone was cut out without hands, which smote the image upon his feet, which were of iron and clay, and brake them to pieces. Then was the iron, the clay, the brass, the silver, and the gold, broken to pieces together, and became like the chaff of the summer threshing-floors; and the wind carried them away, that no place was found for them: and the stone that smote the image became a great mountain, and filled the whole earth.' Compare those verses with the 44th and 45th verses, 'And in the days of those kings shall the God of heaven set up a kingdom, which shall never be destroyed: and that kingdom shall not be left to other people, but it shall break in pieces and consume all these kingdoms, and it shall stand for ever.' All the kingdoms that are against the kingdom of Christ shall be broken in pieces by this little kingdom. And so likewise in Micah iv., the three last verses, 'Now also many nations are gathered against thee, that say, Let her be defiled, and let our eye look upon Zion. But they know not the thoughts of the Lord, neither understand they his counsel: for he shall gather them as the sheaves into the floor. Arise and thresh, O daughter of Zion; for I will make thine horn iron, and I will make thy hoofs brass; and thou shalt beat in pieces many people'—or rather, as the Hebrew hath it, 'thou shalt stamp to powder multitudes of peoples or nations,'—'and I will consecrate their gain unto the Lord, and their substance unto the Lord of the whole earth.' Many nations are gathered together against thee, that say, Let her be defiled, let her be polluted and profaned, and let our eyes look upon Zion. Oh, but they know not the thoughts of the Lord, what a design God is about, and what a project he hath in hand to advance his name, and to deliver his people and ruin their enemies, and that by the most unlikely and contemptible means that can be!

Therefore, let not men wonder at such and such strange providences as sometimes fall out, but rather consider that God hath, and he will save his people, and ruin their enemies, by very dark and mysterious ways, and by contemptible and unlikely means; and this he will do that no flesh may boast, and that his people may live a life of faith,

[1] Query, 'grape' or 'grain'?—ED.

and that their enemies may be the more dreadfully ashamed and confounded; and mainly that his own name may be alone exalted and magnified.

[6.] Lastly, Right Honourable, it is the earnest desires of the people of God generally, that your hands may further be strengthened, and that your souls may be lifted up in the ways of the Lord, *that justice and righteousness may run down now at the last among us as mighty streams.* Now, as to this, give me only leave to premise these two cautions, and so I shall have done:—

First, Right Honourable, *do justice, but do it with much pity and mercy.* Oh! weep over those wounds that the sword of justice makes; mourn over those bones that the sword of justice breaks; lament over those members that the sword of justice cuts off. Look, as justice and mercy meet in God, and kiss in God, and act harmoniously in God; so let justice and mercy meet, and kiss, and act harmoniously in you.

Secondly, Right Honourable, look to this, *that you do justice from principles of uprightness, and from the love of justice and righteousness.* Otherwise, remember this, that God may revenge that blood that may be shed upon you, if you do not justice out of a love of righteousness, and from principles of uprightness. It is very considerable in Hosea i. 4, 5, 'And the Lord said unto him, Call his name Jezreel; for yet a little while and I will avenge the blood of Jezreel upon the house of Jehu, and will cause to cease the kingdom of the house of Israel.' Right Honourable, consider this, that which Jehu did, God himself bears witness to it: 2 Kings x. 30, 'And the Lord said unto Jehu, Because thou hast done well in executing that which is right in mine eyes, and hast done to the house of Ahab according to all that was in my heart, thy children to the fourth generation shall sit on the throne of Israel.' Observe, Right Honourable, Jehu, for the matter of justice, did that which was right in the sight of the Lord. God here approves of it; but Jehu did not do justice from a love of justice, and a principle of uprightness. The matter was good, but his principles were bad. Therefore God tells him that he will avenge the blood of Jezreel upon the house of Jehu. The Lord make your Honours wise to consider of these things!

What I have here delivered, Right Honourable, hath been in the discharge of my conscience, that I may give up my account at last with joy, and not with grief; and so I shall conclude with that saying of Augustine,[1] 'Not every one that spareth us is a friend, nor every one that striketh us is an enemy.'

[1] Non omnis qui parcit est amicus, nec omnis qui ferit est inimicus.—*Augustine, Serm. 59, de verbis Domini.*

HYPOCRITES DETECTED.

A THANKSGIVING SERMON.

NOTE.

Prefixed to this Sermon is the usual form of Thanks and license to print. It will be found below*: also the title-page.† Historically the Sermon is valuable as shewing the intense feeling against Scotland at the time on occasion of the 'crowning victory' at Dunbar.—G.

* *Die Mercurii*, ix. *Octo.* 1650.

Ordered by the Parliament, that the thanks of this House be given to Mr Brooks for his great pains taken in his Sermon preached yesterday at Margarets, Westminster, being a day set apart for publick thanksgiving; and that he have the like privilege in printing as others in like case have usually had, and that Collonel *Jones* do give Mr *Brooks* the thanks of this House accordingly.

Hen: Scobell:
cler: Parliament.

I appoint Hanna Allen to print this sermon.

THO: BROOKS.

† THE
HYPOCRITE
DETECTED, ANATOMIZED,
Impeached, Arraigned, and Condemned
before the *Parliament* of ENGLAND.

OR,
A WORD IN SEASON.

Shewing Hypocrites to be the prime objects of God's wrath: and the Grounds of it: with the Speciall Lessons that we are to learn from it.

EXPRESSED
In a SERMON Preached before the PARLIAMENT of ENGLAND; upon their last thanksgiving Day, being the 8th of *Octo.* 1650. for that late great Victory that the Lord of Hosts gave our Army over the Scots Army in a battell at Dunbarr *Septemb.* 3. 1650.

By *Thomas Brooks*, a weak and unworthy Teacher of the Gospel at *Thomas Apostles, London.*

The Sinners in Zion are afraid, fearfulness hath surprised the hypocrites: who among us shall dwell with the devouring fire? who among us shall dwell with everlasting burnings? Isa. 33. 14.

Simulata sanctitas est duplex iniquitas. *Aug.*

Multi sunt oves habitu, vulpes actu, crudelitate lupi. *Bernard*

Hypocrita aut esto quod appares, aut appare quod es. *Gregory.*

Hypocritis nihil est crudelius, impatientius & vindicta cupidius, plane sunt serpentes, &c. *Luther.*

London,
Printed by Fr: Neile for Hanna Allen at the Crown in Popes-Head-Alley, 1650.

[4to.—G.]

THE EPISTLE DEDICATORY.

To the Honourable PARLIAMENT OF ENGLAND, assembled at Westminster.

HONOURABLE SENATORS,—The glorious appearances of God in these late times do with open mouth speak out God to be about to manifest himself in some more choice and remarkable way than heretofore. When little worms[1] and dead men do thresh the mountains, and make them smoke and quake, then surely God is a-coming down to 'judge the earth with righteousness and the people with equity,' and to set his mountains high upon the top of all the mountains in the world, and 'to stain the pride of all glory, and to bring into contempt all the honourable of the earth,' Isa. xxiii. 9. This design he is driving on for certain, and will, in spite of all opposition, accomplish it. The wheel of providence runs swiftly, and one glorious providence does but make way for another; which should heighten our hopes, and strengthen our faith, and raise up our souls to lay out all that we have received from God for the helping forward the design of God. Right Honourable, never had any men on earth such glorious advantages and opportunities to act high for God and his saints as you have. Ah, how many be there now triumphing in heaven, that, when they were on earth, would have thought it a heaven to have enjoyed the least of those advantages and opportunities that you enjoy, that so they might have put out themselves for God and his people to the uttermost! Ah, sirs, 'what your hand findeth to do, do it with all your might; for there is no working in the grave,' Eccles. ix. 10. Your time is short, your task is great, your Master is urgent, and your reward is sure. The devil makes all the haste he can to outwork the children of light, in a quick despatch of deeds of darkness, because he knows his time is short. He will not let slip any opportunity whereby he may do mischief. Oh do not you let slip any opportunity[2] wherein you may honour a good God, and be serviceable to your generation. Suetonius reports of Julius Cæsar, that seeing Alexander's statue, he fetched a deep sigh because he at that age had done so little. Ah that none of

[1] Isa. xli. 14. תולעת, *tolagnath*, signifies a little worm.
[2] One day God will require of men, *Non quid legerint, sed quid egerint: nec quid dixerint, sed quomodo vixerint.*

you had cause to sigh, that you have done no more for God, his truth, his ways, his people! Yet let me say, *Beati sunt qui præcepta faciunt, etiam si non perficiunt*, They are blessed that do what they can, though they cannot but underdo, [Aug.] *In libro tuo scribuntur omnes qui quod possunt faciunt*, saith Bernard—They are surely written all in God's book that do what they can, though they cannot but underdo. Oh that you would arise in Christ's strength, and do what possibly you can for God, though you cannot do what you would and what you should!

Worthy Senators, give me leave to breathe forth a few desires before you:—

First, Oh that you would look to your communion with God![1] Keep up that, increase in that, and that will more and more fit you for all that high and hard service that you are and may be put upon. The communion with God, that is the life of your graces, the sweetener of all ordinances, providences, and mercies, the strengthener of your hearts and hands, the soul of your comforts, and the crown of your souls. Nothing like this to fence you against temptations, to sweeten all afflictions, and to make you own God, and stand for God, and cleave to God, in the face of all troubles and oppositions. A man high in communion with God, is a man too big for temptations to conquer, or troubles to bring under. Communion with God, it makes bitter things sweet, and massive things light. Souls that have no communion, or but little communion, with God, they are usually as soon conquered as tempted, as soon vanquished as assaulted.

Secondly, Oh that you would make more quick despatch of businesses that are before you! Julius Cæsar's quick despatch is noted in three words, *Veni, vidi, vici*, I came, I saw, I overcame. The more quick you are in despatch of business, the more angelical you are; and is it not your highest honour to be like those glistering courtiers that attend the King of kings? Prov. iii. 12, 'Hope deferred maketh the heart sick.' The word that is here rendered 'deferred,' signifies to draw out at length. Men are short breathed and short spirited, and when their hopes are drawn out at length, this makes their heart sick. Oh that there were no such sick souls that lie languishing at hope's hospital! It was the saying of Antoni[n]us the emperor, Clemency is a kingdom's best preserver, *Regni clementia custos.*

Thirdly, Oh that you would do good to them that have rendered you evil for good! Such a spirit as this is, is most suitable to the commands of Christ, Rom. xii. 21; Mat. v. 44; and most suitable to the example of Christ, Mat. xxiii. 54. In revenge of injuries, he is the loser that gets the better, saith Basil.[2] Christ weeps over Jerusalem, though it was his and his saints' slaughter-house; and he receives to mercy those three thousand bloody souls that had embrued their villainous hands in his innocent blood, Acts ii. Joseph weeps over those malicious and bloody brethren that would have slain him, and that did sell him for a slave. Moses stands up in the gap for

[1] *Deus est mihi pro omnibus*, says the soul that has found the sweetness of communion with God. Such a soul cries out with Monica, Austin's mother, *Quid hic faciemus? cur non hinc migramus? cur non hinc avolamus?*

[2] *Victo is inferior est, qui victor est*, saith Basil.

those that called and counted him a murderer and a destroyer, though he was their saviour and deliverer. Elisha provided a table for them that had provided a grave for him. Though the Scots had provided graves for you, yet, Honoured Senators, shew bowels of mercy to them, so far as it will stand with the duty of your places, and with the safety of this commonwealth. Though Rome was most unthankful to Camillus for his conquest of the Veii, yet he buried that wrong, and freed it the second time from the Gauls. Thrasybulus, after his return to Athens, from whence he was banished by tyrants, he, with the aid of Lysander, having expelled thirty tyrants out of Athens, called those home that they had banished, and made a law that no man should remember any former injuries done unto him.

Fourthly, Oh that you may rule more for God, and govern more for God! God is all ear to hear, all hand to punish, all power to protect, all wisdom to direct, all goodness to relieve—he is *omnia super omnia*—and all grace to pardon. Is not God *optimum, maximum?*—the best, and the greatest. He is the horn of plenty, and the ocean of beauty, without the least spot of injustice. Oh that you may govern so sweetly and so prudently, that you may be termed *deliciæ humani generis*—The delight of mankind. Nothing is more difficult than to rule for God, nor nothing is more excellent than to rule for God. *Nil difficilius est quam bene imperare*, was Dioclesian's motto. He that rules, but not for God, has his reward here; but he that rules for God shall have a glorious reward at last. 'Well done, good and faithful servant, enter thou into the joy of thy Lord,' Mat. xxv. 21: a joy too big to enter into us; we must enter into it; a joy more meet for the Lord than the servant; and yet the faithful servant shall have the honour and the happiness to enter into it—even into thy Master's joy.

Fifthly, Oh stand constantly upon your watch to avoid evil! Watch to do good, watch to discover your enemies, watch to prevent your enemies, watch to suppress your enemies, watch to countenance and watch to encourage all those that hold to Christ the head, and that walk according to the law of the new creature; watch to discountenance and watch to suppress profaneness and wickedness, watch to heal the wounded, and watch to bind up the broken, and watch to relieve the oppressed, and watch to raise the dejected; watch to do good to all them that are good, and watch to be good among them that are bad, and watch to do good even to them that are bad. Oh watch your eyes that they behold no vanity, and watch your ears that they hearken not to unjust and unrighteous causes, and watch your hands that they touch not the golden wedge, and watch your lives that they cause not God's laws and your own to be slighted and despised; but, above all, watch your souls, that in the day of Christ they may be saved. The soul is a jewel more worth than heaven. Oh watch it! If that be lost, you are eternally lost; if that be lost, all is lost. Of all loss, the loss of the soul is the most incomparable, irreparable, and irrecoverable loss. It is the greatest folly in the world to watch to save a state, and not to watch to save your souls. John the Third, king of Portugal, was advised by one, every day to spend a quarter of an hour's time in meditating upon that scripture, Mat. xvi. 26, 'What shall it profit a man to gain the world, and lose his soul? or what shall a man give in exchange for his soul?' It is and shall be my desire and prayer, that you may watch to save the state, but above all, that you may watch to save your souls.[1]

Honoured Senators, I had other desires to have breathed out before you; but having made too bold, I fear, with your patience, I shall send them up to heaven, hoping and waiting for a comfortable answer from thence. I humbly crave your Honours, and all others that shall read this sermon, to cast a covering of love over all the mistakes of the printer; I having not the least time to wait upon the press to correct what haply may be found amiss. Now, honoured worthies, that you may do gloriously in your generation, that you may prize Christ above all, and live in him as in your all, and triumph through him over all enemies within you and without you, and eternally reign with Christ after all, is and shall be the earnest desire and prayer of him who is, honoured and worthy Senators, your most humble and devout servant in all humble service for Christ,

THOMAS BROOKS.

[1] Læti simus, non securi,'&c.—*Bernard.* He that feasts his body and starves his soul, is like him that feasts his slave and starves his wife, saith Ephraem Syrus.

A SERMON

PREACHED BEFORE THE PARLIAMENT OF ENGLAND ON THEIR LATE DAY OF THANKSGIVING FOR THEIR VICTORY OVER THE SCOTS.

I will send him against an hypocritical nation; and against the people of my wrath will I give him a charge, to take the spoil, and to take the prey, and to tread them down like the mire in the street.—ISA. X. 6.

I WILL not spend that short time that is left me about that which will turn least to your souls' account, therefore I will very briefly open the words of my text: 'I will send thee against an hypocritical nation.' The word that is rendered 'hypocritical' signifies to pollute, or defile. Of all sins, the sin of hypocrisy is the most defiling sin. It defiles men's prayers and praises; it defiles all duties and ordinances. 'I will give him in charge, to take the spoil and to take the prey.' The word that is rendered 'charge' signifies to give command with authority and power, to bind, and to tread them down 'like the mire of the streets,' or rather, as the Hebrew has it, 'to lay there a-treading.'

The main thing the words hold forth is this,—*That of all sorts of sinners God will be most severe in his judgments against hypocrites.* Or thus: *Hypocrites are the proper objects of God's wrath, and such as he will most severely punish.*

I shall, in the handling of this point, briefly point out to you those scriptures that speak out this truth, and then open it to you. The scriptures that speak out this truth are these, Job xv. 34; Isa. xxxiii. 14, and ix. 17; Mat. xxiii., and xxiv. 51.

For the opening of the point, I shall endeavour these two things: First, to give you the reasons of God's severity against hypocrites; and secondly, discover to you who these hypocrites be that are the objects of God's wrath; and thirdly, give you the uses of the point, which is the main thing I intend.

1. Now, first, for the reasons of the point, I shall give you only these six:—

Reason 1. First, Because of all sorts of sinners, hypocrites *are most dangerous to human society.* There are no sorts of sinners upon earth so dangerous to human society as hypocrites are: Job xxxiv.

30, 'That the hypocrites reign not, lest the people be ensnared,'—*mimloch*, from *malach*, [מלך,] 'that the hypocrite king it not.' There are no sorts of men on earth that delight to king it as hypocrites do. 'That the hypocrite king it not, lest the people be ensnared.' There are no men in the world so skilful and careful to lay snares and traps to ensnare the silly birds, as hypocrites are to ensnare the children of men: Prov. xi. 9, 'An hypocrite with his mouth destroyeth his neighbour.' The breath of the hypocrite is poisonous; he breathes out nothing but poison. The word that is rendered 'destroy' signifies utterly to destroy. It is used for corruption both in religion and manners. Hypocrites destroy persons by their vices and corruptions: Mat. xxiii. 13, 'But woe unto you, scribes and Pharisees, hypocrites, for ye shut up the kingdom of heaven against men; for ye neither go in yourselves, neither suffer ye them that are entering to go in.' The great mischief that a hypocrite may do, will sufficiently appear by this history.

Constantia, the widow of Licinius, sister of the emperor Constantine the Great,[1] entertained in [her] house a certain presbyter, who professed the orthodox religion for fear of Constantine, but was in secret an Arian. Several bishops of the Arian sect made use of this man to promote their cause by his sly dissimulation. At length, Constantia, lying sick upon her death-bed, her brother, the emperor, came to visit her. She soon prevailed with him to entertain the presbyter into his court. He soon grew into great credit and favour with Constantine, so that when he died he intrusted him with his last will, whereby he had an opportunity to make himself gracious with Constantius, the emperor's son and successor, which opportunity he did improve. First, he corrupts one Eusebius, a eunuch, the new emperor's chief chamberlain, and by this means other courtiers, and then the empress, and at length the emperor himself, and by degrees brought him to be [a] defender of Arianism, and a great persecutor of the truth which his father had professed, and which himself had been brought up in.

Reason 2. The second reason is this: Because, of all sorts of sinners, there is none *so hardened against the Lord Jesus Christ as hypocrites are.* None stout it against Jesus Christ as hypocrites do. If that Christ call upon the profane man, he hearkens; if he entreats, he yields; if he knock, he opens. But as for the hypocrite, Christ may call and cry, entreat and beseech, and yet the hypocrite will not hear, nor yield, nor open to him: Mat. xxi. 31, 32, 'Verily I say unto you, that the publicans and the harlots go into the kingdom of heaven before you; for John came unto you in the way of righteousness, and yet ye believed him not; but the publicans and the harlots believed him.' Christ comes to the harlot's door, and to the profane man's door, and knocks, and they open to him, and kiss him, and embrace him, and receive him; but as for the hypocrite, though Christ does knock, and call, and cry out to him, yet he will not hear; nay, though he take his soul and hang it over the scotching flames of hell, and say to him, Ah hypocrite! 'is it good to dwell in everlasting burnings?' yet he will not yield; and though he take him and shew him the glory of heaven, and the happiness of sincere souls, yet he will not yield nor

[1] Sozom., lib. iii. cap. 1; Socrat., lib. ii. cap. 2.

open to Christ, though he miss of heaven, and be cast into the hottest and the lowest place in hell.

Reason 3. Because hypocrites *yield the greatest assistance to Christ's grand enemy, to wit, Satan.* One hardened and seared hypocrite is more advantage to carry out Satan's design, than a thousand loose profane persons. A hypocrite is Satan's firstborn; he is Satan's darling; he leans upon the devil's breast, as John did upon Christ's. There are none so active for Satan, nor none have those advantages to carry on his work, as the hypocrite hath, Mat. xxiii. 15. They 'compass sea and land to make a proselyte.' They are very active to enlarge the dominion of Satan, and therefore no wonder God is so severe in his judgments against them.

Reason 4. A fourth reason is, Because hypocrites *are false to the marriage-bed;* and therefore God is so severe against them. They pretend love to Christ, and yet they give up their hearts to other lovers besides Christ, Ezek. xxxiii. 31; Isa. xxix. 13. You know in law nothing gives a man that advantage to put away his wife as falseness to the marriage-bed; and Christ will take that advantage to cast off hypocrites for ever.

Reason 5. Because they are *the very worst of sinners.* They are often in Scripture compared to the very worst of things, to vipers, serpents, wolves, &c., which speaks them out to be the worst of men. They are secret enemies, which are of all enemies the worst; as Leo the emperor said, *Occulti inimici pessimi*, A close enemy is far worse than an open; a close enemy kisses and kills, but an open enemy shoots off his warning-piece before he shoots off his murdering-piece. Again, hypocrites are doomed to the worst of judgments, as that they shall not come before God: Job xiii. 16, 'An hypocrite shall not come before God;' he shall not be taken up into spiritual enjoyment of God on earth, nor into glorious communion with God in heaven. Hypocrites, they are doomed by Christ to the greatest torments in hell: Mat. xxiii. 14, 'Woe unto you, scribes and Pharisees, hypocrites; for ye shall receive the greater damnation.' The darkest and the lowest place in hell is theirs. Hypocrites are hell's free-holders; all other sinners are but inmates to hypocrites. Of all sinners, hypocrites sin against the greatest light, and against the greatest knowledge, against the greatest discovery of God, which speaks them out to be the worst of sinners; yea, though they do know sins against knowledge to be very dangerous, though they know them to be wounding and wasting sins—*peccata vulnerantia et devastantia*—yet hypocrites will hold on in their sin. The hypocrite will rather go to hell with his lusts, than to heaven without his lusts. Though he be convinced that he and his beloved sins must part, or Christ and his soul will never meet, yet the hypocrite will say, Farewell Christ, and welcome sin! A hypocrite will hold on in religious duties, and yet hold on in a resolved way of wickedness, Jer. vii. 9; Ezek. xxxiii. 30–32. A hypocrite will sin and pray, and he will hear and swear, &c.; like Louis the Eleventh, king of France, he would swear, and then kiss the cross, and swear again, and then kiss the cross. And is there any people on earth who are more infamous for this than the Scots, against whose hypocrisy God has given so great a testimony? A hypocrite hath two hands, the one to embrace, and the other to stab with, as Joab; he hath two tongues, with Judas, the one to salute Christ, and another to betray Christ; he hath two faces, with Janus, one looks backward, and the other forward. A hypocrite hath two hearts, with the Israelites, he can cry, 'Hail king Solomon, hail king Adonijah;' like Apuleius' parrot, 'Hail Augustus the emperor, hail Antony,' *Ave Auguste imperator, ave Antoni;* all which speaks them out to be the worst of sinners.

Reason 6. The sixth and last reason is this, Because hypocrites *fight against Christ with his own weapons.* They fight against God with his own gifts that he hath bestowed upon them, as David fought against Goliath with his own sword; or as Jehu fought against Jehoram with his own men. Thus did the scribes and Pharisees, Spira and Judas, fight against Christ to their own eternal overthrow. The hypocrite will fight against God with that knowledge, wisdom, light, and understanding which God hath given him, though he dies eternally for it. Julian the apostate fought against Christ with his own weapons; and through the strength of his parts he prevailed more by persuading than by enforcing, and by enticements than by torments, to the ruin of Christians. Hypocrites fight against God with his own weapons, and dare heaven, and therefore God will cast them to hell.

2. The second thing that I am to do, is to discover to you *what hypocrites are that God is so severe in his judgment against.* The Greek word ʽυποκριτης, signifies stage-players. A hypocrite is a slave in king's robes; he is a devil in angel's apparel; he is a wolf in a sheep's skin. As Cicero saith of Epicurus, that he was no philosopher in truth, but put on the bare name of a philosopher; so I may say, a hypocrite is no saint, no holy man in truth, but one that puts on the name of a saint, and outwardly appears to be a saint, though inwardly he is a devil incarnate. The Hebrew word חנף, that is rendered a hypocrite, signifies to dissemble, and defile, or pollute. Hypocrites are the greatest dissemblers in the world; they dissemble with God, with men, and with their own souls; and as they are the greatest dissemblers, so they are the greatest defilers in the world; they defile all places and company where they come; they defile all duties, mercies, and ordinances they touch. But I shall shew you more fully what he is in these six following things:—

[1.] First, Hypocritical hearts *are proud, vain-glorious hearts.* Every man's silver is but brass to theirs, and every man's light is but darkness to theirs; and no men's duties and abilities are comparable to theirs. The proud and vain-glorious hypocrite, Jehu-like, says, 'Come, see my zeal for the Lord of hosts,' 2 Kings x. 16. A sincere heart loves to do much for Christ, and not to be seen by any but Christ. Jehu's zeal is but the shadow of zeal, as all hypocrites' virtues are but the shadows of virtues, and yet the hypocrite, Narcissus-like, falls in love with his own shadow. The hypocrite loves to see the hat move, and the knee to bow, and men to cry, Rabbi, rabbi, in the market-place, Mat. xxiii. 5–7.[1] Charis, a soldier, was so proud

[1] A sincere heart is like the red rose, which though outwardly it be not so fragrant as the damask, yet inwardly it is far more cordial: a sincere heart is like the violet, which grows low, and hides itself and its own sweetness, as much as can be, with its own leaves.

because of the wound he gave Cyrus, that shortly after he went mad, saith Plutarch; and Menecrates was so proud because he cured many patients which others could not, that he called himself Jupiter; so hypocrites are proud, and swell with the thoughts of their own worth and doings, that they cry up and set up themselves above others: Luke xviii. 11, 12, 'God, I thank thee that I am not as other men are,' &c. 'I fast twice in the week, I give tithes of all that I possess;' Isa. lxv. 5, which say, 'Stand by thyself, come not near to me, for I am holier than thou.'

[2.] Secondly, Hypocrites, they do always *cover their cruel and bloody intentions with specious and religious pretences.* Herod, a notorious hypocrite, covers his intentions of murdering Christ, with pretences of worshipping Christ; and those in Ezra iv. cover their intentions of pulling down the temple, with pretences of help [in] building the temple. They pretend to build the temple, and yet they intended to pull down the temple; and so did Jezebel, in that 1 Kings xxi.; and so Ishmael covers his bloody intention of murdering, with weeping, Jer. xli. A hypocrite will draw a fair glove upon a foul hand; he is like the serpent that stings without hissing; they will kiss, and kill you; they will kiss, and betray you; they will stroke you, and cut your throat. There is nothing more evident in experience and Scripture than that hypocrites have all along covered their bloody and cruel designs with religious pretences. Parsons, when he had plotted that matchless villainy the Powder-plot, he sets out his book of resolutions as if he had been made up all of devotions. Hypocrites are like the Italians, that will hug and embrace you in those arms they intend to imbrue in your dearest blood.

[3.] A hypocritical heart *is a subtle heart, a deceitful heart.* What is said of Jonadab, 2 Sam. xiii. 2, that he was a very subtle man, that may I say of all hypocrites; they are very subtle men; by good words and fair speeches they deceive the hearts of the simple, drawing them unawares into the lion's paw, as Mohammed did. The hypocrite is a cloud without rain, a blossoming tree without fruit, a star without light, a shell without a kernel. The hypocrite is like the fruit of Sodom, that without is very fair, but within is nothing but dust. The hypocrite is like the images Lucian speaks of, that were bravely wrought over with silver and pearl, but within are filled up with the meanest and basest things, as pieces of wood, pitch, mortar, &c.; whereas a sincere heart is like Brutus his staff, thorn without and gold within; or like that ark, gold within and goat's hair without.

[4.] Fourthly, again, Hypocrites *never do good out of love to God, but out of designs to advantage themselves*, Mat. xxiii. 14, and vi. 1–3. The hypocrite very seldom follows Maximilian's counsel, *Tene mensuram et respice finem*, Keep thyself within compass, and always have an eye to the end of thy life and actions. Jehu makes a great deal of stir; he pretends to be very zealous for God; he destroys idolaters, but not idolatry; and all this was only that he might come to the crown. Mr Knox[1] reports of some noblemen in Scotland who seemed very forward for Reformation, but their design was merely for spoil, and for their private commodity; but, saith he, they were

[1] Knox 'History of Scotland,' p. 503.

very licentious, they greedily griped the possessions of the church, and would not lack their part of Christ's coat. And Mr Blair, a great counsellor of Scotland, being under great horrors of conscience, professed that he pretended to religion only to get wealth. I have read of a prince that was of no religion but that which was for his own advantage, and that would advance his own interest. Truly there is no hypocrite that breathes, that doth any good, but he hath some carnal design in it.

[5.] Fifthly, A hypocrite *will not acknowledge God in his own righteous judgments:* Job xxxvi. 13, 'The hypocrite crieth not when God bindeth him.' The Hebrew word, *annegun*, that is here rendered 'cry,' comes from a Hebrew root, which signifies to make no noise. A hypocrite will not acknowledge the justice and the righteousness of God against him; he will not cry, he will make no noise. Although God's hand be sore upon him and against him, he will not say, This is the justice and the righteousness of God; though God's hand be lifted up against him, yet he makes no noise; though God binds him and deals with him as prisoners are bound and dealt with—for so the Hebrew signifies—yet they will make no noise. In Isa. xxvi. 11, 'When thy hand is lifted up, they will not see, but they shall see and be ashamed.' The word, חזה, signifies to 'see' with the greatest exactness and curiosity that can be, to see with the eye and contemplate with the mind: he will not see. Ay, but, saith God, before I have done with him, I will make him see with his eye, and contemplate on my judgments with his mind. He shall see: Jer. v. 10-12, 'Go ye up upon the walls, and destroy; but make not a full end: and take away her battlements; for they are not the Lord's.' The Hebrew word, נטש, *natash*, that is rendered 'battlements,' signifies the young suckers that grow up about a plant; and by a similitude here may be understood the counter-scarf towers and leaning places. The battlements were to compass the house round about, to keep men from falling off; for among the Jews their houses had flat roofs, on which men walked, and from thence they called and spake to the people: to which Christ alludes in Mat. x. 27. The height of the battlement was not to be less than ten hands'-breadths, and it was to be strong, that men might lean thereon, and not fall to maim any. Take away her battlements, take away her succours, her towers, her leaning-places, for they are not the Lord's. But why will God strip them of their strength, and succours, and leaning or resting-places? Ver. 11, 'For the house of Israel and the house of Judah have dealt very treacherously against me, saith the Lord.' 'They have deceived me, they have deceived me;' so it is in the Hebrew, to shew that they have most notoriously and frequently dealt guiltfully, deceitfully, and fraudulently with God. But how does this appear, that they have dealt thus with God? It is answered in ver. 12, 'They have belied the Lord, and said, It is not he; neither shall evil come upon us; neither shall we see sword nor famine.' The Hebrew word that is rendered here 'belied,' 'they have belied the Lord,' [כחש,] signifies 'to deny.' So it is used in Gen. xviii. 15, 'Then Sarah denied, saying, I laughed not.' It is the same word that is here rendered belied. 'They have denied the Lord, and said, It is not he;' they have denied the justice and righteousness and severity of God in his judgments against them; and this is evident in the third verse of this chapter, 'O Lord, are not thine eyes upon the truth? thou hast stricken them.' The Hebrew word signifies 'to smite,' [נכה, *nacha*,] 'to wound,' 'to kill.' Lord, thou hast smitten them, thou hast wounded them, thou hast killed some of them, but they have not grieved. The Hebrew word signifies [*halu a hol*] 'to pain,' 'to make sick.' Though I have dealt thus severely with them, yet they are not pained, they are not sick, but bear up hard against all the blows and wounds I have given them. 'Thou hast consumed them, but they have refused to receive correction.' The Hebrew word that is here rendered 'refused,' signifies to refuse with the greatest pride, disdain, and scorn that may be, Ezek. xvii. 14. Oh! says God, though I have consumed them, yet they proudly, disdainfully, and scornfully refuse to receive correction. The word that is here rendered 'correction' signifies both chastening and teaching, the one being the end of the other. Though my rod has been heavy upon them, yet they have proudly and scornfully refused to be taught by my rod; they have made their faces harder than a rock; they have refused to return.

[6.] Sixthly, Hypocrites *despise those that, in their apprehension, are in outward form below them, and envy those that, in the spirit and power of holiness and godliness, do excel them:* Luke xviii. 11, 12, 'God, I bless thee that I am not as this publican: I fast twice in the week.' He pleads his negative righteousness, and he stands on his comparative goodness, 'I am not as this publican: I fast twice in the week,'—on Thursdays, because on that day Moses went up to mount Sinai; and on Mondays, because on that day he came down, saith Drusius. Hypocrites are better at shewing their worth than their wants; they are as notable at discommending others, as they are at commending themselves; at abasing others, as at exalting themselves; at lessening others, as at greatening themselves. They envy every sun that outshines their own. Let a man excel them in his enjoyments of God, in his communion with God, in acting for God, &c., he shall be envied and hated to the death, John xi. 47, 48. Androgeus, son of Minos, king of Crete, was slain by the Athenians, and Megarenes, for envy, because he overcame all in exercises of arms. So Socrates, that in the judgment of Apollo was the wisest man on earth, and in many moral excellencies did outshine all others, which the eye of envy could not endure, which occasioned him to say, 'My accusers nor my crime cannot kill me, but envy only, which hath and will destroy the worthiest ever.' The emperor Adrian oppressed some, and slew others, that excelled in any art or faculty, that he might be held the only skilful artist. Aristotle is said to have burnt and abolished the books of many philosophers, that he might be the more admired: even so do hypocrites envy all that do excel them in any spiritual or moral excellencies.

There are divers other characters that I might give of those hypocrites that God is so severe in his judgments against: as (1) that they are most zealous about the external part of duties, and regard not the spiritual part of duties, Isa. i. 11–18; Mat. xxiii. 25–27; John xviii. 28. And (2) that they are seemingly for one thing and really for another, as Herod, Pilate, and Judas were. And (3) that they are uneven-carried hearts; they do not carry themselves evenly in all places, nor in all companies, nor at all times. Witness the scribes and pharisees. A sincere heart is like a die, which is every way even, and, like itself, turn it or throw it how you will: but the hypocrite is like the cameleon, that changes his colours—now he is this, and now he is that; sometimes you shall have him an angel at home and a devil abroad, and sometimes a devil at home and an angel abroad. Hypocrites are like Cicero: they will speak to please Pompey and Cæsar too.

(5.) Hypocrites will rather use spectacles to behold other men's sins, than looking-glasses to behold their own, Mat. vii. 3–5. Hypocrites mind not Conradus' motto, *Omnium mores, tuos imprimis, observato*, Observe all men's carriages, but especially thy own.

(6.) Hypocrites trade not with God upon the credit of Christ's love, blood, righteousness, and intercession, but upon the credit of their own prayers, tears, desires, and endeavours, Isa. lviii. 3.

(7.) Hypocrites usually hold not on in religious duties under the want of outward encouragements, and against outward discouragements, John vi. 66; Job xxvii. 10.

(8.) Hypocrites are heartless in all religious duties, Isa. xxix. 13; Hosea vii. 14; Ezek. xxxiii. 31, 32.

(9.) Hypocrites are not only heartless in duties, but they are also partial in duties. The less they will do, the greater they will not do, Mat. xxiii. 23. So Saul, Herod, Judas, and Pilate, &c. It shall suffice that I have named these things. Let us now come to the uses of the point, which is the main thing that I have in my eye.

Beloved, God hath in a very eminent manner made good this truth to a dissembling nation before all the world, even upon them that in the pride of their hearts did say, We have them in Essex's pound, and that did debate what terms to offer to your army for the delivery up of your arms. I confess, God hath all along made my soul tender of them that fear his name in that nation, so that I have improved that interest that I have in heaven for their good; yet I say for the generality of that nation, they are known round about to be a dissembling nation. And truly what I have seen them lately act, is but suitable to that character that is given of them in those parts where I have travelled.

But the main thing that my heart is most upon is to present unto you those choice things that the great and glorious appearance of God against the hypocritical nation, and for your safety, does bespeak of you; and they are these:—

[1.] First, *Thankfulness*. Oh bless that God that hath given you life, when your enemies had passed upon you the sentence of death. Of all the mercies that you have had, is not this the most big-bellied mercy? Ah, the mercies that are in the belly of this mercy, the city mercy, the country's mercy, the family mercies, the soul mercies, that are in the belly of this mercy! Are not all your former mercies, and all future desired mercies, to be found in the belly of this mercy? Besides, is it not an unexpected mercy? Your army at that time did not expect it till they were engaged; many of your friends here did not at that time look for it; and most men, when the first news of it came, could not believe it. And will not you be thankful for it? Was it not a mercy that came in after solemn appeals and prayers made to the God of your mercies, that he would deal with you according to the righteousness of your cause, and according to the uprightness of his people, that were in their sincere desires and endeavours tender of his glory? And will you not be thankful for it? Was it not a mercy given in upon the account of Christ pleading at the right hand of his Father, for them that were as sheep appointed for the slaughter? And will you not be thankful for it? Has not his giving in of this mercy been a means to weaken the hands, the hopes, the counsels, the strength of your enemies? And will you not be thankful for it? Has not the giving in of this mercy given you a further and a greater advantage to honour God, and lift up Christ, and make sure the things that belong to your peace, and to do good to the saints, and to serve your generation? And will you not be thankful for it? Can you look upon it as clothed with all its glorious circumstances, and not be thankful for it? As God looks upon his people's sins, so they should look upon his mercies: he looks upon their sins as clothed with their circumstances; they sinned at the sea, even at the Red Sea, Ps. cvi. 7. In the Hebrew it is at the sea, in the sea, when the waters were as walls, on their right hand and on their left. Now as God looks upon his people's sins as clothed with circumstances, so should you look upon all his mercies as they are clothed with circumstances. O beloved, to have so great a mercy at such a time, when your enemies were strongest, and your army weakest, and under many wants, and temptations, and weaknesses, &c., this should engage you to everlasting thankfulness. That worms and dead men should thresh the mountains, is a mercy that bespeaks the greatest thankfulness; and yet, oh how few are there that return thanks to God for this mercy! Amongst the ten lepers that were cleansed, one returned to give thanks; but were it not well if there were one out of twenty that in good earnest did return thanks for this so great a mercy? A thankful man is worth his weight in gold. Most men are like the philosopher that forgot his own name; so most men in our days forget their own mercies. Too many are like Pythagoras' scholars, that speak not in five years, or rather, like the dumb man in the Gospel, they speak not at all. Many men in our days have a spiritual palsy in their tongues, so as they cannot call mercies mercy; but, with the murmuring Israelites, they call mercies miseries, and saviours destroyers, and deliverers murderers. When the Jews would not be thankful for mercies, the prophet calls out, 'Hear, O heavens, and hearken, O earth,' Isa. i. 2; and Jeremiah calls out, 'O earth, earth, earth,' Jer. xxii. 29; and Micah calls out to the mountains, and the foundations of the earth, chap. vi. 2. And truly if for this mercy you will not be thankful, I think the heavens and the earth, and the foundations thereof, will another day be witness against you. The manifestations of God in his providence are the most precious things in the world; and had we as many tongues as Argus had eyes, they were all too little to set forth the goodness of God for his mercy. It was a good saying[1] of Augustine, 'If God give prosperity, praise him, and it shall be increased; if adversity, praise him, and it shall be removed, or at least sanctified.' It is sad to think that among so many that pretend to the Spirit, there should be so many that have such a spiritual palsy on their tongues, as that they cannot be thankful for the works of the Spirit. The stork is said to leave one of her young ones where she hatcheth them, and the elephant to turn up the first twig toward heaven when she comes to food, and both do this out of some instinct of gratitude: and shall not Christians be thankful for greater mercies? When Tamerlane had taken Bajazet, amongst other questions he asked him whether ever he had given God thanks for making him so great an emperor. He confessed ingenuously he had never thought of it. Ah, it were well if we had none such among us, that do never think of the great things that God has done for them!

[2.] The second thing that the glorious appearances of God for you does bespeak of you, is *to be greatly magnanimous for God.* Right Honourable and beloved, God does expect that you, and all his people in the land, should appear magnanimous for him. God does now expect that all his people should be taken up with those things that have most of God, and most of Christ, and most of heaven in them, and for these his people should be most magnanimous. Your feet should be where other men's heads are. It was a good saying of one, *Vere magnum est magna facere, et teipsum putare nihil,* Great men should do great things, and count themselves nothing, [Euseb.] As Cleopatra said to Mark Antony, It is not for you to be a-fishing for gudgeons, but for towns, and forts, and castles: so I say, It is not for you, for whom God has done such great things, to exercise yourselves about poor, low things, but about high, noble, and honourable things, that may answer to those great things God has done for you. You must not be like the king of Navarre, who told Beza that he would launch no further into the sea, than he might return at pleasure to the shore, though he did shew some countenance to religion. It was an excellent saying of Pacunius, 'I hate the men that are idle in deed and philosophical in word.' God loves, saith Luther, *curistas,* not *quœristas.* When Demosthenes was asked what was the first part of an orator, he answered, Action; what the second, he answered, Action; what the third, he answered, Action. Oh that Severus the emperor's motto might be still in your eye, and still upon your hearts, *Laboremus,* Let us be doing.

[3.] The third thing that the glorious appearance of God for you does bespeak of you, is *to take heed of great sins after these great mercies,* Ezra ix. 13, 14. David, Lot, Solomon, and Noah, fell foulest after great mercies. Of all sins, sin after great mercies are most provoking to the God of mercy: 1 Kings xi. 9, 'The Lord was angry with Solomon, because his heart was turned back from the Lord God of Israel, which had appeared to him twice.' The Hebrew word that is rendered 'angry' is from a root that signifies to snuff and look pale—אנף, *anaph*—with anger, to shew how greatly God was angry with him. O beloved, if God snuff with anger against Solomon,

[1] The ancients used to say, *Ingratum dixeris, omnia dixeris.*

because his heart was turned back from that God who had appeared gloriously to him twice, what tongue can express how the anger of the Lord will burn against you, if your hearts should be turned back from him that hath appeared gloriously, not only twice, but many hundred times to you, and for you? I beseech you seriously consider that great sins after great mercies will cloud the face of God, and make the greatest wounds in conscience, and imbitter present mercies, and prevent future mercies, and cloud your evidences, and weaken your graces, and raise your fears, and heighten your enemies' hopes, and strengthen their hands; and therefore take heed of great sins after great mercies. Boleslaus, king of Poland, when he was to speak or do anything of importance, he would take out a little picture of his father that he carried about him, and kiss it, and say, Dear father, I wish I may do nothing unworthy of thy name. Ah souls! this should be your constant wishes and endeavours, that you may do nothing unworthy of that glorious name that has done such glorious things for you.

[4.] The fourth thing that the glorious appearance of God for you does bespeak of you, is *to own God, and cleave to God in the face of all discouragements, who has owned you in the face of all your weakness and unworthiness and unrighteousness before the whole world.* God, by his owning of you, does with open mouth bespeak you to own him. Caleb owns God, and follows God in the face of all discouragements; and this was to him a praise and an honour, Num. xiv. 24. The word that is rendered 'followed' is taken from a ship under sail —מלא, *male*—which is carried strongly with the wind, as if it feared neither rocks nor sands. So Caleb followed the Lord in the face of all discouragements, without any slavish fears; and this was his crown, and for this he shall enjoy that mercy that most were shut out from. You for whom God has done such great things, must be resolved with Diony sius, come life, come death, to worship none but the God of heaven and earth. Thus did those worthies in Dan. iii. and those in Heb. xi. And thus did Chrysostom, Luther, Calvin, Galeacius [Carraciolus,] and Basil the Great, with many more, own Christ and cleave to Christ in the face of all discouragements. And why should you degenerate from their examples, which is your highest honour to follow? Oh, shall Cleombrotus, in hope of immortality, tumble himself down a hill,[1] and Socrates smile upon his hemlock, and Scævola burn his own hand without ever gnashing his teeth at it, and Marcus Cato scorn his own life because given him by his enemy, and tear off the salve from his bleeding side; and will not you do as much, yea, more, for that glorious God who has wrought so many wonders for you? Oh let not God have cause to say, Lo, here is a parliament, here is a commonwealth, that I have owned in the face of all their sins, unworthiness, and unrighteousness; and they have disowned me when troubles and trials have been upon them. There is nothing that takes God more than men's owning of him in the face of all discouragements: Jer. ii. 2, 'Go and cry in the ears of Jerusalem, saying, Thus saith the Lord, I remember

[1] The philosopher of Ambracia; Callimach., epigr. 60; Cicero, pro *Scaur.* ii. 4; Tusc. i. 34; and Augustine, de Civitate Dei, i. 22. Read a 'high wall,' not a 'high hill.'—G.

the kindness of thy youth, the love of thine espousals, when thou wentest after me in the wilderness, in a land that was not sown.' It is nothing to follow God in a paradise; but it is a glorious, God-taking thing to follow him in a wilderness.

[5.] Fifthly, The glorious appearances of God for you do bespeak you *to set some character of favour and love upon the instruments of your mercy.* I need not tell you that it was the custom of the Romans to reward and crown their soldiers for their good services, but because I understand your hearts have been and are drawn out this way, I shall say no more to this, but sit down satisfied, that you will honour them whom God has honoured, and bless them whom God has blessed, though all the world should slight and curse them.

[6.] Sixthly, The glorious appearances of God for you do bespeak you *to improve your time and opportunities, for the honour and advancement of the glory of that God that hath taken all opportunities to set all his golden wheels, his glorious attributes, at work for your good, and for all our safety and security.* Oh do much for that God in a little time, who hath done exceedingly much for you in so short a time. Time is a jewel more worth than a world. Time is not yours to dispose of as you please; it is a glorious talent that men must be accountable for as well as any other talent. Cato, a heathen, held that an account must be given not only of our labour, but also of our leisure. You have no lease of your lives, and death is not bound to give you warning before it gives you that deadly blow that will send you to everlasting misery or everlasting felicity. Of all talents, time is the hardest well to improve. Chilo, one of the seven sages, being asked what was the hardest thing in the world to be done, answered, To use and employ a man's time well. It was a notorious reproach to Domitian the Roman emperor, that he spent much of his time in killing of flies. And it was a reproach to Artaxerxes, that he spent his time in making hafts for knives, and to Solyman the great Turk that he spent his time in making notches of horn for bows, and to Archimedes that he spent his time in drawing lines in the dust, when he should have been fighting for his life with his sword. Ah, Right Honourable, was their spending their time so vainly such a reproach to them, and will your misspending your time be an honour to you? Oh spend your time so as God may have much honour, the commonwealth much good, and your souls much comfort and boldness when you shall stand before the judgment-seat, where princes must lay their crowns, and parliament-men must put off their robes. Oh, when you have spent your time in the parliament, or in the committees, in shewing your wit and the strength of your parts to oppose and cross one another, when you should have all readily, cheerfully, and willingly agreed together for common justice and righteousness towards all men,—oh then cry out with Titus Vespasian, 'O my friends, I have lost a day! I have lost a day!' Bernard brings in the vain person thus lamenting himself: Oh what a wretch! what a beast! what a mad devil was I! so woefully to waste the marrow and fat of my precious time in sinful pleasures and delights! I have read of one that, upon his dying-bed, would have given a world for time, he crying out day and night, Call time again! oh, call time again! The desires of my soul to God for you shall be, that you may so improve your time, that you may never have cause lamentingly to cry out, 'Call time again! oh, call time again!' Ah, beloved, have not you need to improve your time, who have much work to do in a short time: your souls to save, a God to honour, a Christ to exalt, a hell to escape, a race to run, a crown to win, temptations to withstand, corruptions to conquer, afflictions to bear, mercies to improve, and your generation to serve.

[7.] The glorious appearances of God for you do bespeak you *to rest and rely upon God in future distress, notwithstanding all your unrighteousnesses, weaknesses, and disadvantages.* O beloved, this glorious appearance of God in the mount for you, does for ever bespeak you to rest and rely upon him in your longest day of trouble, and in your darkest night of sorrow. David, in the day of sore distress, does heighten his confidence by former experiences; and so do those worthies in 2 Cor. i. 8–10. There is nothing that engages God to act high for his people when they are low, like resting and relying upon him; as you may see in that 2 Chron. xiii. 16–18 verses compared. It is a scripture worthy to be writ in letters of gold. Abijah and his people slew five hundred thousand chosen men, because they relied upon the Lord God of their fathers. The Hebrew word that is rendered 'relied,' שׁעי, is from a root that signifies to 'lean' or 'rest' upon the Lord, as a man does upon a staff or rest. Oh, nothing does engage God to act for a people like leaning upon God, chap. xiv. 8–15 compared with 7–9th verses of the 16th chapter. Now if you would lean upon God in your distress, then keep open the eye of your faith. So long as faith sees in God a fulness of abundance—*in* [Deo] *plenitudo abundantiæ et plenitudo redundantiæ*—and a fulness of redundancy, the soul cannot but lean on God.

[8.] Eighthly, Another thing that the glorious appearances of God for you do bespeak of you and the whole nation, is to *set light by all worldly glory.* You are not ignorant how that hypocritical nation began to pride themselves, and to exalt themselves, and glory in their arm of flesh; but in the things wherein they did deal proudly, the Lord was above them, and has laid their glory in the dust. Oh it is high time to set light by all earthly glory, when God hath taken counsel to stain the pride of all glory, and to bring into contempt all the honourable of the earth, Isa. xxiii. 9. The word that is rendered 'purposed' may be read counselled: the Lord has agreed upon it in counsel, to stain. In the Hebrew it is 'to *pollute*' the pride of all glory, &c.

Severus the emperor, finding the emptiness and insufficiency of all earthly happiness, cries out at last, *Omnia expertus fui et nihil expedit,* I have tried all things, and find no solid content in anything. Charles the Fifth, in his old age, he curses his honours, and curses his victories, &c., saying, *Abite hinc, abite longe,* Get you hence, get you far away! Severus his soldier could say, when one asked him why he did not wear his crown as the other soldiers did, A Christian ought not to wear his crown in this life; *Non decet Christianum in hac vita coronari.*

[9.] The ninth thing that the glorious appearances of God for you do bespeak of you, is *to live to him that has given you your lives as a prey*. God calls with open mouth upon you, and upon all the saints in England, to live to him who hath with his glorious arm saved you, when your proud enemies had passed the sentence of death upon you. God has therefore given you your lives for a prey, that you may no longer live to yourselves, nor to the lusts of the flesh, but to him who lives for ever, as the apostle speaks in that 2 Cor. i. 8–12; Deut. x. 12, 'And now, O Israel, what doth the Lord thy God require of thee, but to fear the Lord thy God, to walk in all his ways, and to love him, and to serve the Lord thy God with all thy heart and with all thy soul?' The Hebrew word that is rendered 'require,' 'What does the Lord thy God *require* of thee,' signifies to ask, to request, to petition. Oh! God does ask, and request, and as it were petition men that they would live out all his goodness, and live up to all those glorious things that he has done for them. Cyprian, Jerome, and others, complained of the Christians in their time, that they were angels to see to, but wolves in their conversation. *Non in verbis sed in factis res nostra religionis consistunt*, saith Peter Martyr. Oh that we had no cause to complain of such in our days! Noble Mirandola said, it were great madness not to believe the gospel, now it is everywhere believed; yet a greater matter it is not to doubt of the truth of the gospel, and yet to live so as if without all doubt it were false. Plutarch laughed at the folly of such in his time as would be accounted as wise as Plato, and yet would be drunk in the company of Alexander. But oh that our eyes were a fountain of tears, that we might weep for those that pretend to be Christians, and yet live like heathens. Seneca, a heathen, gave this advice to his friend Lucilius, that he should live with men as if God saw him, and pray to God as if men heard him. He liked not such as are always about to live better, but never begin to live better. I shall conclude this with that counsel Periander king of Corinth gave: Live in such sort, saith he, that thou mayest have honour by thy life, and that men may count thee happy after death: *Semper victuri*.

[10.] The tenth thing that the glorious appearances of God for you do bespeak of you, and that is that you *be constantly careful to decline those sins which was the Scots' overthrow and ruin*; and I think that all those that are got above their pride, and passions, and envy, &c., will judge the sins that did usher in their ruin to be these:—(1.) Hypocrisy; (2.) Resting and boasting in an arm of flesh; (3.) Their sinful compliances with those against whom wrath is gone forth: as Isa. xiv. 19–22; Jer. xxxi. 2; (4.) Their hatred and malice against those that in an outward form did differ from them, though they were never so precious to Christ, and eminent in the power and practice of godliness, which sin shall not go unpunished, Isa. lx. 14, lxvi. 5, and xxvi. 10, 11; (5.) Their self-love and covetous desires to enrich themselves, and make themselves great in others' ruins, and under the pretence of being the king and covenant; (6.) Their ingratitude to God, and to the parliament and commonwealth of England, who have so many ways shewed their love to them in the days of their distress, and to that army who was formerly instrumental to pull them as brands out of the fire. As you would avoid their judgments, take heed of their sins. I hope that none of you that hear me this day are of Radbode (?) king of Phrisia's mind, who, coming to the font to be baptized, asked what was to become of all his ancestors? Answer was made, that they died in a fearful state, unbaptized. He replied, that he would rather perish with the multitude, than go to heaven with a few. You are wise, and know how to apply it.

[11.] The next thing that the glorious appearances of God for you do bespeak of you, is *to endeavour with all your might to make a conquest of all those enemies that be within you.* Now the Lord has made so glorious a conquest over those proud enemies that rose up against you, I beseech you consider, of all conquests the conquest of enemies within is the most honourable and the most noble conquest; for in conquering of those enemies that be within, you make a conquest over the devil and hell itself. Of all conquests that is the highest and the greatest that is over enemies within you: Prov. xvi. 32, 'He that is slow to anger is better than the mighty; and he that ruleth his spirit than he that taketh a city.' The word that is rendered 'ruleth,' signifies to 'conquer, and overcome,' (משל, *mashal.*) It is this conquest that lifts a man up above all other men in the world. And as this is the most noble conquest, so it is the most necessary conquest. You must be the death of your sins, or they will be the death of your souls. Sin is a viper, that does always kill where it is not killed. There is nothing gained by making peace with sin, but repentance here, and hell hereafter. Every yielding to sin is a welcoming of Satan into our very bosoms. Alexander and many of the Persian kings conquered and commanded the whole world, and yet were commanded by their concubines, and by enemies within, which was the ruin of their souls.[1] Valentinian the emperor said upon his death-bed, that among all his victories, one only comforted him; and being asked what that was, he answered, 'I have overcome my worst enemy, mine own naughty heart.' Ah! Right Honourable, when you shall lie upon a dying-bed, then no conquest will thoroughly comfort, but the conquest of your own sinful hearts. None were to triumph in Rome that had not got five victories; and he shall never triumph in heaven that subdueth not his five senses, saith Isidorus. Ah, souls! what mercy is it to be delivered from an enemy without, and to be eternally destroyed by an enemy within?

[12.] The next thing that the glorious appearances of God for you do bespeak of you, is *to persevere and hold on in well-doing.* As God holds on in doing you good, so you must hold on in well-doing for his glory: 'Be faithful to the death, and you shall have a crown of life,' Rev. ii. 10. *Vincenti dabo.* 'To him that overcometh will I give to sit down with me in my kingdom: as I overcame, and am set down with my Father in his kingdom,' Rev. iii. 21. It is said of Sceva, that he so long resisted Pompey's army, that he had two hundred and twenty darts sticking in his shield, and lost one of his eyes, and yet gave not over till Cæsar came to his rescue. So, beloved, you must never leave standing for God, and contending for God, and acting for God, who still stands and contends and acts for you against all those that rise up against you. It was a good saying of Mr Bucer, *Pietas quæ finem novit, non est vera pietas,* That piety that has an end is no true piety. He that

[1] Hor., lib. ii.

in a golden game, or in a golden race, shall run after flies or feathers, or faint before he comes to the goal, will lose not only his pains, but also the crown for which he runs. My desires to the Lord shall be, that we may all so run as that we may obtain the crown.

[13.] Lastly, The glorious appearances of God for you do bespeak you *to shew mercy to others.* Now God has shewed such great mercy towards you, oh let 'the sighing of the prisoner' come before you, and the desires, the tears, the cries, the wounds, and the blood of poor distressed souls move your compassion towards them, that so you may do for all to the uttermost what you are able, that so their sorrows may be turned into joy, and sighing and mourning may flee away, and their souls may arise and call you blessed. The only way to have full barns, is to have charitable hands. The gainfullest art is alms-giving, saith Chrysostom. Whatsoever we lay out for them, we do but lay up for ourselves. Whatsoever we scatter to the poor, we gather for ourselves. Not getting, but giving, is the way to wealth. The poor man's hand is Christ's treasury, Christ's bank. Oh let not Christ's hand and Christ's treasury be empty! and yet be careful that what you cast into Christ's treasury be got in Christ's wages. It is better to gratify none, than to grate upon any one, saith Augustine. The Hebrew words signifying 'alms,' צדקה, (*tsedakah,*) properly signifies justice; to intimate to us that the matter of our alms should be goods justly gotten. Hence also the Jews call their alms-box, [*Kuph ashel tsedaka,*] the chest-behest of justice. O Right Honourable, shall the Persians, and many Indians, erect hospitals, not only for lame and diseased men, but also for aged, starved, or hurt birds, beasts, and such like creatures; and will not you do much more for those that have ventured their blood to save yours, and that are the price of the blood of Christ? It is storied up of Stephen, king of Hungary, and of Oswald, sometime king of England, that their right hands, though dead, never putrified, because much exercised in giving and relieving the poor and afflicted. Surely the names and souls of such that do look to *quoad fontem,* and to *quoad finem,* to do this duty from a right principle, to a right end, shall never die, but live for ever; which that all your names and souls may do, shall be my constant desire and prayer at the throne of grace.

A BELIEVER'S LAST DAY IS HIS BEST DAY.

NOTE.

The 'Believer's Last Day his Best Day,' originally published in 1651–52, passed through a great number of editions during the ten subsequent years and onward, though the various reprints are not designated in the title-pages. Our text is that of 1657, compared with another of 1660. The title-page is given below.* Appended to the Sermon was this Notice:—'Christian Reader,—Be pleased to pass by, or to correct with thy pen, the faults that have escaped by reason of the author's absence from the press.' The 'Believer's Last Day' is often found as an appendix to 'Heaven on Earth;' and perhaps nothing proves more completely the popularity of Brooks, than the large circulation and sustained vitality of such merely local and fugitive publications as the 'String of Pearls' and 'Believer's Last Day'—both funeral Sermons. With reference to the former,—'String of Pearls,'—I take this opportunity to give a curious 'Advertisement' concerning it, by Brooks's publisher, which is appended to the seventh edition of the 'Apples of Gold,' (1667.) It is as follows:—

'The Stationer to the Reader.

'This is to give notice that some dishonest booksellers, called land-pirates, who make it their practice to steal impressions of other men's copies—whose sin will surely find them out—have lately printed a false and imperfect impression of Mr Brooks his 'String of Pearls,' and have wronged both the author and me by false printing many words, and leaving out all the table of the chief heads, and of a bad paper and print, and crammed it into eight sheets, the true sort being fifteen sheets, sold by John Hancock, in Broad-street, over against the Church.'—G.

* A
BELIEVERS
Last Day is his *Best Day*.

A
SERMON
Preached at the Funerall of
M[ris] MARTHA RANDOLL,
At *Christs* Church, *London*, June 28. 1651.
By THOMAS BROOKS, Minister of
the Gospel at *Margarets Fish*-street-hill.

Thou wilt guide me by thy Counsell, and after receive me to glory. Psal. 73. 24.
Light is sowne for the righteous, and joy for the upright in heart. Psal. 97. 11.

Ejus est timere mortem, qui ad Christum nolit ire. *Cyp.*
Timor mortis pejor, quam ipsa mors. *Eras.*
Senibus mors in januis, adolescentibus in insidiis. *Ber.*

LONDON:
Printed, and are to be sould by *John Hancock*
at the first Shop in *Popes-head*-Alley,
next to *Cornhill*. 1657.

THE EPISTLE DEDICATORY.

To my worthy and beloved Friends, Mr John Russel, and Mrs Martha, his wife; and to Mr Thomas Randoll; all happiness in this world and that which is to come.

My dear and worthy Friends,—The ensuing sermon was preached upon your importunity, and printed also upon the same account. You know nothing would satisfy your spirits but the printing of it, which at last made me unwillingly willing to answer your desires; not that I did delight to deny your desires, nor because I prized it, but because I thought it not good enough for you, nor worthy of that weight that you laid upon it, it being but the fruit of some short broken meditations. I have now published these notes, which in all love I present to you. They were once in your ear, they are now in your eye, and the Lord keep them ever in your hearts! If there be anything in this sermon worth the having, it is not mine but the Lord's, through grace. I know that my best actions stand in need of sweet sweet odours, a golden censer.

Dear Friends, You know we must all fall in the wilderness of this world, be gathered to our fathers, go hence and be no more seen. Abraham and Sarah must part, Jacob and Rachel must be separated, David and his child must be severed. Our days are numbered, our period of time appointed, and our bounds we cannot pass. 'All flesh is as grass, and the glory thereof as the flower of the field,' Ps. ciii. 15; therefore do not mourn as persons 'without hope,' neither be like Rachel that would 'not be comforted.' To that purpose take this counsel.

1. First, *Dwell much upon the sweet behaviour of others under the loss of their near and dear relations.* When God had passed the sentence of death upon David's child, 2 Sam. xii. 20, he 'arose from the earth, and washed, and anointed himself, and changed his apparel, and came into the house of the Lord, and worshipped; then he came to his own house, and when he required, they set bread before him, and he did eat.' When his servants questioned this action, he answers, 'Now he is dead, wherefore should I fast? Can I bring him back again? I shall go to him, but he shall not return to me,' ver. 23. So when Aaron's sons were destroyed by fire for their offering up strange fire, Lev. x. 22, 23, Aaron holds his peace; he bridled his

passions, and submitted sweetly and quietly to divine justice. So when it was told Anaxagoras that both his sons, which were all he had, were dead, being nothing terrified therewith, he answered, *Sciebam me genuisse mortales*, I knew I begat mortal creatures. Dransi,[1] people in Thrace, bury their children with great joy, but at their birth lament grievously, in regard of the miseries that are like to befall them while they live.

2. Secondly, *In time of crosses, losses, and miseries, it is the wisdom of believers to look more upon the crown than upon the cross, to dwell more upon glory than upon misery, to eye more the brazen serpent that is lifted up, than the fiery serpent that bites and stings.*[2] Basil speaketh of some martyrs that were cast out all night naked in a cold frosty time, and were to be burned the next day, how they comforted themselves in this manner: 'The winter is sharp, but paradise is sweet; here we shiver for cold, but the bosom of Abraham will make amends for all.'[3] Galen writes of a fish called *Uranoscopos*, that hath but one eye, and yet looks continually up to heaven. A Christian under the cross should always have an eye looking up to heaven, that so his soul may not faint, and he may give glory to God in the day of visitation. It is recorded of Lazarus, that after his resurrection from the dead he was never seen to laugh; his thoughts and affections were so fixed in heaven, though his body was on earth, that he could not but slight temporal things, his heart being set upon eternal things.[4] A man, saith one, [Chrysostom,] would dwell in this contemplation of heaven, and be loath to come out of it. Nay, saith another, [Augustine,] a man might age himself in it, and sooner grow old than weary.

3. Thirdly, *Compare your mercies and your losses together, and you shall find that your mercies will wonderfully outweigh your losses.* You have lost one mercy, you enjoy many mercies. What is the loss of a wife, a child, or any other temporal mercy, to a soul's enjoyment of the favour of God, pardon of sin, peace of conscience, hopes of heaven, &c.? Besides, you enjoy many temporal mercies that many of the precious sons of Zion want, &c.

4. Fourthly, *Consider seriously of the reasons of God's stripping his people of their nearest and their dearest mercies;* and they are these:—

[1.] *For a trial of the strength and power of their graces.* It is not every cross nor every loss that tries the strength of a Christian's graces. Job held bravely in the face of many afflictions for a time, but when he was thoroughly wet to the skin, then he acts like a man rather void of grace, than like a man that did excel all others in grace.[5] When God burns up the out-houses but leaves the palace

[1] Query, 'Dolonci' or 'Digeri'?—G.

[2] 2 Cor. iv. 16–18; Heb. x. 34, xi. 24–26, 35, and xii. 1–3.

[3] Basil *ad* XL Martyr. *Tolle cœlum nullus ero*, said the philosopher.

[4] Let heaven be a man's object, and the earth will be his abject.

[5] God tried the strength of Abraham's faith, and the strength of Job's patience, and the strength of Moses' meekness, and the strength of David's zeal, and the strength of Paul's courage, to the utmost. God will not only try the truth, but he will also try the strength of every grace that is in a believer sooner or later, Exod. xii. 27, 30, 31. It is the observation of Theodoret, that when God smote Pharaoh's firstborn, he drew blood off the arm for the cure of the head, which because it mended not, thereupon came all to confusion.

standing, when he takes away the servant but leaves the child, when he gathers here a flower and there a flower out of men's gardens, but leaves the flowers that are the delight of their eyes and the joy of their hearts, they bear it patiently and sweetly; but when he burns up the palace, and takes away the child, and gathers the fairest flower in all our garden, then we usually shew ourselves to be but men, yea, to be weak men, passionately crying out, 'O my son Absalom, my son, my son Absalom! would God I had died for thee, O Absalom, my son, my son!' 2 Sam. xviii. 33.

[2.] *God passes the sentence of death upon men's dearest mercies, that himself may be more dreaded, and that his precious servants and their counsel may be the better minded and regarded.* The Egyptians trembled not under several judgments, nor minded not what Moses and Aaron said, till God smote their firstborn, and then they tremble, and then the servants of the Lord and their counsel found better quarter with them than formerly they had done. Ah, friends! has the Lord smitten your firstborn, as I may say? then look to it, as you tender the honour of God, the advancement of the gospel, the peace of your own consciences, the stopping of the mouths of the wicked, and the gladding of those hearts that God would not have sadded, that God be more dreaded, and that his servants and his services be more owned, loved, and regarded. The people of God, and the ordinances of God, are to God as his firstborn; and they that make light of God's firstborn, God will make as light of their firstborn. These Egyptians had slain Israel, God's firstborn, and therefore God smites their firstborn. My desire and prayer shall be that God's removing and taking away your firstborn, as I may say, may be the making of more room in your bosoms for God, Christ, saints, and ordinances, that so your great loss may be turned into the greatest gain. And certainly, if this physic, this potion that is given you by an outstretched hand from heaven do not work this, the next potion will be far more bitter, John v. 14.

[3.] *God passes the sentence of death upon men's nearest and dearest mercies, that he may win them to a more complete and full dependence upon his blessed self.* Man is a creature apt to hang and rest upon creature props: 'I looked on my right hand, and beheld,' saith the psalmist, 'but there was no man that would know me: refuge failed me; no man cared for my soul,' Ps. cxlii. 4. Well, what does he do now all props fail him? why, now he sweetly leans upon God: ver. 5, 'I cried unto thee, O Lord; I said, Thou art my refuge and my portion in the land of the living.' Cynægeirus, an Athenian captain, used great valour in the Persian war, pursuing his enemies that were laden with the rich spoil of his country, and were ready to set sail and be gone; he held the ship with his right hand, and when that was cut off, he held it with the left, that also being cut off, he held it with the stumps till his arms were cut off, and then he held it with his teeth till his head was cut off.[1] It is the very temper of most men and women in the world—they will hold upon one prop, and if God cut off that, then they will catch hold on another, &c., till God cut off all

[1] Herod. vi. 114; Suidas, *s. v.* Κυναίγειρος; Just. ii. 9; Val. Max. iii. 2, § 22; comp. Sueton. Jul. 68.—G.

their props, and then they will come and rest and centre in God, in whom are all their well-springs, Ps. lxxxvii. 7.

[4.] *God strips his people of their dearest mercies, that he may work their hearts to a more strict and diligent search and examination of their own hearts and ways*, that they may say with the church, 'Let us search and try our ways, and turn to the Lord our God,' Lam. iii. 39, 40, 48. The Hebrew word, חפש, that is rendered 'search,' signifies to search as you would do to find out a disguised person that puts himself into a strange habit that he might not be discovered. When God's hand, when God's rod is upon our backs, our hands must be upon our hearts, and we must cry out, What evil have we done! what evil have we done! Seneca reports of one Sexius,[1] who would every night ask himself three questions—(1.) What evil hast thou healed to-day? (2.) What vice hast thou stood against this day? (3.) In what part art thou bettered this day? When the storm beats strong upon you, you had need to see what Jonah is asleep at the bottom of your souls, that so, he being discovered and cast overboard, your souls may be safe, for in the drowning of your sins lies the security of your soul.

[5.] *He strips his people of their dearest outward mercies, that they may be more compassionate toward those that are or shall be in the same condition with themselves.*[2] The Jews at this day, in their very nuptial feasts and mirth, break a glass with wine in remembrance of Jerusalem, saying, when they throw it down, Thus was Jerusalem broken; and what they spill in wine they fill with tears. Is it not a shame to have the same name, the same faith, the same Christ, the same profession, &c., and to desire always to tread on roses, to be embarked in this great ship of Christianity with so many brave spirits, and to go under hatches, to sleep like the outcasts and scorn of human nature? Saints should be like two lute strings that are tuned one to another; no sooner one is struck but the other trembles.

[6.] *God strips his people of their nearest and dearest outward mercies, that they may the more prize and the better taste spiritual and heavenly mercies.*[3] He takes away uncertain riches, that they may the more prize certain riches; he takes away natural strength, that they may the more prize spiritual strength; he takes away the creature, that they may more prize their Saviour. Spiritual and heavenly things are of nearest and greatest concernment to you. Spirituals will only abide with you in all changes; spirituals can only satisfy your souls. The language of a gracious spirit is this, Ah, Lord! as what I have if offered to thee pleaseth not thee without myself, so the good things I have from thee, though they may refresh me, yet they cannot satisfy me without thyself, John xiv. 8.

5. The fifth and last word of counsel that I shall give you is this, *Consider seriously and frequently, that God's taking away or removing of one mercy is but his making of way for another, and usually for a*

[1] Query, 'Sextus'?—G.

[2] That sentence likes me well for you, that he said of himself, I have no wit but weeping.

[3] Diogenes taxed the folly of the men of his time, that they undervalued the best things but overvalued the worst. Ah that this were not the sin and shame of professors in these days!

better mercy.[1] He took from David a Michal, and gave him a wise Abigail; an Absalom, and gave him a Solomon. He took away the bodily presence of Christ from his disciples, but gave them more abundantly of his spiritual presence, which was far the choicer and the sweeter mercy. God will always make that word good, 'I will not leave you comfortless,' or as the Greek hath it, John xiv. 18, *ὀρφάνους ab ὀρφνῇ*, 'I will not leave you as orphans, or fatherless children;' no, I will come and comfort you on every side, and I will make up all your wants, and be better to you than all your mercies: 'For your brass I will give you silver, and for your iron you shall have gold,' &c., Isa. lx. 17.

To draw to a close, let that dead man or dead woman be lamented whom hell harboureth, whom the devil devoureth, whom divine justice tormenteth; but let those whose departed souls angels accompany, Christ embosometh, and all the court of heaven comes forth to welcome, account immortality a mercy, and be grieved that they are so long detained from the sweet company of Christ, &c.

I desire you, and all others that shall read what is here written, to overlook the mistakes of the printer, if you meet with any, I having no time to wait upon the press to correct what may be found amiss. The perusal and acceptance of what I here present in love, I shall leave [to] your judgments, and rest yours to love and serve in our dearest Lord,

THOMAS BROOKS.

[1] John xvi. 7, 8. *Hujusmodi lucri, dulcis odor*, The smell of this gain is sweet to many.

A SAINT'S LAST DAY IS HIS BEST DAY.

Beloved, I am here at this time to speak a word to the living, my business being not to speak anything of the dead. Be pleased, therefore, to cast your eye upon

ECCLESIASTES VII. 1.

'*A good name is better than precious ointment, and the day of death than the day of one's birth.*'

I shall stand upon the latter part of this verse at this time: 'And the day of death than the day of one's birth.'

The Greeks say, 'that the beginning of a man's nativity is the begetting of his misery.' In Job xiv. 1, 'Man that is born of a woman is born to trouble' and sorrow. The Hebrew word that is there rendered 'born,' ילוד, *jeludh*, signifieth also generated or conceived; to note to us that man is miserable as soon as he is warm in the womb; he comes crying into the world. Before ever the child speaks, he prophesies by his tears of his ensuing sorrows.

And this made Solomon to prefer his coffin before his crown, the day of his dissolution before the day of his coronation. *A fletu vitam auspicatur*, saith Seneca. But not to hold you longer from what is mainly intended, the observation that I shall speak to at this time is this:—

That a believer's last day is his best day; his dying-day is better than his birthday.

This will be a very sweet and useful point to all believers. I shall first demonstrate the truth that it is so, and then make some use of this point to ourselves.

1. The first thing that doth with open mouth speak out this truth is this, *That death is a change of place.* A believer when he dieth, he doth but change his place; he changeth earth for heaven, a wilderness for a Canaan, an Egypt for a land of Goshen, a dunghill for a palace: as it is said of Judas, that 'he went to his place,' Acts i. 25. A soul out of Christ is not in his place, beneath is his place. So when a believer dieth he goes to his place. Heaven, the bosom of Christ, is his place. And that speaks out the truth asserted, that a believer's dying day is his best day.

A believer now is not in his place, 2 Cor. v. 6, but his soul is still working and warring, and he cannot rest till he comes to centre in the bosom of Christ. This Paul well understood when he said, 'I long to be dissolved, and to be with Christ,' Phil. i. 23. I would fain weigh anchor, hoise sail, and away home. And upon this account those precious souls groaned for deliverance, 2 Cor. v. 2, 'For this we groan earnestly, desiring to be clothed with our house which is from heaven.' What is the ground? Why, it is this, 'While we are in the body we are absent from the Lord,' ver. 6. We be not in our place, and therefore we groan to be at home—that is, to be in heaven, to be in the bosom of Christ, which is our proper place, our most desirable home.

2. The second thing which doth demonstrate the truth asserted, is this, *That death is a change of company.* The best that breatheth in this world must live with the wicked, and converse with the wicked, &c.; and this is a part of their misery; it is their hell on this side heaven. This stuck upon the spirit of David: Ps. xii. 5,[1] 'Woe is me that I am constrained to be in Mesech, and to dwell in the tents of Kedar,' &c. And so Jer. ix. 2, 'Oh that I had in the wilderness a lodging-place of wayfaring men, that I might leave my people, and go from them, for they be all adulterers, an assembly of treacherous men.' And this was that that did vex and tear Lot's righteous soul: 2 Peter ii. 7, 8, 'His soul was vexed from day to day with their unlawful deeds.' The word ἐβαστάνιζεν—*vide* Bezam—signifies to 'rack;' he was racked to see their unlawful deeds. Oh, but death is a change of company. A man doth change the company of profane persons, of vile persons, &c., for the company of angels, and the company of weak Christians for the company of just men made perfect. That is a remarkable place, Heb. xii. 22, 23, 'We are come to mount Sion,' saith the apostle, 'and unto the city of the living God, the heavenly Jerusalem, and to an innumerable company of angels, to the general assembly and church of the firstborn, which are written in heaven, and to God the judge of all, and to the spirits of just men made perfect.' Here is a change indeed. Death is a change of company as well as a change of place. And if this be but well weighed, it must needs be granted that a believer's dying day is better than his birth-day.

3. *Death is a change of employment.* A believing soul when he dies, changeth his work and employment. I open it thus: The work of a believer in this world lies in praying, groaning, sighing, mourning, wrestling, and fighting, &c. And we see throughout the Scripture that the choicest saints, that have had the highest visions of God, have driven this trade; they have spent their time in praying, groaning, mourning, wrestling, and fighting: Eph. vi. 12, 'For we wrestle not against flesh and blood, but against principalities, against powers, against rulers of the darkness of this world, against spiritual wickedness in high places.'[2] The truth is, the very life of a believer is a continual warfare, and his business is to be in the field always. They

[1] I have read of a good gentlewoman, who, being near death, cried out, O Lord, let me not go to hell where the wicked are, for thou knowest that I never loved their company in the time of life.

[2] *Probus* a valiant Roman emperor's motto was, *Pra stipe labor*—No fight, no pay. So I say, No fight, no crown; no fight, no heaven. [Probus, M. Aurelius.—G.]

have to deal with subtle enemies, malicious enemies, wakeful enemies, and watchful enemies; with such enemies that threw down Adam in paradise, the most innocent man in the world, and that threw down Moses, the meekest man in the world, and Job, the patientest man in the world, and Joshua, the most courageous man in the world, and Paul, the best apostle in the world, &c. A Christian's life is a warfare. Job saith, 'All the time of my warfare (צבאי) will I wait till my change come,' Job xiv. 14,—I am still a-fighting, saith Job, with lusts and corruptions within, and with devils and men abroad; 'All the time of my warfare will I wait till my change come.' So in the 2 Tim. iv. 8, 'I have fought the good fight of faith,' &c. And so in the 2 Tim. ii. 4, 'No man that warreth entangleth himself with the affairs of this life,' &c.[1] Death is a change of employment. It changeth this hard service, this work that lies in mourning, wrestling, and fighting, for joying and singing hallelujahs to the Almighty. Now no prayers, but praises; no fighting and wrestling, but dancing and triumphing. Can a believing soul look upon this glorious change, and not say, Surely 'better is the day of a believer's death than the day of his birth'? Death is the winding-sheet that wipes away all tears from the believer's eyes, Rev. vii. 9.

4. *Death is a change of enjoyments, as well as a change of employments.* I shall express this in three considerable things:—

(1.) *It is a change of our more dark and obscure enjoyment of God, for a more clear and sweet enjoyment of God.* I say, the best believer that breathes in this world, that doth see and enjoy most of God, and the visions of his glory, yet he enjoys not God so clearly, but that he is much in the dark. The apostle Paul was a man that was high in his enjoyments of God, yet while he was here in the flesh, he did but see as through a glass. 'We see through a glass darkly'—1 Cor. xiii. 12, *αἰνίγματι*, in a riddle—but then face to face; then we shall know even as we are known. God told Moses that he could not see his face and live. The truth is, we are able to bear but little of the discoveries of God, there being such a mighty majesty and glory in all the spiritual discoveries of God. We are weak, and able to take in little of God. We have but dark apprehensions of God. Witness our tears, sighs, groans, and complaints, because we go forward and backward. We look on the right hand and on the left, as Job speaks, Job xxiii. 8, 9, and God hideth himself that we cannot see him. Plutarch tells of Eudoxus, that he would be willing to be burnt up presently by the sun, so he might be admitted to come so near it as to learn the nature of it. This is upon the heart of believers, Lord, let us be burnt up, so we may see thee more in all thy glorious manifestations; let us be poor, let us be anything, so that we may be taken up into a more clear enjoyment of thyself.[2] Ask them that live highest in the

[1] Alexander sent messengers to Mandanius, (?) a famous philosopher, to tell him that if he would do so and so he should be rewarded, and if he did not he should be put to death. The philosopher answered the messengers, That for his gifts he esteemed them worth nothing, seeing his own country could furnish him with necessaries, and as for death he did not fear it, but wish it rather, in that it was a change unto a more happy estate. So far did mere philosophy carry men in the opinion of felicity.

[2] Chrysostom professeth that the want of the enjoyment of God would be a far greater hell to him than the feeling of any punishment.

enjoyment of God, What is your greatest burden? and they will tell you, This is our greatest burden, that our apprehensions of God are no more clear, that we cannot see him face to face whom our souls do dearly love. Oh, but now in heaven saints shall have a clear vision of God: there be no clouds nor mists in heaven.

(2.) *It is a change of our imperfect and incomplete enjoyments of God, for a more complete and perfect enjoyment of him.* As no believer hath a clear sight of God here, so no believer hath a full and perfect sight of God here. In Job xxvi. 14, how little a portion is heard of him—speaking of God—and of that is heard, ah how little a portion is understood![1] So in 1 Cor. xiii. 12, 'Now we see through a glass darkly, but then face to face.' 'Now I know in part, but then shall I know even as also I am known.' The soul, while it is here, dares not but say, I enjoy something of God, and that I would not want for a thousand worlds; yet my enjoyment is not full. If you should say, Souls, why do you wait upon God in this ordinance and that ordinance? they will answer, That we may enjoy God more fully. 'Fly away speedily, my beloved.' What is the meaning of this language but this: 'Oh that I might be filled with the fulness of God!' There is no complaints in heaven, because there is no wants. Oh, when death shall give the fatal stroke, there shall be an exchange of earth for heaven, of imperfect enjoyments for perfect enjoyments of God; then the soul shall be swallowed up with a full enjoyment of God; no corner of the soul shall be left empty, but all shall be filled up with the fulness of God. Here they receive grace for grace, but in heaven they shall receive glory for glory. God keeps the best wine till last; the best of God, Christ, and heaven, is behind. Here we have but some sips, some tastes of God; fulness is reserved for a glorious state. He that sees most of God here sees but his back parts; his face is a jewel of that splendour and glory that no eye can behold but a glorified eye. Our hearts are like a vial-glass, which will not fill on a sudden, though it lie in the midst of the sea, where all fulness is. The best Christian is able to take in but little of God; their hearts are like the widow's vessel, that could receive but a little oil. Sin, the world, and creatures do take up so much room in the best hearts, that God is put upon giving out himself by a little and little, as parents do to their children; but in heaven God will communicate himself fully at once to the soul; grace shall then be swallowed up of glory.

(3.) *It is a change of a more inconstant and transient enjoyment of God, for a more constant and permanent enjoyment of God.* Here the saints' enjoyment of God is inconstant. One day they enjoy God, and another day the soul sits and complains in anguish of spirit. He that should 'comfort my soul stands afar off;' my glass is out, my sun is

[1] דבר, *Dabar, i. e.*, a word or thing. Oh, how little a word, how little a thing, is heard of him. It is an excellent expression that Augustine hath: The good things of eternal life, saith he, are so many, that they exceed number; so precious, that they exceed estimation; so great, that they exceed measure. *Esse Christum cum Paulo, magna securitas; esse Paulum cum Christo, summa felicitas,* [Bernard,]—For Christ to be with Paul was the greatest security, but for Paul to be with Christ was the chiefest felicity. Chrysostom saith, If it were possible that all the sufferings of the saints should be laid upon one man, it were not worth one hour's being in heaven,—such is the greatness and fulness of that glory above. The saints' motto is, *Migremus hinc, migremus hinc*—Let us go hence, let us go hence.

set, and what can make up the want of this sun? As all candle-light, star-light, and torch-light, cannot make up the want of the light of the sun; so when the Sun of righteousness hides his face, it is not all creature-comforts that can make up the want of his countenance.[1] David sometimes could say that 'God was his portion, and his salvation, and his strong tower,' Ps. lxi. 3, and what not; and yet presently cries out, 'Why art thou cast down, O my soul? and why art thou disquieted within me?' Ps. xlii. 5. In one place he saith, 'I shall never be moved,' Ps. xxx. 6; and yet presently it follows, 'Thou hiddest thy face from me, and I was troubled,' ver. 7. And this is the state of a believer in this world. But in heaven there shall no clouds arise between the Lord and a believing heart. God will not one day smile, and another day frown; one day take a soul in his arms, and another day lay that soul at his feet. This is his dealing with his people here. But in heaven there is nothing but kisses and embraces, nothing but a perpetual enjoyment of God. When once God takes the soul unto himself, it shall never be night with it any more—never dark with that soul more, &c.; all tears shall then be wiped away. That is a sweet word in the 1 Thes. iv. 17, 18, 'And so shall we be ever with the Lord; wherefore comfort one another with these words.' There are, saith Musculus, angels and archangels in heaven. Ay, but they do not make heaven; Christ is the most sparkling diamond in the ring of glory. It is heaven and happiness enough to see Christ, and to be for ever with Christ. Now, oh what a glorious change is this! Methinks these things should make us long for our dying-day, and account this life but a lingering death.

5. Consider this: *Death is a change that puts an end to all external and internal changes.* What is the whole life of a man, but a life of changes?[2] Death is a change that puts an end to all external changes. Here you change your joy for sorrow, your health for sickness, your strength for weakness, your honour for dishonour, your plenty for poverty, your beauty for deformity, your friends for foes, your silver for brass, and your gold for copper. Now the comforts of a man are smiling, the next hour they are dying, &c. All temporals are as transitory as a hasty, headlong torrent, a ship, a bird, an arrow, a post, that passeth by. Man himself—the king of these outward comforts—what is he, but a mere nothing?—the dream of a dream, a shadow, a bubble, a flash, a blast. Now death puts an end to all external changes: there shall be no more sickness, no more complaints, no more wants, &c.

And then it puts an end to all internal changes. Now the Lord smiles upon the soul, and anon he frowns upon the soul. Now God gives assistance to conquer sin, anon the man is carried captive by his sin; now he is strengthened against the temptation,

[1] By death saints come to a fixed and invariable eternity. *Nescio quid erit, quid ista vita non erit,* &c., [Augustine,]—*i. e.,* What will that life be, or rather, what will not that life be, since all good either is not at all, or is in such a life,—light which place cannot comprehend, noises and music which time cannot vanish away, odours which are never dissipated, a feast which is never consumed, a blessing which eternity bestoweth, but eternity shall never see at an end.

[2] There is nothing excellent that is not perpetual, saith Gregory Nazianzen. Philosophers could say, that he was never a happy man that might afterwards become miserable. Eternity is that *Unum perpetuum hodie.*

anon he falls before the temptation, &c. Job carried it out bravely in the midst of storms, and speaks like an angel; but when Job was wet to the skin, and the arrows of the Almighty stuck in him, and his day was turned into night, and his rejoicing into mourning, &c., then a man would have thought him a devil incarnate by his cursing. But death puts an end to internal changes, as well as external changes. Now the soul shall be tempted no more, sin no more, be foiled no more. Now ye may judge by this that a Christian's dying-day is his best day. Death is another Moses: it delivers believers out of bondage, and from making brick in Egypt. It is a day or year of jubilee to a gracious spirit—the year wherein he goes out free from all those cruel taskmasters which it had long groaned under. The heathen gods held death to be man's *summum bonum*, his chiefest good; therefore, when one of them had built and dedicated the temple at Delphos, he asked of Apollo for his recompense the thing that was best for man: the oracle told him that he should go home, and within three days he should have it—within which time he died. Thus the very heathens themselves have consented to this truth, that a man's dying-day is his best day.

6. *Death is a change that brings the soul to an unchangeable rest.* It is the bringing of the soul to bed—to a state of eternal rest.[1] That is the last demonstration of the point, that a believer's dying-day is his best day. Now while we are here the soul is in a-toss. The best man in the world—that is highest and clearest in his enjoyments of God—is too often like to Noah's dove that found no rest: either he wants some external mercy or internal mercy, and will do so till the soul be swallowed up in the everlasting enjoyments of God; but death brings a man to an unchangeable rest. In Rev. xiv. 13, 'I heard a voice from heaven saying to me, Write, From henceforth blessed are the dead that died in the Lord.' Why? 'For they rest from their labours,' &c. Oh, saith he, write it down as a thing of worth and weight, 'Blessed are the dead that die in the Lord; for they rest from their labours,' &c. Death brings the soul to unchangeable rest. In Isa. lvii. 1, 2, 'The righteous perish, and no man layeth it to heart, &c. He shall enter into peace: they shall rest in their beds, each one walking in his uprightness.' Oh, death is a change that brings a soul to unchangeable rest; it brings a soul a-bed. This was that that made Paul long 'to be dissolved, and to be with Christ;' and the Corinthians to groan for deliverance.[2] It was a notable saying of blessed Cooper, 'Many a day have I sought death with tears; not out of impatience or distrust,' saith he, 'but because I am weary of sin, and fearful to fall into it.' You know how the martyrs hugged the stake, and welcomed every messenger of death that came to them, and clapped their hands in the midst of the flames. Death is a believer's coronation-day, it is his marriage-day. It is a rest from sin, a rest from sorrow, a rest from afflictions and temptations, &c. Death to a

[1] Death is a rest from the trouble of our particular callings; it is a rest from afflictions, a rest from persecutions, a rest from temptation, a rest from desertion, a rest from sin, and a rest from sorrow, Gen. viii. 8.

[2] Laurence Saunders kissing the stake, said, Welcome the cross of Christ, welcome everlasting life. Funius, the Italian martyr, kissed him that brought him word of his execution. [Query, 'Faninus'?—G.]

believer is an entrance into Abraham's bosom, into paradise, into the 'New Jerusalem,' into the joy of his Lord. And thus much for the doctrinal part. You see that it is clear, by these six things, that a believer's dying-day is his best day, and the day of his death better than the day of his birth.

I might by many other arguments demonstrate this truth to you, but let these suffice; because I would not unwillingly keep you longer from the use and application of the point—application being the life of all teaching. Now the

1. First use shall be this, *Then never mourn immoderately at the death of any believer, let them be the most excellent and useful that ever lived.*[1] Death is to them the greatest gain; and it speaks out much selfishness in us to be more taken with the gain and benefit that redounds to us by their lives, than with the happiness and glory that redounds to them by their deaths. In the primitive times, when God had passed the sentence of death upon their dearest comforts, Christians did carry it at a more high, sweet, and noble rate than now-a-days they do. Remember this, death doth that, I say, in a moment, that no graces, no duties, nor no ordinances could do for a man all his lifetime; it frees a man from those diseases, corruptions, temptations, &c., that no duties, nor graces, nor ordinances could do. When Abraham came to mourn for his deceased Sarah, he mourned moderately for her, Gen. xxiii. 2, as is imported by a small *caph* in the word *Libcothath*, that signifies to weep; in that Hebrew word there is one little letter extraordinary, to note that Abraham wept but a little for her, not because she was old and overworn, as some Rabbins say, but because her dying-day was her best day. When Luther, that famous instrument of God, buried his daughter, he was not seen to shed a tear. So Mr Whately, who was famous in his time, whenas he had preached his own child's funeral sermon upon this subject, 'The will of the Lord be done,' he and his wife laid their own child in the grave.[2] That is the first use, let us not mourn immoderately for any believer's death.

2. Then, in the next place, *Fear not death.* Compose your spirits; say not of death as that wicked prince said to the prophet, 'Hast thou found me, O my enemy?' 1 Kings xxi. 20; but rather long for it, not to be rid of troubles, but that the soul may be taken up to a more clear and full enjoyment of God. Your dying-day is your best day. Good Jacob dies with a sweet composed spirit; he calls for his children, and blesseth and kisseth them, and gathers up his feet into his bed, and dies. Moses, that morning that the messenger came to him, and told him he must die, he goes up the hill, sees the land of Canaan at a distance, and dies. Cato, a heathen man, told Cæsar that he feared

[1] Death is not *mors hominis*, but *mors peccati*, not the death of the man, but the death of his sin.

[2] The people in Thrace mourn and greatly lament at the birth of their children, because of the sorrows and troubles they are born to; and they greatly joy and rejoice at the death of their children, because death is the funeral of all their sorrows. Death is not such as you, as some, would paint it. It was the saying of a heathen man, That the whole life of a man should be nothing else but *meditatio mortis*, a meditation of death. See Deut. xxxii. 29. Alexander the Great did ask the Indian philosopher how long a man should live; saith he, Until he think it better to die than to live. [Whately of Banbury. Died 1639.—G.

his pardon more than the pain that he threatened. Joseph built his sepulchre in his own garden. And some philosophers had their graves always open before their gates, that going out and coming in they might always think of death, for in life they found comforts to be rare, crosses frequent, pleasures momentary, and pains permanent. Believers, your dying-day is your best day. Oh, then, be not afraid of death, and that you may not, remember that it is not such a slight matter as some make it, to be unwilling to die. There is much reproach cast upon God by believers being unwilling to die. You talk much of God, heaven, and glory, &c., and yet when you should come to go and share in this glory, you shrug and say, Spare me a little. Is not this a reproach to the God of glory? But that this counsel may stick upon you, remember these five things:—

[1.] *Christ's death is a meritorious death.* Can a believer think upon the death of Christ as meriting peace with God, pardon of sin, justification, glorification, and yet be afraid to die? What! is the death of Christ thus meritorious, and shall we still be unwilling to depart?

[2.] *Is not death a sword in your Father's hand?* It is true, a sword in a madman's hand, or in an enemy's hand, might make one tremble; but when the sword is in the father's hands, the child doth not fear. Grant that death is a sword, yet why should the child fear and be afraid, when it is in the father's hand, that will be sure to handle it so as he shall not be hurt or cut by it.

[3.] *Remember that Christ's death is a death-conquering death.*[1] He hath taken away the sting of death, that it cannot hurt you; and his death is a death-sanctifying and a death-sweetening death. He hath by his death sanctified and sweetened death to us.

Death is a fall that came by a fall. To die is to be no more unhappy, if we consider death aright. Oh, saith one, that I could see death, not as it was, but as thou, Lord, hast now made it! It is the greatest monarch and the ancientest king of the world. Death reigned from Adam to Moses, saith St Paul. Oh! but the Lord Jesus hath, as it were, disarmed death, and triumphed over death. He hath taken away its sting, so that it cannot sting us, and we may play with it, and put it into our bosoms, as we may a snake whose sting is pulled out. The apostle, upon this consideration, challengeth death, and out-braves death, and bids death do his worst, in that 1 Cor. xv. 56, 57.

[4.] *Did not Christ willingly leave his Father's bosom for your sake?* Did he not willingly die for you? Did Christ plead thus, These robes are too good for me to leave off, this crown too glorious for me to lay aside, I am too great to suffer for such a people? No, but he readily leaves his Father's bosom, he lays down his crown, and puts off his robes, and suffers a cursed, cruel, and ignominious death. Ah,

[1] The fear of death is worse than the pains of death, *Timor mortis ipsa morte pejor*, because fear of death kills us often, whereas death itself can do it but once. *Ejus est timere mortem qui ad Christum nolit ire*, Let him fear death that is loath to go to Christ—Cyprian. *Mori non metuo, sed damnari metuo*, I fear not to die, but I fear to be damned, saith one. *Una guttula plus valet quam cœlum et terra:* Luther, speaking of the blood of Christ, saith, That one little drop is more worth than heaven and earth. If the souls under the altar cry, *Usque quo, Domine?* How long, Lord?—if they solicit for the day of judgment, why not I for the day of death, since death's day is but the eve of God's day? Zeno said, I have no fear but of old age.

souls, you should reason thus, Did Christ die for me that I might live with him? I will not therefore desire to live long from him. All men go willingly to see him whom they love; and shall I be unwilling to die, that I may see him whom my soul loves? Shall Christ lay by all his glory and pomp, and marry a poor soul that had neither portion nor proportion; and shall this soul be unwilling to go home to such a husband? Oh think of it, you souls that are unwilling to die!

Present life is not *vita, sed via ad vitam*, life, but the way to life; for when we cease to be men, we begin to be as angels. They are only creatures of inferior nature that are pleased with the present. Man is a future creature. The eye of his soul looks back. The labourer hastens from his work to his bed, the mariner rows hard to gain the port, the traveller is glad when he is near his inn; so should saints when they are near death, because then they are near heaven, they are near their inn.

[5.] *Are you not complete in Christ?*[1] Why should a believer be afraid to die that stands complete before God in the righteousness of the Lord Jesus? If we should appear in our own righteousness, in our own duties, it would be dreadful to think of dying, but a believer is complete in him, &c. 'Ye are complete in him,' Col. ii. 10. In Rev. xiv. 4, 5, they are said to be 'without fault before the throne of God;' and in Cant. iv. 7, 'Thou art all fair, my love, and there is no spot in thee.' A believer, when he dies, he appears before God in the righteousness of Christ. All the spots and blemishes of his soul are covered with the righteousness of Christ, which is a matchless, spotless, peerless righteousness. Christ's spouse hath perfection of beauty; she is all 'glorious within' and without, she is spotless and blameless, she is the fairest among women, that she may be a meet mate for him that is fairer than all the children of men, Ps. xlv. 2. The saints are as that tree of paradise, Gen. iii., fair to his eye, and pleasant to his palate, or as Absalom, in whom there was no blemish from head to foot. Think of these things to sweeten your last changes, and to make you long to be in the bosom of Christ.

[6.] Sixthly, Consider *that the saints' dying-day is to them the Lord's pay-day.* Every prayer shall then have its answer; all hungerings and thirstings shall be filled and satisfied; every sigh, groan, and tear that hath fallen from the saints' eyes shall then be recompensed.[2] Then they shall be paid and recompensed for all public service, and all family service, and all closet service. Now a crown shall be set upon their heads, and glorious robes put upon their backs, and golden sceptres put into their hands; their dying-day being the Lord's pay-day, they shall hear the Lord saying to them, 'Well done, good and faithful servants, enter into your Master's joy,' Mat. xxv. 21. In that day they shall find that God is not like Antiochus, who promised often but seldom gave; no! Then God will make good all those golden and glorious promises that he hath made to them, especially those that

[1] *Ipse unus erit tibi omnia, quia in ipso uno bono, bona sunt omnia,* One Christ will be to thee instead of all things else, because in him are all good things to be found.—Augustine.

[2] That is not death but life, that joins the dying man to Christ; and that is not life but death, which separates the living man from Christ.

are cited in the margin.[1] Now God will give them gold for brass, and silver for iron, felicity for misery, plenty for poverty, honour for dishonour, freedom for bondage, heaven for earth, an immortal crown for a mortal crown.

[7.] Seventhly, Consider this, *the way to glory is by misery; the way to life is by death.* In this world we are all Benonis, the sons of sorrow. The way to heaven is by Weeping-cross. Christ's passion-week was before his ascension-day; none passeth to paradise but by burning seraphims; we cannot go out of Egypt but through the Red Sea; the children of Israel came to Jerusalem through the valley of tears, and crossed the swift river of Jordan before they came to the sweet waters of Siloam.[2] There is no passing into paradise but under the flaming sword of this angel, death; there is no coming to that glorious city above but through this strait, dark, dirty lane. No wiping all tears from your eyes but with your winding-sheet, which should make you entertain death *non ut hostis, sed ut hospes*, not as a foe, but as a friend, not as a stranger, but as a guest that you had long looked for, and bid welcome death more blessed than your birth.[3] Every man is willing to go to his home, though the way that leads to it be never so dark, dirty, or dangerous; and shall believers be unwilling to go to their homes, because they are to go through a dark entry to those glorious, lightsome, and eternal mansions that Christ hath prepared for them? surely no.

[8.] Eighthly, Consider *that while we are in this world, our weak and imperfect and diseased bodies cast chains, and fetters, restraints, hindrances, and impediments upon the soul, that the soul is hindered from many high and noble actings, which in a state of separation it is free to.* In a state of separation the soul works clearer, and understands better, and discourses wiser, and rejoices louder, and loves nobler, and desires purer, and hopes stronger than it can do here.[4]

It is reported of Apollonius, that he had a familiar spirit engaged[5] in a jewel. Such is the soul of man in the body: the soul, while it is in this body of clay, cannot act like herself, like a spirit whose nature is to soar aloft towards the place whence she came. When the soul is upon the wings for heaven, the body like a lump of lead pulls it down to the earth, &c.

Now the soul cannot look out at the eyes but it will be infected, nor hear by the ears but it will be distracted, nor smell at the nostrils and not be tainted, taste by the tongue and not be allured, and touch by the hand and not be defiled. Every sense and member is too ready upon every occasion and temptation to betray the soul; which should make us willing to die and to long for that day wherein our bodies shall be glorified.[6]

Ah, believers! it will be but as a day before those bodies of yours,

[1] Rev. ii. 10, iii. 4, 12, 22, and vii. 16, 17.

[2] A man will easily swallow a bitter pill to get health. The physician helps us not without pain, and yet we reward him for it.

[3] Death to a believer is the gate of heaven; it is *janua vitæ*, the door of life. It conveys us out of the wilderness into Canaan, out of a troublesome sea into a quiet haven, John xiv. 1–3.

[4] When Plato saw one over-indulgent to his body by high feeding it, he asked him what he meant, to make his prison so strong.

[5] Query, 'encaged' or 'encased'?—G.

[6] The Greeks call the body the soul's bond, the soul's sepulchre.

that are now like a picture out of frame, or a house out of repair, that are now deformed and diseased, &c., shall be agile and nimble, swift and facile in their motion. For clarity and brightness they shall be like Christ's body when it was transfigured, Mat. xvii. 2; they shall be very amiable and beautiful, they shall be impassible and immortal. Here our bodies are still dying. It is more proper to ask when we shall make an end of dying, than to ask when we shall die. Death is a worm that is always feeding at the root of our lives, which should make death more desirable than life.

[9.] Ninthly, *Dwell much upon the readiness and willingness of other saints to die.* Good old Simeon having first laid Christ in his heart, and then taking him up in his arms, he sings, 'Lord, now lettest thou thy servant depart in peace, for mine eyes have seen thy salvation,' Luke ii. 28-30. I have lived enough, I have my life; I have longed enough, I have my love; I have seen enough, I have my sight; I have served enough, I have my reward; I have sorrowed enough, I have my joy. So the believing Corinthians, 2 Cor. v. 4, 8, they groaned earnestly to be clothed upon with their house which is from heaven, they groaned that mortality might be swallowed up of life, and 'that they might be absent from the body, and present with the Lord.' So Paul desires earnestly 'to be dissolved, and to be with Christ, which is best of all,' Phil. i. 23. So those in Peter, 'they look for and hasten the coming of the day of God,' 2 Pet. iii. 12. They are said to hasten the day of God, in respect of their earnest desires after it, and in respect of their preparations for it. So the souls under the altar cry, 'How long, Lord, how long?' &c., Rev. vi. 9, 10.

So Paula, that noble lady, when one did read to her Cant. ii. 11, 'The winter is past, and the singing of birds is come;' Yea, she replied, 'the singing of birds is come,' and so she went singing into heaven. So Jewel, 'Lord, now let thy servant depart in peace; break off all delays; Lord, receive my spirit.' Further he said, 'I have not so lived that I am ashamed to live longer; neither do I fear to die,—because we have a merciful Lord. A crown of righteousness is laid up for me; Christ is my righteousness.' So another being in a swoon, as her friends thought, a little before her end they cried, Give her some *rosa solis;* but she put it back, saying, 'I have *rosa solis* you know not of.' So Mr Pearing,[1] a little before his death, said, 'I find and feel so much inward joy and comfort in my soul, that if I were put to my choice whether to die or live, I would a thousand times rather choose death than life, if it might stand with the holy will of God.[2] So Mr Bolton, lying on his death-bed, said, 'I am by the wonderful mercies of God as full of comfort as my heart can hold, and feel nothing in my soul but Christ, with whom I heartily desire to be.' Ah, Christians! if the exceeding willingness of the saints to die will not make you willing to die, what will?

[10.] Tenthly and lastly, Consider this, *that the Lord will not leave thee, but be with thee in that hour:* 'Yea, though I walk through the

[1] Query, 'Dereing'?—G.

[2] Let all the devils in hell, saith Augustine, beset me round, let fasting macerate my body, let sorrows oppress my mind, let pains consume my flesh, let watching dry me, or heat scorch me, or cold freeze me, let all these—and what can come more—happen unto me, so I may enjoy my Saviour.

valley of the shadow of death, I will fear no evil; for thou art with me; thy rod and thy staff they comfort me,' saith the psalmist, Ps. xxiii. 4. So the apostle, Heb. xiii. 5, 'Let your conversation be without covetousness, and be content with such things as you have, for he hath said, I will never leave thee nor forsake thee.'[1] There are five negatives in the Greek, to assure God's people that he will never forsake them; five times in Scripture is this precious promise renewed, that we may press it till we have pressed the sweetness out of it. Though God may seem to leave thee, thou mayest be confident he will never forsake thee. Why should that man be afraid of death, that may be always confident of the presence of the Lord of life?

3. The next use shall be *to stir you all up to prepare and fit for your dying-day.* Ah, Christians! what is your whole life, but a day to fit for the hour of death? what is your great business in this world, but to prepare and fit for another world? It was a sad speech of Cæsar Borgia, who being sick to death, said, 'When I lived, I provided for everything but death; now I must die, and am unprovided to die.'[2] Ah, Christians! you have need every day to pray with Moses, 'Lord, teach us to number our days, that we may apply our hearts to wisdom,' Ps. xc. 13, and to follow the counsel of the prophet Jeremiah, 'Give glory to the Lord your God, before he cause darkness, and before your feet stumble upon the dark mountains, and while ye look for light he turn it into the shadow of death, and make it gross darkness,' Jer. xiii. 16. Old age is the dark mountain which makes a broad way narrow, and a plain way cragged. It is a high point of heavenly wisdom to consider our latter end: 'Oh that they were wise, that they understood this, that they would consider their latter end!' Deut. xxiii. 19. Jerusalem paid dear for forgetting her latter end. Jerusalem's filthiness was in her skirts, because she remembered not her latter end, therefore also she came down wonderfully. To provoke you to prepare and fit for a dying-day, consider seriously these following things:—

(1.) *He that prepares not for his dying-day, runs the hazard of losing his immortal soul.* Though true repentance be never too late, yet late repentance is seldom true, *aut pœnitendum aut pereundum.* The heathen man could say, 'He that is not ready to repent to-day, will be less ready to-morrow; his understanding will be more dark, his heart more hard, his will more crooked, his affections more distempered, his conscience more benumbed,' &c. Bede tells a story of a certain great man that was admonished in his sickness to repent, who answered, 'That he would not yet, for if he should recover, his companions would laugh at him;' but, growing sicker and sicker, his friends pressed him again to repent, but then he told them it was too late, '*Quia jam judicatus sum et condemnatus;*' 'For now,' said he, 'I am judged and condemned.' It is the greatest wisdom in the world to do that every day that a man would do on a dying-day, and to be afraid to live in such an estate as a man would be afraid to die in.

[1] Maximilian the emperor was so delighted with that sentence, *Si Deus nobiscum?* &c., If God be with us, who shall be against us? that he caused it to be written upon the walls in most rooms of his palace.

[2] As before.—G.

Ah, souls! you are afraid to die in such and such sins; and will you not be afraid to live in those sins?

(2.) Again, *The certainty of death should bespeak you to prepare for death.* When we would affirm anything to be infallibly true, we say, 'As sure as death.' 'It is appointed,' saith the apostle, 'unto men once to die, but after this the judgment,' Heb. ix. 27. The Greek word that is translated 'It is appointed,' signifieth, it lieth as a man's lot.[1] 'Once,' implies two things—[1.] A certainty, it shall once be; [2.] A singularity, it will be but once. 'What man lives and shall not see death?' saith the psalmist,—that is, no man lives and shall not see death. In Job the grave is called 'the house appointed for all the living.' Solomon calls the grave *Baiith Gnolam*, (בת עולם)—*i.e.*, *Domum seculi*, the house of age. The learned translate it 'Long home,' where men must abide for a long time, even till the resurrection. To live without fear of death, is to die living; to labour not to die, is labour in vain. Death hath for its motto, *Nulli cedo*, I yield to none. It is decreed that all must die. Every man's death-day is his doom's-day.

The French have a proverb, 'Three things,' say they, 'agree in the world—the priest, the lawyer, and death.' The priest takes the living and the dead, the lawyer right and wrong, and death the weak and strong. But the Jews have a better: 'In Golgotha are to be seen skulls of all sizes;' that is, death comes on the young as well as the old; the lot is fallen upon all, and therefore all must die. All men are made of one mould and matter,[2] 'Dust thou art, and unto dust thou shalt return,' Gen. iii. 19. 'All have sinned, are fallen short of the glory of God,' Rom. v. 12; and therefore death must pass upon all.

(3.) *The uncertainty of the time of your death does bespeak you with open mouth to be in a constant readiness and preparedness for death.* No man knows when he shall die, nor what kind of death he shall die, whether a natural or a violent death. Augustus died in a compliment, Tiberius in dissimulation, Galba with a sentence, Vespasian with a jest; Zeuxes died laughing at the picture of an old woman which he drew with his own hand; Sophocles was choked with the stone in a grape; Diodorus the logician died for shame that he could not answer a joculary question propounded at the table by Stilpo; Joannes Masius preaching upon the raising of the woman of Naomi's son from the dead, within three hours after died himself; Felix, Earl of Wurtemburgh, sitting at supper with many of his friends, some at the table fell into discourse about Luther, and the people's general receiving [of] his doctrine, upon which the Earl swore a great oath, 'that before he died he would ride up to the spurs in the blood of Lutherans;' but the very same night God stretched out his hand so against him, that he was choked with his own blood.[3]

Consider, in the last place, *That it is a solemn thing to die.* Death is a solemn parting of two near friends, soul and body. Remember,

[1] Heb. ix. 27, ἀπόκειται; Ps. lxxxix. 48; Job xxx. 23; Eccles. xii. 5.

[2] Adam of Adamah, *homo ab humo.*

[3] Bibulus, a Roman general, riding in triumph in all his glory, a tile fell from a house in the street, and beat out his brains.

all other preparations are to no purpose, if a man be not prepared to die. What will it avail a man to prepare this and that for his children, kindred, or friends, &c., when he hath made no preparations for his soul, for his eternal well-being? As death leaves you, so judgment shall find you. If death take you before you expect it, and are prepared for it, it will be the more terrible to you; it will cause your countenance to be changed, your thoughts to be troubled, your loins to be loosed, and your knees to be dashed one against another.[1] Oh the hell of horrors and terrors that attends those souls that have their greatest work to do when they come to die! therefore, as you love your souls, and as you would be happy in death, and everlastingly blessed after death, prepare and fit for death.[2] Look that you build upon nothing below Christ; look that you have a real interest in Christ; look that you die daily to sin, to the world, and to your own righteousness. Look that conscience be always waking, speaking, and tender; look that Christ be your Lord and Master; look that all reckonings stand right betwixt the Lord and your souls; look that you be fruitful, faithful, and watchful, and then your dying-day shall be to you as the day of harvest to the husbandman, as the day of deliverance to the prisoner, as the day of coronation to the king, and as the day of marriage to the bride. Your dying-day shall be a day of triumph and exaltation, a day of freedom and consolation, a day of rest and satisfaction. Then the Lord Jesus shall be as honey in the mouth, ointment in the nostrils, music in the ear, and a jubilee in the heart.

The last use then is this, If a believer's last day be his best day, *then by the rule of contraries, a wicked man's last day must be his worst day*, for he must there lie down with the sins of his youth.[3] Death shall put an end to all the benefits and comforts that now thou enjoyest. Now thou must say, Honours, friends, pleasures, riches, credit, &c., farewell for ever; I shall never have good day more; I shall never be merry more; my sun is set, my glass is out, my hopes fail, my heart fails; all offers of grace are past, the Spirit will never strive with me more, free grace will never move me more, the golden[4] serpent shall never be held forth more; death will be an inlet to judgment, yea, to an eternity of misery.[5] What the voice was of God to Adam upon eating the forbidden fruit; what the coming of the flood was to the profane men of the old world; what the waters of the Red Sea were to Pharaoh and his army; what the fire from heaven was to the captains that came up against Elijah; what the burning furnace was to them that cast in Shadrach, Meshach, and Abednego, the same will be the day of death to profane wicked souls. Ah, sinners, my prayer for you shall be, that the Lord would awaken you, and set up

[1] He that prepares for his body and friends, but neglects his soul, is like him that prepares for his slave, but neglects his wife.

[2] When I was young, saith Seneca the heathen, I then studied *artem bene vivendi*, the art of living well; when age came upon me, I then studied *artem bene moriendi*, the art of dying well.

[3] A great man wrote thus a little before his death: *Spes et fortuna valete*—Hope and fortune farewell.

[4] Query, 'Brazen'?—G.

[5] Sigismund the emperor and Louis the Eleventh of France straitly charged all their servants that they should not dare to name that bitter word *death* when they saw them sick, so dreadful was the very thoughts of death to them.

a choice light in your souls, that you may see where you are, and what you are; that he would give you to break off your sins by repentance, and give you an interest in himself; that so 'for you to live may be Christ, and to die may be gain,' Phil. i. 21; that in life and death Christ may be advantage to you; and that death may be the funeral of all your sins and sorrows, and an inlet to all that joy and pleasure, that blessedness and happiness that is at God's right hand.

A HEAVENLY CORDIAL.

NOTE.

Published in the year of the 'Plague,' (1665,) immediately preceding the 'Fire' of 1666—which destroyed the entire stock of so many books—the 'Heavenly Cordial,' like the 'Experiences' of Mrs Bell, is unknown to Bibliographers, not being found in any of our great libraries. Our own copy seems to have been carefully preserved, along with Brooks's other writings, by some ardent admirer. It would fetch in the market treble the cost of our entire edition of Brooks. The title-page is given below.*—G.

* A

HEAVENLY

CORDIAL.

For all those Servants of the Lord that have had the PLAGUE (and are recovered) or that now have it; also for those that have escaped it, though their Relations and Friends have been either visited, or swept away by it.

OR

Thirteen DIVINE MAXIMES or CONCLUSIONS in respect of the PESTILENCE, which may be as so many supports, comforts, and refreshing springs, both to the visited and preserved people of God in this present day.

ALSO

Ten *Arguments* to prove that in Times of Common Calamity, the people of God do stand upon the advantage ground, as to their outward preservation and protection above all other people under Heaven.

ALSO

Eight *Reasons* why some of the precious Servants of the Lord have fallen by the *Pestilence* in this Day of the Lord's Anger.

By THOMAS BROOKS, late Minister of the Gospel in *London*.

LONDON, Printed for, and are to be sold by *John Hancock*, at the first shop in *Popes*-head Alley, next to *Cornhill.* 1665.

[12mo.—G.]

A HEAVENLY CORDIAL.

I. The first divine maxim or conclusion is this—viz., *When the pestilence is among a people, it is the Lord alone that sends it.*

2 Sam. xxiv. 15, 'So the Lord sent a pestilence upon Israel, from the morning even to the time appointed: and there died of the people, from Dan even to Beer-sheba, seventy thousand men.' Num. xvi. 46, 'Wrath is gone out from the Lord; the plague is begun.' Num. xiv. 12, 'I will smite them with the pestilence, and disinherit them.' Deut. xxviii. 21, 'The Lord shall make the pestilence cleave unto thee, until he hath consumed thee from off the land, whither thou goest to possess it.' Ezek. xiv. 19, 'Or if I send a pestilence into that land, and pour out my fury upon it in blood, to cut off from it man and beast;' ver. 21, 'For thus saith the Lord God, How much more when I send my four sore judgments upon Jerusalem, the sword, and the famine, and the noisome beast, and the pestilence, to cut off from it man and beast?' Amos iv. 10, 'I have sent among you the pestilence, after the manner of Egypt.' Hence it is called, God's arrow, Ps. xci. 5; and when God shoots those arrows into kingdoms, cities, towns, families, Ps. xxxviii. 2, none can pull them out but God himself. The plague is more immediately from God than any other sickness or disease, for it is the immediate stroke of God.[1] The scribe is more properly said to write than the pen, and he that maketh and keepeth the clock is more properly said to make it go and strike than the wheels and poises that hang upon it, and every workman to effect his work, rather than the tools which he useth as instruments. So the Lord of hosts, who is the chief agent and mover in all things and in all actions, may more fitly and properly be said to effect and bring to pass all judgments, yea, all things which are done in the earth, than any inferior or subordinate causes: seeing they are but his tools and instruments, which he rules or guides according to his own will, power, and providence. I know some physicians ascribe it to the heat of the air, and sometimes to the dryness of the air, and sometimes to the corruption of the air, and sometimes to the corruption of men's blood, and sometimes to Satan, and sometimes to the malignancy of the planets; but certainly those are 'physicians of no value' that

[1] Deut. xxxii. 39. Hippocrates calls it το θεῖον, the *Divine disease*, because it comes more immediately from God than other diseases do.

cannot look above second causes to the First Cause, that cannot look to the 'wheel within the wheel,' Ezek. i. The plague is a hidden thing, a secret thing; it is a sickness, a disease, that more immediately comes from God than any other sickness or disease doth. Exod. ix. 3, 'Behold, the hand of the Lord is upon thy cattle which is in the field, upon the horses, upon the asses, upon the camels, upon the oxen, and upon the sheep: there shall be a very grievous murrain.' The word here translated 'murrain' is in chap. v. 3 termed 'pestilence;' and it is one and the same disease. Though when it is applied to cattle it be usually rendered by 'murrain,' yet when it is applied to men, as in the scripture last cited, it is commonly called the 'pestilence.' 'Behold, the hand of the Lord is upon thy cattle,' &c. That is the extraordinary, immediate power and work of God, without the intervening of any second cause or human operation. This open plague, this plague without-doors, that principally fell upon the cattle, was from the immediate hand of God. It is God alone that singles out the nation, the city, the town, the parish, the family, the person that he will strike with the plague; for all second causes are ordered by the First Cause, as every instrument is ruled or overruled by the will and hand of him that holdeth it. When a man goes with his axe to cut down trees in the wood, there is an equal aptness in the axe to cut down one tree as well as another, an oak as well as an ash, &c.; but it is still ruled by the will of him that handles it. So it is here: the noisome pestilence, or the pestilence of grass, as the Hebrew runs in that Ps. xci. 3, hath an equal aptness to cut down one man as well as another, the rich as well as the poor, the honourable as well as the base, the strong as well as the weak, the prince as well as the peasant, the emperor as well as the carter; but it is still overruled by the Lord himself, who gives it a commission to cut off such and such, in this kingdom and that, in this city and that, in this town and that, in this family and that, and to spare, save, and pass by all the rest. In Rev. vi. you shall read of four horses, when the four seals were opened, (1.) a white horse, (2.) a red horse, (3.) a black horse, (4.) a pale horse. After Christ had ridden upon the white horse, propagating the gospel, then follows the red horse, a type of war; then the black horse, a hieroglyphic of famine; and then the pale horse, the emblem of pestilence. Now all these horses, these plagues, were of Christ's sending. From those words, Judges iii. 20, 'I have a message from God unto thee, O king,' said Ehud; lo, his poniard was God's message; from whence one well observeth, that not only the vocal admonitions but the real judgments of God are his errands and instructions to the world, Isa. xxvi. 8–10. It was a mad principle among the Manichees, who referred all the judgments, calamities, and miseries that came upon them to the devil for their author, as if there could be 'any evil in the city, and the Lord have no hand in it,' Amos iii. 6. Now in that it is the Lord alone that sends the pestilence amongst a people, how should this comfort us and quiet us! how should this cool us and calm us! how should this satisfy us and silence us before the Lord, and cause us to lay our hands upon our mouths, as David did, Ps. xxxix. 9, and as Aaron did, Lev. x. 1–3, and as Eli did, 1 Sam. iii. 18, and as the church did, Lam. iii. 26–29.

Solinus (cap. 20) writeth of *Hypanis*, a Scythian river, that the water thereof is very bitter as it passeth through *Exampius*, yet very sweet in the spring.[1] So the cup of trembling which is this day offered to the children of God, is often very bitter at the second hand, or as it appears in second causes; and yet it is sweet at the first hand, yea, it is very sweet as it is reached to them by a hand from heaven; and therefore they may well say, as their head and husband hath done before them, 'Shall we not drink of the cup that our Father hath given us to drink of?' &c., John xviii. 11.

II. The second divine maxim or conclusion is this—viz., *The pestilence and all other judgments of God are limited as to places.*

Hence it comes to pass that God shoots his arrows of pestilence into one city, and not into another; into one town, and not into another; into one family, and not into another; into one kingdom and country, and not into another, Exod. viii. 20–23, and ix. 22–26; 2 Sam. xxiv. 15. Turn to all these scriptures and ponder upon them.

III. The third divine maxim or conclusion is this—viz., *All the judgments of God are limited, not only to places, but also to persons.*

And therefore such and such must fall, when such and such must escape; and such and such must be infected, when such and such are preserved. Hence it is that one is taken in the bed, and the other left; one smitten at the table or in the house, and all the rest preserved in perfect health, &c. God hath numbered so many to the sword, and so many to the famine, and so many to the pestilence, so many to this disease, and so many to that, 2 Sam. xxiv. 15, 16; Ezek. xi. 5–7, v. 12, and vi. 11, 12; Exod. xii. 13; Ps. xci. 3–9; Isa. lxv. 12; Jer. xv. 2; Ezek. xxxiii. 27. Turn to all those scriptures and ponder upon them. God marks out those persons that he intends to shoot the arrow of pestilence amongst. God never shoots at rovers; he never draws his bow at a venture, but he singles out the persons that he purposes to hit, and his arrows fly swiftly and suddenly, yet they hit none but those that God hath set up as a mark to shoot at—as Job speaks, chap. vii. 20.

IV. The fourth divine maxim or conclusion is this—viz., *No man knows divine love or hatred by outward dispensation*, Eccles. ix. 1, 2; Luke xiii. 4, 16; Lam. iv. 6; Dan. ix. 12; Ps. lxxiii. 12–22.

In times of great judgments God sometimes spares those whom his soul hates and abhors, Isa. i. 5; Hosea iv. 14, 17. God sometimes preserves wicked men from great judgments, that they may fall by greater judgments; as you may see in Sodom and her sisters, which were preserved from the slaughter of the four kings, that God might rain down hell out of heaven upon them. And so Sennacherib escapes the stroke of the destroying angel, that he might fall by the sword of his own sons, Isa. xxxvii. 37, 38. And as in times of great judgments God sometimes spares those sinners that his soul hates, so in times of great judgments God takes away those whom his soul dearly loves, 2 Chron. xxxiv. 27, 28. Turn to it. In all the considerable plagues that have been in this nation, how many precious Christians

[1] Rather Hyphasis as in Arrian (*l.c.*) and Diodorus (xvii. 93); for Solinus, cap. 20, read cap. 52; and for *exampius* above, query, *ex campis?* and for Scythia, read India)*Panjab.*)—G.

have fallen by the sword, and by the hand of the destroying angel, when many thousands of Balaks and Balaams, I mean the worst of men, have escaped the sword, the plague, &c.! And is there anything more obvious and notorious this day than this? Surely not.

V. The fifth divine maxim or conclusion is this—viz., *The Lord sometimes takes away his dearest people by some one judgment, that so he may by that means deliver them from many judgments; and sometimes he takes away his people by one great judgment, that so they may escape many other greater judgments that he intends to bring upon the earth.*

And thus good Josiah was slain in battle; yet because he lived not to see the woeful miseries of succeeding times, he is said to go to his grave in peace, 2 Chron. xxxiv. 27, 28. Turn to it. Enoch lived long in a little time, and God took him to heaven before he brought a sweeping flood upon the world; but he foreseeing the flood, named his son Methuselah, that is to say, 'he dieth,' and the dart or flood cometh, and so it fell out; for no sooner was his head laid, but in came the flood. And so Augustine was taken out of the world before Hippo was taken by the Vandals. And so Pareus was gotten to his better country before Heidelberg and the Palatinate was delivered into the power of the enemies. Ambrose is said to have been the walls of Italy, and when he died the Earl Stilico said, 'that his death did threaten destruction to that country;' and when Luther was laid in his grave, then troubles, wars, desolations, and confusions came in upon Germany like a flood. 'The righteous are taken away from the evil to come,' Isa. lvii. 1; and their death is a sad presage of sore and signal calamities that are hastening upon the world. Of late many precious servants of Christ are fallen asleep; but who knows what a day of wrath is coming? When a man cuts down his chiefest timber trees, it is an argument that he intends to part with his land; and how many tall cedars in this our Lebanon hath God lately cut down in the midst of us! Therefore we have eminent cause to be importunate with God, that he would neither part with this nation, nor depart from this nation. When some fatal judgment hovers like a flying fiery scroll over a nation, God many times gathers many of his choice servants unto himself, that he may preserve them from the evil to come.

VI. The sixth divine maxim or conclusion is this—viz., *None of God's judgments upon his people ever make any change or alteration of God's affections towards his people.*

However his hand may be against them, yet his love, his heart, his favour, his affections in Jesus, is still one and the same to them, Isa. liv. 7–10, and xlix. 14–16; Ps. lxxxix. 31–34; Jer. xxxi. 34–37, compared; Mal. iii. 6; John xiii. 3; James i. 17. Ponder seriously upon all those scriptures. So when God sent the plague upon David's people, and that for David's sin too, yet how sweetly, how lovingly, how tenderly, how compassionately, how indulgently, doth the Lord carry it towards David himself! 2 Sam. xxiv. 11–13, 18, 19, and 25 compared. And some learned men are of opinion that Lazarus died of the plague; and yet the text tells us that he was carried by angels into Abraham's bosom. Œcolampadius and many other worthies also died of it. When Munster lay sick, and his friends asked him how he did, and how he felt himself? he pointed to his sores and ulcers, whereof he was full, and said, 'These are God's gems and jewels wherewith he decketh his best friends; and to me they are more precious than all the gold and silver in the world.' God's dear love to his people is not founded upon anything in his people, nor upon anything that is done by his people, but only upon his own free grace and goodness, Deut. vii. 7, 8.

The ethnics[1] feign that their gods and goddesses loved certain trees for some lovely good that was in them: as Jupiter, the oak, for durance; Neptune, the cedar, for stature; Apollo, the laurel, for greenness; Venus, the poplar, for whiteness; Pallas, the vine, for fruitfulness. But what should move the God of gods and the Lord of lords to love us, who are poor, worthless, fruitless fruit-trees, twice dead, and plucked up by the roots, Jude 12; Ezek. xvi. This question is best resolved in three words, *amat quia amat*, he loves us because he loves us. The root of his love to us lieth in himself, and by his communicative goodness the fruit is ours. God's love to his people is a lasting love, yea, an everlasting love, Jer. xxxi. 35–37; it is a love that never decays nor waxes cold. It is like the stone *asbestos*, of which Solinus writes, that being once hot, it can never be cooled again.

VII. The seventh divine maxim or conclusion is this—viz., *Many times when the poor people of God cannot carry it with God for the preservation of a whole land or nation, yet they shall then be sure to have the honour and the happiness to be so potent and so prevalent with God as to prevail with him for their own personal preservation and protection.* Jer. xv. 1; Ezek. xiv. 14–21, compared. So Ezek. ix. 4, 6.

VIII. The eighth divine maxim or conclusion is this—viz., *Sword, famine, and pestilence can only reach our outward man—they only reach our bodies and our bodily concernments, they cannot reach our souls, nor our internal nor our eternal concernments. No outward judgments can reach the favour of God, or the light of his countenance, or our communion with him, or our spiritual enjoyments of him, or the joys of the Spirit, or the teachings of the Spirit, or the leadings of the Spirit, or the earnest of the Spirit, or the witness of the Spirit, or the seekings of the Spirit, or the quickenings of the Spirit, or the peace that passeth understanding, or our secret trade with heaven.*

IX. The ninth divine maxim or conclusion is this—viz., *There are no people upon the earth that in times of common calamity stand upon such fair grounds for their preservation and protection, as the people of God do.*

And this I shall make evident by an induction of ten particulars:—

[1.] First, *They are the only people in all the world that are under divine promises of protection and preservation*, Exod. xv. 26; Job v. 20, 21: Isa. iv. 5, 6, viii. 13, 14, xxvi. 20, 21, xxxi. 5, and xxxii. 1, 2; Ps. xci. throughout. Turn to those sweet promises, and remember that there are no men on earth that can or may lay their hands on these precious promises, and say, these promises are mine, but only the godly man. Those promises are God's bonds, which the godly man may put in suit, and urge God with, and plead hard in

[1] 'Heathen.'—G.

prayer, which no other men may.[1] The promises of God are a Christian's *Magna Charta*, his chief evidences that he hath to shew for his preservation, for his protection, for his salvation. Divine promises are God's deed of gift; they are the only assurance which the saints have to shew for their right and title to Christ, to heaven, and to all the glory and happiness of another world. Oh how highly do men prize their charters and privileges! and how carefully do they keep and lay up the conveyances and assurances of their lands! Oh how should saints then treasure up those precious promises, which are to them instead of all conveyances and assurances for their preservation, protection, maintenance, deliverance, comfort, and everlasting happiness! The promises are a mine of rich treasures; they are a garden full of the choicest and sweetest flowers of paradise; in them are wrapped up all celestial contentments and enjoyments; and therefore study them more than ever, and prize them more than ever, and improve them more than ever.

[2.] Secondly, *If you consider their near and dear relations to God.* They are his servants, his friends, his children, his members, his spouse, &c. By all which it is evident that they stand upon the advantage-ground, for preservation and protection, above all others in the world.

[3.] Thirdly, *If you consider that high value and esteem and price that the Lord puts upon them.* He esteems them as the apple of his eye, Zech. ii. 8; he accounts them as his jewels, Mal. iii. 17; he prizes them as his portion, Deut. xxxii. 9—yea, as his pleasant portion, Jer. xii. 10; he accounts them his crown, yea, his crown of glory, and his royal diadem: Isa. lxii. 3, 'Thou'—speaking of his church—'shalt also be a crown of glory in the hand of the Lord, and a royal diadem in the hand of thy God.' Yea, he prizes one saint above all the world, Heb. xi. 38. By all which it is most evident that they stand upon the advantage-ground, as to their preservation and protection, above all other people in the world; for God accounts all the world besides to be but as dirt, as dust, as chaff, as thorns and briers, that are only fit to be cast into the fire to be consumed and destroyed. When pearls grew common at Rome, they began to be slighted; but saints are such pearls of price, that God will never slight.

[4.] Fourthly, *If you consider that they are the only people in the world that are in covenant with God*, Ps. lxxxix. 30–34; Jer. xxxii. 38–40; Ezek. xx. 37; Deut. xxix. 12; Jer. xxxi. 31–34; Heb. viii. 6–12. Some do derive the word *berith*, which signifies the covenant, from a root which signifies to 'purify,' to 'separate,' and to 'select;' and verily, when the Lord makes a covenant with any, he doth separate them from others, he honours them above all others, and he looks on them and owns them for his peculiar people, and delights in them as the chosen and choicest of all others: 'The whole world lies in wickedness,' 1 John v. 19. By this also it is evident that the people of God stand upon the advantage-ground, for their preservation and protection, above all others in the world.

[1] Sirtorius, as Plutarch observes, paid what he promised with fair words, as courtiers use to do; but so doth not God. Men often eat their words, but God will never eat his. 'Hath he spoken, and shall it not come to pass?' Josh. xxiii. 14; Ezek. xii. 25, and xxiv. 14.

[5.] Fifthly, *If you consider the common carriage and deportment of God towards his people in former times of calamities and great judgments.* Did he not provide an ark for righteous Noah, so that Noah was safer in his ark of three storeys high than Nimrod and his crew were in their tower of Babel, raised to the height of five thousand one hundred and forty-six paces, as is reported?[1] And did he not provide a Zoar for righteous Lot? Hesiod speaks of thirty thousand demi-gods that were keepers of men. But what are so many thousand gods to that one God that neither slumbers nor sleeps, but day and night keeps his people as his jewels, as the apple of his eye; that keepeth them in his pavilion, as a prince keeps his favourite, Ps. cxxi. 3-5; Isa. xxvii. 3; Ps. xxxi. 20. Princes have their retiring rooms and withdrawing chambers, which are sacred places; and so hath God his, and there he shelters the favourites of heaven. God's gracious providence is his golden cabinet, where his children are as safe as if they were in heaven. See Isa. xlix. 2, and xxvi. 20, 21; Jer. xxxvi. 26; Ps. lxxxiii. 3: 'They have consulted against thy hidden ones,'—hidden under the hollow of thy hand, and under the shadow of thy wing, and therefore safe from dangers in the midst of dangers, Jer. xxxix. 16–18. How wonderfully did he preserve the three children, or rather the three non-conformable champions, from burning in the midst of the flames! Dan. iii.; and Daniel from being devoured in the lion's den! chap. vi. And so God's mourning ones were his marked ones, and his saved and preserved ones, when the destroying angel slew old and young, &c., Ezek. ix. 4, 6. And reverend Beza and his family was four several times visited with the plague, and yet as often preserved as they were visited; and this good man was very much refreshed and comforted, under that and other sore afflictions that befell him, by that Psalm xci., which made him the more highly to prize it, and the more dearly to hug it all his days, as himself witnesseth in his writings on this psalm. There is a dialogue between a heathen and a Jew, after the Jews' return from captivity—all nations round about them being enemies to them. The heathen asked the Jew how he and his countrymen could hope for any safety, because, saith he, every one of you is a silly sheep, compassed about with fifty wolves. Ay, but, saith the Jew, we are kept by such a shepherd as can kill all those wolves when he pleaseth. Now by all this, also, it is evident that the people of God stand upon the advantage-ground, as to their preservation and protection, above all other people in the world.

[6.] Sixthly, *If you consider the life-guard of the saints, the ministry of the blessed angels that always attend them:*[2] Ps. xci. 11, 'For he shall give his angels charge over thee in all thy ways;' ver. 12, 'They shall bear thee up in their hands, lest thou dash thy foot against a stone:' Ps. xxxiv. 7, 'The angels of the Lord encampeth round about them that fear him, and delivereth them:' Mat. xviii. 10, 'Take heed that ye despise not one of these little ones: for I say unto you, That in heaven their angels do always behold the face of my Father which

[1] Heylin, Cosm., lib. iii.

[2] Gen. xxxii. 1, 2; Dan. vi. 21, 22; Acts xii. 11, 15, and xxvii. 23; 2 Kings vi. 14–17; Acts v. 18.

is in heaven:' Heb. i. 14, 'Are they not all ministering spirits, sent forth to minister for them who shall be heirs of salvation?' The world may deprive us of many outward comforts, but they can never deprive us of the ministry of the angels.[1] When the servants of God are hated by all men, persecuted by men, and forsaken of men, yet they are then visited and attended by angels. Princes have their guards; but what poor, what weak, what contemptible guards are theirs to those legions of angels that daily guard the saints! When men can clip the wings of angels, and imprison or pinion these heavenly soldiers, then, and not till then, shall they be able to have their wills upon the poor people of God! Oh the honour, the dignity, the safety and security of the saints, in a life-guard so full of state and strength! Well may we say, 'Come and taste and see how gracious the Lord is' in affording his children so glorious an attendance! Now by this argument as well as the rest, it is evident that the people of God stand upon the advantage-ground of their outward preservation and protection above all other people in the world.

[7.] Seventhly, *If you consider that they are the only people that do bear up the name and glory of God in the world*, Deut. iv. 6-9; John iv. 23, 24. They are the only people that worship God in spirit and in truth; and from such worshippers it is that God hath the incomes of his glory. The holy hearts, the holy lives, the holy examples, the holy ways, the holy walkings, and the holy worship that is performed by the saints, are the springs from whence all divine honour rises to the Lord in this world. The people of God are the only people in the world that have chosen him for their God, and that have given themselves up to his service, and thus they honour his goodness, Deut. xxvi. 17, 18; Ps. cxvi. 16; Ps. xxii. 30. The people of God are the only people in the world who, in the times of their fears, doubts, darknesses, distresses, straits, trials, dangers, &c., do consult with God as their great counsellor, as their only counsellor; and thus they honour his admirable wisdom and infinite knowledge, Gen. xxiv. 12; Ps. xlviii. 14. The people of God are the only people in the world that do make God their refuge, their strong tower, their shelter, their hiding-place, in stormy and tempestuous days; and thus they honour the power, all-sufficiency, sovereignty, and authority of God, Ps. xlvi. 1, 7, 11; Prov. xviii. 10; Ps. xxxii. 7, cxix. 114, and xx. 7. Wicked men trust in their chariots and horses, and armies and navies, and revenues and carnal policies, and sinful shifts, devices, and fetches; when the poor people of God do not dare to trust in their swords nor in their bows, nor in their wealth, nor in their wit, nor in their friends, nor in any arm of flesh, as carnal refuges, but in the Lord alone: Isa. xxvi. 3, 4, 'For in the Lord Jehovah is everlasting strength.' The people of God are the only people in the world that do give God the supremacy in their hearts, that do set up God and Christ above themselves and above all their duties, services, privileges, graces, comforts, communions, spiritual enjoyments, and worldly contentments; and

[1] The heathens had some blind notions concerning the angels and their ministry, as may be seen in the writings of Plato and Plutarch. Hesiod the Greek poet could say that there were thirty thousand of them here on earth, keepers of mortal men, and observers of their works.

thus they honour all the excellencies and perfections of God at once, Ps. lxxiii. 25, 26; Phil. iii. 6–9; Rev. iv. 10, 11. And do you think that God will not have a special care of such that are the only promoters of his honour and glory in this world? Doubtless he will. Now by this argument, it is further evident that the people of God do stand upon the advantage-ground, as to their outward preservation and protection, above all other people in the world.

[8.] Eighthly, *If you do but seriously consider what a mighty interest the people of God have in the grand favourite of heaven*—viz., the Lord Jesus, who lies in the bosom of the Father, and who is so near and dear unto him, and so potent and prevalent with him, that he can do what he pleaseth with the Father, and have what he will of the Father, John i. 18; Heb. vii. 25; 1 John ii. 1, 2. Now look, what interest the wife hath in the husband, the child in the father, the members in the head, the subject in his prince, the servant in his lord, the branches in the root, the building in the foundation, that the believer hath in Christ, and much more. Christ is not like the bramble, that receives good but yields none; but he is like the fig-tree, the vine, the olive. All that are interested in him, that pertain to him, are the better for him; they 'all receive of his fulness grace for grace,' John i. 16; Col. i. 19. Now, doubtless, all that interest that Jesus Christ hath in God the Father, he will improve to the utmost for their good that have an interest in him. Now, by this argument, it is also evident that the people of God do stand upon the advantage-ground, above all others in the world, as to their outward preservation and protection.

[9.] Ninthly, *If you consider God's tender and fatherly care of his people, and his singular indulgence towards them, of which you may read much in the blessed Scripture.* Among the many choice scriptures which might be produced, take these as a taste: Ps. ciii. 13, 14, 'Like as a father pitieth his children, so the Lord pitieth them that fear him. For he knoweth our frame; he remembereth that we are dust.' There is an ocean of love and pity in the Father's heart towards his children; but it is but a drop to that which is in God. He hit the mark [Bernard] that said, *Tam pius nemo, tam pater nemo*, No father is like our Father. God is *pater miserationum*, He is all bowels. Let God carry it how he pleaseth towards us, yet we must still acknowledge that he is a propitious Father, and say with him, [Augustine,] 'Lord, thou art a Father both when thou strokest and when thou strikest; thou strikest that we may not perish, and thou strokest that we may not faint.' Pity is as essential to God as light is to the sun, or as heat is to the fire. Hence he is called *the Father* by an eminency, as if there were no father to him, none like him, nor none besides him, as indeed there is not originally and properly, James i. 27. So Exod. xix. 4, 'Ye have seen what I did unto the Egyptians, and how I bare you on eagles' wings, and brought you unto myself.' It is an elegant expression to set forth God's admirable care over his people. The eagle fears no bird from above to hurt her young, only the arrow from beneath; therefore she carries them up upon her wings: Deut. xxxii. 9–11, 'The Lord's portion is his people; Jacob is the lot of his inheritance. He found him in a desert land, and in the waste howling wilderness; he led him about, he instructed him, he kept him as the apple of his eye. As an eagle stirreth up her nest, fluttereth over her young, spreadeth abroad her wings, taketh them, beareth them on her wings:' ver. 12, 'So the Lord alone did lead him, and there was no strange god with him.' The eagle carries her young ones upon her wings—not in her talons, for fear of hurting them—openly, safely, choicely, charily, speedily; and so did God his Israel, of whom he was exceeding choice and chary.

The care that God exercises towards his people is,

(1.) *An extensive care:* a care that reaches, that extends itself to all the saints, whether rich or poor, high or low, bond or free, &c., 2 Chron. xvi. 9; Zech. i. 10, 11.

(2.) *It is an intentive*[1] *care:* he cares for all as if he had but one to care for, Zech. i. 14.

(3.) *It is a pleasant and delightful care,* Isa. xxxi. 5; and not a wearying, tearing, tormenting care. It is such a pleasant care as an indulgent father exercises towards a son, an only son, a son that serves him, Mal. iii. 17.

(4.) *It is an effectual care, a prosperous care, a successful care, a flourishing care.* Men many times rise early and go to bed late, and take a great deal of care at home and abroad, and all to no purpose; but the care of God is always successful, Deut. xi. 12.

(5.) *It is a singular care, a peculiar care.* God cares more for them than he doth for all the world besides. The father's care over the child is a peculiar care, and the husband's care over the wife is a peculiar care, and the head's care over the members is a peculiar care, and so is the Lord's care over his people a peculiar care. God's general care extends to the whole creation; but his special care centres in his saints Zeph. iii. 16-20; Ps. xxxvi. 6; Isa. xl. 31.

(6.) *It is a very tender care:* Isa. xl. 11, 'He shall feed his flock like a shepherd; he shall gather the lambs with his arms, and carry them in his bosom, and shall gently lead those that are with young.' Zeph. ii. 8, 'He that toucheth you toucheth the apple of his eye,' or the 'little man' that is in the eye, or the black of the eye, which is the tenderest piece of the tenderest part, to express the inexpressible tenderness of God's care and love towards his people.[2]

(7.) *It is an abiding care, a lasting care; and not a transient care, a momentary care:* Ps. cxxv. 1, 2, 'They that trust in the Lord shall be as mount Zion, which cannot be removed, but abideth for ever. As the mountains are round about Jerusalem, so the Lord is round about his people, from henceforth even for ever.' Jerusalem was surrounded with many great high mountains, which were a great safeguard to it against all winds and storms. Such a shelter, such a safeguard, yea, and a better, will God be to mystical mount Zion, the church, Zech. ii. 5, against all winds and storms of affliction or persecution: Ps. cxxi. 3, 4, 'He that keepeth thee will not slumber: behold, he that keepeth Israel shall neither slumber nor sleep.' He repeats the promise, and sets it forth with a 'behold,' that it may stick the closer,

[1] 'Earnest.'—G.

[2] *Ishon* of *ish* is here called *bath,* the daughter of the eye; because it is as dear to a man as an only daughter.

and warm our hearts the better. The phrase is taken from watchmen, who stand on the walls in time of war to discover the approaching enemies, and accordingly give warning. Now though they may be careless, treacherous, or sleepy; yet the Lord will be so far from sleeping, that he will not so much as slumber, no, he will not so much as fetch one wink of sleep. It hath been a tradition that lions sleep not, yet to think or say that they sleep not at all were absurd; indeed, their eyelids being too little to cover their great eyes, they do sleep with their eyes somewhat open and shining, which hath occasioned some to think that they sleep not at all.[1] But sure I am that the Lion of the tribe of Judah, who is the keeper of Israel, doth neither slumber nor sleep. He never shuts his eyes, but hath them always open upon his people for good; he winks not so much as the twinkling of an eye; he always stands sentinel for his people's safety: Isa. xxvii. 2, 3, 'In that day sing ye unto her, A vineyard of red wine; I, the Lord, do keep it, I will water it every moment'—or, as the Hebrew runs, 'at moments,' or 'by moments'—'lest any hurt it; I will keep it night and day,' that is, constantly, continually, without intermission. And this constant care of God over his people was signified by those two types, the pillar of fire and the pillar of a cloud, that left not Israel till they were in the possession of the land of Canaan, which was a type of heaven, Exod. xiii. 21, 22.

(8.) And lastly, *It is an active care;* a care that puts the Lord upon preserving his people, and protecting of his people, and making provision for his people, and standing by his people, and pleading the cause of his people, and clearing the innocency of his people.[2] God is above his people and beneath them, Deut. xxxiii. 26, 27; he is under them and over them, Cant. ii. 6; he is before them and behind them, Exod. xxxiii. 1, 2; Isa. lii. 12, and lviii. 8. God is in the front of his people, and God is in the rear of his people, he is on the right hand of his people and he is on the left hand of his people, Ps. xvi. 8, cxxi. 5, and cxviii. 15, 16; Exod. xiv. 22. God made the waters as a wall on their right hand and on their left. God is round about his people, Ps. xxxiv. 7, and cxxv. 1, 2; and in the midst of his people, Zech. ii. 5; Ps. xlvi. 5; 'God is in the midst of her,' Isa. xii. 6. Oh how safe are they that are under such a glorious care! God is above his people and beneath them, he is under them and over them, he is before them and behind them, he is in the front and in the rear, he is round about them and in the midst of them. Now what doth all this speak out, but that the care of God toward his people is an active care? If the philosopher could say, being in danger of shipwreck in a light, starry night, 'Surely I shall not perish, there are so many eyes of providence over me,'[3] oh, then, what may the saints say! Now by this argument it is evident that the people of God stand upon the advantage-ground, as to their outward preservation and protection, above all other people in the world.

[10.] Tenthly, and lastly, *If you do but consider God's great anger and deep displeasure against those that afflict, oppose, or oppress his*

[1] Appianus: Pliny, Hist. lib. iii. cap. 3.

[2] It was a strange speech of Socrates, a heathen, 'Since God is so careful for you,' saith he, 'what need you be careful for anything yourselves?'

[3] Plato.—G.

people. God sent his people into Babylon, and their enemies added to all their sorrows and sufferings; but will God put this up at their hands? No: Zech. i. 15, 'And I am very sore displeased with the heathen that are at ease; for I was but a little displeased, and they helped forward the affliction.' 'I am very sorely displeased,' &c., or, as the Hebrew runs,[1] 'I am in such a heat as causeth fuming and foaming.' I am boiling hot, and even ready to draw upon them, and to cut them off from the land of the living. For the original word here used hath great affinity with another word that signifieth 'to cut down and to destroy,' 2 Kings vi. 6, and importeth a higher degree of displeasure, a greater height of heat than either anger or wrath, as may be seen in that signal gradation, Deut. xxix. 28, 'The Lord rooted them out of their land,' *beaph*, 'in anger,' *ubechemah*, 'and in wrath,' *ubeketseph*, 'and in great indignation.' The last of these three is the word in the text, and notes a higher degree of anger than the two former. So Mal. i. 4, 'Whereas Edom saith, We are impoverished, but we will return and build the desolate places; thus saith the Lord of hosts, They shall build, but I will throw down; and they shall call them the border of wickedness, and the people against whom the Lord hath indignation for ever.' The Edomites were very great enemies to the Israelites; they stood looking on, laughing and rejoicing at Israel's destruction. God saw this, and it greatly displeased him, he being highly sensible of the least indignity done to his people; and therefore he is resolved to pay them home in their own coin, Obad. 8th to 19th verse. The very name and memory of the Edomites have long since been extinct and blotted out from under heaven; they were a people of his wrath, Isa. x. 6; and of his curse, Isa. xxxiv. 5.[2] So Amalek was a bitter enemy to God's Israel, but God utterly blots out his remembrance from under heaven; and laying his hand upon his throne, he swears that he would have war with Amalek for ever, Exod. xvii. 14–16; Nahum i. 2, 'God is jealous, and the Lord revengeth; the Lord revengeth, and is furious; the Lord will take vengeance on his adversaries, and he reserveth wrath for his enemies.' The people of God ought to rest satisfied and assured that God sees and smiles, and looks and laughs, at all the counsels and combinations of wicked men against his Son and against his saints, Ps. ii. 2; and when they have done their worst, the counsel of the Lord shall stand, and Christ shall reign in the midst of his enemies, Prov. xix. 21. And that the stone cut out of the mountains without hands shall bring down the golden image with a vengeance, and make it like the chaff of the summer-floor: Dan. ii. 35. Some write of lions, that as they are mindful of courtesies received—witness the story of Androcles, that fugitive servant of Rome—so they will be sure to revenge injuries done to them; they will prey on them that would make a prey of them. When Juba, king of the Moors, marched through the desert of Africa, a young man of his company wounded a lion; but the year following, when Juba returned, the lion again meets the army, and from among them

[1] *Zeketseph*, from *Ketseph*, which properly signifies such anger as causeth foaming and frothing, as the tumultuous water tossed with the wind, Eccles. vi. 17, and Zech. i. 7, boiling or foaming anger. The word signifies a fervour, a fierceness or vehemency of anger.

[2] See Deut. xxv. 17–19; 1 Sam. xv.; 1 Chron. iv. 42, 43; and compare them together.

all singles out the man that hurt him, and tears him in pieces, suffering the rest to pass by in peace and safety. And thus the Lord Jesus, who is the Lion of the tribe of Judah, Rev. v. 5, is always ready to revenge the cause of his people, and to take vengeance on all that have wounded his people or made a prey of his people, as you may clearly and fully see in Ezek. xxv. and xxxv. Now by this argument, as well as by all the rest, it is evident that the people of God stand upon the advantage-ground, as to their outward preservation and protection, above all other people in the world.

Quest. But, if this be so, how comes it to pass that in this time of great mortality, many of the precious people of the Lord have been taken away as well as others, the raging pestilence having carried many pious souls out of this world, 'of whom the world was not worthy'? Heb. xi. 38. The saint as well as the sinner hath fallen by the hand of the destroying angel. In this day we have seen that word made good in Eccles. ix. 2, 'That all things come alike to all; there is one event to the righteous and to the wicked, to the good and to the clean, and to the unclean, to him that sacrificeth and to him that sacrificeth not; as is the good, so is the sinner, and he that sweareth as he that feareth an oath.'

To this question I shall give these eight short answers:—

(1.) First, *God hath smitten some good men of all persuasions, that none might be proud, secure, or censorious*, and that all might take the alarm and prepare to meet their God, and that all may keep humble and tremble, because of his righteous judgments: Ps. cxix. 120, 'My flesh trembleth for fear of thee, and I am afraid of thy judgments.'

(2.) Secondly, The number of those that feared the Lord that have been taken away by the pestilence *are but few, very few*, if compared with the many thousands of others that never knew what it was to set up God as the main object of their fear, and that never knew experimentally what a changed nature, a sanctified frame of heart, an interest in Christ, or a title to heaven, meant. Oh that we had not cause to fear that hell hath had a very large harvest within these few last months!

(3.) Thirdly, *Sometimes God's own people sin with others*, and therefore they smart with others when God takes the rod into his own hand. Thus Moses and Aaron sinned with others, and therefore their carcases fell in the wilderness as well as others, Num. xx. This may sometimes be the reason why some good men fall in a common calamity; but I dare not say that it is always the reason why some good men fall in a common calamity. I believe there are several choice Christians that have been swept away in this day of the Lord's wrath, who have not sinned with the wicked, though they have fallen with the wicked. Many have fallen by this dispensation who yet have kept their garments pure and clean, and are now walking with Christ in white, Rev. iii. 4. I do not think that those saints that have died by the plague were greater sinners than those that have escaped the plague; yea, I have several reasons to persuade me that several of those precious servants of the Lord that have died of the plague, had more grace in their hearts, and less sin in their lives, than many other saints that have been pitied and spared in this day of the Lord's anger, &c.

(4.) Fourthly, *No godly man dies in any common calamity till his glass be run, and his work done, and he prepared and fitted for another world:* Job xiv. 5, 'Seeing his days are determined, the number of his months are with thee; thou hast appointed his bounds that he cannot pass,' Job v. 26; Rev. xi. 6, 7; Acts xiii. 25, 36. God hath set every man both his time and his task. In this scripture, as in a glass, you may see the true reason why some likely to live long die soon, even whilst their bones are 'full of marrow, and their breasts are full of milk;' and others that are more weak and infirm live long, yea, very long. The reason is, because God hath set bounds to every man's life, to a very day, ay, to a very hour: ver. 14, 'All the days of my appointed time of warfare will I wait till my change come,' *i.e.*, till my death. Job calls death a 'change.' Death is not an annihilation or extinction, but a mutation.

[1.] It is the last change that we shall meet with till the resurrection.

[2.] It is a lasting, yea, an everlasting change. It puts every one into an eternal condition of happiness or misery.

[3.] It is a universal change—1. In respect of persons; all must meet with it: 'it is appointed for all men once to die,' Heb. ix. 27. 2. In respect of the whole man, body and soul. Death lodges the body in the grave, and puts the soul into heaven or hell.

[4.] It is a different change according to the quality of the person changed. It is terrible to a sinner: for,

First, It will put a full period to all his outward mercies, comforts, contentments, and enjoyments, Job i. 21. Saladin, a Turkish emperor, the first of that nation that conquered Jerusalem, lying at the point of death, after many glorious victories, commanded that a white sheet should be borne before him to his grave upon the point of a spear, with this proclamation, 'These are the rich spoils which Saladin carrieth away with him; of all his triumphs and victories, of all the riches and realms that he had, now nothing at all is left him but this sheet.'

Secondly, It will put a full period to all his hopes. Now he shall never hope for mercy more, nor never hope for pardon more, nor never hope for heaven more.

Thirdly, It will put a full period to all the means of grace. Now he shall never hear sermons more, nor never read the word more, nor never enjoy the prayers of the people of God more, nor never taste any of the dainties of God's store more, &c.

Fourthly, It will put a full period to the patience, forbearance, and long-suffering of God, Rom. ii. 4, 5.

Fifthly, It will put a full period to all the pleasures of sin. Now the sinner shall never have one merry day more. In hell there is no singing, but howling; no music, but madness; no sporting, but sighing; no dancing, but wringing of hands and gnashing of teeth for evermore, &c.

Sixthly, It will put a full period to all gracious reprieves. The sinner in his lifetime hath had many a reprieve, from many executions of wrath and judgment. Oh! but now he shall never have one reprieve more.

Seventhly, It will put a full period to all the strivings of the Holy Spirit. Now the Spirit shall never strive with the sinner more, 1 Sam. vi. 3; nor Christ will never knock at the sinner's door, at the sinner's heart, more, &c.

Eighthly, and lastly, It will put a full period to all gracious examples. Now the sinner shall never cast his eye upon one gracious example more. The sinner in his lifetime hath had many gracious examples before his eyes, which it may be at times have had an awakening, convincing, silencing, and restraining power in them. Oh! but now he shall never have his eye upon one pious example more. All hell will not afford one good example. In a word, now the sinner shall find by woeful experience that death will be an inlet to three dreadful things: 1. To judgment, Heb. ix. 27; 2. To an irreversible sentence of condemnation, Mat. xxv. 41; 3. To endless, ceaseless, and remediless sufferings. Not many years since, in the town of Yarmouth, there was a young man, who, being very weak and nigh to the grave, and under the apprehensions of the wrath of God, and supposing that he was presently going down to the pit, to hell, he cried out, 'Oh that God would spare me but two days! Oh that God would spare me but two days! Oh that God would spare me but two days!' This poor creature trembled at the very thoughts of wrath to come. Oh who can dwell with everlasting burnings! who can dwell with a devouring fire! Isa. xxxiii. 14. And as death is terrible to the sinner, so it is desirable, comfortable, and joyful to a child of God: Cant. viii. 14; Luke ii. 27-32; 2 Cor. v. 1-8; Phil. i. 23; Rev. xxii. 20. 'I desire death,' saith Melanchthon, 'that I may enjoy the desirable sight of Christ.' And 'when will that blessed hour come? when shall I be dissolved? when shall I be with Christ?' said holy Mr Bolton when he lay on his dying-bed. Jewel was offended at one that in his sickness prayed for his life. One whom I knew well, a little before his death, after a sharp conflict, cried out three times, Victory! victory! victory! He breathed out his soul and his doxology together, 'Thanks be to God for Jesus Christ,' and so conquered Satan in his last encounter.[1] The dying words of my young Lord Harrington were these: 'O my God, when shall I be with thee?'[2] 'Shall I die ever?' saith Austin; 'Yes; or shall I die at all? Yes,' says he: 'Lord, if ever, why not now?' When Modestus, the emperor's lieutenant, threatened to kill Basil, he answered, 'If that be all, I fear not; yea, your master cannot more pleasure me than in sending of me unto my heavenly Father, to whom I now live, and to whom I desire to hasten.' Mr Dereing,[3] a little before his death, being raised up in his bed, and seeing the sun shine, was desired to speak his mind; upon which he said, 'There is but one sun that giveth light to the whole world, but one righteousness, one communion of saints. As concerning death, I see[4] such joy of spirit, that if I should have pardon of life on the one side, and sentence of death on the other, I had rather choose a thousand times to die than to live.' So Mr John

[1] Much more to this purpose you may find in my 'Saint's Portion,' and in my 'String of Pearls.' [Works, Vol. I., as before.—G.]

[2] Cf. Stock's Funeral Sermon on Lord Harrington, as before.—G.

[3] Edward Dereing or Deering—a fine old Puritan writer.—G.

[4] Query, 'feel'?—G.

Holland, lying at the point of death, said, 'What brightness do I see?' and being told it was the sunshine; 'No,' saith he 'my Saviour shines. Now farewell world, welcome heaven; the day-star from on high hath visited me. Preach at my funeral. God dealeth comfortably and familiarly with man: I feel his mercy! I see his majesty! whether in the body or out of the body I cannot tell, God he knoweth; but I see things that are unutterable.'[1] Mr Knox found so much comfort from the Scriptures upon his death-bed, that he would have risen and have gone into the pulpit to tell others what he had felt in his soul. And by that information that I have had from some good hands, several precious Christians that have lately died of the plague have gone to heaven under as high a spirit of joy, of comfort, of assurance, and of a holy triumph, as any of the last-mentioned worthies, or as any other that ever I heard of or read of: the remembrance of which hath been, and still is, a singular cordial to all their relations and friends that yet survive them. But as I was saying, no godly man falls in any common calamity till his glass be run and his work done; so I say of all those dear servants of the Lord that have fallen by the pestilence in the midst of us, their hour was come, and their course was finished, John vii. 30, and viii. 19, 20; 2 Tim. iv. 6, 7. Had God had any further doing-work, or suffering-work, or bearing-work, or witnessing-work for them in this world, it was not all the angels in heaven, nor all the malignant diseases in the world, that could ever have cut them off from 'the land of the living.' When Lazarus was dead, his two sisters, Martha and Mary, came to Christ with tears in their eyes and sad complaints in their mouths: John xi. 21–32, 'Lord, if thou hadst been here, my brother had not died,' said Martha: and 'Lord, if thou hadst been here, my brother had not died,' said Mary. And is not this the common language of many this day, when such and such precious Christians have fallen by the pestilence? Oh! if such a physician had been here they had not died; or if they had been let blood they had not died; or if they had taken such a potion they had not died; or if they had ate but of such or such meats they had not died; or if they had not lived in such a foggy air they had not died; or if they had not been shut up in such close, narrow, nasty rooms and places they had not died; or had they been but so wise and happy as to have applied such or such a remedy, they might have been alive to this day! not considering with Job that 'the days of man are determined, and his bounds appointed, which he cannot pass,' Job xiv. 5. The time and place, and every circumstance of his dissolution, is decreed from all eternity. That one man dies in the field, another in his bed, one at sea, another on the shore, one of an apoplexy in the head, another of a *struma* in the neck, one of a *squinacy*[2] in the throat, another of a cough and consumption of the lungs; that so many thousands dies of obstructions, inflammations, dropsies, gouts, pestilence, it is foreordained in heaven. The hand of the Lord is in all, and he it is that, having brought us into the world at his pleasure, will take us hence at his appointment. The Jews have a saying that 'God hath four keys under his own girdle:

[1] The saintly friend, and editor of the works, of Dr Robert Harris.—G.
[2] 'Quinsy.'—G.

1. The key of the clouds; 2. The key of the womb; 3. The key of the heart; and 4. The key of death, the key of the grave.

(5.) Fifthly, *God sometimes takes away his dearest children in the common calamity in judgment to wicked men.* Because the hand of the Lord hath touched some of his dearest servants in this sore visitation, how do the wicked insult, rejoice, and triumph! They say, Aha! so would we have it! As the fire-fly leaps and dances in the fire, so do wicked men rejoice in the sufferings and death of the people of God. How do many wicked men bless themselves because they have escaped the hand of the destroying angel, when such and such have fallen by it! Oh, how proud, how obdurate, how impudent, are many grown, because they have escaped the present judgment, when many others that have been a thousand times better than themselves have been sent to their graves! Eccles. viii. 11. The Alcoran saith, God created the angels of light, and the devils of the flame. Certainly God's children are of the light, but Satan's children are furious, wrathful children; they are children of the flame. Oh, in what a flame now are many wicked men against the people of God—since the hand of the destroying angel hath not yet reached them—over what they were in when the destroying angel first drew his sword in the midst of us! as if they were spared on purpose to oppress, persecute, and scatter the people of God more than ever. Oh that all such would be but so favourable to their own souls, as seriously to ponder upon Ezek. xxv. and xxxv.! Obad. 8–19; Nahum i. 9–15.[1]

Felix, earl of Wurtemburg, one of the captains of Charles the Fifth, burning in rage and anger against the people of God, he swore, in the presence of divers at supper, that 'before he died he would ride up to the spurs in the blood of the Lutherans;' but God soon cooled his courage, for that very night he was choked and strangled in his own blood. Paul prayeth that he might be delivered from 'unreasonable and wicked men,' 2 Thes. iii. 2. The word is ἀτόποι, *absurd men*, such as put themselves upon ways of opposition against all reason and common sense; yea, such who in their rage and bitterness of spirit make no bones of breaking all the laws both of God and men, so they may but have their wills and lusts satisfied in afflicting, scattering, and tormenting of the people of God. 'Absurd' men, with Judas, kiss Christ, and betray him. They kiss the head and stab the body; or, as one wittily expresseth it, they kiss the mouth and tread upon the toes. Reader, remember this, when the people of the Jews made use of Philo to apologise for them unto Caius the emperor, Caius used him very ruggedly; but when he was come out of his presence the Jews came round about him. 'Well,' saith he, to encourage them, 'surely Caius will arm God against himself for us.' Let the reader apply it as he pleaseth.

(6.) Sixthly, *God sometimes takes away some of his dearest children in the common calamity, that he may deliver them from greater calamities that are coming upon the world.* The Jews have a saying that, 'When good men die it is an ill sign to the world.' When the luminaries of heaven are eclipsed, *Deus avertat omen!* Paulinus

[1] The scales of the leviathan, as Luther makes the comparison, stick close together; and so do wicked men in their counsels, plots, and projects against the people of God.

reports of Ambrose that he would weep bitterly when he heard of any godly minister's death. Whilst Calvin lives, Beza's life is sweet; but when Calvin dies, death is the more acceptable unto Beza. It is dark night when the lights are put out, and when the curtains are drawn, and the windows close shut. Ah, England, England! if this is not thy present case, I know nothing! The clouds gather more and more, and every day they look blacker and blacker, and bloodier and bloodier! Happy are those souls that are now in heaven, and blessed are those souls that are now waiting for the redemption of Israel.

(7.) Seventhly, Notwithstanding any outward promises that the Lord hath made concerning the protection and preservation of his children, *yet he still reserves a liberty to himself to chastise his children with what rod he pleaseth*, Ps. lxxxix. 30–34; Heb. xii. 6–9; Rev. iii. 19. Notwithstanding all the gracious engagements that are upon the Lord to his people, yet he reserves a freedom to himself to make use of the very lives of his people in such ways as may make best for the bringing about of his own ends, and as may make most for the advance of his own glory; and hence it comes to pass that God delights so to carry it towards his dearest people, as that sinners and saints shall be forced to say that 'his judgments are unsearchable,' and that his 'ways are past finding out,' Rom. xi. 33. 'And that his way is in the sea, and that his paths are in the great waters, and that his footsteps are not known,' Ps. lxxvii. 19. If you take a straight stick and put it into the water, it will seem crooked. Why? Because we look upon it through two mediums, air and water. There lies the *deceptio visus;* thence it is that we cannot discern aright. Thus all the proceedings of God in his righteous judgments, which in themselves are just, righteous, and straight, without the least obliquity, seem to us strange and crooked. That the wicked should prosper, and the righteous be afflicted; that good men should be in bonds, when bad men walk at large; that the Israelites should make the bricks, and the Egyptians dwell in the houses; that some of the best of Christians should fall by the pestilence, when many of the worst of sinners have their lives for a prey—these are some of those mysterious providences that many times make some of the best of Christians to stagger in their judgments; and why so, but because they look upon God's proceedings through a double medium, of flesh and spirit; and hence it comes to pass that all things seem to run cross, and that God's most just and righteous proceedings are not so clearly and fully discerned as otherwise they might be. The wheels in a watch or in a clock move contrary one to another—some one way, some another; yet all shew the skill and intent of the workman, to shew the time, or to make the clock to strike; so in this world divine providences seem to run cross to divine promises; the wicked are spared, and the righteous are taken away; yet, in the conclusion, all issues in the will, purpose, and glory of God.

(8.) Eighthly and lastly, *God hath taken several of his own dear children away by the pestilence, to wipe off that reproach which atheists and wicked men are apt to cast upon the Lord, as if he were partial, and his ways not equal*, Ezek. xviii. 25, 29. God, to stop the mouth of iniquity, the mouth of blasphemy, hath taken away several of his dear servants by the raging pestilence, when the wicked walk on every side, yea, when hell seems to be broke loose, and men turned into incarnate devils; and all because they have not been plagued as other men, nor visited as God hath visited some of his dearest children, Ps. lxxiii. 5; 2 Pet. ii. 9; Job xxiv. 12; Ps. l. 21.

Sometimes God's manner is to begin with his own people: 1 Pet. iv. 17, 'Judgment must begin at the house of God;' and the Lord commands his destroying angel to begin at the sanctuary, Ezek. ix. 6. Sometimes when God intends to bring a common and general destruction upon the enemies, oppressors, haters, and persecutors of his people, he is wont first to scourge his own till the blood comes. 'I took the cup at the Lord's hands'—he means the cup of God's fury, Jer. xxv. 17—'and made all the nations to drink'—that is, prophesied that they should certainly drink of it—'unto whom the Lord hath sent me.' But who were to drink first of this cup? Mark, he tells us, ver. 18, 'Jerusalem and the cities of Judah, and the kings thereof, and the princes thereof.' These were to begin in this cup to Egypt and the Philistines, to Edom, and Moab, and the Ammonites, as he shews in the verses following. Now all these were bitter and implacable enemies to the Israel of God. Ah, sinners, sinners! do not insult over the poor people of God because here and there the hand of the Lord hath touched them, and God hath given the cup into their hands; for if God be God, the cup must go round, and he will make good that word, Isa. v. 22, 23, [see ver. 17,] 'Thus saith the Lord, the Lord and thy God, that pleadeth the cause of his people: Behold, I have taken out of thy hand the cup of trembling, even the dregs of the cup of my fury; thou shalt no more drink it again; but I will put it into the hands of them that afflict thee; which have said to thy soul, Bow down, that we may go over; and thou hast laid thy body as the ground, and as the street to them that went over.' And that word, Jer. xlix. 12, 'For thus saith the Lord, Behold, they'—meaning his own peculiar people—'whose judgment was not to drink of the cup'—that is, the cup of my wrath—'have assuredly drunken; and art thou he that shalt altogether go unpunished? thou shalt not go unpunished, but thou shalt surely drink of it,' or 'drinking drink,' as the Hebrew runs. I have not spared my own dear people, saith God, who might have expected this favour at my hands before any people under heaven, upon the account of my relation to them, my affections for them, and my covenant with them all; and do you think that I will spare you? No! drinking you shall drink—that is, you shall certainly drink of this cup of my wrath; and you shall signally and visibly drink of this cup of my wrath. And that word, Isa. xlix. 25, 26, 'But thus saith the Lord, Even the captains of the mighty shall be taken away, and the prey of the terrible shall be delivered; for I will contend with him that contendeth with thee, and I will save thy children; and I will feed them that oppress thee with their own flesh; and they shall be drunken with their own blood, as with sweet wine; and all flesh shall know that the Lord is thy Saviour and thy Redeemer, the mighty One of Jacob.' Oh that those men would lay these scriptures to heart, who rejoice and glory in the sufferings of the poor people of God, and because some of them have fallen by the hand of the destroying angel, considering that the design of God herein is to stop the mouth of iniquity, and that none may say that he is either partial or fond! Such men that have been eye-witnesses of God's impartial dealing with his own people in this day of his wrath should rather be down-in-the-mouth than up in their spirits; they should rather be silent than raving against the people of the Lord; they should rather tremble than rejoice—for if God deal thus with his green trees, how will he deal with the dry? When God cuts down his best timber, will he not either grub up or burn up the old stumps? Surely he will, Luke xxiii. 31. 'If judgment begin at the house of God, where shall the sinner and the ungodly appear?' 1 Pet. iv. 17, 18. If God deal thus with his best friends, how will he deal with his enemies? If God deal thus with his dearest children, servants and slaves have cause to tremble. And thus much for the reasons why some of God's dearest children have fallen by the pestilence in this day of the Lord's anger.

X. The tenth divine maxim or conclusion is this—viz., *That such saints as do fall by the sword or by the pestilence, they receive no loss, no wrong, no injury, by these sad dispensations; they gain much, but they lose nothing; for by these sad providences they are but hastened to heaven, to their Father's house, to their eternal homes, and to those blessed mansions that Christ hath prepared for them*, John xiv. 1–4.

Elijah went to heaven in a fiery chariot, 2 Kings xi. 12; and many thousand of the martyrs went to heaven in fiery chariots, and in bloody chariots; and doubtless many worthies in this day are gone to heaven in a pestilential chariot, as in a chair of state. Heaven is a place of so much pleasure and delight that they are happy that can get thither anyhow. There is laid up in heaven 'an incorruptible crown,' a 'crown of life,' a 'crown of righteousness, a 'crown of immortality,' a 'crown of glory,' 1 Cor. ix. 25; 2 Tim. iv. 8; James i. 12; 1 Pet. v. 4; Rev. ii. 10; and who would not shoot any gulf to come to these crowns? *Nec Christus, nec cœlum patitur hyperbolem*—Neither Christ nor heaven can be hyperbolised. The good things of heaven are so many that they exceed number, and so great that they exceed measure, and so precious that they are above all estimation. What will that life be, or rather what will not that life be, since all good either is not at all, or is in such a life? Here is light which place cannot comprehend, voices and music which time cannot ravish away, odours which are never dissipated, a feast which is never consumed, a blessing which eternity bestoweth, but eternity shall never see at an end; and who would not wade through a Red Sea to come to this heavenly Canaan? What are all the silks of Persia, and all the spices of Egypt, and all the gold of Ophir, and all the treasures of both Indies; yea, what is the glory of ten thousand worlds, to that glory that those saints are now enjoying who have died by the pestilence in the midst of us? When Cyneas, the ambassador of Pyrrhus, after his return from Rome, was asked by his master what he thought of the city and state, he answered that 'it seemed to him to be *respub-*

lica regum—a state of none but great statesmen, and a commonwealth of kings.' Such is heaven—no other than a commonwealth of kings. Every saint in that kingdom is co-heir with Christ, and hath a robe of honour, and a sceptre of power, and a throne of majesty, and a crown of glory, Rom. viii. 17. Now what doth that Christian lose who dies of the pestilence, and by that means is brought to the fruition of all this glory? 'Death,' saith Mr Brightman, 'that was before the devil's sergeant to drag us to hell, is now the Lord's gentleman-usher to conduct us to heaven.'

In the ceremonial law (Lev. xxv.) there was a year they accounted the year of jubilee, and this was with the poor Jews a very delightful and acceptable year, because that every man that had lost or sold his lands, upon the blowing of a trumpet, returned, and had possession of his estate again; and so he was recovered out of all those miseries and extremities in which he lived before. Now our whole life in this world is made up of troubles and trials, of calamities and miseries, of crosses and losses, of reproaches and disgraces; but death is the Christian's *jubilee;* it wipes away all tears from his eyes, it turns his miseries into mercies, his crosses into crowns, and his earthly hell into a glorious heaven. Though death, though the pestilence be to the wicked as the rod in Moses' hand that was turned into a serpent, yet to the godly, death, the pestilence, is like to the wand in Elijah's hand, a means to waft them over into a better life. The heathen gods held death to be man's *summum bonum*, his chiefest good. Solomon upon his throne extolled his coffin above his crown. Death is a fall that came in by a fall. For a saint to die is for a saint to be no more unhappy. By death the saints come to a fixed and invariable eternity. Death is but an entrance into life. That is not death but life, which joins the dying man to Christ; and that is not life but death, which separates the living man from Christ. Death will blow the bud of grace into the flower of glory. Death is a saint's *quietus est.* All fearful disasters, saith Gregory, which rob the saints of life, do but serve as a rough wind to blow them suddenly into their desired haven—I mean heaven. It matters not, saith Austin, whether a burning fever or flash of lightning, or whether a stone in the bladder, or a thunder-stone in thy head, sends thee out of this miserable world; for God minds not, saith he, the immediate occasion of thy coming to him, but the condition and posture that thy soul is in when it cometh before him. The great thing that God will look at is, whether thou art a sheep or a goat, a sinner or a saint, a friend or an enemy, a son or a slave, a believer or an infidel; whether thou art growing on the crab-stock of old Adam, or art engrafted into Christ; whether thou art clothed with the righteousness of his Son, or whether thou standest before him in the ragged righteousness of thine own duties.

XI. The eleventh divine maxim or conclusion is this—viz., *Though a godly man should die of the plague, yet he shall be certainly delivered from the evil of the plague.*

The smartest rod that God lays upon his own people is from a principle of love. Though he be angry with his people's sins, yet he loves their persons, Rev. iii. 19; Prov. iii. 11, 12; Heb. xii. 5-9.

Though the pestilence comes as a judgment upon wicked men, yet it comes only as a chastisement upon the people of God. When the plague comes upon wicked men, it comes upon them by virtue of the first covenant, and as a fruit of the curse; but when it comes upon the godly, it comes upon them by virtue of the second covenant—I mean the covenant of grace—and as a fruit of his love, Ps. lxxxix. 30–34. Hence God is called 'The great and terrible God that keepeth covenant,' Neh. i. 5. But why is he called 'the terrible God that keepeth covenant,' but because as he hath covenanted to keep them from the evil of the world, and to purge away their sins, and to save their souls, and to preserve them to his heavenly kingdom, Ps. cxix. 75; John xvii.; 2 Tim. iv. 17, 18; so he stands bound by his covenant to make use of any terrible dispensations to effect those great and glorious things. As we sometimes preserve those things in salt that we cannot preserve in sugar; so sometimes God preserves his poor people in the salt of afflictions, in the salt of terrible dispensations, when they would not, when they could not, be preserved in the sugar of mercies, &c. Though the plague should come into a godly family, yet God will deliver that family from the evil of the plague: Ps. xci. 10, 'There shall no evil befall thee, neither shall any plague come nigh thy dwelling.' Beloved, though the plague should come into a godly man's house, yet there shall not be any evil in it to the godly man. When the plague comes into a wicked man's family, it always comes in the quality of a curse, Lev. xxvi.; but it never comes into a godly man's family in the quality of a curse, for Christ was made a curse for them, Gal. iii. 13. It never enters into a godly man's family as a fruit of God's revenging justice or wrath, Rom. viii. 18; Jer. xxiv. 5; Isa. liv. 7–10; Jer. xxxi. 3, and xxxiii. 37. When the plague comes upon the wicked, it comes upon them as a fruit of God's judicial wrath; but when it comes upon the godly, it only comes upon them as a fruit of God's fatherly anger. When it comes upon the wicked, it comes upon them as a fruit of God's everlasting wrath; and therefore where it proves fatal, it is but an inlet to eternal torments. But when it comes upon a child of God, it comes upon him but as a fruit of God's momentary wrath, Isa. liv. 7–10. Look, as David gave charge to his soldiers, that they should not kill Absalom, his son, but only restrain his unnatural rebellion, and reduce him to his former obedience; so when God sends the pestilence amongst his people, he lays a law of restraint upon it that it shall not hurt his people, that it shall not destroy their graces, nor ruin their souls. The full commission that God gives to the pestilence is to restrain the sins of his people, and to destroy the soul-rebellions of his people. I have read of a loadstone in Æthiopia which hath two corners; with the one it draws the iron to it, with the other it puts the iron from it; so God hath two arms, the one of mercy, and the other of judgment; two hands, the one of love, the other of wrath; with the one he draweth, with the other he driveth; the one stroketh, the other striketh; and as he hath a right hand of favour wherewith to lead the saints, so he wants not a left hand of fury wherewith to dash the wicked in pieces.

XII. The twelfth divine maxim or conclusion is this—viz., *That*

God knows how to distinguish his people, and how to difference his people from others, when the pestilence rages in the midst of them: as he did between the Israelites and the Egyptians, Exod. viii. 21–23, ix. 22–26, and xi. 7. That of the apostle is a great truth: 2 Tim. ii. 19, 'The Lord knoweth them that are his.' The Lord knows all his people by name; he doth not only know how many be elected, but he also knoweth who they are. He knows the very numerical persons upon whom he hath set his electing love. Though the pestilence doth not know a saint from a sinner, yet the Lord knows a saint from a sinner; though the pestilence doth not know the righteous from the wicked, yet the Lord knows the righteous from the wicked; though the pestilence doth not know him that feareth an oath from him that sweareth, yet the Lord knows him that feareth an oath from him that sweareth; though the pestilence doth not know the clean from the unclean, yet the Lord knows the clean from the unclean; though the pestilence doth not know him that sacrificeth from him that sacrificeth not, yet the Lord knows him that sacrificeth from him that sacrificeth not; though the pestilence doth not know the oppressed from the oppressor, yet the Lord knows the oppressed from the oppressor; though the pestilence doth not know the persecuted from the persecutor, yet the Lord knows the persecuted from the persecutor: 2 Peter ii. 9, 'The Lord knoweth how to deliver the godly out of temptation,' that is, afflictions. Though the godly man do not know how to deliver himself out of temptations, though others do not know how the godly man should be delivered out of temptations, yet the Lord knows how to deliver the godly man out of temptations; and his time is always the best. The physician turns the hour-glass, and resolves the physic shall work so long; the impatient patient cries out, Oh, I am in pain! oh, how I am tormented! oh, what would I not give for a little ease! oh, methinks every hour is a year! but the wise physician, knowing the fittest time, will not suffer him to have any rest or comfort till the physic hath had its proper operation. Thus many times God's dear children, when they are under sore trials, they cry out, How long, Lord, how long shall this rod lie upon our backs? how long shall thy anger smoke? how long shall the judgment continue? but God will turn a deaf ear, and make them wait his time, which is always the best time. And therefore though God knows how to deliver the godly out of temptations, yet he will take his own time to deliver them out of temptations, &c.

XIII. The thirteenth, and last divine maxim or conclusion, is this —viz., *That though the godly are not delivered* from *the plague, yet they are still delivered* by *the plague; by it they shall be delivered from all their sins.*

Death is not *mors hominis*, but *mors peccati*, not the death of the man, but the death of his sin. When Samson died, the Philistines died together with him; so when a believer dies, be it the pestilence or any other disease, his sin dies with him. As death came in by sin, so sin goes out by death. As the worm kills the worm that bred it, so death kills sin that bred it. The Persians had a certain day in the year wherein they used to kill all serpents and venomous creatures; such a day as that will the day of death be to every believer. When the pestilence hath put a period to a Christian's days, then he shall never be proud more, nor passionate more, nor unbelieving more, nor worldly more, nor neglective of duty more, nor grieve the Spirit of God more, nor wound conscience more, nor break the peace with God more, nor sad the hearts of the righteous more, nor open the mouth of blasphemy more. The death of the body shall quite destroy the body of death; so that as sin was the midwife that brought death into the world, so death shall be the grave that shall bury sin in. When the pestilence takes away a godly man, it doth not take him away in his sins, but it takes him away from his sins; and as death, as the pestilence when it kills, rids the believer of all his sins, so it will rid him of all his troubles. Death cures all diseases, the aching head and the unbelieving heart; *ultimus morborum medicus mors.* At Stratford-Bow were burned in Queen Mary's days[1] at one stake a lame man and a blind man; the lame man, after he was chained, casting away his crutch, bade the blind man be of good comfort, for death would cure them both. It will cure thee, saith he, of thy blindness, and me of my lameness. The way to glory is by misery. In this world we are all Benonis, the sons of sorrow. The way to heaven is by Weeping-cross. Christ's passion-week was before his ascension-day. None passes to paradise but by burning seraphims. We cannot go out of Egypt but through the Red Sea. The children of Israel came to Jerusalem through the valley of tears, and crossed the swift river of Jordan before they came to the sweet waters of Siloam. If a godly man die of the pestilence, he shall never be haunted, tempted, and buffeted by Satan more; he shall never see a cloud, a frown, a wrinkle in the face of God more. The chair of pestilence shall be to him a chair of state, by which he shall be brought into the presence of the King of kings. If the plague prove mortal to a godly man or woman, it shall do that for them which all ordinances could never do, and which all their duties could never do, and which all their graces could never do, and which all their experiences could never do for them, and which all the assistances, influences, and incomes of the Holy Spirit could never do for them, &c. It shall at once free them from all their sins, sorrows, tears, temptations, oppressions, oppositions, vexations, and persecutions. Death will cure the believer of all his bodily diseases and distempers at once. And thus I have done with these divine maxims and conclusions: the Lord make them as so many heavenly cordials to the Christian reader!

READER,

If thou art so ingenuous as to be desirous to know what those special lessons are that thou art to learn by that severe rod, the pestilence, that hath been so long amongst us, I must refer thee to my first Epistle before my Treatise on 'Closet Prayer,' where thou wilt find twenty lessons that we are to learn by the smarting rod.[2]

[1] [Foxe] Acts and Monuments, fol. 1733.

[2] See Works, Vol. II., pp. 139, *seq.*—G.

THE

LEGACY OF A DYING MOTHER.

NOTE.

I have not been able to trace another copy besides my own of this interesting and touching little volume. It appears to be wholly unknown to bibliographers. The original title-page will be found below.* The 'Epistle Dedicatory' of Brooks forms a pungent and quickening little treatise on the duty of children to walk in the footsteps of their godly parents. The 'Legacy' or 'Experiences' itself occupies only eighteen out of the sixty-two pages; and as it is experimental, and also furnishes glimpses of 'good men' in America—*e.g.*, Cotton, Shephard, Eliot—of whom very little is known, we have decided to reprint it along with Brooks's 'Epistle Dedicatory.'—G.

* THE
LEGACY
OF A
DYING MOTHER
To Her
Mourning CHILDREN,
Being the
EXPERIENCES
of
Mrs *Susanna Bell*,
Who died MARCH 13. 1672.
With an
EPISTLE DEDICATORY
By
THOMAS BROOKS Minister of the
Gospel.
LONDON,
Printed and are to be sold by *John Hancock*
Senior and *Junior* at the three Bibles in
Popes-Head Alley in *Cornhill*. 1673.
[12mo.—G.]

THE EPISTLE DEDICATORY.

To his Honoured Friends, Mr T. B., I. B., S. B., I. T., Merchants, and to their Wives, and to the rest of the Children of Mrs Susanna Bell, deceased: the Author wisheth all grace, mercy, and peace.

Honoured Friends,—My design in this epistle is not to compliment you, but to benefit you; it is not to tickle your ears, but to better your hearts; nor it is not to blazon her name or fame to the world whose heaven-born soul is now at rest with God, and who is swallowed up in those transcendent enjoyments of that other world which are above the comprehensions of my mind and the expressions and praises of my pen; but it is to allure and draw you to an imitation of what was praiseworthy in her. Shall I hint at a few things?

1. First, *Imitate her in that sincerity and plain-heartedness which was transparent in her.* Sincerity is not a single grace, but the source of all graces, and the interlineary that must run through every grace; for what is faith, if it be not unfeigned? and what is love, if it be not without dissimulation? and what is repentance, if it be not in truth? Sincerity is the soul of all grace; it is the grace of all our graces. What advantage is it to have 'the breastplate of righteousness, the shield of faith, the helmet of hope,' Eph. vi. 13–17, if they be but painted things? It is the 'girdle of sincerity' that makes all the other parts of our armour useful. Was she not a true Nathanael, John i. 47, a person in whom there was no guile—I mean no allowed hypocrisy? and was not this that which carried her through the pangs of death with a great deal of comfort, as it had done Hezekiah, Paul, and other saints before? Isa. xxxviii. 3; 2 Cor. i. 12. A sincere Christian is like the violet, which grows low, and hides itself and its own sweetness as much as may be with its own leaves; or like Brutus' staff, gold within and thorn without; or like the ark, gold within and goats' hair without. The very heathen loved a candid and sincere spirit, as he that wished 'that there was a glass window in his breast, that all the world might see what was in his heart. But,

2. Secondly, *Imitate her in that humility which was a grace she was clothed withal,* 1 Peter v. 5. I ever found her low and little in her

own eyes, much in debasing herself upon all occasions, looking upon herself as below 'the least of mercies,' with Jacob, Gen. xxxii. 10; and as 'dust and ashes,' with Abraham, Gen. xviii. 27; and as 'a poor worm,' with David, Ps. xxii. 6; and 'less than the least of all saints,' with Paul, Eph. iii. 8. And commonly the more high in spiritual worth, the more humble in heart. God delights to pour in grace into humble souls, as men pour in liquor into empty vessels. Humility makes a person peaceable among brethren, fruitful in well-doing, cheerful in suffering, and constant in holy walking. Humility makes a man precious in the eyes of God. Who is little in his own account is always great in God's esteem. It is well observed by some, that those brave creatures, the eagle and the lion, were not offered in sacrifice unto God, but the poor lambs and doves were; to note that God regards not your brave, high, lofty spirits, but poor, meek, and contemptible spirits. Humility is a rare grace. Many, saith Augustine, can more easily give all they have to the poor, than themselves become poor in spirit. Be low in your own eyes, and be content to be low in the eyes of others; and think not of yourselves above what is meet, as ever you would write after your mother's copy, and affect more to be amongst God's 'little ones,' Mat. xviii. 10, than the 'great ones of this world.' Be humble Christians; as ever you would be holy, be humble. Humility is of the essence of the 'new creature.' He is not a Christian that is not humble. The more grace the more humble. Those that have been most high in spiritual worth have always been most humble in heart. Ignatius could say of himself, *Non sum dignus dici minimus,* I am not worthy to be called the least. Lord, I am hell, but thou art heaven, said blessed Hooper. I am a most hypocritical wretch, not worthy that the earth should bear me, said holy Bradford. I have no other name, saith Luther, than 'sinner;' sinner is my name, sinner is my surname. This is the name by which I shall be always known. I have sinned, I do sin, I shall sin *in infinitum.* Ruth was the daughter of the king of Moab, if we may give credit to the general opinion of the Rabbins; or if that be not so probable, yet she was one that we may well suppose to have been one of good quality in her own country, as being wife of Mahlon, the elder brother of the family of the prince Naasson: yet she accounts herself scarce equal to one of the maid-servants in the house of Boaz, Ruth ii. 13. So Abigail, the wit of the time, 1 Sam. xxv. 41. So Elizabeth, though she was the elder and the better woman for outward quality, yet how confounded was she with Mary's visit, as being too great a weight of honour for her to bear, Luke i. 43. So Mary, Luke i. 38. 'If I were asked,' said Austin, 'what is the readiest way to attain true happiness, I would answer, the first, the second, the third thing is humility.' Humility doth not only entitle to happiness, but to the highest degree of happiness, Mat. xviii. 4. Humility is that Jacob's ladder which reaches from earth to heaven.

3. Thirdly, *Imitate her in her charity and mercy towards suffering, needy, and wanting ones.* How seldom did you find her ear or hand shut against charitable motions! She knew that those that did good to the poor and needy for Christ's sake, God would do good to them for the poor's sake, most sure for his Son's sake. She knew that he

who promised they 'should have that asked,' had first commanded such to give unto them that asked; she knew that unmercifulness is a sin which least becomes and worse beseems one that had so largely tasted of the mercies of God, as she had done both in New and Old England. She was much made up of pity and mercy to the poor; the bellies of the hungry, and the back of the naked, did often proclaim her pity and charity. Many ministers, widows, and fatherless ones, have tasted not only of her husband's bounty, but of hers also. Vain persons, when they give, they will cause their kindness to run in a visible channel, they will sound a trumpet, to be seen of men, Mat. vi. 1, 2; but was she not a secret and hidden reliever of God's distressed ones? Did she not refresh the bowels of many with her hid treasures? Will you all learn to write after this copy? Of Midas it is fabled, 'that whatever he touched he turned into gold.' It is most sure that whatever the hand of charity toucheth it turneth into gold, —be it but a cup of cold water,—nay, into heaven itself; cold water, having not fuel to heat it; cold water, which costs not the charge of fire to warm it. Salvian saith that Christ is *mendicorum maximus*, the greatest beggar in the world, as one that shareth in all his saints' necessities, Heb. vi. 10; and will never forget the charitable person, the merciful person. Cicero could say, 'That to be rich is not to possess much, but to use much;' and Seneca could rebuke them that so studied to increase their wealth that they forgot to use it. I have read of one Evagrius, a rich man, that lying upon his death-bed, being importuned by Synesius, a pious bishop, to give something to charitable uses, he yielded at last to give three hundred pounds; but first took bond of the bishop that it should be repaid him in another world before he had been one day dead. He is said to have appeared to the bishop, delivering in the bond cancelled, as thereby acknowledging what was promised was made good, according to that promise: Mat. xix. 29, 'And every one that hath forsaken houses,' &c.

4. Fourthly, *Imitate her in keeping off from the sins and pollutions of the day wherein you live.* Was she not one of God's mourning one's for the abominations of the time? Did not men's abomination in worship and practice vex, grieve, and wound her poor soul? Was it not her great work to live by no rule, to walk by no rule, to worship God by no rule, but by that which she dared to die by, and to stand by in the great day of our Lord Jesus? Ezek. ix. 4, 6: Jer. ix. 1, 2; 2 Pet. ii. 7, 8; Ps. cxix. 53, 136, 158. She knew that worshipping of God in spirit and in truth was the great worship, the only worship that God stood upon, John iv. 23, 24. She did not, she durst not, worship God according to the customs of the world, or the traditions of the elders, Phil. iii. 3, or the examples of great men. She knew that that worship that is not according to the word, is (1.) Worshipping of devils and not God. Those that depart from the true worship of God, and set upon false worship forbidden by God, do not serve God by it, but the devil, what boasting soever they make, as you may evidently see by comparing the scriptures in the margin together.[1] She knew, (2.) That that worship that is not according to the word, is an image of idolatry, which of all sins is most provoking to a holy, jealous

[1] Jer. ix. 20; 2 Chron. xi. 15; Amos v. 25, 26; 1 Cor. x. 20; 1 Tim. iv. 1; Ezek. viii. 3.

God. 'The devil,' saith Synesius, 'is as glad to be worshipped in an idol, as he was by Israel in a calf,' Exod. xxxii. 4: there being nothing that provokes God to destroy poor sinners more than this. The learned Jews have a saying, 'That no punishment ever happened to them in which there was not an ounce of the golden calf,' grounding it on Exod. xxxii. 34, 'Nevertheless I will remember to visit this sin upon them.' The Egyptians worshipped a pied[1] bull, and whereas some thought it strange that when one died, they should have another of the same colour, Austin thinks that the devil, to keep them in idolatry, might do with their cows as Jacob did with the ewes, present to them when they conceived the likeness of such a bull. Certainly Satan will use all the art he can to keep poor sinners in ways of false worship, it being the most compendious way that can be to engage God to destroy them. She knew, (3.) That that worship that is not according to the word hath destroyed the most flourishing churches and nations; witness the church and nation of the Jews, the seven churches of Asia, and the whole eastern parts of the empire: see Hosea viii. 5-7; Rev. ix. 20; Ezek. x. 2; 2 Chron. vii. 20. She knew, (4.) That that worship that is not according to the word is a cursed worship. It is the observation of one well skilled in the Jewish learning, that there is only one verse in the prophecy of the prophet Jeremiah which is written in the Chaldee tongue, all the rest being in Hebrew: and that is Jeremiah x. 11, 'So shalt thou say, Cursed be the gods who made neither heaven nor earth;' and this is done by the Holy Ghost, on purpose that the Jews, when they were in captivity, and exhorted by the Chaldeans to worship false gods, might be able to answer them in their own language, 'Cursed be your gods; we will not worship them, for they made neither heaven nor earth.' That God that made heaven and earth is only to be worshipped according to his own word; for he will own no worship but what he will accept of, no worship but that; he will bless no worship but that, nor he will reward no worship but that. Your glorified mother kept close to instituted worship when she had health and strength; in this it will be your wisdom to write after her fair copy. But,

5. Fifthly, *Imitate her in justifying of the Lord under the sharpest, bitterest, and most afflictive providences and dispensations.* How often have I heard her to justify the Lord, even whilst he has been a-writing bitter things against her; when gall and wormwood hath been put into her cup, hath she not said with Ezra, chap. ix. 13, 'God hath punished us less than our iniquities deserve;' and with Nehemiah, chap. ix. 33, 'Howbeit thou art just in all that is brought upon us; for thou hast done right, but we have done wickedly;' and with Job, chap. i. 21, 'Oh! the Lord gives, and the Lord takes, and blessed be the name of the Lord;' and with Daniel, chap. ix. 14, 'The Lord our God is righteous in all his works which he doth.' You know what afflictive providences she has been under, both in respect of her person, and in the loss of her husband, and in those variety of weaknesses that attended her body, and in the great losses that some of you have met with in the world, besides several other exercises; yet how has she commonly been taken

[1] 'Parti-coloured,' spelled 'pide.'—G.

up in blessing of God, and in justifying of God, and also in admiring the goodness of God, that it has been no worse with her; and here I am satisfied she would not have exchanged her gains by afflictions for all the gains of the world. Stars shine brightest in the darkest night. Torches are better for the beating. Grapes come not to the proof till they come to the press. Spices smell sweetest when pounded. Young trees root the faster for shaking. Vines are the better for bleeding. Gold looks the brighter for scouring. Glow-worms glister best in the dark. Juniper smells sweetest in the fire. Pomander becomes most fragrant for chafing. The palm-tree proves the better for pressing. Camomile, the more you tread it, the more you spread it. Such is the condition of God's children; they are the most triumphant when most distressed, most glorious when most afflicted; as their conflicts, so their conquests; as their tribulations, so their triumphs. God's people are true salamanders, that live best in the furnace of afflictions; so that heavy afflictions are the best benefactors to heavenly affections. When afflictions hang heaviest, then corruptions hang loosest. And grace that is hid in nature, as sweet-water in rose-leaves, is then most fragrant when the fire of affliction is put under to distil it out. But,

6. Sixthly, *Imitate her in the standing, bent, and course of her life and conversation.* No man is to judge of the soundness or sincerity of his spirit by some particular acts, but by the constant frame and bent of his spirit, and by his general conversation in this world. *Una actio non denominat.* If particular actions might determine whether a man had grace or no grace, whether he were in Christ or not in Christ, whether he were a saint or no saint, whether he were sincere or unsound, we should many times conclude that those have no grace who indeed have, and that they were not in Christ who indeed are, and that they are no saints who indeed are, and that they are not sincere who certainly are true Nathanaels. The best saints on this side heaven have had their extravagant motions, and have very foully and sadly miscarried as to particular actions, even then when the constant course and bent of their spirits and main of their conversations have been God-wards, and Christ-wards, and holiness-wards, and heaven-wards, &c. Witness David's murder and adultery, Noah's drunkenness, Lot's incest, Joseph's swearing, Job's cursing, Jonah's vexing, Peter's denying, and Thomas his not believing. Such twinklings do and will accompany the highest and fairest stars. As he that foots it best may be sometimes found all along,[1] and the neatest[2] person may sometimes slip into a slough; he that cannot endure to see a spot upon his clothes, may yet sometimes fall into a quagmire; so the holiest and exactest Christians may sometimes be surprised with many infirmities and unevennesses and sad miscarriages. Certainly particular sinnings are compatible with a gracious frame, though none are with a glorified condition. Our best estate on earth is mixed, and not absolute. Glory annihilates all sinful practices, but grace only weakens them. The most sincere Christian is but an imperfect Christian, and hath daily cause to mourn over his infirmities,

[1] = fallen and 'lying all along.'—G.
[2] 'Cleanliest,' 'most exact.' Cf. Sibbes, Glossary, *s. v.*—G.

as well as he has cause to bless God for his graces and mercies. Look, as every particular stain doth not blemish the universal fineness of the cloth, so neither doth this or that particular fact disprove and deny the general bent of a person's heart or life. Particulars may not decide the estate either way. It is true, a man by a particular sinning is denominated guilty, but by no one particular can a man's estate be challenged either to be good or bad. He that shall judge of a Christian's estate by particular acts, though very bad, will certainly condemn 'the generation of the righteous,' Ps. lxxiii. 15. We must always distinguish betwixt some single good actions and a series of good actions. It is not this or that particular good action, but a continued course of holy actions, that denominates a person holy. Certainly as there is no man so holy but sometimes he falls into this or that particular sin, so there is no man so wicked but he falls in with this or that particular duty, as you may see in Pharaoh, Balaam, Saul, the Ninevites, Felix, Herod, Judas, yea, and the very scribes and pharisees. Now look, as every sin which a godly man falls into, through infirmity, doth not presently denominate him ungodly, so neither will a few good actions done by a wicked man prove him godly. It is what the course and tenor of the life is that must be most diligently and wisely observed; for every man is as his course is. If his course be holy, the man is so; if his course be wicked, the man is so. There is a maxim in logic, viz., that no general rule can be established upon a particular instance; and there is another maxim in logic, viz., that no particular instance can overthrow a general rule. We are never to make a judgment of our estates and conditions by some particular actions, whether they are good or evil, but we are still to make a judgment of our estates and conditions by the general frame, bent, and disposition of our hearts, and by the constant tenor of our lives. Now, I dare appeal to you, and all others that have observed the constant tenor of her life and conversation, whether it has not been such as becomes the gospel, and as hath adorned the doctrine of God our Saviour—human infirmities excepted, Phil. i. 27; Titus ii. 10; Gen. vi. 9. And oh that this might be the mercy of all her children, to walk with God as she hath done, and then I should not doubt but that they would all meet in heaven at last. But,

7. Seventhly, *Imitate her in her love to the saints, to all the saints, in whom she could discern* aliquid Christi, *anything of Christ.* Did she not love, delight, and take pleasure to see the graces of the Holy Spirit sparkling and shining in the hearts, lives, and lips of the saints? 1 John iii. 10, 14; secretly wishing in herself that her soul were but in so noble a case. Were there any men in all the world that were so precious, so lovely, so comely, so excellent, and so honourable in her account, in her eye, as those that had the image of God, of Christ, of grace, of holiness, most clearly, most fairly, and most fully stamped upon them? Ps. xv. 1, 4, and xvi. 3; 1 John v. 1. Did she not love saints as saints? Was it not the image of God that drew out her affection to the people of God? Many, like the Bohemian cur, can fawn upon a good suit; but grace was lovely in her eye, though clothed with rags. Many love godly men, as they are politicians, or potent, or learned, or of a sweet nature, or affable, or

related, or as they have been kind to them; but all this is but natural love; but to love them because they are spiritually lovely, because of the seed of God in them, 1 John iii. 9, because they are all glorious within, Ps. xlv. 13, is to love them as becometh saints, it is to love them at a higher and nobler rate than any hypocrite in the world can reach to. Did she not set the highest price and the greatest value and esteem upon those that were gracious? Had she not an honour in her heart for them that feared the Lord? Did she not value persons according to their worth for another world, and not according to their worldly greatness or grandeur? Prov. xii. 26, and xxviii. 6. Did she not prefer a holy Job upon a dunghill, before a wicked Ahab upon the throne? Did she not set a higher price upon a gracious Lazarus, though clothed with rags and full of sores, than upon a rich and wretched Dives, though he were clothed gloriously, and fared sumptuously every day? Was not her love to the saints universal? to one Christian as well as another, to all as well as any, to poor Lazarus as well as to rich Abraham, to a despised Job as well as to an admired David, to an afflicted Joseph as well as to a raised Jacob, to a despised disciple as well as to an exalted apostle? Phil. i. 21; 1 Pet. ii. 17. Did she not love to see the image and picture of her heavenly Father, though hung in never so poor a frame, and in never so mean a cottage? Without peradventure, he that loves one saint for the image of God that is stamped upon him, he cannot but fall in love with every saint that bears the lovely image of the Father upon him. And oh that this might be all your mercy, to write after this copy that she has set before you! But,

8. Eighthly, *Imitate her in her constancy in the ways of God, with or notwithstanding all the hazards, storms, dangers, and troubles that has attended those ways, especially in those latter days of apostasy, wherein God had cast her lot.* She was not a reed shaken with every wind; she was unchangeable in changeable times. Whatever storms beat upon the ways of God, or the people of God, she remained firm and immovable in the ways of the Lord, Ps. xliv., and cxix. 112; and doubtless such souls as are truly good, they will be good in the worst of times, and in the worst of places, and amongst the worst of persons. Principles of grace and holiness, they are lasting, yea, everlasting. They are not like the morning cloud nor the early dew, 1 John iii. 9; Hosea vi. 4. Let times and places and persons be what they will, a sincere Christian will not dishonour his God, nor change his Master, nor quit his ways, nor blemish his profession, nor wound his conscience to sleep in a whole skin, or to preserve his safety, or to secure his liberty; and was it not thus with her in the most trying times? An upright man is a right man. So ישר, *jashar*, is rendered by the Septuagint, Judges xvii. 6. He is one that won't be bowed or bent by the sinful customs or examples of the times and places where he lives, Gen. vi. 9; Rev. xiv. 4, and iii. 4; Job xvii. 9. Let the times be never so dangerous, licentious, superstitious, idolatrous, and erroneous, yet a sincere, plain-hearted Christian will keep his ground, and hold on in his way; as might be made evident by a cloud of witnesses, Heb. xii. 1; Ps. cxxv. 1, 2. The laurel keeps its freshness and greenness in the winter season; a sincere Christian is *semper*

eadem; let the wind and the world and the times turn which way they will, a sincere soul, for the main, will still be the same. He will be like mount Zion, which cannot be removed; he will stand his ground and hold his own under all changes; he is like the philosopher's good man, *τετραγονος*, four-square; cast him where you will, like a die, he falls always square and sure; so cast a plain-hearted Christian where you will, into what company you will, and into what condition you will, yet still he will fall sure and square for God and godliness. Let the times be never so sad, nor never so bad, yet a plain-hearted Christian will still keep close to God and his ways, and will rather let all go than let his God go, or his religion go, or his integrity go, or ordinances go. Lapidaries tell us of the Chelydonian stone,[1] that it will retain its virtue and lustre no longer than it is enclosed in gold—a fit emblem of an unsound heart, who is only good while he is enclosed in golden prosperity, safety, and felicity. An unsound Christian, like green timber, shrinks when the sun of persecution shines hot upon him. The heat of fiery trials cools the courage of unsound Christians; but a sincere, plain-hearted Christian is like a massive vessel of gold, that keeps its own shape and figure at all times, in all places, and in all companies. When one of the ancient martyrs was greatly threatened by his persecutors, he replied, 'There is nothing,' saith he, 'of things visible, nothing of things invisible, that I fear; I will stand to my profession of the name of Christ, and contend earnestly for the faith once delivered to the saints, come on it what will, in these evil days wherein multitudes have turned aside into crooked paths.' She kept close and constant to the ways of the Lord so long as her natural strength lasted. And oh that all you, her children, would make it your business in this, as well as in other things, to write after your mother's copy! remembering that if you are not faithful unto death, you shall never receive a crown of life, Rev. ii. 10; and that if you do not continue to the end, that is, in well-doing, you shall never be saved, Mat. xxiv. 13. But,

9. Ninthly, *Imitate her in her high valuations of Jesus Christ.* What low and little things were her own graces, duties, services, and mercies, when she cast her eye upon Christ, when she fell into discourses of Christ! Phil. iii. 8–10; Mat. xiii. 44. Christ was her *summum bonum*, chiefest good. What was all the world to a sight of Christ, to a day, yea, to an hour's communion with Christ! They are no believers that do not value Jesus Christ above all the world and all things in the world; 'for unto every one that believes he is precious,' 1 Pet. ii. 7—most precious, only precious, and for ever precious. They value him (1.) Above their lusts, Gal. v. 24. They can pluck out right eyes for Christ, and cut off right hands for Christ. They value him (2.) Above the world. Witness David, Ps. lxxiii. 25, and Dan. vi.; and the disciples, Mat. xix. 27; and Moses, Heb. xi. 25, 26; and the primitive Christians, and the martyrs of a later date. They value him (3.) Above their lives: Rev. xii. 11, 'They loved not their lives unto the death.' So Paul, Acts xx. 22–24, and xxi. 13. So the martyrs. They value him (4.) Above all their relations. 'If all the world were a lump of gold,' said the Dutch

[1] As before; see Index, *s.v.*—G.

martyr, 'and in my hands to dispose of, I would give it to live all my days with my wife and children in a prison; but Christ and his truth is dearer to me than all.' You have thousands of such instances upon record. They value him (5.) Above their goods: Heb. x. 34, 'Ye took joyfully the spoiling of your goods.' So has many thousands since under sharp persecutions. They value him (6.) Above all natural, spiritual, and acquired excellencies, Phil. iii. 7, 8. In all my serious discourses with her about our Lord Jesus Christ, she would still set the crown upon Christ's head. She would lay herself low, very low, that he alone might be exalted. The thoughts of Christ was precious to her, the discourses of Christ were precious to her, the image of Christ was precious to her, the ordinances of Christ were precious to her, the discoveries of Christ were precious to her, the day of Christ was precious to her, the offices of Christ were precious to her, and the rebukes of Christ—whilst she enjoyed his presence under them—was precious to her; but, above all, the person of Christ was most precious to her. In her eye he was 'the chiefest of ten thousand, fairer than the children of men,' Cant. v. 10; Ps. xlv. 1; and all the riches, honours, pleasures, and delights of the world were but dung in comparison of him, Phil. iii. 7, 8. Oh at what a rate has the saints of old prized our Lord Jesus! *Mallem*, said one, *ruere cum Christo quam regnare cum Cæsare:* Luther had rather fall with Christ than stand with Cæsar. The same author elsewhere saith that he had rather be *Christianus rusticus* than *Ethnicus Alexander*, A Christian clown than a pagan emperor. Theodosius, emperor, preferred the title of *Membrum Ecclesiæ* before that of *Caput Imperii*, professing that he had rather be a saint and no king, than a king and no saint. And godly Constantine rejoiced more in being the servant of Christ, than in being the emperor of the world. Bernard saith 'that he had rather be in his chimney-corner with Christ, than in heaven without him.' It was an excellent answer of one of the martyrs when he was offered riches and honours if he would recant, said, 'Do but offer me somewhat that is better than my Lord Jesus Christ, and you shall see what I will say to you.' It was a sweet prayer of one, 'Make thy Son dear, very dear, exceeding dear, only dear and precious, or not at all.' Another good man cried out, 'I had rather have one Christ than a thousand worlds.' I have read of Johannes Mollius,[1] 'that whensoever he spake of the name of Jesus, his eyes dropped tears;' and of another reverend divine, who, being in a deep muse after some discourse that passed of dear Jesus, and tears trickling down his cheeks before he was aware, and being asked the reason of it, he confessed ingenuously, 'It was because he could not draw his dull heart to prize Jesus Christ at that rate he should and fain would.'[2] Christ lay near your mother's heart, and oh that he may be near all your hearts, that so you may be safe and saved for ever! But,

10. Tenthly, *Imitate her in the casting a mantle of love over the infirmities and weaknesses of poor, weak, miscarrying Christians, in the burying of Christians' weaknesses under their graces.* Much I know of this, but some know much more. She was not for blazoning of others' weaknesses, whether they were nearer to her or more remote

[1] Clarke, as before, p. 186.—G. [2] John Welch, as before.—G.

from her. She commonly carried a mantle of love about her to cast over other men's sins; she seemed to live under the power of that word: Prov. x. 12, 'Love covereth all sins:' and that 1 Pet. ix. 8, 'Charity shall cover the multitude of sins.' By covering must be meant (1.) A favourable construction of all things, which in right reason might well be construed; (2.) A passing by smaller infirmities and private offences; (3.) Such a covering as might cure also, for love is wise. Love hath a large mantle, and covers all sins—that is, all private sins, and all such sins as may be concealed with a good conscience both towards God and towards men. Again, it must be understood, not of our own transgressions committed against God, but of other men's sins and transgressions committed against us. Love is not suspicious, but interprets all things in the best sense, Prov. xvii. 9. Love will not publish private injuries, to the dishonour or shame of the party offending: Prov. xii. 6, 'A prudent man covereth shame.' It is recorded to Vespasian's honour, 'that he was more ready to conceal the vices than the virtues of his friends.' To observe and take notice of other men's faults, but not of our own, is the easiest thing in the world, said Thales. Such commonly are best acquainted with other men's infirmities, who are least observant of their own iniquities and irregularities. 'The nature of man is very apt,' saith Seneca, *Utimur perspicillis magis quam speculis*, to use spectacles to behold other men's faults, rather than looking-glasses to behold their own.' Erasmus speaks of one who collected all the lame and defective verses in Homer's works, but passed over all that was excellent. The Donatists of old were more glad to find a fault than to see it amended, and to proclaim it than to cover it; to carp at it than to cure it. 'If I should find a bishop committing adultery,' saith Constantine the Great, 'I would cover that foul fact with mine imperial robe rather than it should come abroad to the scandal of the weak and the scorn of the wicked.' Seneca, unmasking the face of their corrupt state, hath this notable passage, 'The news from Rome take thus: the walls are ruined, the temples are not visited, the priests are fled, the treasuries robbed, old men are dead, young men are mad, vices are lords over all. The dictator blames the consul, the consul checks the censor, the censor chides the prætor, the prætor falls foul upon the ædile, and he casts all the fault upon the quæstor, and because no man will acknowledge himself in fault, we have no hopes of better times.' How applicable this is to our present times, I shall leave others to judge; but by the whole you see that all sorts and ranks of men are more apt to shame and quarrel at other men's faults than with their own. Observable is that of our blessed Saviour: Luke vii. 37, 'There was a woman in the city which was a sinner.' No wonder! what woman is not? We may guess both who the woman was, and what the sin was, and which city it was; but he neither names the city, nor the sin, nor the sinner. Seeing her reformation, he consults her reputation. Oh that you would all labour to write after this copy. When Alexander was painted, the painter laid his finger on his wart, and Apelles covered Venus' mole with his finger, that it might not be spied. As you stand in a near relation one to another, so I could wish that you would lay your fingers upon one another's warts and moles, and not blazon one another's human frailties and infirmities to the world; but love and live as brethren and sisters who are never without a mantle of love to cover infirmities—I say not enormities; to cover weaknesses—I say not wickedness; to cover from the world—I say not from God nor from one another. But,

11. Eleventhly, *Imitate her in her earnest desires and endeavours that others, especially that her nearest and dearest relations, might taste that the Lord is gracious;* that they might all be holy and happy, gracious and glorious; that they might all have changed hearts, renewed natures, and sanctified souls; that they might all be born again, adorned with grace, filled with the Spirit, and fitted for heaven. You know that upon her dying-bed she desired me that when she was asleep in Jesus, 1 Thes. iv. 14, that I would, for the advantage of the living, especially for your sakes, who lay nearest her heart, preach on that Psalm xxxiv. 8, 'Oh taste and see that the Lord is gracious,' which accordingly I did once and again.[1] Now what was her design in this, but that every one of you might share with her in the same favour, love, spirit, grace, merit, righteousness, and goodness that her soul had long tasted of? There is not a soul that ever has had any saving taste of the Lord and of his goodness, but is mighty desirous that others should taste of the same grace and goodness. 'Oh taste and see that the Lord is good;' as if David should have said, I for my part have seen, tasted, and experienced much of God and his goodness, and never more than in my greatest straits. I am loath to eat these heavenly viands and soul-ravishing morsels of contentment alone. 'Come hither, all you that fear God, and I will tell you what God hath done for my soul.'[2] Come, oh come, poor souls! taste and see with me how good the Lord is; how comfortable the embraces of Christ are, and how sweet communion with heaven is. We cannot advantage others more than by declaring and communicating unto them our soul-secrets, our soul-experiments. All the saints own it as their duty to glorify God in their generation: and wherein can they bring more glory to God than in helping souls to heaven? and how can they find out a readier way to effect this great business, than by telling them what God has done for their souls, than by making a faithful narrative of their own conditions by nature and by grace, when and how the goodness of the Lord was made known unto them upon a saving account. Oh tell poor wounded sinners what methods of mercy the Lord used to the healing of your wounds and to the quieting of your consciences, that so they may be encouraged to a serious use of all gospel means, and to a hope of the same grace and goodness of the Lord towards them. Oh labour more and more to convince others by your experiences that grace is the only way to glory, and that 'without holiness no man shall see the Lord,' Heb. xii. 14.[3] Paul had tasted that the Lord was good, and he

[1] The three sermons that I preached on Ps. xxxiv. 8 I have been desired to print, but could not answer friends' expectations in that, because I had not the notes by me of what I said upon that text.

[2] Ps. lxvi. 16: the words are without a copulative in the Hebrew, *venite, audite:* Calvin, 'Come hearken;' like that Gen. xix. 14. It not only imparts an invitation, but the affection also of him that speaks.

[3] See my treatise on this text, ['Crown and Glory of Christ,'] Vol. IV.—G.

wished that both Agrippa and all that heard him were altogether such as he was, except his bonds,' Acts xxvi. 29. As soon as Matthew had tasted that the Lord was good, Luke v. 29, he called together a huge multitude of publicans and others to meet at his house. As soon as Philip had tasted of the sweetness of communion with Christ, he runs to Nathanael to invite him to Christ, saying, 'Come and see,' John i. 45, 46. No sooner had the woman of Samaria tasted of Christ's living waters, but she leaves her water-pot, and posts into the city to call out her friends and neighbours to see and taste how good dear Jesus was, John iv. 28. So those young converts, Zech. viii. 21, 'And the inhabitants of one city shall go to another, saying, Let us go speedily to pray before the Lord, and to seek the Lord of hosts; I will go also:[1] Micah iv. 2, 'And many nations shall come, and say, Come, and let us go up to the mountain of the Lord, and to the house of the God of Jacob; and he will teach us of his ways, and we will walk in his paths: for the law shall go forth of Zion, and the word of the Lord from Jerusalem.' Those blessed converts would not come alone, but draw others along in company with them to worship the Lord, which is lively expressed in a *mimesis* or imitation of the encouragements and invitations they should use one to another, 'I will go also.' Every one was as forward for himself, as zealous for another. Oh blessed frame of spirit! O my friends, it is the nature of true grace to be diffusive and communicative. Grace cannot be concealed. They that have tasted of divine sweetness cannot choose but speak of it to others; their hearts, like bottles of new wine, would be ready to burst if they had not vent. Grace is like fire in the bones. They that have it cannot hide it. All the faculties of the soul, and all the members of the body will still be a-telling of others that there is a treasure of grace in the soul. The blind men that were cured were charged to be silent, but they could not hold their peace. So here, *Lilmor belammed*, we therefore learn that we may teach, is a proverb among the Rabbins: and I do therefore lay in and lay up, saith the heathen, that I may draw forth again and lay out for the good of many. And shall not grace do as much as nature? shall not grace do more than nature? Well, friends, this I shall only say, that the frequent counsels that your glorified mother has given you to taste of divine goodness, and the experiences that she has communicated to you of her taste of divine goodness, both in her health and sickness, both in her living and dying, will certainly either be for you, or else be a dreadful witness against you in the great day of our Lord Jesus. Oh remember not only those experiences of hers that are now presented to your eyes, but those other experiences of hers as to her inward man that has often sounded in your ears. But,

12. Lastly, *Labour to imitate her in her comfortable passage out of this world.* Those words were more worth than a world which she uttered a little before she fell asleep in the Lord, viz., 'Lord, take my aching head, and lay it in thy bosom.' How often did she express her longings to be with Christ, that she might sin nor sorrow no more! Her outward man was full of pain, weakness, and trouble; yet how was

[1] *Vide* Pemble, *in loc.*

her inward man refreshed and quieted in a way of believing, according to that blessed word, Isa. xxvi. 3, 'Thou wilt keep him in perfect peace;'—the Hebrew runs, שלום, שלום, *shalom, shalom*, peace, peace:—'whose mind is stayed on thee, because he trusteth in thee.' Never did the espoused maid long more for the marriage-day, nor the apprentice for his freedom, nor the captive for his ransom, nor the condemned man for his pardon, nor the traveller for his inn, nor the mariner for his haven, nor the sick man for his health, nor the wounded man for his cure, nor the hungry man for his bread, nor the naked for clothes, than she did long to die, and to be with Christ, which for her was best of all, Phil. i. 23. How often were those words in her mouth, Rev. xxii. 20, 'Come, Lord Jesus, come quickly!'[1] The face of none is so comely to the saint's eye, the voice of none so lovely to his ears, the taste of none so pleasant in his mouth, as Jesus Christ. The name of Jesus hath a thousand treasures of joy and comfort in it, saith Chrysostom; and is therefore used by Paul five hundred times, as some have reckoned. The name of a Saviour, saith one, [Bernard,] is honey in the mouth, music in the ear, and a jubilee in the heart. And how often was that blessed word in her mouth, 'Remember, O Lord, I beseech thee, how I have walked before thee in truth, and with a perfect heart; and have done that which is good in thy sight,' Isa. xxxviii. 3. A serious sense of her uprightness in the main, of her walking with God, did yield her more than a little sweetness and comfort when she was upon her bed of pain. One of the last speeches of a dying upright Christian was this, 'Satan may as well pluck God out of heaven, as pluck my soul out of his keeping,' John x. 28–30; 2 Tim. ii. 12. She 'knew him in whom she had believed, and was persuaded that he was able to keep that soul she had committed to him against that day.' A child that hath any precious jewel given him cannot better secure it than by putting it into his father's hands to keep; so neither can we better provide for our souls' safety than by committing them to God. 'Keep that which I have committed;' that is, either my precious soul, which I have committed to his care and custody, to bring it forth glorious at that day of his appearing; or my eternal life, happiness, and crown of glory, which I have, as it were, deposited with him by faith and hope. And thus it was with her. The apostle saith he committed to God's custody a pawn or pledge; but about this pawn or pledge interpreters differ. One saith it is his soul; another saith it is himself; and a third saith it is his works; and a fourth saith it is his sufferings; and a fifth saith it is his salvation. In short, he committed to God his soul, himself, his doings, his sufferings, to be rewarded with life and salvation; and so did she who is now at rest in the Lord. Lord, saith Austin, I will die that I may enjoy thee; I will not live, but I will die; I desire to die that I may see Christ, and refuse to live, that I may live with Christ. The broken rings, contracts, and espousals contents not the true lover, but he longs for the marriage-day; and so did she who has now exchanged a sick-bed for a royal throne, and the company of poor mortals for the presence of God, Christ, angels, and the 'spirits of just men made perfect.'

[1] In all my visits to her, my hardest task was still to work her into a willingness to stay inthis world till all her doing and her suffering work was over.

It was well said of [by] one, 'So far as we tremble at death, so far we want love.' It is sad, when the contract is made between Christ and a Christian, to see a Christian afraid of the making-up of the marriage. But your deceased relation was no such Christian. I know nothing in this world that her heart was so much set upon as the completing of the marriage between Christ and her soul. My eye is upon that text, Isa. lvii. 1, 'The righteous perisheth, and no man layeth it to heart, and merciful men are taken away, none considering that the righteous are taken away from the evil to come.' I have read of one Philo, a Jew, and another, that when they came to any city or town, and heard of the death of any godly man, though never so poor, they would both of them mourn exceedingly, because of the great loss that place had by the death of that godly man, and because it was a warning piece from God of evil approaching. But ah, how many famous, godly ministers, and how many choice Christians, hath the Lord of hosts taken away from us, and yet who lays it to heart! There is no greater prognostic of an approaching storm, than God's calling home so many worthies, 'of whom the world was not worthy,' as he has lately done. Now oh that God would beautify all your souls with all these twelve jewels, with which your mother was adorned in life and death!

Sir[s], your having signified to me that it was your mother's mind and your desires that her following experiences should be printed, I did think it might be somewhat reasonable to put you all in mind of such things as I had, among many others, observed, and which should be all your ambition to imitate, as you would give up your accounts at last with joy, and be happy with her for ever in the other world.

Considering that these Experiences may fall into other hands besides your own, I thought it meet to let such readers know that these were taken from her by one of you, when she was in a very weakly condition, and had little more strength than to speak; and they are but some of those that lay most warm upon her heart at that time. God began to work upon her in the morning of her days, and had there been a collection of all her most close, inward, spiritual experiences, they would have been greatly multiplied beyond what is now presented to the reader's eye; but that was a task too hard for her under those variety of weaknesses that she was every day contending with. The experiences of old disciples commonly rise high; but the ingenuous reader may easily discern by the twelve jewels with which she was adorned, that she was a woman both of choice and great experiences. Austin observes on Ps. lxvi. 16, 'Come and hear, all ye that fear God, and I will declare what he hath done for my soul;' 'he doth not call them,' saith he, 'to acquaint them with speculations—how wide the earth is, and how far the heavens are stretched out, or what the number of the stars are, or what is the course of the sun;—but come and I will tell you the wonders of his grace, the faithfulness of his promises, and the riches of his mercy to my soul.' Now all ministers and Christians that had any inward acquaintance with her soul concernments, do very well know that she was most taken up with the wonders of God's free, rich, and sovereign grace, and with the sweetness, the freeness, the riches, and the faithfulness of his promises, and with the riches of his mercy in Christ to her soul.

To draw to a close, it is observable that even the holy apostles in their canonical epistles, have spent some good part of their holy lives in the ample commendations of those eminent saints to whom they wrote; as Paul in his to Philemon, and John in that of his to an honourable lady, and that other to a meaner person—viz., Gaius; and that they went not behind the door, as we say, to whisper, but as on the house-top did proclaim the religious and pious practices of those more choice Christians to the imitation of others. And further, when I consider that which the apostle speaketh of Demetrius, a rare and not ordinary testimony: 'Demetrius hath a good report of all men, and of the truth itself: and we also bear record; and we know that our record is true,' 3 John 12. And yet further, when I consider what is recorded of Hezekiah, 'Thus did Hezekiah throughout all Judah, and wrought what was good, and right, and true before his God. And in every work that he began in the service of the house of God, and in the law and commandments, he did it with all his heart, and prospered,' 2 Chron. xxxi. 20, 21. And when I consider what high commendations the apostle bestows upon the churches of Macedonia, 2 Cor. viii. 1–11; and upon the church of Thessalonica, 1 Thes. i. 1-9; and also 2 Thes. i. 3-5. And when I consider that it was the Holy Ghost who writ Jehoiada's epitaph, 'They buried him in the city of David among the kings, because he had done good in Israel, both towards God and toward his house,' 2 Chron. xxiv. 16. It is said also of Josiah, in his commendations by the same Spirit, 'Like unto him there was no king,' 2 Kings xxiii. 25. Moses and Mordecai, Sarah, Deborah, Esther, Elizabeth, and others, after their deaths, have had their due praises. When I consider of these things, I am very well satisfied in what I have said concerning this deceased sister and friend. I do noways doubt but that we may very safely say good of such when dead, whose ordinary course and practice it was to do good while they lived; but in this censorious age, no sooner is dust cast upon some Christians' heads, but there are those that will do what they can to throw dirt in their faces. Augustine doth very fitly compare those to Dives his dogs; they lay licking and sucking Lazarus his sores, but his sounder parts they never meddled with. To trample upon the reputation and stain the glory of them that 'die in the Lord,' argues such persons to be akin to fleas, who bite most when men are asleep. It was one of Solon's laws, that none should dare to speak evil of the dead; and Plutarch tells us, that that was highly commended and duly observed. But is it so now? This I am sure, that it well becomes Christians not to dare to speak evil, if they could, of those who for the main have lived holily and died graciously, as this deceased friend hath done. Let this satisfy us, that she is above the praises and envies of men. It is the good, the profit, the advantage of all your souls and theirs into whose hands this little piece may fall, that has drawn me out to write so large an epistle. If I had only the dead in my eye, a few lines should have served my turn. I doubt not but that you will kindly accept of my endeavours to be serviceable to your immortal souls; and who can tell what fruit may grow upon this tree? I shall improve all the interest I have in heaven, that both the Epistle and your glorified mother's Experiences may be blest to the furtherance of the internal and eternal welfare of all your souls. The 'good-will of him that dwelt in the bush' rest upon you and yours. So I rest, honoured friends, your souls' servant, THOMAS BROOKS.

A TRUE RELATION

OF SOME OF THE

EXPERIENCES OF MRS SUSANNA BELL,

TAKEN FROM HER OWN MOUTH BY A NEAR RELATION OF HERS, A LITTLE BEFORE HER DEATH.

Left as a legacy to her mourning children.

It pleased the Lord to order it so that in my young days I was cast into a family that feared the Lord; and going to hear Mr White[1] preaching from these words, Prov. xv. 15, 'But he that is of a merry heart hath a continual feast;' from these words he did shew how happy a thing a good conscience was, and what a sad thing it was, with Judas, to have a bad conscience. And what a blessed thing it was to have a good conscience from that of Hezekiah: Isa. xxxviii. 3, 'And he said, Remember now, O Lord, I beseech thee, how I have walked before thee in truth, and with a perfect heart, and have done that which is good in thy sight.' This sermon God made useful to me; and after this it pleased the Lord to order it so that I changed my condition, and the Lord provided for me a good husband, 'one that feared him.' And some troubles being here, many of the people of God went for New England, and among them my husband desired to go; but I and my friends were very averse unto it. I having one child, and being big with another, thought it to be very difficult to cross the seas with two small children; some of my neighbours advising me to the contrary, living so well as I did. But I told them that what the Lord would have me to do that I would willingly do; and then it pleased the Lord to bring that scripture to my mind: Eph. v. 22, 'Wives, submit yourselves unto your own husbands, as unto the Lord'—and then my heart was brought off to a quiet submission. But after this, I being well-delivered, and the child well, it pleased the Lord soon after to take my child to himself. Now upon this, so far as it pleased the Lord to help a poor wretch, I begged earnestly of him to know why he took away my child, and it was

[1] Probably the excellent John White of London.—G.

given in to me that it was because I would not go to New England. Upon this the Lord took away all fears from my spirit, and then I told my husband I was willing to go with him; for the Lord had made my way clear to me against any that should oppose. And then my husband went presently upon the work to fit to go. And the Lord was pleased to carry us as upon eagle's wings, according to that Deut. xxxii. 10, 11. We were eight weeks in our passage, and saw nothing but the heavens and waters. I knew that the Lord was a great God upon the shore; but when I was upon the sea I did then see more of his glorious power than ever I had done before, according to that of the psalmist, Ps. cvii. 23, 24. And when the Lord was pleased to bring us in safety on shore, his people gave us the best entertainment they could; and then I thought I could never be thankful enough to the Lord for his goodness in preserving us upon the sea, I being big with child, and my husband sick almost all the voyage. After this my husband would have gone by water higher into the country; but I told him the Lord having been so good in bringing us safe ashore amongst his people, I was not willing to go again to sea. And it was a good providence of God we did not; for most of them that went were undone by it. The first sermon that I heard after I came ashore was out of Jer. ii. 13, 'For my people have committed two evils; they have forsaken me, the fountain of living waters, and hewed them out cisterns, broken cisterns, that can hold no water.' Now the minister did shew that whatever we did build on short of Christ would prove but a broken cistern; and by that sermon the Lord was pleased to shake my foundation. But I being a poor, ignorant creature, thought if I could but get into the fellowship of the people of God, that that would quiet my spirit and answer all my objections; and I did accordingly attempt to join with the church; but they were very faithful to the Lord and my soul, and asked me what promise the Lord had made home in power upon me. And I answered them, Jer. xxxi. 3, 'Yea, I have loved thee with an everlasting love; therefore with loving-kindness have I drawn thee:' but they told me that that was a general promise, that I must look to get some particular dromise made home in power upon me; and persuaded me to wait a little longer to see what God would further do for my poor soul, which accordingly I did. And going to hear Mr Cotton,[1] who did preach out of Rev. ii. 28, 'To him that overcometh I will give the morning star;' from which words he did observe that that star was Christ. And [from] this he came to shew how a soul might know whether it had an interest in Christ or no, and that was by the Lord's giving out such precious promises as these to the poor soul—viz., that 'God was in Christ, reconciling the world to himself,' 2 Cor. v. 19; and that John xvi. 21, 'And your joy shall no man take from you:' and Isa. liv. 22, 'I have blotted out, as a thick cloud, thy transgressions, and as a cloud, thy sins;' and that Isa. xliii. 25; which promises afterwards God made sweet to my soul. After this I went to hear Mr Shepherd,[2]

[1] John Cotton of Boston in Old England, and afterwards of Boston in New England. Died, 1652.

[2] Thomas Shepard of Cambridge, Mass., whose Works—including his celebrated sermons expository of the Parable of the Ten Virgins, mentioned by Mrs Bell—have been collected in 3 vols., cr. 8vo, 1853, (Boston.)—G.

and he was preaching out of the parable of the ten virgins, Mat. xxv. 1–13. In his discourse he shewed that all were professors, but the foolish had nothing but lamps without oil, a profession without grace in their hearts; but that the wise had got grace in their hearts, and so were ready-prepared to meet the Bridegroom when he came. Now by that discourse of his the Lord was pleased to convince me that I was a foolish virgin, and that I made a profession, but wanted the oil of grace in my heart, and by this means I was brought into a very sad condition. For I did not experimentally know what it was to have oil in my lamp, grace in my heart, nor what it was to have union with Christ, that being a mystery to me. And then I did think myself guilty of breaking all the commandments of God except the sixth. For I thought I had never desired, wished, or endeavoured any man's death. But then the Lord shewed me that if I were saved by Christ my sins had murdered him, according to that Acts iii. 15, and iv. 10. And that did greatly aggravate my sin the more unto me. Now one of my neighbours, observing that I was in a distressed condition, told me that she had been a-hearing, and that the minister she heard was a-shewing that the Lord had more glory in the salvation than in the damnation of sinners. For in their salvation his mercy and his justice were both glorified, but in their destruction only his justice was glorified. Hearing of this the Lord was pleased to draw out my heart to plead with him, that if he might receive more glory in my salvation than in my destruction, that then his mercy might be manifested to me. For I thought, although I had many worldly comforts, yet I had no interest in Christ, and that if I should die presently, hell would be my portion; and in this sad and sore distress the Lord was pleased to imprint that scripture upon my mind: Job x. 2, 'I will say unto God, Do not condemn me: shew me wherefore thou contendest with me:' Job xl. 2, 'Shall he that contendeth with the Almighty instruct him? he that reproveth God, let him answer it;' and that word of the apostle's: Rom. ix. 20, 21, 'Nay but thou, O man, who art thou that repliest against God? Shall the thing formed say to him that formed it, Why hast thou made me thus? Hath not the potter power over the clay, of the same lump to make one vessel unto honour, and another unto dishonour?' After this it pleased God that Mr Eliot[1] and some other of the people of God, seeing me in this sad condition, [sent to] tell me the church would have me come in to be a member with them; but I did reply that all church-fellowship would do me no good. Then Mr Eliot asked me, what would do me good? and I told him, nothing but an interest in Christ. His answer was, that I was already in the pangs of the new birth, and he did believe it would not be long before the Lord spoke peace to my poor soul. After that, reading a book of Dr Preston's,[2] where he did shew 'that when the Lord joined himself to a believer, he did first comprehend the soul, and then enabling [enable] the soul by faith to apprehend him,' which double act of faith I then knew not. About fourteen days after, considering what a distressed condition I

[1] The venerable apostle of the Indians, John Eliot, born 1604, died 1690.—G.

[2] Sibbes's great friend. Died 1628. Probably his 'Breastplate of Faith,' is referred to.—G.

was in, I was bemoaning myself before the Lord, and the Lord was pleased to bring that scripture to my remembrance in John xvi., 'I will give you that joy that no man taketh from you.' And then I thought with myself that it was Christ that I did want, and not joy. But the Lord brought that scripture to me that Christ was tidings of great joy, Luke ii. 10, 11; and I thought, how could this be to such a poor wretch as I was, and the Lord was pleased to bring that scripture to my mind, that he looked not as man looked, 1 Sam. xvi. 7, and that he was God and not man, Hosea xi. 9; and by this means he took away all my fears. And then the Lord did help me to discern that this was a mystery indeed, and did so quiet my heart that all the world seemed as nothing unto me. For I never heard such a voice before, blessed be his name. And then the people of God would have me come into fellowship with them, and soon after I was admitted a babe in Christ among them. Afterwards being to hear Mr Cotton on 1 Pet. ii. 2, 'As new-born babes, desire the sincere milk of the word, that you may grow thereby;' and from thence he shewed that if it were a living babe it would cry out for nourishment, and that the soul that did once really taste of Christ was never satisfied, but would still be crying out for more and more of Christ. When such a soul came to any ordinance as hearing, prayer, the Lord's supper, and did get nothing of Christ, they were all as lost ordinances to it.

It so fell out that the next Lord's day was the day of sitting down at the Lord's table, and the Lord did put it into my thoughts that if we received nothing but a piece of bread and a sip of wine, it would be but a poor empty thing; and so the Lord did help me to beg that if what he had been pleased to speak to my soul before were a true manifestation of himself, that he would be pleased to speak again unto my soul, for a threefold cord is not easily broken, Eccles. iv. 12. Being at the ordinance, the bread and wine coming about, I was thus sighing unto the Lord, What! shall I have nothing but a bit of bread and a sip of wine this day? and the Lord was pleased to bring that scripture to my mind: John vi. 55, 'For my flesh is meat indeed, and my blood is drink indeed.' And so the Lord was pleased to give something more of himself to my poor soul at that time. After this, a sad providence attended one of my neighbours. I was full of fears that her condition might be mine; but the Lord brought that scripture to my mind: Jer. xxix. 11, 'For I know the thoughts that I think towards you, saith the Lord, thoughts of peace and not of evil, to give you an expected end;' and thereby the Lord stayed my heart in trusting upon himself, and giving me a safe delivery. And being up again, I went to hear Mr Cotton, and he was shewing what assurance was, and how happy that soul was that could say as Job did, chap. xix. 25; and with David, Ps. cxix. 89, 'For ever, Lord, thy word is settled in the heavens;' and so the Lord was pleased to shew me what a mercy I had that had assurance. Then I went to speak to Mr Cotton, to ask him what he thought of the work of God upon my poor soul, and he told me that he was satisfied that it was a real work of God. And he did counsel me to walk humbly and thankfully, and to take heed of grieving that Spirit of God by which I was sealed up to the day of redemption, and to walk humbly towards those that God had not revealed so much of himself to as he had to me. And then the Lord was pleased by his providence to call my husband to come for England, and he did tell me that he should so order business that I should have less of the world to trouble me. I was glad to hear it from him, and desired him to go. And then the Lord was pleased to help me to consider whether I had not got a better husband, and the Lord did quiet my heart in himself; my soul being espoused to him, 2 Cor. xi. 2. After he was gone from me, we did hear of a war broke forth in England, and friends told me my husband would be in danger of his life if taken. I told them the best I knew, and the worst I knew; and that if God should take my husband out of the world, I should have a husband in heaven, which was best of all. And Mr John Eliot did visit me in his absence, and asked me how the Lord did bear up my heart in my husband's absence; and I did tell him that the Lord was as well able to bring him to me in safety as he did to carry him out. And he answered me, I believe the Lord will say unto thee as he did to the Canaanitish woman, Mat. xv. 28, 'Be it unto thee according to thy faith.' And the Lord was pleased to keep me, and all that I had, and to preserve him, and to bring him home in safety unto me. And then, instead of having less of the world, which I desired, the Lord did cast in more of it. After this, my husband told me that he must go again to England, and I was very unwilling to it; but he told me if he did not, the name of God would suffer. To prevent which, I consented, and it pleased God to bring him home in safety to me; and in a few years after he brought me over to England, and God shewed much of his goodness to me.

At my coming ashore, he brought that scripture to my remembrance, Deut. xxxiii. 26, 27, 'There is none like unto thee, O God of Jeshurun, who rideth upon the heaven in thy help, and in his excellency on the sky. The eternal God is thy refuge, and underneath are the everlasting arms.'

After it had pleased God to bring me back to my native country, I was much troubled that there was no better observation of the Lord's day—it being our practice in New England to begin it at sunset the evening before, as it is recorded in Genesis 'that the evening and the morning was the first day;' and that scripture was brought to my memory, Prov. xiv. 10, 'The heart knows its own bitterness, but no man intermeddles with its joy.' Many trials the Lord hath been pleased to exercise me with, but in the midst of all God hath made that word sweet to my soul, Isa. liv. 10, 'For the mountains shall depart, and the hills be removed; but my kindness shall not depart from thee, neither shall the covenant of my peace be removed, saith the Lord that hath mercy on thee.' It pleased the Lord after a year or two to exercise me with much weakness; but then he made that word sweet unto me, Isa. l. 8, 'He is near that justifies me: who will contend with me?' and that word, Job xv. 11, 'Are the consolations of God small unto thee?' After these things, when I was in a very great strait upon the apprehension of some public dangers that seemed to threaten us, the Lord was pleased to bring to my mind that scripture, Zech. ix. 12, 'Turn to your strongholds, you prisoners of hope.'

And since, in the midst of my many bodily infirmities, God hath made that word sweet to my soul, Ps. cxvi. 7, 'Return unto thy rest, O my soul, for the Lord hath dealt bountifully with thee;' and that word, Ps. xxiii. 4, 'Though I walk through the valley of the shadow of death, I will fear no evil, for thou art with me, thy rod and thy staff they comfort me.' I still remain as a 'prisoner of hope,' waiting for a fruition of that happiness which the Lord Jesus Christ hath prepared for me, 'for I know that he that hath the Son hath life,' 1 John v. 12. 'And if the Son make us free, then are we free indeed,' John viii. 36. And 'blessed is that people that knows the joyful sound: they shall walk, O Lord, in the light of thy countenance,' Ps. lxxxix. 15. I find the Lord Jesus very free in the tenders of his love to poor sinners; and that love hath in a great measure been manifested to my poor soul.

After this it pleased the Lord to visit one of my daughters with a great sickness, upon which my heart was drawn out to seek the Lord on her behalf; then that scripture was brought to my mind, John xi. 21, 'Then said Martha unto Jesus, Lord, if thou hadst been here, my brother had not died. But I know that now, whatsoever thou wilt ask of God, God will give it to thee. Jesus saith unto her, Thy brother shall rise again. Martha saith unto him, I know that he shall rise again at the last day. Jesus saith unto her, I am the resurrection and the life: and he that believeth in me shall never die.' And it pleased the Lord to give me her life as an answer of prayer.

It pleased the Lord after this to visit this land with the pestilence; a severe stroke of his that swept away many thousands; and under that sad providence of his, the Lord did help me to rely alone upon himself from that scripture, Ps. xci. 7, 'A thousand shall fall at thy side, and ten thousand at thy right hand; but it shall not come nigh thee.' And according to my faith, it pleased the Lord to preserve both myself and all my relations from that sad stroke, though some of them were often in the midst of danger; blessed be his name.

The next year after the Lord did again, for our sins, visit us, and that by a dreadful fire, which reduced to ashes many thousand houses; and yet his love was then manifested to me in the preservation of my habitation, when many better than myself were burned out. Therefore unto my God shall I, who am less than the least of all his mercies, render that praise which is due unto his name.

Since that, whilst I was upon a languishing bed, and death even knocking at the door, it pleased the Lord once again to alarm me in that weak condition, by a dreadful fire which broke out very near us; and at that time it pleased my good God to support and strengthen my spirit with that scripture, Isa. xliii. 2, 'When thou passest through the waters, I will be with thee; and through the rivers, they shall not overflow thee: when thou walkest through the fire, thou shalt not be burnt; neither shall the flame kindle upon thee;' and that scripture, Isa. liv. 5, 'For thy Maker is thy husband; the Lord of hosts is his name; and thy Redeemer the Holy One of Israel; the God of the whole earth shall he be called.' And this second time also the Lord was graciously pleased to preserve me and my house from that amazing stroke which did so much threaten us. And oh that all those new and old experiences might be high obligations upon me and mine to holiness and fruitfulness all our days!

Whilst I remained in New England there happened a great earthquake, which did shake all in the house, and my son being by me, asked me what it was; I told him our neighbours were all amazed at it, and knew not but that the world might then be at an end, and did run up and down very much affrighted at it, but I sat still, and did think with myself what a Christ was worth to my poor soul at that time. And then God made these scriptures sweet refreshings, supporting and quieting my soul: Ps. xviii. 46, 'The Lord liveth: and blessed be my Rock; and let the God of my salvation be exalted;' Heb. xi. 13, 'These all died in faith, not having received the promises, but having seen them afar off, and were persuaded of them, and embraced them, and confessed they were strangers and pilgrims on the earth;' Rev. vii. 9, 'After this I beheld, and lo, a great multitude, which no man could number, of all nations, and kindred, and people, and tongues, stood before the throne, and before the Lamb, clothed with white robes, and palms in their hands;' ver. 11, 'And he said to me, These are they which came out of great tribulation, and have washed their robes, and made them white in the blood of the Lamb.'

INDEXES, &c.

I.—TEXTS.

NOTE.—In this Index will be found the whole of those Texts of Scripture which are discussed fully in Treatise or Sermon, together with all such as are incidentally explained; but as in Sibbes, there are thousands of others adduced in proof of given points, which it was impossible to include. These will be readily traced under the *Index of Subjects*. It has been our endeavour to give every Text on which anything considerable or noticeable is said by Brooks.—G.

1 'Apples of Gold.'

2 'Mute Christian.'

3 See under Heb. x. 6-8.

4 'God's Delight in the Progress of the Upright.'

1 'Hypocrites Discovered.'
2 'A Believer's Last Day his Best Day.'
3 'London's Lamentations.'
4 See 'Epistle to Closet Prayer.'
5 'Ark for all God's Noahs.'
6 'Privy-Key of Heaven.'

1 'Heaven on Earth.'
2 'Precious Remedies.'
3 'Unsearchable Riches.'
4 'Glorious Day of the Saints' Appearance.'
5 'A word in Season.'
6 See under Ps. xl. 6-8.
7 'Crown and Glory of Christianity.'

	CHAP.	VER.	VOL.	PAGE
1 Peter	1.	4	1.	409-468[1]
,,	1.	5	5.	245
,,	1.	8, 9	2.	518
,,	1.	8, 9	5.	109
,,	2.	9	1.	343
,,	2.	9	3.	131, 132
,,	2.	15	3.	144
,,	2.	24	5.	169
,,	3.	12	5.	404-406
,,	3.	18	5.	79-81
,,	3.	19, 20	5.	123
,,	4.	15	5.	425
,,	5.	5	3.	30, 31
,,	5.	5	4.	310
,,	5.	8	1.	160, 172
2 Peter	1.	5-11	2.	429
,,	1.	12-15	4.	445
,,	1.	13	2.	325

	CHAP.	VER.	VOL.	PAGE
2 Peter	2.	7, 8	4.	130
1 John	1.	5	2.	18,19 seq
,,	3.	3	2.	509, 510
,,	5.	13	1.	95
Jude		6, 13	6.	205, 206
,,		23	1.	39
Rev.	1.	8	5.	152, 153
,,	2.	10	6.	227
,,	2.	17	2.	230, 231 345, 346
,,	2.	17	5.	35
,,	2.	24	1.	12
,,	3.	19	1.	52
,,	3.	20	3.	205
,,	4.	5	6.	10
,,	9.	7	1.	201
,,	9.	11	5.	118
,,	17.	14	3.	194

	CHAP.	VER.	VOL.	PAGE
Rev.	19.	8	5.	231, seq
,,	22.		5.	403, seq

APOCRYPHA.

	CHAP.	VER.	VOL.	PAGE
Eccles.	3.	26, 27	1.	249
,,	7.	36	4.	205, 206
,,	25.	3	1.	190
1 Macc.	6.	34	1.	315
2 Macc.	6.	24	5.	419, 420
,,	6.	18-31	5.	438
Wisd.	2.	—	5.	56
,,	3.	7	1.	434
,,	5.	1-8	2.	18
,,	5.	1-10	5.	56
Tobit	1.	21	6.	232
,,	2.	24	6.	310

II.—GLOSSARY.

This Glossary is given in fulfilment of our promise in the Preface, (Vol. I., page xvii.) *As a rule*, we have not given separate references to the different grammatical forms of the words, *i.e.*, noun, verb, adjective, &c., but have placed all under one form. In nearly every case the references guide to explanations *in the place*. See Index of Names, &c., under 'Shakesperean words,' for a number of interesting old-English words.—G.

Abates, i. 303.
Accidental, iv. 374; v. 465.
Acting, v. 470.
Admiration, i. 188, 193; ii. 225.
Advertisement, i. 26.
Affect, i. 61; iv. 36; vi. 438.
Affecting, i. 227.
Affectionate, i. 226.
Alas! i. 19; ii. 206, 532; iii. 5, 177.
Along-all, vi. 441.
Amort, i. 375; iv. 433.
Amuse and amusing, ii. 288, 350; iv. 399; v. 13; vi. 49.
Anawares, i. 11.
Angels, iii. 113; iv. 12, 115.
Anguish, i. 317.
Anonywar, i. 11.
Apricock, iii. 460.
Artifices, i. 116.
Artificial, i. 164; iii. 85, 468; vi. 169.
Assay and Assays, i. 172; iv. 261.

Baby=doll, ii. 35; iii. 57, 121; iv. 55; vi. 51.
Banded, iii. 160.
Bartholomew-babies, vi. 51.
Bavin, iv. 388.
Bedlams, i. 317.
Bed-rool, iv. 157.
Begged, iv. 30.
Being, ii. 141.
Bib, iii. 355; iv. 141.
Blades, iv. 186.
Blue-bottle, iv. 23.
Bonity, iii. 225.
Boulter, i. 288.
Bounce, i. 390.
Brave, i. 256.
Bravery, i. 3, 63.
Butt-mark, i. 45.
Button-up, ii. 364; iii. 83.

Carriage, i. 213, 257.
Charms, iii. 178.
Chineses, ii. 442.
Chock, iv. 113, 210.
Civility, iv. 127.
Cloddered, clods=clots, v. 92; vi. 39.
Conceited, v. 5.
Contemptible, vi. 438.
Coprice, v. 560.
Counterpain, ii. 522; iii. 345; iv. 24.
Cozen, i. 199.
Crassy, v. 86.
Criminous, iv. 311.

Debasing, vi. 437.
Deboist, iii. 217.
Decline, i. 98.
Dedi-gift, iv. 44.
Delightfully, i. 370.
Deordination, v. 65.
Diapary, iv. 56.
Die, vi. 444.
Dispose, iii. 167, 168.
Drabbing, i. 182, 199.
Dromish, iii. 105.
Droyled, iv. 316.

Earl, iv. 83.
Egregious, ii. 449; iii. 289.
Entireness, i. 39.
Ephemeron, i. 426.
Ethnicks, ii. 39; iii. 177; iv. 150; vi. 415.
Eutical, i. 294.
Exigents, i. 286.
Experiments, i. 194.
Experiments, i. 405; iii. 407; vi. 447.

Factors, ii. 398; iv. 127.
Fare, ii. 508.
Feathers-purple, vi. 88.
Festraw, i. 213.
File, ii. 191.
Flaunt, iv. 87.
Forgeries, iv. 39.
Fraughted, iv. 432.
Fray-bugs, iv. 361.
Frontless, iii. 412.

Gad, i. 199.
Gaggling, i. 250.
Galliard, iii. 130.
Garbidge, ii. 38.
Gashly, gashful, v. 215; vi. 170
Gastred, v. 92.
Grate, i. 288.
Gripe, i. 3; ii. 420.

Hansel, I. lxxv.
Happily, iv. 257.
Hatcht, vi. 104.
Haws, ii. 23.
Hempton, ii. 488.
Heteroclites, iii. 416.
Honararies, iii. 295.
Horn-book, iii. 63.
Hudgin, i. 297.
Humorous, i. 387.
Husbandry, i. 16.
Hushed, v. 409.

Idiot, ii. 187.
Immarcessible, v. 519.
Impertinent, i. 169.

[1] 'String of Pearls.'

III.—NAMES AND AUTHORITIES QUOTED OR REFERRED TO.

[1] For this reference see Becanus, Origines Antwerpianæ, lib. v.; Indoscythica, p. 500; and cf. Pownall's Treatise of Antiquities, p. 139.—G.

[1] Wrongly queried: being Holcot, as in other reference, *supra*.—G.

[1] As under this reference the Index is pointed to, the present opportunity is embraced of placing here a little note which was accidentally dropped out from 'Precious Remedies,' [Vol. I., 5, footnote 1,] and, as above, inadvertently alluded to, as if inserted. For the comparison of Satan with pirates, compare Leighton on the Temptation of Christ, as recorded in Matthew, near beginning. Brooks preceded the Archbishop, but both had a common authority in the Mediæva lpreachers.—G.

[1] Adv. Hermogenes, cap. 22. –G.

IV.—GENERAL INDEX OF MATTERS.

THE END.

BALLANTYNE AND COMPANY, PRINTERS, EDINBURGH.

www.ingramcontent.com/pod-product-compliance
Lightning Source LLC
Chambersburg PA
CBHW070942150426
42812CB00063B/2717